macOS Catalina

the missing manual®

The book that should have been in the box®

macOS Catalina

the missing manual®

The book that should have been in the box®

David Pogue

O'REILLY®

Beijing | Boston | Farnham | Sebastopol | Tokyo

macOS Catalina: The Missing Manual
by David Pogue

Copyright © 2019 David Pogue. All rights reserved.
Printed in the United States of America.

Editor: Julie Van Keuren
Proofreaders: Diana D'Abruzzo, Kellee Katagi, and Judy Le
Illustrator: David Pogue
Interior book designer: Julie Van Keuren (based on a design by Phil Simpson)
Indexer: Julie Van Keuren

Published by O'Reilly Media, Inc.,
1005 Gravenstein Highway North, Sebastopol, CA 95472.

O'Reilly books may be purchased for educational, business, or sales promotional use. Online editions are also available for most titles at *http://oreilly.com*. For more information, contact our corporate/institutional sales department: 800-998-9938 or *corporate@oreilly.com*.

December 2019: First Edition.

ISBN: 978-1-492-07506-6
[LSCH] [12/19]

Table of Contents

Part Four: The Technologies of macOS

TABLE OF CONTENTS

The Missing Credits

About the Author

 David Pogue (author, illustrator) writes the "Crowdwise" column for *The New York Times,* where he was the weekly tech columnist from 2000 to 2013. (Somewhere in there, he took a five-year detour at Yahoo Finance.)

He's also a five-time Emmy-winning correspondent for *CBS News Sunday Morning,* the host of several *NOVA* miniseries on PBS, and the creator of the Missing Manual series. He's written or co-written more than 100 books, including dozens in this series; six in the *For Dummies* line (including *Macs, Magic, Opera,* and *Classical Music*); two novels (one for middle-schoolers); *The World According to Twitter;* and three books of essential tips and shortcuts: *Pogue's Basics: Tech, Pogue's Basics: Life,* and *Pogue's Basics: Money.* In his other life, David is a former Broadway show conductor, a magician, and a funny public speaker. He lives in Connecticut with his wife, Nicki, and three awesome children.

You can find a complete list of David's columns and videos, and sign up to get them by email, at *authory.com/davidpogue.* His website is *davidpogue.com.* He welcomes feedback about his books by email at *david@pogueman.com.*

About the Creative Team

Julie Van Keuren (editor, indexer, interior book designer) spent 14 years in print journalism before deciding to upend her life, move to Montana, and live the freelancing dream. She now works for a variety of terrific clients who understand that skilled editing, writing, book layout, and indexing don't have to come from inside a cubicle. She and her husband have two adult sons. Email: *JulieVanK@gmail.com.*

Diana D'Abruzzo (proofreader) is a Virginia-based freelance editor with more than 20 years of experience in the journalism and book publishing industries. More information on her life and work can be found at *dianadabruzzo.com.*

Kellee Katagi (proofreader) has devoted most of her 20-plus-year writing and editing career to covering fitness, nutrition, travel, and outdoor sports. A former managing editor of SKI magazine, she now smiths words from her Colorado home, where she lives with her husband and three kids. Email: *kelkatagi@gmail.com.*

Judy Le (proofreader) is a magazine editor and newly elected school board member in Virginia, where she lives in a near-constant state of amazement with her husband and their son.

Acknowledgments

Over the years, over the many editions of this book, many friends and colleagues have contributed enthusiasm, expertise, and even prose to this Missing Manual. They include Tom Gewecke, Zachary Brass, Kirill Voronin, Dan Pourhadi, Rich Koster, J.D. Biersdorfer, Teresa Noelle Roberts, Ben Waldie, Brian Sawyer, Phil Simpson, and Lesa Snider.

I owe debts of thanks to O'Reilly's Missing Manuals editor-in-chief, Nan Barber; to Apple's Todd Benjamin and Bill Evans for going beyond the call of duty to chase down tweaky tech answers; and to Julie Van Keuren, whose Missing Manual role over the past decade has grown from humble copy editor to full-blown editorial and design factory.

I also wish I could send out an "I Made the Book Better!" T-shirt to every reader who ever took the time to write with corrections, suggestions, tips, and tricks. And thanks, as always, to David Rogelberg for believing in the idea.

Above all, this book owes its existence to the patience and affection of Nicki, Kelly, Tia, and Jeffrey. They make these books—and everything else—possible.

—*David Pogue*

About The Missing Manuals

Missing Manuals are witty, well-written guides to computer products that don't come with printed manuals (which is just about all of them). Each book features a hand-crafted index, cross-references to specific page numbers (not just "see Chapter 14"), and an ironclad promise never to put an apostrophe in the possessive pronoun "its."

Also by David Pogue:

- *iPhone: The Missing Manual*

- *Windows 10: The Missing Manual*

- *David Pogue's Digital Photography: The Missing Manual*

- *Pogue's Basics: Tech*

- *Pogue's Basics: Money*

- *Pogue's Basics: Life*

Introduction

MacOS Catalina is the 16th major version of Apple's operating system. It's got very little in common with the original Mac OS, the one that saw Apple through the 1980s and 1990s. Apple dumped that in 2001, when CEO Steve Jobs decided it was time for a change. Apple had spent too many years piling new features onto a software foundation originally poured in 1984. Programmers and customers complained of the "spaghetti code" the Mac OS had become.

So today, underneath macOS's classy, shining desktop is Unix, the industrial-strength, rock-solid OS that drives many a website and university. It's not new by any means; in fact, it's decades old and has been polished by generations of programmers.

Note: Beginning with Sierra in 2016, Apple stopped calling the Mac operating system "OS X." It's now "macOS." That's partly because Apple sought consistency with the software in its other products—iOS and watchOS—and partly, no doubt, because it was tired of hearing people pronounce it "oh ess sex."

What's New in Catalina

Having run out of big cat species (Cheetah, Puma, Jaguar, Panther, Tiger, Leopard, Snow Leopard, Lion, and Mountain Lion), Apple started naming its Mac operating systems after places in California. There was the surfing site Mavericks, followed by Yosemite, El Capitan, Sierra, High Sierra, and Mojave. And now there's Catalina, named after Santa Catalina, a rocky island off the coast of Southern California.

The changes in Catalina are either "thoughtful and strategic" or "ridiculously minor," depending on your generosity of thought toward Apple products.

Herewith: a list of what's new.

Death of iTunes

The bloated behemoth program called iTunes is gone. In its place are smaller, simpler apps called TV, Music, and Podcasts. (The iTunes Store, however, still exists and is where you can continue to buy music.)

Why did Apple bother? Partly because people had been complaining for years that iTunes was trying to do too many things and becoming too complex in the process. And partly because, with every passing year, Apple adapts more of its popular iOS apps into Mac apps. By maintaining essentially the same program on two kinds of machines, Apple saves time and effort; and because you get identical apps with the same features on phone/tablet/Mac, you have less to learn.

And what about syncing your iPhone or iPad with the Mac, another duty of iTunes? Now you do that right in the Finder; see page 420.

Sidecar

If you own a recent iPad, you can now prop it up off to the side of your Mac—and marvel as it acts as a second screen, either wirelessly or over a cable. It displays either a duplicate of the Mac's screen or an extension of it. It works with the Apple Pencil, meaning that you can use your iPad as a graphics tablet for Mac software. And because Apple gives you a few essential Mac buttons on the iPad screen, you can relax on the couch with the iPad on your lap, operating, for the first time in history, Mac software.

Screen Time

The Catalina update continues Apple's Quest to Make the Mac More Like iOS. It blesses the Mac with Screen Time, the iPhone/iPad feature that's designed to help us with our digital addictions. Or at least our kids'.

Screen Time is a series of graphs that show how much time you've spent on the Mac, how much time you spend in each app, how many times you wake your Mac a day, and so on.

It incorporates limits that replace the old Parental Controls feature on the Mac. For example, Downtime lets you schedule periods when you're not allowed to use your Mac, except for certain apps that you designate. App Limits are daily time limits for categories of apps, like Games, Entertainment, and Social Networking. You can also block raunchy or violent movies, music, games, and so on.

You can opt to apply these restrictions to your Mac or to a child's Mac, have it apply to all your devices or only the one in front of you, require a password to override the blockades, manage the kids' limits remotely from your own phone or Mac, and so on.

Voice Control

It's now possible to do everything on the Mac by voice alone—an enormous engineering accomplishment. You can click buttons, drag things, scroll, dictate, make text edits—all with natural voice commands, all hands-free. This feature is primarily intended for people who can't use the mouse or keyboard, but it turns out to be useful

in all kinds of situations, especially when you're trying to fix dictation mistakes. You can say, for example, "Replace 'Mr. Trannidy' with 'missed her train today.'"

This feature, too, has been inherited from the iPhone/iPad. It's not quite as comprehensive, but it's still amazing.

Security Tweaks

Truth be told, there isn't much in the way of Mac malware. Even so, Apple continues to ruggedize the Mac against the bad guys on the internet.

- **Gatekeeper,** the feature that warns you when you open a program that didn't come from Apple's sanitized, inspected App Store, has been beefed up; now it actually scans all new apps for viruses and malware before you open them.

- **Any time a program tries** to access data in your Documents, Desktop, or Downloads folders; your iCloud Drive (or similar services like Dropbox); or external or removable drives, you get a dialog box asking you for permission to proceed. That warning puts a big damper on the activities of nefarious badware.

- **Any time a program tries** to record your keystrokes or take a screen capture of the screen (still or video), a message alerts you and asks for permission.

- **Until now, somebody who steals** your laptop could just erase it and use it as their own—or sell it. Thanks to the new Activation lock feature (inherited from the iPhone), that's become impossible, at least on Macs that contain the T2 security chip (Macs introduced in 2018 or later, plus the iMac Pro).

 Here's how it works. Once you're signed into your iCloud account and you've turned on Find My Mac (page 658), your Mac is essentially un-erasable. Nobody can wipe it without your iCloud login information.

- **When you install macOS Catalina,** it partitions off a chunk of your internal drive to use as its own private "system volume"—a read-only disk that can't be changed or tampered with, just for the operating system itself. It's completely separate from your programs and your files—and unavailable to any badness you download.

Radical Photos Redesign

The Photos app, too, has been iPhone-ized. The main browsing mode now presents AI-chosen representative photos for Years, Months, and Days, with easy zooming in and out of these times.

New Notes

With every passing year, the Notes app becomes more mighty. In Catalina, you can view your notes as a gallery of thumbnail miniatures instead of a list; share entire notes folders, rather than one note at a time; share notes or folders either in "view only" or "go ahead and make changes" mode; and search for words *even inside scanned images* you've attached to your notes.

New Reminders

Reminders, too, has had a huge upgrade—in fact, it's been fully replaced by a new app. This one features reminder groups, subtasks, attachments, the automatic parsing of phrases like "Poker Tuesday nights at seven," and more.

Lots of Misc.

Some of the smaller tweaks:

- **Safari.** The Start page (which appears before you've entered a web address) has a new design. It features icons for websites in your browsing history, sites you've recently visited, bookmarks, your reading list, and even links people sent to you in Messages.

- **Mail.** When you get an email from a commercial mailing list, there's an Unsubscribe button right there above the body. A new Block Sender command auto-deletes incoming messages from somebody who's annoying you. And there's a Mute Thread option that stifles notifications for a particularly overactive email conversation.

- **Continuity Sketch.** If you have a recent iPad and an Apple Pencil stylus, you can sign or annotate PDF documents that are on your Mac. And you can draw something on the iPad and drop it directly into a Mac document.

- **Find My.** The Find My Mac and Find My Friends apps have been combined into a single app. And when you're trying to find your lost device, you can now see where it is even if it's offline, using some Bluetooth passerby magic (page 660).

- **Unlock with Apple Watch.** Often, your Mac displays a message asking for your password, just to confirm that you're you and that you know what you're doing. Now, if you have an Apple Watch, you can just double-click its side button to authenticate yourself instead of typing your password. That comes into play when, for example, you want to make a change in System Preferences, view your Safari passwords, unlock a note, OK the installation of a new app, and so on.

- **Apple ID in System Preferences.** A new icon, Apple ID, at the top of System Preferences gives you direct access to all things Apple: your iCloud settings; your name, contact, and payment info; your subscriptions and purchases; your Family Sharing settings; and so on. You can also view a list of all your Apple gadgets and their statuses.

- **QuickTime Player tweaks.** You can now play back a video Picture-in-Picture style: as a floating mini-window that keeps playing while you do other things. You can also create a video from a folder full of sequentially numbered images.

- **HomeKit video recordings.** If you have an Apple TV or a HomePod, your HomeKit home security camera can record a clip automatically when it detects movement. You can get notified, and you can view the clips in the Home app on your Mac or online.

- **International goodness.** The keyboard prediction feature now offers Cantonese suggestions; there are 34 new fonts for Indian languages; Thai-English and

Vietnamese-English dictionaries are on board; and there are new, more natural-sounding Indian voices for Siri.

- **Un-upgrading.** If, within 24 hours of installing Catalina, you decide you hate it, you can "rewind" your Mac to its condition before the upgrade.

The Dearly Departed

You may discover a few familiar features that are gone in Catalina:

- **32-bit apps don't run.** This one might be painful. In Catalina, ancient, "32-bit" apps (including years-old versions of Microsoft Office and Photoshop) don't even open. See page 163 for details.

- **Dashboard.** That weird screen full of "widgets" (floating windowlets showing stocks, weather, Stickies, and so on) has finally bitten the dust.

- **iTunes.** Yep, that old dinosaur's functions have been split into individual apps for TV, Music, and Podcasts.

About This Book

To find your way around macOS Catalina, you're expected to use Apple's online help system. As you'll quickly discover, these help pages are tersely written, offer very little technical depth, lack useful examples, and provide no tutorials whatsoever. You can't mark your place, underline, or read them in the bathroom.

The purpose of this book, then, is to serve as the manual that should have accompanied macOS—version 10.15 in particular. Whether you have an antique, hand-cranked 2012 iMac or a shiny new model, this is your guide.

MacOS Catalina: The Missing Manual is designed to accommodate readers at every technical level. The primary discussions are written for advanced-beginner or intermediate Mac fans. But if you're a Mac first-timer, miniature sidebar articles called "Up to Speed" provide the introductory information you need to understand the topic at hand. If you're a Mac veteran, on the other hand, keep your eye out for similar shaded boxes called "Power Users' Clinic." They offer more-technical tips, tricks, and shortcuts.

When you write a book like this, you do a lot of soul-searching about how much to cover. Of course, a thinner book, or at least a thinner-looking one, is always preferable; plenty of readers are intimidated by a book that dwarfs the Tokyo White Pages. On the other hand, Apple keeps adding features and rarely takes them away.

That's why some chapters come with free downloadable appendixes—PDF documents, available on this book's "Missing CD" page at *missingmanuals.com*—that go into further detail on some of the tweakiest features. (You'll see references to them sprinkled throughout the book.)

Maybe this idea will save a few trees—and a few back muscles when you try to pick this book up.

About the Outline

MacOS Catalina: The Missing Manual is divided into six parts, each containing several chapters:

- **Part One: The macOS Desktop** covers everything you see on the screen when you turn on a Mac: folders, windows, icons, the Dock, the Sidebar, Spotlight, Spaces, Mission Control, Launchpad, Time Machine, menus, scroll bars, the Trash, aliases, the menu, and so on.

- **Part Two: Programs in macOS** is dedicated to the proposition that an operating system is little more than a launchpad for *programs*—the actual applications you use: email programs, web browsers, word processors, graphics suites, and so on. These chapters describe how to work with applications—how to open them, switch among them, swap data between them, and use them to create and open files. And there's also, of course, a chapter about Siri (and other ways to have a conversation with your Mac).

- **Part Three: The Components of macOS** is an item-by-item discussion of the software nuggets that make up this operating system—the 30-ish panels of System Preferences and the 50-some programs in your Applications and Utilities folders.

- **Part Four: The Technologies of macOS** treads in more advanced territory, like networking and file sharing. These chapters also cover the visual talents of the Mac (photos, fonts, printing, graphics) and its multimedia gifts (sound, movies).

- **Part Five: macOS Online** covers all the internet features, including the Mail email program and the Safari web browser; Messages for instant messaging and audio or video chats; internet sharing; Apple's free, online iCloud services; and connecting to and controlling your Mac from across the wires.

- **Part Six: Appendixes.** This book's appendixes include guidance on installing this operating system, a troubleshooting handbook, a Windows-to-Mac dictionary (to help Windows refugees find the new locations of familiar features in macOS), and a master list of all the keyboard shortcuts and trackpad/mouse gestures on your Mac.

About MissingManuals.com

To get the most out of this book, visit *missingmanuals.com*. Click the "Missing CDs" link—and then this book's title—to reveal a neat, organized, chapter-by-chapter list of the shareware and freeware mentioned in this book.

The website also offers book corrections and updates. (To see them, click the book's title, and then click View/Submit Errata.) In fact, please submit such corrections and updates yourself! In an effort to keep the book as up-to-date and accurate as possible, each time we print more copies of it, we'll make any confirmed corrections you've suggested. We'll also note such changes on the website so you can mark important corrections into your own copy of the book, if you like. And we'll keep the book current as Apple releases more macOS 10.15 updates.

About→These→Arrows

Throughout this book, you'll find sentences like this one: "Open the System folder→Library→Fonts folder." That's shorthand for a much longer instruction that directs you to open three nested folders in sequence, like this:

"On your hard drive, you'll find a folder called System. Open that. Inside the System folder window is a folder called Library; double-click to open it. Inside *that* folder is yet another one called Fonts. Double-click to open it, too." See Figure I-1.

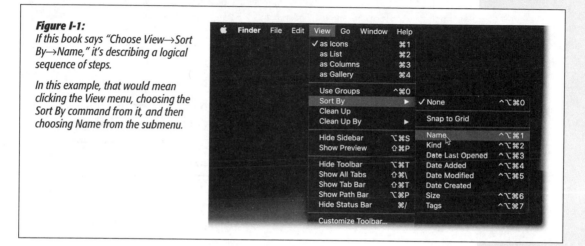

Figure I-1:
If this book says "Choose View→Sort By→Name," it's describing a logical sequence of steps.

In this example, that would mean clicking the View menu, choosing the Sort By command from it, and then choosing Name from the submenu.

The Very Basics

To use this book, and indeed to use a Mac, you need to know some basics. This book assumes you're familiar with a few terms and concepts:

- **Clicking.** To *click* means to point the arrow cursor at something on the screen and then—without moving the cursor—press and release the clicker button on the mouse or trackpad. To *double-click,* of course, means to click twice in rapid succession, again without moving the cursor at all. And to *drag* means to move the cursor while holding down the mouse button.

 When you're told to ⌘-*click* something, you click while pressing the ⌘ key (which is next to the space bar). *Shift-clicking, Option-clicking,* and *Control-clicking* work the same way—just click while pressing the corresponding key. (There's also *right-clicking.* That very important topic is described in depth on page 233.)

- **Menus.** The *menus* are the words at the top of your screen: , File, Edit, and so on. Click one to make a list of commands appear.

 Some people click once to open a menu and then, after reading the choices, click again on the one they want. Other people like to hold down the mouse button continuously after the initial click on the menu title, drag down the list to the desired command, and only then release the mouse button. Either method works fine.

- **Keyboard shortcuts.** If you're typing along in a burst of creative energy, it's disruptive to have to grab the mouse to use a menu. That's why many Mac fans prefer to trigger menu commands by pressing key combinations. For example, in word processors, you can press ⌘-B to produce a boldface word. When you read an instruction like "Press ⌘-B," start by pressing the ⌘ key, and then, while it's down, type the letter B, and finally release both keys.

Tip: You know what's really nice? The keystroke to open the Preferences dialog box in every Apple program—Mail, Safari, iMovie, Photos, TextEdit, Preview, and on and on—is always the same: ⌘-comma. Better yet, that standard is catching on in other apps, too, like Word, Excel, and PowerPoint.

- **Gestures.** A *gesture* is a swipe across your trackpad (on your laptop, or on an external Apple trackpad) or across the top surface of the Apple Magic Mouse. Gestures have been given huge importance in macOS. Page 805 contains a handy list of them.

- **Dialog boxes.** See Figure I-2 for a tour of the onscreen elements you'll frequently be asked to use, such as checkboxes, radio buttons, tabs, and so on.

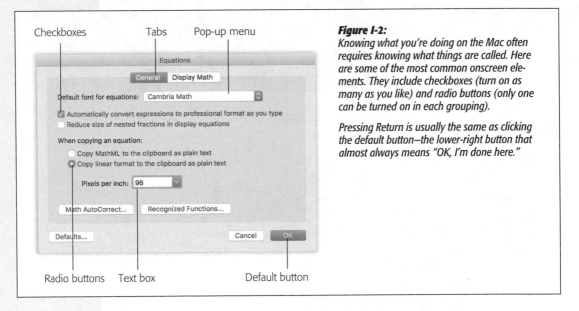

Figure I-2:
Knowing what you're doing on the Mac often requires knowing what things are called. Here are some of the most common onscreen elements. They include checkboxes (turn on as many as you like) and radio buttons (only one can be turned on in each grouping).

Pressing Return is usually the same as clicking the default button—the lower-right button that almost always means "OK, I'm done here."

- **Icons.** The colorful inch-tall pictures that appear in your various desktop folders are the graphic symbols that represent each program, disk, and document on your computer. If you click an icon one time, it darkens, indicating that you've just *highlighted* or *selected* it. Now you're ready to manipulate it by using, for example, a menu command. (If you double-click an icon, it opens.)

A few more tips on using the Mac keyboard appear at the beginning of Chapter 6. Otherwise, if you've mastered this much information, then you have all the technical background you need to enjoy *macOS Catalina: The Missing Manual.*

Part One:
The macOS Desktop

1

Folders, Windows & Finder Tabs

These days, the graphic user interface (icons, windows, trash cans) is standard. MacOS, Windows, Chrome OS, Android, iOS—every operating system is fundamentally the same, and a very long way from the lines of typed commands that defined the earliest computers.

That's not to say that the graphic interface hasn't evolved, though; it has. Herewith: a grand tour of the state of the art in computer desktops—the one in Catalina.

Getting into macOS

When you first turn on a Mac running macOS, an Apple logo greets you, soon joined by a skinny progress bar that lets you know how much longer you have to wait.

Logging In

What happens next depends on whether you're the Mac's sole proprietor or have to share it with other people in an office, school, or household.

- **If it's your own Mac,** a password box awaits you, as shown in the inset of Figure 1-1. Log in; you arrive at the macOS desktop.

- **If it's a shared Mac,** you may encounter a choice of accounts, shown in Figure 1-1. It's like a portrait gallery, set against a blurry version of your usual desktop picture. Click your icon.

 Enter your password and then click Log In (or press Return). You arrive at the desktop. Or, if your Mac has a Touch Bar (page 227) and you've registered your fingerprint, just touch that finger to the sensor at the right end of the bar.

Chapter 12 offers much more on this business of accounts and logging in.

Note: In certain especially paranoid workplaces, you may not see the rogues' gallery shown in Figure 1-1. You may just get two text boxes, where you're supposed to type in your name and password. Without the icons of known account holders, an evil hacker's job is that much more difficult.

Figure 1-1:
On Macs used by multiple people, this is one of the first things you see upon turning on the computer. Click your name. (If the list is long, you may have to swipe the trackpad to find your name—or just type its first few letters.)

Inset: At this point, you're asked to type in your password. Type it, and then click Log In (or press Return). If you type the wrong password, the box vibrates, in effect shaking its little dialog-box head, suggesting that you guess again.

The Elements of the macOS Desktop

The desktop is the shimmering, three-dimensional macOS landscape shown in Figure 1-2. On a new Mac, it's covered by a photo of a spectacular rocky island off the coast of Long Beach, California: Catalina Island (get it?). If you upgraded from an earlier version of macOS, you keep whatever desktop picture you had before.

If you've ever used a computer before, most of the objects on your screen are nothing more than updated versions of familiar elements. Here's a quick tour.

The Dock

This translucent row of colorful icons (Figure 1-2, bottom) is a launcher for the programs, files, folders, and disks you use often—and an indicator to let you know which programs are already open. They appear to rest on a sheet of transparent, smoked glass.

In principle, the Dock is very simple:

- **It has three sections.** Programs are the left side. The icons of recently used programs live in the middle. Everything else goes on the right, including documents, folders, and disks.

- **You can add a new icon to the Dock by dragging it there.** Rearrange Dock icons by dragging them. Remove a Dock icon by dragging it away from the Dock.

- **Click something once to open it.** When you click a program's icon, a tiny black dot appears under it to let you know it's open.

 When you click a folder's icon, you get a *stack*—an arcing row of icons, or a grid of them, that indicates what's inside. See page 136 for more on stacks.

- **Each Dock icon sprouts a pop-up menu.** To see the menu, hold the mouse button down on a Dock icon—or right-click or two-finger click it. A shortcut menu of useful commands pops right out.

- **If you have a trackpad, you can view miniatures of all open windows in a program by pointing to its Dock icon and then swiping down with three fingers.** Details on how to turn on this feature are on page 186.

Figure 1-2:
The macOS landscape looks like a more futuristic version of the operating systems you know and love. This is just a starting point, however. You can dress it up with a different background picture, adjust your windows in a million ways, and of course fill the Dock with only the programs, disks, folders, and files you need.

Apple menu Menu bar Desktop Menulets

Dock Trash

Because the Dock is such a critical component of macOS, Apple has decked it out with enough customization controls to keep you busy experimenting for months. You can change its size, move it to the sides of your screen, hide it entirely, and so on. Chapter 4 contains complete instructions for using and understanding the Dock.

The menu

The menu houses important Mac-wide commands like Sleep, Restart, and Shut Down. They're always available, no matter which program you're using.

The menu bar

Every popular operating system saves space by concealing its most important commands in menus that drop down. MacOS's menus are especially refined:

- **They stay down.** MacOS menus stay open until you click the mouse, trigger a command from the keyboard, or buy a new computer, whichever comes first.

- **They're consistently arranged.** The first menu in every program, which appears in bold lettering, tells you at a glance what program you're in (Safari, Microsoft Word, whatever). The commands in this Application menu include About (which indicates what version of the program you're using), Preferences, and Quit, as well as commands like Hide Others and Show All (which control window clutter, as described on page 192). In short, all the Application menu's commands actually pertain to the application you're using.

 The File and Edit menus come next. The File menu contains commands for opening, saving, and closing files. (See the logic?) The Edit menu contains the Cut, Copy, and Paste commands.

 The last menu is almost always Help. It opens a miniature web browser that lets you search the online Mac help files for explanatory text.

- **You can operate them from the keyboard.** Once you've clicked open a menu, you can highlight any command in it just by typing the first letter (*g* for Get Info, for example). It's especially great for "Your country" pop-up menus on websites, where "United States" is about 200 countries down in the list. You can type *united s* to jump right to it.

 You can also press Tab to open the next menu, Shift-Tab to open the previous one, and Return to "click" the highlighted command.

- **They can hide themselves.** You can set things up so the menu bar disappears completely when you're not using it. You get a little more room on your screen. The on/off switch for this menu-hiding feature is in System Preferences→General; turn on "Automatically hide and show the menu bar." Then, when you do want to open a menu manually, just move your cursor to the top edge of the screen; the menu bar reappears.

Disk icons on the desktop

For years, Apple has encouraged its flock to keep a clean desktop, to get rid of all the icons that many of us leave strewn around. Especially the hard drive icon, which had appeared in the upper-right corner of the screen since the original 1984 Mac.

Today, the Macintosh HD icon doesn't normally appear on the screen. "Look," Apple seems to be saying, "if you want access to your files and folders, just open them directly—from the Dock or your Home folder (page 70). Most of the stuff on the hard drive is system files of no interest to you, so let's just get that icon out of your way."

If you'd prefer that the disk icons return to your desktop, then choose Finder→Preferences, click General, and turn on the checkboxes of the disks whose icons you want on the desktop: hard disks, external disks, CDs, and so on.

Windows and How to Work Them

In designing macOS, one of Apple's key goals was to address the window-proliferation problem. As you create more files, stash them in more folders, and launch more programs, it's easy to wind up paralyzed before a screen awash with overlapping rectangles.

That's the problem addressed by Mission Control, described on page 177. But some clutter and navigation controls are built into the windows themselves, too:

The Sidebar

The Sidebar (Figure 1-3) is the pane at the left side of every Finder window, unless you've hidden it. (It's also at the left side of every Open dialog box and every full-sized Save dialog box.) It's slightly translucent—your desktop picture shines through just a little bit.

The Sidebar has as many as four sections, each preceded by a collapsible heading.

Figure 1-3:
Good things to put in the Sidebar: favorite programs, disks on a network you often connect to, a document you're working on every day, and so on. You can drag a document onto a folder icon to file it there, drag a document onto a program's icon to open it with the "wrong" program, and so on.

Tip: If you point to a heading without clicking, a tiny Hide or Show button appears. Click it to collapse or expand that heading's contents.

Here are the headings you'll soon know and love:

- **Favorites.** This primary section of the Sidebar is the place to stash things for easy access. You can stock this list with the icons of disks, files, programs, folders, and the virtual, self-updating folders called *saved searches.* Click something to open it.

 Here, too, you'll find the icon for AirDrop, the instant file-sharing feature described on page 528. (The All My Files "folder" is gone; see the box below.)

- **iCloud.** This heading offers the fantastic iCloud Drive, a Dropbox-like feature that's described on page 210.

UP TO SPEED

What Happened to "All My Files"?

It was there for years on the Mac, at the top of the Sidebar: the All My Files folder. It was a super-convenient, massive, searchable, sortable list of every human-useful file on the computer: documents, pictures, movies, music. No matter what folders they were *actually* in, they appeared in this single window.

People could use All My Files to find, for example, all the presentation files on the Mac, just by sorting the list by Kind. Or, when running out of disk space, they could sort it by file size, making it easy to see which files were eating up the most space.

What's with the past tense? The All My Files folder is gone. The Mysterious Minds of Apple decided to replace it with a folder called Recents.

You might expect that this Recents folder lists every file that you've recently interacted with. In fact, though, it lists only files you've *opened* recently. Files you just *created or down-loaded* don't appear here (because you haven't *opened* them), much to the confusion of everyone.

If you miss All My Files, it's easy to recreate the effect. The trick is to create a smart folder (page 132.) Set it up as shown here, where the Kind is "Document" and the sub-criteria rows list anything opened, modified, or created in the past 90 days (or whatever time you specify). (See page 124 for details on setting up this kind of query, and remember to Option-click the ⊕ button to open the "Any of the following are true" rows.)

Save this Smart Folder, name it "All My Files," turn on "Add to Sidebar," and boom—you're back in business.

Oh—and then choose Finder→Preferences→Sidebar and *turn off* Recents.

- **Locations.** Here's a complete list of *containers*: other computers on your network (Chapter 13), hard drives, iPhones, iPads, CDs, DVDs, memory cards, USB flash drives, and so on. (Your main hard drive doesn't usually appear, but you can drag it here, or turn it on in Finder→Preferences→Sidebar.) The removable ones (like memory cards, flash drives, and disks) bear a ⏏ logo, which means Eject.

 In Catalina, iPhones and iPads can show up here, too, so you can fiddle around with their contents. See page 420.

- **Tags.** This section lists all your Finder *tags* (color-coded keywords). See page 89 for more on tags.

Note: If you remove everything listed under one of these headings, the heading itself disappears to save space. It reappears the next time you put something in its category back into the Sidebar.

Fine-tuning the Sidebar

The beauty of this parking lot for containers is that it's so easy to set up with your favorite places. For example:

- **Remove an icon** by dragging it out of the Sidebar. It vanishes. You haven't actually removed anything from your Mac; you've just unhitched its alias from the Sidebar.

Tip: If you drag a Locations item out of the list, you'll have to choose Finder→Preferences→Sidebar and then turn on the appropriate checkbox to put it back in.

- **Rearrange the icons** by dragging them up or down in the list. For example, hard drives don't appear at the top of the Sidebar as in the olden days, but you're free to drag them back into those coveted spots.

- **Rearrange the sections** by dragging *them* up or down. For example, you can drag Favorites to the bottom but promote the Locations category.

- **Install a new icon** by dragging it off your desktop (or out of a window) into any spot in the Favorites list of the Sidebar; a horizontal line shows where it will land after you let go. You can't drag icons into any section of the Sidebar—just Favorites.

Tip: You can also highlight an icon wherever it happens to be and then choose File→Add to Sidebar, or just press Control-⌘-T.

- **Adjust the width** of the Sidebar by dragging its right edge—either the skinny divider line or the extreme right edge of the vertical scroll bar, if there is one. You "feel" a snap at the point where the line covers up about half of each icon's name. Any covered-up names sprout ellipses (…) to let you know there's more (as in "Secret Salaries Spreadsh…").

- **Hide the Sidebar** by pressing Option-⌘-S, which is the shortcut for the View→Hide Sidebar command. Bring the Sidebar back into view by pressing the same key combination (or by using the Show Sidebar command).

Tip: You can hide and show the Sidebar manually, too: To hide it, drag its right edge all the way to the left edge of the window. Unhide it by dragging the left edge of the window to the right again.

Then again, why would you ever want to hide the Sidebar? It's one of the handiest navigation aids since the invention of the steering wheel. For example:

- **It takes a lot of pressure off the Dock.** Instead of filling up your Dock with folder icons (all of which look frustratingly alike and are unlabeled), use the Sidebar to store them. You leave the Dock that much more room for programs and documents.

- **It's better than the Dock.** In some ways, the Sidebar is a lot like the Dock, in that you can stash favorite icons of any sort there. But the Sidebar reveals the names of these icons, and the Dock doesn't until you use the mouse to point there.

- **It makes ejecting easy.** Just click the ⏏ button next to any removable disk to make it pop out.

- **You can drag onto its folders and disks.** That is, you can drag icons onto Sidebar icons, just as though they were the real disks, folders, and programs they represent.

- **It simplifies connecting to networked disks.** Park your other computers' shared folder and disk icons here, as described in Chapter 13, to shave several steps off the usual connecting-via-network ritual.

Title Bar

The title bar (Figure 1-4) has several functions. First, when a bunch of windows are open, the darkened title bar, window name, mini-icon, and colored left-corner buttons tell you which window is active—in front. (In background windows, these elements

UP TO SPEED

Fixing the Sidebar

Anything you drag out of the Sidebar can be dragged back in again, including the big-ticket items like Applications and Pictures. That's good to know if you drag something important out of the Sidebar and then change your mind.

Even so, there's a quicker way to restore the Sidebar to its factory settings.

If you choose Finder→Preferences and then click the Sidebar button, you discover

the checkboxes shown here. They let you put back the Apple-installed icons you may have removed in haste. Just turn on a checkbox to restore its icon to your Sidebar. So if something you expect to see in your Sidebar isn't there, check back here.

On the other hand, you may as well streamline your computing life by turning *off* the checkboxes of icons you *never* want to see filling your Sidebar.

appear dimmed and colorless.) Second, the title bar acts as a handle that lets you move the window around on the screen.

You can also move a window by dragging the solid gray strip on the bottom, assuming you've made it appear (choose View→Show Status Bar).

Tip: Here's a nifty keyboard shortcut: You can cycle through the different open windows in one program without using the mouse. Just press ⌘-~ (that is, the tilde key, to the left of the number 1 key on U.S. keyboards). With each press, you bring a different window forward within the current program. It works both in the Finder and in your everyday programs, and it beats the pants off using the mouse to choose a name from the Window menu. (Note the difference from ⌘-Tab, which cycles through different open *programs*.)

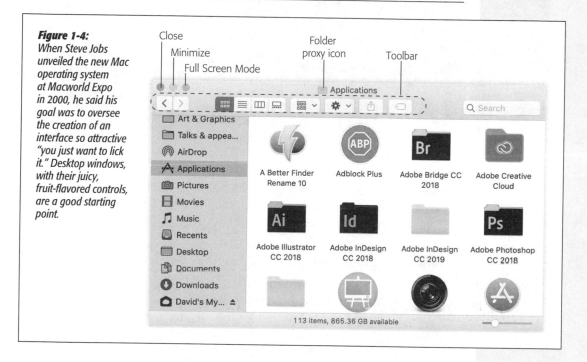

Figure 1-4:
When Steve Jobs unveiled the new Mac operating system at Macworld Expo in 2000, he said his goal was to oversee the creation of an interface so attractive "you just want to lick it." Desktop windows, with their juicy, fruit-flavored controls, are a good starting point.

After you've opened one folder that's inside another, the title bar's secret folder hierarchy menu is an efficient way to backtrack—to return to the enclosing window. Get into the habit of right-clicking (or two-finger clicking, or Control-clicking, or ⌘-clicking) the name of the window to access the menu shown in Figure 1-5. (You can release the Control or ⌘ key immediately after clicking.)

By choosing the name of a folder from this menu, you open the corresponding window. When browsing the contents of the Users folder, for example, you can return to the main hard drive window by right-clicking or two-finger clicking the folder name "Users" and then choosing Macintosh HD from the menu.

Tip: Keyboard lovers, take note. Instead of using the title bar menu, you can also jump to the enclosing window by pressing ⌘-▲ (up arrow), which is the shortcut for the Go→Enclosing Folder command. Pressing ⌘-▼ (down arrow) takes you back into the folder you started in, assuming that it's still highlighted. (This makes more sense when you try it than when you read it.)

Figure 1-5:
Right-click or two-finger click a Finder window's title bar to summon the folder hierarchy menu. This trick also works in most other programs. For example, you can right-click a document window's title to find out where the document is saved on your hard drive.

Once you've mastered dragging, you're ready for these title bar tips:

- **Pressing the ⌘ key** lets you drag the title bar of an inactive window—one that's partly covered by a window in front—without bringing it to the front. (Drag any empty part of the title bar—not the title itself.)

 By the way, you can close, minimize, or full-screenize a background window without the help of the ⌘ key. Just click one of those three corresponding title-bar buttons normally, even if the window you're working on is in front of it.

- **Double-clicking the title bar** is a special technique: It *zooms* the window, enlarging it enough to reveal all the icons inside it (or, in programs, large enough to reveal all the text, graphics, or music). If your monitor isn't big enough to show all the icons in a window, then the window grows to show as many as possible.

 With a quick visit to System Preferences→Dock, though, you can change things up. You can turn on "Double-click a window's title bar to minimize." Now double-clicking the title bar makes the window collapse into the Dock, exactly as though you had clicked the Minimize button.

Tip: If you've turned on that "minimize" option, then you can minimize *all* desktop windows, sending them flying to the Dock, when you double-click the title bar while pressing the Option key.

Close Button

As the tip of your cursor crosses the three buttons at the upper-left corner of a window, tiny symbols appear inside them: ⊗, ⊖, and ⊙. Ignore the gossip that these symbols

were added to help color-blind people who can't distinguish the colors red, yellow, and green. Color-blind people are perfectly capable of distinguishing the buttons by their positions, just as they do with traffic lights.

But for people who aren't paying attention to button position, these cues distinguish the buttons even further. They also signal when it's time to click. For example, as described in the previous section, you can use these three buttons even when the window is not at the front. You know the buttons are ripe for the clicking when you see the little symbols appear under your cursor.

The most important window gadget is the Close button, the red, droplet-like button in the upper-left corner (see Figure 1-4). Clicking it closes the window, which collapses back into the icon from which it came.

Tip: If, while working on a document, you see a tiny dot in the center of the Close button, macOS is trying to tell you that you haven't yet saved your work. (It doesn't appear in Auto Save programs like TextEdit.) The dot goes away when you save the document.

The universal keyboard equivalent of the Close button is ⌘-W (for window)—a keystroke well worth memorizing. If you get into the habit of dismissing windows with that deft flick of your left hand, you'll find it far easier to close several windows in a row, because you won't have to aim for successive Close buttons.

In many programs, something special happens if you're pressing the Option key when using the Close button or its ⌘-W equivalent: You close all open windows. This trick is especially useful in the Finder, where a quest for a particular document may have left your screen plastered with open windows for which you have no further use. Option-clicking the Close button of any one window (or pressing Option-⌘-W) closes all of them.

The Option-key trick doesn't close all windows in *every* program—only those in the *current* program. Option-closing a Microsoft Word document closes all Word windows, but your Finder windows remain open.

Moreover, Option-closing doesn't work in all programs.

Minimize Button

Click this yellow dot to minimize any Mac window, sending it shrinking, with a genie-like animated effect, into the right end of the Dock, where it then appears as an icon. The window isn't gone. It's just out of your way for the moment, as though you've set it on a shelf. To bring it back, click the newly created Dock icon; see Figure 1-6. Chapter 4 has more on the Dock.

Minimizing is a great window-management tool. In the Finder, minimizing a window lets you see whatever icons were hiding behind it. In a web browser, minimizing lets you hide a window that has to remain open (because you're waiting for some task to finish) so you can read something else in the meantime.

And now, some Minimize button micro-goodies:

- **If you enjoy the ability to roll up your windows in this way,** remember that you actually have a bigger target than the tiny Minimize button. (You can make the entire title bar a giant Minimize button, as described on page 20.)

Figure 1-6:
Clicking the Minimize button sends a window sliding down to the Dock, collapsing in on itself as though being forced through a tiny, invisible funnel. A little icon appears on the lower-right corner of its minimized image to identify the program it's running in.

POWER USERS' CLINIC

Adjusting the Genie Speed

Apple has a name for the animation you see when you minimize, open, or close a window: the *genie effect*, because it so closely resembles the way Barbara Eden, Robin Williams, and other TV and movie genies entered and exited their magic lamps and bottles.

You don't have to watch the "genie" animation in precisely the same way, day in and day out. There's no keystroke for making the animation go faster, but you can substitute a faster *style* of minimizing animation.

To do so, choose System Preferences→Dock. From the "Minimize windows using" pop-up menu, choose Scale Effect, and then close the window. Now, instead of collapsing through an invisible funnel, minimized windows simply shrink as they fly down to the Dock, remaining rectangular. The time you

save isn't going to get you home an hour earlier each day, but at least you have the illusion of greater speed.

There's a third animation style, too, but there's a trick to unleashing it: You need the free utility called TinkerTool. It's available from this book's "Missing CD" page at *missingmanuals.com.*

Nostalgia moment: When Steve Jobs first demonstrated Mac OS X, one of his favorite bits was slowing down the animation so everyone could see it in graceful slow motion. How did he do that?

For years, you could Shift-click a window's Minimize button to make it collapse into the Dock at about one-tenth its usual speed. Alas, Apple's No Fun Committee removed this feature from macOS. Ah, the cost of progress.

Better yet, you can also minimize the frontmost window of almost any program (including the Finder) from the keyboard by pressing ⌘-M. That's a keystroke worth memorizing on your first day with the Mac.

- **Option-clicking one minimized window on the Dock** un-minimizes all a program's windows.

Tip: MacOS can change menu commands as you press modifier keys. For example, open a couple of Finder windows and then click the Window menu. Focus on the Minimize Window command. Now press Option and watch both the wording and the listed keyboard equivalent change instantly to Minimize All (Option-⌘-M).

The Option key works wonders on the File menu, too.

- **In the bad old days (up to late 2009)**, minimizing a bunch of documents could get really messy. Each one flew onto the Dock, putting a new icon there, creating a tighter and tighter squeeze, shrinking the Dock's icons until they were the size of Tic Tacs.

Nowadays, your document windows can minimize themselves into their programs' Dock icons, rather than creating new Dock icons for themselves. That way, your Dock doesn't get any more crowded, and the icons on it don't keep shrinking away to atoms.

To turn on this feature, choose System Preferences→Dock. Turn on "Minimize windows into application icon."

So how do you get those windows back out of the Dock icon? You use Dock Exposé, which is described on page 188.

Full Screen Button

A click on the third dot, the green one, on every window's title bar (in most programs, anyway), throws the window into *Full Screen mode*, in which the menu bars and window edges disappear, in the name of making your window fill your screen edge to edge. See page 173 for details.

As your cursor approaches this green dot, a little indicator appears inside it: ⊙. That's the hint that you're about to enter Full Screen mode.

And once you're in Full Screen mode, you can push your cursor to the top of the screen to reveal the window controls. When it passes over the green dot, it changes to this: ⊕. That's right: It's the universal symbol for "Click me to *exit* Full Screen mode."

If you *Option*-click this button, your window grows just large enough to reveal all the icons inside it—or, in programs, large enough to reveal all the text, graphics, or music. It's almost like Full Screen mode, except that you don't lose your menu bar and all your other windows. A second Option-click restores the window to its previous size. (At the desktop, the Window→Zoom command does the same thing, and so does double-clicking the title bar of a Finder window.)

Note: Not all programs permit you to full-screenize their windows. In those apps, this green button displays the ⊕ button and, when clicked, merely zooms the window.

The Folder Proxy Icon

In the Finder, there's a tiny icon next to the window's name (Figure 1-7). It's a stand-in—a proxy—for that window's folder itself. By dragging this tiny icon, you can move or copy the folder into a different folder or disk, into the Sidebar, into the Trash, or into the Dock without having to first close the window.

Tip: You have to hold down the mouse button on the folder proxy icon until the icon darkens before dragging. (It darkens in a fraction of a second.)

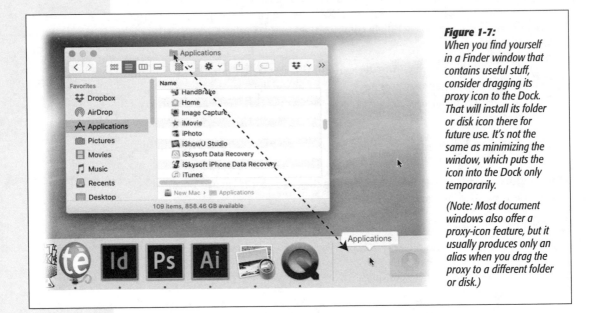

Figure 1-7:
When you find yourself in a Finder window that contains useful stuff, consider dragging its proxy icon to the Dock. That will install its folder or disk icon there for future use. It's not the same as minimizing the window, which puts the icon into the Dock only temporarily.

(Note: Most document windows also offer a proxy-icon feature, but it usually produces only an alias when you drag the proxy to a different folder or disk.)

When you drag this proxy icon to a different place on the same disk, the usual folder-dragging rules apply: Hold down the Option key if you want to copy the original disk or folder; ignore the Option key to move it. (You'll find details on moving and copying icons in the next chapter.)

Many programs, including Microsoft Word, Preview, TextEdit, and others, offer the same mini-icon in open document windows. Once again, you can use it as a handle to drag a document into a new folder or onto a new disk. Sometimes, doing that really does move the document—but more often you just get an alias of it in the new location.

Two Clicks, One Window

Double-clicking a folder in a window doesn't leave you with two open windows. Instead, it makes the contents of the original window disappear (Figure 1-8).

Tip: If you Option-double-click a folder, you don't simply replace the contents of a fixed window that remains onscreen; you actually switch windows, as evidenced by their changing sizes and shapes.

So what if you've now opened Inner Folder B, and you want to backtrack to Outer Folder A? In that case, just click the tiny ‹ button—the Back button—in the upper-left corner of the window, or use one of these alternatives:

- Choose Go→Back.

- Press ⌘-[(left bracket).

- Press ⌘-▲ (up arrow).

- Choose Go→Enclosing Folder.

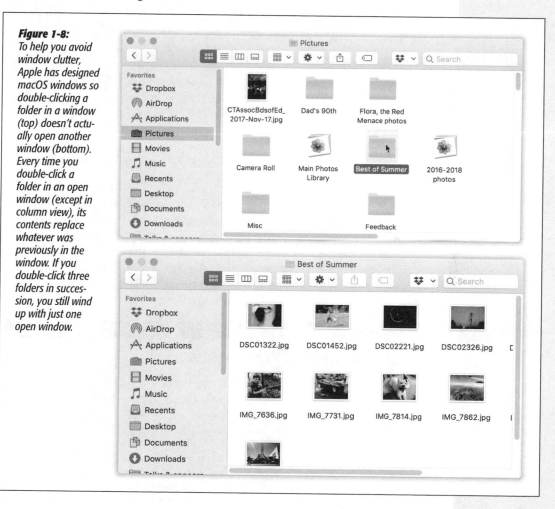

Figure 1-8:
To help you avoid window clutter, Apple has designed macOS windows so double-clicking a folder in a window (top) doesn't actually open another window (bottom). Every time you double-click a folder in an open window (except in column view), its contents replace whatever was previously in the window. If you double-click three folders in succession, you still wind up with just one open window.

None of that helps you, however, if you want to move a file from one folder into the other, or to compare the contents of two windows. In that case, you probably want to see both windows open at the same time.

You can open a second window using any of these techniques:

- **Choose File→New Finder Window (⌘-N).**

Tip: What folder contents fill the "new" window that appears when you use this command? Usually, it's the Recents folder (page 16)—but it can be any window you want. Choose Finder→Preferences→General. Change the "New Finder windows show" pop-up menu to whatever folder you'd like to use as the starting point for your computing life. Your Home folder (page 70) is a good choice. But you're also free to choose your Documents folder, your iDisk, or any folder at all. Now every new Finder window shows you that specified folder, which is a useful arrangement.

- **Double-click a folder or disk icon** on your desktop.

The Finder Toolbar

Page 147 describes this fascinating desktop-window element in great detail.

Scroll Bars

On the modern Mac, scroll bars don't appear nearly as often as they used to. A scroll bar, of course, is the traditional window-edge slider that lets you move through a document that's too big for the window. Without scroll bars, for example, you'd never be able to write a letter that's taller than your screen.

On the very first Macs, scroll bars were a necessary evil; those computers were too underpowered to manage visibly moving the contents of the window. That's why scroll bars were invented in the first place: to give you some feedback about how far you were moving into a document, because the window itself went pure white when you dragged the handle. Today, though, you can manipulate the contents of a window and see where you are. Nobody questions the absence of scroll bars on an iPad, right? Because you just push the contents of a window around with your fingers to scroll.

NOSTALGIA CORNER

How the Scroll Bar Used to Work

If you are that rare, special individual who still operates the scroll bar by clicking it with the mouse, the old-style controls are still around.

For example: Ordinarily, when you click in the scroll bar track above or below the dark-gray handle bar, the window scrolls by one screenful. But another option awaits when you choose System Preferences→General and turn on "Jump to the spot that's clicked." Now when you click the scroll-bar track, the Mac considers the entire scroll bar a proportional map of the document and jumps precisely to the spot you clicked. That is, if you click the very bottom of the scroll-bar track, you see the very last page.

No matter which scrolling option you choose, you can always override your decision on a case-by-case basis by *Option*-clicking the scroll-bar track. In other words, if you've selected the "Jump to the spot that's clicked" option, you can produce a "Jump to the next page" scroll by Option-clicking in the scroll-bar track.

In macOS, you scroll by pushing two fingers up the trackpad (or one finger up the Magic Mouse) or by turning your mouse's scroll wheel. You almost never use the antiquated method of dragging the scroll bar's handle manually, with the mouse.

Tip: You can also scroll using the keyboard. Your Page Up and Page Down keys let you scroll up and down, one screen at a time, without ever having to take your hands off the keyboard. The Home and End keys are generally useful for jumping directly to the top or bottom of your document (or Finder window). And, if you've bought a mouse that has a scroll wheel on the top, you can use it to scroll windows without pressing any keys at all.

That's a long-winded way of explaining why, in most programs, the scroll bars are hidden. See Figure 1-9 for details.

Note: If the missing scroll bars leave you jittery and disoriented, you can bring them back. Open System Preferences→General and then turn on "Show scroll bars: Always."

Figure 1-9:
Scroll bars don't appear at all while you're working (right); you have more screen area dedicated to your work. If you begin to scroll by sliding your fingers up or down the trackpad or Magic Mouse, the scroll-bar handle appears, so you know where you are (middle).

At that point, if you point to the scroll bar, it fattens up so you can grab it (left).

And what if you're such an old-timer that the modern Mac's scrolling direction feels backward to you? When you slide your fingers upward on your laptop's trackpad, you wish the page would scroll *up*, like it used to.

You can put things back to the way they used to be. Open System Preferences. Then:

- **For a trackpad:** Click Trackpad, click Scroll & Zoom, and then turn off "Scroll direction: natural."

- **For a Magic Mouse:** Click Mouse, click Point & Click, and then turn off "Scroll direction: natural."

Note: If you have a non-Apple mouse with a scroll wheel, the Mouse pane may not offer this scroll-direction option. You can still reverse the logic, though, if you're handy in Terminal (macOS's command line program).

Open Terminal and type *defaults write ~/Library/Preferences/.GlobalPreferences com.apple.swipescrolldirection -bool false*. When you press Return and log out, you'll find that the time-honored scroll directions have been restored.

Insta–Full Screen

Why drag a window manually? That's so 2015! Let the software do the dragging for you.

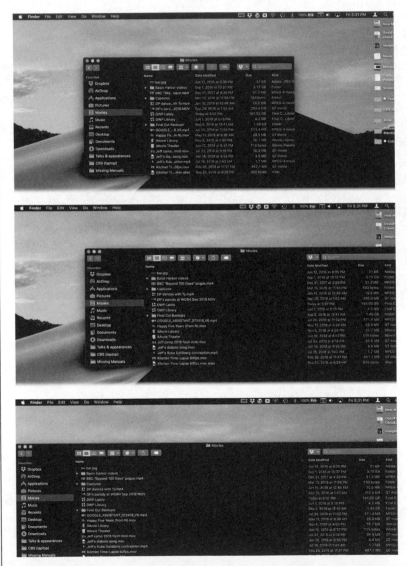

Figure 1-10:

Top: Suppose you've got a window. Hey–it could happen. You double-click the right edge of it, and boom: You've extended the window all the way to the right edge of the screen (middle).

Bottom: If you press Option at the same time, you extend the window all the way to both edges of the screen. This feature works in Apple's own programs (Finder, Mail, TextEdit, and so on), but not in programs that have their own weird ways of doing things (Microsoft Word, for example).

Turns out that if you *double-click* any edge of a window, it snaps to the full width of your screen in that direction: left, right, top, or bottom (see Figure 1-10). And if you double-click any edge while pressing Option, the window expands to the full height or width of the monitor in both directions (Figure 1-10, bottom).

Tip: In macOS Catalina, the green ⊙ button at the top left of most windows offers a less hidden way to achieve these arrangements. When you point to it without clicking, you get not only the Enter Full Screen mode option, but also Tile Window to Left of Screen and, of course, Tile Window to Right of Screen.

Old Finder Mode

Old Finder Mode (not its real name) was designed for people who came to the Mac from a much older version, like Mac OS 9, and lost half their hair when they discovered how different things were. In this mode, there are two big differences that make macOS more like its predecessors:

- **The Sidebar and the toolbar** blink out of sight.

- **Double-clicking a folder** now works like it did back in 2000. Every time you double-click a folder, you open a new window for it.

To invoke Old Finder Mode, press Option-⌘-T, the equivalent for the View→Hide Toolbar command. (Repeat that keystroke or command to turn Old Finder Mode off again.) This won't work if your Finder window has multiple tabs open, but that's not going to be a problem if you're yearning for the days of yore.

Resizable Edges

You can drag *any* edge of a window to change its shape. Just move the pointer carefully to the exact top, bottom, left, or right edge; once the pointer changes to a double-headed arrow, you can drag to move that window's edge in or out.

Tip: There are a few cool, totally undocumented variations on the window-edge-dragging business. First, if you press the Option key while dragging, you resize the *opposite edge* simultaneously. For example, if you Option-drag the bottom edge upward, the top edge simultaneously collapses downward. If you press Shift as you drag, you resize the *entire* window, retaining its proportions. And if you Shift-Option-drag, you resize the window around its center, rather than from its edges.

Snappable Windows

It's easy to position windows tightly against each other, side by side, for comparison or copying. As you slowly drag a window (by its title bar, for example), you'll notice that its edge *sticks* momentarily to any other window edge it passes.

This feature works only in Apple's own programs—and it doesn't happen if you're dragging *quickly*.

Tip: Pressing the Option key as you drag eliminates the moment of stickiness. Great when you're in a hurry.

Path Bar

Choose View→Show Path Bar to see a tiny map at the bottom of the window, showing where you are in the folder hierarchy. If it says Casey→Pictures→Picnic, well, then, by golly, you're looking at the contents of the Picnic folder, which is inside Pictures, which is inside your Home folder (assuming your name is Casey).

Tip: Each tiny folder icon in this display is fully operational. You can double-click it to open it, right-click or two-finger click it to open a shortcut menu, or even drag things into it.

Status Bar

MacOS hides yet another information strip at the bottom of a window: the status bar, which tells you how many icons are in the window ("14 items," for example) and the free space remaining on the disk. To make it appear, choose View→Show Status Bar.

POWER USERS' CLINIC

The Go to Folder Command

Sometimes a Unix tentacle pokes through the macOS interface and you find a place where you can use Unix shortcuts. One classic example is the Go→Go to Folder command (Shift-⌘-G). It brings up a box like the one shown here. Its purpose is to let you jump directly to a folder on your Mac by typing its Unix *folder path.*

For example, if you want to open Documents in your Home folder, you can choose Go→Go to Folder and type */Users/casey/Documents*. Then click Go or press Return. (In this example, of course, *casey* is your short account name.)

In other words, you're telling the Mac to open the Users folder in your main hard drive window, your Home folder inside that, and then the Documents folder inside that. Each slash means "and then open." (You can leave off the name of your hard drive; that's implied by the opening slash.) When you press Return, the folder you specified pops open.

Of course, if you really wanted to jump to your Documents folder, you'd be wasting your time by typing all that. Unix offers a handy shortcut that means "home folder." It's the tilde (~) at the upper-left corner of the U.S. keyboard.

To see what's in your Home folder, then, you could type just that ~ symbol into the Go to Folder box and press Return. Or

you could add some slashes to it to specify a folder inside your Home folder, like this: *~/Documents*

You can even jump to someone *else's* Home folder by typing a name after the symbol, like this: *~chris*

If you get into this sort of thing, here's another shortcut worth noting: If you type nothing but a slash (/) and then press Return, you jump to the main hard drive window.

Note, too, that you don't have to type out the full path—only the part that drills down from the *window you're in.* If your Home folder window is already open, for example, you can open the Pictures folder just by typing *Pictures.*

But Go to Folder really turns into a time-saver if you use *autocompletion.* Here's how it works: After each slash, you can type only enough letters of a folder's name to give macOS the idea—*de* instead of *desktop,* for example—and then wait a fraction of a second or press the Tab key). MacOS fills in the rest of the folder's name. It even auto-capitalizes the folder names for you. (In Unix, capitalization matters.)

For example, instead of typing */Applications/Microsoft Office/clipart/standard,* you could type nothing more than */ap/mi/cl/st,* remembering to press Tab after each pair of letters. Now *that's* a way to feel like a Unix programmer.

Tip: The status bar shows you disk-space information for the entire disk, but not how much disk space *this particular window's* contents occupy.

To find out *that* piece of information, make sure no icon in the window is highlighted. Then choose File→Get Info (or press ⌘-I). The resulting Info window, which is described starting on page 97, shows the size of the folder or disk whose window you're browsing, along with other useful statistics.

The Preview Pane

There's even a way to park more information on the right side of any window, by choosing View→Show Preview; see page 54.

The Four Window Views

You can view the files and folders in a desktop window in any of four ways: as icons; as a single, tidy list; in a series of neat columns; or in gallery view, where you can

Figure 1-11:
From the top: the same window in icon view, list view, column view, and gallery view. Very full folders are best navigated in list or column views, but you may prefer to view emptier folders in icon or gallery views, because larger icons are easier to preview and click. Remember that in any view (icon, list, column, or gallery), you can highlight an icon by typing the first few letters of its name. In icon, list, or gallery views, you can also press Tab to highlight the next icon (in alphabetical order), or Shift-Tab to highlight the previous one.

flip through giant document icons like they're CDs in a music-store bin. Figure 1-11 shows the four views.

Every window remembers its view settings independently. You might prefer to look over your Applications folder in list view (because it's crammed with files and folders) but view the Pictures folder in icon or gallery view, where the larger icons serve as previews of the photos.

To switch a window from one view to another, just click one of the four corresponding icons in the window's toolbar (Figure 1-11).

You can also switch views by choosing View→as Icons (or View→as List, or View→as Columns, or View→as Gallery), which can be handy if you've hidden the toolbar. Or, for less mousing and more hard-bodied efficiency, press ⌘-1 for icon view, ⌘-2 for list view, ⌘-3 for column view, or ⌘-4 for gallery view.

Or, if your Mac has a Touch Bar, you can install a View Options button onto it (page 231).

The following pages cover each of these views in greater detail.

Note: One common thread in the following discussions is the availability of the View Options palette, which lets you set up the sorting, text size, icon size, and other features of each view, either one window at a time or for all windows. To open View Options, choose View→Show View Options, or press ⌘-J, or choose Show View Options from the ✿ menu at the top of every window.

Icon View

In icon view, every file, folder, and disk is represented by a small picture—an icon. This humble image, a visual representation of electronic bits and bytes, is the cornerstone of the entire Mac religion. (Maybe that's why it's called an icon.)

GEM IN THE ROUGH

Multiple Views, Same Folder

If you read this chapter carefully, you may discover a peculiar quirk of the macOS Finder: By choosing File→New Finder Window, you open a second, completely independent Finder window. Therefore, if you stop to think about it, there's nothing to stop you from opening a third, fourth, or fifth copy of *the same folder window.* Once they're open, you can even switch them into different views.

Try this, for example: Choose Go→Applications. Choose File→ New Finder Window (⌘ -N), and then choose Go→Applications *again.* Using the View menu or the

controls in the toolbar, put one of these windows into list view and the other into icon view.

This ability has its advantages. For example, you might decide to open the same window twice while doing some hard-drive housekeeping. By keeping a list view open, you can check the Size column as you move your files into different folders (so you can make sure the folders fit onto a blank CD, for example). By keeping a *column* view open, on the other hand, you gain quicker navigational access to the stuff on your drive.

Icon Size

If you choose View→Show Status Bar so that the bottom-edge strip shown in Figure 1-12 appears, you get a size slider that you can drag to the right or left to make that window's icons larger or smaller. (For added fun, make little cartoon sounds with your mouth.)

Figure 1-12:
Once you make the status bar appear, you can choose an icon size to suit your personality. For picture folders, it can often be very handy to pick a jumbo size, in effect creating a slide-sorter "light table" effect. Icons can be an almost ridiculously large 512 pixels square.

Icon Previews

The Mac expands the notion that "an icon is a representation of its contents" to an impressive extreme. As you can see in Figure 1-13, each icon actually looks like a miniature of the first page of the real document.

Because you can make icons so enormous, you can actually watch movies, or read PDF and text documents, right from their icons.

To check out this feature, point to an icon without clicking. A Play button (▶) appears on any movie or sound file; as shown in Figure 1-13, ◐ and ◑ page buttons appear on multipage documents (like PDFs, Pages files, or even presentation documents like PowerPoint and Keynote). You can actually page through one of these documents right there on its icon without having to open the program!

Tip: If you Option-click the little ⊖ and ⊕ buttons on a PDF, PowerPoint, or Keynote icon preview, you jump to the first or last page or slide in the document.

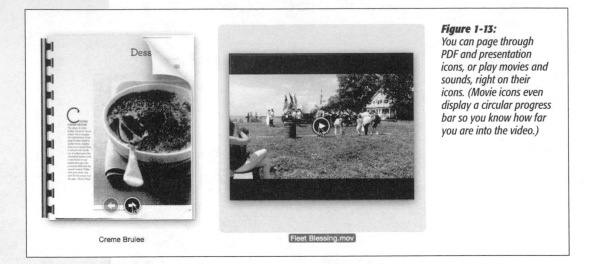

Figure 1-13:
You can page through PDF and presentation icons, or play movies and sounds, right on their icons. (Movie icons even display a circular progress bar so you know how far you are into the video.)

Icon-View Options

MacOS offers a number of useful icon-view options, all of which are worth exploring. Start by opening any icon-view window, and then choose View→Show View Options (⌘-J). (You can put a View Options button onto your Touch Bar, if you have one, too; see page 231.)

The dialog box shown in Figure 1-14 appears.

Always open in icon view

It's easy—almost scarily easy—to set up your preferred look for all folder windows on your entire system. With one click on the Use as Defaults button (described on page 39), you can change the window view of 20,000 folders at once—to icon view, list view, or whatever you like.

Note: The wording of this item in the View Options dialog box changes according to the view you're in at the moment. In a list-view window, it says "Always open in list view." In a gallery-view window, it's "Always open in gallery view." And so on. But the function is the same: to override the default (master) setting.

The "Always open in icon view" option lets you override that master setting, just for one window. For example, you might generally prefer a neat list view with large text. But for your Pictures folder, it probably makes more sense to set up icon view, so you can see a thumbnail of each photo without having to open it.

That's the idea here. Open Pictures, change it to icon view, and then turn on "Always open in icon view." Now every folder on your Mac is in list view except Pictures.

Browse in icon view

This option makes sure that any folders inside the current window open up into icon view, too, even if you'd previously set them to open into some other view. So if you're looking at your Pictures folder in icon view and you open the Grand Canyon Jaw-Droppers folder inside it, then that folder also will be in icon view.

Group By, Sort By

For a discussion of these pop-up menus, see page 39.

Icon size

It's super-easy to make all your icons bigger or smaller; just drag the "Icon size" slider in the lower-right corner of the window. (To make the slider appear, turn on View→ Show Status Bar.) But for the benefit of old-timers who expect to find that slider in the View Options window, well, there's an identical slider there.

Grid spacing

You can control how closely icons are spaced in a window. Figure 1-14 shows all.

Figure 1-14:
Drag the "Grid spacing" slider to specify how tightly packed you want your icons to be. At the minimum setting, they're so crammed it's almost ridiculous; you may not even be able to see their full names. But sometimes you don't really need to. At a more spacious setting (bottom), you get a lot more blank space.

Text size

Your choices range only from 10 to 16 points, and you can't choose a different font for your icons' names. But using this pop-up menu, you can adjust the type size. And for people with especially big or especially small screens—or for people with aging retinas—this feature is much better than nothing.

In fact, you can actually specify a different type size for every window on your machine. (Why would you want to adjust the point size independently in different windows? Well, because you might want smaller type to fit more into a crammed list view without scrolling, while you can afford larger type in less densely populated windows.)

Label position

Click either Bottom or Right to indicate where you want an icon's name to appear, relative to its icon. As shown in Figure 1-15 at bottom, this option lets you create, in effect, a multiple-column list view in a single window.

Show item info

While you've got the View Options palette open, try turning on "Show item info." Suddenly you get a new line of information (in tiny blue type) for certain icons, saving you the effort of opening up the folder or file to find out what's in it. For example:

- **Folders.** The info line lets you know how many icons are inside each without having to open it up. Now you can spot empties at a glance.

- **Graphics files.** Certain other kinds of files may show a helpful info line, too. For example, graphics files display their dimensions in pixels.

- **Sounds and QuickTime movies.** The light-blue bonus line tells you how long the sound or movie takes to play. An MP3 file might say "03' 08" " (three minutes, eight seconds).

- **.zip files.** On compressed archives like .zip files, you get to see an archive's total size (like "48.9 MB").

Show icon preview

This option is what makes icons display their contents. If you turn it off, then icons no longer look like miniature versions of their contents (tiny photos, tiny PDF files, and so on). Everything takes on generic icons.

You might prefer this arrangement when, for example, you want to be able to pick out all the PDF files in a window full of mixed document types. Thanks to the matching icons, it's easy now.

Background

Here's a luxury that other operating systems can only dream about: You can fill the background of any icon-view window on your Mac with a certain color—or even a photo.

Color coordinating or "wallpapering" certain windows is more than just a gimmick. In fact, it can serve as a time-saving visual cue. Once you've gotten used to the fact that your main Documents folder has a sky-blue background, you can look at a screen filled with open windows and pick it out like a sharpshooter. Color-coded Finder windows are also especially easy to distinguish at a glance when you've minimized them to the Dock.

Note: Background colors and pictures show up only in icon view.

Once a window is open, choose View→Show View Options (⌘-J). The bottom of the resulting dialog box offers three choices:

- **Default.** This is the standard option (white).

- **Color.** When you click this button, you see a small rectangular button beside the word "Color." Click it to open the Color Picker, which you can use to choose a new background color for the window (Figure 1-15, top). Unless it's April Fools' Day, pick a light color. If you choose a dark one—like black—you won't be able to make out the lettering of the icons' names.

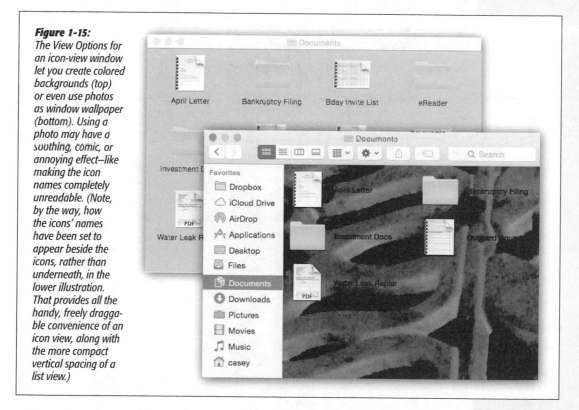

Figure 1-15:
The View Options for an icon-view window let you create colored backgrounds (top) or even use photos as window wallpaper (bottom). Using a photo may have a soothing, comic, or annoying effect—like making the icon names completely unreadable. (Note, by the way, how the icons' names have been set to appear beside the icons, rather than underneath, in the lower illustration. That provides all the handy, freely dragga-ble convenience of an icon view, along with the more compact vertical spacing of a list view.)

• **Picture.** If you choose this option, a "Drag image here" square appears. Now find a graphics file—one of Apple's in the Desktop Pictures folder, or one of your own, whatever—and drag it into that "well."

You see that macOS has superimposed the window's icons on the photo. As you can see in Figure 1-15, bottom, low-contrast or light-background photos work best for legibility.

The Color Picker

Here and there—in System Preferences, iMovie, TextEdit, Microsoft Office, and many other programs—macOS offers you the opportunity to choose a *color* for some element: your desktop background, a window, and so on.

The dialog box that appears offers a miniature color lab that lets you dial in any color in the Mac's rainbow—several color labs, actually, arrayed across the top, each designed to make color choosing easier in certain circumstances:

Color wheel. Drag the scroll bar horizontally to adjust the brightness, and then drag your cursor around the ball to pick the shade.

Color sliders. From the pop-up menu, choose the color-mixing method you prefer. CMYK stands for cyan, magenta, yellow, and black. People in the printing industry will feel immediately at home, because these four colors are the component inks for color printing. (These people may also be able to explain why K stands for black.)

RGB is how a TV or computer monitor thinks of colors: as proportions of red, green, and blue light. Grayscale means shades of gray, like a black-and-white TV. And HSB stands for hue, saturation, and brightness—a favorite color-specifying scheme in scientific circles.

In each case, just drag the sliders to mix up the color you want, or type in the percentages of each component.

Color palettes. This option presents canned sets of color swatches. They're primarily for programmers who want

quick access to the standard colors in macOS. The Web Safe Colors list is useful for web designers, too; they can use it to ensure that the colors they choose will display properly on other computers.

Image palettes. Here's the visible rainbow arrayed yet another way: in cloudy, color-arranged streaks. (Cool tip: If you drag a graphics file directly into the dialog box, it appears in the spectrum's place. That's a handy trick if you're trying to identify the color of a certain spot on an image, for example.)

Colored pencils. Now this is a good user interface. You can click each pencil to see its color name: Mocha, Fern, Cayenne, and so on. (Some interior decorator in Cupertino had a field day naming these things.)

In any of these color pickers, you can also "sample" a color that's outside the dialog box—a color you found on a web page, for example. Just click the eyedropper icon and then move your cursor around the screen. You'll see the sliders and numbers change inside the dialog box automatically when you click.

Finally, note that you can store frequently used (or frequently admired) colors in the tiny palette squares at the bottom. To do that, drag the big rectangular color swatch (next to the eyedropper) directly over into one of the little squares, where it will stay fresh for weeks.

If you don't have space for all the colors you want at the bottom of the window, you can grab the line above the eyedropper and drag it up to make room for more.

Incidentally, the Mac has no idea what sizes and shapes your window may assume in its lifetime. Therefore, it makes no attempt to scale down a selected photo to fit neatly into the window. If you have a high-res digital camera, therefore, you may see only the upper-left corner of your photo in the window. For better results, use a graphics program to scale the picture down to something smaller than your screen resolution.

Use as Defaults

This harmless-looking button can actually wreak havoc on your kingdom—or restore order to it—with a single click. It applies the changes you've just made in the View Options dialog box to all icon-view windows on your Mac (instead of only the front-most window). If you set up the frontmost window with a colored background, big icons, small text, and a tight grid, and then you click Use as Defaults, you'll see that look in every disk or folder window you open. You've been warned.

Fortunately, there are two auxiliary controls that can give you a break from all the sameness:

- **First, you can set up individual windows** to be exceptions to the rule; see page 34.

- **Second, you can remove any departures** from the default window view—after a round of disappointing experimentation on a particular window, for example—using a secret button. Choose View→Show View Options to open the View Options dialog box. Now hold down the Option key. The Use as Defaults button magically changes to Restore to Defaults, which means "Abandon all the changes I've foolishly made to the look of this window."

Tip: In the View Options for your Home folder, a checkbox appears: Show Library Folder. The Library folder is usually hidden, to prevent clueless newbies from wreaking havoc on important files. But macOS is willing to give it back to you—if you know about this sneaky little trick.

Group By and Sort By

You can wield two different kinds of control over the layout of files in a Finder window: grouping and sorting.

Note: You can perform all these obsessive reorganizations in *any view:* icon view, list view, column view, or gallery view.

Grouping

Grouping files means "Put my files into related clumps, separated by headings that identify them." For example, you can arrange your documents into Application groups (meaning which program opens each one); now you can see at a glance which files will open in, say, Music when you double-click them. Or you can organize your Pictures folder into Date Added groups, with headings like "Today," "Last 7 Days," and "Earlier."

To use groups, turn on View→Use Groups. Then use the View→Group By submenu to specify how you want your icons grouped. There are some incredibly useful options here; Figure 1-16 shows a few examples.

Tip: In icon view, the icons under each heading appear in a *single row*, scrolling off endlessly to the right. Use the usual sideways-scrolling gesture to flip through a row. (That is, swipe to the left on a trackpad with two fingers, or with one finger on a Magic Mouse.)

If you're not into gestures, or if you don't have a swipeable input device, then click the tiny Show All button at the right end of a row. Now you've turned off that one-row-per-heading thing, and all the icons under that heading appear in the usual rows and columns; scroll down to see them all.

Figure 1-16:
You can view your Finder-window files in neat little groups, separated by headings.

Top: The Applications window, in icon view, grouped by Application Category.

Middle: The Documents folder, in list view, grouped by Application (meaning "which program opens this document").

Bottom: A pictures folder, in column view, grouped by Date Added.

Apple wants to make extra, extra sure you're aware of the Group commands. It gives you four different ways to find them:

- **Choose View→Group By.** Choose one of the criteria from the submenu. Your options are Name (alphabetically); Kind (type of file, like Images, Movies, and Documents); Application (which program opens which documents); Date (Last Opened, Added [to the window], Modified, or Created); Size; or Tags (Finder Tag colors, described on page 89). Marvel as the Finder puts your files into tidy categorized groups.

Note: When you're looking at the Applications folder, you get a special choice: Application Category. It clumps your programs by what they do: Productivity, Social Networking, Music, Video, Board Games, Entertainment, Utilities, Reference, Photography, and so on. Pretty cool, actually.

- **Choose from the** ⊞ **icon.** This icon appears in the toolbar of every Finder window. It contains the same options listed in the previous bullet.

- **Right-click or two-finger click an empty spot in an icon-view window; choose from the Group By shortcut menu.** Yep, it's those same commands again.

- **In the View Options palette (seen in Figure 1-14), use the Group By pop-up menu.** Yes, it's a fourth place to find the same options.

In each case, you can choose None to turn off the grouping altogether.

Tip: On the desktop, macOS offers a supercharged way to group your icons: desktop stacks, described on page 74.

Remember, grouping (clumping) is not sorting. You can, in fact, sort the icons differently within each arranged group; read on.

Sorting

Sorting means just what it says: You can sort your files alphabetically (by Name), chronologically (by Date), in order of hugeness (by Size), and so on. See Figure 1-17.

You can sort a window whether or not you've also grouped it. You can even sort by different criteria. For example, you might have the programs in your Applications folder grouped by category but sorted alphabetically within each category.

Figure 1-17:
You can use either the View menu or the View Options window (right) to turn on permanent cleanliness mode. You've told the Mac to keep these icons on the invisible grid, sorted the way you requested. Just don't get frustrated when you try to drag an icon and discover that it won't budge.

Once again, Apple gives you four ways to sort:

- Option-click the ⊞ icon in the toolbar of the Finder window.

- Choose View→Sort By.

- Right-click or two-finger click an empty spot in an icon-view window.

- In the View Options palette, use the Sort By pop-up menu.

In each case, you've opened a menu of sorting criteria: Name, Kind, Date, Size, and so on.

Tip: In icon view, you get an additional option: Snap to Grid (see Figure 1-17). It means "Let me drag these icons into any sequence I want." When you release each drag, the icon jumps into the nearest position on the underlying spacing grid (unless you press the ⌘ key, which gives you full manual control over the icon's position).

In general, this option disappears if you're using one of the Group By options. After all, if you've asked the Mac to arrange your icons into groups, then you've relinquished control of their grid spacing. (The exception: You can still move icons when they're grouped by name—but only if you're dragging into gaps that maintain alphabetical order.)

Free dragging—and grid spacing

Whenever you've applied a Group or Sort to an icon view, the icons remain rooted to an invisible underlying rows-and-columns grid. You can't budge them.

Tip: You can, however, control how tight or loose that grid is, using the "Grid spacing" slider described on page 35.

But there are two situations when you're allowed to drag icons freely into any order you want:

- **Icons never snap to the grid.** If both Group By and Sort By are set to None, then you can go nuts, freely dragging icons into sloppy, off-the-grid positions.

 If, later, you become overwhelmed by shame at your untidiness, you can choose View→Clean Up. Now all the icons in the window jump to the closest positions on the invisible underlying grid.

 This same command appears in the shortcut menu when you right-click or two-finger click anywhere inside an icon-view window, which is handier if you have a huge monitor. There's even a Clean Up By submenu in the View menu and the shortcut menu. These commands don't just put icons back onto the closest grid positions; they put the icons into their proper sorted positions among the other icons—by name, size, date, and so on.

- **Icons always snap to the grid.** If Group By is set to None but Sort By is set to Snap to Grid, then you can drag icons into any order you like (that is, not in any particular sorted order)—but they'll snap to the grid when you let go of the mouse button.

Tip: If you press the ⌘ key as you release the drag, you can reverse the snapping logic. That is, the icons *will* snap to the grid if Sort By is set to None, but you can drag them freely if it's set to Snap to Grid. (Don't press the key until after you've begun to drag.)

Although it doesn't occur to most people, you can also apply any of the commands described in this section—Clean Up, Group, Sort—to icons lying loose on your desktop. Even though they don't seem to be in any window at all, you can specify small or large icons, automatic alphabetical arrangement, and so on. Just click the desktop before using the View menu or the View Options dialog box.

Note: There's only one View Options dialog box. Once it's open, you can adjust the icon sizes or arrangement options of other windows just by clicking them. Each time you click inside a window, the View Options dialog box remains in front, changing to reflect the settings of the window you just clicked.

Incidentally, you can get rid of the View Options box the same way you summoned it: by pressing ⌘-J.

List View

In windows that contain a lot of icons, list view is a powerful weapon in the battle against chaos. It shows you a tidy table of your files' names, dates, sizes, and so on (Figure 1-18). You get to decide how wide your columns should be, which of them should appear, and in what order (except that Name is always the first column). Here's how to master these columns.

Sorting the List

Most of the world's list-view fans like their files listed alphabetically. It's occasionally useful, however, to view the newest files first, largest ones first, or whatever.

When a desktop window displays its icons in list view, a convenient strip of column headings appears. These headings aren't just signposts; they're buttons, too. Click Name for alphabetical order, Date Modified to view the newest first, Size to view the largest files at the top, and so on.

Don't miss the tiny ∧ or ∨ that appears in the column you've most recently clicked. It shows you which way the list is being sorted. When it's ∧, then the oldest files, smallest files, or files beginning with numbers (or the letter A) appear at the top of the list, depending on which sorting criterion you selected (see Figure 1-18).

Tip: It may help you to remember that when the smallest portion of the triangle is at the top (∧), the smallest files are listed first when viewed in size order.

To reverse the sorting order, click the column heading again. Now the ∨ shows you that the newest files, largest files, or files beginning with the letter Z appear at the top of the list.

Note: You can also change the sorting order using the Sort By command described earlier. But, honestly, clicking the column headings is much faster.

Figure 1-18:
You control the sorting order of a list view by clicking the column headings (top). Click a second time to reverse the sorting order (bottom). You'll find the ∧ or ∨ triangles—indicating the identical information—in email programs, Music, and anywhere else where reversing the sorting order of a list can be useful.

Grouping the List

You can arrange your list view into groups by name, date, kind, and so on, with tidy headings that help you make sense of it all. This unsung feature is described under "Group By and Sort By" on page 39.

Flippy Triangles

One of the Mac's most attractive features is the tiny triangle that appears to the left of a folder's name in a list view. In its official documents, Apple calls these buttons *disclosure triangles;* internally, the programmers call them *flippy triangles.* (They don't appear if you've sorted the window using the View→Group By menu.)

When you click one, the list view turns into an outline, showing the contents of the folder in an indented list, as shown in Figure 1-19. Click the triangle again to collapse the folder listing. You're saved the trouble and clutter of opening a new window just to view the folder's contents.

By selectively clicking flippy triangles, you can in effect peer inside two or more folders simultaneously, all within a single list-view window. You can move files around by dragging them onto the tiny folder icons.

Figure 1-19:
Click a "flippy triangle" (left) to see the list of the folders and files inside that folder (right). Or press the equivalent keystrokes: ▶ (to open) and ◀ (to close).

GEM IN THE ROUGH

Flippy Triangle Keystrokes

The keystrokes that let you open and close flippy triangles in a list view are worth committing to memory.

First, pressing the Option key when you click a flippy triangle lets you view a folder's contents *and* the contents of any folders inside it. The result, in other words, is a longer list that may involve several levels of indentation.

If you prefer to use the keyboard, substitute ▶ (to expand a selected folder's flippy triangle) or ◀ (to collapse the folder listing again). Here again, adding the Option key expands or collapses *all* levels of folders within the selected one.

Suppose, for example, that you want to find out how many files are in your Pictures folder. The trouble is, you've organized your graphics files within that folder in several category folders. And you realize that the "how many items" statistic in the status bar shows only how many icons are

visible in the window. In other words, you won't know your total photo count until you've expanded all the folders within the Pictures folder.

You could perform the entire routine from the keyboard like this: Get to your Home folder by pressing Shift-⌘-H. Select the Pictures folder by typing the letter P. Open it by pressing ⌘-O (the shortcut for File→Open) or ⌘-▼. Switch to list view, if necessary, with a quick ⌘-2. Highlight the entire contents by pressing ⌘-A (short for Edit→Select All).

Now that all folders are highlighted, press Option-▶. You may have to wait a moment for the Mac to open every subfolder of every subfolder. But, eventually, the massive list appears, complete with many levels of indentation. At last, the "items" statistic in the status bar gives you a complete, updated tally of how many files and folders, combined, are in the window.

Tip: Once you've expanded a folder by clicking its flippy triangle, you can even drag a file icon out of the folder so it's loose in the list-view window. To do so, drag it directly upward onto the column headings area (where it says Name, for example). When you release the mouse, you see that the file is no longer inside the expanded folder.

Your Choice of Columns

Choose View→Show View Options. In the dialog box that appears, you're offered on/off checkboxes for the different columns of information macOS can show you, as illustrated in Figure 1-20:

- **iCloud Status.** This checkbox is dimmed for every folder except what's in your iCloud Drive folder (page 210). If you turn it on, you'll get a column that indicates whether or not each file has been downloaded from iCloud to your Mac.

- **Date Modified.** This date-and-time stamp indicates when a document was last saved. Its accuracy, of course, depends on the accuracy of your Mac's built-in clock.

Note: Many an up-to-date file has been lost because someone spotted a very old date on a folder and assumed that the files inside were equally old. That's because the modification date shown for a folder doesn't reflect the age of its contents. Instead, the date on a folder indicates only when items were last moved into or out of that folder. The actual files inside may be much older, or much more recent.

- **Date Created.** This date-and-time stamp shows when a document was *first* saved.

- **Date Last Opened.** Just what it sounds like.

- **Date Added.** This option shows when a file was added to this folder or window.

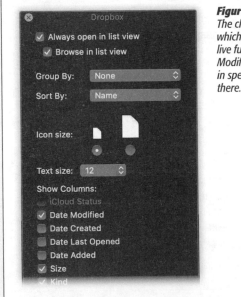

Figure 1-20:
The checkboxes you turn on in the View Options dialog box determine which columns of information appear in a list-view window. Many people live full and satisfying lives with only the three default columns—Date Modified, Size, and Kind—turned on. But the other columns can be helpful in special circumstances; the trick is knowing what information appears there.

- **Size.** With a glance, you can tell from this column how much disk space each of your files and folders is taking up in kilobytes, megabytes, gigabytes, or terabytes—whichever the Mac thinks you'll find most helpful.

Tip: For disks and folders, you see only dashes—at first. You can, however, instruct the Mac to reveal their sizes, as described on page 48.

- **Kind.** In this column, you can read what kind of file each icon represents. You may see, for example, Folder, JPEG Image, Application, and so on.

- **Version.** This column displays the version numbers of your programs. For folders and documents, you just see dashes.

- **Comments.** This rarely seen column (Figure 1-21) can actually be among the most useful. Suppose you're a person who uses the Comments feature (highlight an icon, choose File→Get Info, type notes about that item into the Comments box). This column displays the first line of those comments about each icon, which comes in handy when tracking multiple versions of your documents.

Figure 1-21:
If your screen is big enough, you can expand the Comments column to show several paragraphs, all in a single line. (To enter some comments about an icon, type into the Comments box in its Get Info box, as shown here at right.)

- **Tag.** Tags are colors and identifying phrases you can slap onto icons, wherever they appear, to help you categorize and group them. For details, see page 89.

 Even with this column turned off, you can still see an icon's color, of course. But only by turning on this column do you get to see the text phrase you've associated with each label.

Other View Options

The View Options for a list view include several other useful settings; choose View→ Show View Options or press ⌘-J.

- **Always open in list view.** Turn on this option to override your system-wide preference setting for all windows. See page 34 for details.

- **Browse in list view.** Ensures that any folder inside this one will also open up in list view, even if its regularly scheduled view is something else.

- **Icon size.** These two buttons offer you a choice of icon sizes for the current window: either tiny or standard. Unlike icon view, list view doesn't give you a size slider.

 Fortunately, even the tiny icons aren't so small that they show up blank. You still get a general idea of what they're supposed to look like.

- **Text size.** You can change the type size for your icon labels, either globally or one window at a time.

- **Show columns.** Turn on the columns you'd like to appear in the current window's list view, as described in the previous section.

- **Use relative dates.** In a list view, the Date Modified, Date Added, Date Last Opened, and Date Created columns generally display information in a format like this: "December 24, 2018 at 11:01 AM." (The Mac uses shorter date formats as the column gets narrower.) But when the "Use relative dates" option is turned on, it substitutes the words "Yesterday" or "Today" where appropriate, making recent files easier to spot.

- **Calculate all sizes.** See the box below.

- **Show icon preview.** Exactly as in icon view, this option turns the icons of graphics files into miniatures of the photos or images within.

FREQUENTLY ASKED QUESTION

Calculate All Sizes

When I sort my list view by size, I see only dashes for folder sizes. What am I doing wrong?

Nothing at all; that's normal. When viewing a Finder window, you see a Size statistic for each file. For folders and disks, however, you sometimes see only uninformative dashes.

Most Mac fans study this anomaly momentarily, scratch their chins, and then get back to their work. (Former Windows people don't even scratch their chins; Windows PCs *never* show folder-size or disk-size information in list views.)

Here's what's going on: In the olden days (like 2016), it could take a computer a long time to add up the sizes of all files inside a folder. Your System→Library folder alone, for example, contains over 100,000 files. Instead of making you wait while it did all the addition, the Mac simply showed you dashes in the folder's Size column.

On occasion, however, you really did want to see how big your folders were. In such cases, you could choose View→ Show View Options and turn on "Calculate all sizes." You'd see the folder sizes slowly begin to pop onto the screen, from the top of the window down, as the Mac crunched the numbers on the files within.

In fact, you could even turn on the "Calculate all sizes" option *globally*—that is, for all windows.

The "Calculate all sizes" option is still there in macOS, and you can still turn it on or off. But a lot has changed now, thanks to the Apple File System (page 471). Among the virtues of this filing system, it makes turning on "Calculate all sizes" instantaneous for all but the largest folders. There's really no reason not to have it turned on for all folders, all the time.

- **Use as Defaults.** Click to make your changes in the View Options box apply to all windows in that view on your Mac. (Option-click this button to restore a wayward window back to your defaults.)

Rearranging Columns

You're stuck with the Name column at the far left of a window. However, you can rearrange the other columns just by dragging their gray column headers horizontally. If the Mac thinks you intend to drop a column to, say, the left of the column it overlaps, you'll actually see an animated movement—indicating a column reshuffling—even before you release the mouse button.

Adjusting Column Widths

If you place your cursor carefully on the dividing line between two column headings, you'll find that you can drag the divider line horizontally. Doing so makes the column to the left of your cursor wider or narrower.

What's delightful about this activity is watching macOS scramble to rewrite its information to fit the space you give it. For example, as you make the Date Modified (or Created) column narrower, "March 7, 2020 at 2:22 PM" shrinks first to "Mar 7, 2020 at 2:22 PM," then to "3/7/20, 2:22 PM," and finally to a terse "3/7/20."

If you make a column too narrow, macOS shortens the file names by removing text from the middle. An ellipsis (…) appears to show you where the missing text would have appeared. (Apple reasoned that truncating the ends of file names would hide useful information, like the numbers at the end of "Letter to Marge 1," "Letter to Marge 2," and so on. It would also hide the extensions, such as Thesis.doc, that may appear on file names in macOS.)

For example, suppose you've named a Word document "Kim Kardashian A Major Force for Righteousness and Cure for Depression, Acne, and Migraine Headache." (Yes, file names really can be that long.) If the Name column is too narrow, you might see only "Kim Kardashian—A Major…Migraine Headache."

Tip: You don't have to make the column mega-wide to read the full text of a file whose name has been shortened. Just point to the icon's name without clicking. After a moment, a floating balloon appears—something like a tooltip in Microsoft programs—to identify the full name.

In fact, you can hover your mouse up or down a list over truncated file names, and their tooltip balloons appear instantaneously. (This trick works in list, column, and gallery views—and in Save and Open dialog boxes, for that matter.)

Column View

The goal of column view is simple: to let you burrow down through nested folders without leaving a trail of messy, overlapping windows in your wake. The solution is

shown in Figure 1-22. It's a list view that's divided into vertical panes. The first pane (not counting the Sidebar) shows whatever disk or folder you first opened.

When you click a disk or folder in this list (once), the second pane shows a list of everything in it. Each time you click a folder in one pane, the pane to its right shows what's inside. The other panes slide to the left, sometimes out of view. (Use the horizontal scroll bar to bring them back.) You can keep clicking until you're looking at the file icons inside the most deeply nested folder.

If you discover that your hunt for a particular file has taken you down a blind alley, it's not a big deal to backtrack, since the trail of folders you've followed to get here is still sitting before you on the screen. As soon as you click a different folder in one of the earlier panes, the panes to its right suddenly change, so you can burrow down a different rabbit hole.

Figure 1-22:
If the rightmost folder contains pictures, sounds, Office documents, or movies, then you can look at them or play them right there in the Finder. You can drag this jumbo preview icon anywhere—into another folder or to the Trash, for example.

The beauty of column view is that, first of all, it keeps your screen tidy. It effectively shows you several simultaneous folder levels but contains them within a single window. With a quick ⌘-W, you can close the window, panes and all. Second, column view provides an excellent sense of where you are. Because your trail is visible at all times, it's much harder to get lost—wondering what folder you're in and how you got there—than in any other window view.

Column View by Keyboard

Efficiency fans can operate this entire process by keyboard alone. For example:

• **You can jump from one column** to the next by pressing the ◀ or ▶ keys.

- **You can use the Go menu,** or the icons in the Sidebar, to fill your columns with the contents of the corresponding folder—Home, Favorites, Applications, and so on.

- **The Back command** (clicking the ‹ button on the toolbar, pressing ⌘-[, or choosing Go→Back) works as it does in a web browser: It retraces your steps backward. Once you've gone back, in fact, you can then go forward again; choose Go→Forward, click the › button on the toolbar, or press ⌘-].

- **Within a highlighted column,** press the ▲ or ▼ keys to highlight successive icons in the list. Or type the first couple of letters of an icon's name to jump directly to it.

- **When you finally highlight the icon you've been looking for,** press ⌘-O or ⌘-▼ to open it (or double-click it, of course). You can open anything in any column; you don't have to wait until you've reached the rightmost column.

Manipulating the Columns

The number of columns you can see without scrolling depends on the width of the window. That's not to say, however, that you're limited to four columns (or whatever fits on your monitor). You can make the columns wider or narrower—either individually or all at once—to suit the situation, according to this scheme:

- **To make a single column wider or narrower,** drag the vertical dividing line at its right edge (see Figure 1-23). To adjust all the columns simultaneously, press the Option key as you drag the handle.

Figure 1-23:
When you move your cursor close to the divider line between columns, you get a double-headed arrow. That's a sign that you can now drag that line to adjust the width of the column to its left.

- **To make a column precisely as wide as necessary** to reveal all the names of its contents, double-click the handle on its right side.

- **To make *all* columns as wide as required**—when you absolutely, positively don't want any names truncated—Option-double-click a column's right-side handle.

Tip: If you're having trouble remembering all those key and click combinations, you're not alone. Fortunately, if you right-click or two-finger click the handle at the right side of a column, you get a shortcut menu that offers these commands: Right Size This Column (make it exactly as wide as necessary), Right Size All Columns Individually (make *every* column exactly as wide as necessary), and Right Size All Columns Equally (make all columns *the same width,* based on whatever width is necessary to see all the names in the *narrowest* one).

Grouping the Column Contents

The Group commands are available to column view, too; you can add those category headings to the clumps of files in each window. It all works exactly as described starting on page 39.

View Options

Just as in icon and list views, you can choose View→Show View Options to open a dialog box—a spartan one, in this case—offering additional control over your column views.

- **Always open in column view.** Once again, this option lets you override your system-wide preference setting for all windows. See page 34 for details.

- **Browse in column view.** Ensures that any folder inside this one will open up in column view when double-clicked.

- **Group By, Sort By.** You can put column-view icons into arranged groups—and sort them within those groups—just as described starting on page 39.

- **Text size** affects the type used for icons in all column views.

- **Show icons.** For maximum speed, turn off this option. Now you see only file names—not the tiny icons next to them—in all column views. Weird!

- **Show icon preview.** Turn off this option if you don't want the tiny icons in column view to display their actual contents—photos showing their images, Word and PDF documents showing their first pages, and so on. You get generic, identical icons for each file type (text, photo, or whatever).

- **Show preview column.** The far-right preview column can be handy when you're browsing graphics, sounds, or movie files. Feel free to enlarge this final column when you want a better view of the picture or movie; you can make it really big.

 The rest of the time, though, the preview column can get in the way, slightly slowing down the works and pushing other, more useful columns off to the left side of the window. If you turn off this checkbox, then the preview column will be empty.

Tip: No matter what view you're in, remember this: If you ever start dragging an icon and then change your mind, just press the Esc key or ⌘-period, even while the mouse button is still down. The icon flies back to its precise starting place. Or, if you've already dragged something to a new window and now you regret it, press ⌘-Z (for Undo). Too bad real life doesn't have a similar feature.

Gallery View

The old Cover Flow view has received a tweak. It still displays a jumbo preview of each icon as you arrow-key your way through the items in a folder. But now the icons themselves appear in a horizontal row instead of in a list view (Figure 1-24). And you no longer get to see the icons' names (unless you're pointing to one).

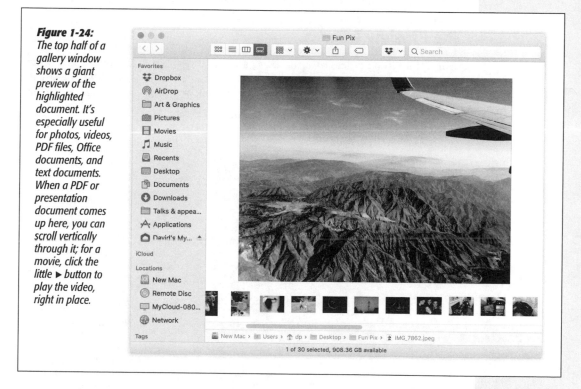

Figure 1-24:
The top half of a gallery window shows a giant preview of the highlighted document. It's especially useful for photos, videos, PDF files, Office documents, and text documents. When a PDF or presentation document comes up here, you can scroll vertically through it; for a movie, click the little ▶ button to play the video, right in place.

In any case, gallery view is ideal for perusing folders full of pictures. It lets you get a good, clear view of each file without actually having to open it.

To fire up gallery view, open a window. Then click the Gallery button (▦) in the toolbar. Or choose View→as Gallery, or press ⌘-4.

Now the window splits. On the bottom: a scrolling row of icons. On the top: the giant preview of whichever one is highlighted. It's probably not something you'd want to set up for every folder, because browsing is a pretty inefficient way to find something.

But in folders that contain photos or movies (and aren't filled with hundreds of files), gallery view can be a handy and satisfying way to browse.

And now, notes on gallery view:

- **Multipage documents, presentation files, movies, and sounds are special.** When you point to one, you get the ▶ button and a scrubber bar. For a Keynote or PowerPoint file, you get a vertical scroll bar to move through the slides. If it's a PDF document, you can use your trackpad or mouse wheel to move through the pages vertically.

- **The previews are actual icons.** When you're looking at a gallery view mini-document, you can drag it with your mouse—you've got the world's biggest target—anywhere you'd like: another folder, the Trash, wherever.

The Preview Pane

In any of the four Finder views, there's yet another way to see instant previews of what's in each file you highlight (the words in a Word file, the image in a JPEG photo, the numbers in an Excel spreadsheet, and so on). It's called the preview pane (Figure 1-25).

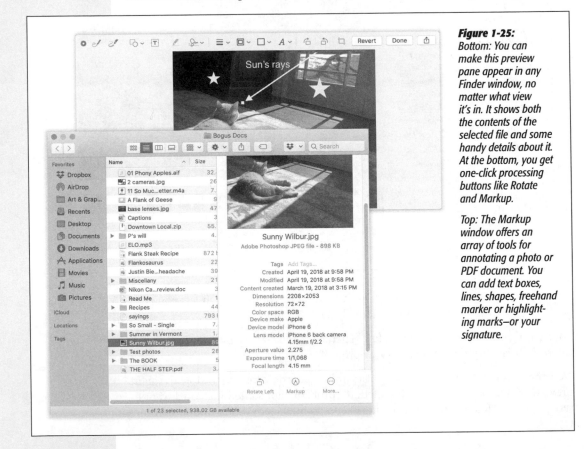

Figure 1-25:
Bottom: You can make this preview pane appear in any Finder window, no matter what view it's in. It shows both the contents of the selected file and some handy details about it. At the bottom, you get one-click processing buttons like Rotate and Markup.

Top: The Markup window offers an array of tools for annotating a photo or PDF document. You can add text boxes, lines, shapes, freehand marker or highlighting marks—or your signature.

To see it, choose View→Show Preview (or press Shift-⌘-P). Now there's a full-height preview pane at the right side of the window. It shows the contents of the highlighted file, along with a dossier of details about it. Depending on the kind of file it is, you may see its name, date, and size; author (Word documents); number of pages and level of security (PDF files); album name, audio channels, and duration (music files); aperture, shutter speed, resolution, lens, and focal length (photos); and so on.

At the bottom, you'll find Quick Actions buttons, relevant to the kind of file you've clicked. For a photo, the buttons are Rotate, Markup, and (when you click the More ⊙ button) Create PDF. For a PDF document, it's Markup and maybe Add Password. For an audio or video file, there's a Trim button.

Tip: These Quick Actions commands also show up in the shortcut menu that appears when you right-click or two-finger click an icon. They're also on the MacBook Pro's Touch Bar, and in every Quick Look window.

In every case, the More ⊙ menu offers a Customize command. In the resulting box, you're treated to a master list of every Quick Actions button the preview pane can display. At the outset, it's not such a big list: Rotate, Markup, Create PDF, and Trim.

Fortunately, other apps can add to this list, and so can you, if you're handy with Automator. (See the Automator.pdf appendix on this book's page at *missingmanuals.com*; when you create your new workflow in Automator, choose Contextual Workflow as the file type.)

In general, you'll probably wind up using the preview pane, and those Quick Actions buttons, mostly for working through folders of photos, and maybe PDF files.

To turn off the pane, choose View→Hide Preview.

Quick Look

As the preceding several thousand pages make clear, there are lots of ways to view and manage the teeming mass of files and folders on a typical hard drive. Some of them actually let you see what's in a document without having to open it—the preview column in column view, the giant icons in gallery, the preview pane, and so on.

Quick Look takes this idea to another level. It lets you open and browse a document at nearly full size—without switching window views or opening any new programs (see Figure 1-26). You highlight an icon (or several) and then do one of these things:

- **Press the space bar.** This is by far the best technique to learn. After all, unless you're editing a file's name, what has the space bar ever done for you in the Finder? Nothing. But in macOS, you can highlight any icon and then tap the space bar for an instant preview.

- **Choose File→Quick Look, or press ⌘-Y, or click the ◉ icon at the top of the window.** The space bar is still better.

- **Right-click or two-finger click an icon; choose Quick Look.**

• Tap the 👁 icon on your Touch Bar (page 227), if you have one.

You exit Quick Look in any one of these same ways.

Note: Whenever Quick Look appears in a menu or shortcut menu, its wording changes to reflect the name of the icon. For example, it might say "Quick Look 'Secret Diary.doc.' "

In any case, the Quick Look window now opens, showing a gigantic preview of the document (Figure 1-26). Rather nice, eh?

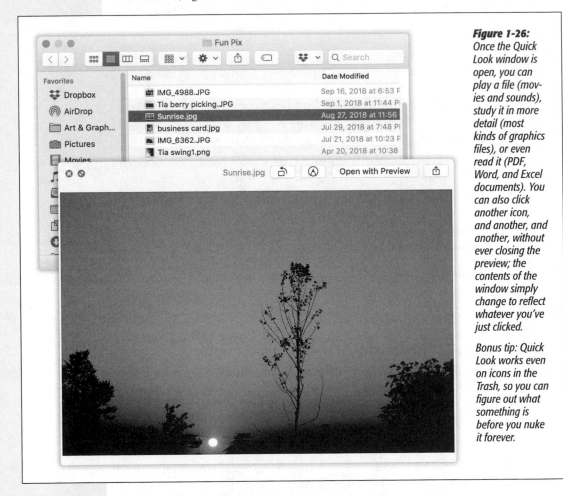

Figure 1-26:
Once the Quick Look window is open, you can play a file (movies and sounds), study it in more detail (most kinds of graphics files), or even read it (PDF, Word, and Excel documents). You can also click another icon, and another, and another, without ever closing the preview; the contents of the window simply change to reflect whatever you've just clicked.

Bonus tip: Quick Look works even on icons in the Trash, so you can figure out what something is before you nuke it forever.

The idea here is that you can check out a document without having to wait for it to open in the traditional way—at full size. For example, you can read the text in a Word or PowerPoint document without actually having to open Word or PowerPoint, which saves you about 45 minutes.

You may even be able to edit your document right in the Quick Look pane. Tucked along the top of the window, you'll find the same Quick Actions buttons described on page 55: for pictures, Rotate and Markup; for PDF documents, Markup; and so on.

Tip: You can use the usual "next page" gesture (two-finger swipe up or down on a trackpad, one-finger swipe on the Magic Mouse) to page through PDF or iWork documents, or to move among photos if you've highlighted a whole bunch.

It's astonishing how few Mac fans are aware of this useful feature. Learn it!

What Quick Look Knows

Quick Look doesn't recognize all documents. If you try to preview, for example, a Final Cut Pro video project, a sheet-music file, a .zip archive, or a database file, all you'll see is a 6-inch-tall version of its generic icon. You won't see what's inside.

People can write plug-ins for those nonrecognized programs. For example, plug-ins that let you see what's inside folders and .zip files await at *quicklookplugins.com*. In the meantime, here's what Quick Look recognizes right out of the box:

- **Graphics files and photos.** This is where Quick Look can really shine, because it's often useful to get a quick look at a photo without having to haul Photos or Photoshop out of bed. Quick Look recognizes all common graphics formats, including TIFF, JPEG, GIF, PNG, RAW, and Photoshop documents.

- **PDF and text files.** Using the scroll bar or a two-finger swipe, you can page through multipage documents, right there in the Quick Look window.

- **Audio and movie files.** These begin to play instantly when you open them into the Quick Look window. Most popular formats work (MP3, AIFF, AAC, MPEG-4, H.264, and so on). A scroll bar appears so you can jump around.

- **Pages, Numbers, Keynote, and TextEdit documents.** Naturally, since these are Apple programs, Quick Look understands the document formats.

- **Microsoft Word, Excel, and PowerPoint documents.** Move through the pages using the vertical scroll bar or a two-finger swipe; switch to a different Excel spreadsheet page using the Sheet tabs at the bottom.

- **Fonts.** Totally cool. When you open a font file in Quick Look, you get a crystal-clear, huge sampler that shows every letter of the alphabet in that typeface.

- **vCards.** A vCard is an address-book entry that people can send by email to save time in updating their Rolodexes. When you drag a name out of Apple's or Microsoft's address books and onto the desktop, for example, it turns into a vCard document. In Quick Look, the vCard opens up as a handsomely formatted index card that displays all that person's contact information.

- **HTML (web pages) and Safari archived pages.** If you've saved some web pages to your hard drive, here's a great way to inspect them without firing up your web browser.

In fact, Quick Look has started seeping into other programs—not just the Finder. For example, you can preview any of the following:

- **A link in a Mail message.** In Mail, a tiny ▾ appears next to each web link when you hover your mouse over it. Click it to view the actual web page it leads to, right there in a pop-up bubble!

- **An address in Mail.** If you ever see a street address in an email message, click the ▾ that appears next to it when you hover your mouse. You're offered the chance to add this person to your address book or to see a map of that address in Maps.

- **Files in the Open dialog box.** From within any program, whenever you choose File→Open to view the list of files and folders on your drive, you can tap the space bar to get an instant preview of each.

- **An address in Contacts.** In the Contacts program, click the label for an address (like "Work" or "Home"); from the shortcut menu, choose Open in Maps.

- **Anything in Mission Control or a Dock menu.** You can also tap the space bar to get a Quick Look preview of anything in the Mission Control view (page 177) or the stack, list, or grid of a Dock folder (page 136).

And you were alive to see the day!

The Quick Look Slideshow

The Mac is supposed to be all about graphics and other visual delights. No wonder, then, that it offers a built-in, full-screen slideshow feature.

Figure 1-27:
Once the slideshow is underway, you can use this control bar. It lets you pause, move forward or backward, enlarge the "slide" to fill the screen, or end the show. The Index Sheet view (▫▫) is especially handy. (You can press ⌘-Return to "click" the Index Sheet button.) It displays an array of miniatures, all at once—a sort of Exposé for Quick Look. Click a thumbnail to jump directly to the Quick Look document you want to inspect.

It works like this: Highlight a bunch of icons, and then open Quick Look. Click the ⊙ (Full Screen) button in the top-left corner. Click the Play button. The screen goes black, and the documents begin their slideshow. Each image appears on the screen for about three seconds before the next one appears. (Press the Esc key to end the show.) It plays all documents it recognizes, not just graphics. Use the control bar shown in Figure 1-27 to manage the playback.

It's a useful feature when you've just downloaded or imported a bunch of photos or Office documents and want a quick look through them.

Note: This same slideshow mechanism is available for graphics in Preview and Mail; Preview even offers crossfades between pictures.

Fun with Quick Look

Here are some stunts that make Quick Look even more interesting:

- **Full screen.** When you click the Full Screen button (the gray ⊙), the Quick Look window expands to fill your screen. Keep this trick in mind when you're trying to read Word, Excel, or PDF documents, since the text is usually too small to read otherwise. (When you're finished with the close-up, click the ⊙ button in the control bar to restore the original Quick Look window, or the ✖ button to exit Quick Look altogether.)

Tip: How's this for an undocumented shortcut? If you highlight an icon and then press Option-space bar, or Option-click the eyeball icon, you go straight into Full Screen mode without having to open the smaller Quick Look window first. Kewl.

(OK, this is actually part of the slideshow feature, but it's also good for super-enlarging a single icon.)

- **Share it.** Click the ⬆ in the title bar to open the Share pop-up menu—a quick way to send this document on to somebody or to post it online.

- **Open with [program name].** This button shows up at the top-right corner of your Quick Look window. It might say, for example, Open with Preview.

 Handy, really. It says: "Oh, so you've been Quick Looking to find a particular document, and this is the one you wanted? Click me to jump directly into the program that opens it, so you can get to work reading or editing. I've just saved your having to close the window and double-click the icon."

Tip: Actually, you have a much bigger target than the "Open with" button in the corner. You can double-click *anywhere in the Quick Look window* to open the document (in whatever program is named on the "Open with" button).

Better yet: If you click and hold your cursor on that "Open with" button, then you get a secret pop-up menu of other programs that could open the file you're looking at.

• **Keep it going.** Once you've opened Quick Look for one icon, you don't have to close it before inspecting another icon. Just keep clicking different icons (or pressing the arrow keys to walk through them); the Quick Look window changes instantly with each click to reflect the new document.

• **Fix the size.** Quick Look tries to display an entire picture or document in a single small window. To view it at actual size, hold down the Option key.

Keep Folders on Top

Hiding away in Finder→Preferences→Advanced, "Keep folders on top" awaits. It turns out to be incredibly useful (see Figure 1-28).

Figure 1-28:
Left: Ordinarily, folders (high-lighted here for clarity) appear sorted alphabet-ically into lists of loose files.

Right: But the "Keep folders on top in windows when sorting by name" option places them into their own neigh-borhood above the list.

• **In windows when sorting by name.** When you've sorted a window's contents alphabetically, all the folders now appear at the top of the list, in their own little alphabetical grouping. (Otherwise they appear mixed in with the loose files, all in one alphabetical list.) This "folders first" arrangement is how things work in Windows—and, although Apple may not have wanted to admit it for 30 years, it's pretty handy.

• **On Desktop.** This option applies the same idea to icons on your desktop: Folders appear first, and then loose files after them. (The checkbox has no effect if you have *not* opted to sort your desktop icons.)

Finder Tabs

The world discovered the miracle of tabs in *web browsers* years ago. It was a simple software design idea, modeled after the tabs of paper file folders, that let you keep multiple web pages open at once in a single window. What convenience! What cleanliness!

But it took until 2013 for someone to realize that tabs might be useful at the desktop, too. That's when Apple added tabs to Finder windows.

They do exactly the same job they do in Safari: They let you keep open the windows of several different containers—folders or disks—in a single window frame. That makes it easy to move icons back and forth between them (Figure 1-29), or even to view the same window twice in different views.

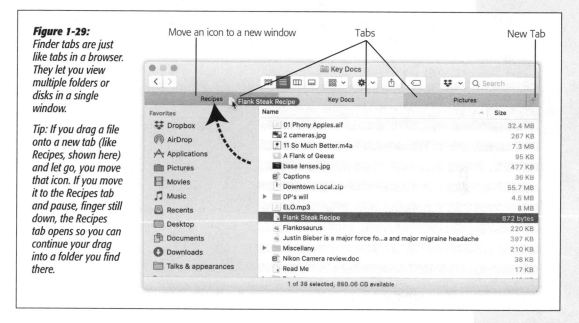

Figure 1-29:
Finder tabs are just like tabs in a browser. They let you view multiple folders or disks in a single window.

Tip: If you drag a file onto a new tab (like Recipes, shown here) and let go, you move that icon. If you move it to the Recipes tab and pause, finger still down, the Recipes tab opens so you can continue your drag into a folder you find there.

As a convenience, Apple designed the commands, keystrokes, and clicks to work exactly as they do in Safari.

Creating Tabs

There are almost as many ways to open new tabs as there are people:

- **Press the ⌘ key as you open a folder or disk.** (That shouldn't come as a shock; you ⌘-click a link to open a new tab in Safari, too.)

Tip: You can ⌘-click the names of places in the Sidebar of a Finder window, too, like Documents or Pictures.

- **Right-click or two-finger click a folder or disk.** From the shortcut menu, choose Open in New Tab.

- **If you already have some tabs, then click the + button at the far right.** (Even if you haven't created any tabs yet, that button appears if you've made the tab bar visible; choose View→Show Tab Bar.)

- **Drag a disk or folder icon onto the + button at the far right of the tab bar.**

- **Select a folder or disk (or several).** From the ✿ menu, choose Open in New Tab(s)—or press Control-⌘-O.

- **Choose File→New Tab,** or press ⌘-T.

Tip: And what will it show? Whatever you've chosen in the Finder→Preferences→General→"New Finder windows show" pop-up menu. It's usually your Recents window, or maybe the desktop's contents.

- **A New Tab button is also available to install onto your Touch Bar,** if you have one of those on your MacBook Pro (page 231).

Using Tabs

So why bother opening tabs? Because you can perform a few power-usery stunts now that you couldn't before. Like this:

- **Move files around.** You can drag a file or folder icon into another tab, as shown in Figure 1-29.

- **View the same window twice.** Put one copy of the window in list view, another in icon view. Or view different sections of a long list of files in two side-by-side tabs.

- **Live in a desktop-free world.** Click the green ⊙ button (upper-left corner) to put your Finder window into Full Screen mode. (See page 173 for more on Full Screen mode.)

Now you can work in tabs, manipulating your files, without ever seeing the desktop.

Tab Management

Once you've got some tabs adorning your window, you can operate them thusly:

- **To switch tabs,** click one, or press Control-Tab. (Add the Shift key to cycle through the tabs in reverse.) If you forget these important keystrokes, they're listed for you as commands in the Window menu.

- **Rearrange tabs** by dragging them horizontally.

- **Turn a tab into a stand-alone window** by dragging it away from the other tabs. (Or choose Window→Move Tab to New Window.)

Tip: There's no built-in keyboard shortcut for the Window-menu commands like Move Tab to New Window and Merge All Windows. But it's easy enough to add a shortcut of your own, as described on page 200.

- **Move a tab into a different window** by dragging it. That is, you can drag a tab from one window to another.

- **Round up a bunch of open windows** into a single tabbed window: Choose Window→Merge All Windows. That's a good one.

- **To close a tab,** press the usual "close window" keystroke, ⌘-W. (Or, if it's a slow day at work, choose File→Close Tab. Or move your cursor onto the tab itself and click the tiny ✕ that appears.)

- **To close all tabs,** add the Option key. For example, press Option-⌘-W or Option-click the Close button on one of the tabs.

Tabs in Other Apps

Apparently, you just can't keep a good idea down. Tabbed windows, which did so well in web browsers, eventually made their way to the Finder—and now they're in six *other* Apple programs: Mail, Maps, TextEdit, Pages, Keynote, and Numbers. Some non-Apple apps that are "document-based" (you work in multiple windows, each containing a different document) also have tabs.

For one reason or another, you *don't* get tabbed windowing in any other built-in Apple apps. And you don't get it in Microsoft programs.

If you're using one of the anointed apps, start by opening at least two windows. (Some apps, like Mail, create a new tab when you choose File→New Tab.) Choose Window→Merge All Windows to turn them into tabs. At this point, a + button appears at the top right of the window, so you can create a new blank tab.

Tip: If you like, those apps can open a new tab, rather than a separate window, every time you create a new document. In System Preferences→Dock, the "Prefer tabs when opening documents" pop-up menu offers three choices. "Always" means *every* new document will appear in a tab. "In Full Screen Only" means that new documents become tabs only when you're in Full Screen mode (page 173). And "Manually" means that new tabs appear only when you use the New Tab command.

At that point, you can switch tabs, rearrange them, close them, and separate them exactly as described already.

Logging Out, Shutting Down

If you're the only person who uses your Mac, finishing up a work session is simple. You can either turn off the machine or simply let it go to sleep, in any of several ways.

Sleep Mode

If you're still shutting down your Mac every night, you may be doing a lot more waiting than necessary. Sleep mode consumes very little power, keeps everything you were doing open and available, and wakes up almost immediately.

To make your machine sleep, do one of the following:

- **Close the lid.** (Hint: This works primarily on laptops.)

- **Press the power button (⏻) on your Mac.** Tapping that button (for about a half-second) makes any kind of Mac drop off to sleep instantly.

- **Hold down the power button (⏻) for two seconds.** You get the box shown in Figure 1-30; hit Sleep (or type S) or wait 60 seconds.

- **Choose →Sleep.** Or press Option-⌘-⏏.

- **Press Control-⏏.** In the dialog box shown in Figure 1-30, click Sleep (or type *S*).

- **Tap the Sleep button on your Touch Bar,** if you have one (and if you've installed the Sleep button there; see page 231).

- **Just walk away,** confident that the Energy Saver setting in System Preferences will send the machine off to dreamland automatically at the specified time.

Tip: Ordinarily, closing your MacBook's lid means cutting it off from the world. But the Power Nap feature lets your Mac stay connected to your network and to the internet, even while it's otherwise sleeping. It can download email, back up your stuff, download software updates, and so on. For details, see page 346.

Restart

You shouldn't have to restart the Mac very often—only in times of severe trouble-shooting mystification, in fact. Here are a few ways to do it:

- **Choose →Restart.** A confirmation box appears; click Restart (or press Return).

Tip: If you press Option as you release the mouse on the →Restart command, you won't be bothered by an "Are you sure?" confirmation box.

- **Press Control-⌘-⏏.**

- **Press Control-⏏** (or hold down the ⏻ button) to summon the dialog box shown in Figure 1-30; click Restart (or type *R*).

Shut Down

To shut down your machine completely (when you don't plan to use it for more than a couple of days, when you plan to transport it, and so on), do one of the following:

- **Choose →Shut Down.** A simple confirmation dialog box appears; click Shut Down (or press Return).

Tip: Once again, if you press Option as you release the mouse, no confirmation box appears.

Are you sure you want to shut down your computer now?

If you do nothing, the computer will shut down automatically in 54 seconds.

☐ Reopen windows when logging back in

Cancel Shut Down

Figure 1-30:
Once the Shut Down dialog box appears, you can press the S key instead of clicking Sleep, R for Restart, Esc for Cancel, or Return for Shut Down.

- **Press Control-Option-⌘-⏏.** (It's not as complex as it looks—the first three keys are all in a tidy row to the left of the space bar.)

- **Press Control-⏏** (or hold down the ⏻ button) to summon the dialog box shown in Figure 1-30. Click Shut Down (or press Return).

- **Wait.** If you've set up the Energy Saver preferences (page 344) to shut down the Mac automatically at a specified time, then you don't have to do anything.

The "Reopen Windows" Option

In Figure 1-30, you'll notice a checkbox called "Reopen windows when logging back in." That option does something very useful: The next time you start up your Mac, every running program, and every open window, will reopen exactly as they were at the moment you used the Restart or Shut Down command. This saves you a lot of reopening the next time you sit down to work.

If you turn off that checkbox when you click Restart or Shut Down, then your next startup will take you to the desktop, with no programs running, as though this were still some year between 1984 and 2010. And if you want the Mac to stop asking—if you never want your programs and windows to reopen—then open System Preferences→General, and turn on "Close windows when quitting an app."

Log Out

If you share your Mac, then you should log out when you're done. Doing so ensures that your stuff is safe from the evil and the clueless, even when you're out of the room. To do it, choose ﹩→Log Out [your name], or press Shift-⌘-Q.

When the confirmation dialog box appears, click Log Out (or press Return) or just wait for one minute (a message performs the countdown for you). The Mac hides your world from view and displays the Log In dialog box, ready for its next victim.

Tip: One more time: If you press Option as you release the mouse on the ﹩→Log Out command, you squelch the "Are you sure?" box.

Logging out is described in much more detail starting on page 502.

Getting Help in macOS

It's a good thing you've got a book about macOS in your hands, because the only manual you get with it is the Help menu, a browser-like program that reads a set of help files that reside in your System→Library folder.

Note: In fact, you may not even be that lucky. The general-information help page about each topic is on your Mac, but thousands of the more technical pages reside online and require an internet connection to read.

You're expected to find the topic you want in one of these three ways:

• **Use the search box.** The first "command" in the Help menu in any window is, in fact, a search box (Figure 1-31). You can type a few words here to specify what you want help with: "setting up printer," "disk space," whatever.

Figure 1-31:
You don't have to open the Help program to begin a search. No matter what program you're in, typing a search phrase into the box shown here produces an instantaneous list of help topics, ready to read.

GEM IN THE ROUGH

Menu Help in the Help Menu

MacOS contains a weird, wonderful little enhancement to its online help system. It helps you find menu commands.

You're floundering in some program. You're *sure* there's a page-numbering command. But there are 11 menus, and 143 submenus, hiding in those menus, and you haven't got time for the pain. That's when you should think of using the Help menu. When you type *page number* (or whatever) into its search box, the results menu lists, at the top, the names of any menu commands that contain the words you typed. Better still, it actually *opens that menu* for you, and displays a big, blue, animated, floating arrow pointing to the command you wanted. Slide your cursor over, click the command you wanted, and get on with your life.

Supertip: This feature is especially helpful in web browsers like Safari and Firefox, because it even finds entries in your Bookmarks and History menus! In Safari, for example, you can pluck a recently visited site out of the hundreds in the daily History submenus. You've just saved yourself a *lot* of poking around menus, trying to find the name of a site you know you've seen recently.

Ultratip: If you think about it, this feature also means that you have complete keyboard power over every menu in every program in the world. Hit Shift-⌘-/ (that is, ⌘-?) to open the Help search box, type a bit of the command's name, and then use the arrow keys to walk down the results. Hit Return to trigger the command you want.

Tip: You can also hit Shift-⌘-/ (that is, ⌘-?) to open the Help search box. And you can change that keystroke, if you like, in System Preferences→Keyboard→Shortcuts→App Shortcuts.

After a moment, the menu becomes a list of topics pertaining to your search. Click one to open the Help browser; you've just saved some time and a couple of steps.

Tip: The results menu doesn't show all of Help's results—only the ones Apple considers relevant. If you choose Show All Help Topics, the Help browser opens with a more complete list of Help search results.

- **Drill down.** Alternatively, you can begin your quest for assistance the old-fashioned way: by opening the Help browser first. To do that, choose Help→macOS Help. (In other programs, it might say, for example, "Mail Help." Either way, this command appears only when nothing is typed in the search box.)

After a moment, you arrive at the Help browser shown at top in Figure 1-32. The starting screen offers several "quick click" topics like "Everyday tasks made easy" and "Protect your data and your Mac"—presumably the issues that trigger the

Figure 1-32:
Mac Help likes to help with big-ticket tasks like joining a network, setting up email, or browsing the web. Once you perform a search for some topic, or use the left-side topic list to drill down (bottom), you get a details page that offers a list of finely grained step-by-steps.

most help-hotline calls to Apple. Keep clicking text headings until you find a topic you want to read.

Or click "Table of Contents" to see the left-side list of topics, which you can use to drill down to the subject you need (Figure 1-32, bottom).

You can backtrack by clicking the ⟨ button at the top of the window.

Tip: Annoyingly, the help window insists on floating in front of all other windows; you can't send it to the back like you can any normal program. Therefore, consider making the help window tall and skinny, so you can put it alongside the program you're working in. Drag any edge of the box to change the window's shape.

- **Use the search box in the Help program.** Type the phrase you want, like *printing* or *switching applications,* into the search box at the top of the window, and then press Return. As you type, a list of proposed matches drops down from the search box. When you click the closest match, you're shown a list of help-screen topics that may pertain to what you need; see Figure 1-32 for details.

Organizing Your Stuff

O ver the years, the Finder has grown in size, scope, features, and complexity. Today, its occupants—those humble little icons that represent every scrap of your work on that computer—have become more talented than the cast of Cirque du Soleil. You can rename them, delete them, move them, copy them, tag them, get info on them—and, of course, file them away in folders. This chapter is your guide to life with icons.

The macOS Folder Structure

For the first 20 years of the Mac's existence, you began your workday by double-clicking the Macintosh HD icon in the upper-right corner of the screen. That's where you kept your files.

These days, though, you'll be disappointed if you do that. All you'll find in the Macintosh HD window is a set of folders called Applications, Library, Users, and so on—folders *you* didn't put there.

Most of these folders aren't very useful to you, the Mac's human companion. They're there for macOS's own use—which is why, today, the Macintosh HD icon doesn't even appear on the screen. (At least not at first; you can choose Finder→Preferences and turn the "Hard disks" checkbox on if you really want to.)

Think of your main hard drive window as storage for the operating system itself, which you'll access only for occasional administrative purposes. To open it, choose Go→Computer and double-click Macintosh HD.

Your Home Folder

Everything of yours on this computer lives in the *Home folder*. That's a folder bearing your name (or whatever name you typed in when you installed macOS).

MacOS is rife with shortcuts for opening this all-important folder:

- **Choose Go→Home,** or press Shift-⌘-H.

- **In the Sidebar** (page 15), click the ⌂ icon that bears your name. (If you don't see it, choose Finder→Preferences, navigate to the Sidebar tab, and turn on the ⌂ icon.)

You might also consider adding your Home folder to the Dock (page 133) or making it the window that appears when you press ⌘-N or choose File→New Finder Window (see page 26).

All these steps open your Home folder directly.

If you're the compulsive sort, you can also navigate to it the long way: In the Macintosh HD window, double-click the Users folder and then double-click the folder inside it that bears your name and looks like a house (see Figure 2-1).

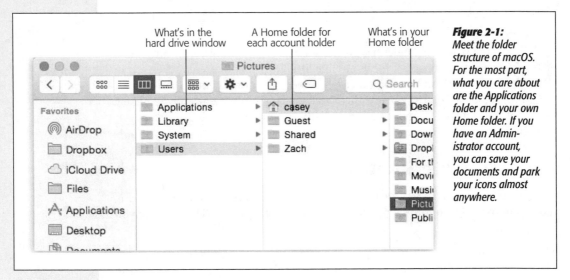

What's in the
hard drive window

A Home folder for
each account holder

What's in your
Home folder

Figure 2-1:
Meet the folder structure of macOS. For the most part, what you care about are the Applications folder and your own Home folder. If you have an Administrator account, you can save your documents and park your icons almost anywhere.

So why has Apple demoted your files to a folder three levels deep? MacOS has been designed from the ground up for *computer sharing*. It's ideal for any situation where different family members, students, or workers share the same Mac.

Each person who uses the computer will turn on the machine to find her own separate desktop picture, set of files, web bookmarks, font collection, and preference settings. (You'll find much more about accounts in Chapter 12.)

Like it or not, macOS considers you one of these people. If you're the only one who uses this Mac, fine—simply ignore the sharing features. (You can also ignore all that business at the beginning of Chapter 1 about logging in.) But in its little software

head, macOS still considers you an account holder and stands ready to accommodate any others who should come along.

In any case, now you should see the importance of the Users folder in the main hard drive window. Inside are folders—the Home folders—named for the different people who use this Mac. In general, nobody is allowed to touch what's inside anybody else's folder.

If you're the sole proprietor of the machine, of course, there's only one Home folder in the Users folder—named for you. (The Shared folder doesn't count; it's described on page 504.)

Yes, macOS imposes a fairly rigid folder structure. But by keeping such tight control over which files go where, macOS keeps itself pure—and very, very stable. Furthermore, keeping all your stuff in a single folder makes it easy for you to back up your universe. It also makes life easier when you try to connect to your machine from elsewhere in the office (over the network) or elsewhere in the world (over the internet), as described in Chapter 13.

What's on Your Hard Drive

If you *did* want to explore the entirety of macOS, to examine the contents of your hard drive, you'd find the following folders in the main hard drive window:

- **Applications.** This folder contains the complete collection of macOS programs on your Mac (not counting the invisible Unix ones). Even so, you'll rarely open programs by opening this folder; the Dock is a far more efficient launcher, as described in Chapter 4.

- **Library.** This folder bears more than a passing resemblance to the System Folder subfolders of Macs gone by, or the Windows folder on PCs. It stores components for the operating system and your programs (sounds, fonts, preferences, help files, printer drivers, modem scripts, and so on).

UP TO SPEED

The Wacky Keystrokes of macOS

MacOS offers a glorious assortment of predefined keystrokes for jumping to the most important locations on your Mac: your Home folder, the Applications folder, the Utilities folder, the Computer window, your iCloud Drive, and so on.

Better yet, the keystrokes are incredibly simple to memorize: Just press Shift-⌘ and the first letter of the location you want. Shift-⌘-H opens your Home folder, Shift-⌘-A opens the Applications folder, and so on. You learn one, you've learned 'em all. The point here is that Shift-⌘ means *places*.

The other system-wide key combo, Option-⌘, means *functions*. For example, Option-⌘-D hides or shows the Dock, Option-⌘-H is the Hide Others command, Option-⌘-= magnifies the screen (if you've turned on this feature in System Preferences→Accessibility), Option-⌘-Esc brings up the Force Quit dialog box, and so on.

You can find a full list of macOS keyboard shortcuts in Appendix D, but consistency is always nice.

- **System.** This is Unix, baby. These are the actual files that turn on your Mac and control its operations. You'll rarely have any business messing with this folder.

- **Users.** As noted earlier, this folder stores the Home folders for everyone who uses this machine.

What's in Your Home Folder

Within the folder that bears your name, you'll find another set of standard Mac folders. They have special logos on their folder icons, and you can't rename them.

- **Desktop.** When you drag an icon out of a window and onto your macOS desktop, it may *appear* to show up on the desktop. But that's just an optical illusion, a visual convenience. In truth, nothing in macOS is really *on* the desktop. It's in this Desktop folder and mirrored on the desktop area.

 The reason is simple enough: Everyone who shares your machine will, upon logging in, see his own stuff sitting on the desktop. Now you know how macOS does it: There's a separate Desktop folder in every person's Home folder.

Tip: The fact that the desktop is actually a folder is handy, because it gives you a sneaky way to jump to your Home folder from anywhere. Simply click the desktop background and then press ⌘-▲ (which is the keystroke for Go→Enclosing Folder). Because that keystroke means "Open whatever folder contains the one I'm examining," it instantly opens your Home folder. (Your Home folder is, of course, the "parent" of your Desktop folder.)

- **Documents.** Apple suggests you keep your actual work files in this folder. Sure enough, whenever you save a new document (when you're working in Keynote or Word, for example), the Save As box proposes storing the new file in this folder.

 Your programs may also create folders of their own here. For example, you may find a Microsoft User Data folder for your Outlook email, a Virtual Machines folder for use with VMware Fusion, and so on.

Note: You can opt to keep your Desktop and Documents folders in iCloud Drive, using iCloud Desktop & Documents (page 214); if you've done that, these folders no longer appear in your Home folder.

- **Downloads.** All the files you download—from your web browser, from AirDrop, and so on—wind up here, for easy finding later.

- **Library.** As noted earlier, the *main* Library folder (the one in your main hard drive window) contains folders for fonts, preferences, help files, and so on.

 You have your own Library folder, too, in your Home folder. It stores the same kinds of things—but they're *your* fonts, *your* preferences.

Note: Your own Library folder starts out invisible. But as you'll soon learn from this book, having access to it is frequently useful. That's why Apple gave you a sneaky way to open it even when it's invisible: Press the Option key as you open the Go menu in the Finder; choose Library (which doesn't appear in the menu until you press Option). Or make it stay unhidden permanently; see page 39.

Once again, this setup may seem redundant if you're the only person who uses your Mac. But it makes perfect sense in the context of families, schools, or offices where many people share a single machine. Because you have your own Library folder, you can have a font collection that's "installed" on the Mac only when *you're* using it. Each person's program preference files (the files that determine where Photoshop's palettes appear and so on) are stored independently, too. And each person, of course, sees her own email when launching macOS's Mail program—because mail, too, is generally stored in your personal Library folder.

Other Library folders store your Bookmarks, web browser plug-ins, cached web pages, keyboard layouts, sound files, and so on.

- **Movies, Music, Pictures.** The various macOS programs that deal with movies, music, and pictures will propose these specialized folders as storage locations. For example, when you plug a digital camera into a Mac, the Photos program automatically begins to download the photos on it—and stores them in the Pictures folder. Similarly, iMovie is programmed to look for the Movies folder when saving its files, and Music stores its audio files in the Music folder.

- **Public.** If you're on a network, or if others use the same Mac when you're not around, this folder can be handy: It's the "Any of you guys can look at these files" folder. Other people on your network, as well as other people who sit down at this machine, are allowed to see whatever you've put in here, even if they don't have your password. Details on networking and sharing the Mac are in Chapter 13.

- **Sites.** MacOS used to have a built-in *web server,* software that turns your Mac into a website that people on your network—or, via the internet, all over the world—can connect to. This macOS feature relied on a program called the Apache web server,

UP TO SPEED

The Computer Window

In your explorations of the Finder's Go menu, you may have wondered about the command called Computer (Shift-⌘-C). ("Go to Computer? Jeez, I thought I was already *at* my computer!")

As in Microsoft Windows, the Computer window holds the icons for all the disks connected to your machine—the hard drive, a CD that you've inserted, a flash drive, another external hard drive, and so on—as well as an icon called Network. (The Network icon appears even if you're not, in fact, on a network.) This is the topmost level of your Mac. This is the stuff that can't be put into any folder at all.

So what's it for? In some ways, the Computer window is redundant. After all, macOS displays your disk icons on the desktop *and* in the Sidebar. But some people, particularly Windows refugees, don't care for that icons-on-the-desktop feature. In the interest of creating a neater, cleaner desktop, they turn it off (by choosing Finder→Preferences and turning off the checkboxes under "Show these items on the desktop").

Furthermore, in the interest of creating neater windows, some people also *hide* the Sidebar. In that case, the Computer window still provides access to all your disks.

Otherwise, the Computer window really doesn't serve much purpose except as a familiar landmark to Windows veterans and Mac fans who grew used to it in the era before the Sidebar came along.

which is so highly regarded in the Unix community that programmers lower their voices when they mention it.

The web server is gone now. If you have a Sites folder, it's where you put the actual web pages you wanted to make available to the internet at large—in a previous version of the Mac operating system.

Desktop Stacks

It doesn't matter that Apple has provided us with folders, windows, and other organizational tools; some of us will always use the *desktop* as our organizational structure (Figure 2-2, top). We leave our icons there, sometimes dozens of them in a seething chaotic array, with the vague rationalization that it takes too much effort to file them away in folders (and the vague fear that we'll never find them again).

Apple, with a big corporate sigh, has given in. "OK, fine," it seems to say. "You insist upon leaving everything strewn across your desktop? Then at least let us help you tidy it all up."

When you turn on the View→Use Stacks command, your desktop icons auto-clump into related piles (Figure 2-2, bottom), auto-sorted by date created, date added, date last opened, date modified, tags, or kind (for example, Documents and Images). The result: far fewer icons on your desktop, and far less clutter. You've created more order without expending any time or effort.

Figure 2-2:
There's a huge difference between a messy desktop (left) and one with Stacks turned on (right). Click one of the stacks to expand the contents of that folder for easier access.

So how do you find what you need? Just click one of the stacks to expand its contents, pushing the others out of the way if necessary. Now that your inner icons are exposed, you can use them as usual: Double-click to open, tap the space bar for Quick Look (page 55), and so on.

Close the stack again by clicking it.

Note, by the way, that the View→Group Stacks By command lets you change *how* macOS creates the stacks:

- **Kind** clumps them by file type: Images, Documents, Music, PDF Documents, Spreadsheets, Presentations, and so on.

- **Date Last Opened, Date Created, Date Added [to the desktop], and Date Modified** create Stacks for Today, Yesterday, Previous 7 Days, Previous 30 Days, and so on.

- **Tags,** of course, creates a Stack for each of your colored tags (page 89).

If you're a soldier in the Leave-Stuff-Out-on-the-Desktop Army, rejoice. After all, why should your real-world desktop be the only surface with piles of stuff?

Icon Names

Every document, program, folder, and disk on your Mac is represented by an *icon*: a colorful little picture that you can move, copy, or double-click to open. In macOS, you can scale them to practically any size.

An icon's name can have up to 255 letters and spaces. If you're accustomed to the 31-character or even 8-character limits of older computers, that's a luxurious ceiling.

You can name your files using letters, numbers, punctuation—in fact, any symbol except the colon (:), which the Mac uses behind the scenes for its own folder-hierarchy designation purposes. And you can't use a period to *begin* a file's name.

Rename One File

To rename a file, click its name or icon (to highlight it) and then press Return. (Or, if you have time to kill, click once on the name, wait a moment, and then click a second time. Or right-click or two-finger click the icon; from the shortcut menu, choose Rename.)

In any case, a rectangle appears around the name (Figure 2-3). At this point, the existing name is highlighted; just begin typing to replace it. If you type a very long name, the rectangle grows vertically to accommodate new lines of text.

Tip: If you simply want to add letters to the beginning or end of the file's existing name, press the ◄ or ► key after pressing Return. The insertion point jumps to the beginning or end of the file name.

You can give more than one file or folder the same name, as long as they're not in the same folder. For example, you can have as many files named "Chocolate Cake Recipe" as you like, provided that each is in a different folder. And, of course, files called Recipe.doc and Recipe.xls can coexist in a folder, too.

As you edit a file's name, remember that you can use the Cut, Copy, and Paste commands in the Edit menu to move selected bits of text around, just as though you were word processing. The Paste command can be useful when, for instance, you're renaming many icons in sequence (Quarterly Estimate 1, Quarterly Estimate 2…).

Figure 2-3:
Click an icon's name (top left) and press Return to produce the renaming rectangle (top right), in which you can edit the file's name. MacOS is kind enough to highlight only the given name and not the suffix (like .jpg or .doc).

Now begin typing to replace the existing name (bottom left). When you're finished typing, press Return or Tab to seal the deal, or just click somewhere else.

And now, a few tips about renaming icons:

- **When the Finder sorts files,** a space is considered alphabetically *before* the letter A. To force a particular file or folder to appear at the top of a list view window, insert a space (or an underscore) before its name.

- **Older operating systems sort files** so the numbers 10 and 100 come before 2, the numbers 30 and 300 come before 4, and so on. You wind up with alphabetically sorted files like this: "1. Big Day," "10. Long Song," "2. Floppy Hat," "20. Dog Bone," "3. Weird Sort," and so on. Generations of people have learned to put zeros in front of their single-digit numbers just to make the sorting look right. In macOS, though, you get exactly the list you'd hope for: "1. Big Day," "2. Floppy Hat," "3. Weird Sort," "10. Long Song," and "20. Dog Bone."

- **In addition to letters and numbers,** macOS also assigns punctuation marks an "alphabetical order," which is this: space, _, -, –, —, comma, semicolon, !, ?, ', ", (,), [,], {, }, @, *, /, &, #, %, ` (the accent mark above the Tab key), ^, +, <, =, ≠, >, |, ~, and $.

Numbers come after punctuation; letters come next; and bringing up the rear are these characters: μ (Option-M), π (Option-P), Ω (Option-Z), and (Shift-Option-K).

Renaming Batches of Files

It's one of macOS's most useful features, and hardly anyone knows it exists: You can rename a whole windowful of files at once—numbering them, correcting spelling in dozens of files at once, deleting a certain phrase from their names, and so on.

To perform this kind of simultaneous name surgery, begin by selecting all the files whose names you want to edit, as described in the next section. Then right-click or two-finger click any one of them; from the shortcut menu, choose "Rename 12 Items" (or whatever the number is).

Now you get the dialog box shown in Figure 2-4. Its pop-up menu offers three choices:

- **Replace Text.** This, ladies and gents, is search and replace for text in your files' names. Fill in the "Find" and "Replace with" boxes; click Rename. *Example:* Change "Mom's Recipes—Fish," "Mom's Recipes—Desserts"…into "My Own Recipes—Fish," "My Own Recipes—Desserts"…

- **Add Text** tacks some text onto the files' original names; use the second pop-up menu to specify *where* (beginning or end). *Example:* Change "Mom's Recipes—Fish," "Mom's Recipes—Desserts"… into "My Mom's Recipes—Fish," "My Mom's Recipes—Desserts"…by typing *My* into the box and selecting "before name."

- **Format** is complicated but powerful. It completely obliterates whatever the files are called now; instead, it gives them all the same base name (like "Recipes"), differentiating them with a number or the date, either before or after their base names.

 Suppose, for example, that you type "Recipes" into the Custom Format box. That's the base name.

Figure 2-4:
MacOS offers a range of sophisticated batch-renaming options. There's search and replace within file names; there's "add the same text to the beginning or end of the file names"; and there's the option shown here, Format.

Here you completely replace the existing file names with new, consecutively numbered names, available in various creative styles.

Now, if you choose "Name and Index" from the second pop-up menu and click Rename, you'll get files named "Recipes 1," "Recipes 2," and so on. You can specify that you want the number (what macOS calls the *index*) either before or after the base name, and what number should begin the sequence. Name and Counter is the same, except that each number is padded out to five digits ("Recipes 00001," "Recipes 00002"…).

Finally, Name and Date adds the current time and date to the end of every file's name, in the form "2019-3-19 at 20.20.05 PM" (which means "March 19, 2019, at 8:20 p.m."). Of course, that means every selected file will have exactly the *same* name ("Recipes 2019-3-19 at 20.20.05 PM"). The Mac will give you an instant error message, therefore, *unless* the original files are in different folders or have different file name extensions (like .jpg, .doc, and so on).

The batch-renaming feature is delicious and awesome, but there is some fine print. Don't search and replace the file name extensions (like .jpg or .doc); you might not be able to open the files afterward. Don't rename system files or your Home folder.

And use a shareware program like A Better Finder Rename if you want even more power and flexibility in mass-renaming files.

Selecting Icons

To highlight a single icon in preparation for printing, opening, duplicating, or deleting, click the icon once. (In a list or column view, you can also click on any visible piece of information about that file—its size, kind, date modified, and so on.) Both the icon and the name darken in a uniquely macOSish way.

Tip: You can change the color of the oval highlighting that appears around the name of a selected icon. Choose →System Preferences, click General, and use the "Highlight color" pop-up menu.

FREQUENTLY ASKED QUESTION

Printing a Window—or a List of Files

How do I print a Finder window? I want a neat list of the files that I can use as a label for a CD I'm going to burn. What's the trick? (The File→Print command prints a selected document, not the list of files in a window.)

It's easy enough to make a list of files for printing. Once the window is open on your screen, choose Edit→Select All. Choose Edit→Copy 3 items (or however many you selected). Now switch to a word processor and paste. (If you're using TextEdit, use Edit→Paste and Match Style instead.) You get a tidy list of all the files in that window, ready to format and print.

This simple file name list isn't the same as printing a window; you don't get the status bar showing how many items are on the disk and how full the disk is. For that purpose, you could always make a screenshot of the window (see page 612) and print that. Of course, that technique is no good if the list of files is taller than the screen itself.

Really, what you want is Print Window, a handy shareware program dedicated to printing out your Finder windows, without these workarounds and limitations. You can download it from this book's "Missing CD" page at *missingmanuals.com*.

That much may seem obvious. But most first-time Mac owners have no idea how to manipulate *more* than one icon at a time—an essential survival skill in a graphic interface like the Mac's.

Selecting by Clicking

To highlight multiple files in preparation for moving or copying, use one of these techniques:

- **Highlight all the icons.** To select all the icons in a window, press ⌘-A (the equivalent of the Edit→Select All command).

- **Highlight several icons by dragging.** You can drag diagonally to highlight a group of nearby icons, as shown in Figure 2-5. In a list view, in fact, you don't even have to drag over the icons themselves—your cursor can touch any part of a file's row, like its modification date or file size.

Tip: If you include a particular icon in your diagonally dragged group by mistake, ⌘-click it to remove it from the selected cluster.

- **Highlight consecutive icons in a list.** If you're looking at the contents of a window in list view or column view, you can drag vertically over the file and folder names to highlight a group of consecutive icons, as described already. (Begin the drag in a blank spot.)

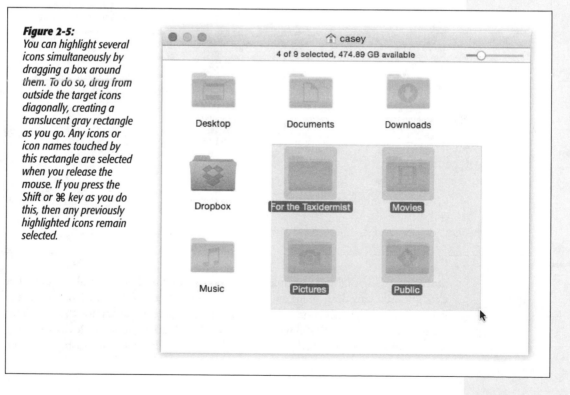

Figure 2-5:
You can highlight several icons simultaneously by dragging a box around them. To do so, drag from outside the target icons diagonally, creating a translucent gray rectangle as you go. Any icons or icon names touched by this rectangle are selected when you release the mouse. If you press the Shift or ⌘ key as you do this, then any previously highlighted icons remain selected.

There's a faster way to do the same thing; see Figure 2-6.

- **Highlight arbitrary icons.** If you want to highlight only the first, third, and seventh icons in a window, for example, start by clicking the first icon. Then ⌘-click each of the others (or ⌘-drag new rectangles around them). Each icon darkens to show that you've selected it.

If you're highlighting a long string of icons and click one by mistake, you don't have to start over. Instead, just ⌘-click it again so the dark highlighting disappears. (If you do want to start over, you can deselect all selected icons by clicking any empty part of the window.) The ⌘ key trick is especially handy if you want to select almost all the icons in a window. Press ⌘-A to select everything in the folder, and then ⌘-click any unwanted icons to deselect them.

Tip: In icon view, you can either Shift-click *or* ⌘-click to select multiple individual icons. But you may as well just learn to use the ⌘ key when selecting individual icons. That way you won't have to use a different key in each view.

Click the first icon...

...and then Shift-click the last one

⌘-click to omit one from the group

Figure 2-6:
Left: To select a block of files in list view, click the first icon. Then, while pressing Shift, click the last one. MacOS highlights those files and all the files in between your clicks. This technique mirrors the way Shift-clicking works in a word processor and in many other kinds of programs.

Right: To remove one of the icons from your selection, ⌘-click it.

Once you've highlighted multiple icons, you can manipulate them all at once. For example, you can drag them en masse to another folder or disk by dragging any *one* of the highlighted icons. All other highlighted icons go along for the ride. This technique is especially useful when you want to back up a bunch of files by dragging them onto a different disk, delete them all by dragging them to the Trash, and so on.

When multiple icons are selected, the commands in the File and Edit menus—like Duplicate, Open, and Make Alias—apply to all of them simultaneously.

Tip: Don't forget that you can instantly highlight all the files in a window (or on the desktop) by choosing Edit→Select All (⌘-A)—no icon-clicking required.

Selecting Icons from the Keyboard

For the speed fanatic, using the mouse to click an icon is a hopeless waste of time. Fortunately, you can also select an icon by typing the first few letters of its name.

When looking at your Home window, for example, you can type *M* to select the Movies folder. And if you actually intended to select the Music folder instead, then press the Tab key to select the next icon in the window alphabetically. Shift-Tab highlights the *previous* icon alphabetically. Or use the arrow keys to highlight a neighboring icon.

(The Tab-key trick works only in icon, list, and gallery views—not in column view, alas. You can always use the ◄ and ► keys to highlight adjacent columns, however.)

After highlighting an icon this way, you can manipulate it using the commands in the File menu or their keyboard equivalents: Open (⌘-O), Move to Trash (⌘-Delete), Get Info (⌘-I), Duplicate (⌘-D), or Make Alias (Control-⌘-A), as described later

GEM IN THE ROUGH

Smart Handling of Identically Named Icons

What if you're dragging a file or folder into some window—and there's already a file or folder there with the same name?

In days of yore, a warning appeared. It let you Stop (the whole operation) or Replace (the existing item with the one you were mov-ing). MacOS today is much smarter. It offers a third option: Keep Both. If you click it, macOS adds "copy" (or "copy 2," or "copy 3"…) to the end of each repeated file's name.

Tip 1: If you press Option, the Keep Both button changes to say Skip (meaning "Don't copy *this* file, but keep going with the others I dragged").

Tip 2: If you're dragging *several* files whose names match existing files, macOS asks you about each one (Stop, Replace, Keep Both?). If you intend to answer the same way for every file, save yourself the insanity by turning on the Apply to All checkbox before answering the question.

> An item named "Secret Prototype Info" with extension ".pdf" already exists in this location. Do you want to replace it with the one you're moving?
>
> Keep Both Stop Replace

There's a related feature that comes into play when you paste a *folder* into a spot where there's another folder with the same name. In this case, the Mac offers to *merge the contents* of the two folders.

It might say: "A folder named 'Notes' already exists in this location. Do you want to merge or replace it with the one you're copying? Merge will combine the two folders, preserving all the newer items such as 'Stealth Projects.doc' and 2 other items." And your choices are Stop, Replace, or Merge. (These options appear only when you're *pasting* a folder into a new window—not dragging it. They also appear when you Option-drag a folder into a new window to copy it there or when you drag it to a different disk.)

If you click Merge, the Finder *combines the contents* of the two folders. The folder you're pasting disappears, but its contents join the contents of the other folder (the one in the destination window) in blissful harmony.

in this chapter. By turning on the special accessibility features described starting on page 320, you can even *move* the highlighted icon using only the keyboard.

If you're a first-time Mac owner, you may find it excessively nerdy to memorize keystrokes for jobs the mouse can do. If you make your living using the Mac, however, memorizing these keystrokes will reward you immeasurably with speed and efficiency.

Moving and Copying Icons

In macOS, there are two ways to move or copy icons from one place to another: by dragging them and by using the Copy and Paste commands.

By Dragging

You can drag icons from one folder to another, from one drive to another, from a drive to a folder on another drive, and so on. (When you've selected several icons, drag any *one* of them; the others tag along.) As you drag, you see the images of all the selected icons moving with your cursor. And the cursor itself sprouts a circled number that reminds you how many files you're moving.

Understanding when the Mac *copies* a dragged icon and when it *moves* it bewilders many a beginner. However, the scheme is fairly simple:

- **On a single disk,** dragging from one folder to another *moves* the icon.

- **Dragging from one disk** (or disk partition) to another *copies* the folder or file. (You can drag icons either into an open window or directly onto a disk or folder icon.)

- **If you press the Option key** as you release an icon you've dragged, you *copy* the icon instead of moving it. Doing so within a single folder produces a duplicate of the file called "[Whatever its name was] 2."

- **If you press the ⌘ key** as you release an icon you've dragged from one disk to another, you *move* the file or folder, in the process deleting it from the original disk.

Note: This business of pressing Option or ⌘ *after* you begin dragging is a tad awkward, but it has its charms. For example, it means you can change your mind about the purpose of your drag in mid-movement, without having to drag back and start over.

And if it turns out you just dragged something into the wrong window or folder, a quick ⌘-Z (the shortcut for Edit→Undo) puts it right back where it came from.

Tip: You can tell the copying is underway even if the progress bar is hidden. A tiny progress bar appears right on the icon of the copied material in its new home. You can cancel the process either by pressing ⌘-period or by clicking the ⊗ in the progress window.

With Copy and Paste

Dragging icons to copy or move them feels good because it's so direct: You actually see your arrow cursor pushing the icons into the new location.

But you pay a price for this satisfying illusion. You may have to spend a moment or two fiddling with your windows to create a clear "line of drag" between the icon to be moved and the destination folder. (A background window will courteously pop to the foreground to accept your drag. But if it wasn't open to begin with, you're out of luck.)

There's a better way. Use Copy and Paste to move or copy icons from one window into another. The routine goes like this:

1. **Highlight the icon or icons you want to move.**

 Use any of the techniques described starting on page 78.

2. **Choose Edit→Copy.**

 Or press the keyboard shortcut: ⌘-C.

Tip: You can combine steps 1 and 2 by right-clicking or two-finger clicking an icon and choosing the Copy command from the shortcut menu that appears—or by using the ✿ menu. If you've selected several icons, say five, then the command says "Copy 5 Items."

3. **Open the window where you want to put the icons. Choose Edit→Paste.**

 Once again, you may prefer to use the keyboard equivalent: ⌘-V. And once again, you can also right-click or two-finger click inside the window and then choose Paste from the shortcut menu that appears—or use the ✿ menu.

 If you add the Option key—press Option-⌘-V—you *move* the icons to the new window instead of copying them. That is, the originals disappear after they appear in the new location. (This might make more sense if you use the menu way: If you open the Edit menu and press Option, you'll see that the Paste Items command changes to say Move Items Here.)

 You can press ⌘-period to interrupt the process. When the progress bar goes away, it means you've successfully transferred the icons, which now appear in the new window.

Icon's Progress: The Least-Marketed Feature

Here's an unsung little feature: When you're copying a file or a folder, a tiny progress bar or circle appears right on the icons as they sit in their new location. Animated and everything!

Doesn't matter if it's list view, icon view, or what—you'll see how your operation is progressing.

In icon view, you'll also see the little ⊗ button at the top-left corner. That, of course, means "Click me to cancel this

Blurbs, Brochures, Notes 2

copying job, since you obviously don't know about the ⌘-period keystroke."

Think of it as a little bit of mistake-recovery insurance, finally on the Mac after almost 30 years.

Oh, and one more happy bit of news: If the Mac happens to get shut down before the copying is complete, the process resumes automatically when it comes to life again.

Dragging from the Title Bar

You may remember from Chapter 1 that the title bar of every Finder window harbors a secret pop-up menu. When you ⌘-click it, you're shown a little ladder that delineates your current position in the folder hierarchy. You may also remember that the tiny icon just to the left of the window's name is actually a handle that you can drag to move a folder into a different window.

In many programs, you get the same features in *document* windows, as shown in Figure 2-7. For example, by dragging the tiny document icon next to the document's name, you can perform these three interesting stunts:

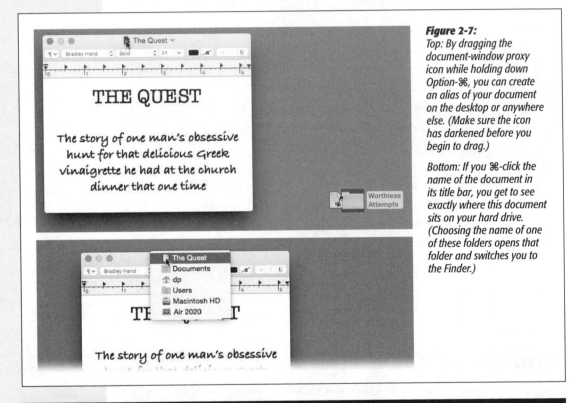

Figure 2-7:
Top: By dragging the document-window proxy icon while holding down Option-⌘, you can create an alias of your document on the desktop or anywhere else. (Make sure the icon has darkened before you begin to drag.)

Bottom: If you ⌘-click the name of the document in its title bar, you get to see exactly where this document sits on your hard drive. (Choosing the name of one of these folders opens that folder and switches you to the Finder.)

Dragging to Copy a Disk

Help! I'm trying to copy a CD onto my hard drive. When I drag it onto the hard drive icon, I get only an alias—not a copy of the CD.

Sure enough, dragging a disk onto a disk creates an alias. But producing a copy of the dragged icon is easy enough: Just press Option or ⌘ as you drag.

Honestly, though: Why are you trying to copy a CD this way in the first place?

Using Disk Utility (page 469) instead saves space, lets you assign a password, and usually fools whatever software was on the CD into thinking that it's still *on* the original CD.

- **Create an alias on the desktop or the Dock.** By dragging this icon to the desktop or onto a folder or disk icon while holding down Option-⌘, you create an instant alias of the document you're working on. (If you drag into the right end of the Dock, you can park the document's icon there, too, without holding down any keys.) Before the Resume Windows feature came along, this was useful when, for example, you were about to knock off for the night and wanted easy access to the file you'd been working on when you returned the next day.

- **Attach a file to an email message.** You can drag a document (using its proxy icon as a handle) onto the icon of an email program like Mail or Outlook. That process creates a new, outgoing message with the file you dragged already attached. (If an outgoing message is already open in that program, then you can drag the file directly into its window, too.) In either case, use the ⌘-Tab app switcher (page 173) in mid-drag to switch programs.

- **Launch from a Dock icon.** By dragging this title-bar icon onto another program's *Dock icon,* you open your document in that other program. For example, if you're in TextEdit working on a memo and you decide you'll need the full strength of Microsoft Word to dress it up, you can drag its title-bar icon directly onto the Word icon in the Dock. Word then launches and opens up the TextEdit document, ready for editing.

Note to struggling writers: Unfortunately, you can't drag an open document directly into the Trash.

Spring-Loaded Folders: Dragging Icons into Closed Folders

You want to drag an icon not just into a folder, but into a folder *inside* that folder. This challenge would ordinarily require you to open the folder, open the inner folder, drag the icon in, and then close both windows. As you can imagine, the process is even messier if you want to drag an icon into a sub-subfolder or a *sub*-sub-subfolder.

Instead of fiddling around with all those windows, you can instead use the *spring-loaded folders* feature. Figure 2-8 shows you how it's done.

Tip: You can even drag icons onto disks or folders whose icons appear in the Sidebar (Chapter 1). When you do so, the main part of the window flashes to reveal the contents of the disk or folder you've dragged onto.

In short, the Sidebar and spring-loaded folders make a terrific drag-and-drop way to file an icon from anywhere to anywhere—without having to open or close any windows at all.

When you finally release the mouse, you're left facing the final window. All the previous windows closed along the way. You've placed the icon into the depths of the nested folders.

Making Spring-Loaded Folders Work

That spring-loaded folder technique sounds good in theory, but it can be disconcerting in practice. For most people, the long wait before the first folder opens is almost

enough wasted time to negate the value of the feature altogether. Furthermore, when the first window finally does open, you're often caught by surprise. Suddenly your cursor—mouse button still down—is inside a window, sometimes directly on top of another folder you never intended to open.

Figure 2-8:
Top: To make spring-loaded folders work, start by dragging an icon onto a folder or disk icon. Don't release the mouse button. Wait for the window to open automatically around your cursor.

Bottom: Now you can either let go of the mouse button to release the file in its new window or drag it onto yet another, inner folder. It, too, will open. As long as you don't release the mouse button, you can continue until you've reached your folder-within-a-folder destination.

Fortunately, you can regain control of spring-loaded folders using these tricks:

- **Choose System Preferences→Accessibility.** In the Pointer Control pane, adjust the "Spring-loading delay" slider to a setting that drives you less crazy. For example, if the first folder takes too long to open, then drag the slider toward the Short setting.

- **You can turn off this feature entirely** by choosing System Preferences→Accessibility→Pointer Control, and turning off the "Spring-loading delay" checkbox.

- **Tap the space bar to make the folder spring open at your command.** That is, even with the slider set to the Long delay setting, you can force each folder to spring open when *you* are ready by tapping the space bar as you hold down the mouse button. True, you need two hands to master this one, but the control you regain is immeasurable.

Tip: The space bar trick works even when the "Spring-loading delay" checkbox (in System Preferences→
Accessibility→Pointer Control) is turned off. That's a handy arrangement, because it means folder windows
never pop open accidentally.

- **Whenever a folder springs open into a window,** twitch your mouse up to the newly
opened window's title bar or down to its information strip. Doing so ensures that
your cursor won't wind up hovering on, and accidentally opening, an inner folder.
With the cursor parked on the gradient gray, you can take your time to survey
the newly opened window's contents and plunge into an inner folder only after
gaining your bearings.

Tip: Email programs like Outlook and Mail have spring-loaded folders, too. You can drag a message out of
the list and into one of your filing folders, wait for the folder to spring open and reveal its subfolders, and
then drag it directly into one of them.

Aliases: Icons in Two Places at Once

Highlighting an icon and then choosing File→Make Alias (or pressing Control-⌘-A)
generates an *alias,* a specially branded duplicate of the original icon (Figure 2-9). It's
not a duplicate of the *file*—just of the *icon*—so it requires negligible storage space.
When you double-click the alias, the original file opens. (A Macintosh alias is essen-
tially the same as a Windows *shortcut.*)

You can create as many aliases as you want of a single file; therefore, in effect, aliases
let you stash that file in many different folder locations simultaneously. Double-click
any one of them, and you open the original file, wherever it may be on your system.

Tip: You can also create an alias of an icon by Option-⌘-dragging it out of its window. (Aliases you create
this way lack the word *alias* on the file name—a delight to those who find the suffix redundant and annoying.)
You can also create an alias by right-clicking or two-finger clicking a normal icon and choosing Make Alias from
the shortcut menu that appears, or by highlighting an icon and then choosing Make Alias from the ✿ menu.

What's Good About Aliases

An alias takes up very little disk space, even if the original file is enormous. Aliases
are smart, too: Even if you rename the alias, rename the original file, move the alias,
and move the original around on the disk, double-clicking the alias still opens the
original file.

And that's just the beginning of alias intelligence. Suppose you make an alias of a file
that's on a removable disc, like a flash drive. When you double-click the alias on your
hard drive, the Mac requests that particular flash drive by name. And if you double-
click the alias of a file on a different machine on the network, your Mac attempts
to connect to the appropriate machine, prompting you for a password—even if the
other machine is thousands of miles away and your Mac must go online to connect.

Here are a couple of ways you can put aliases to work:

- **You can file a document you're working on** in several different folders, or place a particular folder in several different locations, for convenience.

- **You can use the alias feature** to save you some of the steps required to access another hard drive on the network. (Those steps begin on page 546.)

Tip: MacOS makes it easy to find the file an alias "points to" without actually having to open it. Just highlight the alias and then choose File→Show Original (Control-Option-⌘-A), or choose Show Original from the ✿ menu. MacOS immediately displays the actual, original file, sitting patiently in its folder, wherever that may be.

Broken Aliases

Don't email an alias to the Tokyo office and then depart for the airport, hoping to give the presentation upon your arrival in Japan. When you double-click the alias, now separated from its original, you'll get the message shown in the dialog box at the bottom of Figure 2-9.

Figure 2-9:
Top: You can identify an alias by the tiny arrow badge on the lower-left corner. (Mac old-timers should note that the name no longer appears in italics.)

Bottom: If the alias can't find the original file, you're offered the chance to hook it up to a different file.

Be grateful the Mac doesn't just show you an error message that says " 'NSA Institutional Ethics Handbook' can't be found." Instead, you can click the Fix Alias button. It opens the Fix Alias dialog box, which you can use to navigate the folders on your Mac. When you click a new icon and then click Choose, you associate the orphaned alias with a different file. From now on, double-clicking the alias opens the new file.

Or you can click Delete Alias (to delete the orphan alias) or OK (to do nothing, leaving it where it is).

Tip: You don't have to wait until the original file no longer exists before choosing a new original for an alias. You can perform alias reassignment surgery anytime you like. Just highlight the alias icon and then choose File→Get Info. In the Get Info dialog box, click Select New Original. In the resulting window, find and double-click the file you'd now like to open whenever you double-click the alias.

Finder Tags

Finder tags offer a way to color-code, or apply a keyword to, your icons (Figure 2-10). They're a lot like the Finder labels that have been on the Mac for decades, with a few differences:

- **You can apply more than one tag** to an icon, in effect letting it be in more than one place or sortable in more than one way. A photo of Aunt Edna in her early days on the farm could be tagged Relatives, Photos, *and* Ancient History.

- **You have more than seven tags available;** in fact, you can have dozens (although you can choose from only seven colors).

- **You can create, assign, and use tags in many more ways,** in many more places, than you could labels. For example, you can assign a tag or two to a new document *as you're naming and saving it.*

- **Tags** *sync.* That is, if you have more than one Mac, and they're signed into the same iCloud account, the same tags are available on all your machines.

What Tags Are Good For

After you've applied tags to icons, you can perform some unique file-management tasks—in some cases on all of them simultaneously, even if they're scattered across multiple hard drives.

For example:

- **Round up files with Find.** Using the Spotlight search command described in Chapter 3, you can round up all the icons with a particular tag, no matter which folders they're in.

- **Sort a list view by tag.** No other Mac sorting method lets you create an arbitrary order for the icons in a window. When you sort by tag, the Mac creates alphabetical clusters *within* each tag grouping.

 This technique might be useful when, for example, your job is to process several different folders of documents; for each folder, you're supposed to convert graphics files, throw out old files, or whatever. As soon as you finish working your way through one folder, flag it with a tag called Done. The folder jumps to the top (or bottom) of the window, safely marked for your reference pleasure, leaving the next unprocessed folder at your fingertips, ready to go.

Tip: In a list view, the quickest way to sort by tag is to first make the tag column visible. Do so by choosing View→Show View Options and then turning on the Tags checkbox.

- **Track progress.** Use different-colored tags to track the status of files in a certain project. For example, the first drafts have no tags at all. Once they've been edited and approved, make them blue. Once they've been sent to the home office, make them purple.

(Heck, you could have all kinds of fun with this: Money-losing projects get red tints; profitable ones get green; things that make you sad get blue. Or not.)

Figure 2-10:
Use the File menu, ◁ menu, or shortcut menu to apply tags to highlighted icons. You can even apply a tag within an icon's Get Info dialog box.

Middle: The same menu is your opportunity to create (and simultaneously apply) a new tag. Just type it.

Bottom: You can also apply a tag—or even create a new one—at the moment you're saving a new document. Just type the new tag names into the Tags box that appears just below the Save As box.

Creating Tags

Apple starts you out with a few handy tags, ready to apply to any files you like. They come with ingenious names like Red, Yellow, Blue, and Gray.

If you upgraded your Mac from an earlier version of the operating system, you'll find your old Finder labels magically reincarnated as tags, too.

But to create a *new* tag, use one of the techniques shown in Figure 2-10. You're simultaneously creating a new tag and applying it to the file(s) in question. The new tag will be available later in the regular Tags menus.

Editing Tag Names and Colors

To change a tag's name, reassign it to a different color, or delete the tag entirely, open the Tags tab of the Preferences dialog box, as shown in Figure 2-11.

Tip: Actually, an identical set of controls appears when you right-click or two-finger click one of the tags that appears in the Sidebar of any Finder window. And if you have a Touch Bar, keep in mind you can add an Edit Tags button to it, too, as described on page 231.

Figure 2-11:
Middle: In Finder→ Preferences→Tags, you can right-click or two-finger click a tag for the shortcut menu shown here. It lets you rename a tag, delete it, or choose a different color.

Left: You can install some favored tags in the Sidebar.

Right: An even smaller set of favorites appears in Finder menus and shortcut menus.

Two Sets of Favorites Tags

Apple is prepared for Tagageddon; it's created a system that could lead some people to create *hundreds* of tags. That number, of course, is a bit unwieldy. Fortunately, Apple also has equipped you with not one but two sets of "favorites."

- **Sidebar favorites.** The Sidebar at the left side of each Finder window has a section reserved exclusively for displaying the tags you use the most (Figure 2-11, left). To

choose which tags you want installed here, open the Preferences dialog box shown in Figure 2-11, center, and make your selections.

- **Menu favorites.** As shown in Figure 2-11 at right, there's room for only a few favorite tags—their colored dots, anyway—right in the File→Tags menu, or the shortcut menu that appears when you right-click or two-finger click an icon.

So how do you choose which tags get these exalted positions? In the dialog box shown in Figure 2-11 (center), drag each favored tag's name into the Favorite Tags box at bottom. (You can remove one by dragging your new favorite tag on top of the dot you want to replace.)

Applying Tags

To apply a tag to a file, highlight the file(s), and then do one of the following:

- **Choose from a menu.** Right-click or two-finger click an icon in the Finder or click the ⬭ button at the top of the Finder window (Figure 2-10, middle). Or choose File→Tags.

In each case, you get to see colored dots representing the "menu favorite" tags in your arsenal, as described already. Or you can click Show All to see the complete scrolling list of dozens. (You can apply multiple tags to a single icon.)

Figure 2-12:
A tag doesn't change the background color of an icon's name, as labels once did. That's because you can now apply more than one tag to a single icon.

Instead, tags show up as colored dots—and if you've applied more than one, they show up as stacked, side-by-side colored dots.

- **Use the Sidebar.** You can drag Finder icons *onto* the names of tags in the Sidebar.

- **Apply while saving.** You can tag a file as you're saving it (Figure 2-10, bottom).

- **Apply in the Get Info box.** See page 97.

- **Apply with the Tag button on the Touch Bar (page 227).** If your laptop has the Touch Bar above the keyboard, then a ⬅⬜ button appears whenever you've selected an icon (or several). Tap the ⬅⬜ to view your list of tags on the Touch Bar; tap the one you want to apply.

- **Apply within the app.** Certain Apple programs, like TextEdit, Pages, Numbers, and Keynote, bear a tiny triangle next to the document's name on the title bar (page 18). You can click it to open a Tags box, which lets you edit a document's tags while you're still working on it.

- **Hit a keystroke.** Page 200 describes how you can assign keystrokes to common Mac menu commands. As it turns out, the File→Tags command is available for assignment, too. Give it, say, Control-T, and from now on you can call up the Tags dialog box without even taking your fingers off the keyboard.

 For the application name, use Finder; for the menu title, type *Tags…* (press Option-semicolon to produce that three-dot ellipsis, not three periods).

Once you've applied a tag, you can see it in the Finder. It's represented as a colored dot next to the file's name; see Figure 2-12.

Using Tags

OK. So you sat up all weekend, painstakingly tagging your thousands of files. Now comes the payoff: *using* tags.

- **Find them all with a click.** Click one of the tag names in the Sidebar (Figure 2-11, left). You've instantly performed a Mac-wide search for all files with that tag. They appear in a single search-results window, regardless of where they're actually sitting on your computer.

Tip: You can drag the name of a tag directly from the Sidebar of any Finder window onto the right (or bottom) side of the Dock. From now on, clicking that Dock icon opens a fan, grid, or list that displays every icon on your entire Mac that you've tagged with that color.

- **Find them all using the search box.** Type a few letters of the tag's name in the search box at the top-right corner of any Finder window. Use the "Tags" search token.

- **Find them all with Spotlight.** Into the Spotlight box (page 107), type *tag:orange* (or whatever the tag name is). The results list shows you all the icons you've tagged that way.

 The beauty of this method is that you can combine search criteria. In the Spotlight box, you could search for *tag:orange* and *kind:movie*, for example.

Detagging Files

To remove a tag from an icon, use any of the same menu commands you used to apply the tag in the first place (right-click or two-finger click, File→Tags, click the ◁▢ menu). In the Tags panel, just delete the tag name.

The Trash

No single element of the Macintosh interface is as recognizable or famous as the Trash can icon, which appears at the end of the Dock. (It's actually a wastebasket, not a can.)

You can discard almost any icon by dragging it onto the Trash icon. As a convenience, macOS even replaces the empty-wastebasket icon with a wastebasket-filled-with-crumpled-up-papers icon, to let you know there's something in there.

It's worth learning the keyboard alternative to dragging something into the Trash: Highlight the icon, and then press ⌘-Delete (which corresponds to the File→Move to Trash command). Or, if your Mac has a Touch Bar (page 227), you can install a Move to Trash button on it, so one tap there does the trick.

Tip: Here's a secret method of trashing something that *bypasses* its visit to the Trash can—and instead deletes it instantly. While pressing the Option key, choose File→Delete Immediately (or press Option-⌘-Delete). When it's all over, that icon is gone—and the Trash was never even involved.

The keyboard and Touch Bar techniques are not only far faster than dragging, but they also require far less precision. MacOS does all the Trash-targeting for you.

Note: If a file is locked, a message appears to let you know; it offers you the chance to fling it into the Trash anyway. You don't have to unlock the file before you trash it.

Rescuing Files and Folders from the Trash

File and folder icons sit in the Trash forever—or until you choose Finder→Empty Trash, whichever comes first.

GEM IN THE ROUGH

Opening Things in the Trash

Now and then, it's useful to see what some document in the Trash *is* before committing it to oblivion—and the only way to do that is to open it. Trouble is, you can't open it by double-clicking; you'll get nothing but an error message.

Or at least that's what Apple *wants* you to think.

First of all, you can use Quick Look (page 55) to inspect something in the Trash.

But if Quick Look can't open the file—or if you want to *edit* it instead of just reading it—then drag the document onto the icon of a program that can open it. That is, if a file called Don't Read Me.txt is in the Trash, you can drag it onto, say, the Word or TextEdit icon in your Dock.

The document dutifully pops open on the screen. Inspect, close, and *then* empty the Trash (or rescue the document).

If you haven't yet emptied the Trash, you can open its window by clicking the waste-basket icon once. Now you can review its contents: icons you've placed on the waiting list for extinction. Here's how you can change your mind about one of them:

- **Use the Put Back command.** This feature flings the trashed item back into whatever folder it came from, even if that was weeks ago.

 You'll find the Put Back command wherever fine shortcut menus are sold. For example, it appears when you two-finger click the icon, right-click it, or click the icon and then open the ✿ menu.

Tip: The same keystroke you use to hurl something *into* the trash (⌘-Delete) also works to hurl it *out* again. That is, you can highlight something in the Trash and press ⌘-Delete to put it back where it once belonged.

- **Hit Undo.** If dragging a file to the Trash was something you just did, you can press ⌘-Z—the keyboard shortcut for the Edit→Undo command. (The Finder offers a five-level Undo, meaning that you can retrace your past five actions.)

 Undo not only removes a file from the Trash, but it also returns it to the folder from which it came. This trick works even if the Trash window isn't open.

- **Drag it manually.** Of course, you can also drag any icon out of the Trash with the mouse, which gives you the option of putting it somewhere new.

Emptying the Trash I: Quick and Easy

If you're confident that the items in the Trash window are worth deleting, use any of these three options to empty it:

- **Choose Finder→Empty Trash, or press Shift-⌘-Delete.** Or, if you'd just as soon not bother with the "Are you sure?" message, throw the Option key in there, too.

- **Right-click the wastebasket icon** (or two-finger click it, or just click it and hold the mouse button down for a moment); choose Empty Trash from the shortcut menu.

The Mac asks you to confirm your decision. (Figure 2-13 shows this message.) If you click Empty Trash (or press Return), macOS deletes those files from your hard drive.

Tip: If you'd rather not be interrupted for confirmation every time you empty the Trash, you can suppress this message permanently. To do that, choose Finder>Preferences, click Advanced, and then turn off "Show warning before emptying the Trash."

Emptying the Trash II: Even Easier

The Mac can empty the Trash automatically after 30 days, just as Windows has been able to do for years. (Well, technically, it removes *individual items* from the trash after each has sat there for 30 days.)

If you turn on this option in Finder→Preferences→Advanced ("Remove items from the Trash after 30 days"), then you can forget about having to empty the Trash

manually. You can just think of it as a 30-day safety net for things you're pretty sure you want to ditch.

Locked Files: The Next Generation

By highlighting a file or folder, choosing File→Get Info, and turning on the Locked checkbox, you protect that file or folder from accidental deletion (see Figure 2-13 at bottom). A little ⊝ appears on the corner of the full-size icon, also shown in Figure 2-13.

Figure 2-13:
Top: Your last warning. MacOS doesn't tell you how many items are in the Trash or how much disk space they take up.

Bottom: This is the Get Info window for a locked file. Locking a file in this way isn't military-level security by any stretch—any passing evildoer can unlock the file in the same way you locked it. But it does trigger a warning when you try to put it into the Trash, providing at least one layer of protection against losing or deleting it.

Locked files these days behave quite differently than they did in early Mac versions:

- **Dragging the file into another folder makes a copy;** the original stays put.

- **Putting the icon into the Trash produces a warning message:** "Item 'Shopping List' is locked. Do you want to move it to the Trash anyway?" If so, click Continue.

- **Once a locked file is in the Trash, you don't get any more warnings.** When you empty the Trash, that item gets erased right along with everything else.

You can unlock files easily enough. Press ⌘-I (or choose File→Get Info). Turn off the Locked checkbox in the resulting info window. (Yes, you can lock or unlock a mass of files at once.)

Get Info

By clicking an icon and then choosing File→Get Info (or pressing ⌘-I, or touching Get Info on the Touch Bar [page 227], if you've installed one there), you open an important window like the one shown in Figure 2-14. It's a collapsible, multipanel screen that provides a wealth of information about a highlighted icon. For example:

- **For a document icon,** you see when it was created and modified, and what programs it "belongs" to.

- **For an alias,** you learn the location of the actual icon it refers to.

- **For a disk icon,** you get statistics about its capacity and how much of it is full.

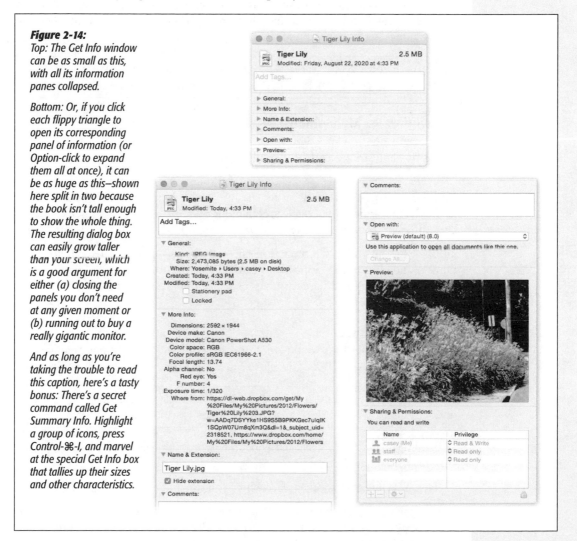

Figure 2-14:
Top: The Get Info window can be as small as this, with all its information panes collapsed.

Bottom: Or, if you click each flippy triangle to open its corresponding panel of information (or Option-click to expand them all at once), it can be as huge as this—shown here split in two because the book isn't tall enough to show the whole thing. The resulting dialog box can easily grow taller than your screen, which is a good argument for either (a) closing the panels you don't need at any given moment or (b) running out to buy a really gigantic monitor.

And as long as you're taking the trouble to read this caption, here's a tasty bonus: There's a secret command called Get Summary Info. Highlight a group of icons, press Control-⌘-I, and marvel at the special Get Info box that tallies up their sizes and other characteristics.

- If *nothing* is selected, you get information about the desktop itself (or the open window), including the amount of disk space consumed by everything on or in it.

- If you highlight so many icons simultaneously that their Get Info windows would overwhelm your screen, macOS thoughtfully tallies up their information into a single summary window. It shows you how many icons you highlighted, breaks them down by type ("23 documents, 3 folders," for example), and adds up their file sizes. That's a great opportunity to change certain file characteristics on numerous files simultaneously, such as locking or unlocking them, hiding or showing their file name suffixes, changing their ownership or permissions (page 534), and so on.

How many icons do you have to highlight to trigger this Multiple Item Info box? That depends on the size of your screen; bigger monitors can hold more Get Info boxes. If you highlight fewer than that magic number of icons, macOS opens up individual Get Info windows for each one.

Tip: You can force the Multiple Item Info dialog box to appear, though, even if you've highlighted only a couple of icons. Just press Control-⌘-I. (The Option-⌘-I trick described next works for this purpose, too.)

Uniwindow vs. Multiwindow

Ordinarily, when you click a bunch of icons and then choose File→Get Info, a new dialog box appears for each icon (unless you've highlighted a lot of icons, as just described).

But there's a useful variation on the Get Info dialog box called the Inspector. It's a single Get Info window that *changes,* even though it remains open on the screen, as you click different icons. It's a clutter-free way to explore different files, icons, and disks.

To open the Inspector, select an icon and then press Option-⌘-I (or hold down Option and choose File→Show Inspector). The Get Info Inspector window that appears looks slightly different (it has a smaller title bar), and it changes to reflect whatever icons you now click.

The Get Info Panels

Apple built the Get Info window out of a series of collapsed "flippy triangles," as shown in Figure 2-14. Click a triangle to expand a corresponding information panel.

Tip: The title-bar hierarchical menu described on page 19 works in the Get Info dialog box, too. That is, ⌘-click the Get Info window's title bar to reveal where this icon is in your folder hierarchy.

Depending on whether you clicked a document, program, disk, alias, or whatever, the various panels may include the following:

- **Tags.** Yes, here's yet another place where you can add or delete tags for a file.

- **Comments.** Here you can type in comments for your own reference. Later, you can view these remarks in any list view if you display the Comments column—and you can find them when you conduct Spotlight searches (Chapter 3).

- **General.** Here's where you can view the name of the icon and also see its size, creation date, most recent change date, locked status, and so on.

 If you click a disk, this info window shows you its capacity and how full it is. If you click the Trash, you see how much stuff is in it. If you click an alias, this panel shows you a Select New Original button and reveals where the original file is. The General panel always opens the first time you summon the Get Info window.

- **More Info.** Just as the name implies, here you'll find more info, most often the dimensions and color format (graphics only) and when the icon was last opened. These morsels are also easily Spotlight-searchable.

- **Name & Extension.** On this panel, you can read and edit the name of the icon in question. The "Hide extension" checkbox refers to the suffix on macOS file names (the last three letters of Letter to Congress.doc, for example).

 Many documents, behind the scenes, have file name extensions of this kind—but macOS comes factory-set to hide them. By turning off this checkbox, you can make the suffix appear for an individual file. (Conversely, if you've elected to have macOS *show* all extensions, this checkbox lets you hide them on individual icons.)

- **Open with.** This section is available for documents only. Use the controls on this screen to specify which program will open when you double-click this document, or any document of its type.

- **Preview.** When you're examining pictures, text files, PDF files, Microsoft Office files, sounds, clippings, and movies, you see a magnified thumbnail version of what's actually *in* that document. This preview is like a tiny version of Quick Look (page 55). A controller lets you play sounds and movies where appropriate.

- **Sharing & Permissions.** This panel is available for all kinds of icons. If other people have access to your Mac (either from across the network or when logging in, in person), this panel lets you specify who is allowed to open or change this particular icon. See Chapter 13 for a complete discussion of this hairy topic.

Shortcut Menus, Action Menus

It's part of the Mac's user-friendly heritage: You can do practically everything using only the mouse. Everything is out front, unhidden, and clickable, whether it's an icon, a button, or a menu.

But as in rival operating systems, you can shave seconds and steps off your workload if you master *shortcut menus*: short menus that sprout out of things you click, offering commands the software thinks you might want to invoke at the moment, as shown in Figure 2-15.

To summon one, just right-click or two-finger click something—an icon, the desktop, a window, a link in Safari, text in a word processor, whatever. You can also trigger these shortcut menus with special clicks on your trackpad or Magic Mouse; see page 233 for additional options.

In any case, a menu drops down listing relevant commands: Get Info, Move to Trash, Copy, and so on. You can click the command you want, or type the first couple of letters of it and then tap the space bar.

These menus become more useful the more you get to know them. That's why Apple provided a second way to access them. At the top of every Finder window, you'll find a ✿ pop-up menu, technically called the *Action menu* (Figure 2-15, right).

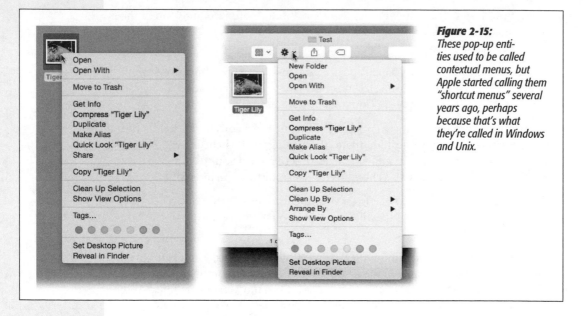

Figure 2-15:
*These pop-up enti-
ties used to be called
contextual menus, but
Apple started calling them
"shortcut menus" several
years ago, perhaps
because that's what
they're called in Windows
and Unix.*

It lists the same sorts of commands you'd find in the shortcut menus, but it's *visible*, so novices stand a better chance of stumbling onto it.

The Finder shortcut menus offer some of the most useful Mac features ever. Don't miss the two described in the next sections in particular.

New Folder with Selection

Imagine this: You've got a bunch of icons scattered on your desktop, or a mass of related files in a window. You can highlight all of them; right-click or two-finger click any one of them; and from the shortcut menu, choose "New Folder with Selection (12 items)" (or whatever the number of icons is).

Note: If your Mac has a Touch Bar, there's a New Folder with Selection button available to install there (see page 231).

With a cool animation, the Finder throws the selected icons into a brand-new folder. It's initially named New Folder With Items (duh), but the hard part is over. All you have to do is rename it—and be grateful that you were spared the 736 steps it would have taken you to do the same job manually.

Share ⬆

Here's a handy menu of ways to send whatever's highlighted to somebody else.

Note: You don't actually have to open a shortcut menu to find the ⬆ button; it's also sitting right there in every Finder window toolbar. And if your Mac has a Touch Bar, there's a Share button available to install there, too (page 231).

In the case of selected Finder icons, you can use these methods (see Figure 2-16):

- **Mail** whips open and creates a new, outgoing message with the selected file(s) already attached. Address and send, and make a sacrifice to the right-clicky gods.

- **AirDrop** is a slick, simple way to shoot a file to another Mac, or an iPhone or iPad, without involving any setup, settings, or user accounts; see page 528.

 You don't even have to budge from your current window. Click the file(s) you want to send, click Share→AirDrop, click the name of the nearby destination Mac, iPhone, or iPad, and click Send. Off it goes!

- **Notes** adds the contents of the file to a new page in your Notes app. (A note can hold graphics, movies, sounds—and even icons from the Finder. See page 429.)

- **Messages** sends the file to somebody's iPhone. Type a little message and then click Send. Off it goes, just as though you'd sent it from the Messages app (Chapter 20).

- **Add to Photos.** If you've selected a photo (or several), this command sends your masterpieces directly into your photo-organizing program.

- **More.** This command opens up a dialog box where you can rearrange the commands in your Share menu, turn off the ones you don't use, and so on; see page 260.

Figure 2-16:
The Share command in every Finder window offers direct access to several ways of transmitting a file. As a handy bonus, it remembers how you sent the last few files (and to whom), so you can send something new without having to readdress anything.

Optimized Storage

Your Mac sits at the unhappy pinch point between two opposing trends: the growing size of today's files (videos, photos, music) and the shrunken size of our available storage (the non-hard disks on today's Mac laptops).

But macOS can solve that problem rather neatly, by reclaiming huge swaths of wasted space on your drive.

It begins with the window shown in Figure 2-17. To see it, choose →About This Mac; in the dialog box, click Storage. You get a handsome graph that shows the breakdown of the junk that's clogging up your drive(s): Apps, Documents, System, and so on (Figure 2-17, top).

Note: Purgeable means "expendable." These are files that are on your Mac but don't need to be. They're files that you can download again whenever you need them, like photos and email attachments that are backed up on iCloud; Asian-language fonts and dictionaries you've never used; and movies you've already watched. This notion of "purgeable" will become clearer once you read "Store in iCloud," next.

By the way: When you see the Finder report showing how much free space is available on your drive, it's *including* the purgeable space. If you actually try to copy a file onto your nearly full drive, the Mac will nuke the purgeable files instantly to make room.

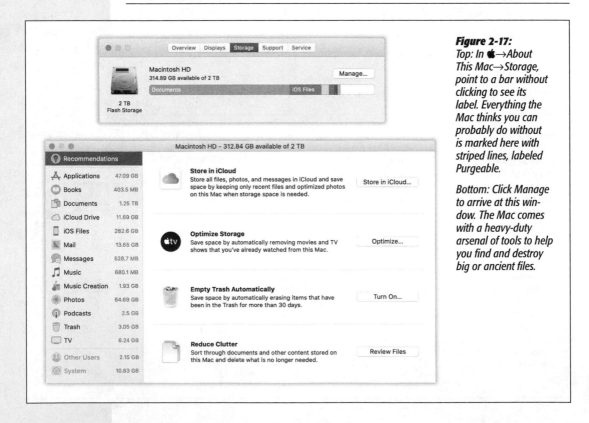

Figure 2-17:
Top: In →About This Mac→Storage, point to a bar without clicking to see its label. Everything the Mac thinks you can probably do without is marked here with striped lines, labeled Purgeable.

Bottom: Click Manage to arrive at this window. The Mac comes with a heavy-duty arsenal of tools to help you find and destroy big or ancient files.

If, in that dialog box, you click Manage, you arrive at the impressive window shown at bottom in Figure 2-17. It's the Manage Storage dialog box—a blessing to anyone whose hard drive has ever been full. It contains no fewer than four tools for freeing up space. Ready?

Note: The Manage Storage dialog box duplicates several on/off switches that sit in the Preferences of various apps. In the following sections, you'll see where to find them.

Store in iCloud

If you click this button, you're offered three checkboxes:

- **Desktop and Documents**. If you turn this item on, the Mac copies everything on your desktop and in your Documents folder to Apple's iCloud servers online. (See page 214 for more on iCloud Desktop & Documents.)

- **Photos**. This item copies all your original photos and videos to Apple's iCloud servers.

Later, as your Mac begins to run out of space, it quietly and automatically *deletes the originals* of these files to free up room. You can download your originals, which are safely stored online, whenever you need them—but in the meantime, you're not carrying around a bunch of huge files that you never use.

When iCloud has deleted a desktop or Documents-folder file, for example, it leaves behind an icon marked with a ☁ badge. If you ever need that file, just double-click its icon as usual to download it (and open it). Seamless as could be.

Similarly, what you'll see in Photos are screen-sized versions of your pictures—maybe 1 megapixel instead of 20. But if you ever want the original, just double-click to open it. (To be clear: No files are deleted from your Mac *until you're running low on space*.)

UP TO SPEED

Compressing, Zipping, and Archiving

MacOS comes with a built-in command that compresses a file or folder down to a single, smaller icon—an archive—suitable for storing or emailing. It creates .zip files, the same compression format used in Windows. That means you can now send .zip files back and forth to PC owners without worrying that they won't be able to open them.

To compress something, right-click or two-finger click a file or folder and choose "Compress [the icon's name]" from the shortcut menu. (Of course, you can use the File menu or the ✿ menu instead.) MacOS thoughtfully creates a .zip archive, but it leaves the original behind so you can continue working with it. Behind the scenes, the Mac relies on a little app called Archive Utility. Sometimes it remains open after the unzipping process; don't be alarmed. Just scold it and then quit it.

Opening a .zip file somebody sends you is equally easy: Just double-click it. Zip!—it opens.

• **Messages.** This item stores all your messages and attachments online, as described on page 753.

Of course, using these options requires a lot more space on the iCloud service than the measly 5 GB you get for free. You'll have to sign up for one of Apple's more expensive plans, like $12 a year for 50 GB of storage, or $120 a year for 2 TB.

It's a solid, if pricey, way to be free of storage worries.

Note: Once you've turned on these options, you can't turn them off again here. Instead, open System Preferences→Apple ID→iCloud→iCloud Drive Options to change the settings for Desktop & Documents, Photos→Preferences to control iCloud Photo Library, and Messages→Preferences to turn off Messages in iCloud.

Optimize

The Optimize button presents you with a single option, which might be better called "Automatically remove movies and TV shows once you've watched them." When your drive gets low on space (under 10 GB), this feature zaps movie and TV-show files on your Mac that you've already watched. (You're always free to re-download them at no charge.) Video files are huge, so you may find some real gold here.

Note: Even after it regains some space, the Mac will continue to delete these video files after you've watched them—at least until you turn the feature off in the TV app (choose Preferences→Advanced).

Empty Trash Automatically

This item does just what it says—it's another way to turn on the feature described on page 95. (The master switch is in Finder→Preferences→Advanced.)

Reduce Clutter

Clicking Review Files auto-clicks the Documents category (in the left-side panel), which opens a fairly amazing set of lists (Figure 2-18):

• **Large Files.** On this tab, the Mac lists all the biggest files on your drive. You're supposed to look them over, scanning for whoppers you don't really need anymore.

If you right-click or two-finger click on one of the files, you get the option to Delete. Clicking that brings up the "Are you sure?" box, which notes that once you delete the item, you can't get it back.

If you're *not* sure, you can press the space bar for a Quick Look at it (page 55).

• **Downloads.** Here's everything in your Downloads folder. Chances are pretty good that you've got some installers and other stuff you don't need anymore.

• **Unsupported Apps.** New in Catalina, this tab shows you all the apps it can't run anyway—mostly because they're 32-bit programs (see page 163). You might as well not have them junking up your machine.

- **File Browser.** This column-view list shows the entire contents of your drive, with the biggest folders listed at the top. It's easy to spot what's eating up space unnecessarily.

Note: To delete a file in the list, you have to right-click or two-finger click its name and, from the shortcut menu, choose Move to Trash.

More to Delete

The left side of the Manage Storage window lists other categories of large files. Click one of these headings to see, in the main window, the gunk within.

- **Applications.** Most programs you've downloaded or installed yourself appear here, presented for deletion. Really, now: When was the last time you ran BeeKeeper Pro?

- **Books, Podcasts, TV.** These are lists of the individual ebooks, podcast episodes, and TV/movie files you've bought from the iTunes Store. Each shows you how much space it's occupying and offers a Delete button.

- **Documents.** This view is identical to the File Browser described in the previous section (Figure 2-18).

Figure 2-18:
The Documents category presents four tabs. Some, like Large Files, offer buttons for each item that let you insta-delete them or find them in the Finder.

- **Music Creation.** The instrument sounds and music-instruction videos in Garage-Band, Apple's music-creation program, take up many gigabytes of storage. This option offers a Remove GarageBand Sound Library file, so you can delete them all in a swoop. (You can always re-download them later.)

- **iCloud Drive.** Here's another road into the Store in iCloud option, where everything on your desktop and in your Documents folder gets copied to iCloud. When your drive fills up, the originals get deleted from your Mac. (See page 214.)

- **iOS Files.** This item (Figure 2-18, top) really should be called "iOS Backups." Each time you back up an iPhone, iPad, or iPod Touch on your Mac, it creates a huge backup file. You might be surprised to find ancient backups still clogging up your drive—duplicate backups, or backups of i-devices you sold long ago.

- **Mail** simply shows you the grand total of all your email and attachments. From here, it's up to you to use one of the file-attachment removal options described already.

- **Messages.** A list of every file attachment you've received in Messages, complete with its size—and a Delete button for each.

- **Music.** A list of music videos, for your removal pleasure. Also an Open Music button that takes you into the Music app, where you can delete songs themselves.

- **Music Creation** refers to instrument-sound files you've downloaded for use in GarageBand. They're huge. If you don't use GarageBand much, delete away; you can always re-download them.

- **Photos** shows your total photos-and-videos space tally; the Open Photos button opens the app so you can go on a deleting binge.

- **Trash.** Here's what's in your Trash. You can look over these things—you even get to see how long they've been in the Trash—and delete them individually or all at once.

- **Other Users.** If other people have accounts on your Mac, this item shows how much space *their* stuff is eating up.

- **System.** MacOS itself eats up many gigabytes of your drive, but unfortunately, there's nothing you can do about it; the Mac needs all those bits. That's why this item is listed in gray.

Spotlight

Every computer offers a way to find files. But Spotlight, a star feature of macOS, shows matches for your search beyond your Mac; it can fetch results from the web, from Apple's app and music stores, from the Maps app, from movie theaters, and so on. It's also the world's most flexible calculator. It can not only do math, but it can also *convert* things: kilometers to miles, Celsius to Fahrenheit, euros to dollars, and so on. And it can pull down even more information from the internet, like sports scores, weather, stock quotes, and lists of Vimeo and YouTube videos.

Even better, it understands "natural language" searches. That is, you can type out plain-English queries that describe what you're looking for, like "files I worked on in January," "slides from 2019 containing WidgeTech," or "images from last year."

Note: Spotlight also understands plain French, Italian, German, Simplified Chinese, and Spanish, if one of those is more your thing.

The Spotlight Menu

See the little Q in the right corner of your menu bar? That's the mousey way to open the Spotlight search box. The other way is to press ⌘-space bar. If you can memorize only one keystroke on your Mac, that's the one to learn. It works both at the desktop and when you're in apps.

In any case, the Spotlight text box appears just below your menu bar (Figure 3-1). Feel free to drag it around your screen. As soon as you begin typing what you're looking for, a list of results appears below the search box. This is a live, interactive search; that is, Spotlight modifies the menu of search results *as you type*.

Tip: You can make the results window taller (drag downward on its bottom edge) or move it around the screen (drag its top bar). Bonus tip: To restore the Spotlight window to its original size and position, hold the cursor down on the Q icon at the top of your screen.

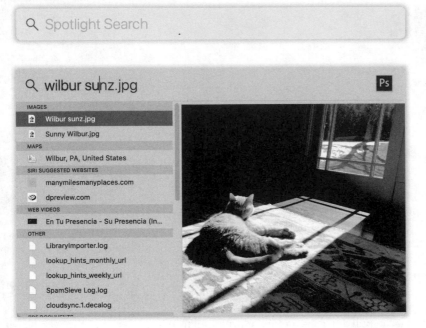

Figure 3-1:
Press ⌘-space bar, or click the Q icon, to make the search box appear.

As you type, Spotlight builds the list of every match it can find, neatly organized by type: programs, documents, folders, images, PDF files, and so on. Better yet, if you're not sure what something is, click its name—or pause on it as you walk down the list with the arrow keys. A preview pops out to the right. It shows exactly what's in that movie, picture, document, web page, or whatever.

Searching Your Mac

As you'd expect, Spotlight can round up anything with an icon on your Mac. Any file, folder, program, picture, movie, PDF document, music file, Microsoft Office document, and even font, regardless of its name or folder location. Spotlight can also find things according to their file types (type *.docx* to find Word files), download source (type *cnet.com* to find programs you downloaded from that site), sender (a name or email address), or Finder tag (page 89).

In the Spotlight search box, you can type part of its name or some text that appears *inside* the document you want. For example, if you're trying to find a file called *Pokémon Fantasy League.doc,* typing just *pok* or *leag* would probably suffice. (The search box doesn't find text in the *middles* of words, though; it searches from the beginnings of words.)

Spotlight also finds matching information within many of your Mac programs: every email message, Contacts entry, calendar appointment, web bookmark, System Preferences panel, To Do item, chat transcript, dictionary definition, and website in your History list. Spotlight can even find photos according to *who's in them* (using the Faces

feature in Photos) or where they were taken (using its Places feature). If you use Messages (Chapter 20), Spotlight can also find the lucky members of your buddies lists.

Tip: The Spotlight menu is a full-blown English dictionary, too. Or, more specifically, it's wired directly into macOS's own dictionary, which sits in your Applications folder.

So if you type a word—say, *myrmecophile*—into the search box, you see the Dictionary definition in the results. Click it to see the full-blown entry in the preview pane. (In this example, that would be "n: an invertebrate or plant which has a symbiotic relationship with ants.")

You can also type out, in plain English, a description of files you're trying to find. You can use any combination of file types (*documents, movies, images, presentations, email*), dates and times (*2020, last year, this week, last month, in February*), the names of email senders or recipients (*simon jary, halle franklin*), plus the words and phrases inside each file.

In other words, you can search for things like these: *files I worked on last week, slides from 2019 containing EduMotion, images from last year, messages from Xerxes, photos of tia, files I created yesterday, emails from Bob last year that contain documents,* or *the presentation I was working on yesterday.*

Searching the Internet

Spotlight is also a Google wannabe. It can bring up results from the web for all kinds of common information, saving you the trouble of opening your web browser and doing a search.

You'll often find, for example, a Wikipedia entry in the results, or Twitter results, along with matches from the App Store, the iTunes Store, Apple TV, the Maps app's database of restaurants and businesses, movies now playing, and so on.

Here are the kinds of things Spotlight knows about:

- **General information.** Spotlight uses Google to provide lists of web links it thinks you'll find useful. The beauty of Spotlight is that, often, you get the answers you need right in the Spotlight box, without having to venture any further afield on the web.

- **Music.** Spotlight can find anything in the iTunes music store. Type the name of a performer, album, or song.

- **Restaurants, businesses, points of interest.** Spotlight is hooked into macOS's Maps program and everything it knows about the world. You can quickly look up landmarks like *empire state building* or *washington monument*, business names like *home depot*, and business categories like *sushi, pizza,* or *gas station.*

 In each case, the preview pane shows you a snippet of that location's map, plus handy buttons like Directions and Call. (The Directions button hands you off to the Maps app to complete the task.) Spotlight may not be able to find some smaller locations and companies, but it knows quite a bit.

If you search for the name of a nearby restaurant or shop, the results include driving directions, photos, hours of operation, Yelp reviews, and contact information.

- **Movies.** When you type the name of a movie—past or present—the preview panel shows you a handy dossier about that flick: its year of release; rating (like PG-13 or R); plot summary; cast and crew lists; and even a button that takes you to the TV app, where you can rent, buy, or preorder the movie (Figure 3-2).

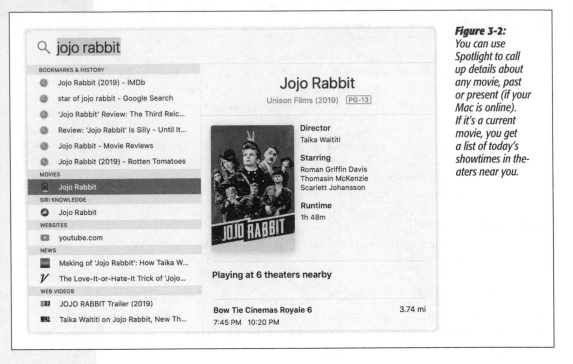

Figure 3-2:
You can use Spotlight to call up details about any movie, past or present (if your Mac is online). If it's a current movie, you get a list of today's showtimes in theaters near you.

- **Stocks.** Type a stock abbreviation (*AAPL* or *NFLX*) or a wordier phrase (*Microsoft stock*) to see an info panel of its current price, its rise or fall today, and its 52-week high and low.

- **Weather.** Need a forecast? Type "weather" plus the city name (*weather boston*).

- **Tweets and hashtags.** A hashtag is a searchable keyword preceded by a # symbol, like *#firstworldproblems* or *#StanleyCup*. When you search for one, Spotlight shows you a few matching tweets—a great way to find out what's happening in the world.

- **iTunes Store and Apple TV.** Want to know if Apple sells or rents a certain movie or TV show or has a certain album for sale? Use Spotlight. It searches Apple's online stores without your having to open any other programs. (Only the biggest names show up in these searches; Spotlight doesn't search the entire music and movie stores.)

- **Web videos.** Spotlight can find a video from YouTube or Vimeo. You get a link that takes you to the video, but you can't actually play it in the Spotlight box.

- **Flight info.** Spotlight can find you the latest information about any flight. Just type in the airline and the flight number to get a map of the flight, status, and other details.

- **Sports scores, standings, and info.** Spotlight is the world's most smug sports know-it-all; see Figure 3-3.

Figure 3-3:
You can search for team scores or schedules (sf giants schedule), team lineups (knicks roster), league standings (marlins standings), or player stats (lebron james). You can click within the preview pane to open a web page with further details.

Calculations and Conversions

Yes, Spotlight is great for searching your Mac and the internet. But it also has a third skill: It can do math for you. Get into the habit of hitting ⌘-space when you have a quick question about any of the following:

- **Calculations.** Spotlight is a tiny pocket calculator, always at the ready. Press ⌘-space, type or paste 38*48.2-7+55, and marvel at the first result in the Spotlight menu: 1879.6. There's your answer—and you didn't even have to fire up the Calculator.

 Use the asterisk (*) to mean "times" and the slash (/) as "divided by."

 And Spotlight is not just a four-function calculator, either. It works with square roots: Type *sqrt(25),* and you'll get the answer 5. It also works with functions like $\log(x)$, $\exp(x)$, $\sin(x)$, $\sinh(x)$, and e. You can even type *pi* to represent, you know, pi.

- **Conversions.** This handy feature (see Figure 3-4) converts units of measurement for you. It converts time, temperature, mass (weight), length, and even currency.

 Usually, you don't have to type anything more than the amount you want to convert; Spotlight instantly converts it to the five most likely other units. For example, if you type *338 feet,* the preview pane shows you the same distance in meters, yards, kilometers, miles, and inches.

But what if what you really wanted was to know how many *centimeters* that is? Just keep typing. If you type *338 feet in centimeters,* you get the answer: 10,302.2 centimeters.

In the same way, you can convert volume (teaspoons, tablespoons, cups, pints, quarts, gallons, cubic feet, fluid ounces, centiliters, milliliters, liters, cubic feet, cubic meters); weight and mass (pounds, ounces, kilograms, grams, milligrams, short tons, metric tonnes, long tons); area (acres, hectares, square feet, square yards, square meters, square kilometers); temperature (Fahrenheit, Celsius, Kelvin—you can abbreviate F, C, or K); force (joules, calories, foot pounds, newton meters, BTUs); or power (watts, kilowatts, BTUs per minute). And those are just a few examples.

If you have an internet connection, you can even convert currencies. Type *134 euros,* for example, and you may find out that that's 148.64 in U.S. dollars—a lot for a hamburger. The preview pane also offers the same figure in British pounds, Japanese yen, Canadian dollars, and Swiss francs. If you want a different unit, say so. Type *134 euros in yuan,* for example, to find out how much it's worth in China.

Note: Spotlight doesn't offer to convert the lesser-known units, like furlongs, leagues, cubits, and spans. It leaves those conversions to the lucrative market already serving biblical scholars and sea captains.

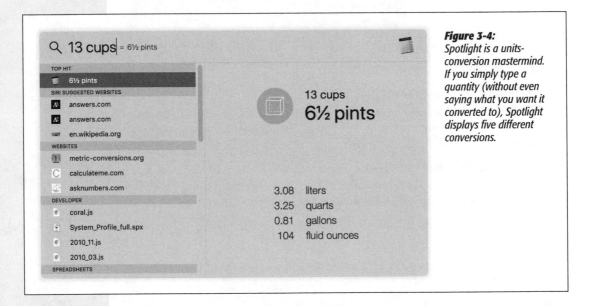

Figure 3-4:
Spotlight is a units-conversion mastermind. If you simply type a quantity (without even saying what you want it converted to), Spotlight displays five different conversions.

The Preview Pane

Spotlight's window is divided in half. The left side is the list of results.

On the right, though, is a preview pane that shows what's *in* each result. When you click an item in the results list—or use the arrow keys to walk down that list—the preview pane bursts to life, presenting a visual display of that result (Figure 3-5).

Plenty of times, your quest for information *ends* with a glance at the preview pane. If you were hoping to find a dictionary definition, a phone number, an email address, a unit conversion, the address of a business from Maps, or the rating or plot summary of a current movie, for example, that information is now attractively arrayed before you. No need to open anything from here.

In the same way, you can grab yourself a Quick Look preview of what's inside a document. That is, you can see the actual photo when you highlight a JPEG file's name, or you can read the actual text when you highlight a Word document's name.

Tip: You can even copy material out of the preview pane. Just drag through it and then press ⌘-C.

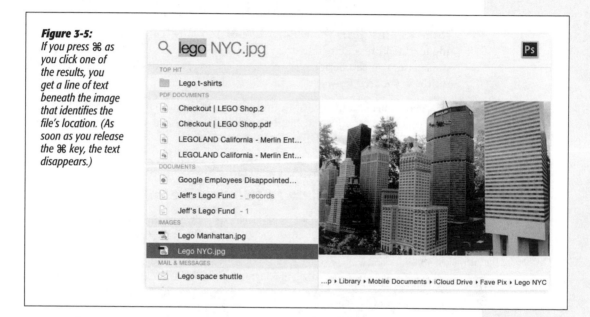

Figure 3-5:
If you press ⌘ as you click one of the results, you get a line of text beneath the image that identifies the file's location. (As soon as you release the ⌘ key, the text disappears.)

Opening a Result

If you're using Spotlight to find and open an app or a document, double-click it to open it. Or use the arrow keys to walk down the menu, and then press Return to open the one you want.

If you click an application, it opens. If you select a System Preferences panel, System Preferences opens to that panel. If you choose an appointment, the Calendar program opens, already set to the appropriate day and time. Selecting an email message opens that message in Mail or Outlook. And so on.

Spotlight is so fast it eliminates a lot of the folders-in-folders business that's a side effect of modern computing. Why burrow around in folders when you can open any file or program with a couple of keystrokes?

Spotlight Results Tips

It should be no surprise that a feature as important as Spotlight comes loaded with options, tips, and tricks. Here it is—the official, unexpurgated Spotlight Tip-O-Rama:

- **You may wonder why Spotlight bothers** to display, in big gray lettering, the name of each item you highlight in the results list. It's because sometimes the item's name doesn't match your search term. You might search for *kumquats*, for example, and find it inside a file called "Frank's Favorite Fruits." The lettering tells you the document name.

 The same sort of thing happens when you see a website's name in the results. The results list might show the ".com" name for the site (like *amazon.com*), and the gray lettering might say "Top Sellers in Electronics."

- **If the very first item—sometimes labeled Top Hit—is** the icon you were looking for, then press Return to open it. This is a huge deal, because it means that in most cases you can perform the entire operation without ever taking your hands off the keyboard.

 To open Safari in a hurry, for example, press ⌘-space bar (to open the Spotlight search box), type *safa*, and hit Return, all in rapid-fire sequence, without even looking. Presto: Safari is before you.

UP TO SPEED

What Spotlight Knows About Your Files

The beauty of Spotlight is that it doesn't just find files whose names match what you've typed. That would be *so 2004!*

No, Spotlight actually looks *inside* the files. It can read and search the contents of text files, RTF and PDF documents, documents from Keynote, Pages, Photoshop, Microsoft Office (Word, Excel, Outlook, and PowerPoint), and so on.

Software companies can release bits of add-on software—plug-ins—that make their documents searchable by Spotlight, too. Check periodically by Googling, for example, *spotlight plug-in* and the kind of software you use. For example, free Spotlight plug-ins are available for OmniGraffle, OmniOutliner, MacDraft, Corel Painter, and many others.

But that's only the beginning. Spotlight searches files not only for the text inside them, but also for over 125 other bits of text—a staggering collection of information tidbits, including the names of the layers in a Photoshop document, the tempo of an MP3 file, the shutter speed of a digital-camera photo, a movie's copyright holder, a document's page size, and on and on. Technically, this sort of secondary information

is called *metadata*. It's usually invisible, although a lot of it shows up in the Get Info dialog box described on page 97.

You might think typing something into the Spotlight search box triggers a search. But to be technically correct, Spotlight has already done its searching. In the first 15 to 30 minutes after you install macOS—or in the minutes after you attach a new hard drive—Spotlight invisibly collects information about everything on your hard drive.

Like a kid cramming for an exam, it reads, takes notes on, and memorizes the contents of all your files. (During this time, if you click the 🔍 icon on the menu bar, you'll be told that Spotlight is indexing the drives.) Once it has indexed your hard drive in this way, Spotlight can produce search results in seconds.

After that initial indexing process, Spotlight continues to monitor what's on your hard drive, indexing new and changed files in the background, in the microseconds between your keystrokes and clicks in other programs.

And what, exactly, is the Top Hit? MacOS chooses it based on its *relevance* (the importance of your search term inside that item) and timeliness (when you last opened it).

Tip: Spotlight makes a spectacular application launcher. That's because Job One for Spotlight is to display the names of matching *programs* in the results menu. Their names appear in the list nearly instantly—long before Spotlight has built the rest of the menu of search results.

If some program on your hard drive doesn't have a Dock icon, for example—or even if it does, actually—there's no faster way to open it than to use Spotlight.

- **To find out where something is on your hard drive**—that is, to see its folder path (page 128)—⌘-click its name. The folder path appears at the bottom of the preview pane (Figure 3-5).

- **To jump to (highlight) a search result's Finder icon** instead of opening it, ⌘-*double*-click its name. Or arrow-key your way to the result's name and then press ⌘-Return, or just ⌘-R. (If it's information from a program, like an email message, calendar appointment, or address-book entry, then it opens in Mail, Calendar, or Contacts instead.)

- **Spotlight's menu shows you, at most,** a couple dozen of the most likely suspects, evenly divided among the categories (Documents, Applications, and so on). To see the complete list, you have to open the Spotlight *searching window* (page 119). Scroll to the bottom of the list and double-click "Show all in Finder."

- **It's easy to open something in the results list** from the keyboard. Just press ⌘-▲ (or ⌘-▼) to jump from category to category. Once you've highlighted the first result in a category, you can walk through the remaining ones by pressing the arrow key by itself. Then, once you've highlighted what you want, press Return to open it.

 In other words, you can get to anything in the Spotlight menu with only a few keystrokes.

- **The Esc key (top-left corner of your keyboard)** offers a two-stage "back out of this" method. Tap it once to close the Spotlight menu and erase what you've typed, so you're all ready to type in something different. Tap Esc a *second* time to close the Spotlight text box entirely, having given up on the whole idea of searching. (If you've managed to lose your Esc key, then ⌘-period does the same thing.)

- **You can drag things out of the results**—either to the desktop, where it becomes an icon, or onto an app's icon on the Dock to open it. For example, you might drag a JPEG graphic from the results list directly onto the Dock icon for Photoshop Elements to open it with that program (instead of whatever program would have opened when you double-clicked the result).

- **Think of Spotlight as your little black book.** When you need to look up a number in Contacts, don't bother opening Contacts; it's faster to use Spotlight. You can type somebody's name or even part of someone's phone number.

- **Among a million other things,** Spotlight tracks the keywords, descriptions, faces, and places you've applied to your pictures in Photos. As a result, you can find, open, or insert any photo at any time, no matter what program you're using, just by calling up the Spotlight box (⌘-space bar)! This is a great way to grab a photo to insert into an email message, a presentation, or a web page you're designing. The Photos program doesn't even have to be running.

- **Spotlight is also a quick way to adjust** one of your Mac's preference settings. Instead of opening the System Preferences program, type the first few letters of, say, *mouse* or *network* or *security* into Spotlight. The Spotlight menu lists the appropriate System Preferences panel, so you can jump directly to it.

- **When something is selected in the results list,** you can press ⌘-B to summon a Google search of that term and ⌘-K to see the Wikipedia entry for it.

Spotlight's menu lists only a couple of dozen found items. In the following pages, you'll learn about how to see the rest of the stuff. But, for now, note that you can eliminate some of the categories that show up here (like PDF files or bookmarks)to permit more of the *other* kinds of things to enjoy those limited seats of honor. Details are on page 130.

- **Spotlight shows you only the matches from** *your account* and the public areas of the Mac (like the System and Applications folders)—but not what's in anyone else's Home folder. If you were hoping to search your spouse's email for phrases like "meet you at midnight," forget it.

- **If Spotlight finds a different version** of something on each of two hard drives, it lets you know by displaying a faint gray hard drive name after each item in the menu.

- **Spotlight works by storing an** *index*—a private, multimegabyte Dewey Decimal System—on each hard drive, disk partition, or USB flash (memory) drive. If you have some oddball type of disk, like a hard drive that's been formatted for Windows, Spotlight doesn't ordinarily index it—but you can turn on indexing by using the File→Get Info command on that drive's icon.

Tip: Spotlight can even find words inside files on other computers on your network—as long as they're also Macs. If not, Spotlight can search only for the names of files on other networked computers.

Advanced Menu Searches

Most people just type the words they're looking for into the Spotlight box. But if that's all you type, you're missing out on a lot of the power of this feature.

Use quotes

If you're searching for a phrase where the words really belong together, put quotes around them. You'll save yourself from having to wade through hundreds of results where the words appear *separately*.

For example, searching for *military intelligence* rounds up documents that contain those two words, but not necessarily side by side. Searching for *"military intelligence"* finds documents that contain that exact phrase. (Insert your own joke here.)

Limit by kind

You can confine your search to certain categories using a simple code. For example, to find all photos, type *kind:image*. If you're looking for a presentation document but you're not sure whether you used Keynote or PowerPoint to create it, type *kind:presentation* into the box. And so on.

Here's the complete list of kinds. Remember to precede each keyword type with *kind* and a colon.

To find this:	Use one of these keywords:
A program	app, application, applications
Someone in your address book	contact, contacts
A folder or disk	folder, folders
A message in Mail	email, emails, mail message, mail messages
A Calendar appointment	event, events
A Calendar task	to do, to dos, todo, todos
A graphic	image, images
A movie	movie, movies
A music file	music
An audio file	audio
A PDF file	pdf, pdfs
A System Preferences control	preferences, system preferences
A Safari bookmark	bookmark, bookmarks
A font	font, fonts
A presentation (PowerPoint, Keynote)	presentation, presentations

You can combine these codes with the text you're seeking, too. For example, if you're pretty sure you had a photo called "Naked Mole Rat," you could cut directly to it by typing *mole kind:images* or *kind:images mole* (the order doesn't matter).

Limit by recent date

You can use a similar code to restrict the search by chronology. If you type *date:yesterday*, then Spotlight limits its hunt to items you last opened yesterday.

Here's the complete list of date keywords you can use: *this year, this month, this week, yesterday, today, tomorrow, next week, next month, next year*. (The last four items are useful only for finding upcoming Calendar appointments. Even Spotlight can't show you files you haven't created yet.)

Limit by tag

Round up everything with a certain tag (page 89) using "tag:" as the search prefix. For example, to find everything you've tagged as Important, you'd search for *tag:important*.

Limit by metadata

If your brain is already on the verge of exploding, then you might want to take a short break before reading on.

These days, you can limit Spotlight searches by *any* of the 175 different info-morsels that may be stored as part of the files on your Mac: author, audio bit rate, city, composer, camera model, pixel width, and so on. Page 126 has a complete discussion of these so-called *metadata* types. (Metadata means "data about the data"—that is, descriptive info-bites about the files themselves.)

Here are a few examples:

- *author:casey.* Finds all documents with "casey" in the Author field. (This presumes that you've actually *entered* the name Casey into the document's Author box. Microsoft Word, for example, has a place to store this information.)

- *width:800.* Finds all graphics that are 800 pixels wide.

- *flash:1.* Finds all photos that were taken with the camera's flash on. (To find photos taken with the flash *off*, you'd type *flash:0*. A number of the yes/no criteria work this way: Use 1 for yes, 0 for no.)

- *modified:3/7/19-3/10/19.* Finds all documents modified between March 7 and 10, 2019. You can also type *created:6/1/19* to find all the files you created on June 1, 2019. Type *modified:<=3/9/19* to find all documents you edited *on or before* March 9, 2019.

 As you can see, three range-finding symbols are available for your queries: <, >, and - (hyphen). The < means "before" or "less than"; the > means "after" or "greater than"; and the hyphen indicates a range (of dates, sizes, or whatever).

Tip: Here again, you can string words together. To find all PDFs you opened today, use *date:today kind:PDF*. And if you're looking for a PDF document you created on July 4, 2018, containing the word "wombat," you can type *created:7/4/18 kind:pdf wombat*—although, at this point, you're not saving all that much time.

Now, those examples are just a few representative searches out of the dozens that macOS makes available. To see the complete list of searchable metadata options, choose Other in the Spotlight Searching window (read on). You'll probably be stunned and amused by the tweakiness of the things you can search for. (Altitude? Tempo? Year recorded? Due date?)

Boolean searches

What comp sci professors call *Boolean* searches are terms that round up results containing *either* of two search terms, *both* search terms, or one term but *not* another.

To go Boolean, you're supposed to incorporate terms like *AND, OR,* or *NOT* into your search queries.

For example, you can round up a list of files that match *two* terms by typing, say, *vacation AND kids.* (That's also how you'd find documents co-authored by two

people—you and a pal, for example. You'd search for *author:Casey AND author:Chris.* Yes, you have to type Boolean terms in all capitals.)

Tip: You can use parentheses instead of AND, if you like. That is, typing *(vacation kids)* finds documents that contain both words, not necessarily together. But the truth is, Spotlight runs an AND search whenever you type two terms, like *vacation kids*—neither parentheses nor *AND* is required.

If you use OR, you can find items that match *either* of two search criteria. Typing *kind:jpeg OR kind:pdf* turns up photos and PDF files in a single list.

The minus sign (hyphen) works, too. If you did a search for *dolphins,* hoping to turn up sea-mammal documents, but instead find your results contaminated by football-team listings, then by all means repeat the search with *dolphins -miami.* MacOS eliminates all documents containing "Miami."

Tip: The word *NOT* works the same way. You could type *dolphins NOT miami* to achieve the same effect. But the hyphen is faster to type.

The Searching Window

As you may have noticed, the Spotlight window doesn't list *every* match on your hard drive. Unless you own one of those extremely rare 60-inch Apple Skyscraper Displays, there just isn't room.

Instead, Spotlight uses some fancy behind-the-scenes analysis to display the *most likely* matches for what you typed. But at the bottom of the results list, you usually see that there are other matches; it says "Show all in Finder," meaning there are other candidates.

There is, however, a second, more powerful way into the Spotlight labyrinth. And that's to use the *Searching* window, shown in Figure 3-6.

You can open the Searching window in either of two ways.

From Spotlight

If the Spotlight results list—its Most Likely to Succeed list—doesn't include what you're looking for, click "Show all in Finder" at the bottom. You've just opened the Searching window.

Now you have access to the *complete* list of matches, neatly listed in what appears to be a standard Finder window.

From the Finder

When you're in the Finder, you can also open the Searching window *directly,* without using the Spotlight window as a trigger. Actually, there are three ways to get there:

- ⌘-F (for *Find,* get it?). When you choose File→Find (⌘-F), you get an *empty* Searching window, ready to fill in for your search.

Tip: When the Find window opens, what folder does it intend to search?

That's up to you. Choose Finder→Preferences→Advanced. From the "When performing a search" pop-up menu, you can choose Search This Mac, Search the Current Folder (usually what you want), or Use the Previous Search Scope (that is, either "the whole Mac" or "the current folder," whichever you set up last time).

Figure 3-6:
When you type your search term, macOS presents a pop-up menu of suggestions. For example, when you type excel*, it's asking: "Would you like me to limit the search to Excel spreadsheets?" If you ignore the suggestions, the window shows you all matches— including files with the word "excel" inside them.*

- **Option-⌘-space bar.** This keystroke opens the same window. But it always comes set to search the *currently open window*, rather than everything on your Mac, regardless of the setting you made in Preferences (as described in the previous Tip).

- **Open any desktop window, and type something into the search box at upper right.** Presto—the mild-mannered folder window turns into the Searching window, complete with search results.

Tip: You can change the Find keystrokes to just about anything you like. See page 200.

The Basic Search

When the Searching window opens, you can start typing whatever you're looking for into the search box at the top. As you type, the window fills with a list of the files and folders whose names contain what you typed. It's just like the Spotlight results, but without the item-count limit (Figure 3-6).

Where to look

The phrases at the top of the window—This Mac, [Folder Name], and Shared—are buttons. Click one to tell the Mac where to search:

- **This Mac** means your *entire* computer, including secondary disks attached to it (or installed inside)—minus other people's files, of course.

- **"Letters to Congress"** (or whatever the current window is) limits the search to whatever window was open. So if you want to search your Pictures folder, open it first and *then* hit ⌘-F. You'll see the "Pictures" button at the top of the window, and you can click it to restrict the search to that folder.

- **Shared.** Click this button to expand the search to your *entire network* and all the computers on it. (This assumes, of course, that you've brought their icons to your screen as described in Chapter 13.)

 If the other computers are Macs running Leopard (OS X 10.5) or later, then the Searching window can search their files just the way it does on your own Mac—finding words inside the files, for example. If they're any other kind of computer, Spotlight can search for files only by name.

Tip: If the object of your quest doesn't show up, you can adjust the scope of the search with one quick click on another button at the top of the window, like This Mac or Shared. The Mac updates the results list.

The suggestions list

When you search, macOS tries to figure out whether you're looking for *file names* or *words inside files.* The Searching window may show you both in the same results list.

But more important, it offers a suggestions pop-up menu, shown in Figure 3-7. Its purpose is to help you narrow down the results list with one quick click. Whatever you click here is instantly immortalized as a search token, as described in the next section.

Figure 3-7:
Each time you add a criterion by clicking the drop-down list of suggestions, the Mac adds a new token (criterion bubble) to the search box.

Or you can just type what you're seeking instead of using the bubbles. For example, pictures of chris from january 2018.

You may see any of these headings in the suggestions list:

- **Filenames.** The top option is always Filenames; click it to search by the files' names only. If you type *chris* into the box, you want files whose *names* contain that word.

- **Kinds.** If you type *image,* the Kinds option here offers you choices like "Image" (any kind), "JPEG image," "GIF image," or "PNG Image." If you type *document,* you get options like "Word Document" and "PDF Document." If you search for *photo,* the menu lets you pinpoint files whose *file type* contains "photo"—like photo libraries or Adobe Photoshop files. And so on.

- **Downloaded From.** You see this option when what you type is a web address. If you type *Macworld* into the search box, then "Downloaded From Macworld.com" appears in the results list—a handy way to round up all the files you've downloaded from a specific site.

- **Dates.** If you type a month (*august* or *august 2019)* or a year into the search box, the suggestions pop-up menu says "Dates: August 2019" (or whatever). Clicking it lets you do a quick roundup of all files you created, modified, last opened, or added during that period.

- **Tags.** Here's yet another way to use the file tags described on page 89. When you type a search term that matches one of your tags (for example, *green*), the suggestions menu includes "Tags: Green."

In each case, the suggestions in this menu reflect only files that actually *exist* on your Mac. If you search for "green," but green isn't one of your Finder tags, then the Tags suggestion doesn't appear. If you haven't downloaded anything from *Macworld.com*, then that option doesn't appear. And so on.

Once you learn to actually start *using* these suggestions—once you get the hang of the kinds of things they offer—you can get a lot of mileage out of them. If, on the other hand, you just find them confusing, no big deal. Click the ✖ to close the suggestions list and reveal the existing Searching window.

Power Searches with Tokens

The real beauty of the Searching window is that it can hunt down icons via more specific searches than you could using the main Spotlight feature. For example, a feature called *tokens* lets you combine criteria so you can find only *music* files sent to you by *Casey.* (A token, in Apple's usage, means "a visual representation of a search criterion.")

Here, for example, is how you might search for pictures of Chris that were last opened in January.

Note: Before you get too invested in this tokens business, remember that you can do the same thing using Spotlight's plain-English searches. You can just type, for example, *photos of chris from january.*

1. **In the Finder, press ⌘-F.**

 The Searching window opens.

2. **In the search box, type *image.***

 Sure enough: The window now shows everything on your Mac that *is* an image, *contains* the word "image" in its name, or even contains the word "image" within the file. But the list of suggestions (Figure 3-6) wants to know: Which do you really want? Files that are images? Or files with the word "image" in their names?

3. **In the suggestions menu, under Kinds, click *Image.***

 You've just pared down the list of results. Now it shows only the files that *are* photos.

Note, too, that the first *token* has appeared. Each time you click a refinement criterion, as you did in this step, macOS enshrines it in the search box as a shaded bubble. In this case, it created a token that says "Kind: Image." (You can see it in Figure 3-7.)

Note: See the tiny ▾ next to the search token's name? You can click it to see a very short pop-up menu of options: the criterion you selected (like "Kind:" or "Date:") and another command that says "Everything." Choosing it undoes the filtering effect of the suggestion, so this token searches for *any* attribute of your file (like the words inside it).

Why do you need an "Everything" option here? If you'd wanted to search all attributes on your Mac, you could have just typed directly into the search box without even using the suggestions menu.

Three reasons. First, you might want to expand the scope (from "Kind" to "Everything," for example) without having to retype the search term. Second, because you might want to make this token part of a smart folder—a saved search—described starting on page 132. Finally, you might want to go on to add another search criterion—another search token—that builds on this search for "Everything."

Now you need to narrow the quest to files containing the word "Chris."

4. Continue typing in the search box. This time, type *chris.*

The suggestions appear again, offering options for file names and, probably, a Sent By list that lists everyone named Chris who's ever sent you messages or files. What you want is images whose names contain the *word* "Chris."

5. Click *Filename.*

The list of files is much smaller now. It shows only image files with "Chris" in their names.

For your final stunt, you'll screen out all but the January images.

6. Continue typing in the search box. This time, type *january.*

The suggestions list offers dates like *January 2018*. You can see the result so far in Figure 3-7.

7. Click the month you want.

And voilà: The results list shows you only the January photos of Chris.

To delete a token, click it and then press the Delete key, or backspace over it. You can also edit one: Double-click the right side of the token bubble; now you can retype the search term.

Note: This same feature is also in Mail, where it's even more useful; you have search options like Subjects, People, and so on.

Power Searching the Old Way

Search tokens are supposed to make multi-criteria searches easier than they used to be. But they're not as powerful as the Old Way, which is still around.

Using the Old Way of power searching, you can set up a search that finds a document whose name begins with the letters *Cro,* is over a megabyte in size, was created after 10/1/19 but before the end of the year, was changed within the past week, has the file name suffix *.doc,* and contains the phrase "attitude adjustment." (Of course, if you knew *that* much about a file, you'd probably know where it *was,* too. But you get the picture.)

In all, the Old Way lets you specify more than 125 different search criteria: date modified, file size, the "last opened" date, tag, copyright holder's name, ISO speed (of a digital photo), tempo (of a music file), and so on. Figure 3-8 illustrates how detailed this kind of search can be.

Figure 3-8:
By repeatedly clicking the ⊕ button, you can turn on as many criteria as you like; each additional row further narrows the search. To delete a row, click the ⊖ button at its right end.

To set up a complex search like this, use the second row of controls at the top of the window. And the third, and the fourth, and the fifth. Each time you click one of the ⊕ buttons at the right end of the window, a new criterion row appears; use its pop-up menus to specify *what* date, *what* file size, and so on.

Tip: If you press Option, the ⊕ button changes into a ⊖ button. When you click it, you get sub-rows of parameters for a single criterion. A pop-up menu lets you choose Any, All, or None, so you can build what are called exclusionary searches.

The idea here is that you can set up a search for documents created between November 1 and 7 or between November 10 and 14. Or files named Complaint that are also either Word or InDesign files.

The mind boggles.

Here's a rundown of the ways you can restrict your search, according to the options in the first pop-up menu of a row. Note that after you choose from that first pop-up

menu ("Last opened date," for example), you're supposed to use the additional pop-up menus to narrow the choice ("within last," "2," and "weeks," for example), as you'll read in a moment.

Note: It may surprise you that choosing something from the Kind pop-up menu triggers the search instantly. As soon as you choose Applications, for example, the window fills with a list of every program on your hard drive. Want a quick list of every folder on your entire machine? Choose Folders. (Want to see which folders you've opened in the past couple of days? Add another row.)

If you also type something into the search box at the very top of the window—before or after you've used one of these pop-up menus—the list pares itself down to items that match what you've typed.

Kind

When the first pop-up menu says Kind, you can use the second pop-up menu to indicate what kind of file you're looking for: Applications, Documents, Folders, Images, Movies, Music, PDF files, Presentations, Text files, or Other.

For example, when you're trying to free up some space on your drive, you could round up all your movie files, which tend to be huge.

And what if the item you're looking for isn't among those 10 canned choices? What if it's an alias, or a Photoshop plug-in, or some other type? That's what the Other option is all about. Here you can type in almost anything that specifies a kind of file: *Word, Excel, TIFF, JPEG, AAC, final cut, alias,* or whatever.

Last opened date/Last modified date/Created date

When you choose one of these options, the second pop-up menu lets you isolate files, programs, and folders according to the last time you opened them, the last time you changed them, or when they were created:

- **Today, yesterday, this week, this month, this year.** This second pop-up menu offers quick, canned time-limiting options.

- **Within last, exactly, before, after.** If you choose "before," "after," or "exactly," then your criterion row sprouts a month/day/year control that lets you round up items that you last opened or changed before, after, or on a specific day, like 5/27/19. If you choose "within last," then you can limit the search to things you've opened or changed within a specified number of days, weeks, months, or years.

 These are awesomely useful controls, because they let you specify a chronological window for whatever you're looking for.

Tip: You're allowed to add two Date rows—a great trick that lets you round up files you created or edited between two dates. Set up the first Date row to say "is after" and the second one to say "is before."

Science!

Name

Spotlight likes to find text *anywhere* inside your files, no matter what their *names* are. But when you want to search for an icon by the text that's in only its *name,* this is your ticket. (Capitalization doesn't matter.)

Wouldn't it be faster just to click Filenames in the suggestions pop-up menu (Figure 3-6)? Yes—but using the Searching window gives you far more control, thanks to the second pop-up menu that offers these options:

- **Matches.** You'll see files whose names contain entire words you're looking for. If you search for *peas,* you'll find files called "Peas & Crackers" and "Snow Peas"—but not "Appeasement."

- **Contains.** The position of the letters you type doesn't matter. If you type *then,* you find files with names like "Then and Now," "Authentic Cajun Recipes" and "Lovable Heathen."

- **Begins with.** The Find program finds only files beginning with the letters you type. If you type *then,* you find "Then and Now," but not "Authentic Cajun Recipes," or "Lovable Heathen."

- **Ends with.** If you type *then,* you find "Lovable Heathen," but not "Then and Now" or "Authentic Cajun Recipes."

- **Is.** This option finds only files named *precisely* what you type (except that capitalization still doesn't matter). Typing *then* won't find any of the file names in the previous examples. It would unearth only a file called simply "Then." In fact, a file with a file name suffix, like "Then.doc," doesn't even qualify.

- **Is not** finds items that *don't* contain what you've typed—handy for excluding items from a search that has other criteria.

Contents

You can think of this option as the opposite of Name. It finds *only* the text that's inside your files and completely ignores their icon names. That's a handy function when, for example, a document's name doesn't match its contents. Maybe a marauding toddler whacking the keys renamed your doctoral thesis "xggrjpO#$5%////." Or maybe you just can't remember what you called something.

Other

If this were a math equation, it might look like this: *options × options = overwhelming.*

Choosing Other from the first pop-up menu opens a special dialog box containing more than 125 *other* criteria. Not just the big kahunas like Name, File, Size, and Kind, but far more targeted (and obscure) criteria like "Bits per sample" (so you can round up MP3 music files of a certain quality), "Device make" (so you can round up all digital photos taken with, say, a Canon Rebel camera), "Key signature" (so you can find all the GarageBand songs you wrote in the key of F-sharp), "Pages" (so you can find all Word documents that are really long), and so on. As you can see in Figure 3-9, each one comes with a short description.

You may think Spotlight is offering you a staggering array of file-type criteria. In fact, though, big bunches of information categories (technically called *metadata)* are all hooks for a relatively small number of document types. For example:

- **Digital photos and other graphics files** account for the metadata types alpha channel, aperture value, color space, device make, device model, EXIF version, exposure mode, exposure program, exposure time, flash, f number, focal length, ISO speed, max aperture, metering mode, orientation, pixel height, pixel width, red eye, resolution height, resolution width, and white balance.

- **Digital music files** have searchable metadata categories like album, audio bit rate, bits per sample, composer, duration, General MIDI sequence, key signature, lyricist, musical genre, recording date, sample rate, tempo, time signature, track number, and year recorded. There's even a special set of parameters for GarageBand and Soundtrack documents, including instrument category, instrument name, loop descriptors, loop file type, loop original key, and loop scale type.

- **Microsoft Office documents** can contain info bits like authors, contributors, fonts, languages, pages, publishers, and contact keywords (name, phone number, and so on).

This massive list also harbors a few criteria you may use more often, like File Size, File label, and File invisible (which lets you see all the invisible files on your hard drive).

Now, you could argue that in the time it takes you to set up a search for such a specific kind of data, you could have just rooted through your files and found what you wanted manually. But, hey—you never know. Someday you may remember *nothing* about a photo except that you used the flash and an f-stop of 1.8.

Figure 3-9:
Here's the master list of search criteria. Turn on the In Menu checkboxes of the ones you'll want to reuse often. Once you've added some of these to the menu, you'll get an appropriate set of "find what?" controls ("Greater than" and "Less than" pop-up menus, for example).

Select a search attribute:

Attribute	Description	In Menu
Album	Title for a collection of media, such as a record album	☑
Alpha channel	Whether the image has an Alpha channel	☐
Alternate display nam...	Alternate names of the file	☐
Alternatives	Alternatives contained in Logic project	☐
Altitude	The altitude of the item in meters above sea level, express...	☑
Aperture value	Size of the lens aperture as a log-scale APEX value	☐
Application Categories	Categories application is a member of	☐
Arranger	Arranger of the song in this Finale Notation File	☐
Attachment Names	A list of the names of attachments associated with a mess...	☐
Attachment Types	A list of the types for attachments associated with a messa...	☐
Audiences	Who the document is intended for	☐
Audio bit rate	Bit rate of the audio in the media	☑
Audio channels	Number of channels in the file's audio data	☐
Audio encoding appli	Name of the application that encoded the data in the audio	☐

Cancel OK

Tip: Don't miss the search box in this dialog box. It makes it super-easy to pluck one useful criterion needle—File Size, say—out of the haystack. Also don't forget about the In Menu checkbox in the right column. It lets you add one of these criteria to the main pop-up menu, so you don't have to go burrowing into Other again the next time.

What to Do with Search Results

The results window is a regular old Finder window, with all the familiar views and controls (Figure 3-10).

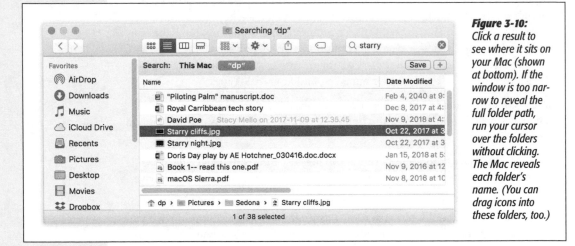

Figure 3-10:
Click a result to see where it sits on your Mac (shown at bottom). If the window is too narrow to reveal the full folder path, run your cursor over the folders without clicking. The Mac reveals each folder's name. (You can drag icons into these folders, too.)

You can work with anything in the results window exactly as though it were in a regular Finder window: drag something to the Trash, rename something, press the space bar for a Quick Look at it, drag something to the desktop to move it there, drag something onto a Dock icon to open it with a certain program, Option-⌘-drag it to the desktop to create an alias, and so on.

You can move up or down the list by pressing the arrow keys, scroll a "page" at a time with the Page Up and Page Down keys, and so on. You can also highlight multiple icons simultaneously, the same way you would in a Finder list view: Highlight all of them by choosing Edit→Select All, highlight individual items by ⌘-clicking them, drag diagonally to enclose a cluster of found items, and so on.

Or you can proceed in any of these ways:

- **Change the view (list, column, and so on)** by clicking one of the View icons or choosing from the View menu as described in Chapter 1. Actually, gallery view is a *great* one for search results; since this list is culled from folders all over the computer, you otherwise have very little sense of context as you examine the file names.

- **Sort the results** by clicking the column headings (in list view).

- **Arrange the results** by using the Group pop-up menu button (⊞▾). That way, you can group the results as described on page 39. It can be especially useful to clump them by Kind, so similar file types are clustered together (Documents, Images, Messages, and so on), or to sort by Date Last Opened, so the list is chronological.

- **Change the view options.** Press ⌘-J (or choose View→Show View Options) to open the View Options panel for the results window. Here you can add a couple of additional columns (Date Modified, Date Created); change the icon size or text size; or turn on the "always" checkbox at the top, so future results windows will have the look you've set up here.

- **Get more information** about a result by selecting it and then choosing File→Get Info (⌘-I). The normal Get Info window appears, complete with date, size, and location information.

- **Find out where the file is.** It's nice to see all the search results in one list, but you're not actually seeing them in their native habitats: the Finder folder windows where they physically reside.

 If you click once on an icon in the results, the bottom edge of the window becomes a folder map that shows you where that item is. For example, in Figure 3-10, the notation in the Path strip means: "The 'Starry cliffs' icon you found is in the Sedona folder, which is in the Pictures folder, which is in dp's Home folder."

 To get your hands on the icon in its home window, choose File→Show in Enclosing Folder (Control-Option-⌘-A). MacOS highlights the icon in question, sitting there in its window wherever it happens to be on your hard drive.

- **Open the file (or one of the folders it's in).** If one of the found files is the one you were looking for, double-click it to open it (or highlight it and press either ⌘-O or ⌘-▼). In many cases, you don't know or care where the file was—you just want to get into it.

Tip: You can also double-click to open any of the folders in the folder map at the bottom of the window. For example, in Figure 3-10, you could double-click the "Starry cliffs" file to open it, or the Sedona folder to open *it*, and so on.

- **Move or delete the file.** You can drag an item directly out of the found-files list and into a different folder, window, or disk—or straight to the Dock or the Trash. If you click something else and then re-click the dragged item in the results list, the folder map at the bottom of the window updates itself to reflect the file's new location.

- **Start over.** If you'd like to repeat the search using a different phrase, just edit the text in the search box. (Click away from the window and then press ⌘-F to get an empty the search box and Searching window.)

- **Give up.** If none of these avenues suits your fancy, you can close the window as you would any other (⌘-W).

Customizing Spotlight

You've just read about how Spotlight works fresh out of the box. But you can tailor its behavior, both for security reasons and to adapt it to the kinds of work you do. Here are two ways to open the Spotlight preferences center:

- **Use Spotlight itself.** Hit ⌘-space bar, type *spotl*, and press Return.

- **Choose →System Preferences. Click Spotlight.**

In any case, you wind up face-to-face with the dialog box shown in Figure 3-11.

Figure 3-11:
Here's where you can specify what categories of icons you want Spotlight to search and—via the Keyboard Shortcuts button at lower left— choose what keystroke you want to use for highlighting the Spotlight search box.

(You can no longer drag these items up and down to control how the categories appear in the Spotlight results, as you could in some previous versions.)

You can tweak Spotlight in two ways here, both very useful:

- **Turn off categories.** The checkboxes identify what Spotlight tracks. If you find that it uses up menu space by listing, say, web bookmarks or fonts—stuff you don't need very often—turn off their checkboxes.

 This can be especially useful if you don't use Spotlight's internet-searching features. "I'm perfectly capable of looking up movies online," you might say. "I don't need to clutter my Spotlight results list with movie names." Fine—turn off Movies.

- **Change the keystroke.** Ordinarily, pressing ⌘-space bar highlights Spotlight in your menu bar, and Option-⌘-space bar opens the Searching window. If these

keystrokes clash with some other key assignment in your software, though, you can reassign them to almost any other keystroke you like.

To do that, click Keyboard Shortcuts; you jump directly to the System Preferences→Keyboard→Shortcuts tab. Here you can specify a new keystroke, as described on page 200. Apple assumes no responsibility for your choosing a keystroke that messes up some other function. ⌘-S, for example, would not be a good choice.

Privacy Settings

You can hide certain folders from Spotlight searches. Maybe you have privacy concerns—for example, you don't want your spouse Spotlighting your stuff while you're away from your desk. Maybe you just want to create more focused Spotlight searches, removing a lot of old, extraneous junk from its database.

Either way, the steps are simple. Open the Spotlight panel of System Preferences, as described previously. Click the Privacy tab. Figure 3-12 explains the remaining steps.

Tip: When you mark a disk or folder as non-searchable, Spotlight actually deletes its entire *index* (its invisible card-catalog filing system) from that disk. If Spotlight ever seems to be acting wackily, you can use this function to make it rebuild its own index file on the problem disk. Just drag the disk into the Privacy list and then remove it again. Spotlight deletes, and then rebuilds, the index for that disk.

(Don't forget the part about "remove it again," though. If you add a disk to the Privacy list, Spotlight is no longer able to find *anything* on it, even if you can see it right in front of you.)

Once you've built up the list of private disks and folders, close System Preferences. Spotlight now pretends the private items don't even exist.

Figure 3-12:
You can add disks, partitions, or folders to the list of non-searchable items by dragging them into this window. Or, if the private items aren't visible at the moment, click +, navigate to your hard drive, select the item, and then click Choose. To remove something from this list, click it and then press the Delete key or click the − button.

Smart Folders

A *smart folder* is a self-updating folder. It always contains exactly the items that match criteria you've specified in advance. (Smart folders are a lot like smart albums in Music, smart mailboxes in Mail, and so on.) The key to creating one is the little Save button in the upper-right corner of the Searching window when you've built a search request.

Here's a common example. You choose File→Find. You set up the pop-up menus to say "Last opened date" and "this week." You click Save. You name the smart folder something like Current Crises, and you turn on Add To Sidebar (Figure 3-13).

Note: Behind the scenes, smart folders are special files in your Home→Library→Saved Searches folder.

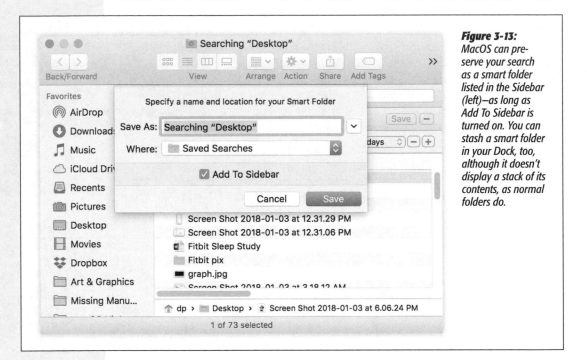

Figure 3-13:
MacOS can preserve your search as a smart folder listed in the Sidebar (left)—as long as Add To Sidebar is turned on. You can stash a smart folder in your Dock, too, although it doesn't display a stack of its contents, as normal folders do.

From now on, whenever you click that smart folder, it reveals all the files you've worked on in the past week or so. These items' *real* locations may be scattered around your Mac and your network. But through the magic of the smart folder, they appear as though they're all in one neat folder.

Tip: If your original search criteria need a little fine-tuning, click the smart folder. From the ✿ menu, choose Show Search Criteria. You're back on the original setting-up-the-search window. Use the pop-up menus and other controls to tweak your search setup, and then click the Save button once again. To delete a smart folder, just drag its icon out of the Sidebar. (Or if it's anywhere else, like on your desktop, then drag it to the Trash like any other folder.)

Dock, Desktop & Toolbars

When you fire up a Mac, the first thing you see is the *desktop*—the great-great-grandchild of the original Mac's home-base screen that changed the world in 1984. There's the Dock, full of colorful icons on a see-through shelf. There are those Finder windows, slick and textureless with their solid-gray title bars. And then there's the shimmering backdrop of the desktop itself.

This chapter shows you how to use and control these most dramatic elements of macOS Catalina's home base.

The Dock

For years, most operating systems maintained two lists of programs. One listed unopened programs until you needed them, like the Start menu (Windows) or the Launcher (Mac OS 9). The other kept track of which programs were open at the moment for easy switching, like the taskbar (Windows) or the Application menu (Mac OS 9).

In macOS, Apple combined both functions into a single strip of icons called the Dock.

Apple's thinking goes like this: Why must you know whether a program is already running? That's the computer's problem, not yours. In an ideal world, this distinction should be irrelevant. A program should appear when you click its icon, whether it's open or not—just as on an iPhone or an iPad.

"Which programs are open" approaches unimportance in macOS, where sophisticated memory-management features make it hard to run out of memory. You can have dozens of programs open at once.

And that's why the Dock combines the launcher and status functions of a modern operating system. Only a tiny black dot beneath a program's icon tells you that it's open—and you can even hide that, if you want. (Choose System Preferences→Dock, and turn off "Show indicators for open applications.")

Apple has made it as easy as possible to like the Dock. You can customize the thing to within an inch of its life, use it to control and manipulate windows in elaborate ways, or even get rid of it completely. This section explains everything you need to know.

Setting Up the Dock

Apple starts the Dock off with a few icons it doesn't want you to miss: Finder, Siri, News, App Store, Mail, the Safari web browser, and so on. But using your Mac without putting your own favorite icons in the Dock is like buying an expensive suit and then turning down the free alteration service. At the first opportunity, you should make the Dock your own.

The concept of the Dock is simple: Any icon you drag onto it (Figure 4-1) is installed there as a button. You can even drag an open window onto the Dock—a Microsoft Word document you're editing, say—using its proxy icon (page 24) as a handle.

Tip: If you right-click or two-finger click a folder, or any other icon, in the *Sidebar* (page 15), you get an Add to Dock command for that icon. Bet you can't guess what it does.

Programs Recent apps Everything else

Open programs Minimized document

Figure 4-1:
To add an icon to the Dock, drag it there. You haven't moved the original file. You've just installed a pointer—like a Mac alias or a Windows shortcut.

A single click, not a double-click, opens the corresponding icon. In other words, the Dock is an ideal parking lot for the icons of disks, folders, documents, programs, and internet bookmarks you access frequently.

Tip: When you click an application icon in the Dock, its icon jumps up and down a few times as the program launches, as though with excitement at having been selected. If you find the icon-bouncing a bit over the top, try this: Choose System Preferences→Dock. Turn off "Animate opening applications." From now on, your icons won't actually bounce—instead, the little dot underneath it will simply *pulse* as the application opens.

You can even install batches of icons onto the Dock all at once—just drag them as a group. That's something you can't do with the other parking places for favorite icons, like the Sidebar and the Finder toolbar.

Here are a few aspects of the Dock that may throw you at first:

- **It has three sections.** See the divider lines (Figure 4-1)? Everything on the left side is an application—a program. Then, in the middle, you get the icons for the apps you've most recently used. (If one of those apps is already represented on the Dock, it doesn't appear here.)

Note: In System Preferences→Dock, you can turn off "Show recent applications in Dock" (the middle section), making more room for other Dock icons.

Everything else goes on the right side: files, documents, folders, disks, and minimized windows.

Remember this division. If you try to drag an application to the middle or right sections, for example, the Mac teasingly refuses to accept it.

- **Its icon names are hidden.** To see the name of a Dock icon, point to it without clicking. The name appears above the icon.

- **Folders and disks sprout *stacks*.** If you click a folder or a disk icon on the right side of the Dock, a list of its contents sprouts from the icon. It's like X-ray vision without the awkward moral implications. Read on for details on stacks.

Tip: If you press Shift as you click, the stack opens in slow motion. Amaze your friends.

- **Programs appear there unsolicited.** You can put stuff on the *right* side of the Dock, but not the left or middle. Program icons appear on the left side automatically whenever you open one and stay there for as long as they're running.

Organizing and Removing Dock Icons

You can move the tiles of the Dock around by dragging them horizontally. As you drag, the other icons scoot aside to make room. When you're satisfied with its new position, drop the icon you've just dragged.

To remove a Dock icon, just drag it away. (You can't remove the icons of the Finder, the Trash, or any minimized document window.) Once your cursor has cleared the Dock, release the mouse button. The icon disappears, and the other Dock icons slide together to close the gap.

Something weird happens if you drag away a Dock program's icon while that program is running. You don't see any change immediately. But when you quit the program, its previously installed icon disappears from the Dock.

Pop-Up Dock Folders ("Stacks")

When you click a disk or folder icon on the Dock, you witness the effect shown in Figure 4-2. In essence, macOS is fanning out the folder's contents so you can see all of them. If it could talk, it would be saying, "Pick a card, any card."

Tip: You can change how the icons in a particular stack are sorted: alphabetically, chronologically, or whatever. Use the "Sort by" section of the shortcut menu.

List view

Fan view

Grid view

Figure 4-2:
What happens when you click a folder in the Dock? You see its contents in one of three views. Here's how you choose the file you're looking for in each:

Top left: In list view, the folder contents appear as a pop-up menu; you can "drill down" into subfolders, and you can open something by clicking its name.

Top right: In fan view, click an icon to open it.

Bottom: In grid view, many more icons appear than can fit in fan view. Click one to open it.

In any of the views, you can get a quick look at a document's contents by using Quick Look. That is, highlight the icon (point without clicking, or use the keyboard to select it), and then press the space bar. A window sprouts, showing the actual document contents.

Click a folder to see what's in it; click the icon you want inside; and you're off and running, without having had to open, manage, and close a window.

Fan vs. grid vs. list

When you click a disk or folder icon on the Dock, what happens? You see its contents, arrayed in your choice of four displays:

- **Fan.** The fan is a single, gently curved column of icons. It's ideal for folders that contain very few icons, because there's room for only a handful of items in a fan (the exact number depends on your screen size). After the first few, you see only a "31 More in Finder" button, which you can click to see everything in that folder—but now you've wasted time, not saved it.

Note: When your Dock is positioned on a side of the screen instead of the bottom, the fan option isn't available.

- **Grid.** If you've set a folder to open as a grid, you get to see all the icons in a big rectangular window. File names often get abbreviated because there's not enough horizontal room, but you get to see many more icons this way. Actually, thanks to the scroll bar, you get to see all the icons this way.

Tip: A cool highlighting effect is available that makes it easier to see which icon you're pointing to as you move your mouse around in a grid or a fan. To make it appear, click-and-hold a folder on the Dock—and then, without releasing the mouse, slide onto the grid or fan. The highlighting follows your cursor.

Alternatively, as soon as the grid or fan appears, press the arrow keys on your keyboard to move from icon to icon—complete with ghostly selection square.

- **List.** You can also opt for a simple list of the folder's contents, like a pop-up menu; you actually see little icons for the files and folders within. The list appears much faster than a fan or a grid does. There's no scroll bar, but you can scroll the list nonetheless just by pointing to the top or bottom of it with your mouse.

GEM IN THE ROUGH

Living Icons

The Mac brought to life a terrific idea, later adopted by other mainstream operating systems: icons that *tell* you something. If the Dock is big enough, you can often tell documents apart just by looking at their icons. Some program icons even change over time.

The Mail icon, for example (Chapter 18), bears a live counter that indicates how many new email messages are waiting for you. (After all, why should you switch into the Mail program only to be disappointed?) The Messages icon lets you know how many chat responses are waiting. You can make your Activity Monitor graph show up right on its icon.

Think of the possibilities. One day the Safari icon could let you know when interesting new web pages have appeared, the Quicken icon could display your bank balance, and the Microsoft Word icon could change every time Microsoft posts a bug fix.

Tip: The list view also displays a little ▶ to the right of each folder within the Dock folder. That is, it's a hierarchical list, meaning you can burrow into folders within folders, all from the original Dock icon, and all without opening a single new window. You can stick your entire Home folder, or even your whole hard drive icon, onto the Dock; now you have complete menu access to everything inside, right from the Dock.

- **Automatic.** There's a fourth option in the shortcut menu for a Dock folder, too: Automatic. If you turn this on, macOS chooses either fan or grid view, depending on how many icons are in the folder.

So how do you choose which display you want? Right-click or two-finger click the Dock folder's icon, and make a selection from the shortcut menu. Each disk or folder icon remembers its own fan/grid/list setting.

The finer points of pop-up Dock folders

Those were the basics of pop-up Dock folders. Here's the advanced course:

- **Ever-Changing Folder-Icon Syndrome (ECFIS).** When you add a folder or disk icon to the Dock, you might notice something disorienting: Its icon keeps changing to resemble whatever you most recently put into it. Your Downloads folder might look like an Excel spreadsheet icon today, a PDF file tonight, and a photo icon tomorrow—but never a folder. You can't get to know a folder by its icon.

 Fortunately, this problem is easy to fix. Right-click or two-finger click the Dock folder. From the shortcut menu, in the "Display as" section, choose either Folder (which looks like a folder forever) or Stack (which changes to reflect its contents).

- **Ready-made pop-up folders.** When you install macOS, you get a couple of starter Dock folders, just to get you psyched. One is Downloads; the other is Documents. (Both of these folders are physically inside your Home folder. But you may well do most of your interacting with them on the Dock.)

 The Downloads folder collects all kinds of online arrivals: files you download from the web using Safari, files you receive in a Messages file-transfer session, file attachments you get via Mail, files sent to you using AirDrop (page 528), and so on. Unless you intervene, they're sorted by the date you downloaded them.

 It's handy to know where to find your downloads—and nice not to have them all cluttering your desktop.

Tip: Once you've opened a stack's fan or grid, you can drag any of the icons right *out* of the fan or grid. Just drag your chosen icon onto the desktop or into any visible disk or folder. In other words, what lands in the Downloads folder doesn't have to stay there. (You can't drag out of a list, however.)

- **Hierarchical folders.** The lists and grids are hierarchical—that is, you can drill down from their folders into their folders. Figure 4-3 makes this concept clearer.

Tip: Figure 4-3 shows you how to open a folder in a grid using the mouse—but you can do it all from the keyboard, too. Once a folder is selected, press Return, ⌘-O, or ⌘-▼ to see what's inside it; press ⌘-▲ to backtrack to the original display. When a folder is highlighted, you can press ⌘-Return to open it in a Finder window; add the Option key to open that Finder window without closing the grid or list.

Figure 4-3:
If you spot a folder inside a grid (left), click it once. You're now looking at a grid of its contents (right). You can go on burrowing like this as deeply as your folders go. You can also "back out" again by clicking the Back button (<) in the upper-left corner.

- **Type-selecting.** Once a list, fan, or grid is on the screen, you can highlight any icon in it by typing the first few letters of its name. For example, once you've popped open your Applications folder, you can highlight Safari by typing *sa*. (Press Return to open the highlighted icon.)

Tip: Alternatively, you can "walk" through the fan, grid, or list by pressing the arrow keys. A highlighting effect makes it crystal clear which icon you're selecting. Once an icon is selected, press Return to open it.

- **Two ways to bypass the pop-up.** If you just want to see what's in a folder, without the graphic overkill of the fan or the grid, then right-click or two-finger click the Dock folder's icon and choose the first command—Open "Applications" (or whatever the folder's name is)—from the shortcut menu. You go straight to the corresponding window.

 Actually, if you *really* value your time, you'll learn the shortcut: Option-⌘-click the Dock folder's icon. That accomplishes the same thing.

Tip: Alternatively, you can ⌘-click a folder on the Dock—or, indeed, any icon on the Dock—to jump to the window that contains that folder's icon. (Bonus: This same ⌘-clicking trick also works in the list of Spotlight search results.)

Three Ways to Get the Dock Out of Your Hair

The bottom of the screen isn't necessarily the ideal location for the Dock. All Mac screens are wider than they are tall, so the Dock eats into your limited vertical screen space. You have three alternatives: Hide the Dock, shrink it, or rotate it 90 degrees.

Auto-hiding the Dock

To turn on the Dock's auto-hiding feature, press Option-⌘-D. (Or, if it's a slow day at work, choose System Preferences→Dock→"Automatically hide and show the Dock.")

When the Dock is hidden, it appears only when you move your cursor to the Dock's edge of the screen. (Individual Dock icons may still occasionally shoot upward into desktop territory when an app needs attention—cute, very cute.)

In practice, you may prefer to hide and show the Dock at will by pressing the hide/show keystroke, Option-⌘-D. This method makes the Dock pop on and off the screen without requiring you to move the cursor.

Shrinking and enlarging the Dock

Depending on your screen's size, you may prefer smaller or larger Dock buttons. The official way to resize them is shown in Figure 4-4.

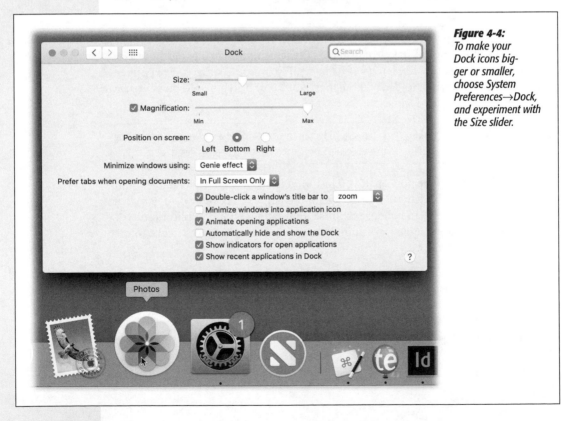

Figure 4-4:
To make your Dock icons bigger or smaller, choose System Preferences→Dock, and experiment with the Size slider.

There's a much faster way to resize the Dock, though: Just position your cursor carefully on the Dock's divider line so it turns into a double-headed arrow (shown in Figure 4-5). Now drag up or down to enlarge or shrink the Dock.

Tip: If you press Option as you drag, the Dock snaps to certain canned icon sizes—those the programmer actually drew. (You won't see the in-between sizes that macOS generally calculates on the fly.)

Figure 4-5:
Look closely—you can see the secret cursor that resizes the Dock. If you don't see any change in the Dock size as you drag upward, you've reached the size limit.

You may not be able to enlarge the Dock if it's already at its size limit. But you can make it almost infinitely smaller. This may make you wonder: How can you distinguish among icons if they're the size of molecules?

The answer lies in the Magnification option (see Figure 4-4). Now your Dock icons balloon to a much larger size as your cursor passes over them.

Tip: You can get Dock magnification à la carte, too. If you press Shift-Control as your cursor approaches the Dock, you temporarily reverse the magnification setting. That is, if magnification is turned off, the icons now swell into magnification mode—and vice versa.

Moving the Dock to the sides of the screen

Yet another approach to getting the Dock out of your way is to rotate it, so it sits vertically against a side of your screen. You can rotate it in either of two ways:

- **The long way.** Choose System Preferences→Dock, and choose Left, Bottom, or Right, as you see fit.

- **The mouse way.** While pressing Shift, drag the Dock's divider line, like a handle, to the side of the screen you want.

You'll probably find that the right side of your screen works better than the left. Most macOS programs put their document windows against the left edge of the screen, where the Dock and its labels might get in the way.

Note: When you position your Dock vertically, the "right" side of the Dock becomes the bottom of the Dock. In other words, the Trash now appears at the bottom of the vertical Dock. So, in this book, mentally substitute the phrase "bottom part of the Dock" when you read references to the "right side of the Dock."

Using the Dock

Most of the time, you'll use the Dock as either a launcher (you click an icon once to open the corresponding program, file, folder, or disk) or as a status indicator (the tiny spots identified in Figure 4-1 indicate which programs are running).

But the Dock has more tricks than that up its sleeve. You can use it, for example, to pull off any of the following stunts.

Switch Applications

The Dock isn't just a launcher; it's also a switcher. Here are some of the tricks it lets you do:

- **Jump among your open programs** by clicking their icons.

- **Drag a document** (such as a text file) onto a Dock application (such as the Microsoft Word icon) to open the former with the latter. If the program balks at opening the document, yet you're sure the program should be able to open it, then add the ⌘ and Option keys as you drag. See the box below.

- **Hide all windows of the program you're in** by Option-clicking another Dock icon.

- **Hide all other programs' windows** by Option-⌘-clicking the Dock icon of the program you do want (even if it's already in front).

GEM IN THE ROUGH

Using the Dock or Sidebar for Drag-and-Drop

The Mac is smart about the relationship between documents and applications. If you double-click a TextEdit document icon, for example, TextEdit opens automatically and shows you the document.

But it's occasionally useful to open a document using a program other than the one that created it. Perhaps, as is often the case with downloaded internet graphics, you don't *have* the program that created it, or you don't know which one was used. This technique is also useful if you want to open a ReadMe file into your word processor, such as Word, instead of the usual TextEdit program.

In such cases, the Dock is handy: Just drag the mystery document onto one of the Dock's tiles, as shown here. Doing so forces the program to open the document—if it

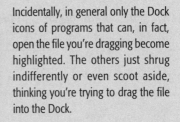

can. (Dragging onto a program's icon in the Sidebar or even the Finder toolbar works the same way.)

Incidentally, in general only the Dock icons of programs that can, in fact, open the file you're dragging become highlighted. The others just shrug indifferently or even scoot aside, thinking you're trying to drag the file into the Dock.

Pressing Option-⌘ as you drag forces Dock icons to be more tolerant. Now they all "light up" as your document touches them, indicating that they'll *try* to open your file. Even so, a "could not be opened" error message may result.

As they say in Cupertino, sometimes what a can really needs is a can opener.

- **Switch windows in one program** by pointing to that program's Dock icon without clicking and then doing a three-finger downward swipe on your trackpad. (This feature, called App Exposé, doesn't work until you turn it on in System Preferences→Trackpad→More Gestures.)

Tip: This trick—the three-finger downswipe—works even on the Dock icons of Apple programs that aren't running. In those situations, you get the effect shown on page 187. For some Apple programs, at least, it's a quick way to get to the icons of recently opened documents.

Operate the Dock by Keyboard Control

If you turn on keyboard navigation, you can operate the Dock entirely from the keyboard; see page 197.

Find Secret Menus

If you right-click, two-finger click, or click-and-hold on a Dock icon, you see its very useful shortcut menu (Figure 4-6).

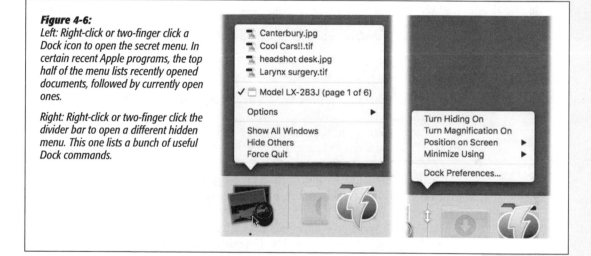

Figure 4-6:
Left: Right-click or two-finger click a Dock icon to open the secret menu. In certain recent Apple programs, the top half of the menu lists recently opened documents, followed by currently open ones.

Right: Right-click or two-finger click the divider bar to open a different hidden menu. This one lists a bunch of useful Dock commands.

If you've clicked a minimized window icon, this shortcut menu says only Open (and possibly also Close). But if you've clicked any other kind of icon, you get some very useful hidden commands. For example:

- **[Window names].** The secret Dock menu of a running program usually lists one or more tiny, neatly labeled window icons, like those shown in Figure 4-6. This useful feature means you can jump directly not only to a certain program but also to a certain open window in that program.

 For example, suppose you've been using Word to edit three different chapters. You can use Word's Dock icon as a Window menu to pull forward one particular chapter or (if it's been minimized) to pull it up—even if a different program is in

front of Word. (The checkmark indicates the *frontmost* window, even if the entire program is in the background. A diamond symbol means the window is minimized and therefore not visible on the screen at the moment.)

In certain Apple showcase programs like TextEdit and the iWork suite, there are actually two lists of documents, separated by a horizontal line. (You can see the effect in Figure 4-6.) The top group lists files you've recently opened in that program; the next batch lists currently open documents.

Tip: The Finder tile that's always at the beginning of the Dock is, in effect, its own Window menu. Its shortcut menu lists all open desktop windows. The Window menu at the top of the Finder screen does the same thing, but the Dock is available no matter what program you're using.

- **Show All Windows/Show Recents.** When a program on the Dock is open, this command says Show All Windows; when it's not running, it says Show Recents. Either way, it takes you to a screen where the icons of recently opened documents appear for easy clicking and reopening. (Well, they *may* appear. Only some apps, including TextEdit and Pages, show these recent icons.) To exit the screen, press Esc or click an empty spot on your desktop.

- **Options.** This submenu contains a bunch of miscellaneous commands:

 Options→Keep in Dock. Whenever you open a program, macOS puts its icon in the Dock—marked with a dot—even if you don't normally keep its icon there.

 As soon as you quit the program, its icon disappears again from the Dock.

Tip: You can get rid of that "running program" indicator dot, if you like. Open System Preferences→Dock and turn off "Show indicators for open applications."

If you understand that much, then the Keep in Dock command makes a lot of sense. It means, "Hello, I'm this program's icon. I know you don't normally keep me in your Dock, but I *could* stay here even after you quit my program. Just say the word." If you find you've been using, for example, Terminal a lot more often than you thought you would, this command may be the ticket.

Tip: Actually, there's a faster way to tell a running application to remain in the Dock from now on. Just drag its icon off the Dock and then right back onto it—yes, while the program is running. You have to try it to believe it.

If you don't want a program's icon to appear in the Dock when it's not running, choose this command again so the checkmark disappears.

Note: If the program is already running, turning off Keep in Dock doesn't *immediately* remove its icon from the Dock. That's because a program always appears in the Dock when it's open. What you're doing here is saying, "Disappear from the Dock when you're *not* running"—and you'll see the proof as soon as you quit that program.

Options→Open at Login. This command lets you specify that you want this icon to open itself automatically each time you log into your account. It's a great way to make sure your email inbox, your calendar, or the Microsoft Word thesis you've been working on is fired up and waiting on the screen when you sit down to work.

To make this item *stop* auto-opening, choose this command again so the checkmark no longer appears.

Options→Show in Finder. This command highlights the actual icon (in whatever folder window it happens to sit) of the application, alias, folder, or document you've clicked. You might want to do this when, for example, you're using a program that you can't quite figure out, and you want to jump to its desktop folder in hopes of finding a ReadMe file there.

- **Hide/Show.** You can hide all traces of the program you're using by choosing Hide from its Dock icon. (You could accomplish the same thing in many other ways, of course; see page 21.)

What's cool here is that (a) you can even hide the Finder and all *its* windows, and (b) if you press Option, the command changes to say Hide Others. This, in its way, is a much more powerful command. It tells all the programs you're *not* using—the ones in the background—to get out of your face. They hide themselves instantly.

Note: Once you've hidden a program's windows, this command changes to say Show, which is how you make them reappear.

- **Quit.** You can quit almost any program directly from its Dock shortcut menu. (Finder, Launchpad, and Mission Control are exceptions.) The beauty of this feature is that you don't have to switch into a program to get to its Quit command.

(If you get nothing but a beep when you use this Quit command, it's because you've hidden the windows of that program, and one of them has unsaved changes. Click the program's icon, save your document, and then try to quit again.)

Tip: If you hold down the Option key—even after you've opened the pop-up menu—the Quit command changes to say Force Quit. That's your emergency hatch for jettisoning a locked-up program.

- **Miscellaneous.** You might find other commands in Dock shortcut menus; software companies are free to add specialty options to their programs.

For example, the Finder icon's shortcut menu offers direct access to commands like Find, Connect to Server, and New Finder Window. Microsoft Office programs (Word, Excel, and so on) come with an Open Recent command, with a list of documents you've opened recently. The Mail icon offers Get New Mail and Compose New Message commands. The Safari icon has a New Window command. The System Preferences icon sprouts a complete list of the preference panes (Sound, Keyboard, Trackpad, and so on). You get the idea.

Tip: If you Control-⌘-click a program's Dock icon, you get an abbreviated shortcut menu. It lists *only* the Options, Hide, and Quit commands and maybe some recent documents—not the full list of commands. If all you want to do is quit a program or something, this abbreviated menu is faster and easier to comprehend.

Drag and Drop

Dock icons are spring-loaded. That is, if you drag any icon onto a Dock folder or disk icon and pause—or, if you're in a hurry, tap the space bar—the Dock icon opens to receive the dragged file.

Note: It opens, that is, *if* the spring-loading delay feature is turned on in System Preferences→Accessibility→Mouse & Trackpad.

This technique is most useful in these situations:

- **Dragging a document icon onto a Dock folder icon.** The folder's Finder window pops open so you can continue the drag into a subfolder.

- **Dragging a document into an application.** The classic example is dragging a photo onto the Photos icon. When you tap the space bar, Photos opens automatically. Since your mouse button is still down, and you're technically still in mid-drag, you can now drop the photo directly into the appropriate Photos album or Event.

 You can drag an MP3 file into an attachment into Mail or Outlook in the same way.

Do Your Filing

Once you've tried stashing a few important folders on the right side of your Dock, you'll never look back. You can mostly forget all the other navigation tricks you've learned in macOS. The folders you care about are always there, ready for opening with a single click.

Better yet, they're easily accessible for putting away files; you can drag them directly into the Dock's folder icons as though they were regular folders.

In fact, you can even drag a file into a subfolder in a Dock folder. That's because, again, Dock folders are spring-loaded. When you drag an icon onto a Dock folder and pause, the folder's window appears around your cursor, so you can continue the drag into an inner folder (and an *inner* inner folder, and so on). Page 85 has the details on spring-loaded folders.

Tip: When you try to drag something into a folder on the Dock, the Dock icons scoot out of the way—and you may end up playing a frustrating game of chase-the-folder. The trick to getting everything to hold still is pressing the ⌘ key as you drag.

Find Great Things to Put in Your Dock

Now that you know what the Dock is about, it's time to set up shop, installing the programs, folders, and disks you'll be using most often.

They can be whatever you want, of course, but don't miss these opportunities:

- **Your Home folder.** Many people immediately drag their hard drive icons—or, perhaps more practically, their Home folders—onto the right side of the Dock. Now they have quick access to every file in every folder they ever use.

- **The Applications folder.** Here's a no-brainer: Stash the Applications folder here so you'll have quick pop-up-menu access to any program on your machine.

- *Your* **Applications folder.** As an even more efficient corollary, create a new folder of your own. Fill it with the aliases of just the programs you use most often and park it in the Dock. Now you've got an even more useful Applications folder that opens as a stack.

- **The Shared folder.** If you're using the Mac's accounts feature (Chapter 12), this is your wormhole to all the accounts—the one place you can put files where everybody can access them (page 504).

- **A tag.** You know those color-coded Finder tags (page 89)? You can drag one directly out of a Finder window's Sidebar and onto the right side of the Dock. When you click its Dock icon, you get a window that displays the icons of everything on your Mac you've tagged that way.

The Finder Toolbar

At the top of every Finder window is a small set of function icons, all in a gradient-gray row (Figure 4-7). The first time you run macOS, you'll find only these icons on the toolbar:

- **Back (<), Forward (>).** The Finder works something like a web browser. Only a single window remains open as you navigate the various folders on your hard drive.

 The Back button (<) returns you to whichever folder you were just looking at. (Instead of clicking <, you can also press ⌘-[, or choose Go→Back—particularly handy if the toolbar is *hidden*, as described in the next section.)

 The Forward button (>) springs to life only after you've used the Back button. Clicking it (or pressing ⌘-]) returns you to the window you've just backed out of.

- **View controls.** The four tiny View buttons switch the current window into icon, list, column, or gallery view, respectively. And, remember, if the toolbar is hidden, you can get by with the equivalent commands in the View menu at the top of the screen—or by pressing ⌘-1 for icon view, ⌘-2 for list view, ⌘-3 for column view, or ⌘-4 for gallery view.

- **Group (▦).** This pop-up menu groups files in a window by date, name, or other criteria; see page 39.

- **Action (⚙).** See page 99.

- **Share (⬆).** See page 258.

- **Tags** (). Here's the Tags menu described on page 89.

- **Search box.** This little round-ended text box is yet another entry point for the Spotlight feature described in Chapter 3. It's a handy way to search your Mac for some file, folder, disk, or program.

Figure 4-7:
If you right-click or two-finger click a blank spot on the toolbar, you get a pop-up menu that offers you a choice of three looks for the buttons here: Icon and Text, Icon Only, or Text Only. (Well, four looks, if you count Customize Toolbar.)

In Text Only mode (bottom), the four View buttons are replaced by a little pop-up menu called View. Furthermore, the search box turns into a one-word button called Search. Clicking it brings up the search window.

Hiding or Shrinking the Toolbar

With the toolbar, the Dock, the Sidebar, and the large icons of macOS, it almost seems like there's an Apple conspiracy to sell big screens.

Fortunately, the toolbar doesn't have to contribute to that impression. You can hide it by choosing View→Hide Toolbar or by pressing Option-⌘-T. (That will work only if you don't have multiple tabs in that Finder window.) That same keystroke, or choosing View→Show Toolbar, brings it back. You can also just make it smaller by hiding the labels (or the icons), as shown in Figure 4-7.

Customizing the Icons on the Toolbar

MacOS offers a collection of beautifully designed icons for alternate (or additional) toolbar buttons. But you can also add anything to the toolbar, turning it into a supplementary Dock or Sidebar. This is great news for people who've run out of space for stashing favorite icons in the Dock or the Sidebar. (Of course, if that's your problem, you do need a bigger monitor.)

Apple's toolbar-icon collection

The first step in tweaking the toolbar is choosing View→Customize Toolbar. The window shown in Figure 4-8 appears.

This is your chance to rearrange the existing toolbar icons or delete the ones you don't use. You can also add any of Apple's buttons to the toolbar by dragging them from the "gallery" onto the toolbar itself. The existing icons scoot out of your cursor's way, if necessary.

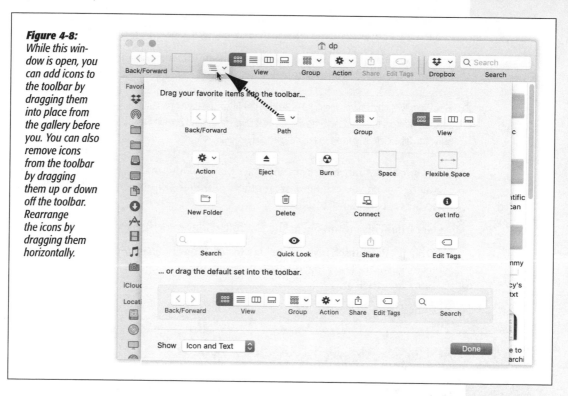

Figure 4-8:
While this window is open, you can add icons to the toolbar by dragging them into place from the gallery before you. You can also remove icons from the toolbar by dragging them up or down off the toolbar. Rearrange the icons by dragging them horizontally.

Most of the options in the gallery duplicate the functions of menu commands. Here are a few that don't appear on the standard toolbar:

- **Path.** Most of the gallery elements are buttons, but this one creates a pop-up menu on the toolbar. When clicked, it reveals (and lets you navigate) the hierarchy— the path—of folders you open to reach whichever window is open. (Equivalent: ⌘-clicking a window's title.)

- **Eject.** This button ejects whichever disk or disk image is currently highlighted. (Equivalent: the File→Eject command, or holding down the ⏏ key, if you have it on your keyboard.)

- **Burn.** This button burns a blank CD or DVD with the folders and files you've dragged onto it. (Equivalent: the File→Burn [Thing Name] to Disc command.)

- **Space.** By dragging this mysterious-looking item into the toolbar, you add a gap between it and whatever icon is to its left. The gap is about as wide as one icon. (The fine, dark, rectangular outline that appears when you drag it doesn't actually show up once you click Done.)

- **Flexible Space.** This icon, too, creates a gap between the toolbar buttons. But this one expands as you make the window wider. Now you know how Apple got the search box to appear off to the right of the standard toolbar, a long way from its clustered comrades to the left.

- **New Folder.** Clicking this button creates a new folder in whichever window you're viewing. (Equivalent: the File→New Folder command, or the Shift-⌘-N keystroke.)

- **Delete.** This option puts the highlighted file or folder icons into the Trash. (Equivalent: the File→Move to Trash command, or the ⌘-Delete keystroke.)

Tip: Weirdly enough, if you highlight an icon in the Trash and then press ⌘-Delete, you trigger the Put Back function—flinging the icon back into the folder it came from (and opening that folder to show you). That is, using the ⌘-Delete keystroke in this case actually *un*deletes.

- **Connect.** If you're on a home or office network, this opens the Connect to Server dialog box so you can tap into another computer. (Equivalent: the Go→Connect to Server command, or ⌘-K.)

- **Get Info.** This button opens the Get Info window for whatever's selected.

- **Drag the default set.** If you've made a mess of your toolbar, you can always reinstate its original Apple arrangement by dragging this rectangular strip directly upward onto your toolbar.

- **Quick Look.** Triggers a preview of the icon (page 55).

Figure 4-9:
You don't need to choose View→Customize Toolbar to add your own icons to the toolbar. Just hold down the ⌘ and Option keys, and then drag an icon from the desktop or any folder window directly onto the toolbar at any time.

To remove the icon later, press ⌘ as you drag it away from the toolbar.

If the window ever gets too narrow to show all the icons you've added to the toolbar, the right end of the toolbar sprouts a **»** symbol. Click it for a pop-up menu that names whichever icons don't fit at the moment. (You'll find this toolbar behavior in many macOS programs, not just the Finder: Safari, Mail, and so on.)

Adding your own stuff

Millions of Mac fans never realize that they can drag *any icons at all* onto the toolbar—files, folders, disks, programs, or whatever—to turn them into one-click buttons.

In short, you can think of the Finder toolbar as yet another Dock or Sidebar (Figure 4-9).

Rearranging or Removing Toolbar Icons

You can drag toolbar icons around, rearranging them horizontally, by pressing ⌘ as you drag. Taking an icon off the toolbar is equally easy. While pressing the ⌘ key, just drag the icon clear away from the toolbar. (If the Customize Toolbar sheet is open, you can perform either step without the ⌘ key. You can also get rid of a toolbar icon by right-clicking or two-finger clicking it and choosing Remove Item from the shortcut menu.)

Designing Your Desktop

In some ways, just buying a Mac was already a renegade act of self-expression. But that's only the beginning. Now it's time to fashion the computer screen itself according to your personal sense of design and fashion.

Backgrounds and Screen Savers

Cosmetically speaking, macOS offers two dramatic full-screen features: desktop backgrounds and screen savers. For details, see page 335.

Accent Colors

For years, macOS has offered a choice of accent colors—used for scroll-bar handles, progress bars, OK buttons, highlighted menu names and commands, and so on.

Well, it wasn't a *huge* choice. You could choose either the standard blue or Graphite (gray). Graphite was intended to pacify Apple's core constituency: artists and graphic designers, some of whom complained that the lively, brightly colored look of the Mac threw off their color judgment.

Graphite is now only one of eight available accent colors. Choose System Preferences→ General, and then choose from the "Accent color" dots.

While you're here, say hello to the "Highlight color" pop-up menu. This is an accent color, too—the background color of highlighted text, the colored oval that appears around highlighted icon names, and a window's "lining" as you drag an icon into it.

Dark Mode

The System Preferences panel just described (General) offers another option, too—one of the most arresting and radical design changes in Mac history. It's Dark mode (Figure 4-10). You're also offered the chance to turn it on during the installation process.

Dark mode is a dark-gray color scheme. Once you turn it on, most of Apple's built-in apps—Finder, Mail, Calendar, Photos, Messages, Notes, Xcode, and so on—take on a stunning, white-on-black appearance.

Here's what *doesn't* change in Dark mode:

- **Your desktop picture.** Or any pictures at all, for that matter.

- **Web pages in Safari.**

- **Preexisting non-Apple apps.** Software companies have to update their programs if they want them to take on Dark mode's dusky hues.

Figure 4-10:
Some people argue that Dark mode blasts less obnoxious light from the screen to your sleeping partner when you're working in bed. Others say Dark mode makes photos stand out more, or that it's less fatiguing to your eyes.

FREQUENTLY ASKED QUESTION

Desktop Fonts

How do I change the fonts used by the macOS Finder?

In Mac versions gone by, you could choose any font you liked for your icon labels. You even had a choice of fonts for use in your menus.

Nowadays, that flexibility is gone. The font used by your menus and icon labels is a modified version of Helvetica Neue called San Francisco—and you can love it or leave it.

For now, Apple intends to remain conservative with the look of macOS—both for "branding" reasons (to make macOS instantly recognizable) and for technical ones (to make sure it doesn't open a Pandora's box of interface hacks that wind up destabilizing the machine).

In general, you'd really have to stretch to say Dark mode helps with your productivity. Mainly it's just cool-looking.

Note: If you're using one of the two dynamic wallpaper options (page 335), then turning on Dark mode also jumps to the nighttime versions of those images.

Desktop Sounds

Desktop sounds are the tiny sound effects that accompany certain mouse drags. And we're talking tiny: a little plink/crunch when you drop an icon onto the Trash, a boingy thud when you drag something into a folder, and so on. The little thud you hear at the end of a file-copying job is actually useful, because it alerts you that the task is complete.

You can turn those sounds off in System Preferences→Sound→"Play user interface sound effects."

And if you decide to leave them turned on, please—use discretion when working in a library, church, or neurosurgical operating room.

Menulets: The Missing Manual

See the menu-bar icons in Figure 4-11? Apple calls them Menu Extras, but Mac fans on the internet have named them "menulets." Each is both an indicator and a menu that provides direct access to certain settings: sound, monitor resolution, Wi-Fi, and so on.

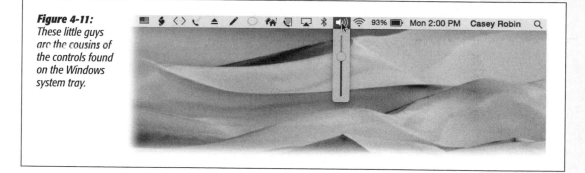

Figure 4-11:
These little guys are the cousins of the controls found on the Windows system tray.

To make the various menulets appear, you generally visit a certain pane of System Preferences (Chapter 9) and turn on a checkbox called, for example, "Show volume in menu bar." Here's a rundown of the various Apple menulets you may encounter, complete with instructions on where to find the magic on/off checkbox for each.

Along the way, you'll discover that secondary, hidden features lurk in many of these menulets, if you happen to know the secret: Press the Option key.

Tip: The following descriptions indicate the official, authorized steps for installing a menulet. There is, however, a folder on your hard drive that contains about 20 of them in a single window, so you can install one with a quick double-click. To find them, open your hard drive→System→Library→CoreServices→Menu Extras folder.

- **Battery** (━) shows how much power remains in your laptop's battery, how much time is left to charge it, whether it's plugged in, and more. You can choose Show Percentage to add a percentage-remaining readout (43%) to the menu bar.

 The Battery menu also shows a list of the most power-hungry open programs ("Using Significant Energy"). That's handy when you're trying to eke out every last drop of battery life for your laptop. *To find the Show checkbox:* Open System Preferences→Energy Saver.

Tip: If you Option-click the Battery menulet, you get to see the status of your battery's health. A Condition command appears. It might say, for example, "Condition: Normal," "Service Battery," "Replace Soon," or "Replace Now." Of course, we all know laptop batteries don't last forever; they begin to hold less of a charge as they approach 500 or 1,000 recharges, depending on the model.

Is Apple looking out for you, or just trying to goose the sale of replacement batteries? You decide.

- **Bluetooth** (✲) connects to Bluetooth devices, "pairs" your Mac with a cellphone, lets you send or receive files wirelessly (without the hassle of setting up a wireless network), and so on. *To find the Show checkbox:* Open System Preferences→Bluetooth.

Tip: You can Option-click this menulet to see three additional lines of nerdy details about your Bluetooth setup: the Bluetooth software version you're using, the name of your Mac (which is helpful when you're trying to make it show up on another Bluetooth gadget), and its Bluetooth MAC (hardware) address.

- **Clock** is the menu-bar clock that sits at the upper-right corner of your screen. Click it to open a menu where you can check today's date, convert the menu-bar display to a tiny analog clock, and so on. *To find the Show checkbox:* Open System Preferences→Date & Time. On the Clock tab, turn on "Show date and time in menu bar."

- **Displays** (▭) adjusts screen resolution. On Macs with a projector or second monitor attached, it lets you turn *screen mirroring* on or off—a tremendous convenience to anyone who gives PowerPoint or Keynote presentations. And if you have an Apple TV, this menulet also lets you turn AirPlay on or off—meaning that you can send the Mac's screen image to a TV. The menulet turns blue when you're projecting. *To find the Show checkbox:* Open System Preferences→Displays→Display tab.

- **Eject** (⏏) is a relic of the days when Macs had DVD drives. There's no checkbox in System Preferences to make this menulet appear. The fact that it even exists is something of a secret, but if you ever buy an external DVD drive, you'll be glad to know it does.

To make it appear, open your System→Library→CoreServices→Menu Extras folder as already described, and then double-click the Eject menu icon. That's it! The ⏏ menulet appears.

You'll discover that its wording changes—"Open Combo Drive," "Close DVD-ROM Drive," "Eject [Name of Disc]," or whatever—to reflect your particular drive type and what's in it at the moment.

- **Text Input** (▦) switches among different text input modes. For example, if your language uses a different alphabet, like Russian, or thousands of characters, like Chinese, this menulet summons and dismisses the alternative keyboards and input methods you need. Details start on page 241. *To find the Show checkbox:* Open System Preferences→Keyboard→Input Sources.

- **Time Machine** (⟲) lets you start and stop Time Machine backups (see page 260). *To find the Show checkbox:* Open System Preferences→Time Machine.

- **Universal Access** (⊕) offers on/off status indicators for features designed to help with visual, hearing, and muscle impairments. Chapter 9 has a rundown of what they do. *To find the Show checkbox:* Open System Preferences→Accessibility.

- **User** (👤) identifies the account holder (Chapter 12) who's logged in at the moment. To make this menulet appear (at the far-right end of the menu bar), turn on *fast user switching,* which is described on page 506.

- **Volume** (◀))), of course, adjusts your Mac's speaker or headphone volume. The menu lists all the different speaker sources—like internal speakers, AirPods wireless earbuds, or an Apple TV—so you can choose which should be the Mac's "voice" at the moment. *To find the Show checkbox:* Open System Preferences→Sound.

Tip: If you Option-click this menulet, you also get to see a list of *input* sources, like the built-in microphone or an external one you've plugged in.

- **VPN** (▥) stands for virtual private networking, which allows you to tap into a corporation's network so you can, for example, check your work email from home. You can use the menulet to connect and disconnect, for example. *To find the Show checkbox:* Open System Preferences→Network. Click the name of your VPN.

- **Wi-Fi** (📶) lets you turn your Wi-Fi (wireless networking) circuitry on or off, join existing wireless networks, and create your own private ones. *To find the Show checkbox:* Open System Preferences→Network. Click Wi-Fi.

Tip: Once you've installed this menulet, you can Option-click it to produce a secret menu full of details about the wireless network you're on right now. You see its channel number, password-security method (WEP, WPA, None, whatever), speed, and such geeky details as the MCS Index and RSSI.

- **WWAN** (.ıll) is useful only if you have a *cellular modem* from Verizon, Sprint, AT&T, or T-Mobile. This menulet lets you start and stop that connection. *To find*

the Show checkbox: Open System Preferences→Network. Click the name of your cellular modem.

Note: A few other items may lurk in the Menu Extras folder: PPPoE, Ink, IrDA, and ExpressCard. Most are relics of an earlier age, when laptops had features like card slots and infrared lenses.

To remove a menulet, ⌘-drag it off your menu bar, or turn off the corresponding checkbox in System Preferences. You can also rearrange menulets by ⌘-dragging them horizontally. You can even ⌘-drag the menulets from other companies to move them around—not just the standard Apple ones.

These little guys are useful, good-looking, and respectful of your screen space. The world could use more inventions like menulets.

Part Two:
Programs in macOS

2

Documents, Programs & Mission Control

The whole point of owning a computer, of course, is to run *programs*—or, as all the kids call them, apps. This chapter covers Apple's Way of Running Programs, and all its Capitalized Elements: the Mac App Store, Launchpad, Mission Control, Full Screen, Auto Save, Versions, and more.

The Mac App Store

For years, people installed software onto their computers by buying disks: floppies, CDs, and, later, DVDs.

But starting with the iPhone, people installed software onto their phones by downloading it directly from the internet. Once everybody saw how convenient (and profitable) that system was, it didn't take Apple long to realize it could bring the same convenience to the Mac.

So now there's the Mac App Store—or, as the program is called in your Applications folder, just App Store (Figure 5-1). It's an online catalog of software from huge software companies, tiny one-person software companies, and everything in between. You can read about the programs, check out customer reviews, and download them directly to your Mac. (As you probably know, Catalina itself is an App Store download.)

There are some huge advantages to this system. Since there's no box, disc, registration card, shipping, or stocking, the software can cost a lot less; Apple's own programs certainly reflect this price advantage. Plenty of programs in the App Store are actually free.

Furthermore, Apple controls the transaction on both ends—it knows who you are—so there are no serial numbers to type in. The installation no longer interrupts you with warnings like "Please enter your password to install this software" or "This software

appears to have been downloaded from the internet." Once you click Buy, the software downloads and installs itself *automatically*, without any interaction from you.

And there are no discs to store and hunt down later. If you ever get a new Mac, or if you ever need to reinstall a program from the App Store, you just re-download it from the Purchases tab; the App Store remembers that you're a legitimate owner. Better yet, you'll be downloading the latest version of that program; you won't have to install all the ".01" patches that have come along since.

Tip: To hide an app you've bought so it no longer appears, click your account icon (lower left); in Purchased, click 😀 and, from the menu, choose Hide Purchase. (To unhide it later, click "View Information" on the same page; under Hidden Items, click Manage.)

Figure 5-1:
Top: Mastering the App Store won't take you long; just about everything you need is in the sidebar, including a search box and buttons like Discover, Create, and Categories, which are meant to help you dive into the catalog of Mac software. Click your own icon (lower left) to see everything you've bought, for easy re-downloading. Updates is new versions of your apps.

Bottom: You can read reviews of each piece of software, written by other people who've tried it.

And speaking of updates: Since Apple knows what programs you have, it can let you know when new versions are available. And it does: A numbered badge appears next to the →App Store command. The updates are small files, so they download quickly; the App Store delivers only the pieces that have actually changed.

Some details:

- **You can opt to have new versions of your programs** quietly and automatically downloaded and installed in the background, so you're never bugged about their arrival. (In App Store→Preferences, the Automatic Updates checkbox takes care of that.)

- **"Automatically download apps purchased on other Macs"** (also in Preferences) ensures that when you download an app on one Mac, it auto-downloads on all your other ones, too (assuming they're logged in with the same iCloud account). Handy, really.

One final advantage of the App Store concept: If you decide to use Launchpad, described starting on page 165, then anything you've bought from the App Store is easy to delete with a single click.

In general, the App Store works exactly like the iPhone/iPad App Store. Click a program's icon to open its details page. Here you'll find reviews and ratings from other people, a description, pictures (screenshots) of the program, and much more information to help you make a good buying decision. See Figure 5-1 for more details.

When you buy an app, Launchpad opens automatically, so you can see where it went.

Note: In Catalina, the App Store's sidebar now offers Arcade, Apple's $5-a-month, all-the-games-you-can-play subscription service. You (and five family members) can download and play hundreds of games that have been made part of the program. There are no ads or extra charges.

Other Ways to Get Mac Software

Most people, most of the time, get their Mac software from the App Store. Occasionally, though, you'll get an app from a website that's *not* controlled by Apple.

Those apps generally arrive in an encoded, compressed form (Figure 5-2). And unless you've changed the settings, they arrive in the Downloads folder on your Dock.

The downloaded file's name usually has a file name extension like .zip (the standard compression file format for Windows and Mac files) or .dmg (a disk image file, described next).

Fortunately, you generally don't have to worry about any of this; most web browsers, including Safari, automatically unzip and unstuff downloads of all types.

Disk Images (.dmg Files)

Once you've downloaded a program, it often takes the form of a disk image file (middle top in Figure 5-2).

All you have to do is double-click the .dmg icon. After a moment, it magically turns into a disk icon on your desktop, which you can work with just as though it were a real disk (top right in Figure 5-2). For example:

- **Double-click it to open it.** The software you downloaded is inside.

- **Remove it from your desktop** by dragging it to the Trash (whose icon turns into a big silver ⏏ key as you drag), selecting it and pressing ⌘-E (the shortcut for File→Eject), clicking its ⏏ button in the Sidebar, or right-clicking or two-finger clicking it and then choosing Eject from the shortcut menu.

When you've finished unzipping or unstuffing a downloaded file, you may have several icons on your desktop or in the Downloads folder. It's generally safe to throw them away—the .sit file you originally downloaded, for example, or the .dmg icon.

The disk image icon, the one that contains the actual software or its installer (top right in Figure 5-2), is a phantom drive, held in memory, that will go away by itself when you log out. So after installing its software, feel free to drag it to the Trash (or select it and press ⌘-E to "eject" it).

Figure 5-2:
A: This is the down-loaded compressed file. Double-click to get…

B: The .dmg (disk image) file. Double-click it to "mount" the disk image.

C: And now, the disk image itself. Double-click to open the installer window. (Dismiss the warning that the software came from the internet.) "Eject" it after the installation is complete.

D: Here's the actual installer.

After the installation, you can delete all this stuff (except maybe the .dmg file, if you think you might want to install the software again later).

Performing the Installation

Once you've got a disk icon on your desktop—either a pseudo-disk from a disk image or a CD or DVD you've inserted—you're ready to install the software. You can install many macOS programs just by dragging their icons or folders to your hard drive (usually the Applications folder). Others offer a traditional installer program that requires you to double-click, read and accept a license agreement, and so on.

Uninstalling Software

If you got a program from the App Store, it's easy to delete from the Launchpad (page 165).

If you got it from some other source, well, there's generally no Uninstall program. To uninstall a program, you just drag it (or its folder) to the Trash.

Some programs leave harmless scraps of themselves behind; to check for them, look for preference files or folders bearing the dearly departed program's name in your Library folders (especially in Application Support) and in your Home→Library→Preferences folder.

The Death of 32-Bit Programs

32-bit programs no longer run in Catalina.

These ancient programs, so named because of the number of data bits they can transmit simultaneously, are badly out of date; Macs have been 64-bit machines for over a decade. 64-bit apps, the current kind, run faster and can access more memory.

For years, Apple has been warning its customers, and the world's software companies, that this day would come. Beginning in 2017's macOS High Sierra, for example, opening any 32-bit program produced a message that said: "[This app] will not work with future versions of macOS and needs to be updated."

No longer. Trying to open one of these apps in Catalina produces the message shown in Figure 5-3. You're simply out of luck.

Figure 5-3:
In macOS Catalina, Apple has gotten serious about blocking 32-bit apps from running. Running them requires installing a "virtual machine" program like Parallels Desktop, or possibly dual-booting your Mac between Catalina and macOS Mojave—both awkward solutions.

"App" needs to be updated.

The developer of this app needs to update it to work with this version of macOS. Contact the developer for more information.

Learn More... OK

Here's a partial list of 32-bit apps that won't run on Catalina. The version numbers are important; that is, newer versions run fine: Microsoft Office 11, Photoshop CS5, Illustrator CS5, InDesign CS5 and CS6, Aperture, iWork '09, Final Cut Pro 10.3.4, lots of old Apsyr game versions (Call of Duty 4, Doom 3, Tomb Raider 2), QuickBooks 2015, and so on.

There's a complete list at *https://roaringapps.com/collections/list-of-32-bit-macos-apps*.

A huge list of very old audio and video formats don't work anymore, either: Cinepak, DivX; Flash Video; Motion JPEG A and B; RealVideo; Sorenson 3; Windows Media Video 7, 8, and 9; and many others. All of them were based on QuickTime 7, which is dead in Catalina.

You can convert them to Catalina-compatible formats *while you're still using macOS Mojave*; once you're in Catalina, your opportunity is gone.

To do so, while you're still running macOS Mojave, open them (or libraries that use them) in the latest version of iMovie or Final Cut Pro. You're offered the chance to convert them automatically to the H.264 format (iMovie) or Apple ProRes format (Final Cut), which keeps them compatible with Catalina and whatever comes next.

Before you install Catalina, you can look over your own machine and see how much 32-bit trouble you'll be in. Choose About This Mac from the menu; click System Report; click Legacy Software in the sidebar. Everything in the resulting list is 32-bit software.

The Catalina installer (Appendix A) interrupts itself to display a similar list while there's still time to back out of the installation.

Opening macOS Programs

You can launch (open) an application in any of several ways:

- **Single-click an icon on the Launchpad,** described on the following pages.

- **Single-click a program's icon on the Dock, the Sidebar, or the Finder toolbar.**

- **Use Spotlight.** Hit ⌘-space bar, type the first letters of the program's name, and then press Return.

- **Double-click an app's icon in the Finder.**

- **If you've added the Applications folder to your Dock,** then click the Dock icon to open the pop-up fan, grid, or list of icons. Then click the program you want (or even type the first few letters of its name and then press Return).

FREQUENTLY ASKED QUESTION

What's with the Big "Duh"?

So I double-click an Excel document, and the Mac asks me: "You are opening Microsoft Excel for the first time. Do you want to continue?" Well, HELLO! I double-clicked the icon, didn't I? Does Apple think I'm some kind of idiot?

It's not you Apple is worried about. It's the silent parade of evil hackers, lurking out there in Internet Land, waiting for the right moment to bring down the Mac.

See, spyware authors have to be sneaky about how they install their stuff on your computer. You wouldn't be so stupid as to double-click an application called Spyware Installer™, of course. So the spyware *tricks* you into running its installer. In the Windows world, it commandeers a certain document type (like MP3 or JPEG), reassigning it to its installer. You innocently double-click some document, but an unanticipated program opens—and you've just opened Pandora's box.

In macOS, that can't happen. When you double-click some document that opens a program for the first time, this dialog box appears, just to let you know what's about to happen. If the program that's about to open isn't the one you were expecting, well, you've got a chance to back out of it.

And if it *is* the program you were expecting, click Continue. You won't be asked again about this version of this particular program.

- **Select an application icon** and then press ⌘-O (short for File→Open) or ⌘-▼.
- **Use the submenus** of the menu's Recent Items→Applications command.

Tip: Once you've opened the Recent Items→Applications submenu, you can hold down the ⌘ key to witness a startling sight: All the program names (Preview, Photoshop, and so on) change to say "*Show* Preview in Finder," "*Show* Photoshop in Finder," and so on. The Recent Items command, in other words, now gives you a direct way to jump to the icon of a program you might want to open, huddling in Applications or whatever window it's in.

- **Open a *document* icon in any of these ways,** or drag a document onto the icon of a program that can open it (whether in the Dock, the Finder toolbar, the Sidebar, or a folder window).

Tip: If you press Option as you open an application (or anything else) in the Finder, you automatically close the window that contains its icon. Later, when you return to the Finder, you find a neat, clean desktop—no loitering windows.

Launchpad

The Launchpad app presents a dark background with evenly spaced icons that represent all your programs (Figure 5-4). You can open one with a single click.

Why did Apple feel the need to create yet *another* way to open programs?

First, because Launchpad fits right into a general Apple effort to make the Mac look and work more like the iPad. Launchpad is a dead ringer for the Home screens of an iPad, iPhone, or iPod Touch.

Second, it's a much less intimidating place for technophobes to learn to love than, say, the Applications folder.

And, third, it's a lot quicker to get to than the Applications folder. You can summon it instantly, using any of these methods:

- **Put four fingers on your trackpad and pinch them together.** The Launchpad appears instantly, no matter what program you were in; you don't have to duck back into the Finder, navigate to the Applications folder, and so on.

- **Press the Launchpad key on your keyboard** (F4, or ⊞).

- **Click its icon on the Dock** (◉).

- **Move the cursor into one of the screen's four corners.** To set up these options, open System Preferences→Mission Control. Click Hot Corners to choose a corner of the screen for Launchpad.

- **Open it as you would any other program.** It's in your Applications folder.

Sooner or later, you'll wind up in Launchpad. Only three visual elements appear there:

- **Icons.** Each icon represents one of your programs. Apple's programs are listed first, in alphabetical order: App Store, Automator, Calculator, and so on. Then come all your other programs, again in A-to-Z order. Click one to open that program.

 Sparkly animated twinkles surround any new app you've installed. (You can see them at bottom in Figure 5-4.)

Note: The only program icon that *doesn't* appear in Launchpad...is Launchpad's. That's a good thing. You wouldn't want to wind up in an infinite loop.

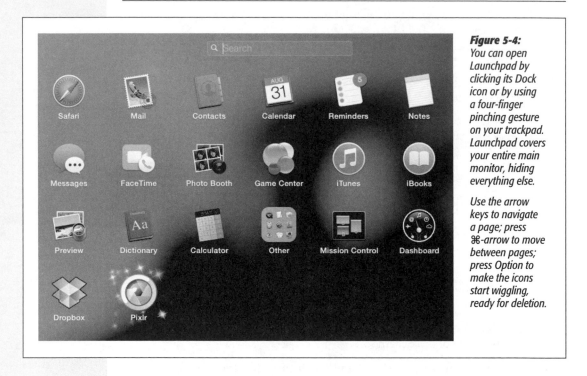

Figure 5-4:
You can open Launchpad by clicking its Dock icon or by using a four-finger pinching gesture on your trackpad. Launchpad covers your entire main monitor, hiding everything else.

Use the arrow keys to navigate a page; press ⌘-arrow to move between pages; press Option to make the icons start wiggling, ready for deletion.

- **The search box** lets you pluck one needle from your haystack of apps, no matter what page it's on. You don't have to click there first—just start typing when Launchpad is before you. With each letter you type, Launchpad hides everything but the matching app icons.

- **Home-page dots.** As you install more and more programs, Launchpad makes room for them by creating additional screens. You can spread your new programs' icons across an unlimited number of launch screens.

 The little white dots are your map. Each represents one Launchpad screen. If the third one is "lit up," then you're on the third screen.

To move among the screens, press ⌘-arrow keys, or swipe horizontally with two fingers on the trackpad (Magic Mouse: one finger). Or tap directly on one of the little dots to jump to the corresponding screen.

Tip: To exit Launchpad without opening anything, click a blank spot, tap the Esc key, or—most fun of all—*spread* the same four fingers on the trackpad.

Redesigning the Launchpad Screens

If you use Launchpad a lot, it's worth taking a moment to arrange its icons into logical categories or a sensible sequence. As it turns out, you can freely drag them into new spots; the other icons scoot aside to make room.

Tip: You can even drag an icon directly to the Dock to install it there for quicker access.

You can create additional screens, too. To do that, drag an icon to the right edge of the screen; keep your mouse button down. The first screen slides off to the left, leaving you on a new, blank one where you can deposit the icon.

You can organize your icons on these Home pages by category, frequency of use, color, or whatever tickles your fancy.

Folders

The Launchpad just wouldn't be like the iPad if it didn't also let you organize your apps into *folders.* Folders let you organize your apps, de-emphasize the ones you don't use often, and restore order to that horribly flat, multipage display of icons.

To create a folder, drag one app's icon *on top of another.* MacOS puts both of them into a single new folder (Figure 5-5). If they're the same kind of app, it even tries to figure out what category they both belong to—and names the new folder accordingly

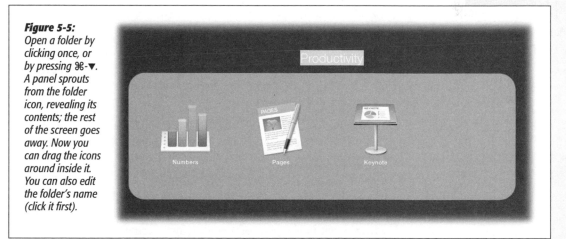

Figure 5-5:
Open a folder by clicking once, or by pressing ⌘-▼. A panel sprouts from the folder icon, revealing its contents; the rest of the screen goes away. Now you can drag the icons around inside it. You can also edit the folder's name (click it first).

("Music," "Photos," "Games," or whatever). This new name is only a proposal; an editing window also appears so you can type a custom name you prefer.

A folder can hold several rows' worth of icons; if you add more apps than that, Launchpad adds additional "pages" that you scroll horizontally. (Little white dots indicate which page you're on.)

Take an app out of a folder by dragging its icon anywhere else on the screen. The other icons scoot aside to make room. If you remove all but one app from a folder, the folder disappears.

Move a folder around by dragging, as you would any other icon.

Deleting App Store Programs

If you've downloaded some apps from the App Store, you'll find a bonus feature here in Launchpad: They're especially fun to delete.

Start by holding the mouse down on any icon until, after about a second, all the icons begin to—what's the correct term?—*wiggle*. (If you have an iPhone, iPad, or iPod Touch, this should look familiar.)

Tip: You can also just press the Option key to trigger the wiggling. Sometimes, every second counts.

At this point, you may notice that some of them have sprouted little red ⊗'s. Those are the ones you downloaded from the App Store.

To delete an App Store program you don't need anymore, click that ⊗ to make it say bye-bye—instantly and for good. It doesn't even have a layover in the Trash.

Note: You can't delete non–App Store apps this way, so no ⊗ appears on those icons. Why not? Because this deletion method is so fast and permanent. It's not much of a risk for App Store apps, because you can always download them again—but that would not be true of other apps.

Windows That Auto-Reopen

For decades, opening a program on the Mac presented exactly the same thing every time: a blank screen, or maybe a welcome screen. It was up to you to specify what *document* you then wanted to work on.

Now, though, whatever documents were open when you last quit that program magically *re*open, ready for you to get back to work. Everything is *exactly* as it was, including your window and palette positions. Incredibly, any text that was highlighted when you last quit the program is still highlighted, and the insertion point is just where you left it.

This is all handy if you tend to work on the same documents day after day; the auto-reopened document serves as a refresher on what you were in the middle of doing. You can skip fussing with the Open command, remembering what you were doing, rearranging the windows the way you like them, and so on.

Then again, maybe you can't stand this feature.

Fortunately, it's easy to turn it off, either globally, on a per-program basis, or on a per-Quit basis:

- **Turn off auto-reopen for good.** Open System Preferences→General. Turn on "Close windows when quitting an app."

- **Prevent your current setup from being memorized.** You can also prevent just *one particular* program from reopening its documents the next time—at the time you're quitting it. To do that, press Option while you quit the program (for example, when you choose Safari→Quit or press ⌘-Q). The Quit command magically changes to Quit and Close All Windows. The next time you open the program, it will have forgotten all about your window setup.

 (On the other hand, if you've turned *off* the "Restore windows" feature in System Preferences, then pressing the Option key makes the Quit command say Quit and *Keep* Windows.)

- **Make a program forget its window setup as you reopen it.** If it's too late for the tip in the previous paragraph, you can force a program to start up in its empty, virginal state by pressing the Shift key as it opens. That forces the program to forget the previous window setup.

POWER USERS' CLINIC

Shutting Down One Program's Window Memorizing

MacOS stashes information about your window setup in a "saved state" folder for each program. This data is in your Home→Library→Saved Application State folder.

The thing is, your Library folder is ordinarily invisible, which makes it a little tough to see the Saved Application State folder inside. Fortunately, you can jump directly to its contents by pressing Option as you choose Go→Library. Then open the Saved Application State folder within.

You get something like the window shown here: a folder for each program you use. You can delete one of these folders manually, but of course the Mac will recreate it the next time you run that program.

So if you want the Mac to stop memorizing a program's setup for good, find its Saved State folder. For Safari, for example, it's called *com.apple.Safari.savedState.*

Open the Saved State folder and empty it out; you've just made it forget the most recent settings. Now close the folder.

With the folder still highlighted, choose File→Get Info and, in the Get Info box, turn on the Locked checkbox. From now on, the Mac won't be able to record that program's window setup. (To undo your surgery later, you can just turn the Locked checkbox off again.)

- **Turn off auto-open for one program.** Suppose you like the auto-window-reopening feature in *most* programs. But there's one particular program that you *never* want to memorize your window setup—maybe for security reasons, or maybe because you use that app for something different every day.

Before long, some shareware program will crop up to make that easy. For now, though, you can do the job manually. It's a quick, one-time step, but it does involve mucking around with one of the Mac's invisible folders. See the box on the previous page.

The Application Menu

In every app, the very first menu (to the right of the menu) appears with bold lettering and identifies the program you're using. It might say Music, or Microsoft Word, or Stickies.

This Application menu (Figure 5-6) offers a number of commands pertaining to the entire program and its windows, including About, Quit, and Hide.

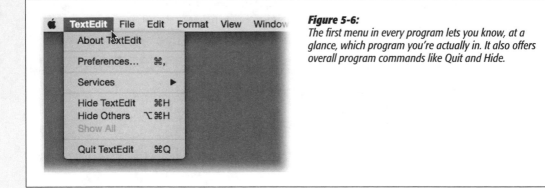

Figure 5-6:
The first menu in every program lets you know, at a glance, which program you're actually in. It also offers overall program commands like Quit and Hide.

Quitting Programs

You quit a program by pressing ⌘-Q, the keyboard equivalent of the Quit command. (The Quit command is always at the bottom of the Application menu.)

But macOS offers two much more fun ways to quit a program:

- **Right-click or two-finger click a program's Dock icon** to make its shortcut menu appear. Then choose Quit. (Or, if you do the *click-and-hold* thing on a program's Dock icon, a Quit button appears just above your cursor.)

- **When you've pressed ⌘-Tab** to summon the app switcher (read on), type the letter Q without releasing the ⌘ key. The highlighted program quits without further ado.

Force-Quitting Programs

MacOS is a rock-solid operating system, but that doesn't mean that *programs* never screw up. Individual programs are as likely as ever to freeze—or, rather, to *hang* (lock

up and display the "spinning beachball of death" cursor). In such cases, you have no choice but to *force-quit* the program—the computer equivalent of terminating it with a blunt instrument.

Doing so doesn't destabilize your Mac; you don't have to restart it. In fact, you can usually reopen the very same program and get on with your life.

You can force-quit a stuck program in any of several ways:

- **Click-and-hold on the program's Dock icon,** or two-finger click it, or right-click it. A Quit button appears just above your cursor. Press the Option key to make the button say Force Quit. Click it. Bingo—that program is outta here.

UP TO SPEED

When Programs Are Actually Folders

MacOS programs don't seem to have 50,000 support files strewn across your hard drive. Most programs just sit there, naked and shivering, in your Applications folder—seemingly unaccompanied by libraries, dictionaries, foreign language components, and other support files and folders.

The question is: Where did all those support files go?

MacOS features *packages* or *bundles*, which are folders that behave like single files. Every properly written macOS program looks like a single, double-clickable application icon. Yet to the Mac, it's actually a folder that contains both the actual application icon and all its hidden support files. (Even documents can be packages, including iDVD project files, Keynote files, and some TextEdit documents.)

If you'd like to prove this to yourself, try this experiment: Choose Go→Applications. See the Calculator program? Right-click or two-finger click it. From the shortcut menu, choose Show Package Contents. You're asking macOS to show you what's inside the Calculator's "application icon" folder.

The Calculator package window opens, revealing a Contents folder you've never seen before. If you open this folder, you'll find a handful of strange-looking, Unix-named folders and files that are, behind the scenes, pieces of the Calculator program itself.

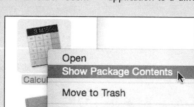

The application-as-folder trick is convenient for you, of course, because it means you're generally free to move the application to a different window—or to uninstall the program by dragging this single icon to the Trash—without worrying that you're leaving behind its entourage of support files. It's also convenient for programmers, because they can update certain aspects of their applications just by replacing one of these component files, without having to rewrite the entire program.

You can try out this programmery benefit for yourself. In the case of the Calculator and many other macOS programs, the Resources folder contains individual graphics files—PDF or TIFF files—that serve as the graphic elements you see when using the program. For example, the file lcd.tiff in the Calculator's Resources folder contains the image of the calculator's screen (where the numbers appear as you punch the calculator buttons).

Using a graphics program, you can change the background of this light-yellow calculator screen to, say, light blue. The next time you double-click Calculator—which you now realize is actually a folder behind the scenes—you'll see your modified calculator design.

(P.S. There are still hundreds or thousands of support files that aren't embedded within their programs' icons. They're sitting in your Library→Application Support folder, organized by software company.)

• **Press Option-⌘-Esc,** the traditional Mac force-quit keystroke, or choose →Force Quit. Either way, proceed as shown in Figure 5-7.

The only downside to force-quitting a program is that you lose any unsaved changes to your open documents, along with any preference settings you may have changed while the program was open.

Figure 5-7:
When you press Option-⌘-Esc or choose Force Quit from the menu, a tidy box listing all open programs appears. Just click the one you want to abort, click Force Quit, and click Force Quit again in the confirmation box. (Using more technical tools like the Unix kill command, there are other ways to jettison programs. But this is often the most convenient.)

NOSTALGIA CORNER

Window Layering

MacOS takes a layered approach to your programs' windows. They're not all in front or all in back; it's entirely possible to wind up with the windows of different programs sandwiched and layered, front to back.

Suppose, for example, you have Microsoft Excel in the foreground but Word in the background. If you click within a visible portion of a background window, you bring only that window of Word to the front.

The remedy for this situation, if it bothers you, is the Window→Bring All to Front command, which appears in the Finder and many other programs. It brings all of a program's windows to the front. (You can do the same thing

by simply clicking the program's Dock icon, or using the ⌘-Tab "heads-up" display.)

Layered windows shine when you're comparing two documents in two different programs, because they free you of the window clutter of other open documents.

But the time will come when you're ready to bring all of a background program's windows to the front. Get into the habit of clicking its Dock icon, or pressing ⌘-Tab to select its icon, rather than clicking inside one window. When you do that, all open windows in that application come forward, from wherever they may be.

The App Switcher

Only one program can be in front, or active, at a time.

To switch to a different program, you could click or double-click its icon (in the Dock, the Applications folder, Launchpad, or wherever). But the fastest method is often to use the ⌘-Tab keystroke (Figure 5-8).

Figure 5-8:
Apple once called this row of open program icons a "heads-up display," named after the projected data screen on a Navy jet windshield that lets pilots avoid having to look down at their instruments.

You can use this feature in three different ways, which are well worth learning:

- **If you keep the ⌘ key pressed,** then each press of the Tab key highlights the Dock icon of another program, in left-to-right Dock order. Release both keys when you reach the one you want. MacOS brings the corresponding program to the front. (To move *backward* through the open programs, press *Shift-*⌘-Tab.)

- **If you leave the ⌘ key pressed,** you can choose a program by clicking its icon with your mouse or by pressing the ◄ or ► keys.

- **A single press of ⌘-Tab** takes you to the program you used most recently, and another, separate ⌘-Tab bounces back to the program you started in.

 Imagine, for example, that you're doing a lot of switching between two programs, like your web browser and your email program. If you have five other programs open, you don't want to waste your time ⌘-tabbing your way through all the open programs just to get back to your web browser.

Tip: Here's a related keystroke, equally awesome. If you press ⌘-~ (the tilde key next to the number 1), you switch to the next window in the *same* program.

Full Screen Mode

Features are great and all. But the more of them your software accumulates, the more toolbars and icon panels fill the screen, and the bigger the clutter problem becomes. After a while, all that "chrome" (as software designers call it) winds up crowding out the document you're actually trying to work on.

That's why Apple invented Full Screen mode. It's not available in all programs, but it's in almost all Apple programs: App Store, Calendar, Chess, Final Cut Pro, Font Book, GarageBand, Books, iMovie, Keynote, Mail, Maps, Messages, Music, Notes, Photo Booth, Photos, Preview, Safari, TV, and so on.

To take a program into Full Screen mode, click the Full Screen button: the round, green dot in the upper-left corner of the document window. (As your cursor approaches, the green dot button looks like this: ⊗. If it's a ⊕ instead, then the app isn't eligible for Full Screening.)

When you click the green ⊗, the Mac hides the menu bar, scroll bars, Dock, status bars, and any other bars or palettes surrounding your work area. The window's edges expand all the way to the edges of the screen (Figure 5-9, bottom).

Tip: You may as well learn the keyboard shortcut to enter Full Screen mode: Control-⌘-F. The same keystroke *leaves* Full Screen mode, but you can also tap the Esc key for that purpose.

Figure 5-9:
Top: So much for the glorious web. You're seeing a web page segment, swimming in an ocean of toolbars, scroll bars, status bars, menu bars, and distracting desktop.

Bottom: In Full Screen mode, Safari stretches to the very edges of your screen, and everything else disappears. (Your address bar and tab bars are still available in this case.)

Each full-screen app becomes its own desktop in Mission Control. And you can put a full-screen app on each of your monitors, too.

To leave Full Screen mode, move your cursor to the top of the screen so the menu bar reappears. Click the green dot once again (top left of your document window).

The menu bar is available—it's just hidden. Move the pointer to the top of the screen to make it reappear.

To *exit* Full Screen mode, make the menu bar appear, and then click that green dot in the upper-left corner of the window (which now looks like this: ⊕).

Split Screen Mode

Once Apple gave us Full Screen mode, the next step was obvious: *split* Full Screen mode. In this arrangement, two windows fill the screen, edge to edge and top to bottom (Figure 5-10). Now *two* apps are now sharing that big monitor canvas.

Figure 5-10:
Here's the complete tutorial for turning on Split Screen mode.

Top: Point to the green ⊕ button in the first app. Choose "Tile Window to Left of Screen."

Second from top: That window now fills half your entire screen. Meanwhile, all other open windows appear in miniature. (There may be a little pile of additional window cards at the bottom corner. These are apps whose software companies have been too lazy to make them compatible with the Full Screen/Split Screen feature.)

Click the one you want to fill the other half of the screen.

Bottom: And voilà: Two apps, perfectly splitting your screen's full height and width. Feel free to drag the divider line sideways to adjust the proportions.

If you like, you can now grab the divider line and drag it, thereby adjusting the proportion of the screen occupied by each app.

This combination works very well when you want to keep a continuously updating app visible—Twitter, Mail, or FaceTime, for example—while continuing to do work in a second app. It's also handy when you're referring to one app (a recipe in your web browser) and making notes in another (an ingredients list in Notes).

Once again, though, Split Screen doesn't work in all apps—only the ones that work in Full Screen mode.

Starting Split Screen Mode, Method 1

There are two ways to get in and out of Split Screen mode. The method shown in Figure 5-10 is quickest; it involves the Tile Window to Left of Screen command (or Right of Screen), which is new in Catalina.

Starting Split Screen Mode, Method 2

The second method makes sense only after you've read about Mission Control and Spaces, starting on the next page. Bookmark this spot, go read that, and then return here.

Back so soon? OK, great!

Now that you know what the Spaces bar is, here's the tip: You can drag a second window onto an existing full-screen app's thumbnail in the Spaces bar; see Figure 5-11 for details.

Figure 5-11:
Drag a window onto an existing Full Screen–mode window's thumbnail. The + shows you which side of the screen this new window will occupy in Split Screen mode. Release the mouse, and then click the split thumbnail to make it fill your screen.

Exiting Split Screen Mode

Just as there are two ways to enter Split Screen mode, there are also two ways to exit it.

- **The title-bar method.** Move your cursor to the top edge of either window and pause; its title bar appears. Now click the green ⊕ button.

That window becomes a normal floating window. (The *other* window remains in Full Screen mode, on its own desktop; you can switch to it as described on page 183.)

- **Mission Control method.** Enter Mission Control, as described next. (For example, press the ⌘ key on your keyboard.) Move your cursor to the top of the screen to make the Spaces bar expand. Point to the desktop icon that contains the split screen; click the ⊗ in the top left.

In this case, *both* windows exit Full Screen and become floating windows again.

Mission Control: Death to Window Clutter

These days, managing all the open windows in all the open programs can be like herding cats. Off you go, burrowing through the microscopic pop-up menus of your Dock, trying to find the window you want. And heaven help you if you need to duck back to the desktop—to find a newly downloaded file, for example, or to eject a disk. You have to fight your way through 50,000 other windows on the way to the bottom of the "deck."

Mission Control tackles this problem in a fresh way. The concept is delicious: With one mouse click, keystroke, or finger gesture, you shrink all windows in all programs to a size that fits on the screen (Figure 5-12), like index cards on a bulletin board. Now you feel like an air-traffic controller, with all your screens arrayed before you. You click the window you want, and you're there. It's efficient, animated, and a lot of fun.

Tip: If you use Mission Control a lot, the zooming animation might get a little tiresome. Fortunately, you can turn that off. Open System Preferences→Accessibility→Display, and turn on Reduce Motion. From now on, Mission Control simply *pops* to the screen instead of zooming.

The window miniatures are scattered all over your screen. The placement isn't entirely random; macOS tries to place the thumbnails on the screen relative to their full-size windows' positions, relative to the top, bottom, and sides of your monitor.

You can impose a little more order on all of this, though. Open System Preferences→Mission Control, and turn on "Group windows by application." The windows still don't overlap, but at least the windows of each program are laid out near one another in Mission Control.

Starting and Stopping Mission Control

Mission Control is a program, just like any other. So you can open it with a click on its Dock icon, from Launchpad, from the Applications folder, and so on.

But it's really meant to be opened quickly, fluidly, naturally, whenever the mood seizes you—with a *gesture*. On the trackpad, that's a swipe upward with three fingers. (On the Magic Mouse, it's a double-tap with *two* fingers—taps, not clicks.)

Or you can press the dedicated 🎛 key (formerly the Exposé key), if you have one, on the top row of your keyboard.

Or you can press Control-▲.

And even that's just the beginning of the ways you can open Mission Control; read on.

Figure 5-12:
Top: Quick! Where's the Finder in all this mess?

Bottom: With a three- or four-finger upward swipe on the trackpad, you can open Mission Control and spot every window, shrunken but not overlapped. These aren't static snapshots of the windows at the moment you Mission Controlled them. They're live, still-updating windows, as you'll discover if one of them contains a QuickTime movie or a web page that's still loading.

Note: To *exit* Mission Control without clicking any of your windows or virtual screens, swipe *down* with three fingers. Or tap the Esc key. Or click a spot in the empty background.

Mission Control keystrokes

You can reassign the Mission Control functions to a huge range of other keys, with or without modifiers like Shift, Control, and Option. To view your options, choose ⌘→System Preferences and then click the Mission Control icon.

Here you'll find three pop-up menus (Figure 5-13). The first, Mission Control, lets you specify how you want to open Mission Control. The other two—Application windows and Show Desktop—correspond to the two functions of the older Exposé feature, described later in this chapter.

Figure 5-13:
You can trigger Mission Control in any of five ways: by clicking its icon, with a finger gesture, by twitching your cursor into a certain corner of the screen (Hot Corners), by pressing a key (bottom half of this box), or by clicking the extra buttons on a multibutton mouse, including the Apple Mouse. Of course, there's nothing to stop you from setting up all of these ways, so you can press or swipe in some situations and twitch or click in others.

Within each pop-up menu, for example, you'll discover that all your F-keys—F1, F2, F3, and so on—are available as triggers. If, while the pop-up menu is open, you press one or more of your modifier keys (Shift, Option, Control, or ⌘), then all these F-key choices *change* to reflect the key you're pressing; now the pop-up menu says Shift-F1, Shift-F2, Shift-F3, and so on. That's how you can make *Shift*-F1 trigger Mission Control, for example.

These pop-up menus also contain choices like Left Shift, which refers to the Shift key on the left side of your keyboard. That is, instead of pressing F9 to open Mission Control, you could simply tap the Shift key.

Note: This is only an example. Repeat: This is only an example. *Actually* using the Shift key to open Mission Control is a terrible, terrible idea, as you'll quickly discover the next time you try to type a capital letter. This feature is intended exclusively for hunt-and-peck typists who never use the Shift key on one side.

If you have a laptop, you'll also find out that you can tap the fn key alone for Mission Control—and this time, it's a great choice, because fn otherwise has very little direction in life.

If your mouse has more than one button, you'll see a second column of pop-up menus in System Preferences (Figure 5-13). Each pop-up menu offers choices like Right Mouse Button and Middle Mouse Button. Use these pop-up menus to assign Mission Control (or Exposé) to the various clickers on your mouse: right-click to hide all windows, middle-click to reveal the desktop, and so on.

Note, by the way, that on a laptop, the wording isn't "right mouse button"—it's "secondary mouse button." Which means "right-click." Which means that on a laptop, you can set it up so a "right-click" *trackpad gesture* triggers one of these functions. See page 233 for all the different ways you can trigger a right-click.

Screen corners

If you click Hot Corners, you see something like Figure 9-11 (page 339). The four corners here represent the corners of your screen. Using these menus, you can assign a window-management feature to each corner; for example, if you choose Mission Control from the first pop-up menu, then when your pointer hits the upper-left corner of the screen, you'll open Mission Control. (Launchpad and Notification Center are options here, too.)

Depending on the size of your screen, this option can feel awkward at first. But if you've run out of keystrokes that aren't assigned to other functions, be glad that Apple offers you this alternative.

Note: In previous versions of the operating system, whipping the pointer into a corner was one good way to turn on your *screen saver.* Apple hasn't forgotten about that, which is why you'll also find commands called Start Screen Saver and Disable Screen Saver in the pop-up menus. Apple wants to make sure you don't get confused and assign two different functions to the same corner.

Managing Windows in Mission Control

Once you open Mission Control, you can click any window's thumbnail to open it.

Tip: Try holding down the Shift key as you do it. You'll enjoy watching all your windows shift around with macOS's patented slow-motion animation, which can be quite a sight.

Or, if you decide to abandon ship and return to whatever you were doing, swipe *downward* with three fingers on the trackpad (two on the Magic Mouse), or press the Esc key.

The trouble with miniaturized windows is that, well, they're miniaturized. The more windows you have open, the smaller they are, and the harder it is to see what's in them.

If you need a little help identifying a window miniature, you have three options:

- **Point to a window thumbnail without clicking.** MacOS displays a label for that window.

- **If that's not enough information, press the space bar.** That, of course, is the Quick Look keystroke, and it works here, too. It magnifies the window you're pointing to, making it full size—big enough for you to read its contents and identify it.

- **Press ⌘-~.** That keystroke takes you into Exposé, described later in this chapter.

Spaces (Virtual Desktops)

Mission Control's other star feature, Spaces, gives you up to 16 *full-size monitors*. Ordinarily, of course, attaching so many screens to a single computer would be a massively expensive proposition, not to mention detrimental to your living space and personal relationships.

Fortunately, Spaces monitors are *virtual*. They exist only in the Mac's little head. You see only one at a time; you switch using Mission Control or a gesture.

But just because the Spaces screens are simulated doesn't mean they're not useful. You can dedicate each one to a different program or *kind* of program. Screen 1 might contain your email and chat windows, arranged just the way you like them. Screen 2 can hold Photoshop, with an open document and the palettes carefully arrayed. On Screen 3: your web browser in Full Screen mode.

You can also have the *same* program running on multiple screens—but with different documents or projects open on each one.

These desktops are also essential to macOS's *full-screen apps* feature, because each full-screen app gets its own Spaces desktop.

Now, virtual screens aren't a new idea—this sort of software has been available for years. But the Mac was the first to make it a standard feature of a consumer operating system.

It's still what most people would consider an advanced feature, and it's definitely confusing at first. But it'll be here when you're ready for it.

Creating a Desktop

Mission Control generally starts you off with just one Space (or "desktop," as it's labeled)—the one you've been using all along. If you've clicked the ⊕ button in an app to make it full screen, it fills an additional desktop unto itself.

To create another desktop, enter Mission Control. At the top edge of the screen, the gray strip—the Spaces bar—is the command center for creating, deleting, rearranging, and configuring your virtual desktops.

Note: To save space, the Spaces bar starts out as a very thin strip bearing only the names of your desktops (Figure 5-14, top). Move your cursor into this strip to expand it vertically, so you can now see the actual thumbnail images of your desktops (Figure 5-14, bottom).

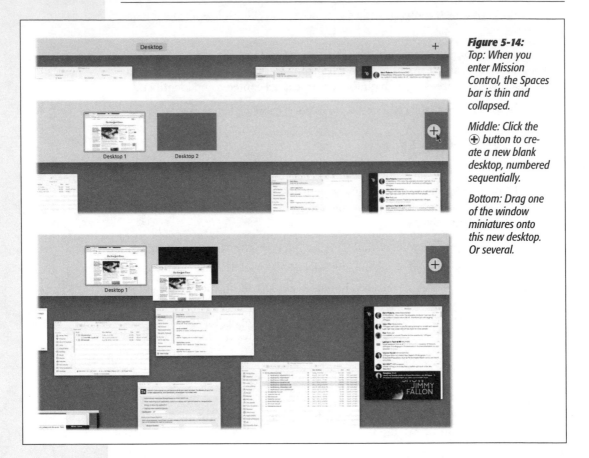

Figure 5-14:
Top: When you enter Mission Control, the Spaces bar is thin and collapsed.

Middle: Click the ⊕ button to create a new blank desktop, numbered sequentially.

Bottom: Drag one of the window miniatures onto this new desktop. Or several.

Once you're in Mission Control, you can proceed in either of two ways:

- **The long way.** See Figure 5-14 for the step-by-steps of clicking the + button in the upper-right corner.

Note: If you've positioned your Dock against the right side of the screen, then the + button appears when you point to the upper-*left* corner. And to create a new screen by dragging a window's icon (see "The short way," next), drag to the upper-*left* corner of the screen.

- **The short way.** Drag one window thumbnail onto any blank spot on the Spaces bar. The Mac creates a new desktop to hold it.

Switching Spaces

Once you've got Spaces set up and turned on, the fun begins. Start by moving to the virtual screen you want; it's like changing the channel. Here are some ways to do that:

- **Swipe horizontally on your trackpad with three fingers.** (On the Magic Mouse, it's two fingers.) If you have a trackpad or a Magic Mouse, this is definitely the method to learn; it's fast, fluid, and happy.

 You can change this gesture so that it requires an additional finger, if you like, in System Preferences→Trackpad (or Mouse)→More Gestures.

Tip: *If you perform this swipe slowly, you can drag the next Space only partway onto the screen. That's sometimes handy when you want to get your bearings or to just peek into the next screen.*

- **While pressing the Control key,** type the number of the desktop you want. For example, hit Control-3 to jump to your third screen. (You have to turn on this feature first, though. See Figure 5-15.)

- **Enter Mission Control,** and then click the desktop you want.

- **Press Control-◄ or Control-►** to rotate to the previous or next desktop.

Figure 5-15:
To control Spaces from the keyboard, open System Preferences→ Keyboard. Click Keyboard Shortcuts and then Mission Control. As shown here, Apple has preassigned keyboard shortcuts to your various Spaces— but they're not turned on yet. Turn on the checkboxes for the shortcuts you want. (You can change those shortcuts here, too.)

When you make a switch, you see a flash of animation as one screen flies away and another appears. Now that you're "on" the screen you want, open programs and arrange windows onto it as usual.

Tip: What if you're using Spaces, and you want to drag something from one screen (like a photo in Photos) into a window that's on a different screen (like an outgoing email message)?

There are two ways; take your pick. First, you can start dragging whatever it is—and then, in mid-drag, press the keystroke for Mission Control (usually fn-F9); complete the drag directly onto the other Space, and even into the relevant window *in* that Space.

Another approach: Start dragging. With the mouse button still down, press ⌘-Tab to open the application switcher. Continue the drag onto the *icon* of the receiving program, and still keep the mouse button down. MacOS switches to the appropriate virtual screen automatically.

Deleting a Desktop

To delete a desktop, enter Mission Control. Point to one of the screen thumbnails without clicking until a ⊗ appears in its corner; click it. The desktop disappears, and whatever windows were on it get shoved onto your main desktop.

Tip: If you don't have the 1½ seconds to wait for the ⊗ to appear, then press Option as you point. The Close button appears instantly.

In apps using Full Screen mode, the symbol is different; instead of ⊗, it looks like this: ⊗. When you click, the desktop flies off the Spaces bar into the main part of your screen. That app is now a plain-vanilla window thumbnail, just like all the others in Mission Control.

The Finer Points of Spaces

Yes, Spaces is an advanced feature. But there are actually advanced features *within* this advanced feature. For example:

- **Rearrange your Spaces.** Open Mission Control, and then drag the Space thumbnails around horizontally.

- **Multiple monitors.** If you have a second monitor connected to your Mac (or even several), each one can have its own set of Spaces.

 If "Displays have separate Spaces" is turned on in the Mission Control panel of System Preferences (Figure 5-13), then each monitor has its own set of Spaces. When you use one of the gestures or keystrokes for switching Spaces, you affect the Spaces on only one monitor: the one that contains your cursor at the moment.

- **Move a window to a different Space.** Of course, you can always move a window to a different Space by dragging its tiny icon within Mission Control. But there are two faster ways.

First, you can drag a window (using its title bar as a handle) all the way to the edge of the screen. Stay there with the mouse button still down. After about a second, the adjacent screen slides into view; you've just moved the window.

Second, switch to the new Space. Hold your mouse down on the app's Dock icon; from the shortcut menu, choose Options→Assign To→This Desktop. The Mac whisks that app's windows from whatever *other* screen they're on to *this* screen.

- **Move a window to all Spaces.** Usually, you slap each app (or each window) onto only *one* Spaces desktop. Your web browser on Space 1. Email on Space 2. And so on.

Sometimes, though, you might want one app's windows on *all* your desktops— perhaps because you use it so often, you want it always with you. The Finder and System Preferences are great examples. Or maybe your calendar app, your browser, or your email program.

To do that, hold the mouse button down on the program's Dock icon until the short-cut menu appears. From this menu, choose Options→Assign To→All Desktops.

- **Wallpaper for every desktop.** Coolly enough, though, you can set a different wall-paper photo (desktop photo) to each Space. You might find it easier to get your bearings that way. When you restart the computer, the Mac will remember not just which Spaces you had open and what was on them, but also what pictures lay behind them.

You can go about assigning desktop pictures in two ways. First switch to the Space whose picture you want to change. Then either open System Preferences→Desktop & Screen Saver→Desktop, or right-click or two-finger click a blank spot on the existing desktop background, and choose Change Desktop Background.

Note: In both cases, you may have to move the System Preferences window onto your current Space. You can do that by popping into Mission Control.

Either way, you wind up in the Preferences panel for choosing desktop wallpaper. Click the backdrop you want for this screen. Then switch to the next Space and repeat.

Two Eccentric Spaces Settings

In System Preferences→Mission Control, two settings govern the way Spaces works:

- **Automatically rearrange Spaces based on most recent use.** If this option is turned on, macOS will constantly rearrange your virtual desktops so the most recently used ones are first. (The most recent one becomes Desktop #2, since Desktop #1 is always your main desktop.)

The point, of course, is to make it quick and easy to return to whatever you were doing most recently. But if you find it disorienting to have your desktops constantly changing their sequence, you can turn this option off.

- **When switching to an application, switch to a Space with open windows for the application.** There must be some clearer way to write this checkbox.

In any case, it means that when you click the Dock icon for a running program, you jump to the Space that contains that program's open windows already, instead of leaving you on the current Space.

For example, suppose you're working in your browser on Desktop #3. Then you click the Mail icon on the Dock. If this option is turned on, you jump to Desktop #2 (or wherever you've been already working in Mail). If it's not turned on, Mail jumps to the foreground, but you won't see any windows—they're stranded back on Desktop #2.

Note: Know what's not part of Mission Control anymore? The Dashboard. For years, that bizarre screen full of hybrid micro-windows that Apple called *widgets* hung out on a virtual desktop to the left of all others in Mission Control.

Apple felt that the Dashboard was too similar to the more modern Today panel (page 377), which also shows stocks, weather, your calendar, and so on. So in macOS Catalina, the Dashboard has finally gone to the great app store in the sky.

Exposé

Before Mission Control, there was Exposé. It was flexible, it was novel, it was a little confusing. A few years ago, Apple incorporated the main functions of Exposé into Mission Control—but Apple didn't want to break all those Exposé fans' hearts. So Exposé is still there, for the benefit of old-timers who don't like change.

Well, it's *mostly* there. There used to be three different Exposé modes. One showed you miniatures of all windows in all programs, one showed you miniatures of all windows in just one program (Figure 5-16, top), and one hid all windows in all programs so you could see the desktop (Figure 5-16, bottom).

These days, only the second and third Exposé functions still exist. (The first one— showing *all* windows in *all* programs—is what Mission Control is for.)

You can trigger both of these modes using different combinations of the mouse and keyboard. The following pages cover all of them, but of course you're not expected to learn all that. Just find the *one* trigger that seems most convenient, and stick with it.

One-App Exposé

When you trigger Mission Control, you see the thumbnails of *all* windows in *all* apps.

But sometimes it's useful to see only the windows of *one* app arrayed before you—the app you're *using.*

That's great when you're web browsing or word processing. This Exposé function makes the program's windows spread out, and shrink if necessary, so you can click the one you want (Figure 5-16, top).

Here's how Apple intends for most people to trigger this option:

- **Swipe down on your trackpad with three fingers.** You're shown the miniatures of your current app's windows. If you point to an icon *on the Dock* before you swipe, you trigger Exposé for that app instead. (There's no equivalent on the Magic Mouse—although if you install the free BetterTouchTool, available on this book's "Missing CD" at *missingmanuals.com*, you can dream up a gesture of your own.)

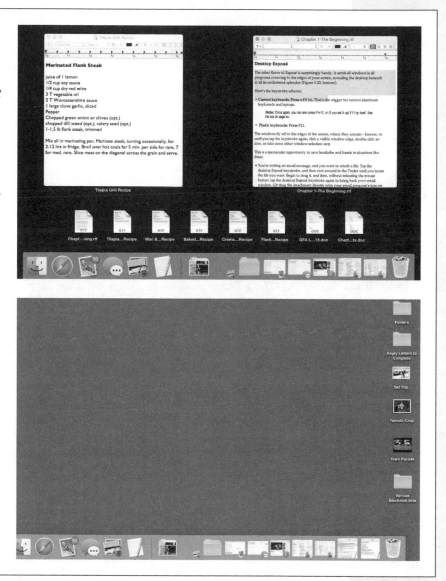

Figure 5-16:

Top: When you trigger one-app Exposé, you get a clear shot at any window in the current program (TextEdit, in this example). In the meantime, the rest of your screen attractively dims. In model Apple apps, like TextEdit and Preview, you even get a little row of icons at the bottom. They represent recently opened files, ready for clicking.

Bottom: Trigger desktop Exposé when you need to duck back to the desktop for a quick administrative chore. Here's your chance to find a file, throw something away, eject a disk, or whatever, without having to disturb your application windows.

Tap the same key again to turn off Exposé.

Note: You have to turn this feature on in System Preferences→Trackpad→More Gestures. Once you've done that, you can change this gesture to four fingers on the trackpad using the pop-up menu—handy if you find yourself triggering the function by accident.

- **Press Control-F3 (⌷).** That's the keystroke on aluminum keyboards. (If you have a plastic keyboard, press F10.)

Tip: As noted in the box below, you can also press fn-F10 or, with some tweaking, F10 alone. Or you can change the keystroke altogether, as described on page 200.

- **Enter Exposé from the heads-up display.** The heads-up display is the macOS application switcher—the row of "These are your open programs" icons—which appears when you press ⌘-Tab.

 The cool thing is that once you've got that heads-up display open, you can press ▲ or ▼ to enter Exposé for whatever program's icon is highlighted! From there, release the keys and hit Tab to cycle through your open apps.

- **Use Dock Exposé.** Click the program's Dock icon and hold the button down for half a second. (Or, for faster service, right-click or two-finger click the program's Dock icon.)

 This feature has one chief advantage over the keystroke method: You can Exposé-ize *any* program's windows, not just the one you're using at the moment.

TROUBLESHOOTING MOMENT

A Tedious Side Note About the Aluminum Apple Keyboards

In the beginning, you could trigger the three Exposé modes described on these pages with three simple keystrokes: F9, F10, and F11.

Then Apple's aluminum keyboards and laptops came along. On these, Apple devoted the F3 key to Exposé functions—and reassigned the F9, F10, and F11 keys to speaker-volume control!

You *can* make them operate as in the days of yore—by adding the fn key. That is: fn-F9 for Mission Control, fn-F10 for one-app Exposé, and fn-F11 for desktop Exposé. (Details on the fn key appear on page 224.)

So here's the point: On modern Macs, you have a choice of two Exposé keystroke suites: the F3 key (by itself, with Control, and with ⌘)—or the fn key plus F9, F10, and F11.

Actually, it's even more complicated than that. If you find yourself using Exposé more than you use the volume keys, then you can get rid of the requirement to press fn. Open System Preferences→Keyboard→Keyboard. Here you'll find a checkbox that reverses this logic. It's called "Use all F1, F2, etc. keys as standard function keys."

If that checkbox is *on,* then you can use F9, F10, and F11 to trigger Mission Control and Exposé. Now you need the fn key only when you want those keys to adjust the *volume.*

- **Shove your mouse into whatever corner of the screen you've chosen.** See page 180 for instructions.

Once you've triggered Exposé, you're not quite finished yet. As shown in Figure 5-16, beneath the window thumbnails, you get to see the icons of documents you've worked on recently in this app (at least in enlightened Apple programs like TextEdit).

Desktop Exposé

The other flavor of Exposé is surprisingly handy. It sends *all* windows in *all* programs cowering to the edges of your screen, revealing the desktop beneath in all its uncluttered splendor (Figure 5-16, bottom).

Here's the keystroke scheme:

- **Current keyboards: Press ⌘-F3 (▣).** That's the trigger for current aluminum keyboards and laptops.

Note: Once again, you can also press fn-F11, or (if you set it up) F11 by itself. See the box on the facing page. You can also install a Show Desktop button on the Touch Bar, if you have one (page 227).

- **Plastic keyboards: Press F11.**

The windows fly off to the edges of the screen, where they remain—forever or until you tap the keystroke again, click a visible window edge, double-click an icon, or take some other window-selection step.

This trick saves headache and hassle in situations like these:

- **You're writing an email message, and you want to attach a file.** Tap the desktop Exposé keystroke, and then root around in the Finder until you locate the file you want. Begin to drag it, and then, without releasing the mouse button, tap the desktop Exposé keystroke again to bring back your email window. (Or drag the attachment directly onto your email program's icon on the Dock and pause until its window thumbnails appear.)

 Move your cursor, with the file in mid-drag, directly over the outgoing message window; release the cursor to create the attachment. You've just added an attachment from the desktop in one smooth motion.

Tip: You can apply the same life-changing shortcut to dragging a graphic into a page-layout program, a folder of photos into Photos, a sound or graphic into iMovie, and so on.

- **You want to open a different document.** For many people, having access to the entire Finder beats having to use the Open dialog box. Double-clicking the icon you want automatically opens it and turns off Exposé.

- **You're on the web, and you want to see if some file has finished downloading.** Trigger desktop Exposé to survey the situation on your desktop.

If the layer of open programs is the atmosphere, the Finder is the earth below—and the ability to teleport back and forth is a huge time-saver.

Exposé Tip-O-Rama

Just having your world o' windows spread out like index cards is magic enough. But these windows are *live.* You can work with them. Let us count the ways:

- **Tab through Exposé'd apps.** Once you've started one-app Exposé and a program's windows are arrayed before you, *press the Tab key.* With each tap, you cycle through the open apps, each getting the Exposé treatment in turn. It's an informative way to inspect what's happening in each open program without losing your way. (Pressing ⌘-~ does the same thing.) Shift-Tab, as usual, cycles through the programs in the opposite direction.

Tip: You can also switch to another app's microwindows by clicking its Dock icon.

- **Hold down instead of two presses.** Most of the time, you'll probably use Exposé in two steps. You'll tap the keystroke once to get the windows out of the way and again to bring them back (if, indeed, you haven't *clicked* a window to bring them back).

 In some cases, though, you may find it easier to *hold down* the relevant key. For example, hold down ⌘-F3 (Show Desktop) to see if a file is finished copying to the desktop, and then release the keys to bring back all the windows. (Actually, you can let go of the ⌘ key as soon as you've entered Exposé.) For quick window-clearing situations, that method saves you the step of having to press the keystroke a second time to turn off Exposé.

- **Use the spring-loaded Dock.** This trick is great when you want to drop a file from one program into a particular window belonging to another.

 The most common example: You want to add an attachment to an outgoing email message. In the Finder, locate the file's icon. Drag it directly onto your email program's Dock icon—and *pause* with your finger still on the button. After a half-second, Exposé happens, showing all your email program's open windows. Now continue your drag onto the miniaturized window of the outgoing message so it's highlighted, tap the space bar to open it, and then release. Presto! The file is attached.

 This trick also works great when you want to drop a photo into a newsletter, for example, or a text clipping into a word-processing document.

- **Dip into Quick Look.** Once you've got shrunken windows on the screen, tap your arrow keys to highlight a window (or point with your mouse at one without clicking). A bright-blue border moves from window to window.

 At any point, you can press the space bar to make that one window return to life size. You haven't really activated it—you can't edit it—but at least you can see it at full size.

 And here's the very cool part: Once you've triggered Quick Look like this, you can press the arrow keys to zap *other* miniwindows back to full size, without having to

exit Quick Look. Or, again, point to other windows without clicking. Each zooms in to 100 percent size. (All of this is much easier to do than to imagine.)

You can keep examining your windows at full size until you spot the one you're after; now tap Return (or click the mouse in the window) to exit Quick Look *and* Exposé. You've just opened that window, and you're ready to roll.

Tip: Keep in mind that you can change all of these Exposé triggers—keyboard shortcuts, hot corners, and so on. See page 179.

Hiding Programs the Old-Fashioned Way

When it comes to getting windows out of your way, nothing can touch Mission Control and Exposé for speed and entertainment value. Once you've mastered those features, the traditional rituals of hiding windows will seem charmingly quaint. "When I was your age," you'll tell your grandchildren, "we used to have to *hold down the Option key* to hide windows!"

But you know the drill at software companies: They giveth, but they never taketh away. All the old techniques are still around for the benefit of Mac fans who use them by force of habit.

Hiding the Program You're Using

For the purposes of this discussion, when a program is *hidden,* all its windows, tool palettes, and button bars disappear. You can bring them back only by bringing the program to the front again (by clicking its Dock icon, for example).

If your aim is to hide only the frontmost program, macOS offers a whole raft of approaches. Many of them involve the Option key, as listed here:

- **Option-click any visible portion of the desktop.** The program you were in vanishes, along with all its windows.

- **Option-click any other program's icon on the Dock.** You open that program (or bring its windows to the front) *and* hide all the windows of the one you were using.

- **Option-click any visible portion of another program's windows.** Once again, you switch programs, hiding the one you were using.

- **From the Application menu, choose Hide Photos (or whatever the program is).** The Application menu is the boldfaced menu that bears the program's name.

- **From the program's Dock icon shortcut menu, choose Hide.** You open the shortcut menu, of course, by right-clicking or two-finger clicking. You also get a Hide button if you click-and-hold on the Dock icon for half a second.

- **When you've highlighted a program's icon by pressing ⌘-Tab to rotate through the running programs, press the letter H key.** The program hides itself instantly. Leave the ⌘ key down the whole time and, after pressing the H, press Tab again

to move on to the next program. If you release the keys while "stopped" on the program instead, you'll bring it forward rather than hiding it.

- **Press ⌘-H.** This may be the easiest and most useful trick of all (although it doesn't work in a few oddball programs). Doing so hides the program you're in; you then "fall down" into the next running program.

Tip: Consider this radical time-saving proposal: Never quit the programs you use frequently. Instead, simply hit ⌘-H whenever you're finished working in a program. That way, the next time you need it, the program launches with zero wait time.

In general, macOS's virtual-memory scheme is so good that there's almost no downside to leaving your programs open all the time.

To unhide a program and its windows, click its Dock icon again, choose the Show All command in the Application menu, or press ⌘-Tab to summon the heads-up application display.

Tip: The Dock continues to display the icons of all running programs without any indication that you've hidden them. Fortunately, that's easy enough to fix. All you need is the free program TinkerTool, which is available on this book's "Missing CD" page at *missingmanuals.com*. It offers a simple checkbox that makes hidden programs appear with transparent Dock icons.

Hiding All Other Programs

Choosing Hide Others from your program's Application menu means, of course, "Hide the windows of every program but this one." It even hides your Finder (desktop) windows, although desktop icons remain visible.

Better yet, there's a keystroke for this command: Option-⌘-H. That's one small step for keystrokes, one giant leap for productivity geeks.

Tip: If you right-click or two-finger click a program's Dock icon, you get its shortcut menu, including a Hide command. If you press Option, it changes to say Hide Others. It's a lot more work than the methods described already, but…you know. One strives for thoroughness.

If this trick interests you, then you might also enjoy its corollary, described next.

The Bring-Forward, Hide-All-Others Trick

Here's a terrific technique that lets you bring one program to the front (along with all its open windows) and hide all other windows of all *other* open programs—with one click.

You might think of it as Hero mode, or Front-and-Center mode, or Clear My Calendar mode.

In any case, the trick is to Option-⌘-click the lucky program's icon on the Dock. As it jumps to the fore, all other windows on your Mac are instantly hidden. (You can bring them back, of course, by clicking the appropriate Dock icons.)

Hiding (Minimizing) Individual Windows

You can also hide or show *individual windows* of a single program. In fact, Apple must believe that hiding a window will become one of your favorite activities, because it offers at least three ways to do it:

- **Choose Window→Minimize Window,** if your program offers such a command, or press ⌘-M.

- **Click the Minimize button** on the window's title bar.

- **Double-click the window's title bar.** (If this doesn't work, choose System Preferences→Dock. Make sure "Double-click a window's title bar to minimize" is turned on.)

In any case, the affected window shrinks down until it becomes a new icon on the right side of the Dock. Click that icon to bring the window back.

How Documents Know Their Parents

Every operating system needs a mechanism to associate documents with the applications that created them. When you double-click a Microsoft Word document icon, for example, it's clear that you want Microsoft Word to launch and open the document.

So how does macOS know how to find a document's mommy?

It actually has two different mechanisms:

- **File name extensions.** A *file name extension* is a suffix following a period in the file's name, as in *Letter to Mom.doc.* (It's usually three letters long, but it doesn't have to be.) These play a role in determining which documents open into which programs.

 That's how Windows identifies its documents, too. If you double-click something called *memo.doc,* it opens in Microsoft Word. If you double-click *memo.wri,* it opens in Microsoft Write, and so on.

Note: MacOS comes set to hide most file name extensions, on the premise that they make the operating system look more technical and threatening. If you'd like to see them, however, then choose Finder→Preferences, click the Advanced button, and then turn on "Show all filename extensions." Now examine a few of your documents; you'll see that their names display the previously hidden suffixes.

You can hide or show these suffixes on an icon-at-a-time basis, too (or a clump-at-a-time basis). Just highlight the icon or icons you want to affect, and then choose File→Get Info. In the resulting Info window, proceed as shown in Figure 5-17.

• **Your preferences.** If you've used the Always Open With command to *specify* which program opens your document, then that's the one that opens; this preference overrides the file name extension system. MacOS memorizes that new pairing.

It's possible to live a long and happy life without knowing anything about these suffixes and relationships. But if you're prepared for a little bit of technical bushwhacking, you may discover that understanding document-program relationships can be useful in troubleshooting, keeping your files private, and appreciating how macOS works.

Figure 5-17:
Top: In the Info window, open the Name & Extension pane. Now you can see what macOS really thinks your file is called. Turn on "Hide extension" if you'd rather not see the file name suffix in the Finder.

Bottom: If you try to add a suffix of your own, macOS objects, in effect saying, "Hey—I've already got a file name extension for this, even if you can't see it. Are you sure you know what you're doing?" (And you can turn off this warning, if you like. Choose Finder→Preferences→Advanced pane. Turn off "Show warning before changing an extension.")

Reassigning Documents to Programs

Unfortunately, file name extensions aren't always especially specific. Suppose you've downloaded a graphic called Sunset.jpg. Well, almost any program these days can open a JPEG graphic—Photoshop, Pages, Word, Preview, Safari, and so on. How does macOS know which of these programs to open when you double-click the file?

Fortunately, *you* can decide. You can *reassign* a document (or all documents of its kind) to a specific program. Here's the rundown.

Reassigning a certain document—just once

Double-clicking a graphics file generally opens it in Preview (page 589). Most of the time, that's a perfectly good arrangement. But Preview has limited editing powers. What if you decide to edit a graphics file more substantially? You'd want it to open, just this once, into a different program—Photoshop Elements, for example.

To do so, you must access the Open With command. You can find it in three places:

- **Highlight the icon and then choose** File→Open With (Figure 5-18).

- **Highlight the icon and then open** the ✿ menu. In the menu, choose Open With.

- **Right-click or two-finger click** the file's icon. From the shortcut menu, choose Open With.

Study the submenu for a moment (Figure 5-18, top). The program whose name says "(default)" indicates which program *usually* opens this kind of document. From this pop-up menu, choose the name of the program you'd *rather* open this particular file, right now, just this once.

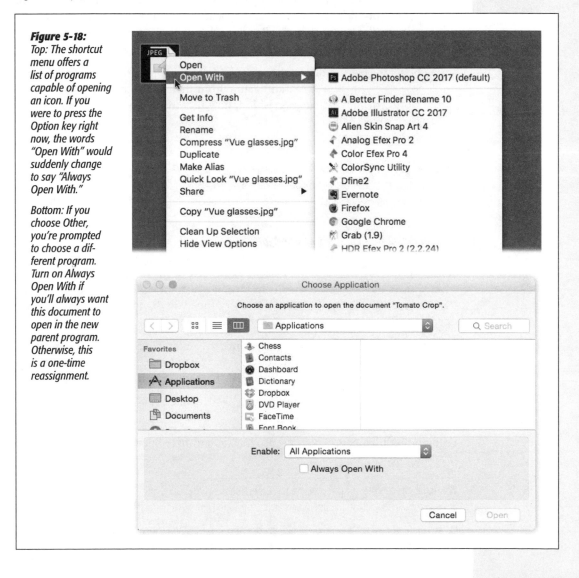

Figure 5-18:
Top: The shortcut menu offers a list of programs capable of opening an icon. If you were to press the Option key right now, the words "Open With" would suddenly change to say "Always Open With."

Bottom: If you choose Other, you're prompted to choose a different program. Turn on Always Open With if you'll always want this document to open in the new parent program. Otherwise, this is a one-time reassignment.

Reassigning a certain document–permanently

After opening a TIFF file in, say, Photoshop Elements for editing, you haven't really made any changes in the fabric of your Mac universe. The next time you double-click that file, it opens once again in Preview.

If you wish this particular file would *always* open in Photoshop Elements, the steps are slightly different. In fact, there are three different ways:

- **In the Choose an Application dialog box** (the one that appears when you double-click a document whose "parent" program isn't clear), turn on Always Open With (shown at bottom in Figure 5-18).

- **Start out with one of the previously described techniques** (for example, File→Open With, or right-click the file's icon and choose Open With)—but after you see the menu, press the Option key, too. Before your very eyes, the Open With command changes to say *Always* Open With.

- **Highlight the icon, and then choose File→Get Info.** Open the "Open with" panel. Choose a new "parent" program's name from the pop-up menu. You'll see that the word "(default)" changes position, now tacking itself onto the name of the program you've chosen.

Tip: You can use a similar trick to reassign the parenthood of a whole *flock* of selected icons at once. Once you've selected them, keep the Option key pressed as you choose File→Show Inspector. In the "Open with" section of this specialized Get Info window, choose a new program from the pop-up menu. The message at the top of the window—"22 items," for example—reminds you that you're changing the whole batch at once.

Reassigning all documents of one type

So much for reassigning one document (or a group of documents) at a time. What if you're writing, say, a book about macOS, and you've been taking a lot of screenshots? MacOS saves each captured screen illustration as a graphics file in something called PNG format. That's all fine, except that every time you double-click one of these, it opens into Preview, where you can't paint out unwanted details.

You could reassign all these files, one at a time, to a different program, but your grandchildren would have grandchildren by the time you finished. In this case, you want to tell macOS, "For heaven's sake, make *all* PNG files open in Photoshop from now on!"

To make it happen, start by highlighting *any* PNG file. Choose File→Get Info. (The shortcut menus won't help you in this case.) Open the "Open with" panel.

From its pop-up menu, choose the program you want to open this kind of document from now on.

Tip: If the one you prefer isn't listed, use the Other option, which opens the "Choose an application" dialog box so you can navigate to the one you want, as shown in Figure 5-18. Find and double-click the program.

Or, instead of choosing Other, you can also choose App Store. It's Apple's way of saying, "Hey–if you don't have a program that can open this document, maybe you should just *go buy one right now!*"

This time, follow up by clicking Change All beneath the pop-up menu. (This button is dimmed until you've actually selected a different program from the pop-up menu.) Confirm by clicking Continue or pressing Return.

From now on, double-clicking any similar kind of document opens it in the newly selected program.

Keyboard Control

MacOS offers a fantastic feature for anyone who believes life is short: keyboard-controllable menus, dialog boxes, pop-up menus, and even Dock pop-up menus. You can operate every menu in every program without the mouse.

In fact, you can operate every control in every dialog box from the keyboard, including pop-up menus and checkboxes. And you can even redefine many of the built-in macOS keystrokes, like Shift-⌘-3 to capture the screen as a graphic.

In fact, you can add or change *any menu command in any program*. If you're a keyboard-shortcut lover, your cup runneth over.

Here are some of the ways you can control your Mac mouselessly. In the following descriptions, you'll encounter the factory settings for the keystrokes that do the magic—but as you'll see in a moment, you can change these key combos to anything you like. (The System Preferences→Keyboard→Shortcuts tab contains the on/off switches for these features.)

Note: On modern-day aluminum keyboards, the keystrokes described below may not work unless you also press the fn key simultaneously.

If that seems clumsy, you can eliminate the fn-key requirement either by using the "Use all F1, F2, etc. keys as standard function keys" option described in the box on page 188—or by choosing a different keystroke altogether (page 200).

Control the Menus

When you press Control-F2, the menu is highlighted. At this point, you can "walk" to another menu by pressing the ◀ or ▶ keys (or Tab and Shift-Tab). When you reach the menu you want, open it by pressing ▼, space, or Return.

Walk down the commands in the menu by pressing ▲ or ▼, or jump directly to a command in the menu by typing the first couple of letters of its name. Finally, "click" a menu command by pressing Return or the space bar.

You can also close the menu without making a selection by pressing Esc or ⌘-period.

Control the Dock

Once you've pressed Control-F3, you can highlight *any* icon on the Dock by pressing the appropriate arrow keys (or, once again, Tab and Shift-Tab).

Then, once you've highlighted a Dock icon, you "click" it by pressing Return or the space bar. Again, if you change your mind, press Esc or ⌘-period.

Tip: Once you've highlighted a disk or folder icon, you can press the ▲ or ▼ keys to make its shortcut menu appear. (If you've positioned the Dock vertically, then use ◄ or ► instead.)

Cycle Through Your Windows

Every time you press Control-F4, you bring the next window forward, eventually cycling through *every window in every open program*. Add the Shift key to cycle through them in the opposite order.

You may remember that macOS offers a different keystroke for cycling through the different windows in your *current* program (it's ⌘-~, the tilde symbol at the upper left on your keyboard). Control-F4, on the other hand, tours all windows in *all* programs. Both keystrokes are useful in different situations.

Control Tool Palettes

In a few programs that feature floating tool palettes, you can highlight the frontmost palette by pressing Control-F6. At this point, use the arrow keys to highlight the various buttons on the palette. You can see the effect when, for example, you're editing text in TextEdit and you've also opened the Font palette. Pressing Control-F6 highlights the Font palette, taking the "focus" off your document.

Control Menulets

Here's a gem you may not have heard about: You can operate *menulets*—those menu-bar status indicators for your speaker volume, wireless networks, and so on—from the keyboard, too.

This time, the trick is to hit Control-F8. That highlights the leftmost Apple menulet. Now you can use your ◄ and ► arrow keys to move around the menu bar; when you've highlighted the one you want, press Return or the space bar to "click" that menu and open it.

Control Dialog Boxes

You can also navigate and manipulate any *dialog box* from the keyboard.

See the dialog box shown in Figure 5-19? If you turn on "All controls" at the bottom, then pressing the Tab key highlights the next control of any type, whatever it may be—radio button, pop-up menu, and so on. Press the space bar to "click" a button or to open a pop-up menu. Once a menu is open, use the arrow keys (or type letter keys) to highlight commands on it, and use the space bar to "click" your choice.

Changing a Menu Keyboard Shortcut

Suppose you love Photos (and who doesn't?). But one thing drives you crazy: The Revert to Original command, which discards all the changes you've ever made since taking the photo, has no keyboard shortcut. You must trek up to the menu bar every time you need that command.

This is why macOS lets you add keyboard shortcuts to menu commands that lack them—or change the commands in programs whose key assignments break with tradition. (It works in any program that uses the standard macOS menu software, which rules out older versions of Microsoft Office.) Here's the routine:

1. **Choose System Preferences→Keyboard. Click the Shortcuts tab, and then click App Shortcuts in the left-side list.**

 You're shown a list of any keyboard assignments you've created so far.

2. **Click the ＋ button just beneath the list.**

 The dialog box shown in Figure 5-19 appears.

Figure 5-19:
If you choose All Applications from the top pop-up menu, you can change the keyboard combo for a certain command wherever it appears. You could, for example, change the keystroke for Page Setup in every program at once. (Beware the tiny yellow triangles; they let you know if a chosen keystroke conflicts with another macOS keystroke.)

3. **Indicate which program needs behavior modification.**

 In this example, you'd choose Photos from the Application pop-up menu. (If the program's name doesn't appear in the pop-up menu, then choose Other; navigate to, and double-click, the program you want.)

4. **Carefully type in the name of the menu command whose keyboard shortcut you want to change or add.**

 Type it *exactly* as it appears in the menu, complete with capitalization and the little ellipsis (…) that may follow it. (You make the ellipsis character by pressing Option-semicolon.)

5. **Click in the Keyboard Shortcut box. Press the new or revised key combo you want.**

For example, press Control-R for Photos' Revert to Original command. You'll see the Mac's notation of your keystroke appear in the Keyboard Shortcut box—unless, of course, the combo you selected is already in use within that program. In that case, you hear only an error sound that means "Try again."

6. **Click Add.**

The dialog box closes. By scrolling down in your Keyboard Shortcuts list, you see that the keystroke you selected has now been written down for posterity under the appropriate program's flippy triangle. (To get rid of it, click its name and then click the — button beneath the list.)

Tip: To delete or change one of your custom menu shortcuts, open System Preferences→Keyboard→Shortcuts. Click App Shortcuts in the list at left. Click the command you'd like to edit. Press Delete to get rid of it; or, to try a different key combo, click where the existing keyboard shortcut appears and then press a new one.

Redefining a Keystroke

As you've no doubt become painfully aware, there are *hundreds* of keyboard combinations for the various macOS functions and settings. That's good, because keyboard shortcuts are efficient and quicker than using the mouse. But that's also bad, because there's no *way* you'll be able to remember all of them—and some of the most useful shortcuts are ridiculous, multikey affairs that you'll never remember at all.

In the keyboard-shortcut center, shown in Figure 5-20, you can look over all the common macOS hidden keyboard functions—for Mission Control, Exposé, Spotlight, the Dock, and many others—and *change them.*

Here's how it goes:

1. **Choose ◆→System Preferences. Click Keyboard. Click the Shortcuts tab.**

You arrive at the dialog box shown in Figure 5-20.

2. **In the left-side list, click the category or function you want.**

Your choices include Launchpad & Dock, Mission Control, Keyboard, and so on. When you click a category name, you see the available shortcuts.

Tip: You don't have to be content with *changing* one of these keyboard shortcuts. You can also *turn it off* by clicking the corresponding checkbox. That's great if one of Apple's predefined keystrokes–for a function you don't even use–is interfering with one in a program you like.

3. **Click the command you want to change. Then click the current keyboard combination (or the "add shortcut" button, if there is no existing shortcut).**

Suppose, for example, that you wish the Show Desktop Exposé keystroke were something easier to remember, like Control-D. So in step 2, you'd click Mission

Control. In this example, you'd click Show Desktop. Then you'd click where it currently says "F11."

4. Press a new key combination.

In this example, you'd press Control-D.

Be careful, though. MacOS keystrokes take precedence over *all others.* So if you choose a keystroke like ⌘-P for something, well, by golly, you'll no longer be able to use ⌘-P to print anything in any of your programs. Think before you assign. Run a couple of tests afterward.

Figure 5-20:
The keyboard-shortcut center lets you redefine the keystrokes that trigger many basic macOS features, menu commands in your programs, and software you've built yourself using Automator.

The Save and Open Dialog Boxes

When you choose File→Save, you're asked where you want the new document stored on your hard drive, what you want to call it, and what Finder tags (page 89) you want applied to it. The resulting dialog box is a miniature Finder. All the skills you've picked up working at the desktop come into play here.

To give it a try, launch any program that has a Save or Export command—TextEdit, for example. Type a couple of words, and then choose File→Save. The Save sheet appears (Figure 5-21).

Tip: In most programs, a glance at the Close button in the upper-left corner of a document window tells you whether it's been saved. When a small dot appears in the red button, it means you've made changes to the document that you haven't saved yet. (Time to press ⌘-S!) The dot disappears as soon as you save your work.

In programs that offer the Auto Save and Versions features described later in this chapter, like TextEdit, the red-dot convention has been retired. Instead, when you've made changes to a document since saving it, you see the light-gray word *Edited* in the title bar.

Compact Save sheet

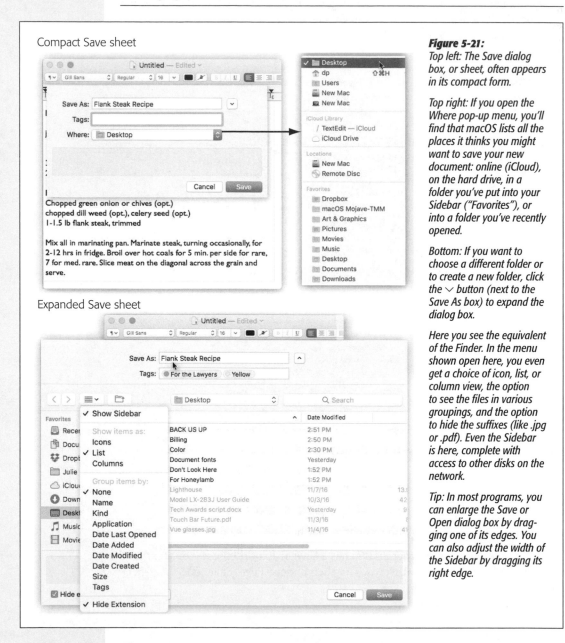

Expanded Save sheet

Figure 5-21:

Top left: The Save dialog box, or sheet, often appears in its compact form.

Top right: If you open the Where pop-up menu, you'll find that macOS lists all the places it thinks you might want to save your new document: online (iCloud), on the hard drive, in a folder you've put into your Sidebar ("Favorites"), or into a folder you've recently opened.

Bottom: If you want to choose a different folder or to create a new folder, click the ⌄ button (next to the Save As box) to expand the dialog box.

Here you see the equivalent of the Finder. In the menu shown open here, you even get a choice of icon, list, or column view, the option to see the files in various groupings, and the option to hide the suffixes (like .jpg or .pdf). Even the Sidebar is here, complete with access to other disks on the network.

Tip: In most programs, you can enlarge the Save or Open dialog box by dragging one of its edges. You can also adjust the width of the Sidebar by dragging its right edge.

Sheets

In the days of operating systems gone by, the Save dialog box appeared dead center on the screen, where it commandeered your entire operation. Moreover, because it seemed stuck to your *screen* rather than to a particular *document,* you couldn't actually tell which document you were saving—a real problem when you quit out of a program that had three unsaved documents open.

In most Mac programs, there's no mystery regarding which document you're saving, because a little Save dialog box called a *sheet* slides directly out of the document's title bar.

Better still, this Save box is a sticky note attached *to the document*. It stays there, neatly attached and waiting, even if you switch to another program, another document, the desktop, or wherever. When you finally return to the document, the Save sheet is still there, waiting for you to type a file name and save the document.

The Mini-Finder

Of course *you,* O savvy reader, have probably never saved a document into some deeply nested folder by accident, never to see it again. But millions of novices (and even a few experts) have fallen into this trap.

When the Save sheet appears, a pop-up menu shows you precisely where the Mac proposes to put your newly created document: usually in the Documents folder of your own Home folder. For most people, this is an excellent suggestion. If you keep everything in your Documents folder, it will be extremely easy to find, and you'll be able to back up your work just by dragging that single folder to a backup disk.

As shown at top in Figure 5-21, the Where pop-up menu gives you access to some other places where you might want to save a newly created file. (The keystrokes for the most important folders work here, too—Shift-⌘-H for your Home folder, for example.)

In any case, when you save a file, the options in the Where pop-up menu have you covered 90 percent of the time. Most people work with a limited set of folders for active documents.

But when you want to save a new document into a new folder, or when you want to navigate to a folder that isn't listed in the Where pop-up menu, all is not lost. Click the ⌄ button mentioned in Figure 5-21. The Save sheet expands into a very familiar sight: a miniature version of the Finder.

Tip: You can switch back and forth between the compact and expanded versions of this dialog box by pressing the undocumented shortcut ⌘-=.

You might be shocked to find out just how many Finder features are available, all within this little Save dialog box. The whole Save box is getting to be more Findery every year. For example:

- **Navigate with the Sidebar.** It's here, complete with access to the other computers on your network and your iCloud Drive.

- **Navigate with keystrokes.** All the usual keyboard shortcuts for navigating your Mac work within the Open and Save boxes. You can press ⌘-D to see what's on your desktop, Shift-⌘-H for your Home folder, Shift-⌘-A for your Applications folder, and so on.

- **Switch views** (icon, list, column), as shown in Figure 5-21 at bottom.

Tip: In column view, your first instinct should be to widen this window, making more columns available. Do so by carefully dragging either edge of the dialog box. The Mac remembers the size for this Save sheet independently in each program.

And in list view, how's this for a tip? If you right-click or two-finger click one of the column headings, like Name or Date Modified, you get a secret pop-up menu of column names: Last Opened, Size, Kind, Label, and so on. That's right: You can customize the list view within an Open or Save dialog box. You can sort, too, by clicking one of the column headings, just as at the desktop.

- **Search for files.** The search box at the top of the Open or Save dialog box is a clone of the Finder's search box (Chapter 3). Press ⌘-F to make your insertion point jump there. Type a few letters of the name of the file or folder you're looking for, and up it pops, regardless of its actual hard-disk location.

- **Delete a document or folder** right from this list. Just right-click or two-finger click it and choose Move to Trash.

- **Rename a document or folder.** Right-click or two-finger click it; from the shortcut menu, choose Rename.

- **Create a new folder.** Click the New Folder button (or press the usual New Folder keystroke, Shift-⌘-N) to create a new folder *inside* the folder you're looking at. You're asked to type the new name for the folder. After you've done so, click Create (or press Return). The new folder appears and opens before you, empty. You can now proceed with saving your new document into it, if you like.

- **Use Quick Look** (page 55). Select a file or folder in the list and tap the space bar to view it in a full-size window.

- **Add folders to the left-side Favorites list.** Drag them into the Sidebar here, either from the desktop, if it's visible, or right out of the dialog box in front of you. You can remove things from the Sidebar, too; just drag them away.

- **Navigate from the keyboard.** Most of the familiar Finder navigation shortcuts work here, too. Press the ◀ and ▶ keys to navigate the columns, or the ▲ and ▼ keys to highlight the disk and folder names *within* a column. Once you've highlighted a column, you can also type to select the first letters of disk or folder names.

- **Get Info.** Even in the Save or Open dialog box, you can highlight an icon (or several) and then press ⌘-I. You switch back to the Finder, where the Get Info box is waiting with the date, size, and other details about the selected icons.

When you're finished playing around, open the folder where you want to save your newly created document and then click Save to store it there.

Tip: Here's one of the weirdest tricks yet. When the Open or Save dialog box is open before you, you can press Shift-⌘-period to make all your Mac's *hidden* files appear. (As a Unix-based outfit, macOS is crawling with these invisible files, which are of interest primarily to technical types.) Press that keystroke again to re-hide the hidden files. Fun for geeks! If you use a non-American number-formatting system (where one thousand is 1.000, for example), use Shift-⌘-comma instead.

The next time you save a new document, the Save sheet reappears in whatever condition you left it. That is, if you used column view the last time, it's still in column view. You can collapse it into simplified view, shown at top in Figure 5-21, by clicking the ∧ button to the right of the Save As pop-up menu.

Tip: For years, there's been a keyboard shortcut for the Don't Save button that appears when you close a new document without saving it: ⌘-D. But in some modern Apple programs, including TextEdit, Preview, Grab, Pages, and Keynote, the button says Delete instead of Don't Save. In those cases, press ⌘-Delete to "click" it instead of using the mouse.

Insta-Jumping to a Folder Location

Whether you're using the mini-sheet or the expanded view, you can save yourself some folder-burrowing time by following this very weird tip: You can specify a folder location by dragging the icon of any folder or disk *from your desktop* directly into the Save or Open sheet. MacOS instantly displays the contents of that folder or disk. This feature is totally undocumented—but well worth learning.

Tip: If, when the Save box is in its expanded condition, you click the name of an existing file, macOS thoughtfully copies the name of the clicked file into the Save As text box (which otherwise said "Untitled" or was blank).

This trick can save you time when you're saving a second document with a slightly modified name ("Oprah and Me: The Inside Story, Chapter 1" and then "Oprah and Me: The Inside Story, Chapter 2"). It's also useful if you want to replace the original file with the new one you're saving. Instead of having to type out the entire name of the file, you can just click it.

The File Format Pop-Up Menu

The Save dialog box in many programs offers a pop-up menu of file formats below the Save As box. Use this menu when preparing a document for use by somebody else—somebody whose computer doesn't have the same software. For example, if you've used a graphics program to prepare a photograph for use on the web, this menu is where you specify JPEG format (the standard web format for photos).

The Open Dialog Box

The dialog box that appears when you choose File→Open is almost identical to the expanded Save File sheet. Because you encounter it only when you're opening an existing file, this dialog box lacks a Save button, a Tags box, a file name field, and so on.

Note: Furthermore, the Open dialog box gives you access only to disks, folders, and documents that you can actually open at this moment. For example, when you're using GarageBand, picture files show up dimmed.

But the Open box adds a special Sidebar category called Media (see Figure 5-22), which gives you direct access to all your photos, music, and movies. Apple figures you might want to import these items *into* a document you're working on.

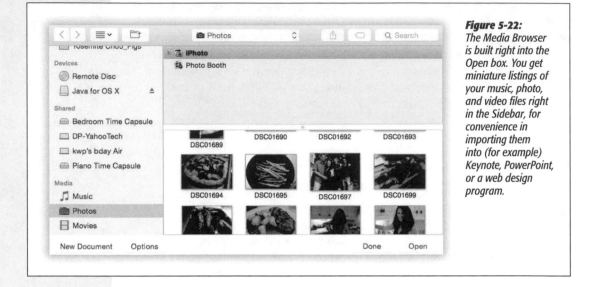

Figure 5-22:
The Media Browser is built right into the Open box. You get miniature listings of your music, photo, and video files right in the Sidebar, for convenience in importing them into (for example) Keynote, PowerPoint, or a web design program.

Most of the other Save File dialog box controls are equally useful here. That handy Spotlight search bar is still there, only a ⌘-F away. Once again, you can begin your navigation by seeing what's on the desktop (press ⌘-D) or in your Home folder (Shift-⌘-H).

Once again, you can find a folder or a disk by beginning your quest with the Sidebar and then navigate using icon, list, or column view. And, once again, you can drag a folder, disk, or file icon off your desktop and directly into the dialog box to specify where you want to look. (If you drag a *file* icon, you're shown the folder that contains it.)

When you've finally located the file you want to open, double-click it or highlight it (which you can do from the keyboard), and then press Return or ⌘-O.

In general, most people don't encounter the Open File dialog box nearly as often as the Save File dialog box. That's because the Mac offers many more convenient ways to *open* a file—double-clicking its icon in the Finder, choosing its name from ⌘→Recent Items, and so on—but only a single way to *save* a new file.

Auto Save and Versions

In the beginning, Jobs created the Save command—because computers were slow.

Every time you saved, your work was interrupted for a few seconds (or a lot of seconds) as the very slow program on your very slow computer saved your work onto a very slow floppy disk.

And *that,* ladies and gentlemen, is why most programs still don't autosave: because the interruptions were just too annoying.

Apple figured it was high time the world revisit that scenario. Computers now have plenty of horsepower. They could be saving your work *continuously,* and you'd never even know it. Why shouldn't *all* programs save your work as you go, automatically and invisibly? As long as you also have the option to rewind and take your document in a different direction, what could possibly be the harm?

And so it is that, in macOS today, Auto Save is here. Unfortunately, it's available in only a few programs. You'll find it in Apple's showcase programs: Pages, Keynote, Numbers, Preview, and TextEdit.

In these programs, your document is saved every time there's even the tiniest pause in your typing or working—in the background. No progress bar, no interruption. If you quit or close the document without remembering to save, no problem: Your work will be there when you open the document again later.

Note: "But wait a minute," cry the masses, "I *like* being able to close a document without saving changes! Sometimes all I wanted to do was fool around, play 'what-if' games—and then close it without saving changes!"

Just for you, Apple offers a pair of sneaky little checkboxes in System Preferences→General. First, "Ask to keep changes when closing documents." If that's turned on, then when you close a document with unsaved changes, the Mac asks if you want to keep the edits, just as it does in all other programs.

But if you *quit* the program without saving, your changes *are* auto-preserved; Auto Save apps autosave your documents when you quit their programs, so you can pick up where you left off the next time. You can override that, too, if you like; turn on "Close windows when quitting an app," also in System Preferences→General. Now you'll get the "Save changes?" box when you quit the app with unsaved changes.

Versions

In those enlightened programs that work with Auto Save, there's a more complicated but more powerful feature at work: Versions. It's an invisible paper trail of every in-progress condition of your document—and you can return to any earlier version at any time. You can even return to an earlier version and copy just a *chunk* of it into the current version, which is great when one paragraph of your previous draft was gold but the rest was junk.

The Versions world of document management is quite a bit different from the old setup. Here's what you need to know:

- **All the version information is stored in the same original document file.** (It's not like there's a rat's nest of icons for each thing you're working on.) But when you send the document to somebody else (by email or network, for example), the Mac sends only the current version, stripping out all the history. Nobody will ever know how much you labored over your work (or how little).

Note: Behind the scenes, the various versions of each document are saved in an invisible folder on your hard drive called *.DocumentRevisions-V100*. But you probably guessed that.

- **MacOS creates a new snapshot of your document once an hour.** You can also create new snapshots manually at even shorter intervals—by using the File→Save command (⌘-S), as you always have.

 These snapshots, or *versions,* represent rewind points that you can return to later, even months or years after you first created the document. Thoughtfully enough, the Mac records, invisibly, only what's *changed* between versions, so your files don't get all big and bloated.

Note: All right, you don't have *total* time-rewinding control. MacOS stores hourly versions for a day, daily versions for a month, and weekly versions for all previous months.

- **There's a secret menu in the title bar.** Point to the name of your document. In Auto Save–compatible files, a little ∨ appears in the title bar (Figure 5-23).

- **The Save As command is hidden in these programs.** It appears in the File menu only when you hold down the Option key.

 Apple is hoping you'll learn to use the new way. When you want to spin off a version of a document—to experiment with taking it into a new direction, for example— choose File→Duplicate. Before your very eyes, a copy of the open window springs into existence. If the original was called "Kumquat Tarts," then the new one is called "Kumquat Tarts copy"—but that name is highlighted, selected, right in the title bar.

 To leave your duplicated document in the same folder as the original, just type a new name and press Return. To file it in a different folder, choose File→Save. You get the standard Save dialog box, where you can choose a name and a folder for it.

Tip: You can also choose to move a document to a different folder later right there in the program. Just choose File→Move To and choose a new storage bin for it. (You can even store it in iCloud at this point; see page 210.) Or use the secret menu-bar menu shown in Figure 5-23.

Figure 5-23:
Point to the title of your document to see this secret menu. It lets you rename the document, change its tags, or file it into a new folder, without ever leaving the window.

Rewinding to an earlier version

The point of all this, of course, is to make it easy to go back in time—to undo the mediocre work you've done, or to resurrect some genius work that you later deleted.

The quick way is to choose File→Revert to→Last Saved (or Last Opened). That command restores the document to the last snapshot version (or to the way it was when you most recently opened it, if no new versions have been created).

You can revert your document to *any* snapshot, even an ancient one from weeks or months ago. To do that, choose File→Revert to→Browse All Versions.

After a moment, you see the stunning display shown in Figure 5-24. On the left, you see your document in its current condition. On the right, you see a stack of windows that represent all the different snapshots of your document, going back in time.

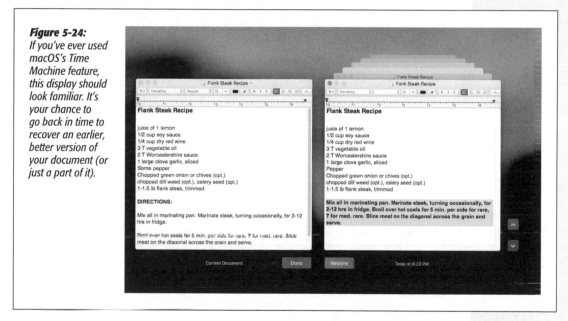

Figure 5-24:
If you've ever used macOS's Time Machine feature, this display should look familiar. It's your chance to go back in time to recover an earlier, better version of your document (or just a part of it).

You can have all kinds of productive fun in this version browser:

- **Compare the current version (on the left) with the next-most-recent one (on the right).** These are live documents, so you can scroll through them as necessary. If you decide to stick with the latest edition on the left, just click Done. You leave the version-history world and go back to editing.

- **Zoom back in time to inspect older versions (snapshots) of your document.** On the right side of the screen, you see earlier versions of the document—maybe even dozens of them, stretching back in time.

 You can click individual windows' title bars to see what's in them. You can also click or drag your cursor through the notches at the right side. It's like a time ruler that flies through the windows into the past. (As you go, the time/date stamp below

the right-side window identifies where you are in time—that is, which version you're examining.)

- **Restore an earlier version.** If you finally find the incarnation of the document you consider superior to your current one, click Restore. You leave Blurry Versionland and return to your document, which has now been rewound to its earlier condition.

 If you later decide you should not have gone back to that earlier version, no problem. Your later version—the one you started out with—is still in the version browser, too. So you can fast-forward back to it, if necessary.

Tip: If you press Option, the Restore button changes to say Restore a Copy. In other words, you'll create a previous-version duplicate of the document, without disturbing the current condition of the one you've just been working on.

- **Restore *part* of an earlier version.** Often, the current version of your work is *generally* good, but you really wish you could recover *one* magical sentence or paragraph or section—something you've since edited or deleted.

 You can do that in Blurry Versionland, too, because Copy and Paste work here!

 Use the time ruler to find the earlier edition of your document, the one containing the good stuff. Then drag through the desired text or graphics in the window on the right, as shown in Figure 5-24. Now copy the highlighted material (either press ⌘-C, or move your mouse to the top of the screen so the menu bar appears, and choose Edit→Copy). Click in the *current* version of the document, the one at left, and now paste (⌘-V, or use the menu bar). Click Done to complete this astonishing act of salvation.

- **Delete a version.** Once you've found a draft you never want to see again, move your cursor to the top of the screen; the menu bar appears. Choose File→Revert To→Delete This Version.

Tip: If you press Option, the command changes to Delete Old Versions; it gets rid of *all* old versions of the file.

Revert

Even though Auto Save is constantly backing up your document, it also remembers how the file looked the moment you opened it. And you want to know what's crazy? It can revert to that condition even if you've been manually saving your work all along! That's better than the old Revert command ever was. Just choose File→Revert to→Last Saved (or Last Opened).

iCloud Drive

Truth is, "cloud" is an annoying buzzword. Most of the time, when people say "in the cloud," they mean "online" or "on the internet"—terms that have served us perfectly well for years.

In any case, you can save your files online, into an online "hard drive" called iCloud Drive. The advantage here is that your files are now available for opening or editing from any computer or gadget you use, including iPhones, iPads, and iPod Touches.

iCloud Drive Defined

iCloud Drive, part of Apple's iCloud suite of services, is like a magic folder. In the Finder, it's represented by an iCloud Drive icon (⌂) in the Sidebar of every window.

Whatever you put into it appears, almost instantly, in the iCloud Drive folders on all your other machines: Macs, iPhones, iPads, and even Windows PCs. In fact, your files are even available at *icloud.com*, so you can grab them when you're stranded on a desert island with nothing but somebody else's computer. And internet access.

(If this concept reminds you of the popular free program Dropbox, then you're very wise.) Figure 5-25 shows the idea.

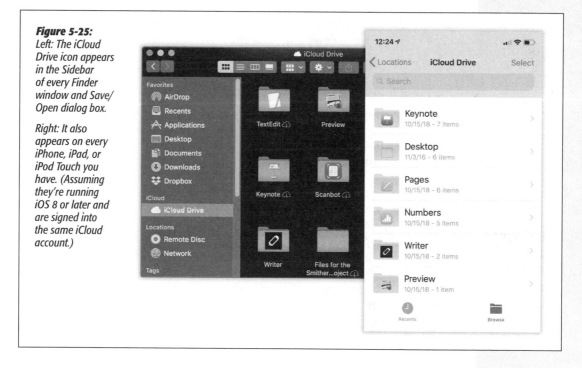

Figure 5-25:
Left: The iCloud Drive icon appears in the Sidebar of every Finder window and Save/ Open dialog box.

Right: It also appears on every iPhone, iPad, or iPod Touch you have. (Assuming they're running iOS 8 or later and are signed into the same iCloud account.)

This is an incredibly useful feature. No more emailing files to yourself. No more carrying things around on a flash drive. After working on some document at the office, you can go home and resume from right where you stopped; the same file is waiting for you, exactly as you left it.

iCloud Drive also makes a gloriously simple, effective backup disk. Anything you drag into this "folder" is instantly copied to all your devices and computers. And, as you know, the more copies that exist of something (and in the more locations), the

better your backup. Even if your main Mac is stolen or burned to aluminum dust, your iCloud Drive files are safe.

Your drive holds 5 gigabytes of files for free. You can pay extra for more space: $1 a month for 50 gigs, $3 a month for 200 gigs, or $10 for 2 terabytes (2,000 gigs).

Putting Files onto the iCloud Drive

On the Mac, you use the iCloud Drive just as you would a folder or a flash drive. Click its name in the Sidebar to see what's in there. Drag files into its window to copy them there. Make folders, add files, delete files, rename them—whatever. Any changes you make are reflected on your other Apple (and Windows) gadgets within seconds.

Inside a program, you can choose File→Save in the usual way. When the Save box appears, click iCloud Drive in the Sidebar. Or choose an iCloud Drive folder's name, if you've made one.

Tip: The window shown in Figure 5-25 shows your iCloud Drive documents and lets you open them, even when you're offline. How? Turns out your Mac stores a secret "local" copy. The changes you make won't update the online copy until you're online again, but at least you're never cut off from your own files.

Sharing iCloud Drive Files

You can also share access to individual files in your iCloud Drive with other people electronically, so you can collaborate across the internet. It's exactly like the same feature in popular services like Dropbox and Google Drive—except that it's available only to people who have iCloud accounts.

Note: Apple says that, in the spring of 2020, an update to macOS Catalina will permit you to share *folders*, too. That will be fantastically useful to co-workers, family, and friends. The steps will be identical to what's described here for individual files.

In the Finder, in the iCloud Drive, click the file. From the ⬆ menu, choose Show People. (The ⬆ option also appears when you right-click or two-finger click the document and, from the shortcut menu, choose Share.) The box shown in Figure 5-26 appears. Here you have three decisions to make:

- **How to invite people.** You can welcome your collaborators to this document by Messages, Email, AirDrop (if they're nearby)—or using the Copy Link button. That command puts a web link on your Clipboard, so you can share it in any other electronic way—in a Facebook post, in Slack, or whatever.

- **Who can access.** Of course, if you post the invitation link online somewhere, you might wind up with hundreds of people descending on your document. If you're posting a flyer advertising a garage sale, maybe that's just what you want. But if you're sharing the first draft of your screenplay, maybe you want to be more selective. That's why, in Share Options, you can specify either that "Only people you invite" have access, or "Anyone with the link."

- **What they can do.** If, from the Permission pop-up menu, you choose "Can make changes," then your document is editable on both ends, and both of you see the changes the other makes. Great for party planning, co-authoring papers, and editing novels. If you choose "View only," well, they can see your document but can't touch it.

Once you click Share, the ball is rolling. An email, text message, or AirDrop notification goes out to your lucky colleagues. Next to the document on your iCloud Drive, the legend "Shared by me" appears, for your reference. As long as you're all online, anyone can make changes to the shared document, and you all see the results almost immediately.

Once Apple gets that iCloud folder sharing working, your collaborators will be able to add new documents to the shared folder (everyone will see the new files) or make changes to the ones already there (everybody will see document changes, along with who made them).

At any time, you can revisit the list of invitees or how much access they have. Right-click or two-finger click the document's icon; this time, choose Share→Show People (that command has nothing to do with Broadway performers). You're right back at the box shown in Figure 5-26, so you can amend the settings, Remove Access for one person (hit •••), or shut off sharing altogether (click Stop Sharing).

Figure 5-26:
Sharing a document from your iCloud Drive means that you can either publish a document to the entire web from the convenience of a desktop folder, or collaborate with co-workers on a single document.

iCloud Drive on Other Devices

If the iCloud Drive behaves just like a folder on your Mac, how does it appear on iPhones, iPads, and Windows computers? Like this:

- **On the iPhone, iPad, or iPod Touch.** iCloud Drive is an app in iOS 9 and 10; in iOS 11 and later, it's called Files. Just open it to see a list of the folders and files on your iCloud Drive (including the Desktop and Documents folders from your Macs).

- **On another Mac.** Click the iCloud Drive icon in the sidebar of any Mac (to which you've logged in with your iCloud ID), and there's your stuff.

- **On the web.** You can pull up *icloud.com*, log in, and click the iCloud Drive icon. Presto: a list of the files and folders on your Drive. (Including Desktop and Documents folders, if you've turned that on.)

- **On a Windows PC.** Your computer requires the iCloud control panel. (You can download it from this book's "Missing CD" page at *missingmanuals.com*.) It does just what you'd expect: It creates an iCloud Drive icon in your File Explorer windows, exactly as on the Mac.

iCloud Desktop & Documents

An optional feature makes everything on your *desktop* and in your *Documents folder* accessible everywhere—on every Mac you own, every iOS device, every Windows PC, and even online, at *icloud.com*.

If you think about it, those are the two places that most people, most of the time, leave their stuff: on the desktop or in the Documents folder. The point of this feature is that you no longer have to *remember* to copy some file or folder you'll need onto the iCloud Drive; if you left it on your desktop or in your Documents folder, it'll just be there. When you need a file you don't have with you, you'll be able to grab it from wherever you are.

Of course, you get only 5 gigabytes of iCloud Drive storage free, which is shared by all of iCloud's features. So to use this system, you'll almost certainly have to pay for additional storage, month after month.

If you didn't turn on iCloud Desktop & Documents when you installed macOS Catalina, you can also turn it on at any time:

- **In System Preferences→iCloud.** Next to the first checkbox, iCloud Drive, click Options; in the resulting dialog box, on the Documents tab, turn on Desktop & Documents Folders. (See Figure 5-27, top.)

- **In About This Mac→Storage→Manage→Store in iCloud (page 103).** Turn on "Store files from Desktop and Documents in iCloud Drive."

If you don't have enough iCloud Drive space, you're cheerfully offered a list of price plans at this moment. The cheapest plan available that will fit your documents is highlighted.

Once that's all set up, you'll discover a few alarming changes to your Mac universe:

- **Everything on your desktop has disappeared.** It's all been swept into a new folder on your desktop called "Desktop - MacBook Air" (or whatever your Mac's name is).

 So why does macOS create a new Desktop folder bearing your Mac's name? Because you might turn on this feature on a *second* Mac that you own, or even a third. The folder-naming system is designed to separate what's on the desktop of *this* Mac from what's on the desktops of those *other* Macs. If you have two computers, then,

you might see folders on your desktop called *Desktop - MacBook Air* and *Desktop - Kitchen iMac.* (Figure 5-27, middle right, shows this effect.)

Of course, if you primarily use only one Mac, the icons you once kept on your desktop are now in a desktop *folder* that seems to be *on* your desktop, which seems silly.

Fortunately, there's nothing to stop you from dragging the contents of "Desktop - MacBook Air" right back onto your actual desktop. The only caution here is that, if you do that on more than one Mac, you wind up with a commingled desktop. All the icons from your laptop desktop *and* all the icons from your iMac desktop are now on the desktops of both machines. You've just duplicated them. And any changes you make—any new icons you save to any desktop—get likewise duplicated to your other Macs.

Figure 5-27:
Top: Here's how you enter the rabbit hole known as iCloud Desktop & Documents.

Middle left: Desktop and Documents are now listed under iCloud Drive. The actual folders have moved, too.

Middle right: You see a separate Desktop folder for each Mac for which you've turned this feature on. (Documents, too.)

Bottom: If you move something from Desktop or Documents into any other folder, you get a warning that you're actually deleting it from your iCloud Drive (assuming that checkbox is turned on in Finder→Preferences→Advanced).

That may be exactly what you want. Just watch out for disk space.

Note: What you see on your iPhone and at *icloud.com*, meanwhile, is identical to what you see on your Mac.

- **Everything in your Documents folder disappears, too.** All *those* icons get shunted into a new folder in your Documents folder called "Documents - MacBook Air."

- **The real Desktop and Documents folders are no longer in your Home folder.** And in the Finder sidebar, they're no longer listed under the Favorites heading; now they're listed under iCloud Drive (Figure 5-27, middle left), to remind you that their new home is online, in the iCloud Drive.

- **You get a warning if you drag something out of Documents or off your desktop.** The warning is alarming (Figure 5-27, bottom), but it's perfectly logical: If you move an icon out of the Documents folder or from your desktop into another folder, you're removing it from the iCloud Drive. (The iCloud Drive's only responsibility is to mirror what's in your *Documents and Desktop* folders.)

- **If you turn off iCloud Desktop & Documents, you get an alarming message.** It says: "If you continue, documents on your Desktop and in your Documents folder will be visible in iCloud Drive only. No documents will be deleted from iCloud Drive."

What this means is that the icons on your desktop, and in your Documents folder, will disappear!

OK, be confused, but don't be hysterical; your files *are* on your Mac. The message makes it sound like you'll have to re-download them from iCloud, but that's not true. They're already on your Mac—in the iCloud Drive folder.

Turning off iCloud Desktop & Documents leaves only an empty Desktop folder on your desktop, and an empty Documents folder in your Documents folder. If you want to put your files back where they belong, you have to drag them there manually—out of the iCloud Drive folders.

Screen Time

It might seem strange that Apple, whose primary business is persuading you to consume more of its goods and services, is concerned that you might be spending *too much* time on your Mac. But it's true: macOS Catalina contains a feature, closely modeled on (and integrated with) the same one for iOS and iPadOS, that's designed to help you set reasonable limits on your screen time.

Or at least on your *kids'* screen time.

In System Preferences→Screen Time, you'll find a vast suite of tools that help you keep track of how much time you're spending on your Macs, iPhones, and iPads; monitor which apps you're using during that time; and set daily limits for how much time you're allowed to spend in each category of app (Figure 5-28).

Or, of course, monitor or limit all this for your kids, students, or employees.

Every Sunday, a Screen Time notification will appear, announcing that your weekly report is available. Open the notification to see a colorful summary, full of bar graphs and stats that show how much you, and your other family members, rotted their brains on their devices, and on which apps, and how many times you lost your will and went over your limits.

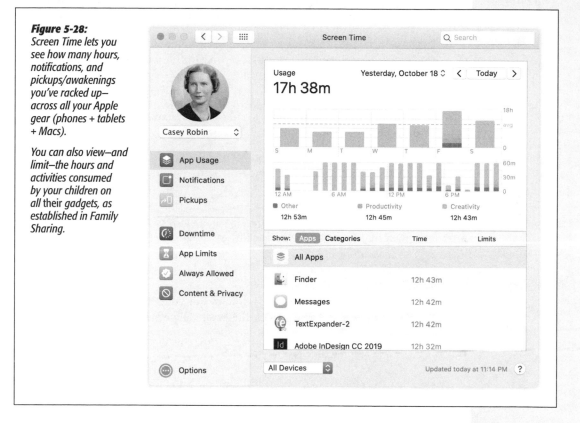

Figure 5-28:
Screen Time lets you see how many hours, notifications, and pickups/awakenings you've racked up—across all your Apple gear (phones + tablets + Macs).

You can also view—and limit—the hours and activities consumed by your children on all their gadgets, as established in Family Sharing.

[Your Name]

This pop-up menu, at top left, appears only if you've set up Family Sharing (page 661). Choose a kid's name to see a replica of *your* Screen Time settings—but this time, you're changing the settings only for that kid. And, yes, that means you can also see the *kid's* graphs.

Here's a tour of the new Screen Time panel, starting with the left side.

Options

This button, at lower left, offers two important options:

- **Share Across Devices.** If you have more than one Apple gadget—say, a Mac and an iPhone—Screen Time is only too happy to add their totals. If the pop-up menu at the bottom says All Devices, then the graph at the top is the grand tally. You can

choose the names of the devices from that pop-up menu to see their individual breakdowns.

This checkbox, therefore, lets you *exclude* the Mac you're now using from the tally that would otherwise include all devices.

- **Use Screen Time Passcode.** Of course, Apple is not about to lock you out of your own gear; these limits are more like friendly reminders. You can choose to ignore the "Time's up!" message when it appears.

 But for your kids, it's another story. Here you can set up a parental password. Without it, your underlings can't bypass the limits you've set up. They can't just open System Preferences and turn off Screen Time (or the individual features within).

 (You may be invited, at this point, to change your account to a Standard account; see page 489 for the difference.)

 Once you've created the code, though, nobody can change Screen Time's settings—or even request more time when the time's up—without it.

Turn On/Turn Off

If you're offended by the entire notion of macOS as a nanny, always harassing you about your computer addiction and sending you judgy reports about your progress, here's your master on/off switch.

App Usage

This big, bold graph shows how much time you or your chosen family member has spent on Mac and other Apple gadgets this week. Hope you're sitting down.

- **Date control:** Click the arrows to move through the days of recorded data, or click Today to jump back to today.

- **Top row:** Bar graphs for each day of the week.

- **Second row:** An hourly breakdown for whichever Day bar you've clicked.

- **Bottom half:** A list of the apps you've been using, sorted by most time eaten. Or, if you click Categories, a list of app *categories*: Productivity, Creativity, and so on. Click a category name to see how much of your bar graphs are made up of each one.

Remember: These are the totals for *all* your Apple gadgets (the ones signed into your iCloud account). Use the pop-up menu at the bottom to see *only* your Mac's usage, only your iPhone, or whatever.

Note: If most of the controls in Screen Time are dimmed, it's because your family is using Family Sharing (page 661), and you're not a designated parent. Sorry, kid!

Notifications

This time, each graph indicates how many *notifications* you got on the selected day, category, or device. Here again, you can view this information by device or by app.

Pickups

These graphs show how many times this day or week you've actually awakened your Mac, phone, and other Apple machines, and which app you used first. Once again, you can view the information as a total of all your Apple devices, or one at a time.

Downtime

For some people, just seeing these startling graphs may be enough to produce a change in behavior—like looking away from your screen now and then. But if you need a little reminder to help curb your addiction, click Downtime, and then Turn On.

Here you're supposed to indicate a slice of the day when you're willing to quit using your devices—during dinner, maybe, or the couple of hours before bed. (Use "Every Day" if the schedule will be the same seven days a week, or "Custom" to set up separate schedules for each day. That's handy if, for example, your kids aren't allowed to play games on school nights.)

At the appointed time, all apps' windows go white and blank, and all apps' icons in the Finder dim.

The only exceptions: You can still use whatever apps you've chosen in Always Allowed, described next.

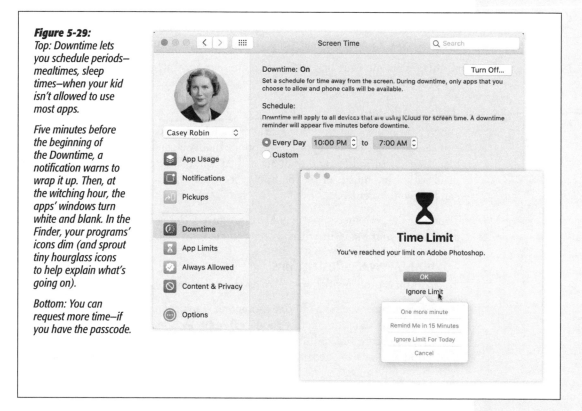

Figure 5-29:
Top: Downtime lets you schedule periods—mealtimes, sleep times—when your kid isn't allowed to use most apps.

Five minutes before the beginning of the Downtime, a notification warns to wrap it up. Then, at the witching hour, the apps' windows turn white and blank. In the Finder, your programs' icons dim (and sprout tiny hourglass icons to help explain what's going on).

Bottom: You can request more time—if you have the passcode.

Of course, it's not so hard to bypass your own Downtime limits. All you have to do is hit Ignore Limit and choose one of the options there, like "One more minute," "Remind Me in 15 Minutes," or "Ignore Limit For Today" (Figure 5-29). Or you could just open System Preferences and turn Downtime off.

So what's the point? First, even a thin obstacle is, psychologically speaking, better than nothing. Second, of course, most people use this feature for their kids—and they add a passcode so Downtime *can't* be turned off, and the Ignore button *isn't* available without the code.

There may be some deep conversations at dinner tonight.

App Limits

You can also set daily time limits for individual app *categories*. Maybe you want to cut back your social-networking habit to an hour a day. Maybe you think three hours a day watching videos is plenty (well, at least for your kid).

When you click App Limits, and then Turn On, and then +, macOS presents app categories like Social Networking, Games, Entertainment, Education, and Health & Fitness. (Who on earth would limit Health & Fitness?)

You can limit either an entire category—or tap the ▶ to see the names of the apps *in* that category, so you can limit them individually. Dial up the number of hours and minutes you want as the maximum per day—once again, either Every Day or on a Custom weekly schedule. When everything looks good, hit Done.

At this point, you can click + to set up another app-category time limit, repeating the process.

Always Allowed

When Downtime is on, your Mac isn't completely bricked. It's still a computer—and you can designate certain apps as exceptions that you can use. It's probably smart to block Messages, Twitter, and Mail before bed. But maybe Spotify is OK, so you can relax with some music, or maybe Books, so you can read. Or maybe Maps, so you can find your hotel.

To choose the permitted apps, click Always Allowed. Here's a master list of every single program on your Mac. Turn on apps you want to be available even during Downtime.

Content & Privacy Restrictions

This section is probably better known as "parental controls" (Figure 5-30).

If you're issuing a Mac to a child, or someone who acts like one, you'll be gratified to discover that Catalina offers a good deal of protection. That's protection of your offspring's delicate sensibilities (it can block pornography and dirty words) and protection of your bank account (it can block purchases of music, movies, and apps without your permission).

The setup is here, in System Preferences→Screen Time→Content & Privacy Restrictions. The master switch is here, at the top (Turn On/Turn Off).

Figure 5-30:
Here's where you can lock down the kid's Mac—and his iPhone and iPad—in one fell swoop. Any changes you make here you'll also see in the Screen Time settings on your own iPhone.

Once Restrictions are on, you can put up data blockades in a number of categories. Many of them may seem baffling, because they pertain to *phones*, not Macs. But remember that Screen Time is synchronized across all Apple gadgets on your account, so it's useful that you can make these changes on either the phone, tablet, *or* Mac:

- **Content.** This is where you can shield impressionable eyes from pornography online. Unrestricted Access means no protection; Limit Adult Websites means Apple will apply its own judgment in blocking dirty websites, using a list it has compiled; and Allowed Websites Only is a "whitelist." It blocks the entire web *except* for the wholesome sites listed here. You can add your own sites to this list (click Customize), but the point is clear: This is the web with training wheels.

 Also on this tab, Explicit Language in Siri & Dictionary lets you plug your Mac's ears when your little monster says unspeakable things to it. Web Search Content in Siri lets you turn off your youngsters' ability to say to Siri, "Look up naked ladies" (or whatever naughty searches they dream up).

 You can restrict or allow Music Profiles & Posts (the discussion within Apple's defunct music service), Multiplayer Games in Game Center (stops your kid from playing games against strangers online), or Adding Friends in Game Center.

- **Stores.** Since every country has its own ratings schemes (for movies, TV shows, games, song lyrics, and so on), you use the Ratings For control to say which country's rating system you want to use.

The Movies, TV Shows, and Apps pop-up menus specify what your kid is allowed to watch, play, read, or listen to. For example, you can choose PG-13 from the Movies pop-up menu; any movies rated "higher," like R or NC-17, won't play.

For some categories, like Books, Music, Podcasts & News, you can turn off Explicit to prevent iTunes Store goods that contain naughty language.

As for Allow on iOS: Is your kid allowed to install apps? Delete them? Buy new levels, weapons, and features within apps? And is your Apple ID required to make a *second* purchase once you've made the first one?

Apps are three Mac features you can block from your kid's use (Camera, Books Store, Siri & Dictation), and 10 iPhone/iPad features you can block.

• **Other.** This tab offers a motley miscellaneous set of further restrictions for your kid. They include Passcode Changes, Account Changes (the email and social-media accounts you've set up), Cellular Data (limits you've set up for various apps on the phone or iPad), Do Not Disturb While Driving (ensures that your underling can't turn off that important iOS safety feature, thereby defeating the entire purpose), TV Provider (makes sure the rapscallion won't attempt to change your cable-TV company), and Background App Activities (which apps are allowed to run when they're not the frontmost).

The Open Privacy Settings button opens the Security & Privacy page of System Preferences.

Data: Typing, Sharing & Backing Up

The original 1984 Mac didn't make jaws drop because of its speed, price, or sleek looks. What amazed people was the simplicity and elegance of the user interface. At some point in every Apple demo, the presenter copied a graphic drawn in a painting program (MacPaint) and pasted it directly into a word processor (MacWrite), where it appeared neatly nestled between typed paragraphs of text.

Today, the Mac is even more adept at helping you enter, move, and share your hard-won data. MacOS offers several ways to move information within a single document, between documents, between programs, and even between Mac and Windows computers. This chapter leads you through this broad cycle of data: from entering it with the mouse and keyboard, to moving it around, to backing it up.

The Mac Keyboard

All through this book, you'll find references to certain keys on Apple's keyboards. "Hold down the ⏏ key," you might read, or "Press Control-F2." If you're coming from Mac OS 9, from Windows, or even from a typewriter, you might be a bit befuddled.

To make any attempt at an explanation even more complicated, Apple's keyboards keep changing. The one you're using right now is probably one of these models:

- **The current keyboards,** where the keys are flat little jobbers that poke up through square holes in the black or silver aluminum (Figure 6-1). That's what you get on current laptops, wired keyboards, and Bluetooth wireless keyboards.

- **The old, plastic desktop keyboards,** or the white or black plastic laptop ones.

Here, then, is a guided tour of the non-typewriter keys on the modern Mac keyboard:

Tip: To see close-ups of Apple's current wired and wireless keyboards, visit *apple.com/keyboard*.

- **fn.** How are you supposed to pronounce fn? Not "function," certainly; after all, the F-keys on the top row are already known as function keys. And not "fun"; goodness knows, the fn key isn't particularly hilarious to press.

 What it *does*, though, is quite clear: It changes the purpose of certain keys. That's a big deal on laptops, which don't have nearly as many keys as desktop keyboards. So for some of the less commonly used functions, you're supposed to press fn and a regular key. (For example, fn turns the ▲ arrow key into a Page Up key, which scrolls upward by one screenful.)

Note: On most Mac keyboards, the fn key is in the lower-left corner. The exception is the full-size Apple desktop keyboard (the one with a numeric keypad); there the fn key is in the little block of keys between the letter keys and the number pad.

Figure 6-1:
On the top row of aluminum Mac keyboards, the F-keys have dual functions. Ordinarily, the F1 through F4 keys correspond to Screen Dimmer (☼), Screen Brighter (☼), Mission Control (⊡), and either Dashboard (⊙, no longer functional) or Launchpad (⬚⬚⬚). Pressing the fn key in the lower-left corner changes their personalities.

You'll find many more fn examples in the following paragraphs.

- **Numeric keypad.** The number-pad keys do exactly the same thing as the numbers at the top of the keyboard. But, with practice, typing things like phone numbers and prices is much faster with the number pad, since you don't have to look down at what you're doing.

 Apple has been quietly eliminating the numeric keypad from most of its keyboards, but you can still find it on some models. And on some old Mac laptops, the numbers 0 through 9 were painted onto a block of *letter* keys near the right side (1, 2, and 3 were J, K, and L, for example). You could turn those letter keys into their numeric alter egos by pressing the fn key with your left hand.

 Eventually, Apple eliminated this embedded-keyboard effect from its laptops, having discovered that almost nobody was using it.

- ☀, ☀ (**F1, F2**). These keys control the brightness of your screen. Usually, you can tone it down a bit when you're in a dark room or when you want to save laptop battery power; you'll want to crank it up in the sun.

Tip: If you hold down the Shift and Option keys, tapping the brightness keys adjusts the brightness by just a little bit—a fraction of one of the larger brightness steps. Control freaks, rejoice.

- ▣ (**F3**). This one fires up Mission Control, the handy window-management feature described starting on page 177.

- ⏱ or ⊞ (**F4**). On recent Macs, the F4 key bears a ⊞ logo. Tapping it opens Launchpad, which is described starting on page 165. On older Macs, the ⏱ key used to open Dashboard, which is now defunct.

- �night, ⏵night (**F5, F6**). Most recent Mac laptops have light-up *keys,* which is very handy indeed when you're typing in the dark. The key lights are supposed to come on automatically when it's dark, but you can also control the illumination yourself by tapping these keys. (On most other Macs, the F5 and F6 keys aren't assigned to anything. They're free for you to use as you see fit, as described on page 200.)

- ◄◄, ►ıı, and ►► (**F7, F8, F9**). These keys work in the programs you'd expect: Music, QuickTime Player, DVD Player, and other programs where it's handy to have Rewind, Play/Pause, and Fast Forward buttons.

Tip: Tap either ◄◄ or ►► to skip to the previous or next track or chapter. Hold one down to rewind or fast-forward.

- ◄, ◄), ◄)) (**F10, F11, F12**). These three keys control your speaker volume. The ◄ key means Mute; tap it once to cut off the sound completely and again to restore its previous level. Tap the ◄) repeatedly to make the sound level lower, the ◄)) key to make it louder.

 With each tap, you see a big white version of each key's symbol on your screen, your Mac's little nod to let you know it understands your efforts.

Tip: If you hold down the Shift and Option keys, then tapping the volume keys adjusts the volume by smaller increments, just as with the brightness keys.

- ⏏. This is the Eject key. When there's a flash drive or a memory card in your Mac (or, less likely, a CD or a DVD), tap this key to make the computer spit it out. (If you don't have this key, then choose File→Eject, or press ⌘-E.)

- **Home, End.** The Home key jumps to the top of a window, the End key to the bottom. If you're looking at a list of files, the Home and End keys jump you to the top or bottom of the list. In Photos, they jump to the first or last photo in your collection. In iMovie, the Home key rewinds your movie to the very beginning. In Safari, it gets you to the top or bottom of the web page.

(In Word, they jump to the beginning or end of the line. But then again, Microsoft has always had its own ways of doing things.)

On keyboards without a dedicated block of number keys, you get these functions by holding down fn as you tap the ◄ and ► keys.

- **Page Up, Page Down.** These keys scroll up or down by one screenful. The idea is to let you scroll through word-processing documents, web pages, and lists without having to use the mouse.

On keyboards without a numeric keypad, you get these functions by pressing fn plus the ▲ and ▼ keys.

- **Clear.** Clear (on the old full-size keyboards only) gets rid of whatever you've highlighted, but without putting a copy on the invisible Clipboard, as the Cut command would do.

- **Esc.** Esc stands for escape, and it means "cancel." It's fantastically useful. It closes dialog boxes, dismisses menus, and exits special modes like Quick Look, slideshows, screen savers, and so on. Get to know it.

- **Delete.** The backspace key.

- **⌦.** Many a Mac fan goes for years without discovering the handiness of this delightful little key: the Forward Delete key. Whereas Delete backspaces over whatever letter is just to the *left* of the insertion point, this one (labeled "Del" on older keyboards) deletes whatever is just to the *right* of the insertion point. It comes in handy when, for example, you've clicked into some text to make an edit—but wound up planting your cursor in just the wrong place.

The old full-size Apple keyboard has a dedicated key for this. On all other keyboards, you get this function by holding down fn as you tap the regular Delete key.

- **Return/Enter.** Most Apple keyboards have a single Return/Enter key. On the old-style wide keyboards, there are separate Return and Enter keys (very few programs treat these keys as different, although Microsoft Excel is one of them). In any case, pressing Return wraps your typing to the next line. When a dialog box is on the screen, tapping the Return key is the same as clicking the confirmation button (like OK or Done).

- **⌘.** This key triggers keyboard shortcuts for menu items.

- **Control.** The Control key (represented by ^ in software menus) triggers shortcut menus, described on the following pages.

- **Option.** The Option key (sometimes labeled Alt, and represented by ⌥ in menus) is sort of a "miscellaneous" key. It's the equivalent of the Alt key in Windows. It lets you access secret features—you'll find them described all through this book—and type special symbols. For example, you press Option-4 to get the ¢ symbol, and Option-Y to get the ¥ (yen) symbol.

- **Help.** In the Finder, Microsoft programs, and a few other places, this key opens up the electronic help screens. But you'd guessed that.

The Complicated Story of the Function Keys

As the previous section makes clear, the F-keys at the top of modern Mac keyboards come with predefined functions: brightness, volume, music playback, and so on.

But they didn't always. Before Apple gave F9, F10, and F11 to the fast-forward and speaker-volume functions, those keys controlled the Exposé window-management function described starting on page 186.

So the question is: What if you don't *want* to trigger the hardware features of these keys? What if you want pressing F1 to mean "F1" (which opens the Help window in some programs)? What if you want F9, F10, and F11 to control Exposé's three modes, as they once did?

For that purpose, you're supposed to press the fn key. The fn key (lower left on small keyboards, center block of keys on the big ones) switches the function of the function keys. In other words, pressing fn *and* F10 triggers an Exposé feature, even though the key has a Mute symbol (◄) painted on it.

But here's the thing: What if you use those F-keys for software features (like Cut, Copy, Paste, and Exposé) *more often* than the hardware features (like brightness and volume)?

In that case, you can reverse the logic, so that pressing the F-keys *alone* triggers software functions and governs brightness and audio only when you're pressing fn. To do that, choose System Preferences→Keyboard. Turn on the cryptically worded checkbox "Use F1, F2, etc. as standard function keys."

And that's it. From now on, you press the fn key to get the functions painted on the keys (◄◄, ►II, ►►, ◄, ◄), ◄))), .⸱⸱⸱., .⸱⸱⸱., and so on).

The Touch Bar + Fingerprint Reader

The 2016 MacBook Pro models introduced an eye-popping feature, a first on computers: Above the keyboard, where the function keys (F1, F2, F3…) once sat, there's a colorful strip of touchscreen. Apple calls it the Touch Bar (Figure 6-2).

Figure 6-2:
Meet the Touch Bar, shown in just a few of its incarnations. Apple decided that touch might be a useful feature— as part of the keyboard, not the screen.

It's a half-inch-tall, high-resolution ("Retina"), 2170×60 pixel, multitouch, OLED screen. It can display whatever programmers want: buttons for functions you might need right now, or a rainbow of color selections, or a timeline of the video you're editing. The Touch Bar is designed to give you quick access to commands and features that are usually hidden in menus—but now you don't have to memorize keystrokes to trigger them.

The controls here *change* according to what you're doing at this moment—what program you're using, and what function within that program.

When you're typing, you might see QuickType (autocomplete buttons for the three words the Mac thinks you're most likely to want to type next). When you're in Safari, you see little buttons for your open page tabs. When you've selected text, you get formatting controls. When you're editing video or reading a Books book, you see a horizontal "map" of your movie or book, for quick navigation with a finger touch.

Note: The Touch Bar fades to black if you haven't used it in a while. Just tap to make the buttons light up again.

All the major programs that come with the Mac have been outfitted with Touch Bar controls, including the Finder, Automator, Calculator, Contacts, GarageBand, Books, iMovie, Keynote, Mail, Maps, Messages, Music, News, Notes, Numbers, Pages, Photos, Podcasts, Preview, QuickTime Player, Reminders, Safari, Stickies, System Preferences, TextEdit, and TV. (Apple has even blessed some of the utility programs with Touch Bar buttons, like Activity Monitor, Script Editor, Terminal, and Xcode.)

Other software companies, including Adobe and Microsoft, have added Touch Bar buttons to their programs, too.

In many programs, you can *customize* what's on the Touch Bar, so the functions you use most often are always glowing there.

The Touch Bar is especially useful when you're in Full Screen mode (page 173), where the whole point is to maximize your document's area on the screen. Now the editing controls you might need are on the Touch Bar, out of the way of the big screen.

There's no feedback when you tap the Touch Bar—no little beep or vibration—so you do have to glance at it to see what you're doing. Fortunately, the Touch Bar image is actually angled, not flat, so it's looking right at you.

The Touch Bar may not revolutionize your work in every program. But you'll probably find some situations where it's a truly helpful work accelerator: navigating a video you're editing without having to fuss with the onscreen scroll bar, for example, or tapping out emoji symbols in Messages.

Oh—and being able to log in without entering a password 65 times a day (thanks to your fingerprint) is a joy; read on.

Tip: If you miss the old function keys (F1, F2, F3...), you can have them back on command. Just hold down the physical fn key on your keyboard; the Touch Bar buttons change to the old F-keys.

The Fingerprint Reader

On Touch Bar laptops, the power button sits at the right end of the Touch Bar—and it's also a Touch ID fingerprint reader, the same sensor that's on the iPhone and iPad. (The 2018 MacBook Air has this button, too, even though it doesn't have a Touch Bar.) Once you've taught the Mac to recognize your fingerprint in System Preferences→ Touch ID, then just resting your finger on this button is enough to unlock the Mac, bypassing the password screen.

In fact, if you've set up your Mac with different accounts, the next person can insta-switch to his account just by clicking the Touch ID sensor himself—no logging out, no menu commands, no other steps.

Finally, your fingerprint can approve App Store purchases, or buy stuff on the web without having to enter your name, address, and credit card info over and over again. That part's called Apple Pay on the Web, and it's described on page 665.

Tip: In Catalina, your Apple Watch can authenticate you, too— for example, when you're making a change to a locked System Preferences panel. Instead of entering your password, you can just double-press the Watch's side button. See page 313 for details.

The Control Strip

Some Touch Bar buttons are always present. At the left end, for example, what Apple calls a System button is always available. Usually, it's the Esc key (page 226). Sometimes the System button says Done or ⊗, but you get the idea.

At the right end, Apple offers something called the Control Strip. You're probably too young to remember the Control Strip (in System 7, which ran Macs from 1991 to 1998). But this is the same idea: a collapsible row of buttons that give you direct access to settings you're likely to want to change without burrowing into System Preferences.

Out of the box, the Control Strip seeks to restore the most essential functions of the F-keys that the Touch Bar replaces: screen brightness and speaker volume (plus a button for Siri), as shown at top in Figure 6-3.

When the Control Strip is collapsed, you have two ways to adjust the brightness and volume:

- **Tap the ☼ or ◀)) button.** A slider springs out to the left of the button. Touch or drag your finger inside the slider to adjust the brightness or volume.

- **Slide from the ☼ or ◀) button.** In other words, you can adjust the brightness or volume with one continuous finger move instead of two—just keep your finger down after the initial tap, and drag within the slider (Figure 6-3, bottom).

Tip: Starting with the 2018 MacBook Pro models, making brightness or volume changes can be a little quicker: You can make little horizontal swipes directly on top of the ☼ or ◀)) buttons. No slider ever appears, and you save a couple of seconds.

Now, not everybody likes change. And some people don't like the way Apple makes changes. Fortunately, the Control Strip is a change you can change.

- **Bring back the function keys temporarily.** If you need the standard full-row set of Mac function keys as described on pages 188 and 227, you can bring them back. Tap the thin ❨ button to the left of the ☀ button. The collapsed Control Strip now expands to stretch the full length of the keyboard, precisely replicating the function keys that used to be painted on the top row of physical keys (Figure 6-3, second from top).

Tip: You can also set things up so that tapping the physical fn key expands the Control Strip temporarily. Open System Preferences→Keyboard and from the "Press Fn key to" pop-up menu, choose Expand Control Strip.

Figure 6-3:
Top: The Control Strip is always present on the right—and usually collapsed, to make room for your programs' buttons in the center of the Touch Bar. To expand the Control Strip to the full width of the keyboard, tap the skinny ❨ button.

Bottom: The Brightness and Volume buttons transform into sliders when you hold your finger down on them.

- **Bring back the function keys permanently.** If you prefer to have the standard function keys at all times, open System Preferences→Keyboard. From the "Touch Bar shows" pop-up menu, choose Expanded Control Strip. At this point, the Touch Bar never changes, never shows you app-specific buttons; it *always* shows the traditional function keys, pictured second from top in Figure 6-3.

- **Get rid of the Control Strip.** On the other hand, maybe you don't adjust your brightness or volume much, or you have another way to do it. And you'd rather have the entire width of the Touch Bar dedicated to app-specific buttons.

In that case, open System Preferences→Keyboard. From the "Touch Bar shows" pop-up menu, choose App Controls. Now the Control Strip is always hidden; you've got a lot more space available for function buttons within each program.

• **Change the buttons on the Control Strip.** Apple's probably correct that the functions most people want most of the time are Brightness, Volume, and Mute. (Siri? Well, maybe in time.) But that doesn't mean you can't add or delete buttons from the collapsed Control Strip if there are other functions you use more often. In fact, you can even customize the *expanded* Control Strip (Figure 6-3, second from top).

The key to making these changes: Open System Preferences→Keyboard; click Customize Control Strip. Now you've opened the weird, wonderful world of Touch Bar customizing, as described in the next section. Note that, in this case, you can expand or collapse the Control Strip during this process, thereby editing either version. For example, you could get rid of the Siri button (there are, after all, other ways to trigger Siri), which makes more room for app-specific buttons. Or maybe you never use the Launcher button in the expanded Control Strip; this is your chance to replace it with, for example, the Screenshot button or the Show Desktop button.

Customizing the Touch Bar

The key to choosing which buttons you want on your Touch Bar is the View→Customize Touch Bar command. You'll find that command in the Finder, Mail, Photos, and a few other major programs. (If the program you're using doesn't let you customize its Touch Bar, then that command doesn't appear.)

The dialog box shown in Figure 6-4 shows what you'd see in the Finder.

Figure 6-4:
When the Customize dialog box is on the screen, you can move, delete, or add buttons on the Touch Bar. All the existing buttons begin gently wiggling to indicate that they're movable or deletable.

Editing your Touch Bar is a strange, delightful procedure. It goes like this:

- **Install a new button.** Inspect the palette of available Touch Bar buttons on your Mac's main screen. You can *drag* one of those buttons downward with your mouse, down off the screen, "through" the laptop's hinge, and onto the Touch Bar.

 If you drag onto a blank spot (anywhere marked by ---- dashes), you can drop it there to install it. If you drag it onto an existing button, then a dotted outline appears; that means that you'll replace the existing button when you let go.

- **Rearrange existing buttons.** Once the Customize dialog box is open, you can use your finger to drag the existing Touch Bar buttons into a new order.

Tip: Truth is, you can use your mouse, too. No cursor appears on the Touch Bar, which is a little weird. But as you move your mouse, the existing buttons light up to show where the cursor *would* be. Once a button is lit up, you can drag it horizontally to move it.

- **Delete a button.** Once the Customize dialog box is open, use your finger to drag the unwanted button all the way to the left; release it on top of the Trash icon that appears there.

Tip: Here again, you can use your mouse to drag a button to the Touch Bar Trash, too. The buttons light up to show the invisible cursor's position.

In each case, hit Done (either at the far left of the Touch Bar, or on your main screen) to wrap it up.

QuickType on the Touch Bar

On a phone, what Apple calls its QuickType keyboard can save you a lot of time, tapping, and errors. As you type a sentence, the software predicts which word you might type next—the three most likely words—and displays them as three buttons above the keyboard. (See Figure 6-5.)

Figure 6-5:
QuickType is autocomplete on steroids. Frankly, it's a rush when it finishes a long word for you.

If you begin the sentence by typing, "I really," then the three suggestions might be *want, don't,* and *like.* But what if you intended to say, "I really hope…"? In that case, type the first letter of "hope." Instantly, the three suggestions change to "*h,*" *hope,* and *hate.* (The first button always shows, in quotes, whatever non-word you've typed so

far, just in case that's what you really intend. To place it into your text, you can tap that button or tap the space bar or some punctuation.)

When someone texts you a question that ends with a choice ("Coffee, tea, or me?"), the QuickType buttons cleverly offer those same choices. Before you've even typed a single letter, the choices say "coffee," "tea," and "you."

QuickType automatically adds a space after each word you select, so you don't have to mess with the space bar. And, sometimes, QuickType offers you several words on a single button, to save you even more time (for example, "up to" or "in the").

Thanks to the Touch Bar, the QuickType suggestions are now on your Mac, too. They're available in any Touch Bar–enabled program where you can type, like Mail, Notes, and TextEdit. (If you don't see the suggestions, they may currently be collapsed. Tap the ⟨▦ button to bring them up.)

Of course, on the Mac, you have a real keyboard; you're not trying to hit keys the size of Tic Tacs on a glass screen. And QuickType means you have to split your focus; you have to pay attention to both the words you're tapping and the text on the main screen.

You could argue, therefore, that QuickType is less important on the Mac than on the iPhone. It might be useful if you're unsure of a word's spelling, or if you're a very slow typist—but if you can type fairly quickly, it's usually faster to just use the keyboard.

In that case, you may want to turn off the QuickType feature entirely, or maybe only for one program.

The key is the "Show typing suggestions" checkbox on the Customize Touch Bar screen (Figure 6-4). If you turn it off (for the program whose Touch Bar you're editing), then the QuickType suggestions no longer appear. There's that much more space for your app-specific function buttons.

Notes on Right-Clicking

In macOS, *shortcut menus* are more important than ever (Figure 6-6).

Figure 6-6:
A shortcut menu pops out of something you're clicking—an icon, a button, a folder. The beauty of it is that its commands are contextual. They bring up commands in exactly the spots where they're most useful.

They're so important, in fact, that it's worth this ink and this paper to explain the different ways you can trigger a "right-click" (or a *secondary click,* as Apple calls it, because not all these methods actually involve a mouse button, and it doesn't *have* to be the right one):

- **Control-click.** For years, you could open the shortcut menu of something on the Mac screen by Control-clicking it—and you still can. That is, while pressing the Control key (bottom row), click the mouse on your target.

- **Right-click.** Experienced computer fans have always preferred the one-handed method: right-clicking. That is, clicking something by pressing the *right* mouse button on a two-button mouse.

Every desktop Mac since late 2005 has come with a two-button mouse—but you might not realize it. Take a look: Is it a white, shiny, plastic capsule with a tiny, gray scrolling track-pea on the far end? Then you have an Apple Mouse. Is it a cordless, flattened capsule instead? Then it's a Magic Mouse. Each has a *secret* right mouse button. It doesn't work until you ask for it.

To do that, choose System Preferences. Click Mouse. There, in all its splendor, is a diagram of the Apple or Magic Mouse.

Your job is to choose Secondary Button from the pop-up menu that identifies the right side of the mouse. (The reason it's not called a "right button" is because left-handers might prefer to reverse the right and left functions.)

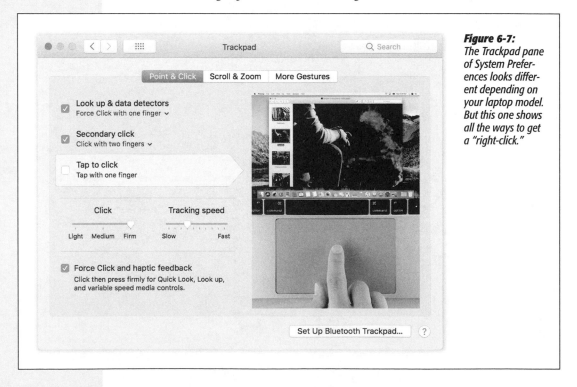

Figure 6-7:
The Trackpad pane of System Preferences looks different depending on your laptop model. But this one shows all the ways to get a "right-click."

From now on, even though there aren't two visible mouse buttons, your Apple Mouse does, in fact, register a left-click or a right-click depending on which side of the mouse you push down. It works a lot more easily than it sounds like it would.

Tip: You can also attach any old $6 USB two-button mouse to the Mac, and it'll work flawlessly. Recycle the one from your old PC, if you like.

- **Use the trackpad.** If you have a trackpad (on a laptop, for example), you can trigger a right-click in all kinds of ways.

 Out of the box, you do it by *clicking the trackpad with two fingers.* The shortcut menu pops right up.

 Or you can point to whatever you want to click. Rest two fingers on the trackpad—and then click with your thumb.

 But even those aren't the end of your options. In System Preferences→Trackpad, you can also turn on even more right-click methods (and watch little videos on how to do them; see Figure 6-7). For example, you can "right-click" by clicking either the lower-right or lower-left corner of the trackpad—one finger only.

When shortcut menus are mentioned throughout this book, rather than repeat this explanation for "101 ways to right-click" over and over, you'll find only the two best methods: right-click (if you have a mouse) or two-finger click (if you have a trackpad).

Power Typing

Something strange has been quietly taking place at Apple: *Typing* has been getting a lot of attention.

It began when Apple created *system-wide* spelling and grammar checkers. For the first time in computer history, the *operating system* took over typos and grammos. You didn't have to maintain a separate spelling checker for each program you used. Now there's just one, and it works in most programs: TextEdit, Stickies, Messages, Mail, Calendar, Safari, Pages, Photos, iMovie, and so on. Add a word to the dictionary in one program, and it's available to all the others.

Today, there's much more. There's text substitution, where you type *addr* and the system types out "Irwina P. McGillicuddy, 1293 Eastport Lane, Harborvilletown, MA 02552." (The same system autocorrects common typos like *teh* instead of *the.*) There's also a case-flipping feature that can change selected text to ALL CAPS, all lowercase, or First Letter Capped. Both of these features are available in most Apple programs and in any other programs that tap into macOS's built-in text-processing circuitry (although not, alas, Microsoft programs).

The Spelling and Grammar Checker

Your Mac can give you live, interactive spelling and grammar checking, just as in Microsoft Word and other word processors. That is, misspelled words or badly

written sentences or fragments get flagged with a dashed red underline (for grammar problems, a green underline) the moment you type them. Here's the crash course:

- **Check the spelling of one word:** Highlight the word. Choose Edit→Spelling and Grammar→Show Spelling and Grammar. The spell-check dialog box opens, with the proposed corrections visible.

- **Check spelling as you type.** Choose Edit→Spelling and Grammar→Check Spelling While Typing. (If Check Grammar With Spelling is turned on in the same submenu, you'll get a grammar check, too.)

Now, as you type, you'll see those red and green underlines on words the Mac thinks represent spelling or grammar mistakes. To fix one, right-click or two-finger click the underlined word, and proceed as shown in Figure 6-8.

Tip: In TextEdit, the factory setting for error-underlining is On. To turn it off for all new documents, choose TextEdit→Preferences, click New Document, and then turn off "Check spelling as you type."

Figure 6-8:
Top: You're never more than a right-click or two-finger click away from more accurate spelling. Once you right-click a questionable word, the suggestions of Apple's built-in dictionary appear right in the shortcut menu, along with the Ignore Spelling and Learn Spelling commands.

Bottom: If you've opted for autocorrected spelling, you get the little iPhoney suggestion bubble when you pause after typing a word. Ignore it to accept the suggestion; click the ✕ in the bubble to keep what you typed.

- **Check spelling after the document is finished.** Choose Edit→Spelling and Grammar→Show Spelling and Grammar (or press ⌘-:). The Spelling dialog box appears. The first error it spots appears in the top box, with the proposed corrections in the bottom one.

If you like one of Apple's proposals, then click it and click Change. If the word was correct already (for example, the guy's last name really is Teh), then click Find Next

("Leave the word as I typed it"), Ignore ("It's OK everywhere in this document"), or Learn ("Never flag this word again").

Handily enough, you can also click Define to look up a highlighted word (one of the spelling suggestions, for example) in the Mac's built-in Dictionary app. Also handily enough, the spelling checker maintains dictionaries for 15 languages. It's often smart enough to recognize, within a single document, which language you're using—but specifying the language in System Preferences→Keyboard→Text→Spelling is generally more reliable.

- **Fix spelling as you type.** Note the difference. *Checking* your spelling just means "finding the misspelled words." *Fixing* means autocorrecting the errors as they occur, as you type. You might not even notice that it's happening!

This most tantalizing option is found in Edit→Spelling and Grammar→Correct Spelling Automatically. And sure enough, when this option is turned on, common typos like *teh* and *frmo* and *dont* get fixed as you type.

Note: If you're typing slowly enough, you might see the suggestion bubble illustrated in Figure 6-8, bottom. That, of course, is a feature Apple brought to the Mac from the iPhone/iPad. It's saying, "Here's the word I *think* you meant—and if you just keep on typing, I'll go ahead and make the change I'm proposing. If you disagree, click on the ✕ in the word bubble to make me shut up and leave what you typed, just as you typed it."

It's not perfect. It doesn't correct all errors (or even most of them). It occasionally even corrects a word you didn't mean to have corrected. (When it makes a mistake,

GEM IN THE ROUGH

The Least-Known Typing Feature

This may come as a shock if you think you know your Mac pretty well, but here goes: MacOS actually offers system-wide autocomplete of big words, just like the iPhone.

We're not talking about the spelling checker, and we're not talking about text substitution. (And we're also not talking about the Touch Bar on newer MacBooks, which performs a similar trick with its QuickType feature.) We're talking, you start typing a word and the Mac finishes it for you. It's ideal when you're in a hurry, when you're not sure how to finish a word (is it "independance" or "independence"?), or

when you're trying to solve a crossword puzzle. It works in all the standard Mac programs (TextEdit, Mail, Safari, Pages, and so on).

Dear Harold,

It has come to our attention

> attention
> attentive
> attentions
> attentively
> attentiveness
> attention's
> attentional

Once you've begun typing a word, press either fn-F5 or Option-Esc to produce the list of possible word completions shown here. If the Mac correctly anticipates the rest of the word, great; press Tab, Return, or the space bar to accept the suggestion, and then keep right on typing. If it guesses wrong, you can either select a different word in the list (using the mouse or the arrow keys), or tap Esc to ignore the suggestions and continue typing.

hit ⌘-Z, the Undo command, to restore what you typed.) And sometimes it doesn't make the change until you're halfway through the sentence.

Still, though. Kind of cool.

Text Substitution (Abbreviation Expansion)

This useful feature autoreplaces *one* thing you type with something else. Why? Because it can do any of these things.

Insert the proper typographical symbols

For example, the Mac can insert attractive "curly quotes" automatically as you type "straight ones," or em dashes—like this—when you type two hyphens (-- like that).

You can see the built-in sample substitution ("omw" for "On my way!")—and create your own—in the System Preferences→Keyboard→Text tab, as shown in Figure 6-9.

Apple doesn't want to drive you nuts, though, so it makes sure *you're* sure you really want these swappings to take place. So you have to turn on each of these features manually, in each program. (These commands are available anywhere you do a *lot* of typing, like TextEdit, Mail, and Stickies. Look for the Edit→Substitutions submenu.)

- **Auto-quotes.** To make the quotes curlify themselves, choose Edit→Substitutions→ Smart Quotes, so that a checkmark appears.

Note: In the System Preferences→Keyboard→Text tab, you can specify which kind of fancy quotation mark you prefer: «this kind,» „this kind," or whatever. You international thing, you!

- **Auto-dashes.** To turn double hyphens into these (—) long dashes, choose Edit→ Substitutions→Smart Dashes, so that a checkmark appears.

- **Smart links.** There's also an option to create smart links, where any web address you type turns into a blue, underlined, *clickable* link to a web page. Turn on Edit→Substitutions→Smart Links.

Tip: You can also choose Edit→Substitutions→Show Substitutions to make a floating panel appear, complete with on/off checkboxes for all these features.

FREQUENTLY ASKED QUESTION

Smart Copy and Paste

Hey, I saw one more autofix feature in the Edit→Substitutions submenu: "Smart Copy/Paste." What's that about?

It's about spaces.

Ordinarily, when you cut or copy a word out of a sentence and then paste it into a new one, you have some cleanup to do. You leave an extra space behind, and you have to add a space after the word when you paste.

Smart Copy/Paste cleans up these spaces for you. If you cut a word out of a sentence, only *one* space gets left between the words where it used to be. And when you paste text, a space is added on either side automatically—but only one.

Replace abbreviations with much longer phrases

You can program *addr* to type your entire return address. Create two-letter abbreviations for big legal or technical words you have to type a lot. Set up *goaway* to type out a polite rejection letter for use in email. And so on.

This feature has been in Microsoft Office forever (called AutoCorrect), and it's always been available as a shareware add-on (TypeIt4Me and TextExpander, for example). But now it's built right into most Apple programs, plus any others that use Apple's text-input plumbing.

You build your list of abbreviations in the System Preferences→Keyboard→Text tab, shown in Figure 6-9. See the list at left? Click the + to create a new row in the scrolling table of substitutions.

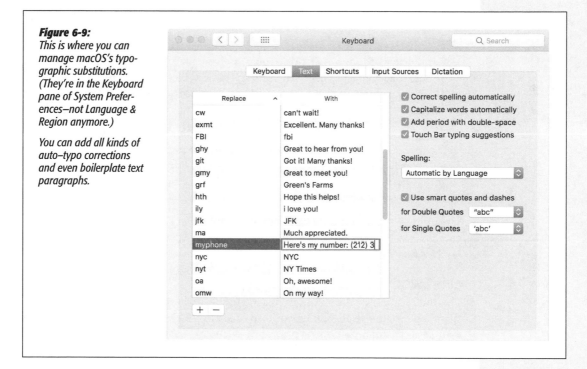

Figure 6-9:
This is where you can manage macOS's typographic substitutions. (They're in the Keyboard pane of System Preferences—not Language & Region anymore.)

You can add all kinds of auto–typo corrections and even boilerplate text paragraphs.

Click in the left column and type the abbreviation you want (for example, *addr*). Click in the right column and type, or paste, the text you want macOS to type instead.

Tip: You're not limited to short snippets. The replacement text can be pages long, which is handy if you're a lawyer and you build your contracts out of boilerplate chunks of canned text.

You can even create multiple paragraphs—but not by hitting Return when you want a new line; Return means "I'm finished entering text" and closes the box. Instead, press Option-Return when you want a paragraph break.

That's it! Now, whenever you type one of the abbreviations you've set up, the Mac instantly replaces it with your substituted text.

And not just the Mac, either; your abbreviations autosync to iPhones, iPads, iPod Touches, and other Macs. If, that is, you've turned on System Preferences→iCloud→ iCloud Drive. (Remember, you can *turn off* the text-replacement feature in individual programs, if you like—TextEdit, Mail, Stickies, and so on. To do that, choose Edit→Substitutions→Text Replacement, so the checkmark disappears.)

Auto-Periods, Auto-Caps

On the iPhone, the software comes to your rescue every time you reach the end of a sentence. All you have to do is tap the space bar twice. The phone automatically gives you a period and a space and capitalizes the first letter of the next sentence.

Believe it or not, those features have now made their way into macOS. In System Preferences→Keyboard→Text, you can now turn on these options:

- **Capitalize words automatically.** You can give your Shift keys a break. From now on, the Mac can capitalize proper nouns (*Ohio, Texas, Pepsi, Bible, Empire State, American Express*) and the first words of sentences *for* you. Just type away, and marvel as those lowercase letters become capitals an instant after you've typed them.

- **Add period with double-space.** Truth is, there's not much point to this feature on the Mac. On an iPhone, it's a godsend because it saves you from having to swap onscreen keyboard layouts every time you want a period. On the Mac, the period key is always there! Still, for the sake of consistency, here it is: the "type two spaces to get a period" option.

Screamingly important note: Sadly, these features don't work in all programs. They have an effect in Apple's apps (Mail, TextEdit, Pages, Notes, and so on), but not in Microsoft or Adobe apps.

Case Swapping

The final feature in macOS's text-massaging tool chest is case swapping—that is, changing text you've already typed (or pasted) from ALL CAPS to lowercase or Just First Letters Capitalized.

This one's simple: Select the text you want to change, and then choose from the Edit→ Transformations submenu. Your options are Make Upper Case (all caps), Make Lower Case (no caps), and Capitalize (first letters, like a movie title).

Keep that in mind the next time some raving lunatic SENDS YOU AN EMAIL THAT WAS TYPED ENTIRELY WITH THE CAPS LOCK KEY DOWN.

Tip: Here's a sneaky one: You can tap a word with three fingers on your trackpad to get a pop-up dictionary and thesaurus definition. (That's a light three-finger *tap,* not a full *click*.) This trick doesn't work in all programs, and it requires you to turn it on in System Preferences→Trackpad→Point & Click. And it's a tad bit finicky.

But once you have it working, check it out: It also works in text documents you're examining in Quick Look!

The Many Languages of macOS Text

Apple has always taken pride in its language-friendliness. You can shift from language to language on the fly, as you type, even in midsentence—without reinstalling the operating system or even restarting the computer.

MacOS's facility with language, though, goes the extra overseas mile. It lets you type vertical Japanese and Chinese text; includes fonts for 23 more non-Roman alphabets (including the ones you need for 10 Indian languages); offers "filtering by tones, ordering and filtering by radical or stroke count, and improved pinyin-han conversion accuracy" (you have to be a Chinese speaker to appreciate those tweaks); and much more.

First, tell your Mac which languages you'd like to have available. Open System Preferences→Language & Region. You see a listing of the languages the Mac can

Figure 6-10:
Top: You can flip your copy of macOS into any of dozens of languages. Click + to see them all— and add them to the list of Preferred Languages. You can also specify the default temperature unit.

Bottom: Here's what your Mac looks like running in Dutch. Actually understanding Dutch would be useful at a time like this—but even if you don't, it can't help but brighten up your workday to choose commands like Spraakfunctie or Knip.

switch into, in the corresponding languages—Français, Español, and so on. (If you don't see the one you want, click the + and choose it from the list.) Just drag one of the languages to the top of the list to select it as your primary language, as shown in Figure 6-10.

Note: You can mix English with right-to-left languages like Hebrew and Arabic. There's even a split-cursor option that makes the pointer flip directions at the boundary between right-to-left and left-to-right text.

Now launch Safari, TextEdit, Mail, or Stickies. Every menu, button, and dialog box is now in the new language you selected! If you log out and back in (or restart) at this point, the entire Finder will be in the new language, too.

Formats

Of course, if you're *really* French (for example), you'll also want to make some formatting changes on the System Preferences→Language & Region panel. First, choose your French-speaking country from the Region pop-up menu, so that time and date formats, number punctuation, and currency symbols also conform to your local customs.

For example, the decimal and thousands separator characters for displaying large numbers differ from country to country. (The number 25,600.99, for example, would be written as "25 600,99" in France, and as "25.600,99" in Spain.) And what appears to an American to be July 4 (the notation "7/4"), to a European indicates April 7.

Similarly, for Calendar purposes, you'll want to specify what you consider to be the first day of the week and which calendar style you observe. (Hint: If you're reading this book, it's probably Gregorian.)

Choose the French *keyboard layout* from the Input Sources tab, as explained next.

Note: MacOS and most Apple apps are localized for only 39 languages, but Calendar app can display the names of months and days in a huge number.

Input Sources

While the Mac can display many different languages, *typing* in those languages is another matter. The symbols you use when you're typing in Swedish aren't the same as when you're typing in English. Apple solved this problem by creating different keyboard layouts for different languages. (Apple calls them *input sources*, because not all of them technically use a keyboard.) Each rearranges the letters that appear when you press the keys. For example, when you use the Swedish layout and press the semicolon key, you don't get a semicolon (;)—you get an ö.

Apple even includes the famous Dvorak layout and the not-very-famous Colemak layout. Both are scientific rearrangements of the standard layout that put the most common letters directly under your fingertips on the home row. Fans of the Dvorak layout, and the more modern Colemak layout, claim greater accuracy, better speed, and less fatigue. To set up an input source, see Figure 6-11.

Note: The icon of the Input menulet changes. It becomes a colorful flag, or some other symbol, to show the currently selected language.

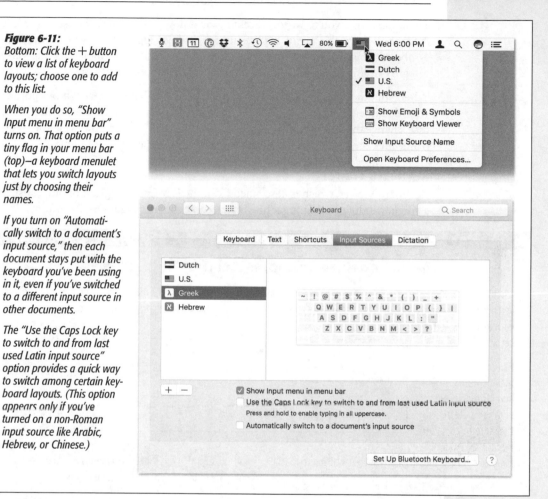

Figure 6-11:
Bottom: Click the + button to view a list of keyboard layouts; choose one to add to this list.

When you do so, "Show Input menu in menu bar" turns on. That option puts a tiny flag in your menu bar (top)—a keyboard menulet that lets you switch layouts just by choosing their names.

If you turn on "Automatically switch to a document's input source," then each document stays put with the keyboard you've been using in it, even if you've switched to a different input source in other documents.

The "Use the Caps Lock key to switch to and from last used Latin input source" option provides a quick way to switch among certain keyboard layouts. (This option appears only if you've turned on a non-Roman input source like Arabic, Hebrew, or Chinese.)

The Character Viewer

There you are, two-thirds of the way through your local matchmaker newsletter, when it hits you that you need a heart symbol. Right now.

You can't help but wish there were an easy way to find those special symbols that hide among your fonts—fancy brackets, math symbols, special stars and asterisks, and so on.

The Keyboard Viewer, described next, can generate a few of them. But to see the full range of symbols available, you need the Characters panel (also called "Emoji & Symbols"). To make it appear, choose Edit→Emoji & Symbols.

Most programs have this command. If yours doesn't, here's the long way: Open System Preferences→Keyboard→Input Sources tab, and then turn on "Show Input menu in menu bar." You've just installed the Keyboard menulet.

Then, next time you're word processing or doing page layout, choose Show Emoji & Symbols from this menu. The resulting window (Figure 6-12, top) rounds up all symbols from all your fonts at once. To find a particular symbol, click the various category headings: Arrows, Bullets/Stars, Math Symbols, and so on.

When you find the symbol you want, double-click it. The correct symbol pops into your document. (If not, you may get the correct character in the wrong font. In that case, change the font of the inserted character manually. To find out what font it came from, click the symbol in the Font Variation panel to see the font name.)

Keyboard Viewer

Keyboard Viewer, which is descended from the Key Caps program of old, consists of a single window containing a tiny onscreen keyboard (Figure 6-12, bottom). When

GEM IN THE ROUGH

Instant Accented Characters, Courtesy of the iPhone

It's been a problem since the dawn of computing: How do you produce accented characters—líké thësë—on a keyboard with only 26 letter keys?

For most of history, the answer has been: You bring up some special palette on the screen, or you memorize key combinations. And, yes, those options are still available in macOS.

But today there's a new option, which Apple stole from its own iPhone software: Hold down the letter you want accented—e, for example. After a moment, you get a pop-up panel of possible accented versions. You can click the one you want, or, if you'd rather not lift your hands off the keyboard, you can type the corresponding number that appears in light gray beneath each letter.

This feature works in almost all programs, although there may be some where it doesn't…pop up.

Now, if you're the kind of person who needs accents from time to time, you're probably delighted with this new, clever way to get them. But if holding down a key produces an accented character, that means holding down a key no longer *repeats* the key, right? It means you can no longer type, "You go, grrrrrrrrrrrl!" or "rated XXXXXXXX" or "I just love you SOOOOOOOOOOOO much!" Right?

Right. A few characters that people routinely type lines of, like ***** and …….and ____, still repeat when you hold them down. But none of the 26 letter keys repeat anymore.

There is, fortunately, a quick and easy way to restore the old key-repeating behavior, if you're a "SOOOOOOOOOOOO much" kind of person.

Open up Terminal (page 479). Type this one line, exactly as it appears here:

```
defaults write -g AplePressAnd-
HoldEnabled -bool false
```

…and then press Return. Log out and back in.

You've just flipped off the switch for the accent picker. Now every key repeats, just as it always used to.

you hold down any of the modifier keys on your keyboard (like ⌘, Option, Shift, or Control), you can see exactly which keys produce which characters. The point, of course, is to help you learn which keys to press when you need special symbols or non-English characters, such as © or ñ, in each keyboard layout.

Note: Keyboard Viewer shows only the symbols you can produce by typing keystrokes. A font may contain thousands of other characters that can't actually be typed; the Character Viewer, accessed by clicking Show Emoji & Symbols, is the only way to see these other symbols.

Figure 6-12:
Top: You can preview variations of the same symbol in the Font Variation panel. Use the search box to find a symbol by name: "heart," "yen" or "asterisk," for example. And if you click the ✿ menu in the top left, you can choose Customize List—and you'll have access to a staggering array of even more symbol categories, including wacky symbols from other alphabets.

Bottom: How do you make a π? Keyboard Viewer reveals the answer. When you press the Option key, the Keyboard Viewer shows that the pi character is mapped to the P key. To insert one into an open document, just click it in the Keyboard Viewer window.

Keyboard Viewer is a great tool—if you can find it. The secret is to open System Preferences→Keyboard→Keyboard tab. Then turn on "Show keyboard and emoji viewers in menu bar." You open the Keyboard Viewer by choosing its name from the new menulet that appears.

To see the effect of pressing the modifier keys, either click the onscreen keys or press them on your actual keyboard. The corresponding keys on the onscreen keyboard light up as they're pressed.

Tip: You're not stuck viewing the characters in a 12-point font size—a good thing, because some of them are hard to read when displayed that small. You can make the Keyboard Viewer window bigger by dragging its lower-right corner. That will magnify the Keyboard Viewer window and its font size.

Ink: Handwriting Recognition

In the same way that your grandmother turned yesterday's dinner into today's sandwich (and tomorrow's soup), Apple recycled the handwriting technology of its failed Newton handheld and added it to macOS. It's now called Ink, and it does exactly what it used to: turn your handwriting into "typed" text in any program. Can Ink replace

GEM IN THE ROUGH

Draw Those Chinese Characters

Apple has made a huge push to appeal to Chinese Mac fans. There's a Chinese dictionary and text input; over a dozen Chinese fonts; compatibility with popular Chinese mail services like QQ, 163, and 126; built-in Safari searching using Baidu (a Chinese Google); and Share button posting directly to Youku Tudou (like YouTube) and Sina Weibo (a microblogging service).

If you want to write in Chinese, you can draw the characters you want, right on your laptop's trackpad. To set this up, open the System Preferences→ Keyboard→Input Sources pane. Click +, and then turn on Chinese–Simplified (or Chinese–Traditional), choose the Chinese writing system you prefer, and then turn on Trackpad Handwriting.

Then, when you're actually writing, use the flag (Input) menulet to choose Show Trackpad Handwriting (or press Shift-Control-space bar) to make the writing panel appear, as shown here. This panel is a full map of your trackpad. Draw your character by dragging on the trackpad; lines appear as you go.

Now, atop the onscreen panel, you see the Mac's interpretations of your character; to choose one, tap the corresponding spot on the edge of your actual trackpad. (Or, to delete your most recent line, tap the upper-left corner of your trackpad.) The Mac drops the character into your document. Press Shift-Control-space bar again to hide the panel, or press Esc to exit it momentarily, and shake your head in wonder.

the keyboard? Not for anything more than quick notes, that's for sure. But it can be handy when you're web surfing, sketching, filling in database forms, and so on.

Ink appears in macOS only if you have a graphics tablet, one of those stylus-and-pad devices found generally only on the desks of graphic artists. (Wacom is the best-known tablet company, but there are a couple of others.) You could count on one hand the number of people with Wacom tablets who use them for handwriting input. And so, to avoid sacrificing any more old-growth trees than absolutely necessary, the how-to for Ink is available as a free downloadable PDF appendix to this chapter. You'll find it on this book's "Missing CD" page at *missingmanuals.com.*

Data Detectors

Here's a cool step-saver that no other computer operating system offers—a little something Apple likes to call *data detectors.*

In short, Mac programs like Mail and TextEdit can recognize commonly used bits of information that may appear in your text: a physical address, a phone number, a date and time, and so on. With one quick click, you can send that information into the appropriate program, like Calendar, Contacts, or your web browser.

Here's how it works: When you spot a name, address, date, or time, point to it without clicking. A dotted rectangle appears around it (Figure 6-13). Right-click or two-finger click inside the rectangle, or click the ▾ at the right side.

Figure 6-13:
When a data detector detects a date and time, it can suggest an appointment on your calendar automatically. It even shows you the proposed new Calendar entry (in dotted lines), in context with all your existing appointments, so you'll know whether to accept or decline the new appointment.

If everything looks good, click Add to Calendar. Or, if Mail's parsing of the appointment needs a little tweaking, click Details; the box expands so you can edit the details.

A shortcut menu appears. Its contents vary depending on what you're pointing to:

- **A date and time.** When you click the ▾, you get the amazing pop-up menu shown in Figure 6-13. It shows you the actual Calendar day view where macOS is proposing adding the appointment. The logic of this feature is overwhelming; after all, when someone emails you to ask if you're free for drinks next Thursday at 10, what's the first thing you usually want to do? Check your calendar, of course.

Tip: If, while working in Calendar, you ever forget where this event came from, double-click it. In the Info panel, you'll see a link that takes you back to the original Mail message that started it all.

- **A mailing address.** You can choose Open in Maps from the shortcut menu; the app opens automatically and shows you that address.

 Alternatively, you can choose Add to Contacts. Like magic, a little editing box sprouts out of the data-detected rectangle, prefilled with the information from the message, so you can create a new Contacts entry or add it to an existing entry.

- **A phone number.** The shortcut menu here offers you things like Add to Contacts, FaceTime, and Message. The Large Type option is great when you want to call this person right now—it displays the phone number in huge type, filling your screen, so you can see it from across your mansion.

- **A flight number.** When you highlight flight information (for example, "AA 152"), the shortcut menu shows you the flight's departure time, arrival time, and other details. It works only if the airline is represented as a two-letter code.

- **A web address.** When you click the ▾ next to a URL, you get a pop-up balloon that contains the *actual web page!* You don't even have to leave your email message.

- **A package tracking number.** When you send a package using a service like FedEx, UPS, or the U.S. Postal Service, you usually get a confirmation email. A data detector can recognize such numbers and, when you click the ▾, show you a pop-up window right there at your cursor, showing the courier company's tracking page for that package, and thereby letting you know exactly where your package is right now.

Tip: In the unlikely event that you don't actually care for data detectors and would rather not see those dotted lines and ▾ buttons, you can shut down the whole feature. To do that, open Terminal (page 479). Carefully type this command, and then press Return:

```
defaults write com.apple.mail DisableDataDetectors YES
```

You can always turn them back on again by repeating that step—and substituting *NO* for the final word.

Moving Data Between Documents

You can't paste a picture into your web browser, and you can't paste MIDI music information into your word processor. But you can put graphics into TextEdit, paste movies into your database, insert text into Photoshop, and combine a surprising variety of seemingly dissimilar kinds of data.

Cut, Copy, and Paste

The original copy-and-paste procedure of 1984—putting a graphic into a word processor—has come a long way. Most experienced Mac fans have learned to trigger the Cut, Copy, and Paste commands from the keyboard, quickly and without even thinking. Here's how the process works:

1. **Highlight some material in a document.**

 Drag through some text in a word processor, for example, or highlight graphic, music, movie, database, or spreadsheet information, depending on the program you're using.

2. **Use the Edit→Cut or Edit→Copy command.**

 Or press the keyboard shortcuts ⌘-X (for Cut—think of the X as a pair of scissors) or ⌘-C (for Copy). The Macintosh memorizes the highlighted material, socking it away on an invisible storage pad called the Clipboard. If you chose Copy, nothing visible happens. If you chose Cut, the highlighted material disappears from the original document.

 At this point, most Mac fans take it on faith that the Cut or Copy command actually worked. But if you're in doubt, switch to the Finder (by clicking its Dock icon, for example), and then choose Edit→Show Clipboard. The Clipboard window appears, showing whatever you've copied.

3. **Click to indicate where you want the material to reappear.**

 This may entail switching to a different program, a different document, or simply a different place in the same document.

4. **Choose the Edit→Paste command (⌘-V).**

 The copy of the material you had originally highlighted now appears at your insertion point—*if* you're pasting into a program that can accept that kind of information. (You won't have much luck pasting, say, a block of spreadsheet numbers into World of Warcraft.)

GEM IN THE ROUGH

Styled Text

When you copy text from, for example, Microsoft Word, and then paste it into another program, such as Mail, you may be pleasantly surprised to note that the formatting of that text—bold, italic, font (size, color, and so on)—appears intact in Mail. You're witnessing one of the Mac's most useful but underpublicized features: its handling of styled text on the Clipboard.

Almost all Mac programs transfer the formatting along with the copied text. Every time you paste formatted text copied from one of these programs, the pasted material appears with the same typographical characteristics it had in the original program. Over time, this tiny time-saver spares us years' worth of cumulative reformatting effort—yet another favor the noble Macintosh does humanity.

The most recently cut or copied material remains on your Clipboard even after you paste, making it possible to paste the same blob repeatedly. Such a trick can be useful when, for example, you've designed a business card in your drawing program and want to duplicate it enough times to fill a letter-sized printout. On the other hand, whenever you next copy or cut something, whatever was already on the Clipboard is lost forever.

Drag-and-Drop

As useful and popular as it is, the Copy/Paste routine doesn't win any awards for speed. After all, it requires four steps. In many cases, you can replace that routine with the far more direct (and enjoyable) drag-and-drop method. Figure 6-14 illustrates how this works.

Note: Most modern Mac programs require you to press the mouse button for a split second before beginning to drag.

Virtually every Apple program works with the drag-and-drop technique, including TextEdit, Stickies, Mail, QuickTime Player, Preview, iMovie, Photos, and System Information, not to mention other popular programs like Microsoft applications, web browsers, and so on.

When to use drag-and-drop

As shown in Figure 6-14, drag-and-drop is ideal for transferring material between windows or between programs—from a web page into Photoshop, for example. It's especially useful when you've already copied something valuable to your Clipboard, since drag-and-drop doesn't involve (and doesn't erase) the Clipboard.

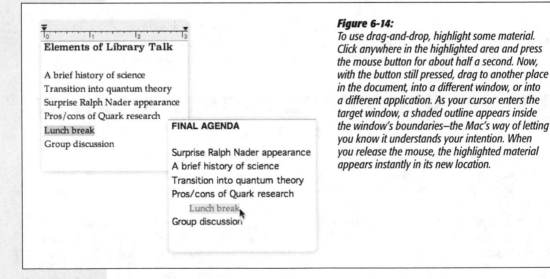

Figure 6-14:
To use drag-and-drop, highlight some material. Click anywhere in the highlighted area and press the mouse button for about half a second. Now, with the button still pressed, drag to another place in the document, into a different window, or into a different application. As your cursor enters the target window, a shaded outline appears inside the window's boundaries–the Mac's way of letting you know it understands your intention. When you release the mouse, the highlighted material appears instantly in its new location.

Its most popular use, however, is rearranging text within a single document. In Word or Pages, for example, you can rearrange entire sections, paragraphs, sentences, or even individual letters, just by dragging them—a wonderfully efficient editing technique.

Tip: When you use drag-and-drop to move text within a document, the Mac moves the highlighted text, deleting the highlighted material from its original location. If you press Option as you drag, however, you make a copy of the highlighted text.

Drag-and-drop to the desktop

You can also use drag-and-drop in the Finder itself. As shown in Figure 6-15, you can drag text, graphics, sounds, and even movie clips out of your document windows and directly onto the desktop. Graphics and movies generally turn into ordinary graphic or movie files; text becomes an icon called a *clipping file*.

Figure 6-15:
When you drag material out of the document window and onto the desktop or into a folder, you get a clipping file. Its icon depends on the kind of material contained within, like a text clipping, picture clipping, or movie clipping. (For easy identification, macOS conveniently titles text clippings by the first line of the text contained inside.) You can view a clipping by double-clicking it; it opens into its own window (left).

Later, you can examine a clipping's contents using Quick Look—just select its icon and then tap the space bar. Or you can double-click a clipping file and then select a portion of the text to copy.

When you drag a clipping from your desktop *back* into an application window, the material in that clipping reappears. Drag-and-drop, in other words, lets you treat your desktop itself as a giant, computer-wide pasteboard—an area where you can temporarily stash pieces of text or graphics as you work.

Tip: When the material you drag to the desktop contains nothing but an internet address, such as an email address or a web page URL, it gets a special icon and a special function: an internet location file. You can stash it in a folder, double-click it for quick access, and so on.

Export/Import

When it comes to transferring large chunks of information—especially address books, spreadsheet cells, and database records—from one program to another, none of the data-transfer methods described so far in this chapter does the trick. For these purposes, use the Export and Import commands found in the File menu of almost every database, spreadsheet, email, and address-book program. (In some programs, the Save As command serves this function.)

These Export/Import commands aren't part of macOS, so the manuals (if any) of the applications in question should be your source for instructions. For now, however, the power and convenience of this feature are worth noting—it means that your four years' worth of collected addresses in, say, some old email program can find their way into a newer program, like Contacts, in a matter of minutes.

Exchanging Data with Other Macs

Considering how many ways there are to move files back and forth between Macs, it seems almost comical that people complained when Apple discontinued built-in floppy disk drives. Here's a catalog of the different ways you can move your files from one computer to another, including some that might not have occurred to you.

By AirDrop or Network

You can shoot a file to another Mac with a single drag-and-drop operation, thanks to AirDrop or another file-sharing method. You can open files from the other drives, copy stuff back and forth—anything you would do with your own disk. (Step-by-step instructions for AirDrop start on page 528.)

Best for files of any size, when the computers are in the same building.

Tip: And for $0 you can create an *ad hoc* network, meaning a tiny wireless network between just two computers (or a handful). Great when you're in the car somewhere, or in the airport waiting lounge, or a hotel lobby, and someone says, "Hey, can I have a copy of that?" Details are on page 525.

By Email

High on convenience; computers can be in different countries. Of course, the traditional problem with email was that it couldn't handle file attachments larger than 5 or 10 megabytes. To get around that limitation, you had to use a free website like *sendthisfile.com*, which can handle enormous files by sending the recipient only a link to them by email.

The world has changed, though. Nowadays, the Mail program can cheerfully send huge file attachments to anyone, no matter what kind of computer she uses. See page 681 for details.

Using Dropbox

Dropbox is a free service, almost universally adored, that lets you create synchronized folders on multiple computers. Add a file to, say, your New Projects folder on your home Mac, and it appears instantly in the matching folder on your Windows folder at work.

You can use Dropbox to share files with other people, too. Just drag a file into a shared folder, and marvel as your associates get an auto-generated email message letting them know. They open the shared folder on their *own* desktops, and there is the file, waiting. (Details are at *dropbox.com/help/19*.)

The great thing about services like Dropbox is that you don't have to worry about the small file-size limits email imposes. (There's a 2-gigabyte storage limit on Dropbox's free accounts, but you can upgrade to larger storage capacities for a fee; you also get more storage granted when you refer a friend to Dropbox.)

Via iCloud Drive

In many ways, iCloud Drive (page 210) is identical to Dropbox. It, too, acts as a magic folder that reproduces itself on as many Macs as you own.

It's a fantastic way to transfer big files among your own computers. And now, thanks to iCloud file sharing, you can even make your big files available to other macOS fans with just a couple of clicks (see page 212).

Via Flash Drive

A flash drive, also called a thumb drive, is one of those keychain-like doodads that plug into your USB jack. Inside is a big chunk of memory that acts like a miniature hard drive. When the flash drive is plugged into your Mac, its icon shows up on the desktop as a disk. Use it as a tiny, 8-gigabyte hard drive (or whatever size you've bought).

The beauty of a flash drive is that it works instantly with any Mac *or* any Windows machine, without software installation or configuration. It's small and light enough to carry around on your keychain…and it's *so darned cool.* If you regularly transfer documents between Macs or between Macs and PCs, a flash drive will change your life.

FireWire Disk Mode/Thunderbolt Disk Mode (Target Disk Mode)

FireWire Disk Mode/Thunderbolt Disk Mode is a brilliant but little-known Macintosh-only feature that lets you turn one Mac into an external hard drive for another. This is by far the fastest method yet for transferring a lot of data—even faster than copying files over a network. It's extremely useful in any of these situations:

- **You're traveling with a laptop.** You want to copy your life onto it from your main Mac, including your entire 5 GB email folder and project files, before taking it on a trip, and then unload it when you return.

- **You have a new Mac.** You want to copy everything off the old one, without having to wait all night.

- **One Mac won't start up.** You want to repair it, using another Mac as a "front end."

Unfortunately, not all Macs have a FireWire or Thunderbolt jack. If you're among the lucky, though, you can use the following trick. (In these steps, suppose your main Mac is an iMac and you want to use a MacBook as an external hard drive for it.)

1. **Connect the FireWire (Thunderbolt) jacks of both computers with a cable.**

 If you have an older Mac with a FireWire 400 jack, you need a *6-pin* FireWire cable—*not* the one that connects a camcorder to a Mac. The one you need has the same large connector on both ends.

 Modern Macs have Apple's FireWire 800 jacks, which require a 9-pin FireWire cable (and give you much greater speed). If only one Mac has a FireWire 800 jack, then use that computer's traditional FireWire 400 connector instead. Otherwise, you need either a special FireWire 800–to–FireWire 400 cable, or the 400-to-800 adapter that came with your Mac.

2. **On the MacBook, choose →System Preferences. Click Startup Disk.**

 The Startup Disk panel opens.

3. **Click Target Disk Mode. In the confirmation box, click Restart.**

 The MacBook turns off and then on again. A giant gray FireWire icon ('ŏ') or Thunderbolt icon (ϟ) bounces around the laptop screen.

 Now take a look at the iMac's screen: Sure enough, there's the MacBook's hard drive icon on the desktop. You're ready to copy files onto or off of it, at extremely high speeds, and go on with your life.

4. **When you're finished working with the MacBook, eject it from the iMac's screen as you would any disk. Then turn off the laptop by pressing the power button.**

The next time you turn on the MacBook, it'll start up from its own copy of macOS, even if the cable is still attached. (You can disconnect the cable whenever you please.)

Note: The steps here describe the modern method of setting up Target Disk Mode. But the old way still works, too. Leave the iMac turned on, but shut down the MacBook. (Make sure it's plugged in. You wouldn't want the battery to die in the middle of this process.) Now turn the MacBook on again, but hold down the T key immediately after the chime. After a moment, you see the big Y-shaped FireWire icon ('ŏ') on the laptop screen, and the laptop's hard drive shows up on the iMac's desktop. Finish with step 4 above.

This method is arguably quicker, because you don't have to open System Preferences. And this method works when the Mac is too sick even to start up.

Via Bluetooth

Bluetooth is a cable-elimination technology. It's designed to let Bluetooth-equipped gadgets communicate within about 30 feet, using radio signals.

Bluetooth comes built into most computers and cellphones, plus the occasional printer, pocket organizer, and even camera or camcorder.

Bluetooth is built into all recent Macs. It's ready, therefore, to connect with Apple's wireless keyboard and mouse, to get on the internet using a Bluetooth cellphone as a cordless modem, to listen to music through wireless headphones or speakers, and to transfer files through the air to similarly equipped gear.

Bluetooth is pretty slow. (You get transfer speeds of 30 to 150 K per second, depending on the distance.) But when you consider the time you'd have taken for wiring, passwords, and configuration using any other connection method, you may find that Bluetooth wins, at least in casual, spur-of-the-moment, airport-seat situations.

And Bluetooth works no matter what the gadget—Mac, Windows, smartphone—so it's great as a universal file-exchange translator, too.

Note: For more details on configuring your Mac for Bluetooth connections, see page 330.

Sending a file

To shoot a file or two across the airwaves to a fellow Bluetooth-equipped Mac fan, first *pair* your Mac with the other Bluetooth machine. In System Preferences→Bluetooth, make sure your Mac is Discoverable. *Discoverable* means "Other Bluetooth gadgets can see me." (Check the receiving gadget, too, to make sure *it's* in Discoverable mode.) Then you're ready to send:

1. **From the Bluetooth ⍟ menulet, choose the device's name—and, from the submenu, "Send file to device" (Figure 6-16).**

 If you don't *have* the Bluetooth menulet on your menu bar, then open System Preferences. Click Bluetooth, and turn on "Show Bluetooth status in the menu bar."

 After a moment, the Select File to Send dialog box appears. (You've actually succeeded in opening a program called Bluetooth File Exchange, which sits in your Applications→Utilities folder.)

Figure 6-16:
Once your Mac is paired with the other gadget, it's easy to shoot a file to it wirelessly. In this example, you'll start by choosing "Send file to device."

2. Navigate to, and select, the files you want to send.

3. Click Send.

What happens now depends on how the receiving machine has been set up. In most cases, a dialog box tells the receiver that files are arriving; if he clicks Accept, then the download proceeds. He's then offered the chance to either (a) open each transferred file or (b) reveal its highlighted icon in the Finder.

Tip: In System Preferences→Sharing→Bluetooth Sharing, you can control what happens when someone sends you files via Bluetooth. Usually, you'll want your Mac to ask whether to accept these files. (That's what "Ask What to Do" means.) You can also specify where you want received files to wind up.

Fetching a file

You can also perform this entire procedure in reverse. That is, you can go fishing through your buddy's files without him explicitly having to send anything.

To make a Mac invadable, the person to be invaded must open System Preferences→ Sharing and turn on Bluetooth Sharing. Here's also where he can specify what folder is available to you for examination (the Mac proposes his Home→Public folder), and what kind of security he wants to set up.

Then all you have to do is choose Browse Files on Device from your own menulet (you can see it in Figure 6-16)—and let the rummaging begin!

Exchanging Data with iPhones or iPads

Apple has dreamed up some clever wireless ways for you to shoot files and information between a Mac and an iOS phone or tablet. These features are part of Continuity, described in Chapter 8.

Exchanging Data with Windows PCs

Documents can take one of several roads between your Mac and a Windows machine: via disk (such as a CD), flash drive, Dropbox, network, email, Bluetooth, iPod, web page, FTP download, and so on.

Preparing the Document for Transfer

The Mac is more Windows-compatible than ever. Still, before sending a document to a colleague who uses Windows, you must be able to answer "yes" to both of the following questions.

Is the document in a file format Windows understands?

Most popular programs are sold in both Mac and Windows flavors, and the documents they create are freely interchangeable. For example, documents created by recent versions of Word, Excel, PowerPoint, FileMaker, Illustrator, Photoshop, Dreamweaver, and

many other Mac programs don't need any conversion. The corresponding Windows versions of those programs open such documents with nary a hiccup.

Files in standard exchange formats don't need conversion, either. These formats include JPEG and PNG (digital photos), GIF (cartoon/logo graphics on web pages), HTML (raw web page documents), Rich Text Format (a word-processor exchange format that maintains bold, italic, and other formatting), plain text (no formatting at all), MP3 and AAC files (for audio), MIDI files (for music synthesizers), and so on.

But what about documents made by Mac programs that don't exist on the typical Windows PC hard drive, like Keynote or Pages? You certainly can't count on your recipient having the application.

Do your recipients the favor of first saving such documents into one of those exchange formats. In Pages, for example, choose File→Export To→Word; the resulting dialog box will confirm your choice. Click Next. Now name this special version of the document (complete with the .docx suffix), and then click Save.

Does the file have the correct file name suffix?

Every document on your hard drive has some kind of tag to tell the computer what program is supposed to open it: either a pair of invisible four-letter codes or a file name suffix like .docx.

Microsoft Windows uses *only* the latter system for identifying documents. Here are some of the most common such codes:

Kind of document	Suffix	Example
Microsoft Word (old)	.doc	Letter to Mom.doc
Microsoft Word	.docx	Letter to Mom.docx
Excel	.xls or .xlsx	Profit Projection.xlsx
PowerPoint	.ppt or. pptx	Slideshow.pptx
JPEG photo	.jpg	Baby Portrait.jpg
GIF graphic	.gif	Logo.gif
Web page	.htm	index.htm

The beauty of macOS is that its programs add these file name suffixes automatically and invisibly, every time you save a new document. You and your Windows comrades can freely exchange documents without ever worrying about this former snag in the Macintosh/Windows relationship.

Notes on Disk Swapping

Once you've created a document destined for a Windows machine, your next challenge is to get it *onto* that machine. One way is to put the file on a disk—a CD you've burned, for example—which you then hand to the Windows owner.

Macs and PCs format *hard drives* differently. The Mac can read Windows disks and flash drives (which use unappetizingly named formatting schemes like FAT32 and NTFS), but Windows can't read Mac hard drives or flash drives. CDs and DVDs use

the same format on both kinds of computers, though, so you should have very little problem moving these between machines.

Network Notes

MacOS can "see" shared disks and folders on Windows PCs that are on the same network. Complete instructions start on page 545.

Via the Internet

Chapter 13 offers details on FTP and web sharing, two ways to make your Mac available to other computers—Windows PCs or not—on the internet. And, of course, you can always email files between Macs and PCs.

The Share Button

The Share button is a quick, one-click way to send something (text, link, photo, video) to somebody else (by email, Twitter, Facebook, text message, AirDrop).

If you've seen an iPhone or iPad, then you've probably seen this icon: ⬆. On the Mac, this button, or a command that just says Share, pops up in all kinds of programs: the Finder's shortcut menus. Quick Look panels. The Open File dialog box in Apple programs. Mac programs like Contacts, Notes, Preview, Safari, Photo Booth, TextEdit, Photos, and so on. Other companies can add it to their programs, too, or install new commands into the Share menu for transmitting stuff to new channels.

To use this feature, select or open some text, a photo, a video, a file icon, a web link, or something else you want to send to friends. When you click this button or command, you're offered various ways to share the selected item. The choices vary according to the program you're using, but here are some examples:

- **Mail.** The Mac copies the selected material into a new, outgoing email message, or attaches the selected file to an outgoing message. Just add a few explanatory notes, address the message, and send.

- **Messages.** Puts the selected material into an outgoing message, ready to send as a text message or an iMessage (page 752). Just address and send.

Tip: In the Finder, the Share command offers a brilliantly simple way to send a file to somebody. Just right-click or two-finger click a file icon, choose Share→Message, and then enter the person's phone number (to send to an iPhone) or Apple ID (to send by iMessage). Click Send—off it goes!

- **AirDrop.** As you can read on page 528, AirDrop lets you shoot Finder files to nearby Macs, iPhones, and iPads—wirelessly, without having to fuss with passwords, file sharing, mounting disks, and so on.

 In the Finder, right-click or two-finger click the file icon (or icons) you want to send to another Mac. From the shortcut menu, choose AirDrop. In a flash, you get the AirDrop share sheet (page 528). It lists every nearby Mac, iPhone, or iPad.

Click the one you want, and then click Send; if the other guy clicks Accept, then the file is on its way to his Apple gadget.

- **Notes.** Anything you've highlighted—text, graphics, links, whatever—gets plopped onto a new page in the beefed-up Notes app (page 429). Figure 6-17 shows the sequence.

- **Reminders.** This option turns the highlighted text (in whatever app) into the entry for a reminder (page 442)—either a new one or an existing one. The process works just as it does for Notes (Figure 6-17).

Figure 6-17:
Top: Here's how you might save some text from Safari into a new Notes page. Right-click or two-finger click the selected text; from the shortcut menu, choose Share→Notes.

Bottom: The Choose Note pop-up menu offers to paste the text into a new note—or one of your pinned notes (page 431), or any existing note in your Notes app. (You may have hundreds of notes, which is why the search box can be especially handy at this point.)

Click Save to finish up.

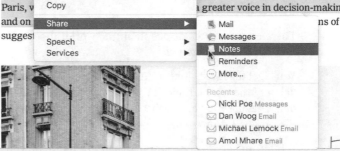

This list of options in the Share menu isn't complete; you may find other oddball options in the Share menus of certain programs. For example, in Photo Booth, you also get choices like Add to Photos and Change Profile Picture—handy things to do with a picture you've just taken with your Mac's built-in camera.

Note: What you don't find here in Catalina anymore are links to Twitter, Facebook, Vimeo, YouTube, or Flickr. Apple removed those options from the Share sheet in hopes of making macOS even more secure.

Editing the Share Menu

You can choose the options in your Share menu, and in which order they appear.

For that, you can thank the pane in System Preferences called Extensions. (One quick way to open it: From the Share menu itself, choose More.) If you click Share Menu in the left-side list, you're treated to a System Preferences box where you can turn off the Share-menu options you never use. You can also drag items' names up or down, so the most useful ones appear at the top of the Share menu from now on. (You're not allowed to turn off the Big Three: Mail, Messages, and AirDrop.) For more on Extensions, see page 348.

Time Machine

There are two kinds of people in the world: those who have a regular backup system—and those who *will*.

You'll get that grisly joke immediately if you've ever known the pain that comes with deleting the wrong folder by accident, or making changes that you regret, or worst of all, having your hard drive die. All those photos, all that music you've ripped over the years, all your email—gone.

Yet the odds are overwhelming that at this moment, you do not have a complete, current, automated backup of your Mac. Despite about a thousand warnings, articles, and cautionary tales a year, guess how many do? About *4 percent*. Everybody else is flying without a net.

If you don't have much to back up—you don't have much in the way of photos, music, or movies—you can get by with using a free online backup system like iCloud Drive, Dropbox, or CrashPlan. But those methods leave most of your Mac unprotected: all your programs and settings.

What you really want, of course, is a backup that's rock-solid, complete, and *automatic*. You don't want to have to remember to do a backup, to insert a disc, and so on. You just want to know you're safe.

That's the idea behind Time Machine, a marquee feature of macOS. It's a silent, set-it-and-forget-it piece of peace of mind. You sleep easy, knowing there's a safety copy of your *entire* system: your system files, programs, settings, music, pictures, videos, document files—*everything*. If your luck runs out, you'll be *so* happy you set up Time Machine.

Setting Up Time Machine

Here's the bad news: Time Machine requires a second hard drive. That's the only way to create a completely safe, automatic backup of your *entire* main hard drive.

That second hard drive can take any of these forms:

- **An external USB, FireWire, or Thunderbolt hard drive.**

- **An AirPort Time Capsule.** That's an AirPort wireless base station/network backup hard drive in one; it's available in gigantic capacities.

- **Another internal hard drive.**

- **A *partition* of any one of those drives.**

- **The hard drive of another Mac on the network** (OS X 10.5 or later) that you've mounted on your screen.

Tip: It's perfectly OK to back up several Macs onto the same external hard drive, as long as it's got enough room. You can also back up onto a hard drive that has other stuff on it, although of course that means you'll have less room for Time Machine backups.

In all cases, the backup disk must be bigger than the drive you're backing up (preferably *much* bigger).

Here's what you *can't* use as the backup disk: a CD or your startup drive.

POWER USERS' CLINIC

Encrypted Time Machine Backups

Time Machine can encrypt your backups.

Without encryption, an evildoer could theoretically bust into your house, steal your backup disk, and have full, unfettered access to all your backed-up files. It's never happened yet, but—you know. It could.

If you're interested in encrypting your backups, there are some prerequisites. The hard drive must use HFS (Journaled) formatting—a Mac hard drive, in other words. The drive has to be physically, directly connected to your Mac using USB, FireWire, or Thunderbolt—or else a wireless Apple Time Capsule.

To turn this feature on, open System Preferences→Time Machine. Click Select Disk. Turn on "Encrypt backup disk." You're asked for a password. Type it in and, whatever you

do, don't forget it! Without that password, you won't be able to recover your files if something goes wrong. Keep that password somewhere safe—on the bottom of the backup drive, for example. (Joke! That's a joke.)

Once you click OK, the encryption begins. It takes a long time. Go away for the weekend.

Once it's done, you won't notice any difference—until the day comes when you need to recover your files. At that point, you'll be asked for your password when you enter Time Machine.

If something serious ever happens to your Mac, you can connect the encrypted Time Machine drive to any other Mac that's running Lion or later. You'll be able to enter your password there and recover your files onto that different Mac.

Note: The backup drive must be a standard Mac-formatted hard drive—yet many new drives come preformatted as Windows disks. Fortunately, Time Machine automatically reformats them to the Mac OS Extended (Journaled) scheme, which it requires. Thoughtful, really.

Sure, it sounds like an Apple plot to sell hard drives. But you'd be surprised at how cheap they are. At this writing, you can buy an external 2-*terabyte* hard drive (2,000 gigabytes) for $50, for goodness' sake—and prices-per-gigabyte go only down.

The first time the Mac sees your second hard drive, it invites you to use it as Time Machine's backup drive ("Do you want to use 'Seagate 2TB Drive' to back up with Time Machine?"). That could be the moment you connect an external drive, or the first time you turn on the Mac after installing an internal drive.

Note: Time Machine still works if there's other stuff on the drive, but life is simpler if you don't use that drive for anything but Time Machine.

If you click Use as Backup Disk, you're taken immediately to the Time Machine pane of System Preferences (Figure 6-18). Here's where you see that Time Machine is turned on and has a drive it can use for backups.

Figure 6-18:
Use the Back Up Automatically checkbox to manage Time Machine activity, although it would be hard to imagine why you'd want to risk leaving it off. You can click Select Backup Disk to choose a different hard drive to represent the mirror of your main drive (after the first one is full, for example).

Soon enough, the Mac starts copying *everything* on your hard drive, including macOS itself, all your programs, and everyone's Home folders. You know that because you see the ↻ symbol in the Sidebar (next to the backup disk's name), and the menu-bar Time Machine icon looks like ↺.

And that, ladies and gentlemen, is the easiest setup for a backup program in history.

Note: Unless you turn on encryption (see the box on page 261), Time Machine doesn't use any compression or encoding; it's copying your files exactly as they sit on your hard drive, for maximum safety and recoverability. On the other hand, it does save some space on the backup drive, because it doesn't bother copying cache files, temporary files, and other files you'll never need to restore.

Now go away and let the Mac do its thing. The first backup can take hours, as the Mac duplicates your entire internal hard drive onto the second drive. The Mac may feel drugged during this time.

Tip: You can create multiple backups on different disks—a great feature if you have a laptop you carry between work and home. You can have a backup drive at both places; Time Machine will seamlessly switch between them. To set this up, just choose another backup disk in System Preferences→Time Machine. Time Machine will automatically back up to that drive, too.

How the Backups Work

From now on, Time Machine quietly checks your Mac once an hour. If any file, folder, or setting has changed, it gets backed up at the end of the hour. These follow-up backups are quick; Time Machine backs up only what's changed. So, should disaster strike, the only files you can lose are those you've changed within the past 59 minutes.

Tip: You can force more frequent backups if you want to. Just choose Back Up Now from the Time Machine menulet. Or choose Back Up Now from the shortcut menu of the Dock's Time Machine icon.

You can pause the backup the same way—if you need to use the backup drive for another quick task, for example. Choose Skip This Backup from the Time Machine menulet, open System Preferences→Time Machine and click the ⊗ next to the backup progress bar, or choose Stop Backing Up from shortcut menu of the Dock's Time Machine icon.

By the end of the day, you'll have 24 hourly backups on that second disk, all taking up space. So at day's end, Time Machine replaces that huge stash with a single *daily* backup. You can no longer rewind your system to 3:00 p.m. last Monday, but you can rewind to the way it was at the *end* of that day.

Similarly, after a month, Time Machine replaces those 30 dailies (for example) with four weekly backups. Now you may not be able to rewind to October 12, but you can rewind to the end of that week. (Apple assumes it won't take you that long to notice that your hard drive has crashed.)

Tip: You can see these backups, if you want. Open your backup drive, open the *Backups.backupdb* folder, and then open the folder named for your computer. Inside, you'll find a huge list of backup folders, bearing names like 2016-07-22-155831. That's the backup from July 22, 2016, at 15:58 (that is, 3:58 p.m.) and 31 seconds.

The point is that Time Machine doesn't just keep *one* copy of your stuff. It keeps *multiple* backups. It remembers how things were in every folder—not just yesterday, but last week, last month, and so on. It keeps on making new snapshots of your hard drive until the backup drive is full.

At that point, the oldest ones get deleted to make room for new ones.

Tip: Ordinarily, Time Machine alerts you when it has to start deleting old backups. If you'd rather have it just do it without bothering you, open System Preferences, click Time Machine, click Options, and then turn off "Notify after old backups are deleted."

By the way, if a backup is interrupted—if you shut down the Mac, put it to sleep, or take your laptop on the road—no big deal. Time Machine can keep working on its own, as you'll see in the next section, and resumes backing up to the backup drive the next time you're connected.

Local Snapshots

If you're among the 75 percent of Mac owners with a laptop, Time Machine used to be something of a bust in one regard: Whenever you were away from your backup disk (at home or the office, for example), you lost the benefits of Time Machine.

POWER USERS' CLINIC

Declaring Stuff Off-Limits to Time Machine

The whole point of Time Machine is to have a backup of your entire hard drive. That's how most people use it.

It's conceivable, though, that you might want to exclude some files or folders from the Time Machine treatment. There are two reasons.

First, you might not want certain, ahem, private materials to be part of your incriminating data trail.

Second, you might want to save space on the backup drive, either because it's not as big as your main drive or because you'd rather dedicate its space to more backups of the essential stuff. For example, you might decide not to back up your collection of downloaded TV shows, since video files are enormous. Or maybe you use an online photo-sharing website as a backup for all your photos, so you don't think it's necessary to include those in the Time Machine backup.

To eliminate certain icons from the backup, open the Time Machine pane of System Preferences. Click Options.

Exclude these items from backups:

/Applications	6.98 GB
~/Desktop/Billing	392.2 MB
~/Desktop/Incriminating photos	1.2 MB
System Files and Applications	3.1 GB

+ − Estimated size of full backup: 184.47 GB

☐ Back up while on battery power
☑ Notify after old backups are deleted

Cancel Save

In the resulting list, click the + button; navigate to your hard drive, and then select the files or folders you don't want backed up. Or just find their actual icons in the Finder and drag them into the list here. (Use the − button to remove items from the list, thereby excluding them from the excluded list.)

If you're strapped for disk space, one logical candidate to exclude is the System folder on your main hard drive—that is, macOS itself. After all, if you lose your hard drive, you already have a copy of macOS: the original App Store installer.

When you add the System folder to the exclusion list, Time Machine makes another space-saving offer: "Would you like to also exclude other files installed with macOS, such as system applications and UNIX tools?"

Agreeing (by clicking Exclude All System Files) saves you another several gigabytes of backup space.

Today, crazy as this may sound, Time Machine keeps on working even on a laptop that's far from home. Thanks to a feature called local snapshots, Time Machine works as usual by making its backups right on the laptop's own hard drive.

Of course, this system won't help you if your hard drive dies; your backup is on the same drive, so you'll lose the originals and the backups simultaneously. But what local snapshots do provide is a safety net—a way to recover a file you deleted or changed during this time away. Better yet, once you're home again, when your laptop rejoins the network, the local snapshots intelligently merge with the master Time Machine backups, as though you'd never been away.

If Time Machine is turned on on your laptop, it makes local snapshots automatically—once an hour, as usual. As time goes on, Time Machine deletes snapshots more than 24 hours old to save disk space.

Note: If your laptop gets really low on disk space, Time Machine stops making new snapshots and may even delete old ones so you can keep using your Mac. When you make more space, snapshots resume automatically.

If you need to recover a file, enter Time Machine as usual. Your local snapshots show up on the same timeline as backups made on your external backup disk, but they're color-coded: pink tick marks for external backups, gray for local ones. If the pink bars are dimmed, it's because you're not hooked up to your Time Machine backup drive.

Tip: To see how much disk space your local snapshots are eating up, choose →About This Mac. Click the Storage tab. The color-coded graph clearly indicates the space being used for backups.

Changing Time Machine Settings

Time Machine has four faces. There's the application itself, which sits in your Applications folder; open it only when you want to enter Restore mode. There's its Dock icon, which also enters Restore mode, but which has a shortcut menu containing useful commands like Back Up Now (and Stop Backing Up).

There's the Time Machine menulet, which may be the handiest of all. It identifies the time and date of the most recent backup, offers Back Up Now/Skip This Backup commands, and has direct access to Time Machine's Restore mode and preferences pane.

Tip: If you Option-click the Time Machine menulet, you get two secret commands: Verify Backups (just in case you're nervous about your backups' integrity) and Browse Other Backup Disks. Yes, it's perfectly possible to back up onto multiple hard drives—to keep one offsite in case of fire, flood, or burglary, for example—and this is how. (Right-clicking or two-finger clicking Time Machine's Dock icon is another way to get this command.)

Finally, there's its System Preferences pane, where you adjust its settings (Figure 6-18). To see it, choose System Preferences→Time Machine. Or choose Time Machine Preferences from Time Machine's Dock icon or menulet.

Recovering Lost or Changed Files

All right, you've got Time Machine on the job. You sleep easy at night, confident that your life is in order—and your stuff is backed up.

Then, one day, it happens: Your hard drive crashes. Or you can't find a file or folder you know you had. Or you save a document in some non–Auto Save program and then wish you could go back to an earlier draft. Some kind of disaster—sunspots, clueless spouse, overtired self—has befallen your files. This is Time Machine's big moment.

Start by pinpointing what you're looking for, in one of these two ways:

- **Open the disk or folder window** where the missing or changed item was.

- **Type what you're looking for** into the search box at the top of any Finder window. Click the location button that makes the most sense: "This Mac" or the name of the window you're in.

 In the case of deleted files or folders, the search will probably come up empty; that's totally OK.

Figure 6-19:
Top: Choose Enter Time Machine from the menulet. (If you don't see this menulet, then turn on "Show Time Machine in menu bar," shown in Figure 6-18.)

Bottom: The starry outer-space background of the old Time Machine is gone, but everything works the same way: You see dozens of copies of the Finder window, representing its condition at each backup, stretching back to the past.

Now click the Time Machine icon on the Dock, or choose Enter Time Machine from the menulet (Figure 6-19, top).

Everything else on your desktop fades away. Front and center is your Finder window—or, rather, dozens of them, stretching back in time (Figure 6-19, bottom). Each is a snapshot of that window at the time of a Time Machine backup.

You have four ways to peruse your backup universe:

- **Click individual windows to see what's in them.**

- **Drag your cursor through the timeline at the right side.** It's like a master dial that flies through the windows into the past.

- **Click one of the two big, flat arrows.** The one pointing into the past means "Jump directly to the most recent window version that's *different* from the way it is right now." In other words, it's often a waste of time to go flipping through the windows one at a time, because your missing or changed file might have been missing or changed for the last 25 backups (or whatever). What you want to know is the last time the contents of this window *changed*. And that's what the big, flat arrows do. They jump from one *changed* version of this window to another. (Or, if you began with a search, the arrow takes you to the most recent backup with a matching result.)

- **Use the search box in the corner of the window.** You can search for whatever you're missing in the current backup.

As you go, the very bottom of the screen identifies where you are in time—that is, which backup you're examining.

Tip: You can let Time Machine take you on a guided tour of folders past, or you can go your own way to find your files. Just open the backup disk itself, whose icon appears on your desktop. Inside, you'll find nested folders, neatly representing every computer, every backup, every day, and every hour—which you can rummage through by hand.

The End of Time

What happens when my backup drive gets full?

The whole idea of Time Machine is that it preserves multiple backups, so that you can rewind a window or a drive not just to *a* backup, but to *any* date in the past. The bigger the hard drive, the farther back those monthly backups are preserved.

Eventually, of course, your backup drive runs out of space. At that point, Time Machine notifies you and offers you a choice: "Your backup disk is now full. The oldest remaining backup disk is…" (and then the date). You can keep using that drive; Time Machine deletes the oldest backups to make room for newer ones. Or you can install a new Time Machine backup drive. New backups will go on that one; your older backups will still be available on the original drive.

If you ever need to retrieve files or folders from the older disk, right-click or two-finger click the Time Machine icon in the Dock; from the shortcut menu, choose Browse Other Time Machine Disks. Choose the older disk. Then click the Time Machine icon on the Dock to enter the Restore mode.

In many ways, the recovery mode is just like the Finder. You can't actually open, edit, rename, or reorganize anything here. But you can use Quick Look to inspect the documents to make sure you've got the right version. And you can use icon, list, column, or gallery views to sort through the files you're seeing.

If you're trying to recover an older *version* of a file or folder, highlight it and then click the flat arrow button that's pointing away from you; Time Machine skips back to the most recent version that's *different* from the current one.

If you're trying to restore a deleted file or folder that you've now located, highlight it and then click Restore (at bottom). Presto: The lost file or folder is back in the window where it belonged.

Note: Time Machine prides itself not just on recovering files and folders, but also on putting them back where they belong. If you recover a different version of something that's still there, macOS asks if you want to replace it with the recovered version—or to keep both versions.

And if you're recovering a document whose original folder no longer exists, Time Machine asks if you want to choose another place for the document or recreate the missing folder, perhaps so the recovered item feels at home. Choose accordingly.

Recovering from Contacts and Mail

The Finder isn't the only program hooked into Time Machine's magic. Contacts and Mail work with Time Machine, too. Other software companies can also revise their own applications to work with it.

In other words, if you want to recover certain addresses or email messages that have been deleted, you don't start in the Finder; you start in Contacts or Mail.

Then click the Time Machine icon on the Dock. Once again, you enter the recovery mode—but this time, you're facing a strange, disembodied, stripped-down copy of Contacts or Mail.

You're ready to find your missing data. Click the Jump Back arrow to open the most recent version of your address book file or email stash that's different from what you've got now. (You can also use the timeline on the right if you remember the date when things went wrong.)

Tip: If you're looking for something particular, specify that before you start clicking. For example, type a name into the Contacts search box first.

At this point, you can select individual Contacts entries or email messages to restore; just click the Restore button. Contacts may discover a lot of duplicate name-and-address entries and invite you to step through them, deciding which ones "win" (the old or the new).

Note: When you finish restoring in Mail, you'll find the restored messages in the On My Mac→Time Machine→Recovered folder at the left side of the window.

Recovering the entire hard drive

Every hard drive will die at some point. You just hope it won't happen while *you* own the computer. But if it does, you, as a Time Machine aficionado, won't care. You'll just repair or replace the hard drive, and then proceed as follows.

1. **Connect the Time Machine backup disk to the Mac. Start the recovery mode.**

 There are actually three ways to recover a dead Mac or a dead hard drive. If the hard drive is fine but it just can't start up your Mac, hold down ⌘-R during startup. If the hard drive is empty, you can restart from the internet itself (if it's a Mac released since Mac OS X Lion came out). And, if all else fails, you can always use the Recovery Disk Assistant that you wisely made long in advance of your horror-story dead-disk day.

 Appendix B covers these recovery modes in more detail. The point is, however, that all three present "Restore from a Time Machine backup" as one of the options.

2. **Choose "Restore from a Time Machine backup." Click Continue.**

 Now you're shown a list of Time Machine backup disks. You probably have only one.

3. **Click your Time Machine backup disk. In the list, click the most recent backup.**

 The installer goes about copying *everything* from the backup disk onto your new, empty hard drive. When it's all over, you'll have a perfect working system, just the way it was before your series of unfortunate events.

Beware, however: Restoring your earlier version also *erases any files* you've created or changed. Back them up manually before you proceed! Then, when you're asked to choose a backup to restore, choose the most recent one. When it's all over, copy the files that you manually backed up back onto the hard drive.

Recovering to another Mac

Weirdly enough, you can also use Time Machine to bring over some or part of any Time Machine backup to a totally different Mac.

On the new machine, connect your backup disk. In the Applications→Utilities folder, open Migration Assistant. Click "From another Mac, PC, Time Machine backup, or other disk." The subsequent screens invite you to choose which backup, which Home folder, and which elements (applications, settings, files) you want to bring over.

Frequently Asked Questions

Time Machine is a very different kind of backup program, and a real departure for longtime Mac addicts. A few questions, therefore, are bound to come up—like these:

- **Can I back up more than one Mac onto the same disk?** Yes. Each Mac's backup is stored in a separate folder on that disk.

- **Can I use more than one backup disk—like one at the office and one at home?** Yes. Just use the Time Machine pane of System Preferences (or the Time Machine Dock icon's shortcut menu) to select the new backup drive each time you switch.

- **Can I delete something from all the backups at once?** Yes. Click the Time Machine icon on the Dock to enter the Restore mode. Find and select the file or folder you want to obliterate. From the ✿ menu, choose Delete All Backups of [the Thing's Name]. (Sneaky, huh? That command is never in the ✿ menu *except* when you're in Time Machine restoring mode.)

Voice Control, Dictation & Siri

I t was a popular sci-fi fantasy for decades: that someday we'd be able to talk to our computers instead of typing into them. But it's been a while since that actually *was* a fantasy.

Dictation—the ability to type by speaking—has long been a Mac and iPhone feature. Siri—the virtual assistant who not only understands what you say but also executes your commands and answers your questions—came a few years later. And now Apple has taken the concept to a whole new level with its brand-new feature, Voice Control.

This chapter covers the Mac's three speech-recognition features—Voice Control, Dictation, and Siri—as well as the Mac's ability to talk back to you.

Voice Control

Voice Control, new in macOS Catalina, lets you operate the entire computer—every button, slider, app, and physical control—by voice. It's absolutely amazing.

Apple's intention, of course, was to make life easier for people who can't use their hands and fingers to manipulate a mouse and keyboard. But when you see how fast, easy, and complete Voice Control is, you might decide it's worth adopting no matter what your physical abilities are.

Voice Control comes turned off. To try it out, open System Preferences→Accessibility→ Voice Control. Turn on Enable Voice Control (Figure 7-1). The first time you do that, the Mac takes a couple of minutes to download a language file from Apple.

Once that's done, a floating microphone palette appears on your screen. Click its Sleep button (or say, "Go to sleep") to make it stop listening for commands, or click its Wake Up button (or say, "Wake up") to make it start again.

You can immediately start to operate the Mac by voice. Anything you say, Voice Control does with amazing speed.

The best part: When you're not talking to the Mac, it's smart enough to ignore you. It executes commands only when you're *saying* commands. If you say, "Hey, buddy, could you toss me a napkin?" nothing happens (at least on the Mac). If you say, "Open Photos," it opens Photos.

After each command, a tiny "hint" bubble appears above the microphone panel, confirming what Voice Control heard.

To see all the commands Voice Control understands, click System Preferences→ Accessibility→Voice Control→Commands. (You can turn off individual commands here, too—a troubleshooting technique when you seem to be triggering a command you don't actually need.)

Tip: When you click one of the commands in this list, you get to see all the *other* voice commands that do the same thing. For example, you don't have to say, "Open Messages." You can instead say, "Show Messages," "Launch Messages," or "Switch to Messages."

Or say, "What can I say?" You get a master list of commands, organized by category and self-adjusting to show only the commands available right now (Figure 7-1).

Figure 7-1:
Welcome to Voice Control!

You can drag the floating "Sleep/Wake Up" panel around the screen (top left).

You turn on and configure Voice Control in System Preferences (right).

And the "What can I say?" commands list changes based on context, so it's always showing the commands you can say right now (bottom left).

Here's a quick sampling of what you'll find there:

- **Clicking things.** "Click Send." "Click Reply." "Click Done." "Click and hold mouse." "Move cursor down 100 pixels." "Double-click." "Click File menu." "Triple-click."

- **Opening things.** "Open Finder." "Launch Photos." "Go back." "Open Siri." "Open Spotlight" (that is, the search box). "Save document." "Quit Maps."

- **Dragging and zooming.** "Scroll up." "Zoom in."

- **Controlling Voice Control.** "Go to sleep" makes the Mac stop listening for commands—except for the phrase "Wake up," which tells it to resume.

Clicking Unlabeled Spots

This all works fast and beautifully. But not everything on the Mac screen has a neat little textual label that you can refer to, as in "Click Send." How are you supposed to click some unlabeled tool in, say, Photos?

You can use one of two techniques:

- **"Show numbers."** Instantly, tiny number tags appear on every clickable item in your current window (shown in Figure 7-1). You don't need to know or care what their official names are. You can now just say, "seven" to click whatever is identified by the 7 tag.

Tip: The number tags appear automatically whenever you open a menu, too. That's to speed you along. You can speak the actual words of the menu command you want, of course ("Click Save As"), but saying "six" may be faster than saying, "Click Smithers Estimated North American Profit-Loss Projections.xls."

And what if there are no identifiable graphic objects that are taggable? What if you're trying to edit a spot on a photo or click a spot in Maps? Voice Control has you covered here, too.

- **"Show grid."** The screen is instantly overlaid with a grid of numbered squares (Figure 7-2, top). The grid starts out by subdividing the entire screen into, say, 50 squares—not nearly fine enough for you to specify a precise click location.

Tip: If you say, "Show window grid," the grid limits itself to the active window, which is often a more precise setup.

What you're supposed to do, therefore, is home in on the spot you want in a series of commands. First, speak the number of the closest grid square to what you want ("eleven"); suddenly, the entire grid crams itself into that one square, giving you much finer control (Figure 7-2, middle).

If you then say one of *those* squares ("nine"), the grid crams entirely into *that* square, which is now so crowded that the Mac displays a magnifier window so you can see what you're zooming into (Figure 7-2, bottom). Eventually, you can zoom all the way into an individual pixel. When you see the exact spot to click,

say, "Click three" (or whatever its number is). You can even say, "Drag three to eleven" to drag something.

Say, "Hide grid" once you're finished with it.

Figure 7-2:
The grid system in Voice Control lets you click (or drag from) any spot on the screen, entirely by voice.

Top: You say, "Show grid" to get this full-screen overlay.

You say "eleven."

Middle: Now you get a mini-grid on square 11.

You say "eighteen."

Bottom: Now you get an even tinier grid within that square.

At this point, the grid numbers would be too small to see, so you get a handy magnified version (lower left) for your reference in speaking the next command.

Speaking Your Text

Whenever your insertion point is in a spot where you can type, all you have to do is speak to type. There's a whole chunk of this chapter dedicated to that process; see page 278.

Editing Text

The Mac's dictation feature is, shall we say, imperfect. You often have to manually correct some words you've dictated before you send your text or email. (Your brain is imperfect, too; you frequently want to correct something you've dictated or typed!)

Using Voice Control, you can perform stunts like these:

- **Deleting.** Say, "Delete that" or "Scratch that" to backspace over the last word or utterance.

- **Moving the insertion point.** Say exactly where you want to move it, using what you've already typed as a reference point: "Move after 'called it macaroni.'"

 You can also say, "Move to end" (or beginning) of whatever you've been writing—a text, for example.

 Or say, "Move to end of word" (or sentence, paragraph, line, or selection). Or "Move forward three characters" (or back—or words, lines, sentences, or paragraphs).

- **Selecting text.** "Select all." "Select 'Yankee Doodle Dandy.'" "Select next word" (or previous—or character, sentence, line, or paragraph). Or specify how many: "Select next four words," for example. And then you can say, "Extend selection back three words." And if you change your mind: "Deselect that."

- **Formatting text.** "Bold that." "Italicize that." "Capitalize 'post office.'"

- **Editing text.** "Replace 'Riding on a pony' with 'Driving in an Uber.'"

 No more mousing and retyping. Just say what you want to fix, and then say what you want it fixed with!

 You can say, "Correct 'went to town,'" or, if the mistake *just* happened, "Correct that." You get a panel of alternative interpretations of the word or phrase you spoke, numbered for your quick-speaking convenience (Figure 7-3).

 You'll also get a lot of mileage out of "Delete that" (whatever you just said) or "Undo that." Even "Delete all."

Figure 7-3:
If Voice Control mis-transcribes what you intended, select the error and then say, "Correct that." You get a pop-up menu that includes alternative transcriptions.

Incredibly, all of this works in Microsoft Word, too—not just Apple apps.

Tip: Voice Control also makes it easy to teach your Mac to recognize weird slang, names, or jargon when you're dictating. Just add them in advance to System Preferences→Accessibility→Voice Control→Vocabulary. Or, after typing or dictating the weird term for the first time, say, "Select that; add to vocabulary." (Alas, the custom vocabulary isn't a syncable iCloud entity. That is, you'll have to create the custom terms again on your iPhone or iPad.)

Putting It All Together

Once you've become familiar with Voice Control, you can do all kinds of stuff with it, hands free. Suppose, for example, you're supposed to find a nice hotel for your mom's birthday trip to Detroit. Make sure Voice Control is listening, and then say:

- **"Open Safari. Search for Detroit luxury hotels. Scroll down. Scroll down."** At this point, you're looking over the search results. But how do you click the one you want?

- **"Show numbers."** The number tags appear. Speak the one next to the search result you want.

- **"50."** Now you're on that hotel's web page. Its address is highlighted.

- **"Copy that. Open Mail. New Item."** (Dumb that you can't say "New *message*," but whatever.) Now address the outgoing message.

- **"Mom. Next field. Next field."** Now you're in the subject line.

- **"The hotel info for your birthday trip. Next field."** Now you're in the body of the email.

- **"Hey Mom. Here's the place I was talking about. Paste that. Click Send."** And it's done.

Voice Control on the Mac isn't nearly as complete and polished as it is on the iPhone and iPad. Its list of commands is far shorter, and its text-editing features sometimes stop working.

But it's so easy and fast, it might be worth using when, for example, your hands are wet or grubby, or you're just kind of lazy.

Mastering Voice Control takes a little time, but you don't have to master it! Just learn a few commands. Even if all you ever use is the "Replace ___ with ___" command for editing text messages, you'll save some frustration 30 times a day.

Custom Commands

If you have even one technical gene in your body, you can extend Voice Control's power by setting up custom commands. You might decide that you want "Crunch numbers" to be the command to open Mathematics Incorporated Spreadsheet Professional Plus, so you don't have to say all that. You can set up Messages so the word "Send" sends what you've just typed, instead of having to say, "Send Message" every

time. You can create the command "Today's bad news" to open *The New York Times* home page in Safari.

If you're handy with Automator (page 382), you can even create voice commands that fire up much longer, more complex operations.

Here's how to build your own command:

1. **Open System Preferences→Accessibility→Voice Control→Commands.**

 Or say, "Open Voice Control preferences."

2. **Click Commands.**

 Or say, "Click Commands." Now you're viewing the master list of commands (Figure 7-4, left).

Figure 7-4:
Here are the seven things a custom voice command can do for you. Of course, each of those seven opens up an infinity of possibilities.

3. **Click +.**

 Or say, "Click Add." Here you're ready to specify the three parameters of any good custom command.

4. **Fill in "When I say" with the spoken command you'll want to trigger the action.**

 It can be a word or a phrase.

5. **Use the "While using" pop-up menu to specify which app you want to listen for this command.**

 If you don't choose anything from this menu, your command will work anywhere, in any app. But narrowing the scope is a good way to limit accidental triggerings.

6. **Use the Perform pop-up menu to set up what you want the command to do. Click Done.**

This last step, of course, is the biggie. Your custom command can perform any of seven different tasks:

- **Open Finder Items.** That is, your command can open *anything* on your Mac—any file, document, or program.

- **Open URL** means "Open a certain website in Safari." This is how you'd create your "Today's bad news" command.

- **Paste Text** pastes a blob of canned text. Maybe it's your home address. Maybe it's a boilerplate legal contract. When you choose this item, you're given a box where you can type or paste the verbiage.

- **Paste Data.** The Paste Text option is all well and good for *text*. But what if you want to paste an image, like your logo? Or a region of spreadsheet cells? That's what this option is for. Copy whatever it is, in whatever program. Then, when you're creating a Paste Data command, you can hit Import from Clipboard to teach your new command what to paste.

- **Press Keyboard Shortcut.** This one is incredibly useful. Now you can speak a command to press any keyboard combination, no matter how twisted. This, for example, is how you'd create a Send command in Messages to transmit what you've just typed; use the Return key, perhaps, as the keyboard shortcut.

- **Select Menu.** Use whatever voice trigger you want to choose whatever menu command you want. That's a huge time-saver, since opening menus and choosing their commands isn't exactly an efficient procedure otherwise. In the Perform box, type the name of the menu command itself. (You don't have to worry about which menu it's in.)

Note: If the command ends with an ellipsis (…), indicating that a dialog box will appear as a result, you must include that in the command name. You can't just type three periods, either; you must make the proper ellipsis symbol, which you get by pressing Option-semicolon (;).

- **Run Workflow.** A *workflow* is a memorized series of steps created in the Automator app (described in a free PDF appendix to this book, "Automator & AppleScript," on the "Missing CD" at *missingmanuals.com*). A single workflow can incorporate multiple apps, menu commands, and operations.

Catalina starts you off with a few ready-to-use workflows, like "Take my picture" and "New screen recording." In macOS 10.15, the first Catalina release, none of these commands actually work—but Apple will surely get around to fixing them. Right?

In the meantime, the workflows *you* make work just fine. If you have a bit of time and technical expertise, Voice Control + Automator = limitless possibilities.

Dictation

Dictation is built into the Mac, just as it is on the latest iPhones and iPads. You can speak to enter text anywhere, into any program, just by speaking. (Behind the scenes,

it's using the same Nuance recognition technology that powers Dragon dictation feature.) You can blather away into an email, fire off a text message, or draft a memo without ever looking at the screen.

Of course, dictation isn't always practical, since everybody around you can hear what you're doing, and voice typing isn't always accurate, either. Very often, you'll have to correct an error or two. (Your accuracy is much, much better when you wear a headset.)

Meanwhile—awkwardly enough—the Mac now has *two different* dictation features. There's the old Dictation feature, and there's Voice Control.

In most ways, the two are identical. Here are the differences:

- **Voice Control offers all the cool** editing-by-voice features described starting on page 274. In regular Dictation, you have to correct errors manually.

- **Voice Control works without an internet connection;** regular Dictation doesn't. (That's because Voice Control does all its work right on the Mac. Your voice is never transferred to Apple's servers somewhere, much to the relief of privacy fans.)

- **Voice Control has no time limit**—you can blabber on until you've dictated your entire dissertation. Regular Dictation stops listening after 30 seconds and writes out what you'd said so far.

- **Regular Dictation works virtually everywhere you can type.** Voice Control has trouble with some programs—for example, it doesn't work in Adobe's apps. That's really the only reason you'd ever want to use regular Dictation instead of Voice Control.

All right—expectations set? Then here's how to type by speaking.

Dictation Step by Step

First, turn on your preferred dictation feature.

- **Voice Control:** Turn on System Preferences→Accessibility→Enable Voice Control. Choose which microphone you want to use, if you have more than one.

- **Regular Dictation:** Open System Preferences→Keyboard→Dictation.

Tip: In either case, you can choose Add Language to specify what the Mac should be listening for. Your options include English in several dialects, plus dozens of other languages.

Now fire up a program where you can type: TextEdit, Mail, Word, whatever.

- **Voice Control:** If you see "Sleep" on the floating microphone palette, the Mac is listening already! Start talking.

- **Regular Dictation:** Press the fn key twice. (You can also choose the Start Dictation command, which appears in almost every program's Edit menu. Or you can choose a different keystroke in System Preferences→Keyboard→Dictation.)

Tip: Here's a shortcut for regular Dictation: You can also *hold down the fn key* on the second click, do your speaking, and then release the key when you're done. In other words, you can use it like a push-to-talk button on a walkie-talkie.

Now you're ready! Say what you have to say. You don't have to speak slowly, loudly, or weirdly; speak normally. Close to your Mac's microphone (or wearing earbuds or a headset) gives the best results.

You have to speak the punctuation, like this: "Dear Dad (colon): Send money (dash)— as much as you can (comma), please (period)." (See the table below.)

After you finish speaking, make the Mac stop listening by:

- **Voice Control:** Say "Go to sleep," or click Sleep on the microphone panel.

- **Regular Dictation:** Press the fn key twice.

The transcribed text appears all at once, in a big blob.

If the transcription contains errors, you can edit them exactly as you would fix an error in something you typed—or, in Voice Control, speak to edit. If the Mac *knows* it made errors, it underlines them, and you can often fix them with a quick click. Or, if the whole thing is a mess, you can press ⌘-Z, the universal keystroke for Undo, or (in Voice Control) say, "Undo that" or "Scratch that."

Usually, you'll find the accuracy pretty darned good, considering that you didn't have to train the software to recognize your voice. You'll also find that the accuracy is better when you dictate complete sentences, and long words fare better than short ones.

Punctuation

Here's a handy table that shows you what punctuation you can say to your Mac, and how to say it.

Say this:	To get this:	For example, saying this:	Types this:
"period" or "full stop"	. [space and capital letter afterward]	"Best (period) date (period) ever (period)"	Best. Date. Ever.
"dot" or "point"	. [no space afterward]	"My email is frank (dot) smith (at sign) gmail (dot) com"	My email is frank. smith@gmail.com
"comma," "semicolon," "colon"	, ; :	"Mom (comma) hear me (colon) I'm dizzy (semicolon) tired"	Mom, hear me: I'm dizzy; tired
"question mark," "exclamation point"	? ! [space and capital letter afterward]	"Ellen (question mark) Hi (exclamation point)"	Ellen? Hi!
"inverted question mark," "inverted exclamation point"	¿ ¡	"(inverted question mark) Que paso (question mark) "	¿Que paso?

Say this:	To get this:	For example, saying this:	Types this:
"ellipsis" or "dot dot dot"	. . .	"Just one (ellipsis) more (ellipsis) step (ellipsis)"	Just one… more… step…
"space bar"	[a space, especially when a hyphen would normally appear]	"He rode the merry (space bar) go (space bar) round"	He rode the merry go round
"open paren" then "close paren" (or "open bracket/close bracket" or "open brace/close brace")	() or [] or { }	"Then she (open paren) the surgeon (close paren) gasped"	Then she (the surgeon) gasped
"new line"	[a press of the Return key]	"milk (new line) bread (new line) quinoa"	Milk Bread Quinoa
"new paragraph"	[two presses of the Return key]	"autumn leaves (new paragraph) softly falling"	Autumn leaves Softly falling
"quote," then "unquote"	" "	"Her perfume screamed (quote) available (unquote)"	Her perfume screamed "available"
"numeral"	[writes the following number as a digit instead of spelling it out]	"Next week she turns (numeral) eight"	Next week she turns 8
"asterisk," "plus sign," "minus sign," "equals sign"	*, +, −, =	"numeral eight (asterisk) two (plus sign) one (minus sign) three (equals sign) fourteen"	8*2+1−3=14
"ampersand," "dash"	&, −	"Cheese (ampersand) ice cream (dash) the best (exclamation point)"	Cheese & ice cream—the best!
"hyphen"	- [without spaces]	"Mine is more of a dumb (hyphen) phone"	Mine is more of a dumb-phone
"backquote"	'	"She was born in (backquote) (numeral) fifty-two"	She was born in '52
"smiley," "frowny," "winky" (or "smiley face," "frowny face," "winky face")	:-) :-(;-)	"I think you know where I'm going with this (winky face)"	I think you know where I'm going with this ;-)

You can also say "percent sign" (%), "at sign" (@), "dollar sign" ($), "cent sign" (¢), "euro sign" (€), "yen sign" (¥), "pounds sterling sign" (£), "section sign" (§), "copyright sign" (©), "registered sign" (®), "trademark sign" (™), "greater-than sign" or "less-than sign" (> or <), "degree sign" (°), "caret sign" (^), "tilde" (~), "vertical bar" (|), and "pound sign" (#).

The software automatically capitalizes the first new word after a period, question mark, or exclamation point. But you can also force it to capitalize words you're dictating by saying "cap" right before the word, like this: "Dear (cap) Mom, I've run away to join (cap) The (cap) Circus (comma), a nonprofit cooperative for runaway jugglers."

Here's another table—this one shows the other commands for capitalization, as well as spacing.

Say this:	To get this:	For example, saying this:	Types this:
"cap" or "capital"	Capitalizes the next word	"Give me the (cap) works"	Give me the Works
"caps on," then "caps off"	Capitalizes the first letter of every word	"Next week (caps on) the new england chicken cooperative (caps off) will hire me"	Next week The New England Chicken Cooperative will hire me
"all caps on," then "all caps off"	Capitalizes everything	"So (all caps on) please please (all caps off) don't tell anyone"	So PLEASE PLEASE don't tell anyone
"all caps"	Types just the next word in all caps	"We (all caps) really don't belong here"	We REALLY don't belong here
"no caps"	Types the next word in lowercase	"See you in (no caps) Texas"	See you in texas
"no caps on," then "no caps off"	Prevents any capital letters	"I'll ask (no caps on) Santa Claus (no caps off) for a pony"	I'll ask santa claus for a pony
"no space"	Runs the next two words together	"Try new mega (no space) berry flavor"	Try new megaberry flavor
"no space on," then "no space off"	Eliminates all spaces	"(No space on) I can't believe you ate all that (no space off) (comma) she said excitedly"	Ican'tbelieveyou ateallthat, she said excitedly
[alphabet letters]	Types the letters out, though usually not very accurately	"The stock symbol is A P P L"	The stock symbol is APPL

You don't always have to dictate these formatting commands, by the way. The Mac automatically inserts hyphens into phone numbers (you say, "2125561000," and it

types "212-556-1000") and handles prices automatically ("six dollars and thirty-two cents" becomes "$6.32"). It formats dates and web addresses well, too; you can even use the nerdy shortcut "dub-dub-dub" when you want the "www" part of a web address.

The Mac recognizes email addresses, too, as long as you remember to say "at sign" at the right spot. You'd say, "harold (underscore) beanfield (at sign) gmail (dot) com" to get harold_beanfield@gmail.com.

Siri on the Mac

Siri is a crisply accurate, astonishingly understanding, uncomplaining, voice-commanded servant. For years, she's made using the phone much easier—and now she's on the Mac.

Older speech-recognition systems work only if you issue certain limited commands with predictable syntax, like "Call 445-2340" or "Open Microsoft Word." But Siri is different. She's been programmed to respond to casual speech, normal speech. It doesn't matter if you say, "What's the weather going to be like in Tucson this week-end?" or "Give me the Tucson weather for this weekend" or "Will I need an umbrella in Tucson?" Siri understands almost any variation.

And she understands dozens of languages.

You can say, "What's Janet's work number?" or "How do I get to the airport?" or "What time is it in Boise?" Siri can also round up files for you: "Show me the presentation I worked on yesterday" or "Show me all the emails about the company picnic." She can round up photos or videos according to their date, location taken, or album name ("Show me all the pictures I took in SeaWorld last year").

You can also ask her questions about movies, sports, and restaurants. Siri displays a beautifully formatted response and speaks in a calm voice. Siri can control HomeKit gadgets in your house ("Siri, turn off the lights downstairs"); show you a password you've forgotten; and answer questions about food, celebrities, and motorsports. You can operate her hands-free, too. With a couple of tweaks in System Preferences, you can teach Siri to respond anytime you say, "Hey Siri."

UP TO SPEED

A Brief History of Siri

In 2010, Apple bought Siri, a company that made a voice-control app (no longer available) for the iPhone. Apple cleaned it up, beefed it up, integrated it with the iPhone's software, and wound up with Siri, your virtual servant.

Believe it or not, Siri is a spin-off from a Department of Defense research project called CALO (Cognitive Assistant that Learns and Organizes), which at one time was the largest artificial-intelligence project ever launched. In a very real way, therefore, Siri represents your tax dollars at work.

The spin-off was run by the Stanford Research Institute (SRI). But that's supposedly not where Siri's name came from. "Siri," it turns out, is a Norwegian name meaning "beautiful woman who leads you to victory." (Co-creator Dag Kittlaus named Siri. He's Norwegian.)

In fact, most of the voice commands that work on the iPhone work on the Mac, too.

It's not *Star Trek*. You can't ask Siri to clean your gutters or teach you French. (Well, you can *ask*.) But, as you'll soon discover, the number of things Siri *can* do for you is rather impressive. Furthermore, Apple continues adding to Siri's intelligence through software updates.

How to Use Siri

To use Siri, you have to turn on the master Siri switch. You were offered that chance the first time you started up Catalina; you can also turn Siri on at any time in System Preferences→Siri→Enable Ask Siri.

Anytime thereafter—well, anytime you have an internet connection—you can put her to work for you. To get Siri's attention, you have four choices:

- **Hold down ⌘+space bar** until you hear a quick double-beep. The beep comes in about a second. (You can change this keystroke, if you like, in System Preferences→Siri.)

- **Click the Siri icon** on the menu bar (Figure 7-5, top).

- **Click the Siri icon on the Dock**, or open the Siri app (in your Applications folder) in any of the ways people open apps.

- **Touch the Siri button** on the Touch Bar, if your Mac has one (page 227).

- **Say, "Hey Siri."** You have to set up this feature in advance, as described on the next page.

Once you hear the double-beep and see the little Siri palette (Figure 7-4, bottom left), Siri is listening. Ask your question or say your command. You don't have to lean up against your Mac; Siri works perfectly well at arm's length.

Note: Apple insists that Siri is neither male nor female. In fact, if you ask Siri her gender, she'll say something noncommittal, like, "Is this relevant?" But that's just political correctness. Any baby-name website—or Norwegian dictionary—will tell you that Siri is a girl's name. In any case, you can change what her gender (and accent!) *sounds* like in System Preferences→Siri.

When you're finished speaking, be quiet for a moment. About a second after you stop speaking, Siri connects with her master brain online and processes your request. After a moment, she presents (and speaks) an attractively formatted response.

Tip: You generally see only the most recent question and response on the Siri screen. But you can scroll up to see all the previous exchanges you've had with Siri during this session.

To cancel your request—maybe because you've decided to rephrase your question—press the Esc key (or press ⌘-period), or click the Siri panel to interrupt Siri's work. Click the swirling Siri icon to trigger your new attempt.

And when you're completely finished talking to Siri, you can make her panel slide away off your screen in any of the following ways:

- **Press the Esc key** (or ⌘-period).

- **Click the** ✖ in the upper-left corner.

- **Trigger Siri again** and say something like "Goodbye," "See you later," or "Adios."

Figure 7-5:
Top: To make Siri start listening, you can click the Siri icon on your menu bar (second icon from right) or click the Siri icon on your Dock (third icon from top).

Center left: Siri's listening! Bottom left: Siri's answering!

Bottom right: If you didn't ask the right thing, or if you want to ask it again differently, you can actually edit the text of your original query. (Here you're about to edit the percentage number.) Siri even offers a couple of other interpretations of what you asked.

"Hey Siri"

On the iPhone, of course, Siri can also accept spoken commands without your clicking anything. That's an ideal feature for use in the car, when your hands and eyes should be focused on driving.

On the Mac, Siri responds to "Hey Siri" only if you have a MacBook Pro (2018 or later), a MacBook Air (2018 or later), or an iMac Pro. On those models, open System Preferences→Siri, and turn on "Listen for 'Hey Siri.' "

The screen asks you to speak a few Siri commands ("Hey Siri, what's the weather?" and "Hey Siri, open my downloads," and so on)—and you're ready to go.

It's possible to use hands-free Siri commands even if you have an older Mac, though. See the free PDF appendix "Hey Siri on Older Macs" on this book's "Missing CD" page at *missingmanuals.com*.

Thanks to "Hey Siri," you now have a front-seat conversationalist, a little software friend who's always happy to listen to what you have to say—and whose knowledge of the world, news, sports, and history can help make those Monday mornings a little less dull.

Type to Siri

You can also *type* your questions and commands to Siri instead of speaking them. Every now and then, that silent method could be preferable to the talk-aloud method—when you've got your laptop in a library, for example, or when your query is of a delicate nature.

To set this up, open System Preferences→Accessibility→Siri. Turn on "Enable Type to Siri."

From now on, when you click the Siri button in your menu bar or press the Siri keystroke, you get a Type to Siri box. Click out your query and then hit Return; Siri shows and speaks her response, exactly as though you had spoken.

What to Say to Siri

Siri comes with a cheat sheet to help you learn her capabilities. To see it, open Siri. After five seconds of silence, Siri begins displaying screen after screen of example commands, under the heading "Some things you can ask me."

Or just open Siri and then say, "What can I say?" or "What can you do?" or "Help me!" The same cheat sheet appears.

Here are the general categories of things you can say to Siri:

- **Opening apps.** Even if you don't learn to use Siri for anything else, learn this one.

 You can say, "Open Calendar" or "Play Angry Birds" or "Launch Calculator."

 Result: The corresponding program opens instantly. It's exactly the same as clicking around to navigate to the app you're looking for and then clicking to open it—but without clicking around to navigate to the app you're looking for and then clicking to open it.

Tip: You can also get apps by voice, with commands like "Search the App Store for time tracking" or "Download the Scrabble app."

- **Changing your settings.** You can make changes to certain basic settings just by speaking your request. You can say, for example, "Turn on Bluetooth," "Turn off Wi-Fi," or "Turn on Do Not Disturb."

You can also make screen and speaker adjustments: "Make the screen brighter." "Dim the screen." "Turn on the screen saver." Or volume adjustments: "Make the volume louder." "Mute the sound." "Make the speaker softer."

Result: Siri makes the requested adjustment, tells you so, and displays the corresponding switch in case she misunderstood your intention.

- **Opening System Preferences panels.** When you need to make tweakier changes, you can open the most important panels by voice. "Open Wi-Fi System Preferences," "Open Notification settings," "Open Sounds settings," "Open wallpaper settings," and so on.

Result: Siri silently opens the corresponding page of System Preferences.

- **Questions about your Mac.** "How much free space do I have on my Mac?" "What version of macOS is running?" "What's this Mac's serial number?" "How fast is my Mac?" "Is Bluetooth on?" "How much memory does this Mac have?" "How much iCloud storage do I have left?"

Result: Siri displays the answer.

- **Navigating your Mac.** "Open the Downloads folder." "Open Documents." "Open the Trash."

Result: The Finder folder pops open. This works even for folders you've created yourself.

- **Wrapping up for the day.** "Put the Mac to sleep." "Shut down the Mac."

Result: Your Mac blinks off. Creepy.

- **Finding photos fast.** Siri is especially handy with files you keep in the Photos app. "Show me the videos from Halloween last year." "Get me the videos from Utah." "Show me the Disney World album." "Open the Panoramas presentation." "Show me the slow-mo videos from Oberlin College." "Give me the pictures from last summer."

Apple knows a lot about what's *in* your photos, too. "Show me photos with dogs," you might say. Or, "Show me pictures of Max from last year in San Francisco." Can you imagine how much time that might save you?

Result: The Photos app opens, with the requested photos already isolated and presented to you.

- **Rounding up files.** This is a big one—and a Mac Special (not on the iPhone): You can use Siri to manage files. "Find the documents I worked on last week." "Show me the PDFs in my Downloads folder." "What was I working on yesterday?" "Show me the Microsoft Word documents I worked on two days ago." "Show me the files I shared with Casey yesterday." "Round up all my Photoshop files." "Where are the files tagged In Progress?" "List all the files with the word 'Asparagus.'" "Let's see the files on my desktop." "Get my Vacation folder." "Show me the file I sent Casey."

Siri remembers context, too, so you can then add, "Just the presentations that Bill sent me."

Result: Siri shows you a tidy list of matching files (Figure 7-6). Double-click one to open it, or drag one into any other window or folder. Or right-click a listing and, from the shortcut menu, choose Open, Reveal in Finder, Quick Look, or Copy.

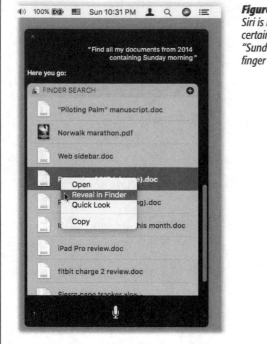

Figure 7-6:
Siri is now the fastest way to get a list of files on your Mac that meet certain criteria—in this example, documents containing the words "Sunday morning" that were created in 2014. Right-click or two-finger click for the shortcut menu shown here.

- **Making FaceTime calls.** Siri can place FaceTime calls for you. "Call Nicole." "Call the office." "Start a FaceTime call with Sheila Withins." "FaceTime Alex."

Result: Siri hands you off to the FaceTime app and places the call. At this point, it's just as though you'd initiated the call yourself. Strangely, Siri can't place *Mac* calls for you, even though the Mac has that capability (see page 304).

- **Clock.** "What time is it?" "What time is it in San Francisco?" "What's today's date?" "What's the date a week from Friday?" Or just "Time."

Result: When you ask about the time, you see the clock app identifying the time in question. (For dates, Siri just talks to you and writes out the date.)

- **Contacts.** You can ask Siri to look up information in your address book (the Contacts app)—and not just addresses. For example, you can say, "What's Gary's work number?" "Give me Sheila Jenkins' office phone." "Show Tia's home email address." "What's Dexter's home address?" "When is my husband's birthday?" "Show Larry Murgatroid." "Who is P.J. Frankenberg?"

Result: A half "page" from your Contacts list. You can click it to jump into that person's full card in Contacts. (If Siri finds multiple listings for the person you named—"Bob," for example—she lists all the matches and asks you to specify which one you meant.)

Tip: In many of the examples on these pages, you'll see that you can identify people by their relationship to you. You can say, "Show my mom's work number," for example, or "Give me directions to my boss's house" or "Call my girlfriend." For details on teaching Siri about these relationships, see "Advanced Siri" on page 298.

- **Email.** Siri can read your email to you. For example, if you say, "Read my latest email" or "Read my new email," Siri reads aloud your most recent email message. (She then offers you the chance to dictate a response.)

 Or you can use the summary-listing commands. When you say, "Read my email," Siri starts walking backward through your Inbox, telling you the subject of each, plus who sent it and when.

 After each listing, Siri asks, "Do you want to hear the next one?" If you say, "Yes," she continues.

 Result: Siri reads aloud.

Tip: You can also use commands like "Any new mail from Chris today?" "Show new mail about the world premiere." "Show yesterday's email from Jan." All of those commands produce a list of the messages, but Siri doesn't read them.

You can also compose a new message by voice; anytime you use the phrase "about," that becomes the subject line for your new message. "Email Mom about the reunion." "Email my boyfriend about the dance on Friday." "New email to Freddie Gershon." "Mail Mom about Saturday's flight." "Email Frank and Cindy Vosshall and Peter Love about the picnic." "Email my assistant and say, 'Thanks for arranging the taxi!'" "Email Gertie and Eugene about their work on the surprise party, and say I really value your friendship."

(If you've indicated only the subject or addressee, Siri prompts you for the rest.)

You can reply to a message Siri has just described, too. "Reply, 'Dear Robin (comma), I'm so sorry about your dog (period). I'll be more careful next time (period).'"

Result: A miniature Mail message, showing you Siri's handiwork before you send it.

- **Calendar.** Siri can make appointments for you. Considering how many tedious clicks it usually takes to schedule an appointment in the Calendar app, this is an enormous improvement. "Make an appointment with Patrick for Thursday at 3 p.m." "Set up a haircut at 9." "Set up a meeting with Charlize this Friday at noon." "Meet Danny Cooper at six." "New appointment with Steve, next Sunday at 7." "Schedule a conference call at 5:30 tonight in my office."

 Result: A slice of that day's calendar appears, filled in the way you requested.

Tip: Siri may also alert you to a conflict, something like this: "Note that you already have an all-day appointment about 'Boston Trip' for this Thursday. Shall I schedule this anyway?" Amazing.

You can also move previously scheduled meetings by voice. For example, "Move my 2:00 meeting to 2:30." "Reschedule my meeting with Charlize to a week from Monday at noon." "Add Frank to my meeting with Harry." "Cancel the conference call on Sunday."

You can even *consult* your calendar by voice. You can say, "What's on my calendar today?" "What does the rest of my day look like?" "What's on my calendar for September 23?" "When's my next appointment?" "When is my meeting with Charlize?" "Where is my next meeting?" "What's my day tomorrow?"

Result: Siri reads you your agenda and displays a tidy Day view of the specified date.

- **Text messages.** "Send a text to Alex Rybeck." "Send a message to Peter saying, 'I no longer require your services.'" "Tell Cindy I'm running late." "Send a message to Jane's mobile asking her to pick me up at the train." "Send a text message to 212-561-2282." "Text Frank and Ralph: Did you pick up the pizza?"

Result: Siri prompts you for the body of the message, if you haven't specified it. Then you see a miniature outgoing text message. Siri asks if you want to send it; say "Yes," "Send," or "Confirm" to proceed. (See Figure 7-7, left.)

If you need to edit the message before sending it, you can say, "Change it to" to re-dictate the message; "Add" to add more to the message; "No, send it to Frank"

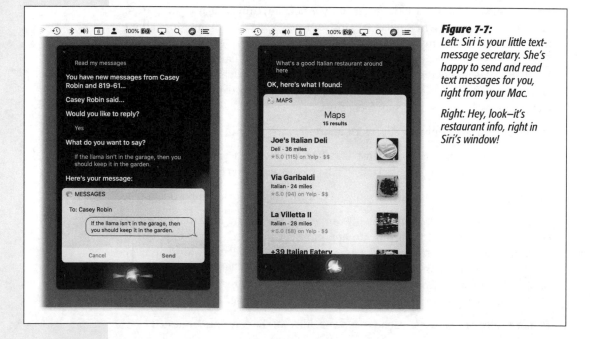

Figure 7-7:
Left: Siri is your little text-message secretary. She's happy to send and read text messages for you, right from your Mac.

Right: Hey, look—it's restaurant info, right in Siri's window!

to change the recipient; "No" to leave the message on the screen without sending it; or "Cancel" to forget the whole thing.

You can also ask Siri to read incoming text messages to you. For example, you can say, "Read my new messages," "Read that again," or "Read my last message from Tia."

You can even have Siri reply to messages she's just read to you. "Reply, 'Congratulations (period). Can't wait to see your trophy (exclamation point)!' " Or: "Tell him I have a flat tire and I'm going to be late."

- **Restaurants.** Siri is also happy to serve as your personal concierge. Try "Good Italian restaurants around here," "Find a good pizza joint in Cleveland," or "Show me the reviews for Olive Garden in Youngstown." (See Figure 7-7, right.) On the Mac, Siri can't book reservations through OpenTable, as she can on the iPhone.

Result: Siri displays a list of matching restaurants—with ratings, distance, prices, and so on. Click a name for more information.

- **Notes.** You create a new note (in the Notes app) by saying things like, "Make a note that my shirt size is 15 and a half" or "Note: Dad will not be coming to the reunion after all." You can even name the note in your request: "Create a 'Movies to Download' note."

But you can also call up a certain note to the screen, like this: "Find my frequent-flyer note." You can even summon a table-of-contents view of all your notes by saying, "Show all my notes."

Result: A miniature Notes page appears, showing your newly dictated text (or the existing note that you've requested).

Tip: You can keep dictating into the note you've just added. Say, "Add 'Return books to library' " (or just say, "Add," and Siri will ask you what to add). She'll keep adding to the same note until you say, "Note that…" or "Start a note" or "Take a note" to begin a fresh note page.

You can add text to an earlier note: "Add *Titanic II: The Voyage Home* to my 'Movies to Download' note." (The first line of any note is also its title—in this case "Movies to Download.")

- **Directions.** Siri can set up the Maps app to answer requests like these: "How do I get to the airport?" "Show me 1500 Broadway, New York City." "Directions to my assistant's house." "Take me home." You just have to make sure Siri can access Location Services; you can do that in the System Preferences→Security & Privacy→Privacy. But, if you don't, Siri will just direct you there the first time you ask for directions. You can ask for directions to the home or work address of anyone in your Contacts list—provided those addresses are *in* your Contacts cards.

Result: Siri fires up the Maps app, with the start and end points of your driving directions already filled in.

- **Reminders.** Siri is a natural match for the Reminders app. She can add items to that list at your spoken command. For example: "Remind me to file my IRS tax

extension." "Remind me to bring the science supplies to school." "Remind me to take my antibiotic tomorrow at 7 a.m."

If you also have an iPhone, the *location-based* reminders are especially amazing. They rely on the phone's GPS to know where you are. So, on the Mac, you can say, "Remind me to visit the drugstore when I leave the office," or "Remind me to water the lawn when I get home," or "Remind me to check in with Nancy when I leave here." Since iCloud magically syncs all of your reminders across devices, the *phone* will pop up a reminder when you reach, or leave, the specified locations.

Result: A miniature entry from the Reminders app, showing you that Siri has understood.

- **Businesses.** Siri is a walking (well, all right, non-walking) Yellow Pages. Go ahead, try it: "Find coffee near me." "Where's the closest Walmart?" "Find some pizza places in Cincinnati." "Search for gas stations." "French restaurants nearby." "I'm in the mood for Chinese food." "Find me a hospital."

Result: Siri displays a handsome list of businesses nearby that match your request.

Tip: She's a sly dog, that Siri. She'll help you out even if your requests are, ahem, somewhat off the straight and narrow. If you say, "I think I'm drunk," she'll offer a "Call me a taxi" button, which produces a list of cab companies. If you indicate that you're craving relief from your drug addiction, she'll provide you with a list of rehab centers.

- **Passwords.** Siri can look up passwords for you. That's a godsend when you're trying to log into a website on a new Mac. "What's my Hulu password?" "Look up my Netflix password." "I need my Citibank password."

Result: The Mac requests proof that you're you—your Mac password or Touch ID—and then displays the Passwords screen in Safari. Super cool. (If you have several passwords for the same item, click the one you mean.)

- **Playing music and podcasts.** Instead of fumbling around in Music, save yourself steps and time by speaking the name of the album, song, or band you want to hear: "Play some Beatles." "Play 'I'm a Barbie Girl.'" "Play some jazz." "Play my jogging playlist." "Play the party mix." "Shuffle my 'Dave's Faves' playlist." "Play." "Skip."

And, of course, podcasts work the same way. "Play podcasts." "Jump back 15 seconds." "Skip ahead two minutes." "Find the 'Undisclosed' podcast in the Podcasts app."

Result: Siri plays (or skips, or shuffles) the music or podcast you asked for—without ever leaving whatever app you were using.

- **Apple Music.** If you subscribe to Apple's $10-a-month Apple Music service, Siri offers a huge range of even more useful voice controls. For example, you can call for any music in Apple's 30 million–song catalog by song name, album, or performer: "Play 'Mr. Blue Sky.'" "Show me some Elton John albums." "Play 'Yesterday' next"

(or "…after this song"). Or ask to have a singer or album played in random order: "Shuffle Taylor Swift."

When you hear a song you like, you can say, "Play more like this." Or "Add this song [or album] to my library." (Or, if you don't like it, "Skip this song.")

If more than one person performed a song, be specific: "Play 'Smooth Criminal' by *Glee*." You can even ask for a song according to the movie it was in. "Play that song from *Frozen*."

Or start one of your playlists by name ("Play 'Jogging' "). Or re-listen to a song: "Play previous." Or ask for one of Apple Music's radio stations: "Play Beats 1" or "Play Charting Now."

While music is playing, Siri's happy to tell you what you're listening to. ("What song is this?" "Who's the singer?" "What album is this from?") You can also tell her, "Like this song" or "Rate this song five stars." She'll note that and offer you more songs like it on the For You screen of the Apple Music app.

You can ask her to play the top hits of any year or decade. ("Play the top song from 1990." "Play the top 35 songs of the 1960s.")

Result: Just what you asked for!

- **Identifying music.** Whenever the Mac is playing music, you can say things like, "What's that song?" or "What song is this?"

Result: Siri identifies whatever song the Mac is playing—song name, singer, album, and so on. At this point, you can (shocker!) say, "Buy this song" or "Add this song to my wish list."

- **Weather.** "What's the weather going to be today?" "What's the forecast for tomorrow?" "Show me the weather this week." "Will it snow in Dallas this weekend?" "Check the forecast for Memphis on Friday." "What's the forecast for tonight?" "Can you give me the wind speed in Kansas City?" "Tell me the windchill in Anchorage." "What's the humidity right now?" "How's the weather in Paris?" "What's the high for Washington on Friday?" "When will Jupiter rise tomorrow?" "When's the moonrise?" "How cold will it be in Houston tomorrow?" "What's the temperature outside?" "Is it windy out there?" "When does the sun rise in London?" "When will the sun set today?" "Should I wear a jacket?"

Result: A miniature Weather display for the date and place you specified.

- **Stocks.** "What's Google's stock price?" "What did Ford close at today?" "How's the Dow doing?" "What's Microsoft's P/E ratio?" "What's Amazon's average volume?" "How are the markets doing?"

Result: A tidy little stock graph, bearing a wealth of up-to-date statistics.

- **Sports.** At last you have a buddy who's just as obsessed with sports trivia as you are (Figure 7-8, left). You can say things like, "How did the Indians do last night?" "What

was the score of the last Yankees game?" "When's the next Cowboys game?" "What baseball games are on today?"

You can also ask questions about individual players, like, "Who has the best batting average?" "Who has scored the most runs against the Red Sox?" "Who has scored the most goals in British soccer?"

Team stats are fair game, too, like, "Show me the roster for the Giants," "Who is pitching for Tampa this season?" and "Is anyone on the Marlins injured right now?"

Apple has, somewhat mystifyingly, put some extra work into Siri's motor-sport answers: current standings, schedules, and stats.

Result: Neat little box scores or factoids, complete with team logos.

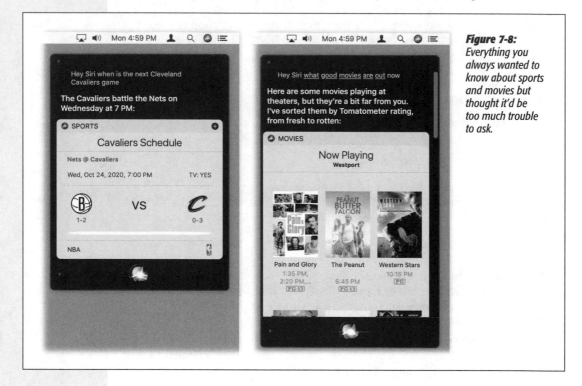

Figure 7-8:
Everything you always wanted to know about sports and movies but thought it'd be too much trouble to ask.

- **Searching the web.** "Search the web for a 2016 Ford Mustang." "Search for healthy smoothie recipes." "Search for news about the Netflix-Amazon merger." "Search the web for pictures of cows."

Tip: Siri uses Google to perform its web searches. If you prefer Bing, just say so. Say, "Bing Benjamin Franklin." (For that matter, you can also ask Siri to "Yahoo" something—for example, "Yahoo low-cal dessert recipes.")

Result: Siri displays the results of your search right on her own screen. Click one of the results to open the corresponding web page in Safari.

- **Facts and figures.** This is a huge category. It represents Siri's partnership with the Wolfram Alpha factual search engine (*wolframalpha.com*). The possibilities here could fill an entire chapter—or an entire encyclopedia.

 You can ask things like, "How many days until Valentine's Day?" "When was Abraham Lincoln born?" "How many teaspoons are in a gallon?" "What's the exchange rate between dollars and euros?" "What's the capital of Belgium?" "How many calories are in a Snickers bar?" "What's a 17 percent tip on 62 dollars for three people?" "What movie won the Oscar for Best Picture in 1985?" "When is the next solar eclipse?" "What's the tallest mountain in the world?" "What's the definition of 'schadenfreude'?" "How much is 23 dollars in pesos?" "Generate a random number." "Graph x equals 3y plus 12." "What flights are overhead?"

 Siri offers great answers about celebrities ("Where was Jennifer Lawrence born?") and food and nutrition ("How much caffeine is in a cup of coffee?" or "How much fat is in an apple?")

 Result: For simple math and conversions, Siri just shows you the answer. For more complex questions, you get a specially formatted table, ripped right out of Wolfram Alpha's knowledge base.

Tip: Siri can also harness the wisdom of Wikipedia. You can say, for example, "Search Wikipedia for Harold Edgerton," or "Tell me about Thomas Jefferson," or "Show me the Wikipedia page about Richard Branson."

- **Movies.** Siri is also the virtual equivalent of an insufferable film buff. She knows *everything*. "Who was the star of *Groundhog Day*?" "Who directed *Chinatown*?" "What is *Waterworld* rated?" "What movie won Best Picture in 1952?"

 It's not just about old movies, either. Siri knows everything about current showtimes in theaters (Figure 7-8, right). "What movies are opening this week?" "What's playing at the Watton Cineplex?" "Give me the reviews for *A Dog's Journey*." "What are today's showtimes for *The Rise of Skywalker*?"

 Result: Tidy tables of movie theaters or movie showtimes. (Click one for details.) Sometimes you get a movie poster filled with facts and a link to watch the trailer.

You may never find the end of the things Siri understands or the ways she can help you. If her repertoire seems intimidating at first, start simple—use her to open apps, find files, send text messages, and take notes. You can build up your bag of tricks as your confidence builds.

When Things Go Wrong

If Siri doesn't have a good enough internet connection to do her thing, she'll tell you so.

If she's working properly but misrecognizes your instructions, you'll know it, because you can see her interpretation of what you said. You can click Siri's interpretation to make corrections by typing.

Tip: You can also correct a misheard command just by speaking the correct version, like this, "I meant Chicago." Siri gets what you mean.

If Siri recognizes what you said but it isn't within her world of comprehension, she offers you a "Search the web" button as a last resort.

Siri's Personality

Siri's understanding of casual spoken commands is so impressive that you might sometimes think she's almost human. And that, of course, is exactly what Apple wants you to think. You can say all kinds of off-kilter things to Siri. Whoever programmed her had a sassy sense of humor.

For example, if you ask her, "What is the meaning of life?" she responds with one of more than a dozen different answers. She might say, "I can't answer that now, but give me some time to write a very long play in which nothing happens." Or: "It's nothing Nietzsche couldn't teach ya." Or: "All evidence to date suggests it's chocolate."

Siri is full of such comebacks, and there are whole websites dedicated to her snark. Here are a few examples. (This list won't ruin the fun, because Siri actually has several different comebacks to most of these questions.)

You: "Who's your daddy?" Siri: "You are. Can we get back to work now?"

You: "Open the pod bay doors, Hal." Siri: "I'm sorry, I'm afraid I can't do that." (Then: "Are you happy now?")

You: "Knock knock." Siri: "Knock knock." You: "Who's there?" Siri: "Joshua." You: "Joshua who?" Siri: "Joshua, I don't do knock-knock jokes."

You: "What are you wearing?" Siri: "You have the wrong personal assistant, Casey."

You: "Who's the boss?" (Siri presents the vital statistics of Bruce Springsteen.)

You: "Beam me up, Siri!" Siri: "Please remove your belt, shoes, and jacket, and empty your pockets."

You: "Show me the money." Siri: "I've found 23 ATMs that are fairly close to you…"

You: "How much wood would a woodchuck chuck if a woodchuck could chuck wood?" Siri: "42 cords of wood, to be exact. Everyone knows that."

You: "Why did the chicken cross the road?" Siri: "I am not perspicacious about the peregrinations of poultry."

You: "Klaatu barada nikto." Siri: "OK, I'll pass the message on to Gort." (You kind of have to know *The Day the Earth Stood Still* to get it.)

You: "Do you have a boyfriend?" Siri: "Why? So we can get ice cream together, and listen to music, and travel across galaxies, only to have it end in slammed doors, heartbreak, and loneliness? Sure, where do I sign up?"

Tip: You may notice that Siri addresses you by name in her *typed* answers, but she doesn't always speak it when she reads those answers out loud.

Ordinarily, she calls you whatever you're called in Contacts. But you can make her call you whatever you like. Say, "Call me Master" or "Call me Frank" or "Call me Ishmael." If you confirm when she asks, then from now on that's what Siri will call you in her typed responses.

Here are a few other things to say to Siri when you get bored:

What does "Siri" mean?

Am I your best friend?

What should I wear for Halloween?

Testing 1, 2, 3.

I'm tired.

What's your secret?

What's your sign?

What do you think of Windows?

You don't understand me.

I'm sorry.

Supercalifragilisticexpialidocious.

Who's on first?

Why are you so awesome?

What's your favorite color?

Where are you?

When is the world going to end?

What's the best computer?

How much do you cost?

What are you doing later?

This statement is false.

Do you believe in Santa Claus?

I don't like your voice.

Blah blah blah.

Are you serious?

You are good to me.

What are the three laws of robotics?

Read me a haiku.

LOL.

Take me to your leader.

Can you sing?

You make me so mad!

What do you want?

Can I borrow some money?

Tell me a joke.

Tell me a story.

I'm cold.

What are you doing?

Beatbox.

Guess what?

You're an idiot.

Have a nice day.

What will be the lottery numbers tomorrow?

I'm cold.

When is your birthday?

What do you want?

What's the best Mac?

What's your favorite song?

Where did I put my keys?

Give me some advice

Can I call you Alexa?

What did you do yesterday?

What is 0 divided by 0?

How do I look?

Who are you voting for?

How many licks does it take to get to the center of a Tootsie Pop?

Pick a card.

Are you smart?

When will hell freeze over?

What to Do with Siri's Results

When you've asked a question about stocks or weather, a ⬚ button appears at the top right of the Siri results panel. If you click it, the Siri result gets pinned to the top of your Today pane (page 377), so you can look at it again later without having to repeat the whole Siri query.

Advanced Siri

With a little setup, you can extend Siri's powers in some intriguing ways.

Teach Siri About Your Relationships

When you say, "Text my mother" or "Call my manager," how does Siri know whom you're talking about? Sure, Siri is powerful artificial intelligence, but she's not actually *magic*. Turns out you teach her by referring to somebody in your Contacts list. Say to her something like, "My assistant is Casey Carpenter" or "Tad Cooper is my boyfriend." When Siri asks for confirmation, say "Yes" or click Confirm.

Or wait for Siri to ask you herself. If you say, "Email my dad," Siri asks, "Who is your dad?" Just say his name; Siri remembers that relationship from now on. (You can add relationships like mother, father, parent, brother, sister, son, daughter, child, friend, spouse, partner, assistant, manager, wife, husband, fiancé, and boss.)

Behind the scenes, Siri lists these relationships on your card in Contacts.

Now that you know that, you can figure out how to edit or delete these relationships. Which is handy—not all relationships, as we know, last forever.

Fix Siri's Name Comprehension

Siri easily understands common names—but if someone in your family, work, or social circle has an unusual name, you may quickly become frustrated. After all, you can't text, call, email, or get directions to someone's house unless Siri understands the person's name when you say it.

One workaround is to use a relationship, as described earlier. That way, you can say, "Call my brother" instead of "Call Ilyich" (or whatever his uncommon name is).

Another is to use Siri's pronunciation-learning feature. It kicks in in several different situations:

- **When you're texting.** If Siri offers the wrong person's name when you try to text someone by voice, say, "Someone else." After you've sent the message, Siri apologetically says, "By the way, sorry I didn't recognize that name. Can you teach me how to say it?"

- **After Siri botches a pronunciation.** Tell her, "That's not how to pronounce his name."

- **Whenever it occurs to you.** You can start the process by saying, "Learn to pronounce Reagann Tsuki's name" or "Learn to pronounce my mom's name."

In each case, with tremendous courtesy, Siri walks you through the process of teaching her the correct pronunciation. She offers you three ▶ buttons; each triggers a different pronunciation. Click Select next to the correct one (or click Tell Siri again if none of the three is correct).

By the end of the process, Siri knows two things: how to speak that person's name aloud and how to recognize that name when *you* say it aloud.

Siri Settings

In System Preferences→Siri, you can fiddle with several Siri settings (Figure 7-9):

- **Listen for "Hey Siri."** This option, available only on the most powerful and recent Macs, is described on page 285.

- **Allow Siri when locked.** If your Mac works with "Hey Siri," you can even ask questions at the password screen, as though it were some kind of Apple-branded Amazon Alexa machine. ("Hey Siri" does not work when the Mac is asleep, though. If the screen is totally dark, you'll first have to slap the space bar to wake it to the Lock screen.)

- **Enable Ask Siri.** If you turn this off, you can no longer command your Mac using the Siri commands described in this chapter.

- **Keyboard Shortcut.** How would you like to make Siri start listening? This pop-up menu starts you off with a key combo to hold down (⌘-space bar), but you can also choose Customize and enter any key combination you like. Of course, it has to be one that's not already "taken" by the Mac, which can be tricky.

- **Language.** What language do you want Siri to speak and recognize? The options here include dozens of languages and dialects.

Figure 7-9:
Why would anyone turn off Siri? One reason: Siri involves transmitting data to Apple, which gives some people the privacy willies. Apple collects everything you say to Siri, the names of your songs and playlists, and the names in your Contacts (so that Siri can recognize them when you refer to them).

Siri

Siri helps you get things done, just by asking. Find files on your Mac, dictate a note, check the weather, and more.

☑ Listen for "Hey Siri"
☑ Allow Siri when locked

Keyboard Shortcut: Hold Command Space

Language: English (United States)

Siri Voice: American (Female)

Voice Feedback: ● On ○ Off

Siri History: Delete Siri & Dictation History

Siri

☑ Enable Ask Siri

☑ Show Siri in menu bar Siri Suggestions & Privacy... ?

- **Siri Voice.** Siri can have either a man's voice or a woman's voice—and she can speak in a selection of accents. Even if you're from Iowa, it's fun to give Siri a cute Australian, South African, Irish, Indian, or British accent.

- **Voice Feedback.** Siri generally replies to your queries with both text and a synthesized voice. Here you can tell Siri not to bother speaking when you're looking at the screen and can read the responses for yourself.

- **Siri History.** Here you can click "Delete Siri & Dictation History," which trashes all interactions associated with your Mac from Apple's servers.

- **Show Siri in menu bar.** Ordinarily, Siri's colorful little icon is at the top right of your screen—a handy clickable way to make her listen. But if you've mastered a keystroke, there's no reason to have that icon cluttering up your menu bar.

- **Siri Suggestions & Privacy.** In Apple's mind, Siri isn't just a voice assistant. "Siri" refers to all kinds of artificial-intelligence features scattered across the Mac. In Mail, for example, when you start typing an address, you may see some suggested addresses under the heading "Siri Found in Apps." You might even see a gray proposed appointment in Calendar that you didn't put there. Siri found it in a Mail message (a flight confirmation, for example) and thinks she's helping you save steps.

 You can make those suggestions stop appearing. There's a clearly labeled checkbox in the Preferences for each of those apps (Mail, Contacts, Calendar, and so on). On this screen, though, you can choose which apps supply those suggestions *to* Mail, Contacts, Calendar, and so on.

The Mac Reads to You

Most Apple programs have a Start Speaking command built right in: Safari, Mail, TextEdit, Stickies, Pages, and so on. Just right-click or two-finger click inside a window full of text and, from the pop-up menu, choose Speech→Start Speaking. How cool is that? Your Mac can read your email or a web article to you—in any of 41 languages—while you're getting dressed.

But that's kid stuff. Truth is, the Mac can read almost anything you like: text you pass your cursor over, alert messages, menus, and *any text document in any program*. It

GEM IN THE ROUGH

Voices to Sing About

The Mac's built-in speaking voices are no end of fun, as noted in Figure 7-10.

Five of the voices, in fact, *sing* rather than speak. Good News sings to the tune of "Pomp and Circumstance," otherwise known as the Graduation March. Bad News sings to the tune of Chopin's *Prelude in C minor,* better known as the

Funeral March. Cellos sings to the tune of Grieg's *Peer Gynt* suite. Pipe Organ sings to the tune of the Alfred Hitchcock TV theme. Bells sings the typical church-bell carillon melody.

In other words, these voices sing whatever words you type to those melodies. (To hear the melody in its entirety, don't use any punctuation.)

can speak in your choice of dozens of voices, ages 8 to 50. Some of the voices (like Alex, Samantha, and Tom) sound scarily like professional human voice-over artists.

Note: This text-reading business is not the same thing as the Mac's VoiceOver feature, which reads *everything* on the screen, including pop-up menus, buttons, and other controls. Details are on page 321.

Setting Up the Mac's Voice

Open System Preferences→Accessibility→Speech tab. Here you can control which of the Mac's voices you want your computer to use, as well as how fast it should speak. As shown in Figure 7-10, though, the Mac comes with a huge range of additional voices that you can add to the pop-up menu here.

Tip: Don't ignore the "international" voices just because you're an American English speaker. There are also voices that speak English with British, South African, Irish, and Australian accents—always fun.

All those voices have to be downloaded, so you can't grab them without an internet connection. They're huge files, so don't be impatient. (They're stored in your System→Library→Speech→Voices folder.)

Here are all the different occasions when the Mac can talk to you.

Figure 7-10:
Top: At the outset, you see only five voices.

Bottom: Choose Customize to see the complete list of voices (including dozens of international voices); turn on the ones you want the Mac to download. Then, for 15 minutes of hilarity, try clicking the voices in turn to hear sample sentences. Drag the slider to affect how fast each one speaks. (Clearly, Apple's programmers had some fun with this assignment.)

Announce when alerts are displayed or applications need your attention

This checkbox makes the Mac read aloud error messages and alert messages that may appear on your screen. If you then click Options, you'll find these useful controls:

- **Voice.** Choose the voice you want reading your error messages. (It doesn't have to be the same as the standard Mac voice that's used for other purposes.)

- **Phrase.** Choose which utterance the Mac speaks before the actual error message—for example, "*Excuse me!* The Trash could not be emptied," or "*Attention!* The document could not be printed."

 If you choose "Next in the phrase list" or "Random from the phrase list," you'll never hear the same expletive twice in a row. Better yet, choose Edit Phrase List to specify your own words of frustration. (Apple Inc. is not liable for any trouble you may get into with people in neighboring cubicles.)

- **Delay.** The ostensible purpose of the Talking Alerts feature is to get your attention if you've wandered away from your Mac—mentally or physically. If you're still sitting there, you may not need the Mac to speak to get your attention; you could simply read the onscreen message. That's why you can set this slider to make the Mac wait, after the error message appears, for up to a minute before trying to flag you with its voice. That way it won't harangue you unnecessarily.

Speak selected text when the key is pressed

As promised, this is the feature that makes the Mac read you any web page, any email message, any sticky note—a welcome break for sore eyes.

The very first time you turn on this checkbox, the Mac offers you the default keystroke, Option-Esc. (You can always change the keystroke by clicking Change Key.)

Now go to the program where you'd like the reading to happen. Highlight some text (or press ⌘-A to select all of it). Then press Option-Esc or the keystroke you specified. The Mac begins reading it aloud immediately. To interrupt the playback, press the same keystroke again.

And be glad you were alive to see the day.

Speak items under the pointer

The Mac can speak the names of items under your cursor, either all the time or only when you use zoom. Using the slider in this window, you can decide whether to have your Mac wait a shorter or longer time before speaking.

Continuity: Mac + iPhone

A pple products have always been designed to work together. Macs, phones, tablets, watches: similar software, design, wording, philosophy. That's nice for you, of course, because you have less to learn and less to troubleshoot. But it's also nice for Apple, because it keeps you in velvet handcuffs; pretty soon, you've got too much invested in its product "ecosystem" to consider wandering over to a rival.

Now, Apple has taken this gadget symbiosis to an astonishing extreme. Your iPhone can be an *accessory* to your Mac. Suddenly the Mac can be a speakerphone, using the iPhone as a wireless antenna. Suddenly the Mac can send and receive regular text messages. Suddenly AirDrop lets you drag files back and forth, wirelessly, from phone to computer. Suddenly a Mac laptop can get onto the internet with one click, even miles from home. And you can even copy and paste between your phone and Mac, or take a picture with the iPhone that appears instantly on your Mac.

Apple's name for this suite of symbiosis is "Continuity." These are the primary rules:

- **You need a Mac running Yosemite or later and an iPhone running iOS 8.1 or later.** (The copy/paste thing requires Sierra or later and iOS 10 or later on the phone. The "take a picture with the iPhone" thing requires at least Mojave and iOS 12.)

- **The Mac and the phone have to be signed into the same iCloud account.** That's a security thing—it proves you're the owner of both machines, and therefore unlikely to pose a risk to yourself. On the Mac, you do that in System Preferences→iCloud. On the phone, you do that in Settings→iCloud, but also make sure you've entered the same iCloud address in Settings→Messages and Settings→FaceTime.

- **Both gadgets must have Wi-Fi and Bluetooth turned on.** The modern Bluetooth— called Bluetooth LE, or low energy—doesn't drain your battery the way it once

did, so it's fine to leave it on. But older Macs don't have Bluetooth LE, so most Continuity features work only on 2012 and later models.

All right. Setup ready? Time to experience some integration!

Mac as Speakerphone

You can now make and take phone calls on your Mac. The iPhone, sitting anywhere in your house, can be the cellular module for your Mac—even if that iPhone is asleep and locked.

When a call comes in to your iPhone's number, your *Mac* plays whatever ringtone your phone is playing. And a notice appears on your Mac's screen (Figure 8-1).

Tip: If your Mac has a Touch Bar (page 227), you get buttons on it that let you Accept or Decline the call.

Figure 8-1:
When a call comes in to your iPhone, a notification appears on your Mac (top). You can click to answer it (or decline it); your Mac's microphone and speaker become your speakerphone (bottom).

You can *place* a call the same way: Just click any phone number you find on the Mac: in Contacts, Safari, an email message, and so on (Figure 8-2).

After that—it just works. Even call-waiting works—if a second call comes in, your Mac notifies you and offers you the chance to put the first one on hold. And on the Mac, the Contacts app now offers Ringtone and Texttone menus, so you can assign custom sounds that play when your *Mac* rings. Crazy.

Tip: You may soon discover that there's no dialing pad on the Mac, so there's no easy way to dial a number that's not already in Contacts. The workaround: Create a temporary fake person in Contacts!

And If It's Not Working

"It just works" is fantastic—when it just works.

If your Mac isn't able to send and receive calls and texts through your phone, here's the checklist. One of these things, you'll discover, isn't set correctly:

- **The iPhone and Mac have to be on the same network** (for example, the same Wi-Fi network).

Note: There's one exception to that requirement, in the form of a feature called Continuity over Cellular. It lets you take calls on your Mac or iPad over the *cellular* network, even if your iPhone is somewhere else in the world! Yes, you can now make calls or send texts from your Mac, even if you left your phone at the office or at your buddy's house. Not all carriers offer it, though; only T-Mobile and AT&T are confirmed.

- **On the phone, open Settings→FaceTime.** Make sure FaceTime, too, is signed into that same iCloud account. Turn on iPhone Cellular Calls.

- **On the phone, open Settings→General→Handoff.** Make sure Handoff is turned on.

- **On the Mac, open System Preferences→General.** Confirm that "Allow Handoff between this Mac and your iCloud devices" is turned on.

- **On the Mac, open the FaceTime program.** Choose FaceTime→Preferences. Confirm that, once again, you're signed in with the same iCloud account, that your phone number's checkbox is turned on, and that "Calls from iPhone" is turned on.

Figure 8-2:
To make Mac dialing work, the iPhone and Mac must be on the same Wi-Fi network. They both have to be signed into the same iCloud account. And you have to open the FaceTime settings on each device and make sure they're both set to use the same iCloud account.

Texting from the Mac

You can send and receive text messages (and picture, audio, and video messages) on your Mac, too. We're not talking about sending texts to other *Apple* people (with iCloud accounts). Those are called iMessages, and they're a special, Apple-only kind

of message. We're talking about something much better: You can type *any* cellphone number and send a regular SMS text message to *anyone*. Or receive them when they're sent to your iPhone number.

Or you can initiate the text conversation by clicking a phone number in Contacts, Calendar, or Safari to send an SMS message. Once again, your iPhone acts as a relay station between the cellular world and your Mac. Here's how to set it up:

1. **On the iPhone, open Settings→Messages. Tap Text Message Forwarding.**

 Your Mac's name appears. Turn on the switch.

2. **Now, on the Mac, open Messages.**

 (If all is going well, its icon is probably popping out of your Dock at this moment, trying to get your attention.) When you open Messages, a code appears. You're supposed to type into the corresponding box on your phone. (This proves, really and truly, that you're the owner of both devices. You wouldn't want some bad guy reading your text messages, would you?)

This same code appears right now on any iPad or iPod Touch you own. They, too, will be able to send and receive texts, with your iPhone doing the relaying.

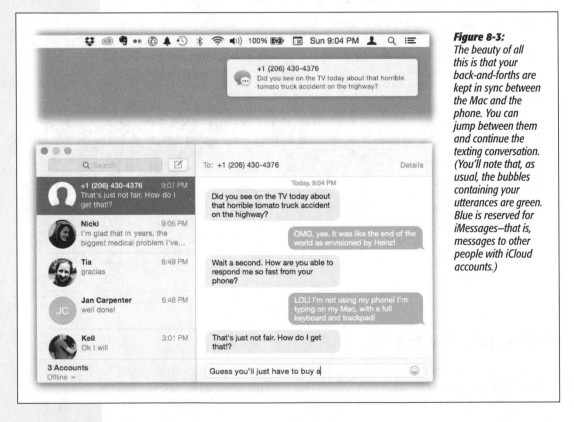

Figure 8-3:
The beauty of all this is that your back-and-forths are kept in sync between the Mac and the phone. You can jump between them and continue the texting conversation. (You'll note that, as usual, the bubbles containing your utterances are green. Blue is reserved for iMessages—that is, messages to other people with iCloud accounts.)

That's it—your gadgets are paired. You can now use Messages to send standard text messages to *any* cellphone. You can also click and hold on a phone number wherever it appears—in Contacts, in a Spotlight search result, in Safari, in Mail—and choose Send Message from there. And when a text message comes in, a standard Mac notification bubble appears at top right (Figure 8-3).

Instant Hotspot

Paying your cell carrier another few bucks every month entitles you to use the iPhone's Personal Hotspot feature. That's where the phone itself acts as a portable Wi-Fi hotspot, so that your laptop (or any other gadgets) can get online almost anywhere.

It used to be kind of a pain to get going. Each time you wanted your laptop to get online, you had to wake your iPhone, unlock it, open Settings, and turn on Personal Hotspot. Then you had to wait about 20 seconds, until the phone's name showed up in your 🛜 menu.

Not anymore.

Now the phone can stay in your pocket. Its name appears in your 🛜 menu, ready for choosing at any time—even if the phone is asleep and locked, and even if Personal Hotspot is turned off! Handily enough, the 🛜 menu also shows the phone's battery and signal status. (As noted in Figure 8-4, things are even easier if the phone's running iOS 13.1 or later.)

Figure 8-4:
Here's how you choose your iPhone's hotspot manually.

Of course, if your iPhone runs iOS 13.1 or later, your Mac invites you to join the phone's hotspot whenever there's no Wi-Fi available. It then stays connected to the hotspot all the time—even when the Mac is asleep, so it can keep getting notifications. Beware—that setup can drain your iPhone's battery in under two hours.

As usual, this works only if the iPhone and Mac both have Bluetooth turned on and are signed into the same iCloud account.

AirDrop

AirDrop is pretty great. It lets you send photos, videos, maps, Contacts cards, PDF files, Word documents—and all kinds of other stuff—from one Apple product to another.

Wirelessly. Without having to set up names, passwords, or permissions. Without even having an internet connection.

Now, the process of using AirDrop from your *Mac* is described on page 528. Below are the instructions for using AirDrop from your *phone*.

To get started, open whatever it is you want to send: a photo, map, website, contact… anything with a ⬆ button.

When you tap ⬆, you see the AirDrop panel—and, after a moment, the icons of any nearby Yosemite or later Macs, iPhones, and iPads show up, too. Including yours (Figure 8-5, top).

If the Mac's icon *doesn't* show up, it's probably because its owner hasn't made the Mac discoverable by AirDrop.

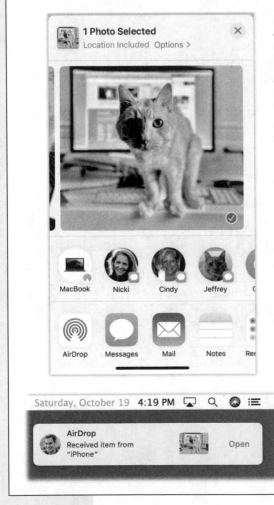

Figure 8-5:
AirDrop goes both ways: from iPhone to Mac (shown here), or Mac to iPhone. Actually, it goes many more ways than that, because the iPad and iPod Touch can do it, too.

A typical transaction works like this: You choose some photos on the phone and then tap the icon representing the nearby Mac/iPhone/iPad/iPod Touch you're sending it to (top).

Bottom: On the receiving device (in this case, a Mac), a notification pops up to let you know files are incoming.

Instruct him to open the AirDrop *window* on his Mac. (Click AirDrop in the Sidebar of any Finder window.) See the small blue control at the bottom? It governs who can "see" this Mac for AirDrop purposes: No One, Contacts Only (that is, people in the Mac's address book), or Everyone.

Once that's set up right, that Mac shows up in the iPhone's AirDrop panel ("MacBook" in Figure 8-5). Send away.

The receiving Mac displays a note like the one shown at bottom in Figure 8-5. Click Accept (to download the incoming item to your Mac's Downloads folder) or Decline (to reject it).

Tip: If the phone and the Mac are both signed into the same iCloud account, you don't encounter that Accept/Decline thing. The file goes directly into your Downloads folder without asking. You do get a notification on the Mac that lets you know how many files arrived, and it offers an Open button (Figure 8-5, bottom).

Apple figures that, since you own both the phone and the Mac, the usual permission routine isn't necessary. You're probably not trying to send yourself some evil virus of death.

For more on AirDrop, see page 528.

Handoff

Handoff is a feature that passes half-finished documents between the phone and the Mac, wirelessly and automatically. Figure 8-6 shows how it works.

It doesn't have to be an email message, either. If you were reading a web page or a map on your phone, then that icon on the Mac opens the same web page or map. If you were working on an entry in Calendar, Contacts, Maps, Mail, Reminders, Safari, Pages, Numbers, or Keynote, you can open the same in-progress item on the Mac. (Some non-Apple apps do the Handoff thing now, too, including Pocket, Wunderlist, and NYTimes.)

Here's the setup: Once again, both gadgets must be signed into your iCloud account. Both must have Bluetooth turned on, and the Mac and phone have to be sitting within Bluetooth range of each other (about 30 feet).

On the Mac, open System Preferences→General; turn on "Allow Handoff between this Mac and your iCloud devices."

On the iPhone, the on/off switch is in Settings→General→Handoff.

Now try it out. Start an email message on your iPhone. Have a look at the Dock on your Mac: There, at the left end, pops up the little icon of whatever program can finish the job.

Watch for the little lower-left icon on your screens to make it work.

And all of it works in the other direction, too. If you're working on something on the Mac, but you're called away, an icon appears on the lower-left corner of your iPhone's app switcher that opens the same item (Figure 8-6, bottom).

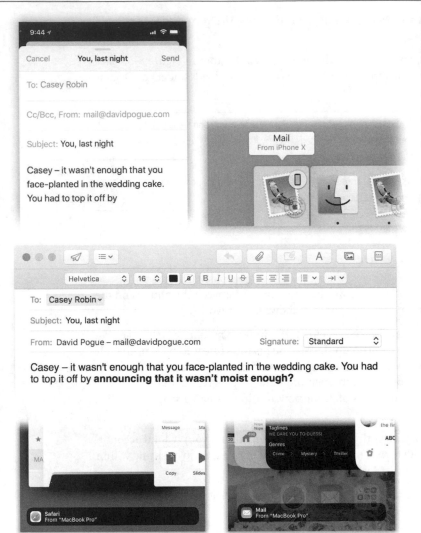

Figure 8-6:

Top left: Suppose you've been writing an email message on your iPhone.

Right: When you arrive home and sit down at the Mac, a new icon appears on the Dock.

(This icon also appears in the standard app switcher described on page 173, the one that appears when you press ⌘-Tab.)

Middle: When you click that icon, Mail opens, and the half-finished message is there, ready to be completed.

Bottom: This all works in the other direction, too. If you're working on something on the Mac, a matching icon appears on the iPhone's app-switcher screen, shown here on the iPhone X (right) and earlier models (left).

Continuity Camera

This cool feature turns your iPhone or iPad into a detached, handheld, wireless camera for your Mac. When you snap a photo, it appears on the Mac a moment later, for incorporating into whatever app you're using. (It requires that iOS 12 or later be running on your phone or tablet.)

The feature is fairly buried, though. Follow along in Figure 8-7:

1. **Open one of the programs that offer this feature.**

 At the moment, they're mostly the built-in Apple apps like Notes, Mail, Messages, Preview, Pages, Keynote, and TextEdit. Non-Apple apps won't offer this feature unless their makers decide to add it.

2. **Right-click or two-finger click a blank spot in your Mac document. From the shortcut menu, choose Take Photo (Figure 8-7, top).**

 On your iPhone or iPad, you'll see that the camera app opens, magically and automatically (Figure 8-7, right).

Tip: If you choose Scan Documents, the iPhone's document-scanning module opens instead, complete with auto-straightening and -clarifying magic for whatever piece of paper you're scanning. Insta-PDF!

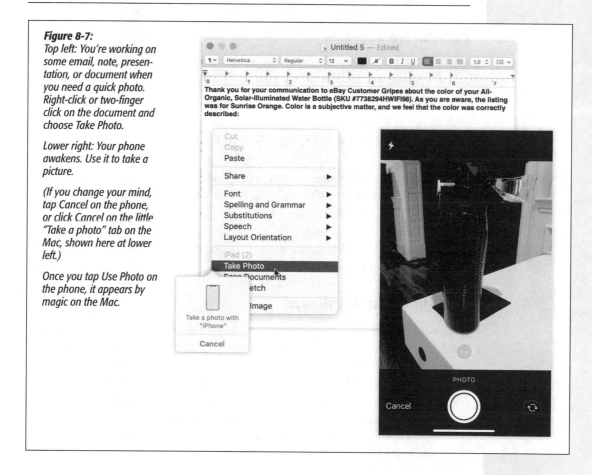

Figure 8-7:
Top left: You're working on some email, note, presentation, or document when you need a quick photo. Right-click or two-finger click on the document and choose Take Photo.

Lower right: Your phone awakens. Use it to take a picture.

(If you change your mind, tap Cancel on the phone, or click Cancel on the little "Take a photo" tab on the Mac, shown here at lower left.)

Once you tap Use Photo on the phone, it appears by magic on the Mac.

3. **On the phone or tablet, frame and take the shot (Figure 8-7, right). If it looks good, tap Use Photo on the iPhone screen.**

 Instantly, that picture appears on your Mac, pasted right into the document.

These features could be brilliant time-savers for researchers and students. If you use Messages on your Mac to do your texting, it's life-changing: Now you can pop a photo into the conversation without any file-transferring nonsense.

Continuity Sketch

New in Catalina: The shortcut menu shown in Figure 8-7 used to offer only Take Photo and Scan Documents. Now there's a third command: Add Sketch.

When you choose it, the drawing tools described on page 597 appear on your iPhone or iPad. Make a sketch; when you tap Done, the drawing pops into your Mac document.

Continuity Markup

Here's another nifty new one in Catalina: You can fling a graphic or a PDF document on your Mac over to your iPhone or iPad for marking up, signing, or annotating with your finger or an Apple Pencil.

This feature is available anywhere the Markup icon (Ⓐ) is available: in an outgoing Mail message, in Notes or TextEdit, in Photos, or in a Quick Look window (page 55), for example.

Once you've clicked Ⓐ, a new button appears on the markup toolbar: 🖍. Click it, and then choose the name of your phone or iPad. The image, complete with markup toolbar, appears on the iOS gadget's screen.

Use your finger (or, on an iPad, an Apple Pencil) to dress it up, sign it, proofread it, whatever. When you tap Done on the iOS device, the markings instantly appear on the Mac version of the graphic or PDF file.

The Universal Clipboard

Now, this is magic—and useful magic, at that. You can copy some text, a picture, or a video on your iPhone, iPad, or iPod Touch—and then, without any further steps, turn to your Mac and paste it. Or go the other way. Somehow, the contents of the Clipboard transfer themselves wirelessly between the two machines (see Figure 8-8).

There's no on/off switch, no extra steps, no visible sign of this feature in Settings or System Preferences. It just works. (Provided, of course, that you've obeyed the Three Laws of Continuity Setup: The Mac and phone have to be on the same Wi-Fi network, both have to have Bluetooth turned on, and both have to be signed into the same iCloud account.)

If you don't paste within two minutes of copying, then macOS restores whatever was already on the Mac's Clipboard, so you don't get confused later.

Figure 8-8:
*Top: On your iPad, you copy
some text (or a picture, or a
video clip).*

*Bottom: If, on your Mac, you
use the Paste command within
two minutes—in any program—
then the material you copied
on the iPad appears!*

Apple Watch Login and Approval

If you have an Apple Watch, you don't need a password to unlock your Mac anymore. The watch on your wrist acts as a wireless master key.

All you have to do is come within 10 feet of your Mac and wake it up. The logging-in takes place instantly and automatically. It may be the lowest-effort security system ever invented.

Note: You still have to enter your Mac's password after shutting it down or restarting it. The watch method works only if the Mac has been sleeping.

Here's the fine print:

- **The watch must be running watchOS 3 or later.** The Sierra or later Mac must have been made since mid-2013. Both devices must have Wi-Fi and Bluetooth turned on.

- **You must have a passcode set up on the watch.** (Open the Apple Watch app on the iPhone; tap General→Apple ID.)

- **You have to set up the feature on the Mac.** In System Preferences→Security & Privacy→General, turn on "Allow your Apple Watch to unlock your Mac."

- **You have to turn on two-factor authentication for your iCloud account.** See page 508.

From now on, everything is automatic. You wake your Mac (open the laptop lid, for example). You see "Unlocked with Apple Watch" flash on the lock screen, you see "[Your Mac] unlocked by this Apple Watch" on the watch's screen—and you're in!

In Catalina (and WatchOS 6), this concept goes a step further.

Every now and then, the Mac asks for your password to confirm that you're you and that you know what you're doing—for example, when you're making a Mac-wide change (like the time zone) in System Preferences, or trying to view your Safari passwords, or unlocking a page of Notes, or approving the installation of a new app.

Now, instead of typing your password, you can just double-click the Watch's side button to authenticate yourself. Wireless, weird, and wonderful.

Part Three:
The Components of macOS

3

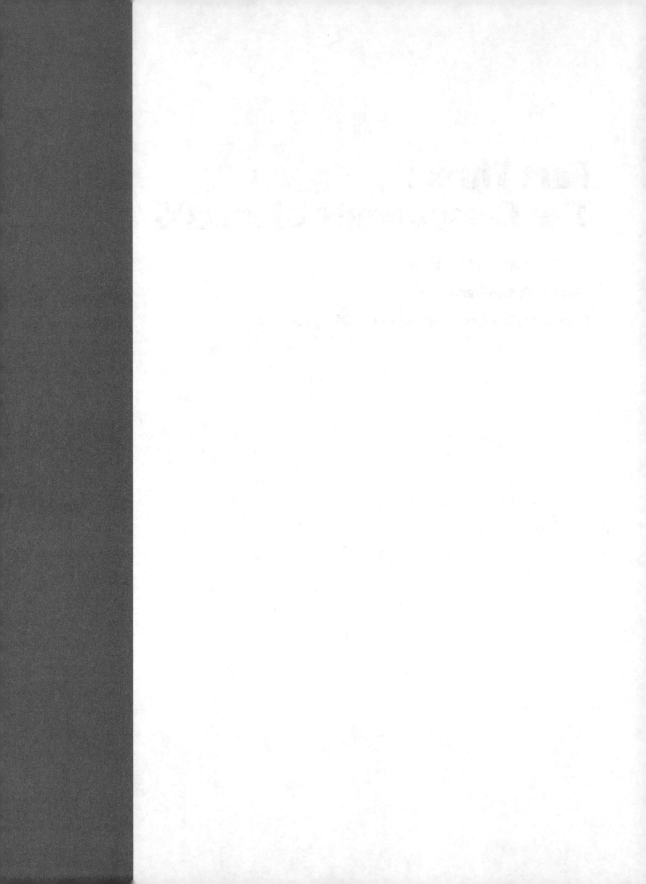

System Preferences

T he hub of Mac customization is System Preferences, the equivalent of the Control Panel (Windows) or the Settings app (iPhone, iPad, Android). Some of its panels are extremely important, because their settings determine whether or not you can connect to a network or go online to exchange email. Others handle the more cosmetic aspects of macOS. In Catalina, its top panel proudly presents your name, icon, and direct access to your iCloud account information.

Note: Only a system administrator (page 488) can change settings that affect everyone who shares a certain machine: most of its Network settings, Energy Saver settings, and so on. If you see a bunch of controls that are dimmed and unavailable, now you know why.

A 🔒 in the lower-left corner is the other telltale sign. If you, a nonadministrator, would like to edit some settings, call an administrator over and ask her to click the 🔒, input her password, and supervise your tweaks.

The System Preferences Window

You can open System Preferences in dozens of ways:

- **Choose its name from the menu.**

- **Jump directly to a System Preferences pane** by pressing Option as you tap keys on the top row of your keyboard: Option-▦ for Mission Control preferences, Option-volume key (◀, ◀), or ◀))) for Sound prefs, Option-brightness keys (☀ or ☀) or Option-keyboard-brightness key (⸫ or ⸫) for the Displays prefs. At that point, you can click ⠿ or press ⌘-L to see the full spread.

- **If you know the name of the Preferences panel** you want, it's quicker to use Spotlight. To open Parental Controls, for example, hit ⌘-space, type *pare,* and then press Return. See Chapter 3 for more on operating Spotlight from the keyboard.

- **If you put the System Preferences icon in your** *Dock* (Chapter 4), you can open it *and* jump to a particular panel in one smooth move: Click-and-hold the System Preferences icon. You get a pop-up menu of every System Preferences panel.

At first, the rows of icons are grouped according to function, as shown in Figure 9-1, top. But you can also view them in tidy alphabetical order, shown at bottom. That can spare you the tedious ritual of hunting around to find a panel icon whose name you already know. (Quick, without looking: Which row is Date & Time in?) This chapter describes the various panels following this alphabetical arrangement.

Figure 9-1:
You can view System Preferences icons alphabetically (bottom), rather than in rows by function (top); just choose View→Organize Alphabetically. Non-Apple panes appear in a final row.

Actually, there are two nearly identical View menus. There's the regularly scheduled View menu at the top of the screen, and there's the Show All button (▦). This button is, believe it or not, also a menu.

Choosing a Preferences Pane

To access a different preferences pane, you have a number of options:

- **Fast:** When System Preferences first opens, the insertion point is blinking in the System Preferences search box. (If the insertion point is *not* blinking there, then

press ⌘-F.) Type a few letters of *volume, resolution, wallpaper, wireless,* or whatever feature you want to adjust. In a literal illustration of Spotlight's name, the System Preferences window darkens *except* for the icons where you'll find relevant controls (Figure 9-2). Click the name or icon of the one that looks the most promising.

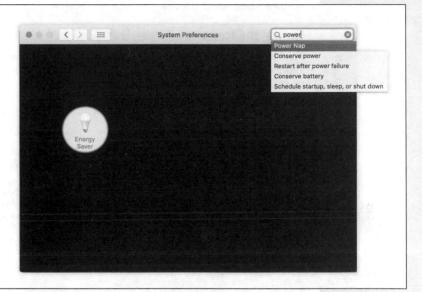

Figure 9-2:
Even if you don't know which System Preferences panel contains the settings you want to change, Spotlight can help. Type into the box at the top, and watch as the "spotlight" shines on the relevant icons.

System Preferences: Under the Hood

The entire System Preferences program is nothing more than a series of graphical front ends for underlying Unix settings. (If you know Unix you can, in fact, use the *defaults* command in macOS's Terminal program to make any of the changes described in this chapter—and many others.)

The individual preferences panes are represented by package icons in your Library folders. For example, the icons Apple supplies are in System→Library→PreferencePanes. MacOS also looks for preferences modules in the Network→Library→PreferencePanes folder, if there is one.

Suppose you've downloaded some new preferences module and you want to install it. Just double-clicking a downloaded System Preferences pane does the trick.

If you prefer manual control, you can put a downloaded module into your Home→Library→PreferencePanes folder. (To get to your Library folder, which is usually invisible, press the Option key; choose Go→Library in the Finder.)

The beauty of this arrangement is that everyone who shares the Mac now can see a different assortment of customized preference panes. If you're an administrator, you can use the PreferencePanes folder in the Mac's main Library folder; it lets everyone with an account on the Mac (Chapter 12) access your newly added panes.

When you install some new System Preferences pane, like TiVo Desktop, it takes the form of a new icon in one of those four PreferencePanes folders. That's good to know if you ever want to remove an add-on pane. Usually, you remove these non-Apple preference panes by right-clicking or two-finger clicking them and choosing Remove Preference Pane from the shortcut menu—but in a pinch, you could also delete one by removing it from one of these special folders.

Within the System Preferences program, any new panes you add this way appear in a new row of icons labeled Other (when you're viewing System Preferences in Category view).

- **Faster:** Click the Show All (⣿) icon in the upper-left corner of the window (or press ⌘-L, a shortcut worth learning). Then click the icon of the new panel you want.

- **Fastest:** You can choose a panel's name from any of three menus. There's the View menu, the Show All button (⣿), or the System Preferences Dock icon pop-up menu described already.

Hiding the Icons You Never Use

Let's face it: Especially for a beginner, System Preferences can be daunting. You just want to change your screen saver, and suddenly you're face-to-face with the space shuttle dashboard.

Fortunately, you can hide the Preferences icons you don't use often (Figure 9-3).

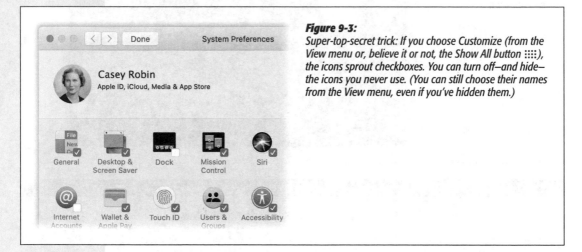

Figure 9-3:
Super-top-secret trick: If you choose Customize (from the View menu or, believe it or not, the Show All button ⣿), the icons sprout checkboxes. You can turn off—and hide—the icons you never use. (You can still choose their names from the View menu, even if you've hidden them.)

All right. What follows, then, is your grand tour of the built-in System Preferences panes. (You may have more if you've installed any non-Apple panes.)

Apple ID, Family Sharing

The Apple ID icon at the top opens what used to be called the iCloud settings panel. It's the master setup page for Apple's iCloud synchronization service, and it's described starting on page 656. Family Sharing appears here if you've turned it on (page 661).

Accessibility

The Accessibility panel is designed for people who, for example, type with one hand, find it difficult to use a mouse, or have trouble seeing or hearing.

Accessibility is a huge focus for Apple. In fact, there's a whole Apple website dedicated to explaining these controls: *apple.com/accessibility*. Here, though, is an overview of the noteworthiest features, broken down according to the tabs at the left side.

Overview Tab

This screen offers a couple of sentences about what Accessibility is all about.

VoiceOver Tab

The Mac has always been able to read stuff on the screen out loud. But Apple has taken this feature light-years further, turning it into a full-blown *screen reader* for the benefit of people who can't see. VoiceOver doesn't just read every scrap of text it finds on the screen; as a precursor to the new Voice Control, it also lets you control everything on the screen (menus, buttons, and so on) without ever needing the mouse.

On a laptop, you can interact with what's visible on the screen by using the trackpad itself as a map of the current window or screen area; in Trackpad Commander mode, VoiceOver speaks whatever is under your finger (represented by a blue ring on the screen). You can flick in any direction to move to the next thing on the screen. It's all in the name of helping you "feel" where everything is.

MacOS can also read entire web pages, navigate tables, hop from link to link, and so on. You can navigate by pressing the arrow keys, by using the mouse, or by using the trackpad.

Learning VoiceOver is a *huge* task that can take days or weeks; there's an entire app (VoiceOver Utility) with *10 pages* of preference settings. But if it's your ticket to being able to use a computer at all, you'll probably be happy to have such a full-fledged monster of a program. Apple offers a complete user's guide at *apple.com/voiceover/info/guide/*.

Zoom Tab

This feature, shown in Figure 9-4, lets you enlarge the area surrounding your cursor in any increment. It's incredibly useful incredibly often, especially if you have over-40 eyes.

You can start enlarging things in either of two ways:

- **From the keyboard.** To set this up, turn on "Use keyboard shortcuts to zoom."

 Next time you want to magnify something, press Option-⌘-8. You've either opened up the magnifying lens or magnified the entire screen. The magnification is 200 percent of original size. At this point, you can increase or decrease the amount of zooming by pressing Option-⌘-plus or Option-⌘-minus (the – key). With each press, the entire screen image (or the image in the magnifying lens, depending on which you've chosen as your zoom style) gets larger or smaller, creating a virtual monitor that follows your cursor around the screen (Figure 9-4, top).

- **With the trackpad or mouse wheel.** To prepare, turn on "Use scroll gesture with modifier keys to zoom."

 To use: While pressing the Control key, drag two fingers up your trackpad, or turn your mouse wheel upward. The amount of dragging or turning controls the degree of magnification.

Once you're zoomed in, you can pan around inside the lens (or pan the entire virtual giant screen) by dragging with two fingers on your trackpad. The lens moves to follow your cursor; in Picture-in-picture mode, the whole screen scrolls when your cursor hits the edge of the magnified area.

Figure 9-4:
Top: You'll be amazed at how much you can zoom using this Accessibility pane. In fact, there's nothing to stop you from zooming in so far that a single pixel nearly fills the entire monitor. (That may not be especially useful for people with limited vision, but it can be handy for graphic designers learning how to reproduce a certain icon, dot by dot.)

The inset window makes it easier for you to keep your bearings. It zooms into the screen only within this window.

Bottom: The Hover Text option magnifies only text, and only when you press the ⌘ key. Great for fine print!

Customizing your zoom

You can tweak the zooming feature to within an inch of its life on this panel:

- **Use scroll gesture with modifier keys to zoom.** You can substitute the Option or ⌘ key, if Control isn't working out for you.

- **Zoom style.** If you choose "Full screen," then zooming magnifies the entire screen. (And that, as many Apple Genius Bar employees can tell you, freaks out a lot of

people who don't know what's happened.) If it's set to "Picture-in-picture," then zooming will produce a movable, rectangular magnifying lens (Figure 9-4, top).

- **Advanced** opens a world of tweaks. They govern exactly how the magnification works: how it follows your cursor, its minimum and maximum range, what keystrokes unlock special features, and so on. If you're really interested, see the free PDF appendix "Advanced Zoom Tweaks," on this book's "Missing CD" page at *missingmanuals.com*.

- **Enable Hover Text.** This feature, new in Catalina, magnifies only the *text* under your cursor, whenever you're pressing the ⌘ key. Ideal for reading fine print or badly designed websites (Figure 9-4, bottom). Click Options to specify the font and size, color schemes, the key to hold down, and so on.

Tip: Tap the ⌘ key three times to lock the text-magnification pane in place, so you don't get tired holding down the key.

- **Enable Touch Bar zoom.** This option appears only on MacBook Pro laptops—those with a Touch Bar (page 227). When you touch the Touch Bar, you see a magnified version of it at the bottom of your screen, so you can better see what you're doing.

Display

If you have trouble seeing the screen, then, boy, does macOS have features for you.

Display tab

- **Invert colors.** By reversing the screen's colors like a film negative (black for white, red for green, blue for yellow), you create a higher-contrast effect that some people find is easier on the eyes.

 It doesn't touch photos, videos, app icons, or dark backgrounds—only light-colored screen elements, making them dark. Unless, that is, you also turn on Classic Invert; that inverts every single pixel, which can create some bizarre-looking photos and videos.

- **Reduce motion** eliminates all of macOS's little animations. Handy if they're making you seasick. This option also gives you a bit of a speed boost, especially in programs like Mission Control.

- **Increase contrast** darkens the lines that form buttons, sliders, and checkboxes on the screen, making them easier to distinguish.

- **Reduce transparency** eliminates all of macOS's translucency; see Figure 9-5.

- **Differentiate without color** was Apple's first attempt to help color-blind people, but it's fairly pointless. The only thing it affects is the "unavailable" status indicators (like "Away" and "Out to lunch") in Messages. They're denoted by red *squares* instead of circles.

- **Display contrast.** As you drag this slider toward Maximum, macOS's gray shades gradually bleach out, becoming closer and closer to pure black and white, which may be easier to see if you have limited vision.

Figure 9-5:
When you turn on "Reduce transparency," those semi-transparent menu bars, window edges, and panels (top) become opaque (bottom). The translucence is a trademark feature of macOS, but it doesn't actually help you use the computer; plenty of people find opaque menus and windows less visually confusing.

Cursor tab

- **Shake mouse pointer to locate.** Year by year, computer screens get bigger, and the resolution (number of dots per inch) gets smaller. But in general the arrow pointer stays the same size: tiny.

 That's why millions of people have gotten into the habit, upon waking up a Mac, of wiggling the mouse or making circles on the trackpad—so they can spot the cursor's movement and thereby see where it is.

 And that's why Apple offers this feature: Anytime you wiggle the cursor or make tight little circles with it, the arrow cursor gets big. Really big. So big you can't miss it.

- **The "Cursor size" slider** is a godsend not only to people with failing vision, but also to anyone using one of Apple's large, super-high-resolution screens; as the pixel density increases, the cursor gets smaller and smaller. This slider lets you make the arrow cursor larger—much larger, if you like—making it easier to find.

Color Filters tab

Turn on Enable Color Filters to see what the pop-up menu can do for you:

- **Grayscale** banishes all color from your screen. This is another feature designed to improve text clarity, but it's also a dandy way to see how a color document will look when printed on a monochrome laser printer.

- **Red/Green filter (Protanopia), Green/Red, and Blue/Yellow.** MacOS can help you if you're color-blind. These screen modes substitute colors you *can* see for colors you *can't*, everywhere on the screen. Choose the various color-blindness types in the list to see how each affects the crayons or color swatches at the top of the screen. Use the Intensity slider to govern the degree of the effect.

 The Color Tint option washes the entire screen with a certain shade (which you choose using the Hue slider that appears); it's designed to help people with Irlen syndrome (visual stress), who may have trouble reading.

 The Mac's colors may now look funny to other people, but you should have an easier time distinguishing colors when it counts— for example, when trying to distinguish different chunks of a chart on a website. (You may even be able to pass some of those Ishihara dot-pattern color-blindness tests online.)

Speech

This panel lets you choose a voice (male, female, British, fast, whatever) for the Mac— when it reads error messages aloud to you. Details are on page 300.

Descriptions

This option, "Play audio descriptions when available," is for internet movies that come, or may someday come, with a narration track that describes the action for the blind.

Audio

If you have trouble hearing the Mac's sounds, the obvious solution is to increase the volume, which is why this panel offers a link to the Sound Preferences pane.

Audio is especially important when the Mac tries to get your attention by beeping. For those situations, turn on "Flash the screen when an alert sound occurs" (an effect you can try out by clicking the Test Flash Screen button). Now you'll see a white flash across the entire monitor whenever the Mac would otherwise beep—not a bad idea on laptops, actually, so you don't miss beeps when you've got the speakers muted.

The "Play stereo audio as mono" option is intended for people with hearing loss in one ear. This way, you won't miss any of the musical mix just because you're listening through only one headphone.

RTT/TTY

A TTY is a teletype or text telephone. It's a machine that lets deaf people make phone calls by typing instead of speaking. RTT (real-time text) is a newer, more reliable, more flexible service along the same lines—and now you don't have to haul around a hardware box to use it.

Of course, your Mac isn't a phone—but if you have an iPhone, it can do the work for you. Make sure RTT and Wi-Fi calling are turned on on your iPhone. For more on using RTT on the Mac, visit Apple's help page at *http://j.mp/2P1E7S4.*

Captions

This option controls the look of subtitles in movies, TV shows, videos, and podcasts you've bought, rented, or streamed from Apple. (Subtitles are an option in TV, Quick-Time, and DVD Player.)

Tip: In the iTunes Store, videos equipped with subtitles bear a small CC icon.

When you first click Captions, you can see that Apple has supplied you with four different caption styles: Transparent Background, Classic, Large Text, and Outline Text; each has its own font, color, and background color. If you click the + button, though, you can whip up a new subtitle style to your own taste; you get an insane number of font, size, opacity, and color options.

A few videos have been subtitled specifically for deaf people. Those subtitles, called closed captioning or SDH (subtitles for the deaf and hard of hearing), are the same thing as regular subtitles, except that they also identify nonspoken sounds ("Glass breaking") and who's speaking ("Captain Picard: Engage!"). If you'd prefer to see these SDH captions instead of just the spoken words, turn on Prefer Closed Captions and SDH.

Voice Control

This new, big-deal Catalina feature is described on page 271.

Keyboard

This panel offers clever features for people who have trouble using the keyboard—or who want a little productivity boost. There are now two panes of this screen.

Hardware

You have two options here:

- **Sticky Keys** lets you press multiple-key shortcuts (involving keys like Shift, Option, Control, and ⌘) one at a time instead of all together.

 To make Sticky Keys work, first turn on Enable Sticky Keys. Then go to work on the Mac, triggering keyboard commands as shown in Figure 9-6.

 If you press a modifier key *twice*, you lock it down. (Its onscreen symbol gets brighter to let you know.) When a key is locked, you can use it for several commands in a row. For example, if a folder icon is highlighted, you could double-press ⌘ to lock it down—and then type O (to open the folder), look around, and then press W (to close the window). Press the ⌘ key a third time to "unpress" it.

Tip: The checkbox called "Press the Shift key five times to toggle Sticky Keys" (click Options to see it) gives you the flexibility of turning Sticky Keys on and off at will, without making a trip to System Preferences. Whenever you want to turn on Sticky Keys, press the Shift key five times in succession. You'll hear a special clacking sound effect alerting you that you just turned on Sticky Keys. (Repeat the five presses to turn Sticky Keys off again.)

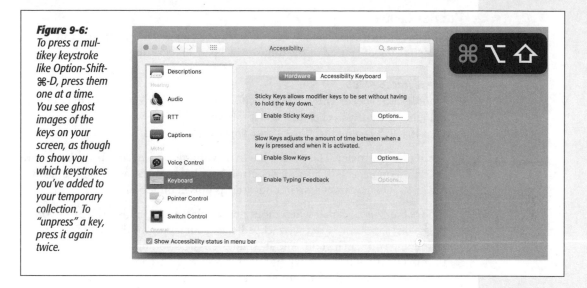

Figure 9-6:
To press a multikey keystroke like Option-Shift-⌘-D, press them one at a time. You see ghost images of the keys on your screen, as though to show you which keystrokes you've added to your temporary collection. To "unpress" a key, press it again twice.

- **Slow Keys,** on the other hand, doesn't register a key press at all until you've held down the key for more than a second or so—a feature designed to screen out accidental key presses.

 If you click Options and then turn on "Use click key sounds," you'll hear a little typing sound each time you press a key—but none of these key presses registers unless you hold the key down for a moment. (Use the Acceptance Delay slider to govern this threshold.) You hear a different sound when the Mac actually accepts the key press—and, of course, you see the letter you typed appear onscreen.

- **Enable Typing Feedback,** new in Catalina, makes the Mac speak each letter, word, or key you press, or speak whatever you select with the mouse.

Accessibility Keyboard

This feature is a classic example of a tool that seems on the surface to appeal to people with disabilities—but turns out to be a powerful utility for almost anyone.

The original idea was to create an onscreen keyboard. If you have trouble typing on a physical keyboard, or if your Mac doesn't *have* a keyboard, you can still enter text and trigger keyboard shortcuts.

This keyboard is infinitely customizable. You can build all kinds of alternate keyboards—floating palettes of your own design, whose buttons can type blobs of text, open apps, run scripts, adjust the brightness or volume, and so on.

To see this keyboard, turn on Enable Accessibility Keyboard. The floating keyboard appears, ready to use, and to customize with the options hiding behind the Options button. For details on what these controls do—and to design your own on-screen keyboard—see the free PDF appendix, "Accessibility Keyboard," on this book's "Missing CD" page at *missingmanuals.com*.

Pointer Control

On this pane (formerly called Mouse & Trackpad), a mass of motley options await, all related to the operation of the mouse, trackpad, and cursor.

Mouse & Trackpad tab

- **Double-click speed.** This setting specifies how much time you have to complete a double-click. If you click too slowly—beyond the time you've allotted yourself with this slider—the Mac "hears" two *single* clicks instead.

- **Spring-loading delay.** This option has to do with *spring-loaded folders,* the feature described on page 85. This slider controls how long a folder waits before springing open (when your cursor, in mid-drag, is poised on top of it).

- **Ignore built-in trackpad when mouse or wireless trackpad is present.** If you've plugged in a mouse or external trackpad, then your laptop's built-in trackpad really isn't doing you much good. And it could even mess you up (for example, if your thumb hits it while you're typing). If this option is turned on, then the built-in trackpad no longer responds to touches.

- **Trackpad Options.** Here you can adjust your Mac's response when you scroll by dragging across the trackpad—do things keep scrolling a little after you lift your finger ("inertia")?

 You can also enable *trackpad dragging,* which means moving things across the screen without having to keep the trackpad button down. To drag, tap *twice* (don't fully click); leave your finger touching the trackpad on the second tap. At this point, your "mouse button" is down. Swipe across the trackpad to move the object. (If "with Drag Lock" is turned on, then the "mouse button" remains down until you repeat the double-tap business. In "without Drag Lock" mode, *one* tap ends the dragging. And "three-finger dragging," of course, means you have to swipe with three fingers to do the moving.)

- **Mouse Options.** This one should really be called *scroll bar* options. It affects how fast a window scrolls when you're holding down the up or down buttons on a vertical scroll bar (or the left/right buttons on a horizontal one).

Alternate Control Methods tab

- **Mouse Keys** is designed to help people who can't use the mouse—or who want more precision when they do. It lets you click, drag, and otherwise manipulate the cursor by pressing the keys on your numeric keypad. (It's not very useful on keyboards that don't *have* separate numeric keypads, like laptops.)

When Mouse Keys is turned on, the 5 key acts as the clicker—hold it down for a moment to "click the mouse," do that twice to double-click, and so on. Hold down the 0 key to lock down the mouse button, and the period key to unlock it. (The amount of time you have to hold them down depends on how you've set the Initial Delay slider.)

Move the cursor around the screen by pressing the eight keys that surround the 5 key. (For example, hold down the 9 key to move the cursor diagonally up and to the right.) If you hold one of these keys down continuously, the cursor, after a pause, begins to move smoothly in that direction—according to the way you've adjusted the sliders called Initial Delay and Maximum Speed.

Tip: The checkbox, in Options, called "Press the Option key five times to toggle Mouse Keys" saves you the trouble of opening System Preferences.

- **Alternate Pointer Actions** lets you set up keystrokes on your keyboard to "click," "right-click," and "double-click" as you choose by hitting Options. If you have a switch (described next), you can use it to "click," too.

Switch Control

Apple has made the Mac accessible to people whose physical skills are limited to very simple gestures, like puffing on an air pipe, pressing a foot switch, blinking an eye, or turning the head, for example. A hardware accessory called a *switch* lets you operate certain gadgets this way.

When you turn on Enable Switch Control, a row of icons appears on a floating bar. They correspond to hardware and software controls you might have trouble operating physically: Keyboard, Pointer, Dock, and so on. (Among them: a Custom item, which lets you build additional floating bars or panels, filled with clickable buttons you might find helpful.)

When you trigger your switch, the Mac sequentially highlights one icon in this panel, or one object on the screen, after another; you're supposed to puff, tap, or blink at the right moment to say, "Yes, *this* one."

If you don't have a physical switch apparatus, you can use the one that came with your keyboard: the space bar (the factory setting). Tap it to begin the sequential highlighting. When the highlighting reaches the button, control, or key you want, tap the space bar.

You can specify how fast the highlighting proceeds, whether or not it pauses on the screen's first item, how many times the highlighting cycles through each screenful, and so on.

Of course, typing or moving the cursor this way can be a very slow process. But for some people, switch control makes the difference between being able to use the Mac slowly or not at all.

For details on adding your own switch and customizing how it works, read *support. apple.com/en-us/HT202865.*

Siri

This panel has only one purpose: to let you turn on Type to Siri (page 286).

Shortcut Tab

Apple assumes that many of the Accessibility features are things you'll want to turn on and off on the fly, as you need them. So in macOS, there's a keyboard shortcut that pulls up a dashboard of Accessibility features and their on/off checkboxes (Figure 9-7): Option-⌘-F5. (If you have a Touch Bar laptop, fast–triple-click the Touch ID fingerprint reader instead. Those should be audible click-downs, not just touches.)

The purpose of *this* dashboard (the General tab) is to choose which checkboxes you want to appear on *that* dashboard. Any checkboxes you turn off here won't appear in the panel shown in Figure 9-7.

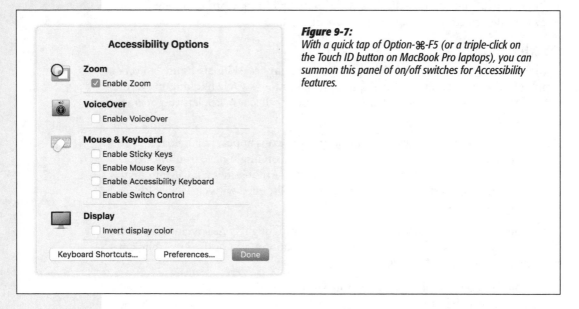

Figure 9-7:
With a quick tap of Option-⌘-F5 (or a triple-click on the Touch ID button on MacBook Pro laptops), you can summon this panel of on/off switches for Accessibility features.

Bluetooth

Bluetooth is a short-range, low-power, wireless *cable-elimination* technology. It's designed to connect gadgets in pairings that make sense, like cellphone+earpiece, Mac+wireless keyboard, phone+portable speaker, or Mac+cellphone. Bluetooth is also the key to the Continuity features described in Chapter 8; it's the wireless link between your Mac and your iPhone.

Pairing

Now, you wouldn't want the guy in the next cubicle to be able to operate *your* Mac using *his* Bluetooth keyboard. So the first step in any Bluetooth relationship is *pairing,*

or formally introducing the two gadgets that will be communicating. Figure 9-8 shows how that goes.

To do that, open System Preferences→Bluetooth. Make sure Bluetooth is On. (The only reason to turn it off is to save laptop battery power.)

You don't have to turn on a Discoverable switch to make the Mac "visible" to other Bluetooth gadgets in range; whenever the Bluetooth pane of System Preferences is open, it's discoverable.

In fact, you don't have to click some Add New Device button, either. When the Bluetooth pane is open, the Mac automatically starts searching for nearby Bluetooth gadgets within range (see Figure 9-8, bottom)—nearby headsets, laptops, cellphones, and so on. Usually, it finds the one you're trying to pair. Just click it, and then click Pair.

When it's all over, the new gadget is listed in the panel, in the list of Bluetooth stuff that you've previously introduced to this Mac. (You can click it and then click ✖ to get rid of the pairing, when that day comes.)

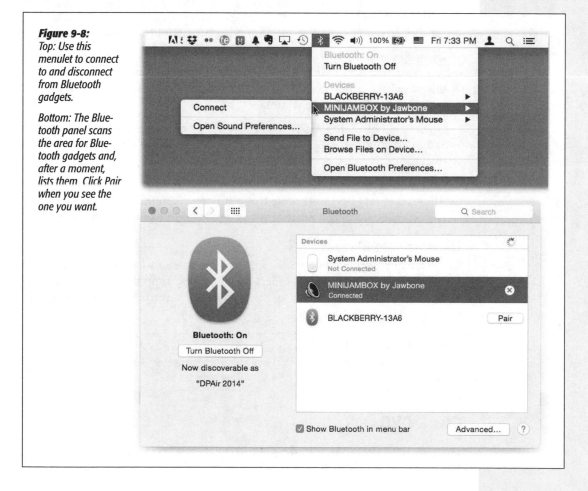

Figure 9-8:
Top: Use this menulet to connect to and disconnect from Bluetooth gadgets.

Bottom: The Bluetooth panel scans the area for Bluetooth gadgets and, after a moment, lists them. Click Pair when you see the one you want.

A few footnotes:

- **If you're pairing a mobile phone** or something else that has a keypad or a keyboard, the Mac may display a large, multiple-digit *passcode*. It's like a password, except that you'll have to input it only this once, to confirm that *you* are the true owner of both the Mac and the gadget. (If it weren't for this passcode business, some guy next to you at the airport could enjoy free laptop internet access through the cellphone in *your* pocket.)

 At this point, the phone, computer, or tablet displays a message to the effect that you have 30 seconds to type that passcode. Do it. When the gadget asks if you want to pair with the Mac and connect to it, say yes. (If you're pairing one Mac with another, just click Continue on both machines; you *see* the same passcode on both but don't have to type it.)

- **If you intend to send a file to another Mac,** set up that other machine by visiting System Preferences→Sharing; turn on Bluetooth Sharing.

Advanced Options

If you click Advanced, you arrive at a few more tweaky Bluetoothisms:

- **Open Bluetooth Setup Assistant at startup if no keyboard is detected.** Here's where you can tell the Bluetooth Setup Assistant to open up automatically when the Mac thinks no keyboard is attached (because it assumes you have a wireless Bluetooth keyboard that has yet to be set up).

- **Open Bluetooth Setup Assistant at startup if no mouse or trackpad is detected.** Same deal, this time suggesting that the assistant will open if the Mac can't find a trackpad or mouse. Once again, the Mac is assuming you'll be wanting to connect a *wireless* one.

- **Allow Bluetooth devices to wake this computer.** Turn this on if you want to be able to wake a sleeping Mac when you press a key, just like a wired keyboard does.

The Bluetooth Menulet

The Bluetooth menulet (Figure 9-8, top) gives you an easy way to turn Bluetooth on and off, to connect to Bluetooth gadgets, to disconnect from them, and to send files to them (page 254). If you don't see this menulet, then turn on "Show Bluetooth in menu bar" (Figure 9-8, bottom).

Tip: If you Option-click the Bluetooth menulet (✳), you get a couple of lines of secret Bluetooth details. The menu reveals the name of your Mac, as it will appear to other Bluetooth wireless gadgets, and the version of Bluetooth you're running.

CDs & DVDs

This pane appears only if your Mac does, in fact, have a DVD drive. It lets you tell the Mac what it should do when it detects that you've inserted a CD or DVD. For example,

when you insert a music CD, you probably want Music to open automatically so you can listen to the songs or convert them to MP3 or AAC files on your hard drive.

Date & Time

Your Mac's conception of what time it is can be very important. Every file you create, save, or even open is stamped with this time, and every email you send or receive is marked with it. As you might expect, setting your Mac's clock is what the Date & Time pane is all about.

Date & Time Tab

Click the Date & Time tab. If "Set date and time automatically" is turned on, then your Mac sets its own clock by consulting a highly accurate online scientific clock. (There's no need to worry about daylight savings time, either; the time servers take that into account.)

Note: You have to authenticate yourself before making any Date & Time adjustments. Click the little 🔒 and enter your administrator's account password.

If you're not online and have no prospect of getting there, you can also set the date and time manually. To change the month, day, or year, click the digit that needs changing and then either (a) type a new number, (b) press the ▲ or ▼ keys on the keyboard, or (c) click the little arrow buttons. Press the Tab key to highlight the next number. (You can also specify the day of the month by clicking a date on the mini-calendar.)

To set the time of day, use the same technique—or, for more geeky fun, you can set the time by dragging the hour, minute, or second hands on the analog clock.

Finally, click Save. (If you get carried away with dragging the clock hands around and lose track of the *real* time, click the Revert button to restore the panel settings.)

Tip: If you prefer seeing 24-hour "military time" notation on your menu bar (that is, *17:30* instead of *5:30 p.m.*)–then click the Clock tab and turn on "Use a 24-hour clock."

Note, however, that this affects only the menu-bar clock. If you'd like to reformat the menu-bar clock *and* all other dates and times (like the ones that show when your files were modified in list views), click the Open Language & Region button at the bottom of the Date & Time pane. Once there, you'll see an Advanced button; its Times tab leads you to a whole new world of time-format customization. You can drag elements of the current time (Hour, Minute, Second, Millisecond, and so on) into any order, and separate them with any desired punctuation. In the Dates tab, you can also set up your date displays in (for example) the European format, expressing April 13 as 13/4 instead of 4/13.

Time Zone Tab

You'd be surprised how important it is to set the time zone for your Mac. If you don't do so, the email and documents you send out—and the Mac's conception of what documents are older and newer—could be hopelessly skewed.

MacOS can set its own time zone *automatically* by consulting the locations of nearby Wi-Fi hotspots. That's a useful feature if you're a laptop warrior who travels a lot.

If you turn on "Set time zone automatically using current location" (Figure 9-9), the Mac will think for a moment. Then, if the Wi-Fi gods are smiling, it will, before your eyes, drop a pin onto the world map to represent your location—and set the time zone automatically. (The world map dims to show that you can no longer set your location manually.)

Often, though, you'll be told that the Mac is "Unable to determine current location at this time." In that case, specify your location manually, as shown in Figure 9-9.

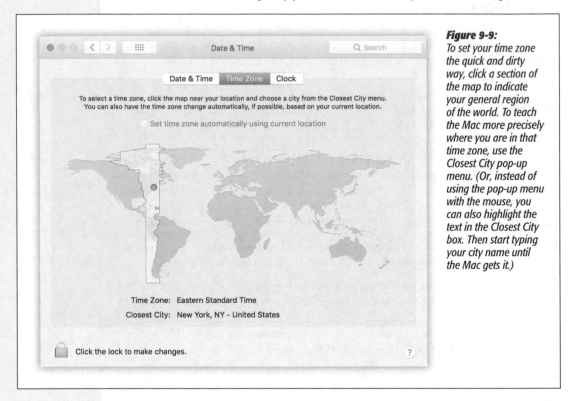

Figure 9-9:
To set your time zone the quick and dirty way, click a section of the map to indicate your general region of the world. To teach the Mac more precisely where you are in that time zone, use the Closest City pop-up menu. (Or, instead of using the pop-up menu with the mouse, you can also highlight the text in the Closest City box. Then start typing your city name until the Mac gets it.)

Clock Tab

In the Clock pane, you can turn the menu-bar clock on or off. You can choose between two clock styles: digital (3:53 p.m.) or analog (a round clock face). You also get several options for the digital clock display: whether to show seconds, designations for a.m. and p.m., the day of the week, a blinking colon, and a 24-hour clock.

Tip: At the bottom of the dialog box, you'll find a feature called "Announce the time." At the intervals you specify, the Mac can speak, out loud, the current time: "It's 10 o'clock." If you tend to get so immersed in "working" that you lose track of time, macOS just removed your last excuse.

The menu-bar clock can show not just the time and day of the week, but also today's *date*. Turn on the "Show the day of the week" and "Show date" checkboxes if you want to see, for example, "Wed May 8 7:32 PM" on your menu bar.

If you decide you don't need all that information—if your menu bar is crowded enough as it is—you can always look up today's day and date just by *clicking* the time on your menu bar. A menu drops down revealing the complete date. The menu also lets you switch between digital and analog clock types and provides a shortcut to the Date & Time Preferences pane.

Tip: This one's for Unix geeks only. Use *sudo*, type *date mmddhhmmyyyy.ss*, and press Return. (Of course, replace that code with the actual date and time you want, such as *040517552019*.00 for April 5, 2019, 5:55 p.m.) You might find this method faster than the System Preferences route.

Desktop & Screen Saver

This panel offers two ways to show off macOS's glamorous graphics features: *desktop pictures* and *screen savers.*

Desktop Pictures

MacOS comes with a mountain of desktop pictures, ranging from plain solid colors to *National Geographic*–style nature photos. To install a new background, first choose one of the image categories in the list at the left side of the window, as shown in Figure 9-10.

Your choices include Desktop Pictures (muted, soft-focus swishes and swirls and lovely nature shots) and solid Colors (simple grays, blues, and greens).

Tip: You can choose *any* solid color—not just one of the preselected shades Apple gives you. Click Custom Color and go nuts.

In the Desktop Pictures category, don't miss the two Dynamic Desktop pictures—images whose lighting *changes through the day*, according to the way the sun would hit it in the real world. One shows a Catalina Island scene. The other is a much less busy color gradient that suggests the sky: a lighter blue during the day, fading to a deep midnight blue at night. It's rather stunning.

Tip: The Catalina Island photo doesn't have to be dynamic. When you select it, a new pop-up menu appears, offering you a choice of Dynamic (changes through the day), Light (Still), and Dark (Still). The latter two are just handsome still photos whose lighting doesn't change.

Using your own pictures

Of course, you may feel that decorating your Mac desktop is much more fun if you use one of your *own* pictures. You can use almost any graphics file: JPEG, GIF, TIFF, Photoshop, and even PDF. (Guess you could use the PDF option to teach yourself your camera's user guide by staring at your desktop every morning.)

That's why icons for your own Pictures folder and Photos albums also appear here, along with a + button that lets you choose *any* folder of pictures. When you click one of these icons, you see thumbnail versions of its contents in the main screen to its right. Just click the thumbnail of any picture to apply it immediately to the desktop. (There's no need to remove the previously installed picture first.)

Tip: If there's a certain picture you like, but it's not in any of the listed sources, you can drag its image file onto the *well* (the miniature desktop displayed in the Desktop panel). A thumbnail instantly appears in the well, and a moment later the picture is plastered across your monitor.

Figure 9-10:
Using the list of picture sources at left, you can preview an entire folder of your own images before installing one as your new desktop picture. Use the + button to select a folder of assorted graphics—or, if you're a Photos veteran, click a Photos album name, as shown here. Clicking one of the thumbnails installs the corresponding picture on the desktop.

Making the picture fit

Unless you've gone to the trouble of editing your chosen photo so that it matches the precise dimensions of your screen (1920 × 1080 pixels, for example), it probably isn't exactly the right size.

Fortunately, macOS offers a number of solutions to this problem. Using the pop-up menu just to the right of the desktop preview well, you can choose any of these options:

- **Fill Screen.** Enlarges or reduces the image so it fills every inch of the desktop. Parts may get chopped off, but this option never distorts the picture.

- **Fit to Screen.** Your photo appears as large as possible without distortion *or* cropping. If the photo doesn't precisely match the proportions of your screen, you get "letterbox bars" on the sides or at top and bottom. Apple provides a color-swatch button next to the "Fit to Screen" pop-up menu. When you click it, the Color Picker appears so you can specify a color for those letterbox bars.

- **Stretch to Fill Screen.** Makes your picture fit the screen exactly, come hell or high water. Larger pictures are squished vertically or horizontally as necessary, and small pictures are drastically blown up *and* squished, usually with grisly results.

- **Center.** Centers the photo neatly on the screen. The edges may be chopped off. If the picture is smaller than the screen, then it sits smack in the center of the monitor at actual size, leaving a swath of empty space all the way around. (Use the swatch button just to the right of the pop-up menu to specify a color for that background.)

- **Tile.** This option makes your picture repeat over and over until the multiple images fill the entire monitor. (If your picture is larger than the screen, no such tiling takes place. You see only the top-center chunk of the image.)

Auto picture changing

The novelty of any desktop picture, no matter how interesting, is likely to fade after several months of viewing. That's why the randomizing function is so delightful.

Turn on "Change picture" at the bottom of the dialog box. From the pop-up menu, specify when you want your background picture to change: "every day," "every 15 minutes," or, if you're *really* having trouble staying awake at your Mac, "every 5 seconds." (The option called "when waking from sleep" refers to the *Mac* waking from sleep, not you.)

Finally, turn on "Random order," if you like. If you leave it off, then your desktop pictures change in alphabetical order by file name.

Now, at the interval you specified, your desktop picture changes automatically, smoothly cross-fading between the pictures like a slideshow. You may never want to open a window, because you'll hate to block your view.

Screen Saver

On the Screen Saver panel, you can create your own screen-saver slideshows—an absolute must if you have a huge screen and a cool Manhattan loft apartment.

Note: Of course, a screen saver doesn't really save your screen. Flat-panel screens, the only kind Apple sells, are incapable of "burning in" a stationary image of the sort that originally inspired the creation of screen savers years ago. No, these screen savers serve two unrelated functions. First, they mask what's on your screen from passersby whenever you leave your desk. Second, they're kind of fun.

When you click a module's name in the Screen Saver list, you see a mini version of it playing back in the preview screen. Click the preview to give the module a dry run on your full screen. When you've had enough of the preview, just move the mouse or press any key.

The screen-saver modules offer two categories of screen savers.

Slideshows

At the top of the scrolling list of icons at left, Apple has installed 12 "slideshows"—attractive animations that gracefully fling photos around in different show-offy ways—that began life in programs like Photos.

At right, use the Source pop-up menu to specify which photos you want included in the slideshow. You can use any of the photo sets Apple provides (Flowers, Landscapes, Colors, Sierras, and Catalina). You can also select Choose Folder to specify some photos of your own from a folder on your Mac, Recent Photos Events to use some photos you've recently imported, or Photo Library to see a list of your Photos albums. Each creates an amazingly dramatic, almost cinematic experience, worthy of setting up to "play" during dinner parties, like the lava lamps of the '70s.

"Shuffle slide order," of course, scrambles the photo sequence so that it's different every time. Wouldn't want you to get bored staring at your screen, now.

Tip: Once a slideshow screen saver kicks in, you can control it as you would a real slideshow. Press the ◄ and ► keys to visit previous or subsequent photos. That's great for those times when someone passing your Mac says, "Hey, what was that?"

Nonphotographic displays

Beneath the list of slideshows, you'll find the icons for seven more-traditional, nonphotographic slideshow displays (Flurry, Arabesque, and so on). Each has options worth exploring. For example, Flurry offers flaming, colorful, undulating arms of fire, which resemble a cross between an octopus and somebody arc welding in the dark. If you click Screen Saver Options, you can control how many streams of fire appear at once, the thickness of the arms, the speed of movement, and the colors.

Similarly, Word of the Day offers a parade of interesting words drawn from the Dictionary program. You're invited to tap the D key to open the dictionary to that entry to read more, or click Options to specify which dictionary you want: the standard *New Oxford American* or the Japanese dictionary.

No matter which screen-saver mode you choose, you can also turn on either of these two options:

- **Show with clock.** This option superimposes the current time on whatever screen saver you've selected. You'd be surprised at how handy it can be to use your Mac as a giant digital clock when you're getting coffee across the room.

- **Use random screen saver.** The Mac chooses a different screen saver each time. Surrender to the power of chance!

Activating the screen saver

You can control when your screen saver takes over your monitor in a couple of ways:

- **After a period of inactivity.** Using the "Start after" pop-up menu, you can set the time that has to pass without keyboard or mouse activity before the screen saver starts. The duration can be as short as one minute or as long as one hour, or you can choose Never to prevent the screen saver from ever turning on by itself.

- **When you park your cursor in the corner of the screen.** If you click the Hot Corners button, you can turn each corner of your monitor into a *hot corner* (Figure 9-11).

Figure 9-11:
This "sheet" lets you set certain corners of your screen as instant-activation spots, or never-come-on spots. Sliding the mouse to the Start Screen Saver corner, for example, turns on your screen saver.

If you work in a business, or in a nosy family, it might be worth noting that you can set things up so that your password is required to exit the screen saver. Visit System Preferences→Security & Privacy, and turn on "Require password immediately after sleep or screen saver begins."

Displays

This is the center of operations for all your monitor settings. Here you set your monitor's resolution, calibrate color balance and brightness, and turn AirPlay on and off—a cool feature that duplicates whatever is on your Mac screen on a TV set. Wirelessly.

Tip: You can open this panel with a quick keystroke from any program on the Mac. Just press Option as you tap one of the screen-brightness keys (☀) on the top row of your keyboard.

The specific controls depend on the kind of monitor you're using, but here are the ones you'll most likely see.

Display Tab

This tab is the main headquarters for your screen controls. It governs these settings:

- **Resolution.** All Mac screens today can make the screen picture larger or smaller, thus accommodating different kinds of work. You perform this magnification or reduction by switching among different *resolutions* (measurements of the number of dots that compose the screen).

When you use a low-resolution setting, such as 800 × 600, the dots of your screen image get larger, enlarging (zooming in on) the picture—but showing a smaller slice of the page. Use this setting when playing a small web movie, for example, so that it fills more of the screen. (Lower resolutions usually look blurry on flat-panel screens, though.) At higher resolutions, such as 1280 × 800, the screen dots get smaller, making your windows and icons smaller, but showing more overall area. You could use this kind of setting when working on two-page spreads in your page-layout program, for example.

If you select "Default for display," then the Mac uses the highest resolution possible for your screen—the one that makes it look sharpest. If you click Scaled, you see a choice of other resolution settings for your built-in monitor—not by number ("1280 × 800" or whatever), but as little representative thumbnails showing the effect you're about to have on text size.

Tip: If you've connected an external monitor or projector, you can *Option-click* the Scaled button to see a scrolling list of additional, less-common display resolutions for that monitor. That's an important trick to remember when you're trying to make some external projector work right.

- **Brightness.** This slider lets you make the screen look good in the prevailing lighting conditions. Of course, most Apple keyboards have brightness-adjustment *keys,* so this software control is included just for the sake of completeness.

- **Automatically adjust brightness.** Your laptop's light sensor dims the screen automatically in dark rooms—*if* this checkbox is turned on.

- **True Tone.** This on/off switch goes beyond the old Auto-Brightness setting. It's Auto-Brightness and Auto-*Tint.* That is, the screen colors actually shift, based on the current lighting color of the room you're in. The idea is to make colors on the screen seem consistent from one lighting condition to another.

 If you find the result off-putting, you can always turn True Tone off. Now the tint never shifts.

- **AirPlay Display.** Read on for details on AirPlay.

- **Show mirroring options in menu bar when available.** Turn on this box if you'd like the Displays menulet to appear automatically whenever you've connected a second monitor or a projector. (Mirroring is described on the following pages.)

Arrangement Tab (Multiple Monitors)

Macs have a terrific feature: They can exploit multiple monitors all plugged into the computer at the same time. Sometimes you want the Mac to project the same thing on both screens (*mirror mode*); that's useful in a classroom when the "external monitor" is a projector. Other times, you want to make one monitor act as an *extension* of the other. For example, you might have your Photoshop image window on your big monitor but keep all the Photoshop controls and tool palettes on a smaller screen. Your cursor passes from one screen to the other as it crosses the boundary.

This is where Sidecar comes in—one of Catalina's star features. If you happen to own an iPad, circa 2018 or later, you can use the iPad as though it's a second monitor for your Mac. It doesn't even have to be connected to the Mac with a cable; it can happen over Wi-Fi. Imagine: a gorgeous external monitor—yours free! See page 357 for all the details on Sidecar.

To connect a second monitor or projector, you have a couple of options.

The wired way

Connect the appropriate cable or adapter to your Mac's video-output jack. This jack may be any of several types. Older Mac laptops and iMacs use a weird, tiny connector called a *Mini DisplayPort*; you'll need an adapter cord to connect it to the VGA, DVI, or HDMI input that most monitors or projectors expect.

More recent Macs also have something called Thunderbolt jacks. You can connect them to a few Thunderbolt-equipped external monitors, notably Apple's.

Current MacBook laptops use USB-C jacks, which Apple calls Thunderbolt 3; you'll need an adapter for these jacks, too, to connect to monitors and projectors.

Finally, there's the black, cylindrical Mac Pro. It also has an HDMI jack, which is the easiest of all to connect to screens and projectors.

To set this up, hook up the monitor or projector. Your Mac should discover (and start projecting to) the external screen automatically; if it doesn't, close and then reopen the lid (if you're using a laptop), or choose Detect Displays from the Displays menulet.

The wireless way to your TV

If you'd shown this feature to the masses in 2005 or so, they'd have fallen down and worshiped it as a god. With one click, you can send whatever is on your Mac's screen to your TV's screen, in high-def. No wires. (This also works for the iPad, but skip to page 357 for that.)

You can make the TV either a mirror of your Mac's screen or an extension of it. You can present photo slideshows on the TV from your laptop. Or play movies you've found online. Or give presentations from PowerPoint or Keynote. Or present software lessons to a class.

To make this work, you need an Apple TV. That's a tiny black box that connects to a high-def TV and lets you watch videos from services like YouTube, Netflix, MLB.TV, NBA, NHL, and Vimeo. It can also play videos, music, and photos from Macs or PCs on the network.

Thanks to AirPlay, the Apple TV (and therefore your TV) can now play anything you can see on your Mac. You can play your music while watching those cool screensavery visualizers on your HDTV. And you can carry your Apple TV around with you to corporate boardrooms to project your pitches, rather than a $1,500 projector.

Tip: If the Apple TV is the third generation or later, the two machines don't even have to be on the same wireless network. This feature, called peer-to-peer AirPlay, is terrific. It makes life so much simpler when you want to give a presentation at some company or school whose Wi-Fi network is complicated and secure; now your Mac doesn't have to be on it at all. (It does, however, have to have Bluetooth turned on.)

Using AirPlay is so simple, it would confuse only an AirHead. The menulet (Figure 9-12) offers controls like these:

- **Connect to: Apple TV.** Here's how you start projecting to your TV. That's all there is to it: The TV lights up as though by magic. The menulet now changes to show:

- **Mirror Built-in Retina Display, Mirror Apple TV, Use As Separate Display.** Your Mac and TV are two screens with two different resolutions (numbers of pixels).

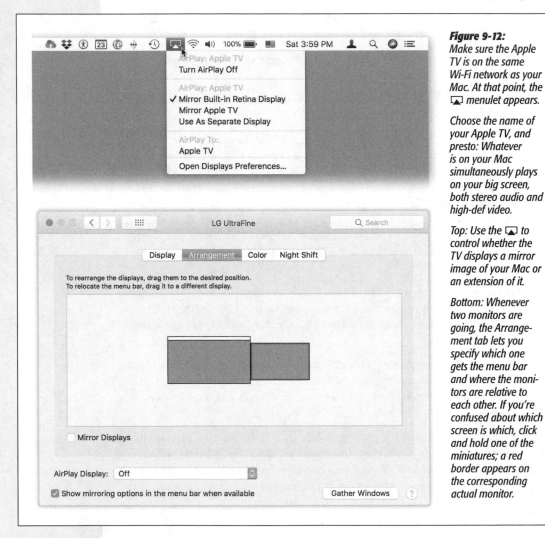

Figure 9-12:
Make sure the Apple TV is on the same Wi-Fi network as your Mac. At that point, the ⌷ menulet appears.

Choose the name of your Apple TV, and presto: Whatever is on your Mac simultaneously plays on your big screen, both stereo audio and high-def video.

Top: Use the ⌷ to control whether the TV displays a mirror image of your Mac or an extension of it.

Bottom: Whenever two monitors are going, the Arrangement tab lets you specify which one gets the menu bar and where the monitors are relative to each other. If you're confused about which screen is which, click and hold one of the miniatures; a red border appears on the corresponding actual monitor.

The question is: If you want them to show the identical image, which one "wins"? Make your choice by choosing one of the two "Mirror" options. (The image on the other screen might look squished, blurry, or letterboxed.)

Or, if you choose "Use As Separate Display," the TV acts as additional screen real estate, off to the right (or left, or top, or bottom) of your Mac's screen.

Arranging multiple monitors

Once you've connected a second screen, with a cable or without, opening the System Preferences→Displays panel makes it appear twice, once on each screen (Figure 9-12, bottom). The idea is that you can change the color and resolution settings independently for each. Your Displays menulet shows two sets of resolutions, too—one for each screen.

Tip: On the Arrangement tab, if you click Gather Windows, then all these separate Displays settings windows appear *together* on the Mac's screen. That's a useful tactic when you're trying to configure an external screen or projector and it's not working, so you can't *see* its Displays window.

And if you hold down the Option key, the Gather Windows button changes to say "Detect Windows." That forces the Mac to look again to see if there's an external monitor—for example, one that you've just plugged in.

The Arrangement tab shows a miniature version of each monitor. By dragging these thumbnails around within the window, you can specify how you want the second monitor's image "attached" to the first. Most people position the second monitor's image to the right of the first, but you're also free to position it on the left, above, below, or even directly on top of the first monitor's icon (the last of which produces a video-mirroring setup). For the least likelihood of going insane, consider placing the real-world monitor in the same position.

For committed multiple-monitor fanatics, the fun doesn't stop there. See the microscopic menu bar on the first-monitor icon? You can drag that tiny strip onto a different monitor icon, if you like, to tell Displays where you'd like your menu bar to appear. (And check out how most screen savers correctly show different stuff on each monitor!)

Tip: If you close your laptop while it's connected to an external monitor and keyboard, the machine doesn't go to sleep. Instead, the laptop remains on, so you can keep right on working, as though the laptop were the brains for a big-screen Mac.

It's worth noting, by the way, that multiple monitors are fairly independent:

- **The Dock** appears on only one screen at a time. As you start working on a different screen, move your cursor to the bottom edge to make the Dock jump there. (That's if you've positioned the Dock at the bottom. If you've placed it on the left or the right, vertically, it stays on the leftmost or rightmost monitor all the time.)

- **Mission Control** appears independently on every screen. That is, when you do the three-finger swipe upward, whatever programs are on each screen shrink down.

You can even create separate sets of Spaces on each screen; it's exactly as though you're using multiple *Macs* and not just multiple screens.

Tip: All these enhancements—multiple menu bars, moving Dock, separate Mission Control and Spaces on each screen—go away when you turn off "Displays have separate Spaces" in System Preferences→Mission Control (and then log out and in again).

Color Tab

This pane offers a list of *color profiles* for your monitor (or, if you turn off "Show profiles for this display only," for *all* monitors). Each profile represents colors slightly differently—a big deal for designers and photo types.

When you Option-click the Calibrate button, the Display Calibrator Assistant opens to walk you through a series of screens, presenting various brightness and color-balance settings on each. Follow the instructions to fine-tune your monitor; at the end of the process, you save your monitor tweaks as a ColorSync profile, which your Mac uses to adjust the screen for improved color accuracy. (If you don't press Option, the Calibrator assistant offers only one settings screen.)

Night Shift

"Many studies have shown that exposure to bright blue light in the evening can affect your circadian rhythms and make it harder to fall asleep," Apple says. You can therefore use this function to give your screen a warmer, less blue tint, either automatically (Sunset to Sunrise), on a bedtime schedule (for example, from 11 p.m. to 6 a.m.), or right now (Turn On Until Tomorrow). You can also tweak the slider to adjust the color temperature (yellowness) of the screen when Night Shift kicks in.

Instead of burrowing into this Settings pane, by the way, you can also tell Siri, "Turn on Night Shift."

All of this works on Macs made in 2012 or later.

Note: Truth is, there's not much research indicating that blue light from screens affects your circadian rhythm. (If using a computer before bed makes it hard to sleep, it's more likely that it's the stimulation of what you're doing or reading.) Sleep scientists have a more universally effective suggestion: Turn off all your screens a couple of hours before bedtime.

Dock

See Chapter 4 for details on the Dock and its System Preferences pane.

Energy Saver

The Energy Saver program helps you and your Mac in a number of ways. By blacking out the screen after a period of inactivity, it prolongs the life of your monitor. By putting the Mac to sleep after you've stopped using it, it cuts down on electricity costs

and pollution. On a laptop, it extends the length of the battery charge by controlling the activity of the hard drive and screen.

Best of all, this pane offers the option to have your computer turn off each night automatically—and turn on again at a specified time in anticipation of your arrival at the desk (Figure 9-13).

Figure 9-13:
Top: Here's what Energy Saver looks like on a laptop. In the "Turn display off after" option, you can specify an independent sleep time for the screen.

Bottom: Here are the Schedule controls–the key to the Mac's self-scheduling abilities.

Energy Saver Q Search

Battery Power Adapter

Turn display off after: ———————————————————

⚠ Never letting your display go to sleep may shorten its life 3 hrs Never

☑ Prevent computer from sleeping automatically when the display is off
☑ Put hard disks to sleep when possible
☑ Wake for Wi-Fi network access
☑ Enable Power Nap while plugged into a power adapter
 While sleeping, your Mac can back up using Time Machine and periodically check for new email, calendar, and other iCloud updates

Current battery charge: 91% Estimated time until full: 0:43 **Restore Defaults**

☑ Sh ☑ Start up or wake Every Day ⬍ at 7:00 AM ⬍ Schedule... ⑦

 ☑ Sleep ⬍ Every Day ⬍ at 8:00 PM ⬍

 Scheduled start up will only occur when a power adapter is connected to your Mac.

⑦ Cancel OK

Sleep Sliders

The Energy Saver controls are different on a laptop Mac and a desktop Mac. In fact, they differ depending on which laptop or desktop model you have.

- **Turn display off after (or Display sleep).** This slider controls when the screen goes black to save power.

- **Computer sleep.** This slider exists only on pre-2013 Macs. (The processors in newer models sleep automatically.) It controls when the *Mac* will automatically go to sleep—anywhere from one minute after your last activity to Never. (Activity can be mouse movement, keyboard action, or internet data transfer; Energy Saver won't put your Mac to sleep in the middle of a download.)

At that time, the screen goes dark, the hard drive stops spinning, and your processor chip slows to a crawl. Your Mac is now in *sleep* mode, using only a fraction of its usual electricity consumption. To wake it up when you return to your desk,

press any key. Everything you were working on, including open programs and documents, is still onscreen, exactly as it was.

Checkbox Options

Below the sliders, you see a selection of additional power-related options. On a laptop, the two tabs at the top of the dialog box let you create different settings for the two states of life for a laptop: when it's plugged in (Power Adapter) and when it's running on battery power (Battery). That's important, because on a laptop, every drop of battery power counts. Here's what you may see:

- **Prevent computer from sleeping automatically when the display is off.** This option (available only on the Power Adapter tab) ensures that even if the screen goes to sleep, the computer itself will keep on chugging.

- **Put hard disks to sleep when possible.** This saves even more juice—and noise—by letting your drives stop spinning when not in use. This option appears on both the Battery and Power Adapter tabs, so you can control it independently for each power source.

- **Slightly dim the display while on battery power.** You see this checkbox only on the Battery tab for a laptop. It means "Don't use full brightness, so I can save power."

Tip: And when your laptop is plugged in, the sudden dimming of the screen becomes a handy signal that you've lost power. Maybe your power cord needs replugging, the power strip went out, or there's a massive blackout in your half of the country.

- **Wake for Wi-Fi network access.** This option (on the Power Adapter tab) lets you access a sleeping Mac from across the network. How is that possible? See the box on the facing page.

Note: The wording of this option reflects how your Mac can connect to a network. If it can connect either over an Ethernet cable or a wireless hotspot, it says "Wake for network access." If it's not a wireless Mac, you'll see "Wake for Ethernet network access." If it's a MacBook without an Ethernet adapter, it says "Wake for Wi-Fi network access." On a laptop, the "wake" feature is available only when the machine's lid is left open and you're plugged into a power outlet.

- **Enable Power Nap.** Power Nap is an ingenious and extremely useful feature for laptops—specifically, flash-storage laptop models introduced in 2012 or later. (On older laptops, it doesn't appear at all.)

 Anyway, when you turn on Enable Power Nap, the Mac keeps updating internet data even while it's closed and asleep. About once every hour, it wakes itself—without activating any fans or lights—long enough to check for mail, calendar updates, Photo Stream updates, software updates, and so on. When you wake the laptop later, you'll be delighted to find it's completely up to date, with new email waiting and all your iCloud programs (Notes, Messages, Reminders, and so on) updated. And the lid was closed the whole time!

Power Nap comes set to work only when your laptop is plugged into a power outlet, but you can make it work on battery power, too (Apple says the battery hit is very slight). You'll find separate on/off switches on each of the Energy Saver tabs. On the Battery tab, it says "Enable Power Nap while on battery power"; on the Power Adapter tab, it says "Enable Power Nap while plugged into a power adapter."

Most of those network functions take place even when the laptop is on battery power. But when it's plugged in, Power Nap also performs two more time-consuming functions: Time Machine backups and App Store software updates.

Of course, Power Nap means your laptop isn't quite as somnolent as it used to be while the lid was closed—it's using a little power.

- **Start up automatically after a power failure.** This checkbox appears only on desktop Macs. It's handy if you leave your Mac unattended and access it remotely, or if you use it as a network file server or web server. It ensures that, if your lonely Mac seizes up or crashes, it will start itself right back up again.

Tip: If you've also turned off (or left off) "Ask to keep changes when closing documents" and "Close windows when quitting an app" in System Preferences→General, then your Mac will both restart *and* restore everything you were doing. You may, in fact, never even realize that a crash or freeze occurred while you were away! (The telltale sign: Any web pages you had logged into, like banking websites, will have logged you out.)

GEM IN THE ROUGH

Auto-Wake for Network Access

You should put your Mac to sleep as much as possible; you'll save power, money, and pollution. Unfortunately, a sleeping Mac is useless on your network. For example, you can't access files on it from another machine.

But Wake on Demand gives you the best of both worlds. It keeps a sleeping Mac available on the network, so you can wake it up remotely when you need it.

How can you do that? Is the Mac sleeping or isn't it?

Yes, it's sleeping. But before it dozes off, it hands over its list of available network services—file sharing, screen sharing, printer sharing, and so on—to your Apple wireless base station. The base station becomes your sleeping Mac's agent, continuing to broadcast the available features of the sleeping Mac (via Apple's Bonjour networking technology) to the rest of the network.

To make this work, you need an AirPort wireless base station or a Time Capsule, running the latest Apple firmware. If

you're using a WPA or WPA2 password on your base station or Time Capsule, it can't be in "bridge mode" (you'd know if you'd turned that on). Only Macs made since late 2008 can be awakened over a wireless network (all Macs can be awakened over an Ethernet wired network). To find out if yours is eligible, open System Information (page 477); under the Network heading, click Wi-Fi and look to see if Wake on Wireless is listed as Supported.

(Longtime Mac nuts may observe that "Wake for network access" has been available in Energy Saver for years. That older method, however, worked only on wired networks, not wireless ones.)

Once you've turned on Wake on Demand, by the way, you might hear brief sounds from the DVD drive, hard drive, or fans, even when the Mac is asleep. That's normal; it means the Mac is checking in with the Bonjour sleep switchboard.

That's right: Even your Mac sometimes stirs in its sleep.

• **Show battery status in menu bar.** This on/off switch (laptops only) controls the battery menulet described in the box below.

Scheduled Startup and Shutdown

By clicking Schedule, you can set up the Mac to shut itself down and turn itself back on automatically (Figure 9-13, bottom).

If you work from 9 to 5, for example, you can set the office Mac to turn itself on at 8:45 a.m. and shut itself down at 5:30 p.m.—an arrangement that conserves electricity, saves money, and reduces pollution but doesn't inconvenience you in the least. In fact, you may come to forget that you've set up the Mac this way, since you'll never actually see it turn itself off.

Note: The Mac doesn't shut down automatically if you've left unsaved documents open onscreen. It will go to sleep, though.

Extensions

One of macOS's unsung features is the ability to install *extensions*. These are add-on features—plug-ins—that expand what your Mac can do. Each is associated with a

GEM IN THE ROUGH

Mysteries of the Battery Menulet

If you've got a laptop, don't miss the checkbox in Energy Saver called "Show battery status in the menu bar." It puts a handy status indicator (▬) in the menu bar.

Without clicking the menulet, all you see is an icon that represents the battery charge. If you turn on Show Percentage from the menulet's actual menu, then the menulet can also show how much charge remains, in percentage form.

Here's what the menulet icon may show:

Lightning bolt in the battery. The laptop is plugged in and the battery is charging or charged.

Superimposed X. The laptop is plugged in, but the battery isn't in right, is missing, or isn't getting a charge.

Emptying black battery. The laptop is on battery power and has at least 25 percent power left. (The width of the bar reveals how much charge remains.)

Emptying red battery. The laptop is running off of battery power but has less than 25 percent charge remaining.

A nearly invisible red bar means you have less than nine minutes left. Save those documents, buddy.

If you click the menulet, you see an estimate of actual time remaining on your battery charge, in hours:minutes form. (If the battery is *charging*, then you see how much time remains until the battery is fully recharged, like this: "0:24 Until Full.") Either way, the readout is counting down (or up) to that joyous moment.

The menu also offers a terrific list: Using Significant Energy. When your battery is running low, it's a great way to see which apps are guzzling down your juice.

Finally, if you Option-click the menulet, you get a health report for your battery. It might say, for example, "Condition: Normal." When the battery needs your attention—when it says "Service Battery," "Replace Soon," "Replace Now," or "Check Battery"—you don't have to press Option. You'll see that message every time you open the menulet.

full-blown program you've installed on your Mac; they can come from Apple or anybody else. This System Preferences panel lists the ones you've got installed so far, and lets you turn off the ones you don't use.

Extensions (Figure 9-14) can modify seven parts of the Mac:

- **Actions, Photos Editing.** You probably have only one item in each of these items, called Markup. That's Apple's own extension, and it lets you mark up attachments in Mail, TextEdit, Photos, and some other programs; page 597 describes these annotation tools. In theory, these extensions do *something* to whatever text or graphics you've selected.

- **Finder Extensions.** These features operate on files at the desktop level. The most common example is Dropbox; its extension adds Dropbox commands (like Share Dropbox Link) to the shortcut menu when you right-click or two-finger click an icon in your Dropbox folder, and adds a green checkmark icon to each file that's been synced with Dropbox online. (Google Drive and Microsoft's OneDrive work similarly.)

- **Share Menu.** You know the Share button that appears all across macOS (page 258)? It produces a list of different ways (Mail, Messages, Facebook) you can share whatever you've got selected (a map, a web page, a photo). Well, that list is extensible. Your programs can insert their own sharing options into it.

Figure 9-14:
Once you click the category name, you can operate on the individual extensions listed within. You can hide or show them by turning their checkboxes off or on, and you can change the order in which they appear in your menus by dragging them up or down.

- **Today.** The Today pane of the Notification Center is described on page 377—but what's fascinating is that you can now install new information chunks (widgets, as Apple calls them) to that display. Everybody can choose from the starter widgets like Calculator, Calendar, and Weather—but other programs can install additional info-bits here.

- **Finder.** Here are the document-editing options known as Quick Actions; Apple starts you off with Rotate, Markup, Create PDF, and Trim. They appear on the preview pane (page 54), the Quick Look window (page 55), and the contextual shortcut menu (page 99) for a selected document. Most people see them only when examining a photo, PDF, audio, or movie file.

- **Touch Bar.** In theory, software companies can add new buttons to the MacBook Pro's Touch Bar (page 227); they'll appear here if you have them.

Each of these extension categories works in the same way, as shown in Figure 9-14.

General

This panel is mostly about how things look on the screen: windows, menus, buttons, scroll bars, and fonts:

- **Appearance** and **Accent color** make a huge difference to the visual character of your Mac's screen elements. They're described on page 151.

- **Highlight color.** When you drag your cursor across text, its background changes color to indicate that you've selected it. *Which* color the background becomes is up to you; choose a shade from the pop-up menu. The Highlight color also affects such subtleties as the lines on the inside of a window as you drag an icon into it.

 If you choose Other, the Color Picker palette appears, from which you can choose any color your Mac is capable of displaying.

- **Sidebar icon size.** This pop-up menu controls the size of the icons in the Sidebar (page 15), as you'd expect. But you might not guess that it also controls the *type size* of those icons. And you'd *definitely* not guess that it simultaneously adjusts the size and type of the mailbox icons in the Mail program.

- **Automatically hide and show the menu bar.** This checkbox has nothing to do with colors, of course. But it can make a big difference on a small screen (this means you, laptoppers). When it's turned on, your menu bar disappears (including the menu-bar clock and other menulets). It reappears only as needed—when you move your cursor to the top of the screen.

- **Show scroll bars.** If you choose "Automatically based on mouse or trackpad," then whether the scroll bars appear or not depends on what you have plugged in.

 If you have a trackpad or a Magic Mouse, for example, Apple assumes you'll scroll by dragging your fingers—so you won't be needing the scroll bars at the edges of the windows. Therefore, the scroll bars appear only when you're actually scrolling (and then only to show you where you are in the window). But if you have no way

of using touch gestures—for example, if you have a regular mouse or the Apple Mouse—then scroll bars are always visible, so you don't freak out.

"When scrolling" means that the scroll bars pop into view during the actual scroll, when your mouse or fingers-on-trackpad are actually in motion. And Always, of course, means the scroll bars never disappear.

- **Click in the scroll bar to.** For details on "Jump to the next page" and "Jump to the spot that's clicked," see the box on page 26.

- **Default web browser.** When you click a link in, for example, an email message— or on Twitter or Facebook—which web browser should open? Safari? Chrome? Firefox? Here's where you decide.

- **Ask to keep changes when closing documents.** This option is for people who liked the old "Save changes before closing?" message that appears when you close a document—instead of the Auto Save feature (page 206). If you turn this item on, Auto Save will still be there in case your program crashes, for example. But when you close that document or its program, you'll be *asked* whether or not you want to preserve the changes you've made since your last manual Save. Auto Save programs like Pages and TextEdit, in other words, will work just like they used to—and the way all other programs do.

- **Close windows when quitting an app.** Here it is: the master on/off switch for the macOS feature responsible for reopening your last-used documents and windows each time you open an app.

Usually, the auto-reopening feature saves you time and helps you resume your mental flow. But if you find it disturbing (or if you're worried about someone else discovering what you're up to), then turn on this checkbox.

- **Number of recent items.** Just how many of your recently opened documents, networked servers, and programs do you want the Mac to show using the Recent Items command in the menu? Pick a number from the pop-up menus.

- **Allow Handoff between this Mac and your iCloud devices.** You know that fantastic synergy you gain if you own both an iPhone and a Mac—the features described starting on page 309? This is the master on/off switch.

- **Use font smoothing when available.** The Mac's built-in text-smoothing (*antialiasing*) feature is supposed to produce smoother, more commercial-looking text anywhere it appears on your Mac: in word-processing documents, email messages, web pages, and so on.

Internet Accounts

For years, this System Preferences pane was called Mail, Contacts & Calendars. It's a single, handy, central place to tell macOS your user names and passwords for all kinds of internet services: Gmail, Yahoo, Exchange, Twitter, Vimeo, Flickr, LinkedIn, and so on.

To get started entering your account names and passwords, click one of the big-name logos (Gmail, Yahoo, whatever) or click the + button below the list. The Mac is smart enough to feed the account information here into the right programs (Mail, Calendar, Contacts, and the Share button described on page 258).

Keyboard

The changes you make on this panel are tiny but can have a cumulatively big impact on your daily typing routine. The options have been organized into five panes: Keyboard, Text, Shortcuts, Input Sources, and Dictation. If your Mac has a Touch Bar, its settings appear here, too.

Keyboard Tab

On this pane, you have these choices:

- **Key Repeat, Delay Until Repeat.** In macOS, holding down letter and number keys doesn't make them repeat, much to the disappointment of people who like to type, for example, "AAAAAARRRRRRGGGGHHH!" Instead, holding down a key produces a palette of alternative accented versions of that letter, like é, è, ê, ë, and so on.

 Only the punctuation keys still repeat, so you can still type ****** or ????? or !!!!!!!.

 There are sneaky ways to make your regular keys repeat, as they did in days gone by; see page 244. In the meantime, these two sliders govern the repeating behavior of the punctuation keys. On the right: a slider that determines how long you must hold down a key before it starts repeating (to prevent triggering repetitions accidentally). On the left: a slider that governs how fast each key spits out characters once the spitting has begun.

- **Adjust keyboard brightness in low light.** Recent Mac laptops' keys light up when you're working in the dark—a showy but useful feature. Here's the on/off switch. (Even if you've turned off the feature here, you can always turn on the keyboard backlighting by tapping the �die and �die keys.)

- **Turn keyboard backlight off after __ seconds of inactivity.** If you're watching a video, those glowing keys can be a distraction. You can use this control to specify how quickly the keyboard backlight fades to black once you've stopped typing or mousing.

- **"Touch Bar shows," "Press Fn key to."** These pop-up menus govern what appears in the Touch Bar, so they appear only if you have one. Details start on page 227.

- **Show keyboard and emoji viewers in menu bar.** You can read all about these special symbol-generating windows on page 347. Here's the on/off switch for the menulet that makes them appear.

- **Use all F1, F2, etc. keys as standard function keys.** This option appears *only* on laptops and aluminum-keyboard Macs. It's complicated, so read page 188 slowly.

- **Customize Control Strip.** This control, too, appears only if your laptop has a Touch Bar. It lets you edit the buttons on the Control Strip, the rightmost, ever-present chunk of system controls. See page 231.

- **Modifier Keys.** This button lets you turn off, or remap, the functions of the Option, Caps Lock, Control, and ⌘ keys. It's for Unix programmers whose pinkies can't adjust to the Mac's modifier-key layout; for anyone using a PC keyboard on which the Option (Alt) and ⊞ (Windows) keys are in the "wrong" positions relative to each other; and for anyone who keeps hitting Caps Lock by accident during everyday typing.

- **Set Up Bluetooth Keyboard.** Yes, you're absolutely right: This button lets you set up a Bluetooth (wireless) keyboard. See page 330.

Text Tab

Here's where you set up the Mac's automatic abbreviation-expansion feature, described on page 238. This is also where you choose a language for spell-checking and autocorrect.

Shortcuts Tab

This pane lets you make up new keystrokes for just about any function on the Mac, like capturing a screenshot, operating the Dock, triggering one of the Services, or operating a menu in *any program* from the keyboard. You can come up with keyboard combinations that, for example, are easier to remember, harder to trigger by accident, or easier to hit with one hand.

Step-by-step instructions for using this pane appear on page 200.

Input Sources

These are the keyboard layouts for various languages. See page 242.

Dictation

This tab is here in Keyboard, even though the entire purpose of the Dictation feature is to *avoid* using the keyboard. Anyway, it's described on page 278.

Language & Region

The primary job of this pane is to set up your Mac to work in other languages. If you bought your Mac already set up in your own language—you're already using the only language, number format, and keyboard layout you'll ever need—then you can ignore most of this panel. But when it comes to showing off macOS to your friends and loved ones, the "wow" factor on the Mac's polyglot features is huge.

Details appear on page 348.

Mission Control

Mission Control, the joint venture of the Exposé and Spaces window-management features, is described in detail on page 177—and so is this joint-venture control panel.

Mouse

This pane (Figure 9-15) looks different depending on what kind of mouse (if any) is attached to your Mac.

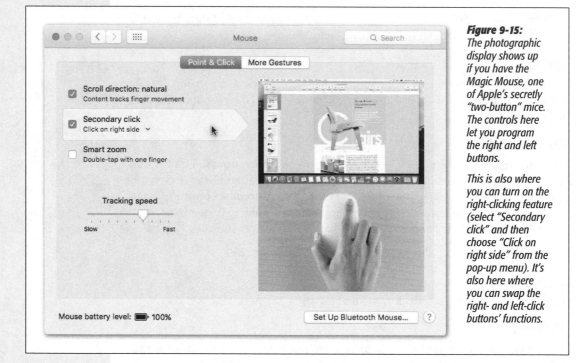

Figure 9-15:
The photographic display shows up if you have the Magic Mouse, one of Apple's secretly "two-button" mice. The controls here let you program the right and left buttons.

This is also where you can turn on the right-clicking feature (select "Secondary click" and then choose "Click on right side" from the pop-up menu). It's also here where you can swap the right- and left-click buttons' functions.

You might have the wireless, Bluetooth Magic Mouse (version 1 or 2), whose flat, broad top surface is also a trackpad. You might have the wired or wireless Apple Mouse, formerly called the *Mighty* Mouse, which has a domed top surface. And, of course, you can connect any old USB or Bluetooth mouse, from a Windows PC or whatever.

Note: On a laptop without any mouse attached, the Mouse pane still appears in System Preferences—but its sole function is to help you "pair" your Mac with a wireless Bluetooth mouse. At that point, the Mouse pane looks just as it does on a desktop Mac.

Scroll Direction

You can make your mouse's scroll wheel make your window scroll what Apple considers the right way ("Natural"), even though that feels *unnatural* to people who've been using mice for a long time. See page 27.

Secondary Click

Just by looking, you'd never know an Apple mouse has both a right button and a left button. Once you turn on the "Secondary click" feature in System Preferences (Figure 9-15), though, each side clicks independently.

Primary Mouse Button

On a two-button mouse, which button (left or right) is the main clicker, and which is the "right-click" that opens shortcut menus? That usually depends on whether you're a righty or a lefty. Anyway, here's where you specify.

Tracking Speed

The cursor on the screen doesn't move 5 inches when you move the mouse 5 inches on the desk. Instead, the cursor moves farther when you move the mouse faster.

How *much* farther depends on how you set the first slider here. The Fast setting is nice if you have an enormous monitor, since you don't need an equally large mouse pad to get from one corner to another. The Slow setting forces you to pick up and put down the mouse frequently as you scoot across the screen. It offers very little acceleration, but it can be great for highly detailed work like pixel-by-pixel editing in Photoshop.

Smart Zoom

This feature, available for Apple's Magic Mouse, lets you double-tap in Safari to magnify only the block of text, or the graphic, that contains your cursor. (These are touches, not full clicks.) It's super-handy if you're over 40 and your eyesight is starting to go.

Scrolling Speed

When you turn the wheel or trackball on the top of a mouse thus equipped, how fast should it affect whatever you're scrolling on the screen?

Double-Click Speed

This option specifies how much time you have to complete a double-click. If you click too slowly—beyond the time you've allotted yourself with this slider—the Mac "hears" two *single* clicks instead.

Network

See Chapter 13 for the settings you need to plug in for networking.

Notifications

Here's where you customize the Notification Center, which gets its own big write-up in Chapter 10.

Printers & Scanners

Chapter 15 describes printing and scanning. This panel offers a centralized list of the printers, scanners, and fax modems you've introduced to the Mac.

Screen Time

Here's one of Catalina's big new features; see page 216.

Security & Privacy

See Chapter 12 for details on locking up your Mac.

Sharing

MacOS is an outstanding, upstanding network citizen, flexible enough to share its contents with other Macs, Windows PCs, people dialing in from the road, and so on. On this panel, you'll find on/off switches for each of these sharing channels.

Many of these features are covered in other chapters. For example, Screen Sharing, File Sharing, and Remote Login are in Chapter 13; Printer Sharing is in Chapter 15; and Internet Sharing is in Chapter 17.

Here's a quick rundown on the other items:

- **Media Sharing.** This option accommodates Mac laptops, which don't have CD/DVD drives. When you sit at a Mac that *does* have a drive and turn on this option, those driveless computers on the network can "see," and borrow, your Mac's DVD drive for the purpose of installing new software or running Mac disk-repair software. (Your drive shows up under the Remote Disc heading in the driveless Mac's Finder Sidebar.)

- **Remote Management.** Lets someone else control your Mac using Apple Remote Desktop, a popular add-on program for teachers and system administrators.

- **Remote Apple Events.** Lets AppleScript gurus send commands to Macs across the network.

- **Bluetooth Sharing.** This pane lets you set up Bluetooth file sharing, a way for other people near you to shoot files over to (or receive files from) your laptop—without hassle, or passwords. Page 254 has the details.

- **Content Caching.** Technical, but cool: If you turn on this checkbox, then your Mac keeps a copy of all the Apple software that *all* Macs on your network download.

That includes macOS updates, App Store apps and their updates, and iCloud photos and documents.

Why? Because the next time one of the *other* Macs needs that app or update, it grabs it from your Mac. That's much faster than re-downloading it from the internet. Note, however, that Apple recommends turning this feature on only if your Mac gets online over a wired Ethernet connection—not Wi-Fi.

Tip: As you can imagine, Content Caching eats up a lot of disk space. If you turn it on and then click Options, you can set a limit to how much software is allowed to pile up on your Mac. Then again, don't worry; if your disk runs out of space, your Mac will auto-delete the cache as needed. (It's part of the purgeable storage described on page 102.)

And if you Option-click that button, it opens Advanced Options: some dizzyingly technical additional settings. Here, for example, you have some control over which other Macs are allowed to access your Mac's cache.

Sidecar

And here it is, a big, fat, supercool windfall for iPad owners. You can use your iPad as an external, second screen for your Mac!

There are all kinds of reasons you might want to use Sidecar (Figure 9-16). Some people just like having a second screen off to the side for reference. That's great for viewing news or social-media feeds, for example, or holding your Mac software's toolbars so there's more room on the Mac's main screen.

Or you can make a Keynote or PowerPoint presentation from the Mac in Presenter View. On the Mac, you see your speaker notes, a timer, and the next slide, but your customer, holding the iPad, sees only the full-screen slides. Or you can edit in Final Cut, with the iPad displaying only the final video without all the palettes and tools.

Other people use the iPad as a graphics tablet, using the pressure-sensitive Apple Pencil as a stylus for *Mac* graphics software.

Figure 9-16:
Sidecar turns your iPad into an external monitor for your Mac. Like any second screen, it can be either a mirror of the Mac's screen or an extension of it. Here you can see a window being dragged from the Mac onto the iPad's screen.

And what a great way to sign contracts!

The sky's the limit, made all the better because the iPad is a *portable* external display.

Before you get all excited, however, note the requirements:

- **A recent Mac.** Sidecar requires these or later models: 2016 MacBook, MacBook Pro, or iMac (the iMac 5K works, too); a 2018 MacBook Air or Mac Mini; or a 2019 Mac Pro.

- **A recent iPad.** 2018 iPad or a 2019 iPad mini or Air, or later. Any model of iPad Pro works, too. Your Mac and iPad have to be logged into the same iCloud account.

You can connect the two with a cable (a Lightning cable or USB-C cable, depending on your model), which gives you the advantage of keeping the iPad charged.

But if you want to carry the iPad across the room, you can do the job wirelessly, too. Each device needs Bluetooth, Wi-Fi, and Handoff turned on.

Starting Sidecar

Once that's all set up—and, presumably, you've found some way to prop the iPad upright—open the iPad menulet (■ or ▦) that suddenly appears on the Mac. Choose the iPad's name (Figure 9-17).

Tip: If the ■ or ▦ doesn't appear, confirm that the iPad is running iOS 13.2 or later. Make sure that, in System Preferences→Displays, "Show mirroring options in the menu bar when available " is turned on. You can also choose the iPad's name using the System Preferences→Sidecar→"Connect to" pop-up menu.

Figure 9-17:
The ▦ menulet lets you broadcast your Mac's screen image either to an Apple TV or to an iPad. And, once you're done, to stop broadcasting.

Like magic, the iPad's screen lights up as an extension of the Mac's screen. Your cursor floats from one screen to the other, no longer stopped by the edge of the Mac's screen. Feel free to drag your programs' windows right off the edge of the Mac screen, through space, and onto the iPad's screen.

Tip: Instead of dragging a window, point to its green ⊙ button (top left) and choose "Move to [iPad Name]." The window jumps over to the iPad, perfectly sized.

Most of the tricks described on page 343 work for the iPad, too. You can position the Mac's menu bar or Dock on either screen, for example.

Mirroring the Screen

At the outset, your iPad's screen displays an *extension* of the Mac's screen, as though your desktop is now twice as wide and crossing the gap between the machines.

You can, if you prefer, turn the iPad into a *duplicate* of the Mac's screen, so that (for example) a fan of your photography can watch a slideshow from the comfort of the couch instead of having to huddle around your iMac on the desk.

To do that, open the ▣ or ◪ menulet. Choose Mirror Built-In Retina Display (or whatever your Mac's screen is called). To switch back, use the same menu to choose Use As Separate Display.

All of this opens up the possibility of using the iPad by itself, away from the Mac. Keep in mind that, while you can read and scroll with your finger, doing actual work pretty much requires an Apple Pencil (read on). You otherwise have no way to "click the mouse"; finger taps don't do anything!

What to Do on the iPad

The iPad works beautifully as a second screen for the Mac next to it. You use your mouse or trackpad as usual, making your cursor slide back and forth between the two screens.

But what about using the iPad to run Mac software when you're *not* next to the Mac? No, you can't tap your finger to click directly on the iPad's screen, but there are a few ways to interact directly with it:

- **Draw, point, and click with the Apple Pencil,** Apple's $130 stylus. Artists and graphic designers use this thing to draw and design on the iPad, enjoying the smoothness of the lines it draws and the way the lines get fatter when you press harder. Now, at last, you can use the iPad as a graphics tablet with actual Mac graphics programs. Photoshop, Illustrator, Final Cut Pro, Maya, ZBrush, and other Mac apps all work with it.

Tip: In System Preferences→Sidecar, you can turn on "Enable double tap on Apple Pencil." That means tapping twice on the barrel of the Apple Pencil 2 with your finger, which has a special shortcut meaning in some Mac programs (like "Go back to the previous tool").

- **Scroll the iPad screen** by dragging with *two* fingers.
- **Adjust settings with the Touch Bar.** As you know from page 227, the Touch Bar is a feature of Apple's pricier laptops. It's a color touchscreen strip above the keyboard, whose buttons offer quick access to common functions, which change according to what you're doing.

 What's fascinating about Sidecar is that it offers you the Touch Bar even if your Mac doesn't have one! That makes sense, since the Touch Bar is especially useful

when you're using Photoshop and other graphics programs, which lend themselves to iPad touchscreen use. In Adobe apps, for example, you can use the Touch Bar to create or open a file, place it, show or hide rulers and guides, change your brush characteristics, and so on, without ever taking your hands off the iPad.

Tip: You can hide or show the Touch Bar using the commands in the ▣ menu. Also, in System Preferences→Sidecar, you can use the Show Touch Bar pop-up menu to move the bar to the top of the screen instead of the bottom—or, again, turn it off.

- **Use the Sidebar.** Yes, there's a Sidebar in Sidecar.

The Sidebar is a skinny column of buttons (shown at right in Figure 9-18). It's intended to give you a few basic controls over your Mac software while you're holding the iPad, to save you the exertion of shifting your body and your focus back and forth between the two machines.

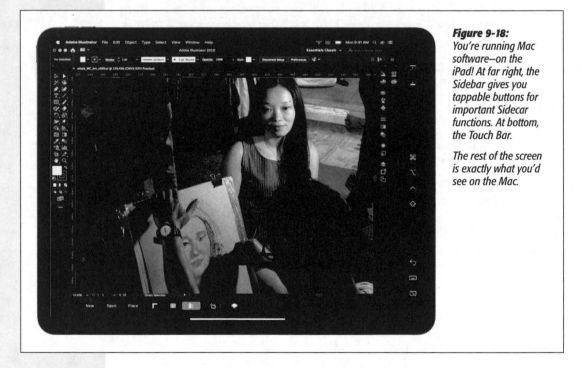

Figure 9-18:
You're running Mac software—on the iPad! At far right, the Sidebar gives you tappable buttons for important Sidecar functions. At bottom, the Touch Bar.

The rest of the screen is exactly what you'd see on the Mac.

At top, you've got ⬚ (show or hide the Mac's menu bar) and ⬚ (show or hide the iPad's Dock).

Next, you've got icons for the Mac's modifier keys: ⌘ (Command), ⌥ (Option), ⌃ (Control), and ⇧ (Shift). These are for use in graphics programs, where holding down a key modifies what a tool does. In Photoshop, for example, you hold down the Option key to draw a rectangle from the center, and in Illustrator, you hold down Shift to resize something proportionally. Now you can do all that on the iPad.

Tip: Double-tap these Sidebar "keys" to lock them down, without having to keep your finger on them.

The Sidebar also includes buttons for ↶ (Undo) and ▦ (show/hide the onscreen keyboard). Finally, the ◻ button disconnects the iPad from the Mac.

You can hide or show the Sidecar Sidebar using the ▣ menu, or you can move it to the other side of the screen in System Preferences→Sidecar.

- **Type.** The onscreen keyboard isn't your only ticket to typing. If you've set up a physical keyboard with your iPad—a Bluetooth one, for example, or a wired one—you can type normally into the Mac app on the iPad screen.

All the standard iPadOS fingers-on-glass gestures work for editing, too. For Copy, pinch on the screen with three fingers. For Cut, do that twice. For Paste, tap where you want to paste, and then un-pinch with three fingers (spread them).

You can now do Undo by swiping left with three fingers, or Redo by swiping right with three fingers.

- **Use iPad apps, too.** Swipe up from the bottom of the screen to reveal the iPad's Dock. Feel free to hop into any of your iPad apps, or even to split the screen between an iPad app and a Mac (Sidecar) app.

To finish a Sidecar session, choose Disconnect from the ▣ menu (on the Mac), or tap ◻ (on the iPad's Sidebar). Next time you connect, the iPad will remember where you had all the windows and tools positioned.

Tip: There's nothing to stop you from using regular external screens with your Mac, in addition to the iPad.

Siri

This pane houses the settings for Siri, as described on page 299.

Software Update

Whenever Apple improves some piece of macOS or some Apple-branded program, the Mac can notify you, download the update, and install it automatically. These updates may include new versions of programs like Photos and Maps; drivers for newly released printers, scanners, cameras, and such; bug fixes and security patches; and so on.

This System Preferences panel governs when and how your Mac auto-downloads new versions of macOS and apps you've acquired from the App Store (page 159). The panel also lets you know the last time updates were automatically installed.

"Automatically keep my Mac up to date" means your Mac will automatically install new macOS versions and new versions of your App Store apps. (In other words, when this is on, the third and fourth checkboxes described next are also on.)

The Advanced checkboxes govern the process:

- **Check for updates.** You grant permission to your Mac to ping the mother ship periodically to see if there are updates available. Turn it off and you're stuck with today's software versions forever.

- **Download new updates when available.** If you leave this option turned on, you'll still be notified before anything gets installed, but you won't have to wait for the downloading—the deed will already be done.

- **Install macOS updates.** If you turn this off, you won't automatically get macOS updates as they come along.

- **Install app updates from the App Store.** If you turn this off, you won't get updates to your apps. It's hard to think of a reason why you wouldn't want the latest, most refined versions of apps. But maybe you want to read about some update online before installing it.

- **Install system data files and security updates.** These files are part of macOS's automatic, ongoing virus protection. If you turn this option off, your Mac won't know how to recognize and fight the latest viruses. Also, you're nuts.

Tip: In case this automatic-update thing feels a little *too* automatic, you can always see a list of what updates were installed while you weren't looking. Open the App Store app and click the Updates tab to see everything that's been installed in the past 30 days.

Sound

At the bottom of this panel, there's an "Output volume" slider—the master volume control for your Mac. (It's a duplicate of the one in the menu bar, and useful only when you've forgotten about the volume keys on your keyboard.)

Using the panes of the Sound panel, you can configure the sound system of your Mac in any of several ways.

Tip: Here's a quick way to jump directly to the Sound panel of System Preferences—from the keyboard, without ever having to open System Preferences or click Sound. Just press Option as you tap the ◀, ◀◦, or ◀)) key on the top row of your Apple keyboard.

Sound Effects Tab

"Sound effects" means *error beeps*—the sound you hear when the Mac wants your attention, or when you click someplace you shouldn't.

Just click the sound of your choice to make it your default system beep. Most of the canned choices here are funny and clever, yet subdued enough to be practical as alert sounds (Figure 9-19).

The other controls on the Sound Effects panel include these:

- **Play sound effects through.** Intriguingly enough, you can specify one sound source (a speaker or headset) for most sound playback—and a different one just for your error beeps. That's the one you specify with this pop-up menu.

- **Alert volume.** The *main* volume slider for your Mac is the "Output volume" slider at the bottom of the Sound pane. The "Alert volume" slider is *just* for error beeps; Apple was kind enough to let you adjust the volume of these error beeps independently.

- **Play user interface sound effects.** This option produces a few subtle sound effects during certain Finder operations: when you drag something off the Dock, into the Trash, or into a folder, or when the Finder finishes a file-copying job.

- **Play feedback when volume is changed.** Each time you press one of the volume keys (◀, ◀), ◀))), the Mac beeps (or, rather, pops) to help you gauge the current volume.

That's all fine when you're working at home. But more than one person has been humiliated in an important meeting when the Mac made a sudden, inappropriately loud sonic outburst—and then amplified that embarrassment by furiously and repeatedly pressing the volume-down key, beeping all the way.

If you turn off this checkbox, then the Mac won't make any sound at all as you adjust its volume. Instead, you'll see only a visual representation of the steadily decreasing (or increasing) volume level.

Figure 9-19:
You can adjust your overall speaker volume independently from the alert-beep volume, thank goodness.

Tip: The Shift key reverses the logic. So if you have "Play feedback" turned *on,* holding down Shift as you tap the volume keys makes them silent. If it's turned *off,* you can force the volume-gauging beeps to play by pressing Shift as you tap the volume keys.

Output Tab

"Output" means speakers or headphones. For most people, this pane lists only Internal Speakers (and a Balance slider for left-to-right stereo balancing).

This panel is more useful when you've connected external speakers, a Bluetooth or USB phone headset, or an AirPlay receiver like an Apple TV—and then clicked its name. All Mac audio now flows to that device. MacOS will even remember your volume setting for each gadget independently.

Tip: Here's a much quicker way to change your audio input or output: Press Option as you click the ◀)) menulet. You get a secret pop-up menu that lists your various microphones, speakers, and headphones, so you can switch things without a visit to System Preferences.

Input Tab

This panel lets you specify which sound source you want the Mac to "listen to," if you have more than one connected: external microphone, internal microphone, line input, USB headset, or whatever. It also lets you adjust the sensitivity of that micro-phone—its *input volume*—by dragging the slider and watching the real-time Input level meter above it change as you speak. Put another way, it's a quick way to see if your microphone is working.

If you'd prefer even more control over your Mac's sound inputs and outputs, don't miss the Audio MIDI Setup program in your Applications→Utilities folder.

Spotlight

Here's how you tell the Mac (a) which categories of files and information you want the Spotlight search feature to search, (b) which folders you *don't* want searched, for privacy reasons, and (c) which key combination you want to use for summoning the Spotlight menu or dialog box. Details are in Chapter 3.

Startup Disk

Use this panel to pick the System folder your Mac will use the next time it starts up—when you're swapping between macOS and Windows (running with Boot Camp), for example. Check out the details on page 467.

Time Machine

Here's the master on/off switch and options panel for Time Machine, which is described on page 260.

Touch ID

As you could probably guess, this panel appears only if your Mac laptop has a Touch ID fingerprint sensor—for example, it's a Touch Bar laptop or a 2018 MacBook Air.

This sensor is built right into the power button (clever!). It reads your finger at any angle. It can't be faked out by a plastic finger or even a chopped-off human one. You can teach it to recognize up to five different fingerprints. They can be a few of your fingers or, for example, you could teach it one finger each for five family members.

Before you can use your fingertip as a password, though, you have to teach the Mac to recognize it, and here's where you do it:

1. **Create a password.**

 That's right: You can't use a fingerprint *instead* of a password; you can only use a fingerprint in addition to one. You'll still need a password from time to time to keep the Mac's security tight. For example, you need to enter your password if you can't make your fingerprint work (maybe it got encased in acrylic in a hideous crafts accident).

 So open System Preferences→Accounts and create a password (page 491), if you haven't already.

Figure 9-20:
Each time you touch your finger to the power button, a little more of the fingerprint map gets filled in. Once you've filled in the fingerprint, the dialog box advises you to keep going, this time tipping the finger a little each time so the sensor gets a better view of your finger's edges.

2. **Teach a fingerprint.**

Click the "Add a fingerprint" button.

Start by entering your account password, to prove you're not a sinister spy. Click OK.

Now place the finger you want to train onto the power button—your index finger is the most logical candidate. You're asked to touch it to the power button over and over, maybe six times. Each time, the gray lines of the onscreen fingerprint darken a little more (Figure 9-20).

Once the registration is complete, the screen says "Touch ID is ready."

3. **Click Done.**

You return to the Touch ID panel, where your fingerprint is now represented by an icon named something like "Finger 1." Feel free to click those words and type a better name ("Right-hand pointer" or whatever). To delete one, point to its icon and then click the ⊗ that appears; click Delete to confirm.

Tip: It's perfectly legal to register the same finger several times. That technique makes Touch ID more reliable if it seems to be having trouble recognizing that finger.

You can register your toes instead of fingers, if that's helpful. Or even patches of your wrist or arm, if you're patient (and weird).

Anyway, you are now ready to start using the fingerprint. Try it: Put the Mac to sleep. Then press the power button with your very special finger. The Mac reads your fingerprint and instantly unlocks itself.

And now, a few notes about using your fingerprint as a password:

- **Apple says the image of your fingerprint is encrypted** and stored in the Touch Bar's dedicated processor chip. It's never transmitted anywhere, it never goes online, and it's never collected by Apple.

- **The Touch ID scanner may have trouble** if your finger is wet, greasy, or scarred.

- **The fingerprint reader isn't just a camera;** it doesn't just look for the image of your fingerprint. It's actually measuring the tiny differences in electrical conductivity between the raised parts of your fingerprint (which aren't conductive) and the skin just beneath the surface (which is). That's why a plastic finger won't work—and even your own finger won't work if it's been chopped off (or if you've passed away).

- **If you've registered fingerprints belonging to several account holders,** then fast user switching (page 506) is *really* fast. All Person B has to do is click the power button with the registered finger, and boom: Person A's account world slides away, and Person B's heaves into view.

Fingerprints for Apps, Websites, and Apple Pay

At the bottom of the System Preferences→Touch ID screen, you see the on/off switches for the three things your fingerprint can do: It can unlock the computer (Unlocking

your Mac), pay for things (Apple Pay—see page 665), and serve as your password when you buy books, music, apps, and videos from Apple's online stores (iTunes & App Store). That last feature is handy: At the moment when you're usually asked to type your iCloud password, you're asked to touch the fingerprint sensor to authorize the purchase instead.

All of this is great news. Most of us would be happy if we never, ever had to type in another password.

Trackpad

You may love your Mac laptop now, but these special features make your laptop *crazy* better. Turns out you can point, click, scroll, right-click, rotate things, enlarge things, hide windows, and switch programs, all on the trackpad itself, without ever having to lift your fingers. (You can do most of this on a desktop Mac, too, if it has an Apple Magic Mouse, or an external trackpad like Apple's Magic Trackpad.)

The options here depend on your Mac model, but usually you see something like Figure 9-21: three tabs. Each governs how you do pointing, clicking, scrolling, and other mouselike maneuvers. Each time you click one, the right half of the dialog box plays a looping movie that shows you that technique clearly and visibly.

Here's what's on the three main tabs.

Figure 9-21:
The Trackpad pane of System Preferences offers hours of entertainment—because each setting triggers a little movie that shows what Apple means.

This is what the pane looks like if you have a Force Touch trackpad (which comes on the latest laptop models).

Point & Click

- **Look up & data detectors.** This gesture lets you tap the trackpad with three fingers simultaneously (*don't* click—just touch the surface) to bring up two kinds of supplementary information. If you're tapping a single word, you get a handy dictionary definition. If you're tapping a web address, map address, block of contact information, or something else the data detectors feature recognizes (page 247), then you get a bubble that proposes opening that item in the corresponding program. (Neither feature works in all programs.)

- **Secondary click.** This means "right-click." As you know, right-clicking is a huge deal on the Mac; it unleashes useful features just about everywhere.

 This pop-up menu offers you three options. You can click with two fingers; click once in the lower-right corner of the trackpad; or click once in the lower-left corner. You can also trigger a right-click by clicking with your thumb while resting your index and middle fingers on the trackpad. Weird, but wonderful.

- **Tap to click.** Usually, you touch your laptop's trackpad only to move the cursor. For clicking and dragging, you're supposed to push down on the clicker (the lower half of the actual trackpad surface). Many people find, however, that it's more direct to tap and drag directly on the trackpad, using the same finger that's been moving the cursor. That's the purpose of this checkbox. When it's on, you can tap the trackpad surface to register a mouse click at the location of the cursor. (Also handy when your trackpad is broken, sticky, or balky.) Double-tap to double-click.

- **Click.** This option appears if you have one of the Force Touch trackpads described on page 370. It lets you adjust *how hard* you have to press to produce a click: Light, Medium, or Firm.

- **Tracking speed.** This is a duplicate of the Tracking Speed slider described on page 355—but it lets you establish an independent tracking speed for the *trackpad*.

- **Silent clicking.** This option appears on older (pre-2016) laptops with Force Touch trackpads. It lets you trigger clicks without actually producing a click sound. Perfect for mousing in bed next to a light sleeper.

- **Force Click and haptic feedback.** This is the on/off switch for the force-clicking features described on page 370.

Scroll & Zoom

- **Scroll direction: natural.** Here's the heart of macOS's once-controversial feature: scrolling *up* when you drag your fingers (or the scroll wheel, or the scroll bar) *up*.

 If you can't stand this arrangement, turn it off here.

- **Zoom in or out.** If you've used an iPhone or iPad, this one will seem familiar. What it means is, "Put two fingers on the trackpad and spread them apart to *enlarge* what's on the screen. Slide two fingers *together* to shrink it down again." It doesn't work

in every program—it affects pictures and PDFs in Preview, photos in Photos, text in Safari, text in a TextEdit window—but it's great when it does.

- **Smart zoom.** You can double-tap a block of text or a graphic on a web page to enlarge just that block to full-screen size. The "smart" element of this is the way the software senses that block's borders and zooms in exactly right. Double-tap your trackpad (touch, don't click) with *two* fingers to do it.

- **Rotate.** Place two fingers on the trackpad, and then twist them around an invisible center point, to rotate a photo or a PDF document. This doesn't work in all programs or in all circumstances, but it's great for turning images upright in Preview, Photos, Image Capture, and so on.

More Gestures

- **Swipe between pages.** Drag two fingers horizontally across the trackpad to skip to the next or previous page or image in a batch. Great for flipping through images or PDF pages in Preview or Photos, or to go back or forward a page in Safari. The tiny pop-up menu here lets you *change* the swiping gesture. You can swipe with two fingers, three fingers, or—if you're a fan of variety—two *or* three fingers.

- **Swipe between full-screen apps.** If you've embraced macOS's Full Screen feature, or its Mission Control feature, you'll want to learn this one. You can flip between full-screen apps with either three or four fingers on the trackpad.

- **Notification Center.** You can summon the Notification Center (page 376) by swiping leftward with two fingers onto the trackpad from beyond its right edge.

- **Mission Control.** This gesture lets you enter and exit Mission Control (page 177) by swiping up or down with three fingers. (You can change it to *four* fingers.)

- **One-app Exposé.** If this checkbox is on, you can trigger one-app Exposé (page 186) by swiping three fingers downward. (You can change the setting to *four* fingers.)

Note: If you study those last two paragraphs carefully, you'll realize that the four-finger swipe has different *levels.* Starting from whatever you're doing, a four-finger swipe *up* takes you into Mission Control. From there, *two* swipes down takes you into one-app Exposé. Similarly, from within one-app Exposé, *two* swipes upward enters Mission Control.

- **Launchpad.** Launchpad (page 165) wouldn't be very useful if it took several steps to open. Fortunately, this option lets you fire up Launchpad by pinching on the trackpad with three fingers and your thumb. (You can also exit Launchpad by *spreading* those four fingers.)

- **Show Desktop.** You can spread three fingers and your thumb to trigger desktop Exposé (page 189). Once there, *pinch* those fingers to return to what you were doing.

Note: Here again, Apple has created *levels* of four-finger pinching. Pinching once opens Launchpad; spread *twice* from there to show the desktop. Likewise, pinching *twice* from Show Desktop takes you straight into Launchpad.

At the bottom of the Trackpad pane, a Set Up Bluetooth Trackpad button appears. Use it to pair your Mac with a wireless external trackpad—like Apple's own Magic Trackpad (version 1 or 2).

The Force Touch Trackpad

The latest MacBook trackpads do a lot more than just click. Apple calls them Force Touch trackpads. (They also come on the external Magic Trackpad, which you can get for any Mac.) Clicking feels pretty much like clicking any other trackpad. But behind the scenes—or, rather, *under* the scenes—it's a totally different story.

Normal trackpads are hinged at the top, so the higher up you press, the harder it is to click. A Force Touch trackpad, on the other hand, doesn't actually move at all. The "click" you feel and hear is a fake-out, created by a vibration module under the pad. Which explains, by the way, why the trackpad doesn't click when the computer is off. There's no power to the click-sound-making unit (what Apple calls the haptic engine).

Force Touch trackpads offer three interesting features: force-click, variable pressure, and "notch" feedback.

Force-click

If you click and then keep pressing harder, you trigger a *second* click, at a "deeper" level.

So what does a force-click do? Lots and lots of things—things that usually require a right-click or a multifinger click:

- **Look up a word.** In Mail or a web browser, you can force-click a highlighted word to open a pop-up window containing a definition or a Wikipedia entry.

- **Look up an address.** Anywhere you've highlighted a street address, in any program, you can force-click it to open a little Maps bubble showing you where it is.

- **Data detectors.** When you see a date (in a Mail or Messages message, for example), you can force-click it to propose adding it to your Calendar, just as shown on page 247. Or, if you see an airplane flight number in a message, or a package-tracking number, force-click it to see details.

- **Web preview.** When you see a link in Mail or Safari, you can force-click it to see a pop-up bubble showing the page itself.

- **Quick Look.** In the Finder, force-click any icon for a Quick Look preview of its contents, as described on page 55.

- **Renaming files.** Force-click an icon's name in the Finder to rename it.

- **One-app Exposé.** Force-click the icon of any open program on your Dock to see all its open windows, arrayed as miniatures (page 186).

- **Mark up PDF files and graphics.** When you're in Mail, creating a message with a picture or PDF attached, force-click its icon to enter Markup mode (page 597).

- **Open the Details pane.** In Messages, force-click a person's name in the left-side conversation list to open the Details pane for her (including a list of all attachments).

- **More details.** In Reminders and Calendar, force-clicking a reminder or an event opens a Details button. In Calendar, force-click the name of someone who's coming to a meeting to see that person's Contacts card.

- **Drop a pin in Maps** by force-clicking that spot.

- **GarageBand.** You can force-click all kinds of things in GarageBand: a region (to rename it), a note (to delete it), an empty Software Instrument track (to create an empty MIDI region), a region while dragging (to zoom in), and so on.

Variable pressure

A Force Touch trackpad can actually tell *how hard* you're pressing. How is that useful?

- **QuickTime, iMovie.** Your finger pressure controls how fast you rewind or fast-forward (on the corresponding buttons).

- **Maps.** Pressing harder zooms in faster.

- **Photos.** When you're moving through photos in an Album or a Moment by pressing the arrow buttons, pressing harder makes you go faster.

"Notch" clicks

Finally, the Force Touch trackpad can make that artificial click sound, complete with a little "click" vibration, to signal certain notch points in onscreen activity. For example, you'll feel that "notch" click when you've dragged a video clip to the maximum length in iMovie, or in Maps when you rotate the compass to north, or in Photos when you're rotating a photo (inside the Crop tool) and it reaches 0 degrees rotation.

Over time, in theory, you'll get used to these little shortcuts—and you'll be more productive with them.

On the other hand, they may just annoy you. In that case, open System Preferences→Trackpad and turn the whole thing off. (The "Force Click and haptic feedback" checkbox is the one you want—or, rather, don't want.)

Tip: Also on the System Preferences→Trackpad screen: a slider that lets you adjust how hard you have to press to generate a simulated click: Light, Medium, or Firm (see Figure 9-21).

Users & Groups

This is the master list of people who are allowed to log into your Mac. (In previous Mac versions it was called Accounts.) It's where you can adjust their passwords, startup pictures, self-opening startup items, permissions to use various features of the Mac, and other security tools. All of this is described in Chapter 12.

Wallet & Apple Pay

This panel is where you can set up Apple Pay, the step-saving feature that lets you complete web purchases without having to type in a credit card number. See page 665 for details.

Notifications

Anotification is an important status message or warning. On a smartphone, you get one every time a text message comes in, an alarm goes off, a calendar appointment is imminent, or your battery is running low. It's no different on your Mac. Mail and Messages might want to let you know a new message has arrived. The Calendar app might want to remind you an important meeting is about to start.

In macOS, you know when some app is trying to get your attention: A message bubble slides into view at the top right of your screen. Some of these alerts slide away again after five seconds; others require you to click a button, like Close, Snooze, or Show (which opens the program that's waving its little hand in your face).

Note: Only apps you got from the Mac App Store can tap into the Notification Center. Other programs use whatever alert mechanisms they always have—pop-up dialog boxes, for example.

You're also notified this way when one of your App Store apps has been automatically updated, or when that update requires you to quit the app or restart the Mac (and you're offered a Later button).

All kinds of warnings—dying battery, failed Time Machine backups, disks ejected improperly—appear in these subtle notification bubbles, rather than bleating their news in showstopping dialog boxes.

Insta-Respond to Bubbles

Some of those notification bubbles aren't just the Mac's way of speaking to you; they're interactive. That's particularly handy when the bubble represents an incoming iMessage, FaceTime call, or email—because you can reply to them. See Figure 10-1.

Shutting Up the Bubbles

Of course, little bubbles sliding into the top-right corner of your screen may not always be what you want, especially if you're trying to beat a deadline.

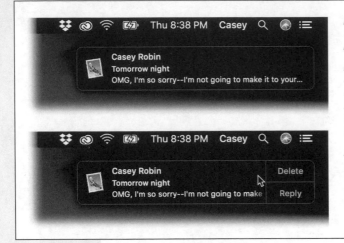

Figure 10-1:
Top: MacOS tries to get your attention using notification bubbles.

Bottom: If you point to a bubble before it disappears, it may offer buttons that let you take action. For example, if it's an incoming instant message, you can hit Reply and then type your response right in the bubble. If it's a FaceTime call, you can answer or decline it.

And if it's email, you can click either Delete or Reply. If you hit Reply, an outgoing, floating message window opens, already addressed, already set up as a response. Just type your reply and hit Send.

Dismiss One Bubble

If you're in a hurry, you can get rid of one of these bubbles with a right-swipe on it (two fingers on a trackpad, one on a Magic Mouse, or just drag it off to the right with your mouse).

Do Not Disturb (Manual)

But to truly shush all notifications, turn on Do Not Disturb (Figure 10-2, top).

Tip: The efficiency nut may prefer to simply Option-click the ☰ button at the right end of the menu bar. It turns gray, indicating that you've stifled all bubbles until midnight (or until you Option-click it again).

When Do Not Disturb is on, your messages quietly pile up in the Notification Center (described in a moment); they don't pop up on your screen individually as they happen, and they certainly don't make any noises.

Do Not Disturb (Automatic)

The Mac can also stifle the bubbles automatically, either according to a daily schedule (like when you're asleep) or when you're giving a presentation.

To see it, open System Preferences→Notifications (Figure 10-2, bottom). You'll find that this version of Do Not Disturb offers all kinds of useful options:

- **On a schedule.** Here you can specify starting and ending hours for Do Not Disturb to kick in automatically. It's handy if you'd like the Mac to go dark during the same hours you do every night. (There's no separate setting for weekends; Do Not Disturb will turn on and off for the same hours every day of the week.)

- **When the display is sleeping.** When the screen is dark, it means you're not at your Mac. You probably don't need passersby seeing your incoming love notes; besides, you're not there to witness them arriving anyway.

- **When mirroring to TVs and projectors.** If you're showing an audience something from your Mac, chances are pretty good you don't want little notice bubbles to interrupt the show. There's nothing worse than an audience of 500 witnessing the embarrassing subject lines of your incoming email.

- **Allow calls from everyone.** If you use your Mac as a speakerphone (page 304), you might still want it to ring for incoming calls. In that case, turn on this option. All other notifications are still silenced when Do Not Disturb is engaged—just not phone calls and FaceTime calls.

- **Allow repeated calls.** If you turn this on, and somebody tries to call you more than once within three minutes, it will ring through. The idea here is that nobody *would* call you multiple times unless it was urgent. You certainly wouldn't want Do Not Disturb to block somebody trying to tell you that there's been an accident, that you've overslept, or that you've just won the lottery.

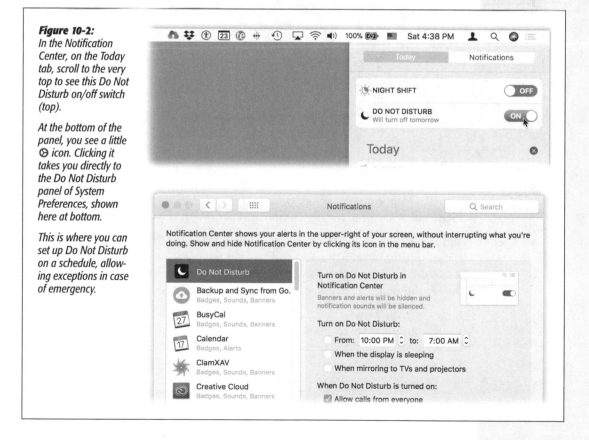

Figure 10-2:
In the Notification Center, on the Today tab, scroll to the very top to see this Do Not Disturb on/off switch (top).

At the bottom of the panel, you see a little ⊗ icon. Clicking it takes you directly to the Do Not Disturb panel of System Preferences, shown here at bottom.

This is where you can set up Do Not Disturb on a schedule, allowing exceptions in case of emergency.

The Notification Center

All right, now you know how to dismiss, stifle, or respond to notification bubbles. But what if you miss one? Or you decide to act on it later?

Thought you'd never ask. All those "Hey you!" messages collect on a single screen called the Notification Center (Figure 10-3).

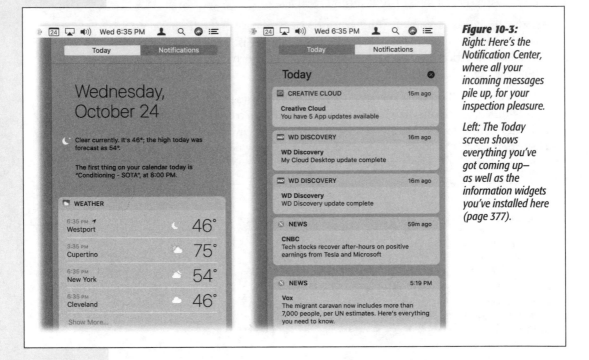

Figure 10-3:
Right: Here's the Notification Center, where all your incoming messages pile up, for your inspection pleasure.

Left: The Today screen shows everything you've got coming up—as well as the information widgets you've installed here (page 377).

To make it appear on a laptop, swipe two fingers *onto* the trackpad from the right. (Start the swipe off to the right of the trackpad. Weird.)

You can also open the Notification Center by clicking the ☰ in the upper-right corner of your screen. That's a handy trick if your Mac doesn't have a trackpad—if it's an iMac, for example. (You can also set up a keystroke or a "hot corner" to open the Notification Center, if you like. See pages 200 and 180.)

Either way, the Notification Center slides onto the screen like a classy gray window shade, showing every recent item of interest.

Tip: To close the Notification Center, swipe the opposite way (left to right) with two fingers. Or click any other part of the screen. Or click the ☰ again. Or just blink really hard.

The Notification Center has two tabs at the top:

- **Today.** On the Today tab (Figure 10-4), you see today's weather, all your upcoming appointments and reminders, and an assortment of widgets (calculator, stock

report, news headlines) that you've installed there. (More on this in a moment.) You also see the answers to any Siri queries you've decided to pin here, as described on page 298.

- **Notifications.** This tab lists all your apps' notifications, as well as all your Mac's messages, reminders, upcoming appointments, and so on.

Each produces a scrolling panel; read on.

Today Tab

The Today panel presents an executive summary of everything you need to know today, in plain English: your upcoming appointments (" 'Personnel meeting' is next up on your calendar, at 2 PM"); reminders coming due; weather and stock information; and

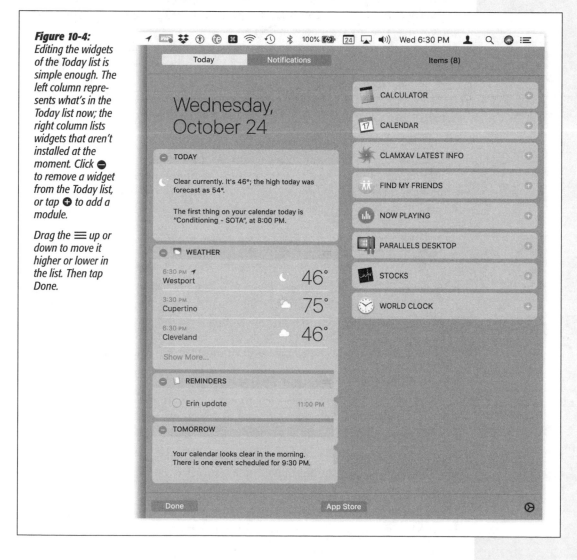

Figure 10-4:
Editing the widgets of the Today list is simple enough. The left column represents what's in the Today list now; the right column lists widgets that aren't installed at the moment. Click ⊖ to remove a widget from the Today list, or tap ⊕ to add a module.

Drag the ≡ up or down to move it higher or lower in the list. Then tap Done.

a preview of your schedule tomorrow. It's identical to the Today panel on the iPhone or iPad, if you're scoring at home.

Each of these little info-panels is called a widget, and there are tons of them available. For example, the Mac comes with ones called Calculator, which puts a calculator at your fingertips, and World Clock, which shows you what time it is anywhere in the world.

To add, remove, or rearrange widgets, click Edit at the bottom of the panel; proceed as described in Figure 10-4.

Intriguingly, Apple also allows apps to add their *own* sections to the Today list. For example, Dropbox can show a list of files that have been added to your Dropbox folder; Evernote can add buttons for creating new notes or reminders; The New York Times, Yahoo Digest, and HuffPost apps can add headlines; the Kindle app offers links to the books you're reading right now; and so on.

Tip: If you're feeling widget-deprived, click App Store. It opens a special section of the Mac App Store dedicated to apps that install widgets on your Today panel.

Notifications Tab

On the Notifications tab (Figure 10-3, right), you can have two kinds of fun:

- **Click an item to open the relevant app for more details.** For example, click an appointment listed there to open its information panel in Calendar. Click the name of a software update to open the Mac App Store program, where you can read about it and download it. Click a message's name to open Mail, where you can read the entire message.

- **Click the little ⊗ to dismiss one day's entire list of notifications**—or one app's worth—once you've seen them. (The ⊗ appears when you point to a notification.)

 So which is it—all the notifications from one app? Or from one day? That's up to you. It depends on how you've set things up in System Preferences→Notifications, as described in the next section. For example, if you've chosen to sort your notifications by Recents, the ⊗ button deletes a *day* of notifications; if you've chosen Recents by App, it deletes all the notifications from a particular *app*.

Customizing the Notification Center

You can (and should) specify *which* apps are allowed to junk up your Notification Center. Open System Preferences→Notifications to see the list of apps that might want to get your attention in the master Notifications list (Figure 10-5).

This is also the place where you can specify the *order* of the various apps' notifications in the center. Use the "Notification Center sort order" pop-up menu at the bottom of the window.

If you choose Recents, the apps with the newest alerts appear at the top. If you choose Recents by App, the notifications are grouped under headings that correspond to the

app generating them. And if you tap Manually by App, you can simply drag the app names up or down in the list to specify their top-to-bottom order on the Notification Center list.

Out of the box, a lot of macOS apps are listed in the Notification Center (along with Do Not Disturb, already described). Here are some of the most significant:

- **Calendar** lets you know about imminent appointments.

- **Facebook** governs the appearance of updates from your Facebook friends.

- **FaceTime** tells you when you've missed an incoming call.

- **Mail** lets you know when you've received a new email message. You can also specify whether or not the notification displays the beginning of the message itself when you're not seated at your Mac, which you may consider to be either useful or a scary privacy violation.

 Mercifully, Mail's Preferences→General tab lets you limit these alerts, so you won't be buried in a barrage of meaningless heads-up bubbles. You can tell Mail to alert you only when somebody in your Contacts list has written to you, only when a message lands in a smart mailbox folder, only when you get email from someone you've designated as a VIP—or whenever any message lands in any mailbox.

- **Messages** lets you know when somebody has sent you an instant message.

- **Safari** allows certain websites, if they're open on your Mac, to send you notifications (known as HTML web notifications).

Other companies' apps may appear in this list, too: BusyCal, Evernote, Skype, and so on.

Now it's time to change the settings for one app at a time. Click an app's name to see its individual Notifications settings (Figure 10-5—the Calendar app, in this case). For example, as hinted above, different apps can get your attention in different ways:

- **None.** If certain apps seem to bug you with news you really don't care about, you can make them shut up forever. They won't bother you with pop-up messages, although they can still insert items into the Notification Center panel.

- **Banners.** This option makes incoming notifications slide quietly and briefly onto the top right of your screen. Each message holds still long enough for you to read it, but it goes away automatically after a few seconds. Banners are a good option for things like Facebook and Twitter updates and incoming email messages.

- **Alerts.** These notifications don't go away until you click a button to dismiss them. Good for important messages, like alarms and flight updates.

At the bottom of the Notifications window, you get more settings for each app:

- **Show notifications on lock screen.** Do you want summaries of all your missed notifications to appear on your Lock screen ("5 email notifications") when you wake the Mac? It's a great feature, as long as you don't mind passing busybodies knowing how popular you are.

- **Show notification preview.** This is a privacy thing. Suppose you've wandered away from your desk. When someone sends you a text, do you want the notification banner to include the message itself, on the Lock screen where anyone can read it? (That's the preview.) Or do you want the banner to indicate only that a person has sent *some* message, which you can read only after unlocking the Mac?

 And it's not just texts. Do you want Uber information to appear in the banner? How about Facebook updates? The name of your alarm or reminder?

 You have two choices here: always (always show the message in the notification banner) or when unlocked (show it only if you're actually *using* the Mac).

- **Show in Notification Center.** Do you want this app's notifications to appear in the Notification Center? If you turn this off for an app, you'll still get its alert messages, but you won't see them listed in the Notification Center panel.

- **Badge app icon.** If you turn this option on, each app's actual icon (in your Launchpad and on your Dock) sprouts a red, circled number. This number lets you know how many times it's tried to flag you about something.

- **Play sound for notifications.** Some apps play a sound when a notification arrives. For example, Calendar dings to remind you of an upcoming event. It's a little insurance that you won't miss a nudge, but here's where you can turn these sounds off.

Figure 10-5:
Here in System Preferences, you can specify which apps are permitted to intrude on the precious billboard that is your Notification Center—and how they're permitted to intrude.

Some individual apps, including Mail and Calendar, offer additional controls in their Preferences boxes. For example, in Calendar, you can turn off notifications from shared calendars and from meeting invitations.

The Free Programs of macOS

R ight out of the box, macOS comes with a healthy assortment of about 50 freebies: programs for reading books, finding your way, writing documents, doing math, even playing games. They're all designed not only to show off some of macOS's most dramatic technologies, but also to let you get real work done without having to invest in additional software.

Some of the programs you'll find in your Applications list are covered in other chapters: App Store (page 159), Launchpad (page 165), Mission Control (page 177), Time Machine (page 260), System Preferences (page 317), Photos (page 457), Preview (page 589), Font Book (page 601) QuickTime Player (page 617), TV (page 626), Music (page 628), Voice Memos (page 637), Mail (page 669), Contacts (page 705), Safari (page 715), and Messages (page 749).

This chapter guides you through the rest of your software library, one program at a time. The important programs sit in the Applications folder in the main hard drive window, and a couple of dozen less frequently used apps await in the Applications→Utilities folder.

Tip: You can jump straight to the Applications folder in the Finder by pressing Shift-⌘-A (the shortcut for Go→Applications), or by clicking the Applications folder icon in the Sidebar. You might consider adding the Application folder's icon to the Dock, too, so you can access it no matter what program you're in. Shift-⌘-U (or Go→Utilities) takes you, of course, to the Utilities folder.

Remember that *your* Applications list may vary. Apple might have blessed your particular Mac model with some bonus programs, or you may have downloaded or installed some on your own.

Automator

This software-robot program is described in a free downloadable PDF appendix to this chapter, "Automator & AppleScript." You can download it from this book's "Missing CD" page at *missingmanuals.com*.

Books

Books (originally called iBooks) is Apple's ebook-reading and audiobook-playing program (Figure 11-1). It lets you carry around dozens or hundreds of books, which, in the pre-ebook days, would have drawn some funny looks in public.

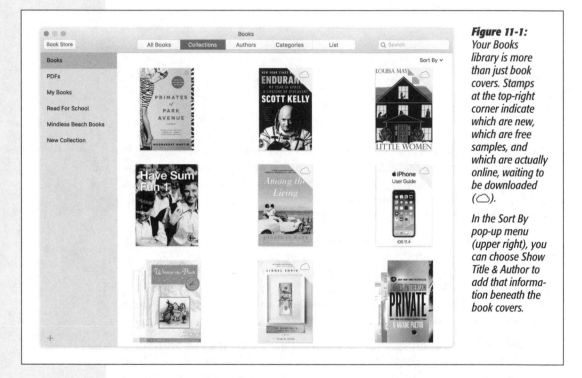

Figure 11-1:
Your Books library is more than just book covers. Stamps at the top-right corner indicate which are new, which are free samples, and which are actually online, waiting to be downloaded (◯).

In the Sort By pop-up menu (upper right), you can choose Show Title & Author to add that information beneath the book covers.

The beauty of all this is iCloud syncing. If you're reading a book on your iPhone in line at the DMV, you'll find that your iPad opens up to exactly the same page when you're on the train home. And when you open your MacBook at home, the book will be on the same page as where you left the iPad. Your books, documents, notes, highlighting, and other details are synced among your Apple gadgets, too. (You can turn that syncing feature off in Books→Preferences→General if it spooks you.)

Most people think of Books as a reader for books that Apple sells on its online bookstore—best-sellers and current fiction, for example—and it does that very well. But you can also load it up with your own PDF documents, as well as thousands of free, older, out-of-copyright books.

Tip: Full disclosure—Amazon's free Kindle app, and Barnes & Noble's free B&N eReader app, are much the same thing—but offer much bigger book libraries at lower prices than Apple's.

Downloading Books

To shop the Books bookstore, open the Books app. Click Book Store; the app becomes the literary equivalent of the App Store, complete with the icons across the top. The links here offer everything you'd need in your bibliographic quest: Bestsellers, Read It Before You Watch It (movie tie-ins), and so on. You can also search by name or click Purchased to see what you've bought.

Note: Once you've bought a book from Apple, you can download it again on other Macs, iPhones, iPod Touches, and iPads. Buy once, read many times. That's the purpose of the Not in My Library tab, which appears when you click Purchased.

But unless you have some kind of privacy concern, you may as well tell Books to download your books *automatically* as you buy them on your other Apple gadgets. Open Books→Preferences→Store and turn on "Download new purchases automatically." That way you'll never forget what you bought on your iPad as you sit down at your Mac.

Once you find a book that looks good, you can click Get Sample to download a free chapter, read ratings and reviews, or click the price itself to buy the book and download it straight to the Mac.

If you see a book cover bearing the ☁ icon, that's a book you own—it's available in your online locker—but you haven't downloaded it to this Mac yet. Click to download.

Audiobooks

Audiobooks can make great listening as you exercise or commute to work. Click the Audiobooks Store to view Apple's online selection of buyable recordings. It works like any of Apple's other stores, complete with free samples, bestseller lists, recommendations, and so on.

Once you've bought an audiobook, it shows up in the Books app alongside your other books. When you play one, the playback controls offer a list of chapters (≡). Not only does Books remember your place from one listening session to another, but it also syncs your place to your other Apple gadgets.

On the same panel, the ⋯ button offers choices like playback speed and a Sleep Timer (shuts off playback automatically after a time you specify).

This corner of Apple's online stores used to be in the now-defunct iTunes software, and a few features got lost along the way in its move to the Books app. For example, you no longer have a choice of hard drives to store your audiobook files on; it has to be your startup drive. Of course, there's nothing to stop you from managing your audiobooks in the Music app instead, which has no such limitation.

Tip: If the Audiobooks Store doesn't offer the book you're interested in, you can find a larger collection (over 50,000 of them) at *audible.com*. This web store sells all kinds of audiobooks, plus recorded periodicals like *The New York Times* and radio shows. To purchase Audible's wares, you have to have either an Audible account or an Amazon account.

Once you've downloaded an Audible audiobook file, you can drag it directly into the Books app to manage and play alongside your other books. If you've ripped audiobooks from their original CDs, you can drag those files into Books, too, right on the Library tab.

ePub Files

Apple's bookstore isn't the only way to get books. You can also load up your ebook reader from your computer, feeding it with ePub files.

ePub is the normal Books format. It's a very popular standard for ebook readers, Apple's and otherwise. The only difference between ePub documents you create and the ones Apple sells is that Apple's are copy-protected.

To add your own ePub documents to your Books library, just drag their icons off the desktop and into the Books window. Or choose File→Add to Library.

And where are you supposed to get all these files? Free (and not free) ebooks in ePub format are everywhere. There are 60,000 free downloadable books at *gutenberg.org*, for example, and over a million at *books.google.com*—oldies, but classic oldies, with lots of Mark Twain, Agatha Christie, Herman Melville, H.G. Wells, and so on. (Lots of these are available in the Free pages of Apple's own Books store, too.)

PDF Files

Books can display and catalog PDF documents (page 587), too. PDFs are everywhere—people send them as attachments, and you can turn any document into a PDF file. (For example, on the Mac, in any program, choose File→Print; in the resulting dialog box, click PDF→Save as PDF.) You bring them into Books by dragging them into its window, or with File→Add to Library.

When you double-click one, though, it doesn't open in Books; it opens into *Preview*. Which is, after all, a program expressly designed for reading PDF documents.

You've been warned.

Your Library

When you open Books, you see your own personal library represented as little book covers (Figure 11-1). Mostly what you'll do here is click a book to open it. But there are all kinds of other activities waiting for you:

- **You can reorganize your bookshelf.** Use the Sort By pop-up menu to choose Most Recent or Title—or Sort Manually, which means you can drag books around into any order you like.

- **You can view your library as a compact list.** Click List at the top to switch the book-cover view to a much more boring (but more compact) list view. The column

headings let you sort the list by author, title, category, and so on. And there's a search box, too, which lets you search your books' titles—helpful if you have an enormous library.

- **To delete a book,** click it and then press the Delete key; confirm in the warning box. Of course, deleting a book from the Mac doesn't delete your safety copy on your other gadgets or online.

- **Organize your books into folders.** In Books, the "folders" are called collections, but it's the same idea. You might have one for school, one for work, and a third for somebody who shares your Mac, for example.

To see your collections, click Collections; the Collections list opens at the left side. Make a new collection by clicking the + button (or choose File→New Collection); type to name it.

Now, to file your books away, select them (you can press ⌘ as you click to select multiple books); then choose File→Add to Collection and choose the name of the collection you want them in.

Reading

But come on—you're a reader, not a librarian. Here's how you read an ebook.

Open the book by double-clicking the cover. Now the book opens, ready for you to read. Looks great, doesn't it (Figure 11-2)? If you're returning to a book you've been reading, Books remembers your place.

Tip: You can open several books at once, you multitasking maniac.

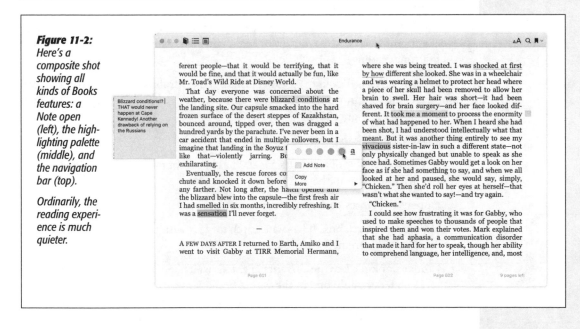

Figure 11-2:
Here's a composite shot showing all kinds of Books features: a Note open (left), the highlighting palette (middle), and the navigation bar (top).

Ordinarily, the reading experience is much quieter.

In general, reading is simple: Just read. Turn pages like this:

- **Press the space bar.** (Add Shift to turn back a page.)

- **Press the ▶ key.** (Press ◀ to turn back.)

- **Point to the right margin;** click the > button that appears. (Left margin to go back.)

- **Swipe two fingers across the trackpad**—to the right (to go forward) or left (to go back a page).

Tip: The Touch Bar, if you have one (page 227), displays a handy "map" of the entire book. By clicking it or dragging your finger through it, you can jump directly to a different spot in the book. As you drag, your main screen shows the page number you're about to open.

What's super-cool is that, after having jumped to that distant spot to check something, the Touch Bar then offers you a ↺ button, which teleports you right back to where you were.

You should also take a moment to adjust your reading environment. For example:

- **Enter Full Screen mode** for the biggest, least distracting view of your book (see page 173).

- **Specify either a one-page or a two-page spread** (use the Single Page or Two Pages commands in the View menu). In Full Screen mode, Single Page isn't available.

- **Adjust the type size using the ₐA button.** That's a huge feature for people with tired or over-40 eyes. And it's something paper books definitely can't do.

 The same pop-out panel offers a Fonts menu, where you can choose from eight typefaces for your book.

- **Adjust the background color.** The ₐA button also offers a choice of four page-background colors: white, sepia (off-white), brown (with white text), or black (for nighttime reading).

While you're reading, Books makes all the onscreen controls fade away so you can read in peace. But if you move your mouse to the top of the window, a row of additional controls appears (Figure 11-2):

- 📕 **takes you back to the bookshelf (Library view).**

- ☰ **opens the Table of Contents panel.** The chapter or page names are "live"— you can click one to jump there.

- 🗐 **opens the Notes pane,** described next.

- 🔍 **opens the search box.** It lets you search for text within the book you're reading, which can be extremely useful.

- 🔖 **adds a bookmark to the current page.** This isn't like a physical bookmark, where there's generally only one in the whole book; you can use these to flag as many pages, for as many reasons, as you like. (The same button appears on your Touch Bar, if you have one.)

Once you've accumulated a bookmark or two, use the ⌄ next to the 🔖 menu to see a list of them—and to jump back to one.

Tip: A Books book can include pictures and even videos. Double-click a picture in a book to zoom in on it.

Notes, Highlighting, and Other Options

Here are some more stunts that you'd have trouble pulling off in a printed book. If you *double-click* a word, you get a graceful, elegant page from Books' built-in dictionary. You know—in the unlikely event that you encounter a word you don't know.

If you drag across some text to highlight it, you get a few surprise options (Figure 11-2):

- **Highlight.** Click one of the colored dots to add tinted, transparent highlighting, or underlining, to the word you clicked. (To remove highlighting, click inside a highlighted area and click Remove Highlighting.)

- **Note.** When you click Add Note, Books creates highlighting on the selected passage *and* opens an empty, colored sticky note so you can type in your own annotations. When you click outside the note, it collapses down to a tiny Post-it square in the margin. Click to reopen it.

 To delete a note, click the highlighted text. Click Remove Note or Remove Highlight & Note.

- **Copy** copies the highlighted text, ready for pasting in some other program.

In the More menu, a few additional options lurk:

- **Search Book** opens the same search box you'd get by clicking the 🔍 icon—except this time the highlighted word is already filled in, saving you a bit of typing.

- **Search Web and Search Wikipedia** hand off the highlighted text to Safari, which searches Google or Wikipedia.

- **Mail, Messages, Notes** opens the share sheet (page 258) so you can send the highlighted material to somebody else by message or email, or add it to a Notes page.

- **Speak** reads the highlighted passage aloud.

Tip: The Mac's speaking feature isn't limited to a blob of text you've highlighted. You can use the Edit→Speech→Start Speaking command to have the *entire book* read to you—in a voice that's only a *little* robotic. Yes, this is exactly the feature that debuted in the Amazon Kindle and was then removed when publishers screamed bloody murder—but somehow, so far, Apple has gotten away with it.

Once you've added bookmarks, notes, and highlighting to your book, they're magically and wirelessly synced to any other copies of that book—on other gadgets, like the iPad or iPod Touch, other iPhones, or other Macs. Very handy indeed.

Furthermore, if you click the 🗒 button, you'll see the Notes pane. It presents a tidy list of all your bookmarked pages, notes, and highlighted passages. You can click one of the listings to jump to the relevant page.

Books Settings

If you've embraced the simple joy of reading electronic books, then you deserve to know where to make settings changes: in Books→Preferences. Here are the options waiting there.

General tab

- **Let lines break naturally.** Ordinarily, Books presents text with ragged-right margins. Select "Justify text" if you like the text to stretch from edge to edge of the screen.

- **Auto-hyphenate words.** Sometimes, typesetting looks better if hyphens allow partial words to appear at the right edge of each line. Especially if you've also turned on "Justify text."

- **Display Sleep.** If you've set your screen to go dark after a period of inactivity (to save power—see page 344), this checkbox adds a 10-minute grace period to your definition of "inactivity." The idea is to prevent the screen from going dark just because you're a slow reader.

- **Sync.** Turn this on if you'd like your bookmarks, highlighting, and book collections to be synced with your other Apple gadgets.

Store tab

See the Note on page 383.

Parental tab

If you're a parent, you might wish to shield your impressionable offspring from smutty reading material—or to shield your credit card from wild teenage book-buying sprees (we should all have that problem!).

Click the 🔒 and enter your administrator's password; now you can turn on "Disable the Book Store" to prevent purchases, or "Restrict books with explicit content" to block the downloading of raunchy material.

Advanced tab

This tab offers exactly one control: a checkbox called "Enable Advanced menu in menu bar." It creates an Advanced menu that itself contains exactly one command: "Add EPUB to Library as Proof."

This is designed to help one very small group: people who create their *own* Apple-format ebooks, and wish to look them over on various Apple gadgets to make sure they look right.

Once you've exported your book as an ePub file (from Pages, Adobe InDesign, or some other app), use this command to add it to Books as a finished book. When you open it, use the Devices button at top right to choose an iPhone or iPad you've connected to your Mac. (The Books app has to be open on that device.) Presto: Your book gets copied to the other gadget, for your proofreading pleasure. The best part: Each time

you make a fix in the ePub document, that change is automatically carried through to the Book versions on the Mac and on iOS.

Calculator

For quick calculations, you don't need any calculator at all. Just ask Siri: "What's 17 percent of 300?" or "What's the square root of 77?" or "What's 35 times 22?"

Tip: The Spotlight menu is a calculator, too. Type or paste an equation into the Spotlight search box; instantly, the answer appears in the results menu.

If you really need to see the numbers, though, you can use this app, which is much more than a simple four-function memory calculator. It can also act as a scientific calculator for students and scientists, a conversion calculator for metric and U.S. measures, and even a currency calculator for world travelers.

The little Calculator widget in the Today pane of the Notification Center is quicker to open, but the stand-alone Calculator program is far more powerful. For example:

- **Calculator has three modes:** Basic, Scientific, and Programmer (Figure 11-3). Switch among them by choosing from the View menu (or pressing ⌘-1 for Basic, ⌘-2 for Scientific, or ⌘-3 for Programmer).

Figure 11-3:
The Calculator program offers a four-function Basic mode, a full-blown scientific calculator mode, and a programmer's calculator (shown here) capable of hex, octal, decimal, and binary notation. The first two modes have a "paper tape" feature (Windows→Paper Tape) that lets you see any errors you may have made way back in a calculation. You can also save the tape as a text file by choosing File→Save Tape As, or print it by selecting File→Print Tape.

- **You can operate Calculator** by clicking the onscreen buttons, but it's much easier to press the corresponding number and symbol keys on your keyboard.

- **Press the C key** to clear the calculator display.

- **As you go, you can make Calculator speak** each key you press. The Mac's voice ensures that you don't mistype as you keep your eyes on the receipts in front of you, typing by touch.

 Just choose Speech→Speak Button Pressed to turn this feature on or off. (You choose *which* voice does the talking in the Accessibility panel of System Preferences.)

- **Once you've calculated a result,** you can copy it (using Edit→Copy, or ⌘-C) and paste it directly into another program.

- **Calculator even offers reverse Polish notation (RPN),** a system of entering numbers that's popular with mathematicians, programmers, and engineers, because it lets them omit parentheses. Choose View→RPN Mode, or ⌘-R, to turn it on and off.

Tip: If your Mac has a Touch Bar (page 227), you can add to it buttons for a few advanced Calculator functions—Sine, Cosine, Tangent, Random Number, Pi, Hyperbolic Tangent, and many others. Choose View→ Customize Touch Bar to get started.

Conversions

Calculator is more than a calculator; it's also a conversion program. No matter what units you're trying to convert—meters, grams, cubic inches, miles per hour, euros—Calculator is ready.

Now, the truth is, asking Siri to convert units for you, or typing (for example) *35 degrees in Celsius* into Spotlight is simpler and quicker to open than this older Calculator feature.

But if you've already got Calculator open, here's the drill: Type in the starting measurement. Then, from the Convert menu, choose the kind of conversion you want (Area, Currency, Temperature, or whatever). In the dialog box, use the pop-up menus to specify which units you want to convert to and from, and then click OK. There's your answer!

The next time you want to make this kind of conversion, you can skip most of those steps. Instead, just choose your desired conversion from the Convert→Recent Conversions submenu.

Calculator is especially amazing when it comes to *currency* conversions—from pesos to American dollars, for example—because it actually goes online to download up-to-the-minute currency rates.

Tip: If you're working with big numbers, don't forget to turn on View→Show Thousands Separators. Calculator will add commas (like 1,242,939) to help you read your big numbers more easily.

Calendar

The calendar program that was called iCal for many years is now called Calendar, so it matches its name on the iPhone and iPad.

Calendar is not so different from those "Hunks of the Midwest Police Stations" paper calendars that people leave hanging on the walls for months past their natural life span.

Tip: Calendar's Dock icon displays today's date—even when Calendar isn't running.

But Calendar offers several advantages over wall calendars:

- **It can automate the process** of entering repeating events, such as weekly staff meetings or gym workouts.

- **It can give you a gentle nudge** (with a sound, a dialog box, or even an email) when an important appointment is approaching.

- **It can share information** with Contacts, with Mail, with your iPhone/iPad/iPod Touch, with other Macs, or with "published" calendars on the internet. Some of these features require one of those iCloud accounts described on page 655. But Calendar also works fine on a single Mac, even without an internet connection.

- **It can subscribe to other people's calendars.** For example, you can subscribe to your spouse's calendar, thereby finding out when you've been committed to after-dinner drinks on the night of the big game. You can also tell Calendar to show your calendars from Google and Yahoo, or even your company's Exchange calendar.

Working with Views

When you open Calendar, you see something like Figure 11-4. By clicking one of the View buttons above the calendar, or by pressing ⌘-1, ⌘-2, ⌘-3, or ⌘-4, you can switch among these views:

- **Day** looks like a day-at-a-time desk calendar. On the left side, you see today's schedule. On the right, you see the details of whichever appointment is selected.

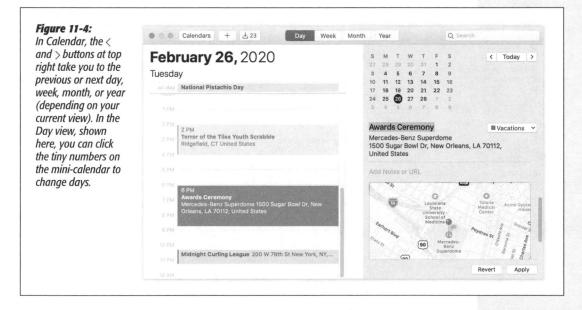

Figure 11-4:
In Calendar, the < and > buttons at top right take you to the previous or next day, week, month, or year (depending on your current view). In the Day view, shown here, you can click the tiny numbers on the mini-calendar to change days.

If you choose Calendar→Preferences, you can specify what hours constitute a workday. This is ideal both for those annoying power-life people who get up at 5 a.m. for calisthenics and for the more reasonable people who sleep until 11.

Tip: Calendar provides four quick ways to get to the current date. Click Today (upper-right corner, between the ‹ and ›), choose View→Go to Today, or press ⌘-T. Or click Today on the Touch Bar, if your Mac has one.

- **Week** fills the main display area with seven columns, reflecting the current week. (You can establish a five-day workweek instead in Calendar→Preferences.)

Tip: If you double-click the date above the calendar, you open the Day view for that day.

- **Month** shows the entire current month. The time of each appointment is listed in gray off to the right of each square.

 If a Month-view square is too small to show everything you've got scheduled that day, you'll see a notation at the bottom of the square, like "3 more…" Sometimes making the window bigger (or full screen) helps make more room, or you can just double-click the date's number to switch to Day view and see everything at once.

Tip: Month view scrolls vertically—and not necessarily a month at a time, either. You can park any week of the month at the top of the screen—not just the first week. That's a refreshing change from paper calendars.

- **Year** view displays the date numbers for the entire year (Figure 11-5).

Figure 11-5:
Year view shows the entire year. In Calendar→Preferences→Advanced, you can turn on "Show events in year view," which actually means "Show me a 'heat map' to indicate how hectic my schedule is."

You can single-click a date number to see a pop-out list of the appointments scheduled for that date.

In Week or Month view, *double-click* an appointment to see more about it, or even make changes to it.

Tip: In Week or Day view, Calendar sprouts a handy horizontal line that shows where you are in time right now. (Look in the hours-of-the-day "ruler" down the left side of the window to see this line's little red bulb.) A nice touch, and a handy visual aid that can tell you at a glance when you're already late for something.

Also, in any view, you can switch into Full Screen mode by clicking the green ⊙ button (top left). See page 173 for more on Full Screen mode.

Tip: Each Calendar view scrolls smoothly and endlessly into the past or future. Day and Week views scroll horizontally; Month and Year views scroll vertically.

Making an Appointment

The basic Calendar is easy to figure out. After all, with the exception of one unfortunate Gregorian incident, we've been using calendars successfully for centuries.

Even so, there are two ways to record a new appointment: using the mouse, or using the Quick Event box.

The mousy way

You can quickly record an appointment using any of several techniques, listed here in order of decreasing efficiency:

- **In Month view,** double-click a blank spot on the date you want. Type the name of the event and a time slot—for example, *Sales meeting 9am-4:30*. (Read on to "The Quick Event way" for details on how Calendar interprets these time notations.)

- **In Day or Week view,** double-click the starting time to create a one-hour appointment. Or drag vertically through the time slots that represent the appointment's duration. Either way, type the event's name inside the newly created colored box.

- **In Day, Week, or Month view,** right-click or two-finger click a date and choose New Event from the shortcut menu. Type the event's name.

 Unless you use the drag-over-hours method, a new event believes itself to be one hour long. But in Day or Week view, you can adjust its duration by dragging the bottom edge vertically. Drag the dark top bar up or down to adjust the start time.

In many cases, that's all there is to it. You've just specified the day, time, and title of the appointment. Now you can get on with your life.

Tip: If the Edit balloon is blocking a part of the calendar you need to see, no biggie: Just drag the balloon out of the way, using any blank spot as a handle. It "tears off" and becomes independent.

The Quick Event way

In the *Quick Event* method, the program spares you the trouble of manually selecting dates, start times, and end times. Instead, Calendar understands notations like "7 pm Friday," and puts your new appointment into the right time slot automatically.

To use this feature, press ⌘-N. Or click ✛ (top left of the window) or choose File→New Event. The Quick Event box appears. Proceed as shown in Figure 11-6.

Note: Calendar proposes adding the new appointment to your *default calendar*—that is, the category you use most often (read on for details on these categories). Supposedly, you've already told it which category is your preferred one by using the Calendar→Preferences→General→Default Calendar pop-up menu.

But as you add a new appointment this way, you can override that setting by *holding down* the ✛ button. You get a pop-up menu of your calendar categories; only after you click one do you see the Quick Event box shown in Figure 11-6.

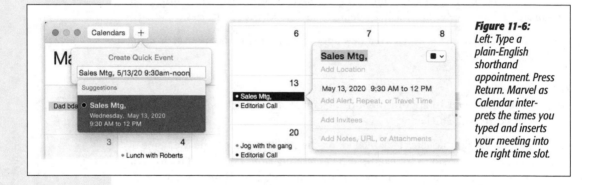

Figure 11-6:
Left: Type a plain-English shorthand appointment. Press Return. Marvel as Calendar interprets the times you typed and inserts your meeting into the right time slot.

Into the Quick Event box, type the name of your appointment and its date and time. For example, you could type *Report deadline Aug 12,* or *"Titanic 2: The Return" Sat 7 pm,* or *Cara date 11-11:15am.* When you press Return, Calendar interprets what you typed, using these rules:

- **If you didn't specify an ending time,** Calendar sets the appointment to one hour.

- **If you didn't enter *any* time information,** Calendar schedules your event for all day.

- **If you typed *breakfast* or *morning,*** Calendar sets the appointment to start at 9 a.m.; *lunch* or *noon,* it starts at 12 p.m.; *dinner* or *night,* it starts at 7 p.m.

- **If you enter a weekday** (for example, *Chicago Monday*), Calendar assumes you mean the very next occurrence of that day. (If that's not what you want, enter the date, like *Chicago Jul 3.)*

- **If you enter a time but not a date or day** (for example, *Fishing 3:30 pm*), Calendar assumes you mean today.

The Quick Event system has a feature that saves you time and typos: As you type, it displays a menu of similar appointments you've entered in the past (Figure 11-6,

left). If you click one, Calendar fills in all the details of the new appointment in one fell swoop, copying them from the earlier event.

As soon as Calendar interprets your shorthand and turns it into a real appointment, its details balloon opens automatically (Figure 11-6, right), so you can clean up any errors and add more details.

Location, alarms, travel time, and other details

No matter which method you use to create the basic event, you're now presented with the information balloon shown at right in Figure 11-6. Here's where you go to town filling in the details. (This same balloon will appear when you double-click any existing appointment later.)

Tip: You can also open the Info balloon by clicking an appointment and then pressing ⌘-E (which is short for Edit→Edit Event).

For each appointment, you can tab your way to the following information areas:

- **subject.** That's the large, bold type at the top—the name of your appointment. For example, you might type *Fly to Phoenix.*

- **calendar.** A *calendar,* in Calendar's terminology, is a subset—a category—into which you can place appointments. You can create one for you, one for family-only events, one for book-club appointments, and so on. You can hide and show these categories at will. Details begin on page 401; for now, note that the tiny colored square in the top-right corner of the Info bubble is a pop-up menu of your calendars.

Tip: Use this same pop-up menu to *change* an appointment's category. If you filed something in "Company Memos" that should have been in "Sweet Nothings for Honey-Poo," then open the event's information balloon and reassign it. Quick.

- **location.** This field makes a lot of sense; almost everyone needs to record *where* a meeting is to take place. You might type a reminder for yourself like *My place,* a specific address like *212 East 23rd,* or some other helpful information, like a contact phone number or flight number.

 As you type, Calendar busily consults Apple's worldwide database of street addresses—and proposes a few matches, as shown in Figure 11-7 (top left). You're under no obligation to choose one of these; you can ignore the suggestions and type "Casey's treehouse," for all Apple cares. But if you *do* choose from Apple's list of proposals, some cool things happen.

 For example, you get a little map (which you can click to open the Maps app for a bigger view), as shown in Figure 11-7 (top right). You get to see the current weather, so you know how much to bundle up. And you get to use the travel-time feature described in a moment.

Note: The next few controls appear only when you expand the Info bubble to see the time and date information. To do that, click whatever time is listed now—or, if you've just tabbed your way to the times, press Return.

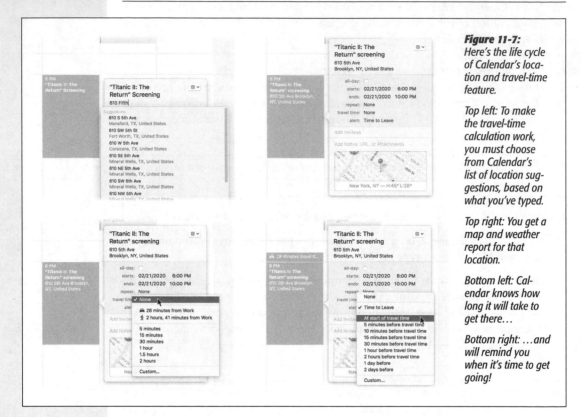

Figure 11-7:
Here's the life cycle of Calendar's location and travel-time feature.

Top left: To make the travel-time calculation work, you must choose from Calendar's list of location suggestions, based on what you've typed.

Top right: You get a map and weather report for that location.

Bottom left: Calendar knows how long it will take to get there…

Bottom right: …and will remind you when it's time to get going!

- **all-day.** An "all-day" event, of course, refers to something that has no specific time of day associated with it: a holiday, a birthday. When you turn on this box, you see the name of the appointment jump to the top of the Calendar screen, in the area reserved for this kind of thing.

- **starts, ends.** You can adjust the times shown here by typing, clicking buttons, or both. Press Tab to jump from one setting to another, and from there to the hours and minutes of the starting time.

Note: The little calendar that pops up when you click the date is handier than typing a date manually.

For example, start by clicking the hour, and then increase or decrease this number either by pressing ▲ and ▼ or by typing a number. Press Tab to highlight the minutes and repeat the arrow-buttons-or-keys business. Finally, press Tab to highlight the AM/PM indicator, and type either *A* or *P*—or press ▲ or ▼—to change it, if necessary.

Tip: If you specify a different ending date, a *banner* appears across the top of the calendar.

- **time zone.** This option appears only after you choose Calendar→Preferences→ Advanced and then turn on "Turn on time zone support." And you would do *that* only if you plan to be traveling on the day this appointment comes to pass.

 Once you've done that, a time zone pop-up menu appears. It starts out with "America/New York" (or whatever your Mac's usual time zone is); if you choose Other, a tiny world map appears. Click the time zone that represents where you'll be when this appointment comes due. From the shortcut menu, choose the major city that's in the same time zone you'll be in.

Tip: The time zone pop-up menu remembers each new city you select. The next time you travel to a city you've visited before, you won't have to do that clicking-the-world-map business.

When you arrive in the distant city, use the time zone pop-up menu at the top-right corner of the Calendar window to tell Calendar where you are. You'll see Calendar's appointments jump, as if by magic, to their correct new time slots.

- **repeat.** The pop-up menu here contains common options for recurring events: every day, every week, and so on. It starts out saying None.

 Once you've made a selection, you get an *end* pop-up menu that lets you specify when this event should *stop* repeating. If you choose "Never," you're stuck seeing this event repeating on your calendar until the end of time (a good choice for recording, say, your anniversary, especially if your spouse might be consulting the same calendar). You can also turn on "After [a certain number of times]," which is a useful option for car and mortgage payments. And if you choose "On date," you can specify the date when the repetitions come to an end; use this option to indicate the last day of school, for example.

 "Custom" lets you specify repeat schedules like "First Monday of the month" or "Every two weeks."

Tip: If you don't see the following items in the editing bubble, click the gray lettering that says "Add Alert, Repeat, or Travel Time" to make them appear.

- **travel time.** This item represents a breakthrough in common sense: It automatically builds travel time into Calendar's understanding of any appointment. After all, it's not very useful to get a reminder like "Lunch with Jenkins at 1 p.m." 10 minutes beforehand if it takes half an hour to get there.

 Now, then: If Calendar is to calculate travel time, it has to know where you're starting out and where you're going.

 To figure out your starting point, the Mac consults your "me" card in the Contacts app (page 705), and uses either your home address or your work address, depending

on the time of day. (How does Calendar know when you're at work? It cleverly uses the "Day starts at" and "Day ends at" settings in Calendar→Preferences→General.)

If you haven't specified home and work addresses on your "me" card, Calendar uses the current location of your Mac as the starting point. (And *that* works only if you've allowed the Mac to track your location; see page 425.)

For the arrival location, the travel-time feature requires that you've accepted one of the Mac's address suggestions, as described in Figure 11-7, top left.

Once all that's done, the travel-time pop-up menu shows you both the driving and walking times to your appointment. You can override these suggestions if you like; you can choose any time interval from five minutes to two hours, or choose Custom to plug in something not listed here.

The real payoff, of course, comes when you set a reminder for yourself; read on.

- **alert.** This pop-up menu tells Calendar to notify you when a certain appointment is about to begin. Choose how much notice you want: "At time of event," "5 minutes before," all the way up to "2 days before." If it's a TV show, a reminder five minutes before airtime is probably fine. If it's a birthday, you might set up a two-day warning so there's time to buy a present.

 Actually, you can get a lot more particular than that. If you choose Custom, you can specify any advance-warning interval at all: "16 minutes before," or "15 days after," or whatever. (Yes, you can set up an alarm to ring *after* the event—great if you want to follow up with something or check the oven.)

 Here in Customland, you can also set any of three kinds of flags to get your attention. Calendar can display a message (with a sound, if you like), send you an email, or open a file on your hard drive. (You could use this unusual option to ensure that you don't forget a work deadline by having Calendar fling the relevant document open in front of your face at the eleventh hour.)

 And if you've used the travel-time feature, Calendar offers choices related to the travel time, such as "at start of travel time" or 5, 15, or 30 minutes before, which may be helpful if you need to plot time for showering. (Figure 11-7, lower right).

Tip: You can set up more than one alarm for the same appointment, each with its own advance-warning interval. Just click the + button to add a new one.

- **show as (busy/free/tentative/out of office).** This little item shows up only if you've subscribed to a calendar server, like an internet-based calendar (in geek-speak, a CalDAV server) or your company's Exchange calendar. It communicates to your colleagues when you might be available for meetings.

Note: If your calendar comes from a CalDAV server, then your only options are "busy" and "free." The factory setting for most appointments is "busy," but for all-day events it's "free." Which is logical; just because it's International Gecko Appreciation Day doesn't mean you're not available for meetings (rats!).

You might think: "Well, *duh*—if I've got something on the calendar, then I'm obviously busy!" But not necessarily. Some Calendar entries might just be placeholders, reminders to self, TV shows you wanted to watch, appointments you'd be willing to change—not things that would necessarily render you unavailable if a better invitation should come along.

• **Add Invitees.** If the appointment is a meeting or some other gathering, you can type the participants' names here. If a name is already in your Contacts program, Calendar proposes autocompleting the name for you.

If you separate several names with commas, Calendar automatically turns each into a shaded button. You can click it for a pop-up menu of commands like Remove Attendee and Send Email. (That last option appears only if the person in Contacts has an email address, or if you typed a name *with* an email address in brackets, like this: *Chris Smith <chris@yahoo.com>*.)

Tip: If you and your invitees are on the same CalDAV or Exchange calendar service—usually, co-workers at the same company—Calendar can show a "time map" of the invitees' days, all in a handy scrolling window, so you can find a time when everybody is free. To see this map, click the Available Meeting Times link beneath the addresses of the invitees you've specified, or choose Window→Availability Panel (see Figure 11-8).

Figure 11-8:
Drag the vertical block (your proposed meeting) to a different time slot, or click Next Available Time to find when everybody's free. Good luck.

Inviting Guests

When you click Send at the bottom of the info balloon, your guests receive your invitation. If they use Calendar, it appears in their Notifications panels. (To open the Notifications panel, click the tiny inbox icon in the top-left corner of the window.) They can click Accept, Decline, or Maybe.

In your Notifications window, you then see the status of each invitee's name: a green checkmark for Accepted, red X for Declined, orange question mark for Maybe, and gray question mark for Not Yet Responded. (Your guests, meanwhile, will be delighted to find that the appointment automatically appears on their calendars once they commit.)

Now, suppose you send an invitation to your sister, who doesn't have a Mac. She just gets an email message that says, "Chris Smith has invited you to the event: Company Hoedown, scheduled for February 04, 2020 at 3:00 PM. To accept or decline this invitation, click the link below." (Unfortunately, there generally *is* no link. She just has to know to open the .ics attachment.)

If she uses a calendar program that understands this attachment, then the appointment appears on her calendar, and her RSVP shows up in your Calendar Notification panel.

Once you've specified some attendees, a Send button appears in the Info box. If you click it, Calendar fires up Mail and prepares messages, each with an *.ics* attachment: a calendar-program invitation file. See the box on the previous page.

- **Add Notes, URL or Attachments.** You can type, paste, or drag any text you like in the note area—driving directions, contact phone numbers, a call history, or whatever.

Your newly scheduled event now shows up on the calendar, complete with the color coding that corresponds to the calendar category you've assigned.

What to Do with an Appointment

Once you've entrusted your agenda to Calendar, you can start putting it to work. Calendar is only too pleased to remind you (via pop-up messages) of your events, reschedule them, print them out, and so on. Here are a few of the possibilities.

Editing events

To edit a calendar event's details, click to open its Info balloon and follow the steps in Figure 11-9).

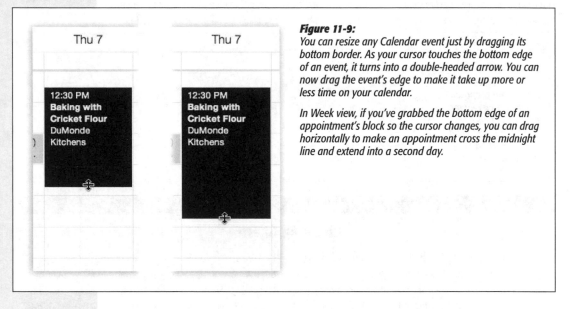

Figure 11-9:
You can resize any Calendar event just by dragging its bottom border. As your cursor touches the bottom edge of an event, it turns into a double-headed arrow. You can now drag the event's edge to make it take up more or less time on your calendar.

In Week view, if you've grabbed the bottom edge of an appointment's block so the cursor changes, you can drag horizontally to make an appointment cross the midnight line and extend into a second day.

And if you want to change only an appointment's "calendar" category, right-click or two-finger click anywhere on the appointment and choose from the resulting Calendar shortcut menu. That way you bypass the need to open the Info balloon.

Rescheduling events

If an event in your life gets rescheduled, you can drag an appointment block vertically in a Day- or Week-view column to make it later or earlier the same day, or horizontally to another date in any view. (If you reschedule a recurring event, Calendar asks if you want to change only *this* occurrence, or this *and* all future ones.)

If something is postponed for, say, a month or two, you can grab it in the Month view and drag it down as the months very slowly scroll by. Or you can open the Info balloon and edit the starting and ending dates or times—or just cut and paste the event to a different date.

Lengthening or shortening events

If a scheduled meeting becomes shorter or your lunch hour becomes a lunch hour-and-a-half (in your dreams), you can change the length of the representative calendar event by dragging the bottom border of its block in any column view (see Figure 11-9).

Printing events

To commit your calendar to paper, choose File→Print, or press ⌘-P. The resulting Print dialog box lets you include only a certain range of dates, only events on certain calendars, with or without To Do lists or mini-month calendars, and so on.

Deleting events

To delete an appointment, click it and then press the Delete key. If you delete a recurring event (like a weekly meeting), Calendar asks whether you want to delete only that instance of the event, or the whole series from that point forward.

Searching for events

When you type into the search box at the top right of the Calendar screen, you're offered some "search tokens" that indicate where you want to search for that phrase (in the name of an event, in its notes, location, and so on). The right-hand column offers a clickable list of search results. Figure 11-10 has the details.

Figure 11-10:
Left: Type into the search box; Calendar sprouts a list of suggestions ("Event contains 'school,' " "Notes contain 'school,' " and so on).

Right: Click one to create a search token exactly like the ones that Spotlight and Mail use. They let you build up complex searches, bubble by bubble. Double-click any row of the list to jump to the corresponding event on the calendar and open its summary balloon.

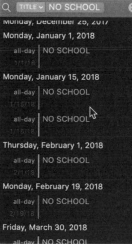

The "Calendar" Category Concept

Calendar has *calendars* that let you organize appointments into subsets. One person might have calendars called Me, Spouse 'n' Me, and Whole Family. A small business could have categories called Deductible Travel, R&D, and R&R.

And now, the Calendar Tip-O-Rama:

- **To create a calendar,** choose File→New Calendar. You have to specify *where* you want this category to live: On My Mac (meaning on your Mac), or on one of your online accounts, like iCloud, Google, Yahoo, or Exchange. Type a name that defines the category in your mind.

Note: When you set up an iCloud account either in System Preferences or when you first run macOS, Calendar automatically transfers your On My Mac categories to iCloud. You can no longer create categories that live only on your Mac. (There's one exception: If you created your iCloud account in Calendar Preferences, then you *can* have an On My Mac category.)

- **To see your list of categories,** click the Calendars button (upper left of the window). A Sidebar list appears, if it wasn't already open.

- **Hide or show an entire category of appointments at once** by turning on or off the appropriate checkbox in the Calendars Sidebar.

- **To change the color of a category,** right-click or two-finger click its name in the Sidebar list. In the pop-up bubble, you choose a new color.

- **To specify your *default* calendar,** choose Calendar→Preferences→General. Choose from the Default Calendar pop-up menu. (The Default calendar is the category every new appointment falls into unless you change it. It's also the category *other* apps, like Mail, propose putting new appointments into.)

- **To assign a new appointment to a calendar,** click the color swatch in the corner of its Info balloon.

- **To change an appointment's calendar category,** right-click or two-finger click the appointment's name and choose a calendar name from the shortcut menu.

- **You may be able to make calendar *groups*, too.** Those are containers that consolidate the appointments from several *other* calendars. For example, you could have a calendar group called Kids, containing the individual calendars for each of your offspring. Super-calendars like this make it easier to manage, hide, show, print, and search subsets of your appointments. (Sadly, this feature is available only for On My Mac categories, as described previously—not for online accounts.)

To create a calendar group, choose File→New Calendar Group. Name the resulting item in the Calendar list; for the most part, it behaves like any other calendar. Drag other calendar names onto it to include them. Click the flippy triangle to hide or show the component calendars.

"Publishing" Calendars to the Web

One of Calendar's best features is its ability to post your calendar on the web, so that other people can subscribe to it, which adds *your* appointments to *their* calendars. Anyone with a web browser—or only people you designate—can also *view* your calendar, right online.

For example, you might use this feature to post the meeting schedule for a club you manage, or to share the agenda for a series of upcoming financial meetings that all your co-workers will need to consult.

Publishing

The steps for sharing a calendar depend on whether or not you have an iCloud account. Observe:

- **If you have an iCloud account:** Proceed as shown in Figure 11-11. Note that you can specify whether each person can just *see* the appointments or be able to edit them, too. That's a delightful, two-way collaboration—a terrific way for a couple or a family to coordinate everyone's calendars, for example.

 Behind the scenes, Calendar sends an invitation to the recipient. If she has a Mac, iPhone, or iPad, she'll see a notification right in Calendar (📥); otherwise, she'll get the invitation by email. Once she clicks the invitation and then Accept, your shared calendar shows up on her machine.

Figure 11-11:

Top: Point to the name of the iCloud calendar you want to publish; click the "share" icon (📶) that appears next to its name.

In the pop-out panel, enter the email address of the lucky recipient (it must be someone in your Contacts). You can invite several people; just keep entering addresses.

The Public Calendar option means the whole internet can see this calendar category (if they know the URL).

Bottom: Use the ⌄ to specify whether a person can see your appointments (View Only) or make changes to them, too (View & Edit).

After the recipient has accepted the invitation, click the 📶 icon again; this time, a green checkmark appears next to the person's name.

Later you can modify the settings (Figure 11-11, bottom). Or you can stop sharing with someone by clicking the ๑ next to a calendar name, clicking a person's name, and then pressing the Delete key.

Tip: You can also share an iCloud calendar at *icloud.com*. Just click the ๑ icon beside a calendar's name.

- **If you don't have an iCloud account:** If you don't have iCloud, then you'll need a website of your own, where your online calendar can be hung. And it has to be a WebDAV-compatible server (ask your web hosting company). You know what? It might just be easier to sign up for a free iCloud account and do it that way.

 In any case, begin by making sure the Calendars list is open. Click the calendar you want to share. Choose Edit→Publish Calendar. (This command doesn't appear if you have an iCloud account, since the sharing mechanism is so much simpler with iCloud.)

Tip: You have to perform this step individually for each calendar category. If you want to publish more than one calendar simultaneously, create a calendar *group* instead and publish *that*.

A dialog box appears. This is where you specify your web address, its password (if necessary), and how your saved calendar is going to look and work. If you turn on "Publish changes automatically," then whenever you edit the calendar, Calendar connects to the internet and updates the copy there. (Otherwise you can right-click or two-finger click the calendar's name and choose Refresh whenever you want to update the web copy.)

When you click Publish, your Mac connects to the web and shows you the web address (the URL) of the finished page, complete with a Send Mail button that lets you fire the URL off to your colleagues.

Tip: Whenever you want to send someone the subscription information, click the calendar category you've published and choose Edit→Send Publication Email. Calendar will prepare an outgoing email message containing details on subscribing to your calendar.

To stop publishing that calendar, click its name in the Calendars pop-up list and then choose Edit→Stop Publishing.

Subscribing

Often, websites publish calendars that you can bring into Calendar. Maybe you use *tripit.com* to manage your flights and hotel reservations. Maybe you've found a calendar you like at *icalshare.com*—a schedule of rocket launches, trade shows, National Hockey League games, NASCAR races, soccer matches, *Survivor* episodes, holidays, or whatever.

Each of these web calendars has its own address. To subscribe, choose File→New Calendar Subscription. In the Subscribe to Calendar dialog box, paste the address of the published calendar.

You can also provide your own name for this category, specify how often you want your copy to be updated (assuming you have a full-time internet connection), and indicate whether you want to be bothered with the publisher's alarms and notes.

When it's all over, you see a new "calendar" category in your left-side list, representing the published appointments.

Google, Yahoo, and Facebook Calendars

If you maintain a calendar online—at Google, Yahoo, or Facebook, for example—you may take particular pleasure in discovering how easy it is to bring those appointments into Calendar. It's one handy way to keep, for example, a husband's and wife's appointments visible on each other's calendars.

Setting this up is ridiculously easy. Choose Calendar→Preferences→Accounts. Click + below the list. Enter your Google, Yahoo, or Facebook address (for example, *psmithers@ gmail.com*) and password. Click Create.

In a minute or so, you'll see all your Google, Yahoo, or Facebook events show up in Calendar. (Each web calendar has its own heading in the left-side list.) Better yet: It's a two-way sync; changes you make to these events in Calendar show up on the web, too.

Syncing Calendar with Your iPhone, iPad, and Other Computers

Here's the real magic of Calendar, iCloud, and the rest of Apple's software archipelago: Your calendar can be autosynced among all your machines, like your iPhone, iPad, and other Macs. Add an appointment on your phone, change an appointment on your iPad, whatever—all your other gadgets are wirelessly and automatically synced to match. See page 656 for details on this amazing setup.

Chess

MacOS comes with only one game, but it's a beauty (Figure 11-12). It's a traditional chess game played on a gorgeously rendered board with a set of realistic 3D pieces.

Note: The program is actually a sophisticated Unix-based chess program, Sjeng, that Apple packaged up in a new wrapper.

Playing a Game of Chess

When you launch Chess, you're presented with a fresh, new game that's set up in Human vs. Computer mode—meaning you, the Human (light-colored pieces) get to play against the Computer (your Mac, on the dark side). Drag the chess piece of your choice into position on the board, and the game is afoot.

If you choose Game→New, however, you're offered a pop-up menu with choices like Human vs. Computer, Human vs. Human, and so on. If you switch the pop-up menu to Computer vs. Human, you and your Mac trade places; the Mac takes the white side of the board and opens the game with the first move, and you play the black side.

Tip: The same New Game dialog box also has a pop-up menu called Variant, which offers three other chess-like games: Crazyhouse, Suicide, and Losers.

Some night when the bowling alley is closed and you're desperate for entertainment, you might also want to try the Computer vs. Computer option, which pits your Mac against itself. Pour yourself a drink, open a bag of chips, and settle in to watch until someone—either the Mac or the Mac—gains victory.

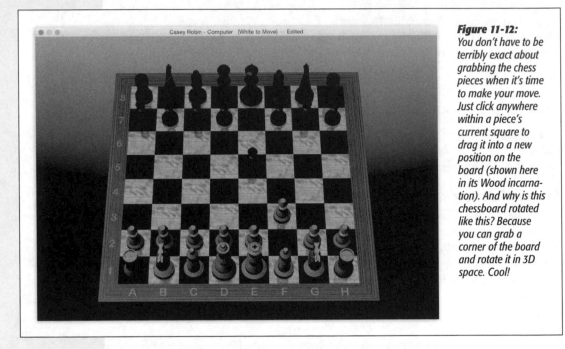

Figure 11-12:
You don't have to be terribly exact about grabbing the chess pieces when it's time to make your move. Just click anywhere within a piece's current square to drag it into a new position on the board (shown here in its Wood incarnation). And why is this chessboard rotated like this? Because you can grab a corner of the board and rotate it in 3D space. Cool!

Studying Your Games

You can choose Game→Save to save any game in progress, so you can resume it later.

To analyze the moves making up a game, use the Moves→Game Log command, which displays the history of your game, move by move. A typical move would be recorded as "Nb8 – c6," meaning the knight on the b8 square moved to the c6 square. With a Chess list document, you could recreate an entire game, move by move.

Tip: If you open this window before you begin a new game, you can see the game log fill in the moves as they happen.

Dictionary

For word nerds everywhere, the Dictionary is a blessing—a handy way to look up definitions, pronunciations, and synonyms (Figure 11-13). To be precise, macOS comes with electronic versions of multiple reference works in one.

Here's what you get:

- **The entire** *New Oxford American Dictionary.* The third edition, actually. You'll note that its entries give you lots of examples, background, and tables that help to differentiate fine shades of meaning (look up "weak" for an example).

- **The complete** *Oxford American Writer's Thesaurus.*

- **Two venerable guides to British English:** the *Oxford Dictionary of English* and *Oxford Thesaurus of English.*

- **A dictionary of Apple terms,** from "Activity" to "Zoom Display."

- **Wikipedia.** This famous citizen-created encyclopedia isn't actually on your Mac. Dictionary just gives you an easy way to search the *online* version and display the results right in the comfy Dictionary window.

- **Foreign language dictionaries:** You also get Japanese, French, Spanish, German, Dutch, Korean, Italian, Chinese, Hindi, Norwegian, Swedish, Portuguese, Russian, Turkish, Thai, Hebrew, and Danish—plus English translation dictionaries for Arabic, Hindi, French, German, Dutch, Italian, Portuguese, Spanish, Russian, Japanese, Korean, Chinese, Thai, and Vietnamese.

Note: You don't ordinarily see these reference books. You have to turn them on in Dictionary→Preferences.

Figure 11-13:
When you open the Dictionary, it generally assumes you want a word's definition (bottom). If you prefer to see the Wikipedia entry first (top), for example, choose Dictionary→ Preferences—and drag Wikipedia upward so that it precedes New Oxford American Dictionary. *That's all there is to it!*

MacOS also comes with about a million other ways to look up a word:

- **Search it in Spotlight.** Press ⌘-space, type the word you want into the Spotlight search box, and marvel as the dictionary entry appears at the bottom of the results list. To read the definition, click it once.

- **If you have a trackpad, point to a word in a basic Mac program, and then double-touch the trackpad (don't actually click) with three fingers.** That's the gesture for the same dictionary panel already described. It doesn't work unless you've turned it on in System Preferences→Trackpad.

- **Double-click the Dictionary icon.** You get the window shown at bottom in Figure 11-13. As you type into the Spotlight-y search box, you home in on matching words; click a word, or highlight it and press Return, to view a full, typographically elegant definition, complete with sample sentence and pronunciation guide.

Tip: And if you don't recognize a word in the definition, click *that word* to look up *its* definition. (Each word turns blue and underlined when you point to it, as a reminder.) You can click again in *that* definition—and on and on and on.

You can use the < and > buttons on the toolbar, or the ⌘-[and ⌘-] keystrokes to go back and forward in your chain of lookups. Hold down the < for a pop-up menu of recent lookups.

It's worth exploring the Dictionary→Preferences dialog box, by the way. There you can choose U.S. or British pronunciations and adjust the font size.

- **Right-click or two-finger click a highlighted word.** From the shortcut menu, choose Look Up [word]. You get a panel that pops out of the highlighted word, showing the Dictionary page for that word.

- **Use the *dict://* prefix in Safari.** This might sound a little odd, but it's actually ultra-convenient, because it puts the dictionary right where you're most likely to need it: on the web.

 You can look up a word (for example, *preposterous*) by typing *dict://preposterous* into the address bar. When you hit Return, Dictionary opens and presents the search results from all its resources (dictionary, thesaurus, Apple terms, and Wikipedia).

- **Point to a word in a basic Mac program, and then press Control-⌘-D.** That keystroke makes the definition panel sprout right from the word you were pointing to. (The advantage here is that you don't have to highlight the word first.) "Basic Mac program," in this case, means one of the Apple standards: Mail, Stickies, Safari, TextEdit, Messages, and so on.

Note: The *New Oxford American Dictionary* you get in the app also includes its *front matter*, the reference section at the beginning. That includes some delicious writers' tools, including guides to spelling, grammar, capitalization, punctuation, chemical elements, and clichés, along with the full text of the Declaration of Independence and the U.S. Constitution. Just choose Go→Front/Back Matter—and marvel that your Mac comes with a built-in college English course.

Tip: Got a big screen or poor eyesight? Bump up the type size. Dictionary's toolbar has bigger/smaller buttons, and there's a Font Size pop-up menu in the Preferences window.

DVD Player

If you're one of the few, the proud, who own a DVD drive, you can play back DVD movies using macOS's aging but perfectly functional—and self-explanatory—DVD Player app.

FaceTime

If you have a Mac laptop or an iMac, it's got a built-in microphone and camera. And that means it's equipped to make free, very high-quality audio and video calls to other Apple computers, phones, and tablets (Figure 11-14). In macOS Mojave 10.14.1 and later, in fact, it can make *group* video calls, with as many as 32 people on the screen at once.

There's very little delay, and it works the first time and every time. Now Grandma can see the baby, or you can help someone shop from afar, or you can supervise brain surgery from thousands of miles away (medical training recommended).

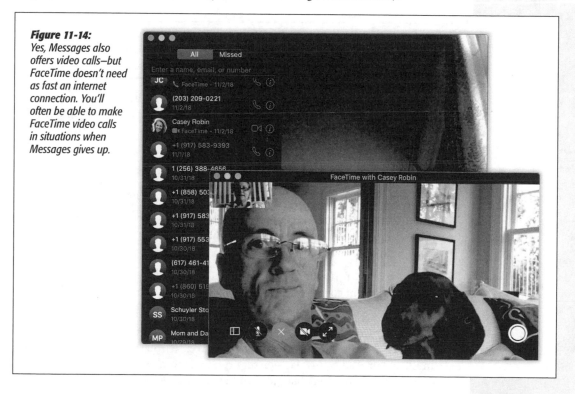

Figure 11-14:
Yes, Messages also offers video calls—but FaceTime doesn't need as fast an internet connection. You'll often be able to make FaceTime video calls in situations when Messages gives up.

From your Mac, you'll probably make FaceTime calls over a Wi-Fi network. But your callees, using iPhones or cellular iPads, can even conduct video chats over the cellular airwaves, when they're out and about.

Placing a Call

The FaceTime experience often begins with a more old-fashioned communication—a phone call or a text message, for example. ("Want to FaceTime now?")

In any case, FaceTime couldn't be easier to fire up—in many different ways:

- **From Contacts.** If you're in the Contacts app, and you've recorded the iPhone number or Apple ID of someone in your Mac's Contacts program, you'll see the ▢◁ button next to that person's name. Click it to place a video call. Or, to place an audio call, click ☏ and then click FaceTime Audio.

- **From the FaceTime app.** This app presents a list of your recent FaceTime calls (Figure 11-14, top left). Click the ▢◁ button next to a name to place a video call. For an audio call, click ☏ next to the person's name.

- **From Messages.** If you're chatting away with somebody by text and you realize typing is no longer appropriate for the conversation, then click Details at the top of the screen. Click ▢◁ (for a video call) or ☏ and then FaceTime (for a FaceTime audio call).

Tip: If you right-click or two-finger click FaceTime's Dock icon, you get a handy pop-up menu of Recent Calls. In other words, if you keep FaceTime in your Dock, you can place a new call to somebody on the spur of the moment, whatever you're doing, without having to open FaceTime first.

At this point, the other guy receives an audio and video message inviting him to chat. If he clicks Accept, then you're on. You're on each other's screens, seeing and hearing each other in real time. (You appear on your own screen, too, in a little inset window. It's spinach-in-your-teeth protection.)

Once the chat has begun, here's some of the fun you can have:

- **Resize the window.** Drag any window edge, or choose Window→Zoom.

- **Go Full Screen.** Click the green ⊙ button or the Full Screen button on your Touch Bar, if you have one (page 227), to make the window fill your entire screen. Click it again to restore the window.

- **Move the inset.** You can drag the little picture-in-picture window showing your face to a different corner of the video window, if you like.

- **Rotate the screen.** FaceTime works in either portrait (upright) or landscape (widescreen) view. Turn Video→Use Landscape on or off to choose, or click the curved arrow in the inset that shows your face. (If you're calling someone using an iPhone or iPad, your Mac's picture rotates automatically when your partner's gadget rotates. You don't have to turn the monitor 90 degrees.)

- **Mute the mike.** Either choose Video→Mute or click the 🎤 button at the bottom of the video window. The video continues. This is handy when you have to make throat-clearing sounds or yell at your kid in the background.

- **Pause the call.** You can also mute (black out) the *video*, for use when you have to perform small acts of personal grooming. To do that, click 📹.

Note: The call is also paused whenever you minimize FaceTime.

When you and your buddy have had quite enough, click ✕ to terminate the call.

Group FaceTime

FaceTime can connect up to 32 people simultaneously, creating a video party line (Figure 11-15)—as long as everyone has macOS Mojave 10.14.1 or later, or iOS 12.1 or later on an iPhone or iPad.

Begin the call

Often, you'll want to dive into a group video call from within Messages, where a group chat is already underway. To do that, click Details at the top of the screen. Click 📹. (Or, for a straight-up audio conference call, hit Audio.)

Each participant gets a special Group FaceTime message, complete with a Join button. Once you click it, that special button in Messages changes to show how long the call has lasted.

Tip: If you're in a group Messages session, that Join button remains yours to click for as long as the group FaceTime call is still going. In other words, you don't have to hop on instantly.

Figure 11-15:
On a group Face-Time call, your icon always appears at lower right. The small icons at left, from left to right, mean: hide/show call list; mute microphone; hang up; mute video; and full screen.

Or you can start in the FaceTime app. Click the + at top right; in the To box, specify the names of the participants. Then click Audio or Video. The other people's phones start ringing, and when they click Accept, the audio or video conference begins!

During the call

In regular FaceTime calls, the other guy's image fills the screen. How are you supposed to conduct a call with dozens of people?

Each face occupies its own rectangle; the more people who join, the smaller the rectangles get (Figure 11-15).

When someone is talking, FaceTime brings that person's rectangle front and center (and makes it bigger) automatically. In a lively conversation, therefore, the four main boxes seem to be constantly inflating and deflating to reflect who's talking.

But even if someone's not speaking, you can bring him to the front on demand, with either of two degrees of prominence:

- **Click his box once.** It comes to the front, gets slightly larger, and reveals his name or iCloud ID.

- **Double-click his box.** Now it gets *much* bigger, shamelessly covering up everyone else's boxes. This is for when you really want to focus on this one person. (Click to enshrink the box again.)

Tip: If you've clicked once, you can click the little ↗ icon to zoom that slightly enlarged box into the fully enlarged version.

The Roster

The FaceTime app can't display big rectangles for more than four people at once. Starting with the fifth joiner, a horizontally scrolling row of faces joins yours at the bottom of the screen—Apple calls it the Roster. But the idea is the same: If one of them speaks, her box jumps into one of the larger four spots on the screen. And even if she's not speaking, you can click or double-click her square to give it one of the two zoom treatments described.

Coming and going

If someone's inviting you to a group call, a notification lets you know. You'll see an option called Join or ◼◀, depending on what you're doing on the Mac. Or, if you're in Messages in a group chat, you'll see a Join button.

If you'd like to add someone to a call that's underway, click the screen, click ⋯, and then click Add Person.

If someone drops off the call (by clicking ✖), everyone else stays on the call, just as with a traditional conference phone call.

FaceTime Audio Calls

Video calling is neat and all, but be honest: Don't you find yourself making regular phone calls more often? Video calling forces us to be "on," neatly dressed and well behaved, because we're on camera. Most of the time, we're perfectly happy (in fact, happier) with audio only.

To place an audio call, you start out exactly as you would when making a video call: in the FaceTime app, Contacts, or Messages. Click ☏, and then click FaceTime Audio (as opposed to whatever phone numbers are listed there).

When you place an audio FaceTime call, the other person's phone, tablet, or Mac rings. If she accepts your call, it's better than being on a phone call in two ways. First, you don't have the usual lag time that throws off your comic timing. And, second, the audio quality is amazing—more like FM radio than cellular. It sounds like the other person is right next to your head; you hear every breath, sniff, and sweater rustle.

Receiving Calls

Life is even simpler when somebody calls *you*. A notification bubble appears on your screen, and you hear an incoming-call sound. (Which ringtone? That's up to you; in the FaceTime app, choose FaceTime→Preferences→Settings. Use the Ringtone pop-up menu.) If music is playing, it pauses automatically. Sweet.

If the Mac is asleep, it wakes; you can even answer the call on the Lock screen, without having to enter your password.

Click Accept to start the call, or Decline if now is not the time. (In that case, the caller will be told you're not available.)

FaceTime doesn't have to be running for you to receive a call. That's generally a cool feature—but if you really don't want to be interrupted, you can hang up a digital "Do Not Disturb" sign in any of these ways:

- **In FaceTime,** choose FaceTime→Turn FaceTime Off.

- **Use the Do Not Disturb feature** (page 374).

- **Sign out of FaceTime.** (Choose FaceTime→Preferences→Settings, and then click Sign Out.)

Find My

No, that's not a typo. The app's name really is missing a direct object. Find My what?

The name of this new Mac app makes a little more sense when you realize that it combines what used to be two iPhone apps: Find My iPhone and Find My Friends. The purpose of both apps was the same—to show where things are on a map. This new uni-app has two tabs: Friends and Devices (Figure 11-16).

People

Find My People is great for keeping tabs on your very young or very old loved ones, for arranging meet-up points in a crowded city, or for making sure nobody's cheating on you. This feature requires transparency and approval on both sides; you can't track people without their permission and awareness.

It may seem backward, but to start tracking someone, you're supposed to first show goodwill by letting them track *you*. They then have the option of letting you track them back.

Suppose, for example, that Juliet wants to monitor Romeo's position. In the app, Juliet clicks Share My Location. She starts typing *romeo* into the To box; she clicks his name in the list and then clicks Send.

The app asks how she wants to broadcast her position to Romeo: Share for One Hour (good for locating a friend downtown), Share Until End of Day (good for finding your colleague at the company off-site), or Share Indefinitely (good for finding your spouse).

At this moment, Romeo sees a notification that says, "Juliet Capulet started sharing location with you. Do you want to share yours?" Romeo, too, can choose either One Hour, End of Day, or Indefinitely (or, if he's still hung up on someone else, Don't Share).

Now Juliet sees a note that Romeo has shared his location, and his name shows up in the People list. She can click his name to see his position on the map.

At that point, she can click the ⓘ next to his name to open an info panel. It offers her buttons to Contact Romeo, get Directions to his location, set up Notifications, add

Figure 11-16:
Find your friends and Apple machinery on a map. Click the ⓘ next to a person's name or gadget's name to send an electronic SOS (or "Hey") to it (inset, right).

or remove him from the Favorites list, stop sharing her location with him, or remove him altogether from this app's list.

Under Notifications, if Juliet clicks Add, the app offers to Notify Me or Notify Romeo. Answering this question is a little baffling for her, since she doesn't yet know what she's asking to be notified about—but here's how it shakes down:

- **Notify Me.** Juliet will get notified when Romeo either arrives at, or departs from, a certain place—either his Current Location or another one she specifies. Yes, it's super-creepy in the wrong hands—but, again, this doesn't work unless he has invited her to know where he is. Also, Romeo will be notified that Juliet has turned this feature on.

- **Notify Romeo.** In this case, Romeo will get notified when Juliet arrives at, or departs from, her Current Location or another address she sets up here.

In each case, she can also choose how often to get these notification bubbles: either Only Once (meaning today only), or Every Time (meaning every time, every day, the person arrives or leaves).

Once you've finished checking out somebody's location, click anywhere on the map to return to the original Find People screen, with the full list of trackees.

Devices

This tab is the new incarnation of the old Find My iPhone app. It lists the Apple gadgets you own (signed into your iCloud account). Click one to see where it is on a map (Figure 11-16, left).

Clicking ⓘ opens a panel with five powerful tools for the panicking gadget owner. Directions opens Maps to guide you to the location of your lost thing. As for Notifications: If Find My can't find your gadget, you'll see its last known location—and, if Notify When Found is on, you'll get an email if it ever pops back online.

Tip: You even get to see where your laptop was the last time it had a charge, just in case you don't realize it's missing until after it's dead.

GarageBand

GarageBand, Apple's do-it-yourself music construction kit, isn't actually part of macOS. If you have a copy, that's because it's part of the iLife suite that comes on every new Mac (along with iMovie and Photos).

Home

HomeKit is Apple's home-automation standard. The Home app (Figure 11-17) lets you control any product whose box says "Works with HomeKit"—all those "smart" or "connected" door locks, security cameras, power outlets, thermostats, doorbells, lightbulbs, leak/freeze/temperature/humidity/air-quality sensors, and so on.

This app is one of several Apple has adapted from iOS. Among other limitations, you can't actually *set up* HomeKit gadgets in the Mac app. You still need an iPhone or iPad for that. The miracle of iCloud syncing brings the information onto the Mac (assuming that System Preferences→iCloud→Home is turned on).

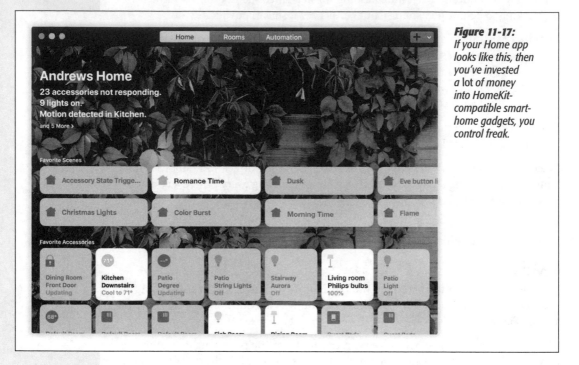

Figure 11-17:
If your Home app looks like this, then you've invested a lot of money into HomeKit-compatible smart-home gadgets, you control freak.

Once you've installed a gadget, you can use this app to:

- **Turn it on and off** by clicking its icon on the Favorites tab. Handy for light bulbs and locks.

Tip: You can do that either in the Home app or by using Siri voice commands ("Lock the front door," "Turn on the downstairs lights," and so on).

- **Adjust its home-control settings,** like the temperature for a thermostat. Double-click the gadget's icon, or right-click it and choose Controls.

- **Adjust its gadget settings,** like its name or which room it's on. Right-click its icon and choose Settings.

This isn't a book about smart-home accessories, but here's some of the fun you can have once you've bought a few (and then read the instructions at *support.apple.com/en-us/HT204893*):

- **Set up rooms.** If you've got a lot of HomeKit accessories—you lucky duck—you may find it easier to keep track of them all by putting their icons on different

screens, named for different rooms of your house. You'll also be able to tell Siri, "Turn off the lights in the living room."

To create or assign a room, double-click the gadget's icon, click Settings at top right, click Room, and either choose a room from the list or hit Create New to establish a new one.

Tip: You can take this concept one step further by putting your rooms into *zones*, which are usually "upstairs" or "downstairs." To get started: On the Rooms tab, choose Edit→Edit Room. At top left, click Rooms to see the complete list of rooms you've got so far. Click one, and then click Zone; choose a zone or hit Create New to make a new one. And voilà: Now you can say, "Turn off the lights upstairs!"

- **Automate your gadgets.** On the Automation tab, you can automate those actions based on the time or when you, or other people, arrive or depart.

- **Create a scene.** A "scene" is a bunch of accessories that you switch on and off simultaneously. You might have one called "Goodnight" that turns off all the lights and locks the doors with a single Siri command. To create one, click +, and then Add Scene, and then Custom, and then Add Accessories. Once the scene is set up, click its icon on the Home tab to trigger it.

- **Control your home by remote control.** It's possible to set things up so you can operate your gadgets from across the internet, when you're not even there. This does, however, require that you also own an Apple home hub, which can take the form of a recent Apple TV, a HomePod speaker, or an iPad.

- **Automate the whole works.** If you do, in fact, have a home hub, you can really smartify your home. You can set things up so that all the lights turn off when you leave the house, or that a certain scene happens at a certain time, or that the temperature goes up when your teenager gets home.

Yes, it can get really complicated. But imagine the magic once you get it all figured out!

Image Capture

This unsung little program was originally designed to download pictures from a camera and then process them automatically (turning them into a web page, scaling them to emailable size, and so on). Of course, soon iPhoto and then Photos came along, generally blowing their predecessor out of the water.

Even so, Apple includes Image Capture with macOS, primarily because it can grab images from scanners, not just cameras. It's also got some great options for insta-sharing newly imported photos—turning them into a web page or a PDF, for example.

You can open Image Capture manually, or you can set it up to open whenever you connect a digital camera and turn it on. To use that arrangement, open Image Capture. Using the "Connecting this camera opens:" pop-up menu, choose Image Capture.

Once Image Capture is open, it looks like Figure 11-18. When you connect your camera, cellphone, or scanner, its name appears in the left-side list. To begin, click it. After a moment, Image Capture displays all the photos on the camera's card, in either list view or icon view (your choice).

Figure 11-18:
In some ways, Image Capture is like a mini Photos app; use the slider in the lower right to change the thumbnail sizes. You can choose the individual pictures you want to download, rotate selected shots (using the lower-left curved-arrow button), or delete shots from the camera.

Import To:

Use this pop-up menu to specify what happens to the imported pictures. Image Capture proposes putting photos, sounds, and movies from the camera into your Home folder's Pictures folder. But you can specify any folder (choose Other from the pop-up menu).

Furthermore, there are some other very cool options here:

- **Photos.** Neat that you can direct photos from your camera to Photos via Image Capture. Might come in handy when you didn't *expect* to want to load photos into your permanent collection, but you change your mind when you actually look them over in Image Capture.

- **Preview** opens the fresh pictures in Preview so you can get a better (and bigger) look at them.

- **Mail** sends the pix directly into the Mac's email program, which can be handy when the whole point of getting the photos off the camera is to send them to friends.

- **Build web page** creates an actual web page of your downloaded shots. Against a dark-gray background, you get thumbnail images of the pictures in a web page document called *index.html*. Just click one of the small images to view it at full size, exactly as your website visitors will be able to do once this page is actually on the web. (Getting it online is up to you.)

Note: Image Capture puts the web page files in a Home folder→Pictures→Webpage on [today's date and time] folder. It contains the graphics files incorporated into this HTML document; you can post the whole thing on your website, if you like.

Image Capture automatically opens this page in your web browser.

- **Make PDF.** When you choose this option, you wind up with what looks like a Preview window, showing thumbnails of your photos. If you choose Save right now, you'll get a beautiful, full-color PDF of the selected photos, ready to print out and then, presumably, cut apart. But if you use the Layout menu, you can choose different layouts for your photos: 3×5, 4×6, 8×10, and so on.

 And what if a photo doesn't precisely fit the proportions you've selected? The Crop commands in the Layout menu (for example, "Crop to 4×6") center each photo within the specified shape and then trim the outer borders if necessary. The Fit commands, on the other hand, *shrink* the photo as necessary to fit into the specified dimensions, sometimes leaving white margins.

Note: The "crop" commands never touch the actual downloaded photos. The downloaded image files themselves retain their full sizes and resolutions.

- **Other.** The beauty of the Image Capture system is that people can, in theory, write additional processing scripts. Once you've written or downloaded them, drop them into your System→Library→Image Capture→Automatic Tasks folder. Then enjoy their presence in the Import To pop-up menu.

Tip: You can set up Image Capture to download everything on the camera *automatically* when you connect it. No muss, no fuss, no options. To do that, connect the camera. Click its name in the Devices list. Then, from the "Connecting this camera opens" pop-up menu, choose AutoImporter. From now on, Image Capture downloads all pictures on the camera each time it's connected. When the process is complete, a little green checkmark appears on the thumbnail of each imported photo.

Import Some, Import All

Clicking Import All, of course, begins the process of downloading the photos to the folder you've selected. A progress dialog box appears, showing you thumbnail images of each picture that flies down the wire.

If you prefer to import only *some* photos, select them first. (In list view, you click and Shift-click to select a bunch of *consecutive* photos, and ⌘-click to add *individual* photos to the selection. In icon view, you can both ⌘-click *and* Shift-click to select individual photos.) Then click Import.

Operating Your Scanner

Image Capture can also operate a scanner, auto-straighten the scanned images, and export them as PDF files, JPEG graphics, and so on. This is *exactly* like using Preview to operate your scanner. Turn on your scanner and click its name in the left-side list. Put your photos or documents into the scanner, and proceed as described on page 589. Clearly Apple saved some time by reusing code.

iMovie

Apple's video-editing program is big enough and complex enough that it gets a book all its own: *iMovie: The Missing Manual*, of course.

iTunes

Just kidding! There is no iTunes in macOS Catalina. After 16 years, Apple finally killed it off. Or, rather, split it into various new apps and locations:

- **Music.** This new app takes over most of the old iTunes program's music-management features (page 628).

UP TO SPEED

iPhone Syncing Without iTunes

In the olden days, you needed a computer to load an iPhone or iPad with music, videos, apps, and other data. Nowadays, all that stuff is wireless. It's perfectly possible to use an iPhone/iPad without even owning a computer.

But Mac syncing is still a great way to get music files onto your phone if you don't want to pay for Apple Music. It's also a free way to back up everything on your phone. (You can back up the phone to iCloud, but that costs money.)

Until Catalina came along, you used iTunes, the program on your Mac, to back up your phone, and to load it up with music, movies, and other files.

But iTunes no longer exists. Instead, when you connect an iPhone to your Mac with a cable, its icon and contents show up right at the desktop, in every Finder window.

(If your iPhone's icon doesn't seem to show up in the left-side Sidebar, confirm that the Sidebar heading Locations is expanded—click the Show button, if it's present. Also open Finder→ Preferences→ General; turn on "External disks" and "CDs, DVDs, and iPods.")

The iPhone window in Catalina looks almost identical to iTunes. The biggest difference is that the tabs (Music, Movies, TV Shows, and so on) appear across the top instead of down the left side.

Once you've connected the phone to the Mac using its Lightning cable, you can set it up to sync wirelessly from now on. For details on that—and for the entire syncing process—see the free PDF appendix to this chapter "Syncing iPhone and iPad with the Mac" on this book's "Missing CD" at *missingmanuals.com*.

- **Subscriptions.** To view and manage subscriptions to apps that require one, you used to use iTunes. Now, instead, you open the App Store app. Choose Store→View My Account, click View Information, scroll down to Manage, and, under Subscriptions, click Manage.

- **Podcasts** have now arrived in a standalone app (page 440).

- **TV and Movies store.** This chunk of iTunes now lives in a new TV app (page 461).

- **Voice Memos** now have their own app, too (page 461).

- **iPhone/iPad management.** When you plug in your iPhone or iPad, it now shows up in the Finder. Click its name in the left side of any window to view an exact copy of the old iTunes system of managing backups and updates—plus music, movies, and other data you want copied from the Mac (see the box on the facing page).

There's one oddball new side effect of the Great iTunes Dismantling: Now, for the first time, you can use a different Apple ID for each app: Books, Music, TV and Movies, and the Mac itself. Don't get confused!

Maps

When Apple brought its Maps app to the iPhone in 2012, the underlying databases had a lot of problems. They didn't include nearly as many points of interest (buildings, stores, landmarks) as Google's. Addresses were sometimes wrong. Satellite view showed bridges and roads melting into the sea. In a remarkable apology letter, Apple CEO Tim Cook recommended using one of Maps' rivals.

But some of Maps' features are pretty great—and now that Maps is a Mac app, too (Figure 11-19), there's some handy synergy with the iPhone and iPad. You can look up an address on the Mac and then wirelessly shoot it over to the phone for navigation in

Figure 11-19:
Maps lets you type in any address or point of interest and see it on a map, with turn-by-turn directions. It also gives you a national Yellow Pages and real-time traffic alerts. You have a choice of a street-map diagram or actual aerial photos, taken by satellite.

the car, for example. Or simply walk over to your Mac; thanks to Handoff (page 309), whatever map was on your phone is now on your Mac. And Maps' smarts are wired into other macOS programs, like Calendar, Contacts, and Safari.

Meet Maps

When you open Maps, you see a blue dot that represents your current location. You can manipulate the map in all the usual ways:

- **Zoom in or out** using the keyboard (press ⌘-plus or ⌘-minus), the mouse (double-click to zoom in, add the Option key to zoom out—or just click the + or − buttons), or the trackpad (pinch two fingers to zoom out; spread them to zoom in).

- **Scroll around the map** using the keyboard (press the arrow keys), the mouse (drag), or the trackpad (swipe two fingers in any direction).

- **Rotate the map** using the mouse (drag the small compass at lower right) or the trackpad (rotate two fingers). You can return the map to "north is up" by pressing ⌘-▲, by clicking the compass, or by double-clicking two fingers on the trackpad.

- **You can tilt into a 3D view,** which makes it look like you're surveying the map at an angle instead of straight down. You can do that with the mouse (click the 3D button), keyboard (press ⌘-0), or the trackpad (press Option and drag with two fingers).

At any time, you can click Satellite (top right) for stunning aerial photos. Using the Show pop-up menu at lower left, you can choose Show Labels to add street names to the aerial views. There's no guarantee that the Satellite view provides a very *recent* photo—the Maps database incorporates photography taken at different times—but it's still very cool.

Finding Yourself

Don't worry if you scroll away and can't find yourself on the map again. Click the ◄ at the top left. A blue dot shows your current location.

Searching the Maps

You're not always interested in finding out where you are; often, you know that much perfectly well. Instead, you want to see where something *else* is. Click in the search box and type what you're seeking—or, if you spot what you want in the list of recently sought addresses, click it there. (If there's already something in the box, then click ⊗ to clear it out.) Here's what Maps can find for you:

- **An address.** You can skip the periods (and usually the commas, too). And you can use abbreviations. Typing *710 w end ave ny ny* will find 710 West End Avenue, New York, New York. (In any of these examples, you can type a zip code instead of a city and state.)

- **An intersection.** Type *57th and lexington, ny ny.* Maps will find the spot where East 57th Street crosses Lexington Avenue in New York City.

- **A city.** Type *chicago* to see that city. You can zoom in from there.

- **A zip code or a neighborhood.** Type *10012* or *greenwich village.*

- **A point of interest.** Type *washington monument* or *niagara falls.*

- **A business type.** Type *drugstores in albany ny* or *hospitals in roanoke va.* (Figure 11-19 shows this idea.)

Tip: Maps is far more useful now that Siri has come to the Mac. You can say things like, "Find pizza near me," "What's the quickest way to JFK Airport?" "Get transit directions to Brooklyn," "Mail these directions to Casey," or "Zoom in on the map."

And if your Mac has a Touch Bar (page 227), then you get one-click buttons for Food, Coffee, Banks, Hotels, Gas, and so on, glowing right at you.

When Maps finds a specific address, an animated, red-topped pushpin comes flying down onto its precise spot on the map. A bubble identifies the location by name. Click outside the bubble to hide it. Click the map pin to bring the bubble back. Click Directions for instant driving directions.

Tip: Or walking directions. Click Walk at the top of the Directions panel.

Click the ⓘ bubble to open the Location page; read on.

The Details Screen

Once you've found something on the map—your current position, say, or something you've searched for—you can drop a pin there for future reference. Choose Edit→ Drop Pin. A purple pushpin appears. (You can drag the pin to move it, if your aim wasn't exact.)

Red pushpins represent addresses you've looked up. And the tiny icons represent restaurants, stores, and other establishments in Apple's (actually Yelp's) database.

All these pushpins and nano-icons are clickable. You get little labels that identify them. And, if you click the label, you open a details screen (Figure 11-20).

Bookmarks, Recents, Contacts

Maps is also plugged into your Contacts list, which makes it especially easy to find a friend's house (or just see how ritzy his neighborhood is).

When you click into the empty search bar at the top of the screen, the Bookmarks/ Recents/Contacts menu appears; it can save you a lot of typing. The list displays Recents (locations you've looked up recently—on your Mac or your iOS gadgets); Favorites (locations you've bookmarked); and Contacts (people whose addresses you've looked up).

When you click an entry in any of these lists, Maps drops a red, animated pushpin onto the map to identify that address.

Finding Friends and Businesses

That pushpin business also comes into play when you use Maps as a glorified national Yellow Pages. If you type, for example, *pharmacy 60609*, those red pushpins show you all the drugstores in that Chicago zip code. It's a great way to find a gas station, a cash machine, or a hospital in a pinch. Click a pushpin to see the name of the corresponding business.

As usual, you can click the pin's ⓘ bubble to open a details screen. If you've searched for a friend, you see the corresponding Contacts card. If you've searched for a business, you get a screen containing its phone number, address, website, and so on; often, you get a beautiful page of Yelp information (photos, reviews, ratings—see Figure 11-20).

Remember that you can click a web address to open it or send the phone number to your phone to dial it. ("Hello, what time do you close today?")

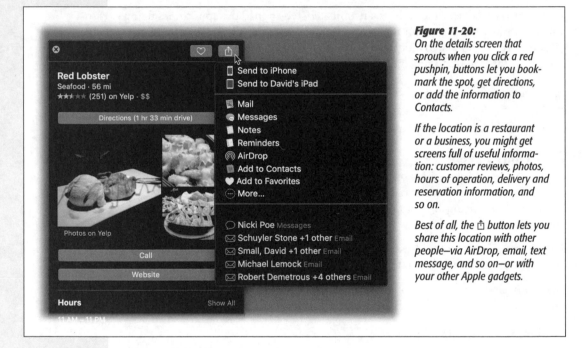

Figure 11-20:
On the details screen that sprouts when you click a red pushpin, buttons let you bookmark the spot, get directions, or add the information to Contacts.

If the location is a restaurant or a business, you might get screens full of useful information: customer reviews, photos, hours of operation, delivery and reservation information, and so on.

Best of all, the ⬆ button lets you share this location with other people—via AirDrop, email, text message, and so on—or with your other Apple gadgets.

Directions

The Directions panel opens when you click the Directions button (top left of Maps), or when you click the Directions button on any location's information panel.

The Directions panel offers *two* search bars: Start and End. Plug in two addresses—the Start address may already say "Current Location"—and let Maps guide you from the first to the second.

Tip: The ↻ button swaps the Start and End points. That's a great way to find your way back after a trip.

When everything looks good, Maps displays an overview of the route you're about to follow. In fact, it may propose several routes on the map, labeled with tags that show how long they'll take: "1 hr 9 min," "1 hr 15 min," and "1 hr 28 min," for example.

If you click one of these routes or tags, the top of the Directions panel lets you know the distance and estimated time for that option and identifies the main roads you'll be on.

Now, nobody expects you to use your Mac as a portable GPS device. You're not going to park it on your dashboard and have it tell you when to turn. What you can do, though, is send your selected directions to an iPhone or an iPad and use *that* as your GPS. Use the Share button highlighted in Figure 11-20.

Or, if you're just planning your trip, click any of the steps in the Directions panel; the map zooms in to that particular turn. Your route looks like it's been drawn in with a highlighter.

Traffic

How's this for a cool feature? Free, real-time traffic reporting. From the Show pop-up menu (bottom of the screen), choose Show Traffic. Now traffic jams appear on the relevant roads, for your stressing pleasure: orange dotted lines for slow traffic, and red ones for true stop-and-go nightmares.

UP TO SPEED

How the Mac Does GPS

When you first open Maps, your current location appears as a blue dot on the map. Now, the Mac doesn't have GPS; how does it do that?

It uses a sneaky trick. Metropolitan areas today are blanketed by overlapping Wi-Fi signals. At a typical Manhattan intersection, you might be in range of 20 base stations. Each one broadcasts its name and unique network address (its MAC address—nothing to do with Mac computers) once every second. Although you'd need to be within 150 feet or so to actually get onto the internet, a laptop or phone can detect this beacon signal from up to 1,500 feet away.

Imagine if you could correlate all those beacon signals with their physical locations. Why, you'd be able to simulate GPS—without the GPS!

So, for years, millions of laptops and iPhones have been quietly logging all those Wi-Fi signals, noting their network addresses and locations. (The Macs and iPhones never have to connect to these base stations. They're just reading the one-way beacon signals.)

At this point, Apple's database knows about millions of hotspots—and the precise longitude and latitude of each.

So your Mac sniffs for Wi-Fi base stations. If it finds any, it transmits their IDs back to Apple—which looks up those network addresses and sends coordinates back to Maps.

That accuracy is good to within only 100 feet, and of course the system fails completely once you're out of populated areas. On the other hand, it works indoors, which GPS definitely doesn't.

By the way: If you'd rather not have your Mac consulting Apple about its location, open System Preferences→Security & Privacy→Privacy and turn off Location Services.

If you don't see any dotted lines, it's either because traffic is moving fine or because Apple doesn't have any information for those roads. Usually, you get traffic info only for highways, and only in metropolitan areas.

Tiny icons also appear, representing accidents, construction sites, closed roads, and general alerts. Click the icon to make a quick description tag appear (like "Accident, Park Ave at State St"); click that tag to read a full-screen account of what's going on.

Public Transportation

Once you've called up some directions, you can click Transit (just below the Start/End box) to see Maps' suggestion of public-transportation methods to get there. Figure 11-21 shows the result.

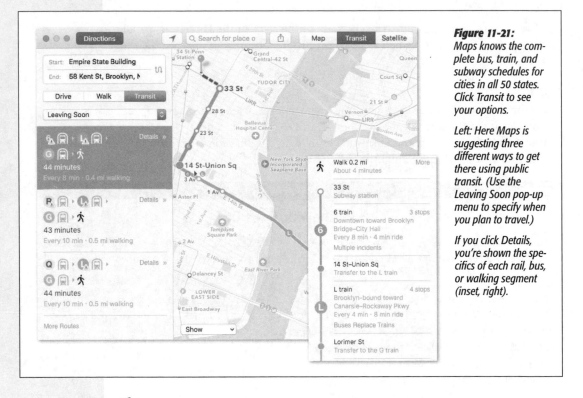

Figure 11-21:
Maps knows the complete bus, train, and subway schedules for cities in all 50 states. Click Transit to see your options.

Left: Here Maps is suggesting three different ways to get there using public transit. (Use the Leaving Soon pop-up menu to specify when you plan to travel.)

If you click Details, you're shown the specifics of each rail, bus, or walking segment (inset, right).

Flyover

You don't need to be headed somewhere to use Flyover, the Maps app's most dazzling feature; it has nothing to do with navigation, really. You can operate it even while you're lying on your couch like a slug; see Figure 11-22.

To engage Flyover, enter a city you'd like to tour, and then switch into Satellite view. Click the 3D logo in the lower-right corner.

Now you can go nuts, conducting your own virtual chopper tour of the city using the zooming and rotating tricks described earlier. Only a couple of things are different:

- **To move around the map,** drag it—or use two fingers on the trackpad.

- **To change your camera angle** relative to the ground, press Option as you use two fingers on the trackpad—or drag up or down on the compass at lower right.

- **To zoom in,** spread two fingers on the trackpad—or click the + and − buttons.

It's immersing, completely amazing, and very unlikely to make you airsick.

Figure 11-22:
Flyover is a dynamic, interactive, photographic 3D model of more than 350 major cities. It looks something like an aerial video, except that you control the virtual camera. You can pan around these scenes, looking over and around buildings to see what's behind them. To create this feature, Apple says, it spent two years filming cities from helicopters.

Flyover Tours

Apple wasn't satisfied with letting you pan around virtual 3D city models using your finger. It's also prepared to give you city *tours* in 3D.

Use the search box to enter the name of a big city or major landmark. (Some examples: San Francisco, New York, Tokyo, London, Paris, Rome, Madrid, Vancouver, San Jose, Cape Town, Stockholm. Or places like Yosemite National Park, the Sydney Opera House, Stonehenge, St. Peter's Basilica, or the Brooklyn Bridge.)

When you hit Search, a new button appears on the map: "3D Flyover Tour." (You can also find the button in the ⓘ Info panel for a city or place.) When you hit Start, you're in for a crazy treat: a fully automated video tour of that city or place. The San Francisco tour shows you the baseball park, the famous Transamerica Pyramid, the Alcatraz prison island, and so on. It's slow, soothing, cool, and definitely something that paper maps never did.

News

The News app (Figure 11-23) does just what Apple promises: It "collects all the stories you want to read, from top news sources, based on topics you're most interested in." Apple employs human editors—rather than software robots—to choose the stories in the Top Stories and Top Videos sections. Everybody sees the same stories here, no matter what their political leanings; in theory, this approach minimizes the triumph of fake news and clickbait.

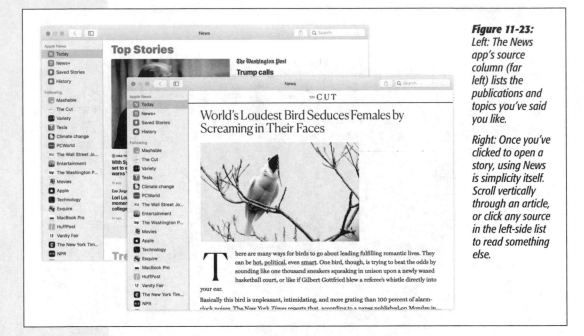

Figure 11-23:
Left: The News app's source column (far left) lists the publications and topics you've said you like.

Right: Once you've clicked to open a story, using News is simplicity itself. Scroll vertically through an article, or click any source in the left-side list to read something else.

If you see a bunch of news headlines right off the bat, well, sweet; you're the beneficiary of iCloud syncing (page 656). News has inherited your taste in journalism from macOS Mojave or some other Apple gadget.

If this is the very first time you've ever opened News, though, click Continue on the welcome screen. You're hit with today's headlines, beautifully laid out. It's been lovingly cobbled together from all sorts of websites, magazines, and newspapers.

This is the Today page. Scroll down far enough, and you'll discover that your "front page" is broken up into sections like Top Stories (chosen by those human editors), Trending Stories (chosen by algorithm based on popularity), For You (stories that match your interests—described in a moment), Top Videos, and so on. Eventually, you scroll down into topic areas like Politics, Sports, and Movies, plus any specialized topics you choose yourself.

Once you've clicked to open a story, using News is simplicity itself. Scroll on through; click < to return to the section from whence you came.

The second source in the left-side list, **News+,** is the home of Apple's $10-a-month "Netflix for magazines" service. It gives you full access to current and past issues of 300 magazines and newspapers: *The Atlantic, Better Homes & Gardens, Entertainment Weekly, Esquire, GQ, National Geographic, New York Magazine, The New Yorker, Parents, People, Runner's World, Sports Illustrated, Vanity Fair, Vogue, The Wall Street Journal, Wired,* and many others.

Saved Stories is where you find articles you've seen and bookmarked. History lists every story you've seen recently. Both of these, like magic, sync with your iPhone or iPad.

The Following section, though, is where you make News your own. Here's where you specify which publications, websites, and topics (tech, business, politics, fashion, and so on) you want to follow in your News app.

Sure, Suggested by Siri offers a few starter categories. But you should choose File→ Discover Channels & Topics. You get a massive, nearly endless list of magazine, newspaper, and website thumbnails. Click each one that looks promising to say, "Yes, please include stories from these pubs in what you show me."

You may as well choose File→Manage Notifications, too, to specify which news outlets are allowed to grab your attention with a notification (Chapter 10).

News no longer offers a list of specific topics that may interest you—the Cleveland Cavaliers, say, or Tesla cars, or seafood recipes. But you can still let it know your preferences in a couple of ways:

- **Use the search box.** At the top of the screen, a search box lets you search for topics, stories, or publications. In the search results, under Channels and under Topics, click **+** for each item you want News to find for you.

- **Just use News.** As you use the News app, it notices which kinds of headlines you click, read, or "favorite" (by choosing File →Suggest More Stories Like This). It will, in other words, learn your interests—and tailor its reporting accordingly.

These operations make new story categories appear on the Today tab.

And that's it: Suddenly, you have a beautiful, infinite, constantly updated, free magazine stand, teeming with stories that have been collated according to your tastes. It's all free, although you're not getting the listed publications in full—usually you're offered just a few selected stories.

Tip: If you anticipate that you'll be spending time in the living hell known as Offline mode (like on a subway, sailboat, or airplane), you can save some stories for reading later. To do that, choose File → Save Story. You'll find your saved stories under– of course–Saved Stories.

Notes

For many years, the Notes app was a simple bucket for pages of text: lists, recipes, driving directions, brainstorms. They all synced effortlessly among your Apple phones, tablets, and other computers.

Today, Notes has sprouted an array of formatting features that practically turn it into OneNote or Evernote. Now there's full type formatting, bulleted lists, checklists, web links, and pasted graphics, videos, or maps. You can collaborate on a Notes page with other people across the internet—or, on the other end of the paranoia scale, you can password-protect certain Notes pages for privacy.

Creating a Note

To create a new page in your digital notepad, choose File→New Note (⌘-N), or click the ☑ button on the top toolbar.

Once the new page appears, type away (Figure 11-24).

Tip: Notes works with Handoff (page 309). So if you're editing a note on your Mac, iPhone, or iPad, you'll be offered the chance to jump to the same note on any *other* Mac, iPhone, or iPad you own (if it's on the same Wi-Fi network).

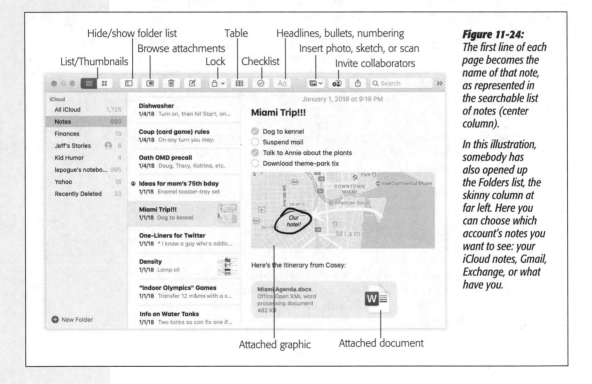

Figure 11-24:
The first line of each page becomes the name of that note, as represented in the searchable list of notes (center column).

In this illustration, somebody has also opened up the Folders list, the skinny column at far left. Here you can choose which account's notes you want to see: your iCloud notes, Gmail, Exchange, or what have you.

As you go, you can dress up your notes with a variety of formatting:

- **Paragraph formatting.** The Aα button gives you one-click access to paragraph styles like Title (big and bold), Heading, or lists with automatic bullets, dashes, or numbering.

- **Text formatting.** You have control over fonts, type sizes, colors, paragraph alignment, and indentation, using the commands in the Format menu.

- **Checklists.** The Checklist button turns any selected paragraphs into a checklist with little circles that you can check off, as shown in Figure 11-24.

- **Tables.** See page 435.

While you work, you can paste or drag photos and other graphics into a note, too—and links, maps, and even documents, like PDF files, Word documents, or Excel spreadsheets. Drag such a document into a note from the desktop; there it becomes an icon you can double-click to open later.

All of this, of course, syncs flawlessly with your iPhone, iPad, or iPod Touch.

Note: To ensure that syncing takes place, make sure Notes is turned on in System Preferences→iCloud (on your Mac), and in Settings→[your name]→iCloud (on your phone or tablet). The rest is automatic.

You can click 🗑 to delete the current note. Or you can click ⬆ to send the note to someone, by email, AirDrop, Messages, or whatever (page 258).

Conversely, the ⬆ button in lots of *other* programs now lists Notes, meaning you can send material (a map, photo, link, text, address, phone number…) directly *to* either a new note page or an existing one.

The Notes List

As you create more pages, the list of pages (at center in Figure 11-24) becomes more useful. It's your table of contents for the Notes app. It's a quick way to jump from one note to another.

Here's how to put it to use:

- **The first lines of your notes,** along with the time or date you last edited them. If there's a photo or sketch on a note—an unlocked one, anyway—you see its thumbnail, too.

 To open a note, click its name. To delete a note, click it and then press the Delete key.

- **Pinned notes.** Ordinarily, your notes appear chronologically, most recent at the top. In Notes→Preferences, you can specify that they be sorted by Date Changed or Title instead.

 But you may have a couple of notes—things you refer to a lot—that you want to appear at the top all the time. Passwords, credit card numbers, or frequent-flyer numbers, for example.

 That's why you can *pin* an individual note to the top of the list, where it won't move. To do that, click a note and then choose File→Pin Note. Or right-click or two-finger click the note and, from the shortcut menu, choose Pin Note.

 You *un*pin a note using the same techniques (but choose Unpin Note instead).

- **Search box.** You can search all your notes instantly. In Catalina, in fact, this search can even find words within the images of documents you've scanned. It's actual optical character recognition, yours free!

- **Gallery view.** New in Catalina: Instead of viewing your notes in a textual list, you can view them as graphic miniatures (thumbnails), which can be very useful if your notes tend to include a lot of formatting, pictures, and other visual elements. See Figure 11-25.

Tip: If you double-click a note's name, it opens into a new window, floating on your screen. You can open multiple notes this way, drag them around the screen, and leave them floating there permanently, as though held by magnets on the great refrigerator door of life.

Figure 11-25:
In the new Notes Gallery view, you get to see miniatures of all your notes instead of just a list.

What you sacrifice, of course, is the ability to see all the notes and an open note simultaneously.

Collaborative Notes

You and a buddy (or several) can edit a page in Notes simultaneously, over the internet. It's great when you and your friends are planning a party and brainstorming about guests and the menu, for example. Also great for adding items to the grocery or to-do list even after your spouse has left the house to get them taken care of.

In Catalina, in fact, you can share an entire folder of notes—a handy way to get started with a project's worth of info (see Figure 11-26).

When you click 👤 at the top of the screen, you're asked if you want to share this note or the entire folder it's in. The menu might say "Share Note [Baked Alaska Recipe]," or "Share Folder [Dessert Recipes]."

On the Add People screen, specify how you want to send the invitation: by message, email, AirDrop, or copying a link that you can send any way you like.

In Catalina, you have another strangely worded choice to make: "Only people you invite can make changes" or "Only people you invite can view." In other words, you can decide whether the people you're inviting are allowed to *see* these notes or *see and edit* them. Hit Share.

Once your collaborators receive and accept the invite, they can begin reading the note(s), or editing them (if you gave permission), right alongside their own notes in Notes.

Once you've shared a note, the icon at the top changes to 👥, and a matching icon appears next to the note's name in the master list. At any time, you can stop sharing the note—or add more people to its collaboration—by clicking that 👥 icon again and editing the sharing panel that appears.

Figure 11-26:
Top: To share a note with someone, click the button shown here by the cursor.

You get a choice: Share this note, or share the entire folder that contains it. (That's new in Catalina.)

Send the invitation by message, email, or whatever.

Also new in Catalina: Before you share, you can specify whether or not the recipients are allowed to make changes to your notes.

Bottom: You see any changes the other person makes highlighted briefly in yellow.

The Attachments Browser

The Attachments Browser in Notes is a single screen showing all attachments from all notes, rounded up on one scrolling screen (see Figure 11-27). It's often incredibly convenient to scan the visual attachments as a way to find a particular note.

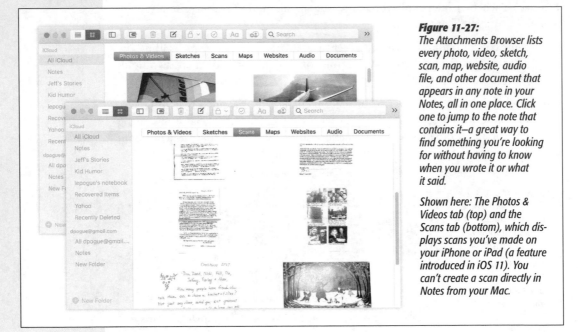

Figure 11-27:
The Attachments Browser lists every photo, video, sketch, scan, map, website, audio file, and other document that appears in any note in your Notes, all in one place. Click one to jump to the note that contains it—a great way to find something you're looking for without having to know when you wrote it or what it said.

Shown here: The Photos & Videos tab (top) and the Scans tab (bottom), which displays scans you've made on your iPhone or iPad (a feature introduced in iOS 11). You can't create a scan directly in Notes from your Mac.

Locking Notes

Locked, hidden, password-protected Notes pages are here at last, suitable for listing birthday presents you intend to get for your nosy kid, the formula for your top-secret invisibility potion, or your illicit lovers' names.

Note: You hide and show all your locked notes with a single password. You can't (that is, don't have to) make up a different password for every note.

To lock a note, click 🔒 in the toolbar; from the shortcut menu, choose Lock Note. Enter a password for locking/unlocking all your notes (or, if you've done this before, enter *the* password).

As long as your locked notes are all unlocked, you can still see and edit them. But when there's any risk of somebody else coming along (on your Mac, iPhone, iPad, or any other synced gadget), click the 🔒 again—and this time choose Close All Locked Notes.

Now all you see of the locked notes are their titles. Everything on them is replaced by a "This note is locked" message (and a password box).

If you correctly enter the password, all your hidden notes are suddenly viewable and editable again. Use your power wisely.

Notes Folders

You can organize your notes into folders, for ease of wading through them. Any folders you create on the Mac also show up on your iPhone/iPad.

The key to understanding this feature is the slide-out Folders list, which you can see at left in Figure 11-24. You can make it appear by choosing View→Show Folders List, or by clicking ▥ on the toolbar. Then you can adjust the Folder list's width by dragging its right edge.

To make a new folder, choose File→New Folder or click New Folder below the list; name the folder and then press Return. You can then drag existing notes into its name in the Folders list. (The usual rules apply: You can select a swath of notes in a list by clicking the first and then Shift-clicking the last. Or you can click individual, nonconsecutive notes by clicking with the ⌘ key pressed.)

Tip: If you press Option as you drag a note, you make a copy of it in the new folder instead of moving the original.

Click a folder's name to see the notes inside it. (Click "All [account name]" to see all the notes in that account. Notes accounts are covered on the next page.)

To create a new note within a folder, click the folder's name first. If you don't click any folder's name before you create the note, it goes into the general Notes category.

You can also rename a folder (right-click or two-finger click its name; choose Rename Folder), delete one (right-click or two-finger click its name; choose Delete Folder), put one inside another (drag its name), and move a folder to a different account—for example, from your iCloud account to your Google one—by dragging it.

Tables

When you click ▦, you get a table with two columns and two rows. Click in a cell and then start typing. To move to the next cell, press Tab on the keyboard (or click the cell).

Poke around long enough, and you can find controls for just about every formatting tool you'd ever need in a table (except the ability to manually adjust column widths and the ability to format the cell borders).

The keys to most of it are the tiny handles (⋯ and ⁝) that appear when you click inside a cell (Figure 11-28, top):

- **Add or delete columns.** Click inside a cell to make the ⋯ and ⁝ buttons appear. Click ⁝ to make the command menu (⌄) appear (Figure 11-24, bottom). It offers commands like Add Column (Before or After the current one), and Delete Column. Click ⋯ and then ⌄ to see equivalent commands for Rows.

 If you're typing in the lower-right cell, pressing Return also makes a new row.

- **Move a row or column.** Click ⋯ or ⁝ to highlight the corresponding row or column; now you can drag it to a new spot.

- **Select cells.** Drag across a couple of cells to make the selection handles appear; you can drag them to expand the highlighting. The usual Edit-menu commands (Cut, Copy, Paste) are now at your disposal. So are the Format-menu commands for bold, italic, underline, and so on.

- **Convert text into a table.** Select the text, and then click the table button (⊞). The selected text winds up in the first column—one cell per paragraph.

- **Convert table into text.** Click inside a cell, and then click ⊞. Choose Convert to Text.

Figure 11-28:
Top: Tables give Notes new information-storing capabilities.

Bottom: The key to adjusting and editing tables? The weird little ⸬ and ⸬ handles on the cells.

Notes Accounts

Notes can show you the contents of the Notes modules on Google, Yahoo, AOL, or another IMAP email account. You'll see each account's notes in the Folder list, as you can see in Figure 11-24—and from there, you can drag notes hither and yon, among accounts, with abandon. (If the Folder list is hidden, click the 🗐 button or choose View→Show Folders.)

To set this up, open System Preferences→Internet Accounts. Click the account you want (Exchange, Gmail, Yahoo, AOL, or whatever); finally, turn the Notes switch On.

That should do it. Now each account's notes appear under their own heading in the Folders list. And your notes are synced, both ways.

This makes life a little more complex, of course. For example, when you create a note, you have to worry about which account it's about to go into. To do that, be sure to

specify an account name (and a folder within it, if necessary) *before* you create the new note.

Numbers, Pages

Numbers and Pages are Apple's spreadsheet and word-processing programs, something like Apple-flavored versions of Microsoft Excel and Microsoft Word. They're part of Apple's iWork suite, which comes preinstalled on every new Mac. And they're complicated enough that there's a whole book about them: *iWork: The Missing Manual.*

Photo Booth

It may be goofy, it may be pointless, but the Photo Booth program is a bigger time drain than Solitaire, the web, and *Dancing with the Stars* put together.

It's a match made in heaven for any Mac with a camera above the screen.

Open this program and then peer into the camera. Photo Booth acts like a digital mirror, showing whatever the camera sees—that is, you.

Figure 11-29:
Some of the Photo Booth effects are simple color filters; others must have been dreamed up one night in the midst of a serious beer party at Apple. They're disturbingly creative. If you decide you really look best without any help from Apple's warped imagery, click the Normal icon in the center.

Click an effect

4-Up | Movie
Still

Finished shots Effects pages

But then click the Effects button (Figure 11-29). You enter a world of special visual effects—and we're talking *very* special. Some make you look like a pinhead, or bulbous, or like a conjoined twin; others simulate Andy Warhol paintings, fisheye lenses, and charcoal sketches. In fact, there are five whole pages of effects, nine previews on a page.

To page through them, click the left or right arrow buttons, or press ◄ or ►, or swipe with two fingers on your trackpad (one finger on the Magic Mouse).

The first page contains eight effects, some of which use sophisticated face-recognition smarts to track your face as it moves around the frame. That's how Dizzy and Love-struck are able to keep the animated birds or hearts circling your head, and how Chipmunk, Nose Twirl, and Bug Out are able to distort your cheeks, nose, and eyeballs even as you move around.

Some of the effects have sliders that govern their intensity; you'll see them appear when you click the preview.

Still Photos

When you find an effect that looks appealing (or unappealing, depending on your goals), click the ⊙ button, or press ⌘-Return. You see and hear a three-second count-down, and then *snap!*—your screen flashes white to add illumination, and the resulting photo appears on your screen. Its thumbnail joins the collection at the bottom.

Tip: Option-click the camera button to eliminate the countdown. You can get rid of the screen flash, too, by *Shift*-clicking. Needless to say, if you press Option *and* Shift, you get neither the countdown nor the flash.

4-Up Photos

If you click the 4-Up button identified at the bottom left of Figure 11-29, then when you click ⊙ (or press ⌘-Return key), the 3-2-1 countdown begins, and then Photo Booth snaps *four* consecutive photos in two seconds. You can exploit the timing just the way you would in a real photo booth—make four different expressions, horse around, whatever.

The result is a single graphic with four panes, kind of like what you get at a shopping mall photo booth. Its icon plops into the row of thumbnails at the bottom of the window, just like the single still photos.

GEM IN THE ROUGH

De-Mirrorizing Your Photos

Technically, Photo Booth acts like a mirror, not a camera. That is, every picture you take is actually flipped, left-to-right. If there's text in the picture—something written on your T-shirt, for example—or if you examine the way your hair is parted, you'll realize that every image is backward.

That's why you can click a thumbnail at the bottom of the window and then choose Edit→Flip Photo (⌘-F). You've just made the photo match what a camera would have seen. Or choose Edit→Auto Flip New Items if you want Photo Booth to do the flipping for you from now on.

Movies

Photo Booth can also record *videos*, complete with those wacky distortion effects. Click the ⊟ below the screen (Figure 11-29), and then click ◼◀ (or press ⌘-T). You get the 3-2-1 countdown—but this time Photo Booth records a video, with sound, until you click ⦿ to stop. (The little digital counter at left reminds you that you're still filming.) When it's over, the movie's icon appears in the row of thumbnails, ready to play or export.

Tip: Want to edit your video? Click its thumbnail and then choose Edit→Trim Movie, or hit ⌘-T. When you do, yellow trim handles appear at both ends of the scroll bar (the same ones you'd see when trimming a video on the iPhone or iPad, or in Photos). Drag them inward to trim off any dead air at the beginning or end of your video clip. Hit the space bar to check your work. If the trim is OK, click the Trim button to confirm.

Exporting Shots and Movies

To look at a photo or movie you've captured, click its thumbnail in the scrolling row at the bottom of the screen. (To return to camera mode, click the ⦿.)

Fortunately, these masterpieces of goofiness and distortion aren't locked in Photo Booth forever. You can share them with your adoring public in any of these ways:

- Click ⬆. The pop-up menu has the usual offerings of the Share menu (page 258): Mail, Messages, and AirDrop, plus Add to Photos and Add to Aperture, if you use those programs.

 There's also a "Change profile picture" command (to make this photo represent you on the Login screen), and a More button that opens the System Preferences→ Extensions screen described on page 348.

- **Click the photo or movie, and then choose File ⟩Export.** (Or just right-click or two-finger click the photo or movie itself; choose Export from the shortcut menu.) You're asked to name and save the exported image or video.

Tip: If you choose File→Export Original instead, the exported photo or video lacks any of the effects you've applied. You get the original, undistorted, underlying photo.

- **Drag a thumbnail out of the window to your desktop.**

Note: These files are stored in a single icon, a package file, that sits in your Home→Pictures folder. Ordinarily, you should never have to mess with it. But if you right-click or two-finger click this icon and choose Show Package Contents→Pictures, you'll find one JPEG apiece for single shots, four JPEG files for every 4-Up, and MOV files for videos.

As you set off on your Photo Booth adventures, a note of caution: Keep it away from children. They won't move from Photo Booth for the next 12 years.

Podcasts

After years of listening to its customers gripe about how the iTunes program had become a bloated, unwieldy monster of spaghetti code, Apple finally did something about it: It split the darned thing up into separate apps. Now you use the TV app (page 626) for buying, renting, managing, and watching TV shows and movies; the Music app (page 628) for buying, managing, and playing music; and this app, Podcasts, for finding and downloading podcasts.

A podcast is a "radio" show that's distributed online. Lots of podcasts begin life as *actual* radio and TV shows; most of NPR's shows are available as podcasts, for example.

But thousands more are recorded just for downloading. Some have millions of listeners and make huge money from ads; some have only a handful of fans. One thing is for sure: There's a podcast out there that precisely matches whatever weird, narrow interests *you* have.

The Podcasts app helps you find, subscribe to, organize, and listen to podcasts. Click Listen Now to see the next episodes of the podcasts you follow (Figure 11-30, top left); Browse to see recommended podcasts; or Top Charts to see what the rest of the world is listening to these days. Or use Search to look for something specific.

Figure 11-30:
Podcasts are for anyone who commutes, works out, works in a garden, works in a kitchen, or otherwise wants entertainment without having to look at a screen.

The Listen Now screen (left) displays your podcast episodes where you left off.

Click any podcast thumbnail to view its details page, which lists its episodes and offers you the chance to play or download them.

Once you've drilled down to a particular episode that seems worthy (Figure 11-30, right), you can listen to it in either of two ways:

- **Stream it.** Point to any episode or series thumbnail image, and then click ▶ to start playing directly from the internet. Podcasts you play like this are never stored on your Mac and don't take up any space, but they do require an internet connection. Generally not what you want for plane rides.

- **Download it.** If you click a podcast series and then click +, you download the podcast to your Mac. It takes up space there (and podcasts can be big)—but you can play it back anytime, anywhere. And, of course, you can delete it when you're done.

Subscribing

Most podcasts are series. Their creators crank them out every week or whatever. If you find one you love, subscribe to it so your phone downloads each new episode automatically. Just click Subscribe on its details page.

The episodes wind up on the Library tab, under Shows. Click a podcast's thumbnail to open its Details screen, where you can find listings for further episodes and reviews. Click ⋯ to find commands for deleting an episode or adding it to the playback queue; and links to share this podcast. You use the same ⋯ menu to unsubscribe.

Settings

There's a lot to control when it comes to podcasts. Do you want new episodes downloaded automatically? Do you want them auto-deleted when you're finished? You make these choices in Podcasts→Preferences. Those are the global settings for podcasts.

But you can also override your preferences for individual shows. On any podcast's details screen, click ⋯ and then Settings to see those options. You can limit how many episodes of this show are stored on your Mac, specify the playback order—oldest first or newest first, and so on.

Listening

Once a podcast is playing, the playback strip at the top reveals all the usual playback controls. There's a scroll bar, plus skip-forward and skip-backward buttons (keyboard shortcuts: ⌘-▶ and ⌘-◀), which are handy for jumping through ads! The factory setting is a 15-second skip per click, but you can change the interval in Podcasts→Preferences.

Using the Controls→Playback Speed, you can make the podcast play back at half speed, or at speeds as fast as 2x. None of this changes the pitch of the voices.

The Queue (Up Next)

When you've got a long drive (or a long run, or a long mowing session) ahead, you can stack up a bunch of episodes that your Mac will play in sequence.

To build this list, click an episode's ⋯ button. From the shortcut menu, you can choose Play Next (adds this episode to the top of your Up Next list) or Play Later (adds it to the *end* of the Up Next list).

At any point, you can click ☰ to see the list you've built of upcoming episodes, and change their sequence by dragging the ☰ handles. To clear the list, start playing any other podcast—and, in the warning box, click Clear Queue.

Reminders

Reminders, which has been dramatically overhauled in Catalina, is a to-do-list program (Figure 11-31). It not only records your life's little tasks, but it also reminds you about them when the time comes. On a laptop, Reminders can even remind you about something based on *where you are,* just as it does on the iPhone. For example, when you arrive home each day, it can remind you to feed your cats—or when you leave your vacation house, it can ask you if you've turned off the gas burners.

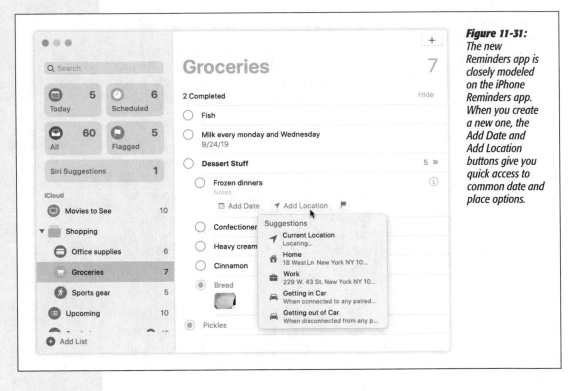

Figure 11-31:
The new Reminders app is closely modeled on the iPhone Reminders app. When you create a new one, the Add Date and Add Location buttons give you quick access to common date and place options.

If you have an iCloud account, your reminders sync across all your gadgets. Create or check off a task on your Mac, and you'll also find it created or checked off on your iPhone, iPad, iPod Touch, or PC. (Yes, PC. See *apple.com/icloud/setup/pc.html*).

(The syncing business also explains why the location feature is useful even if you have a desktop Mac that doesn't move around a lot.)

For Catalina, Apple rewrote the app from scratch, with juicy new features. Unfortunately, you can't have the new features without upgrading your reminders to the new data format.

And once you convert to the new format, you won't be able to open them on any other gadgets unless they, too, have Catalina (or, on the iPhone or iPad, iOS 13). And you won't be able to open them in Windows at all (except by logging in to *icloud.com*).

When you first open Reminders in Catalina, you can click Upgrade Now or Upgrade Later. If you don't upgrade, you can still use Reminders, but without some of the cool new features, like sharing your Reminder lists with other people; setting a reminder to appear when you message someone; and flagging certain items (🚩).

Everything else works as described here.

Tip: Siri and Reminders are a match made in heaven. "Remind me to file the Jenkins report when I get to work." "Remind me to set the TiVo for tonight at 8." "Remind me about Timmy's soccer game a week from Saturday." "Add waffles to my Groceries list." Speech recognition rocks when it comes to leaving notes for yourself. And iCloud will take care of copying those reminders to your iPhone.

The Four Smart Lists

The new Reminders app offers four "smart lists" at the top: one-click bubbles that show you all the reminders due Today, all the ones you've Scheduled for later, all the ones you've flagged as significant, and All, which consolidates all your to-do lists into one massive scrolling one. Click one to open the corresponding list.

Tip: Even within this smart list, you can add items. For example, if you open Scheduled, you'll see your To Dos organized by due date; you can hit ⊕ and add another To Do under the appropriate date.

My Lists

Below the smart list buttons, it should be clear that you can create *more than one* to-do list, each with its own name: a groceries list, kids' chores, a tally of expenses, and so on. It's a great way to log what you eat, or to keep a list of movies people recommend.

Click a list's name to open the to-do list within.

To create a new list, click Add List and type a name. By double-clicking its icon, you can choose a color (for the list's title font and also for the "checked-off" circles once the list is underway), and pick a graphic icon symbol for your new list.

To delete a list, click it and press the Delete key; confirm with the Delete button.

When you're viewing the list of lists, you can rearrange them by dragging their title bars up or down.

Reminder Groups (Sublists)

You can also, in Catalina, *group* your lists. You might, for example, create a group called Shopping, which contains sublists for groceries, sports gear, and office supplies (shown in Figure 11-31). You can expand or collapse the sublists by clicking the little ▶ next to the group's name.

To create a group, select two or more reminder lists (press ⌘ as you click their names), and then choose File→New Group. Type a name for the group. (Later you can rename it by right-clicking or two-finger clicking and choosing Rename Group from the shortcut menu.)

If you right-click or two-finger click a group name and choose Delete Group, you'll be asked whether you want to keep the lists that made up the group.

Creating a Reminder

Once you've opened a list, you create a new reminder in any of these ways:

- **Choose File→New Reminder** (⌘-N), or just click below the existing items. Type your reminder. Feel free, as you type, to specify dates, times, locations, and repeat schedules: "Remind me to feed the cats every day at 8:30 a.m." "Print the Wiggins report when I get to work." "Work out Tuesday and Thursday." As you can see by the text balloon, Reminders correctly recognizes and interprets those where/when phrases. Press Enter.

Tip: Reminders is another app that's greatly accelerated by the Touch Bar, if you have one (page 227). Here you get instant access to the +, ⓘ, and other useful buttons.

- **Use Siri's Add command.** Using Siri, you can say, "Add avocados to my Groceries list." "Add *Titanic 2* to my Movies list." This trick is awesome, because it works no matter what app you're using on the Mac.

Tip: Siri can also *find* these reminders, saving you a lot of navigation. You can say, "Find my reminder about dosage instructions," for example.

- **Use "Remind me about this."** When you're looking at something in one of Apple's apps, you can tell Siri, "Remind me about this later." That might be a text message in Messages, a web page in Safari, an email in Mail, a document in Pages, or whatever. (This command works in Calendar, Contacts, Books, Mail, Maps, Messages, Notes, Numbers, Pages, Phone, Podcasts, Reminders, and Safari. Software companies can upgrade their apps to work with "Remind me about this," too.)

 Instantly, Siri creates a new item on your main Reminders list—named for the precise message, location, web page, document, or thing you were looking at—complete with the icon of the app you were using. Later you can click that icon to open the original app—to the exact spot you were when you issued the command.

 You can also say things like, "Remind me about this tomorrow night at seven" or, "Remind me about this when I get home."

 Put it all together, and you've got an effective system for bookmarking your life. Maybe this feature will, once and for all, end the practice of people emailing stuff to themselves just so they'll remember it.

- **Create a reminder from another app.** You can create a new reminder from within Messages, Mail, Photos, Maps, and other apps. Once you've selected some text (or

a photo, or a location, or whatever), right-click or two-finger click it, and then choose Share→Reminders. You're invited to name this new reminder, specify a list for it, and then hit Add. Behind the scenes, you've just added that material to a new reminder.

Note: When you use Siri to create a reminder, it goes onto the *Default* reminder list, which you choose within the Reminders app in Preferences.

The instant you create a new reminder name in Reminders, four fascinating controls appear:

- **Notes** is a place to record notes: an address, a phone number, details of any kind.

- **Add Date.** Reminders can remind you at a certain time on a certain date. Click this button for a set of quick-click options like Today, Tomorrow, This Weekend, and Custom (which lets you choose any *other* date).

- **Add Time.** Once you've chosen a date, the Add Time button appears. Here again, you can either type any time you like or choose one of the canned options (9am, 12pm, 3pm, 6pm, or 9pm).

- **Add Location.** Your laptop or phone will use its location circuits to remind you of this item when you arrive at a certain place or leave a certain place. (Your laptop will remind you if it's turned on and within a Wi-Fi hotspot. But more often, this option will be useful if you have an iPhone or iPad that's on the same iCloud account. Record the reminder on your Mac—receive the reminder on your phone.)

 The little pop-up menu here proposes Current Location (handy if, for example, you're dropping off your dry cleaning and want to remember to pick it up the next time you're driving by), your Home and Work addresses (as specified in Contacts), Getting in Car, and Getting Out of Car. (Those last two work by detecting when your phone connects to your car's Bluetooth system.) You can also type in an address.

 In each case, you'll get a notification when you arrive at the specified place.

The Info Bubble

The Add Date, Add Location, and other buttons on every new reminder are only meant to be quick-select shortcuts.

If you click the ⓘ at the right end of a reminder's row, you open an Info panel that offers many more options (Figure 11-32):

- **On a Day, At a Time.** These work exactly like the quick-select options described already.

- **At a Location.** Once again, you can choose Current Location, your Home or Work addresses, or type in any address you like. This time, however, you can choose either Arriving *or* Leaving. Later, your iPhone will remind you as you approach (or leave) the address, which is fairly mind-blowing the first few times it happens.

Once you've specified an address, the Location screen shows a map. The diameter of the circle shows the area where your presence will trigger the appearance of the reminder.

Tip: You can adjust the size of this "geofence" by dragging the black handle to adjust the circle. In effect, you're specifying how close you have to be to the specified address for the reminder to pop up. You can adjust the circle's radius anywhere from 328 feet ("Remind me when I'm in that store") to 1,500 miles ("Remind me when I'm in that country").

Figure 11-32:
In the redesigned Reminders app, you never have to leave the main list screen to edit all the tweaky details.

- **repeat.** Reminders can remind you about things that recur in your life, such as quarterly tax payments, haircuts, and anniversaries. Click "repeat" if you want this reminder to appear every day, week, two weeks, month, or year. (This option appears only if you've turned on the On a Day option.)

- **Remind me when messaging** is new in Catalina, and super-useful. Turn it on, hit Choose Person, and select somebody's name from Contacts. The idea is that when you next begin chatting with this person in Messages, a reminder will pop up right there.

 Think of this option every time you're turning out the light and say to yourself, "Dang, I forgot to remind Casey to pay me back that $75."

- **priority.** Click this pop-up menu to specify whether this item has High, Medium, or Low priority—or None. You'll see one, two, or three exclamation marks (!!!)

next to each item in your Reminders list, indicating its urgency. In some of the calendar programs that sync with Reminders, you can sort your task list by priority.

- **URL** stores any web address you want to associate with this item.

- ⚑ lets you flag this reminder. A flag can mean anything you want. It can mean "Front-burner items." It can mean "I've procrastinated on these too long." It can mean "Items I'm gathering up to put into a single new list for the McGillicuddy project." All the flagged Reminders appear, of course, in the Flagged smart list described on page 443.

- **Add Image→Photos** opens a tiny panel of Photos thumbnails, for your image-browsing pleasure. You can drag a thumbnail of a photo directly onto one of your Reminders. It will appear there for quick reference—and you can click to open it full-size.

 If you have an iPhone or iPad nearby, you can use the Take Photo, Scan Documents, and Add Sketch commands, too. Whatever you snap, scan, or draw appears magically and wirelessly on the Mac, in Reminders.

Subtasks

In Catalina's version of Reminders, you can create to-do items within a to-do item. The main reminder might be "Prep for the in-laws' visit," and the indented subtasks might be "Mow lawn," "Paint house," and "Retile roof."

Just drag one reminder underneath another one, indenting it as you go. Use any blank spot on the reminder as a handle. Or click item B, and then choose Edit→Indent Reminder. It indents itself nicely underneath item A.

At this point, the main reminder ("Prep for in-laws' visit") bears a little collapse-o-button (») that hides or shows the subtasks.

Checking Off Reminders

As you go through life being productive, you're supposed to click the little circle next to each item in Reminders that you've completed. At that point, the reminder disappears.

If you ever want to take pride in how much you've accomplished, click Show (above the right side of the list) to bring your checked-off tasks back into view. The button changes to say Hide.

You can select or rearrange reminders if you know *where* to click to select or drag them: on any blank spot to the right of the name. Then:

- **Delete a to-do item altogether, as though it never existed.** Select it, and then press the Delete key.

- **Delete a bunch of items.** ⌘-click a bunch of them, and then press the Delete key.

- **Rearrange the list items.** Drag them up or down the list.

Sharing Lists

You can share your to-do lists with other people electronically, just as you can with notes—a great way for you to share a list of chores with your kids, a gift registry with your wedding guests, a shopping list with your partner, and so on.

Note: This feature works only among machines that are using the upgraded Reminders format (iOS 13 or Catalina).

Point, without clicking, to the reminder list you intend to share; the ⋐ appears. Click it to begin the process of specifying how you want to share the list (by Messages, Mail, or whatever) and with whom. The process is exactly as described on page 403, except that there's no View Only option; once the recipients receive your invitation, you'll all see the progress as you, or they, edit and check off items on the shared list.

Syncing Reminders

Once you've set up a few reminders in Reminders, you'll marvel as it gracefully integrates with the Notification Center when it wants your attention.

But it also auto-synchronizes your to-do lists across other gadgets, like iPhones, iPads, iPod Touches, other Macs, and even Windows PCs. To give it permission for that kind of sharing, open System Preferences→[your name]→iCloud and turn on the Reminders checkbox.

Note, however, that Reminders also can coordinate with the to-do list features of Exchange and so-called CalDAV services (Yahoo is one). To set them up, open System Preferences→Internet Accounts. Click the account you want (like Exchange or Yahoo); finally, turn the Reminders switch On.

That should do it. Now your to-do lists are synced, both ways, although the non-Apple lists won't have the new Catalina features.

Stickies

Even in the age of the far more modern Notes program, the old Stickies app is still creaking along. It creates virtual Post-it notes you can stick anywhere on your screen.

You can use Stickies for quick notes and to-do items, web addresses or phone numbers you need to remember, or any other little scraps and snippets of text you come across. They all show up whenever the Stickies program is running (Figure 11-33).

Creating Sticky Notes

The first time you launch Stickies, a couple of sample notes appear automatically, describing some of the program's features. You can quickly dispose of each sample by clicking the Close button in the upper-left corner of each note or by choosing File→Close (⌘-W). Each time you close a note, a dialog box asks if you want to save it. If you click Delete Note, the note disappears permanently.

To create a new note, choose File→New Note (⌘-N). Then start typing or:

- **Drag text in from any other program.** Or drag text clippings from the desktop directly into your note. You can also drag a graphics file into a note to add a picture. You can even drag a sound or a movie in.

- **Drag the icon of a PDF file into a note.** (Stickies can accommodate multipage PDF files. At first, you see only the first page, but the scroll bar reveals the rest.)

- **Choose File→Import Text** and select any plain text file or RTF (Rich Text Format) document to bring it into a note.

- **Drag URLs** into a note directly from a web browser's address bar.

Tip: If one particular note contains your most important information—your to-do list, say—you can force it to remain in front of all other windows, even if Stickies itself gets shunted to the background. Just click the note, and then choose Note→Floating Window.

Figure 11-33:
In the old days of the Mac, the notes you created with Stickies were text-only, single-font deals. Today, however, you can use a mix of fonts, colors, and styles within each note. You can even paste in graphics, sounds, and movies (like PICT, GIF, JPEG, QuickTime, AIFF, whole PDF files, and so on), creating the world's most elaborate reminders and to-do lists.

After you paste in an image, you can even use the Markup tool to draw, scribble and highlight on it as you would in many other apps. Neat!

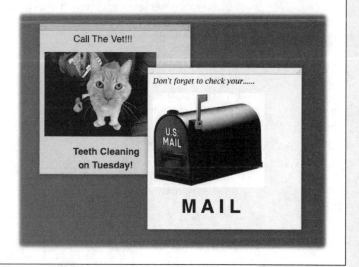

- **In many Apple programs, you can select a chunk of text** and then choose Make New Sticky Note from the program's Services menu, or press Shift-⌘-Y. This command launches Stickies, creates a new note, and fills it with your selected text—all in one step.

Note: All your notes are stored in a file called *StickiesDatabase*, located in your Home→Library folder. You're free to copy it, pass it along, and so on, just as you would any file.

Have a favorite style for your sticky notes? First create a new note, choosing the color and text style you like and setting it to the size you prefer. Then choose Window→Use

as Default. All new notes you create now appear in the size, font, and color you've chosen.

Growing and Shrinking Notes

Stickies includes a few built-in tricks for managing a deskful of notes:

- **Drag any corner of the note** to make it larger or smaller onscreen.

- **Use the small triangle in the upper-right corner** of each note to zoom and shrink note windows with a single click. The first click expands a note nearly to full-screen size. Another click pops it back down to normal size.

- **Double-click anywhere** along the dark strip at the top of each note to collapse it into a compact one-line mini-note. You also can collapse a selected note by choosing Window→Collapse (⌘-M).

Tip: The most efficient way to use Stickies is to keep the notes in their collapsed state. When a note is collapsed, the first line of text shows up in tiny type in the title bar of the note, so you don't have to expand the note to remember what's in it. Plenty of notes can be summed up in a couple of words ("Pick up dry cleaning," "Call Mom"), so you may be able to leave your notes this way.

Formatting Notes

Stickies has word processor–like commands for creating designer sticky notes, with any combination of fonts, colors, and styles (explore the Font menu). You can also choose from six background colors from the Color menu.

Saving Sticky Notes

The notes you create in Stickies last only as long as you keep them open. If you close a note to get it out of the way (and click Delete Note in the confirmation box), it vanishes permanently.

If you want to preserve the information you've stuffed into your notes in a more permanent form, you can do it in one of two ways: Close the note but hit the Save button, or use File→Export Text. Either way, you save the note as a standalone TextEdit document, with the following format options:

- **Plain Text.** This option saves your note as a plain text file, with neither formatting nor pictures.

- **RTF.** RTF stands for Rich Text Format, a special exchange format that preserves most formatting, including fonts, style, and color choices. You can open the resulting RTF file in just about any word processor with all your formatting still intact.

- **RTFD.** RTFD, a strange and powerful variant of RTF, is a Rich Text Format document *with attachments*. How do you "attach" items to an RTFD file? Drag the icon of an actual application (Preview, Calculator, or whatever) or a multipage PDF file, into a sticky note. The icon for the program or document appears in the note, but double-clicking the icon doesn't do anything. When you export the note as an RTFD file, the result is a TextEdit document that has embedded within it the

entire program or document you dragged in. The program icon appears just as it did in the sticky note, but if you double-click the icon, the program actually opens.

You can also paste a graphic into your sticky note. When you export the note as an RTFD document, the resulting *package* file includes a graphics file of the format you pasted.

Stocks

This one's for you, big-time day trader. The Stocks app—a port-over from iOS—tracks the rise and fall of the stocks in your portfolio by downloading the very latest stock prices (see Figure 11-34).

(All right, maybe not the *very* latest. The price updates may be delayed as much as 20 minutes, which is typical of free stock-info services.)

When you first fire it up (and hit Continue to pass the welcome screen), Stocks shows you a handful of sample securities and indexes in the left-side column: the Dow Jones

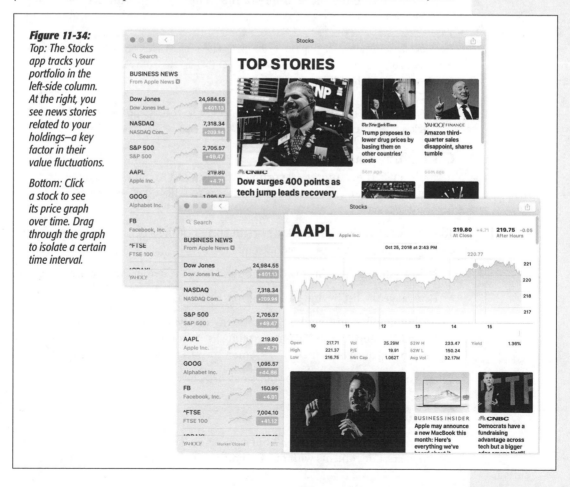

Figure 11-34:
Top: The Stocks app tracks your portfolio in the left-side column. At the right, you see news stories related to your holdings—a key factor in their value fluctuations.

Bottom: Click a stock to see its price graph over time. Drag through the graph to isolate a certain time interval.

Industrial Average, the NASDAQ Composite Index, the S&P 500 Index, Apple, Google, and Facebook, for example.

Next to each, you see a spark graph (a miniature of today's price fluctuations), its current share price, and beneath *that*, how much that price has gone up or down today. As a handy visual gauge to how elated or depressed you should be, this final number appears on a *green* background if it's gone up, or a *red* one if it's gone down. Click this number to cycle the display from a percentage to a dollar amount to current market capitalization ("120.3B," meaning $120.3 billion in total corporate value).

When you click a stock, the top-right part of the screen zooms in for the details on that company. Here's what it contains:

- **A table of statistics.** A capsule summary of today's price and volume statistics for this stock.

- **A graph of the stock's price.** It starts out showing you the graph of today's fluctuations. But by clicking the headings above the chart, you can zoom in or out, from one day (1D) to the entire history of the company (All), with many increments in between.

Tip: Move the cursor across the graph to see the readout for a certain day. Or drag to isolate a certain time period; pop-up labels show how much of a bath you took (or how much of a windfall you received) during the interval you highlighted. Cool!

- **An assortment of relevant headlines,** brought to you by the News app (page 428). Click a headline to read the article.

Customizing Your Portfolio

It's fairly unlikely that *your* stock portfolio contains just Apple, Google, and Facebook. Fortunately, you can customize the list of stocks to reflect the companies you *do* own (or want to track).

To edit the list, click ☰ in the lower-right corner of the stocks list. You arrive at the editing screen, where these choices await:

- **Delete a stock** by clicking the ⊖ button and then the Remove confirmation button.

- **Rearrange the list** by dragging the grip strips on the right side.

- **Add a stock** by clicking + in the top-left corner; in the search box, type in the company's name or symbol for a scrolling list of companies with matching names. Click + for one you want to track. You return to the stocks-list editing screen.

When you're finished setting up your stock list, click Cancel and then Done.

TextEdit

TextEdit is a basic word processor—but it's not nearly as basic as people think it is. You can create real documents with real formatting, using style sheets, colors, automatic

numbering and bullets, tables, and customized line spacing. You can even open, edit, and create Microsoft Word documents. If you had to, you could write a children's book in TextEdit, and it would look pretty decent.

Better yet, TextEdit (Figure 11-35) is now a showcase for macOS's iPaddish features, like Full Screen mode, Auto Save, and Versions (see Chapter 5). It can also save your files into your iCloud locker, as described on page 210.

Figure 11-35:
The text ruler gives you control over tab stops, paragraph justification, and so on. Pressing ⌘-R makes it appear and disappear. On the toolbar, the Style pop-up menu (¶) lists canned sets of character and paragraph formatting, so you can apply them consistently throughout a document.

And TextEdit works with macOS's built-in text-editing features: smart links, smart quotes, smart dashes, smart copy/paste, abbreviation expansion, auto–typo correction, data detectors, and so on. (They're all described in Chapter 6.)

Tip: You can magnify the type of a TextEdit document the way you do on an iPhone or an iPad: by pinching or spreading. That is, spread two fingers on your trackpad to zoom in, or pinch to zoom out. Best. Tip. Ever.

TextEdit's Two Personalities

The one confusing aspect of TextEdit is that it's both a *plain text editor* (no formatting, globally compatible) and a true *word processor* (fonts, sizes, styles; compatible with other word processors). Here's the scheme:

• **You can change a plain text document** to a formatted one by choosing Format→ Make Rich Text or Shift-⌘-T. The ruler appears automatically to remind you that a new world of formatting has just become available.

- **Conversely, you can change a formatted document** (a Word file you've opened, for example) to a plain text document by choosing Format→Make Plain Text (or, again, Shift-⌘-T). An alert message appears to point out that you're about to lose all formatting.

- **If you know what kind of document you *always* want to open,** go to the TextEdit→ Preferences dialog box; on the New Document tab, select Rich Text or Plain Text. That's what you'll get each time you choose File→New.

Tip: Here's where you can turn on all those smart links, smart quotes, smart dashes, and the other smart text-processing features described in Chapter 6.

Working in TextEdit

As you begin typing, all the usual word-processing rules apply, with a few twists:

- **Choose bold, italic, and font sizes** using the formatting toolbar. (You can still use the commands in the Format menu.) You can even create subscripts or superscripts, change the color of the text (Format→Font→Show Colors), and so on.

- **Common paragraph-alignment options**—Align Left, Align Right, Center, Justify— are all available as toolbar buttons and also reside in the Format→Text submenu. Adjust the line spacing (single, double, or any fraction or multiple) using the Spacing pop-up menu in the toolbar.

- **The toolbar also offers automatic bulleting** and numbering of paragraphs. Just choose the numbering style you prefer from the pop-up menu at the right end of the toolbar.

Tip: If your Mac has a Touch Bar (page 227), all these formatting controls appear as glowing buttons—the better to apply styles without lifting your hands from the keyboard.

- **You can select several nonadjacent bits** of text *simultaneously.* To pull this off, highlight your first piece of text by dragging, and then press ⌘ as you use the mouse to select more text. Bingo: You've highlighted two separate chunks of text.

 When you're done selecting bits of text here and there, you can operate on them en masse. For example, you can make them all bold or italic in one fell swoop. You can even use the Cut, Copy, and Paste commands, as described in the next section. When you cut or copy, the command acts upon all your selections at once.

 You can also drag any *one* of the highlighted portions to a new area, confident that the other chunks will come along for the ride. All the selected areas wind up consolidated in their new location.

Tip: If you *Option*-drag one of the highlighted bits, you *copy* all selected chunks, leaving the originals in place.

- **Similarly, you can use the Find command.** To do that, choose Edit→Find→Find (or just press ⌘-F). Fill in the search box; the sought-for term appears highlighted

everywhere in your document at once. (You can also search and *replace,* using the other commands in the Edit→Find submenu.)

- **If you Option-drag vertically,** you can freely select an arbitrary column of text (not necessarily the entire page width). This technique is useful when you want to select only one column in a multicolumn layout, or when you want to select the numbers in a list and format them all at once.

Style Sheets

A *style* is a prepackaged collection of formatting attributes that you can apply and reapply with a click of the mouse (bold, 24-point Optima, double-spaced, centered, for instance). You can create as many styles as you need: chapter headings, sidebar styles, and so on. You end up with a collection of custom-tailored styles for each of the repeating elements of your document.

POWER USERS' CLINIC

Advanced Typography in TextEdit

If you just spewed your coffee upon reading the heading of this sidebar, you're forgiven. Advanced typography in TextEdit? Isn't that a little bit like saying "advanced page layout in Notepad"? Not at all. TextEdit is a gleaming showcase for macOS's typographical smarts.

Most of the commands in the Format→Font submenu should be familiar to you: Bold, Italic, Underline, and so on. But a few were once found only in expensive page-layout programs like InDesign and QuarkXPress. For example:

Kern. Use these commands, such as Tighten and Loosen, to nudge the letters of the selected text closer together or farther apart—an especially useful feature when you're fiddling with headlines and headings.

There are no controls to set how much you want to kern the text, but you can apply these commands repeatedly to the same text selection to intensify them. If you want your text to be very tight, for example, just keep choosing the Tighten command. The characters creep closer and closer together until they crash into one another.

Ligatures. Ligatures are letter pairs, such as fl and ff, that, in fancy typesetting, are conjoined into special combination

characters, as shown here. If you choose Format→Font→Ligatures→Use Default (or Use All), then TextEdit displays these letter pairs with the appropriate ligatures. (This works only if the font you're using has those ligatures built into it. New York, Charcoal, Apple Chancery, and all Adobe Expert fonts do, for example, but many other fonts don't.)

fluffy fluffy

Baseline. The baseline is the imaginary "floor" for text characters in a line of type. You can push text above this line or sink it below the baseline using the Raise and Lower commands in the Baseline submenu. The Superscript and Subscript commands, meanwhile, shift characters far above or below the baseline, so you can write stuff like "H_2O."

Character Shape. In a few fonts, such as Adobe Expert fonts, this submenu offers a choice between Traditional Form and specialized type treatments like Small Caps.

Copy Style/Paste Style. If mastering the Styles pop-up menu is too much effort, you should know that these commands offer another way to copy and paste just the font formatting to other text—the font, color, style, and size, but none of the actual text or paragraph attributes, such as alignment.

Once you've created your styles, you can apply them as you need them, confident in the knowledge that they'll be consistent throughout the document. During the editing process, if you notice that you accidentally styled a *headline* using the *Subhead* style, you can fix the problem by simply reapplying the correct style.

Note: TextEdit doesn't let you *change* a style's formatting and thereby update every occurrence of it. Fortunately, you *can* search for all occurrences of a style and change them all simultaneously (read on).

- **Creating a named style.** To create a style, format some text so it looks the way you like it, complete with font, color, line spacing, tab settings, and so on.

 Then, from the ¶ pop-up menu at the left end of the toolbar, choose Show Styles (Figure 11-36). Click Add To Favorites, type a name for the style, turn on both checkboxes, and then click Add.

Figure 11-36:
Highlight the text you want to format. Then, from the ¶ pop-up menu in the toolbar, choose Show Styles. With each click of the ▶ button, you summon a snippet of the next chunk of formatting. When you find one you like, you can either click Apply (to zap the highlighted text into submission) or Add To Favorites (to reuse this canned style later). In the latter case, you can give the new style a name (bottom).

- **Applying a style.** Later, when you want to reuse the formatting you set up, highlight some text and then choose the appropriate name from the ¶ pop-up menu. TextEdit applies the formatting.

Tip: If you simply click inside a paragraph, applying a style affects only paragraph attributes, like line spacing, tab stops, and alignment. If you highlight a random chunk of text instead, applying a style affects only character attributes, like the font and type size. If you highlight an entire paragraph, however, both text and paragraph formatting appear.

- **Deleting a style.** To delete a superfluous style, choose Show Styles from the ¶ pop-up menu on the toolbar. Click the Favorite Styles button, choose the unwanted style's name from the pop-up menu, and then click Remove From Favorites. (Deleting a style doesn't affect any formatting that's already in your document; it just removes the name from the Styles menu.)

- **Replacing all occurrences.** You can highlight every occurrence of a certain style at once—and then change, copy, or delete them all at once.

To make this work, choose Show Styles from the ¶ pop-up menu. Choose the style you want to work on. (If Document Styles is selected, click the ▶ button to page through the styles; if Favorite Styles is selected, choose from the pop-up menu.) Then click Select.

In the little details sheet that appears, click the options you want, and then click Select. TextEdit highlights every occurrence of that style in the entire document (or selection). At this point, you can use any of the usual text-formatting controls to modify them all simultaneously.

- **Formatting by example.** In TextEdit, you can also use Option-⌘-C and Option-⌘-V (Format→Font→Copy Style and Format→Font→Paste Style) to grab formatting from one place in your document and reuse it elsewhere. (Of course, you can't apply styles in text-only documents.)

UP TO SPEED

The Deal with Microsoft Word

Yes, it's true: Humble TextEdit can open and create Microsoft Word documents! Your savings: the $150 price of Microsoft Office!

Well, sort of.

When you open a Microsoft Word document in TextEdit, most of the formatting comes through alive: bold, italic, font choices, colors, line spacing, alignment, and so on. Even very basic tables make it into TextEdit, although with different column widths.

A lot of Word-specific formatting does not survive crossing the chasm, however: borders, style sheets, footnotes, and the like. Bullets and numbered lists don't make it, either, even though TextEdit can create its own versions of these. And TextEdit doesn't recognize the comments and tracked changes your collaborators might have used to mark up the manuscript.

Saving a new TextEdit document as a Word document is a better bet, because Word understands the many kinds of formatting TextEdit can produce—including bullets, numbering, and tables. (You can create a Word file the first time you save it from TextEdit, or you can convert a document into Word format later by choosing File→Duplicate, and then File→Save.)

The one disappointment is that Word doesn't recognize any style sheets you've set up in TextEdit. The formatting applied by those style names survives—just not the style names themselves.

Even so, a built-in Word-document editor is a huge, huge step for the Mac operating system. It means that, in many cases, you can be a first-class citizen on the playing field of American business. Nobody ever needs to know that you're (a) using a Mac, and (b) not using the real Microsoft Word.

Tables

Tables can make life a lot easier when you want to create a resumé, agenda, program booklet, list, multiple-choice test, web page, or another document where numbers, words, and phrases must be aligned across the page. In the bad old days, people did it by pressing the Tab key to line up columns—a technique that turned into a nightmare as soon as you tried to add or delete text. But using a word processor's *table* feature is light-years easier and more flexible, because each row of a table expands to contain whatever you put into it. Everything else in its row remains aligned.

Tip: Tables are sometimes used for designing web pages. Even though you can't see the table outlines, many a web page is filled with columns of text that are aligned invisibly by tables. Because TextEdit can save your work as an HTML document, it's a viable candidate for designing basic web pages.

- **Create a table** by choosing Format→Table. The floating Table palette appears (Figure 11-37). Use it to specify how many rows and columns you want. The placeholder table in your document adjusts itself in real time.

Figure 11-37:
Note to web designers: TextEdit may not be Dreamweaver, but it's great for spinning out quick web pages, thanks to the table features. Here you can see that a big table forms the underlying structure for this web page, along with a couple of nested ones and color selections.

- **Format the table** using the other controls in the Table palette. The Alignment controls let you specify how the text in the table cells hugs its border. Cell controls the thickness of the line around the selected cells' borders (or, if you enter *0*, makes the

table walls invisible). The color swatch next to Cell specifies the color of the solid lines. The Cell Background controls let you color in the table cells with colors of your choice. (Choose Color Fill from the pop-up menu, and then click the color swatch.) This is an especially valuable option for web designers.

- **Adjust the rows and columns** by dragging the cell borders.

- **Merge two selected cells** by clicking Merge Cells in the Table palette. Once you've done that, you can use the Split Cells button to split them apart again. (Split Cells doesn't work except in cells you've previously merged.)

- **Nest a table inside a cell of another** by clicking in the cell and then clicking Nest Table. Change the numbers in the Row and Columns boxes to set up its dimensions (Figure 11-37).

TextEdit as Web Designer

The Table palette isn't the only clue that Apple intends TextEdit to be a quick-and-dirty web page design program. Consider these other tools:

- **You can easily add graphics to the page** by dragging or pasting them into a document. The program understands many common image formats, including TIFF, PICT, JPEG, and PNG.

- **You can add web-style hyperlinks** by highlighting "Click here" (or whatever the link says), choosing Edit→Add Link (⌘-K), and then entering the web address in the resulting dialog box. Or just drag a link in from Safari, Mail, or another program. (To edit the link later, right-click or two-finger click it, and then choose Edit Link.)

Tip: Of course, you can also have TextEdit convert typed links into clickable ones *automatically* as you type them. That's the purpose of the Smart Links option in TextEdit→Preferences.

- **To save a brand-new document as an HTML** (web page) file, choose File→Save; from the File Format pop-up menu, choose Web Page. (To save an existing TextEdit document as an HTML file, choose File→Duplicate and then File→Save; choose Web Archive Document from the pop-up menu.)

- **Don't miss the HTML options** in TextEdit→Preferences. On the Open and Save tab, you can specify what kind of HTML document you want to produce, what Cascading Style Sheets (CSS) setting you want, and whether or not you want TextEdit to include code to preserve blank areas (white space) in your layout.

Tip: When you open an HTML document—TextEdit is faced with a quandary. Should it open the page as though it's a web page, interpreting the HTML code as though it's a browser? Or should it reveal the underlying HTML code itself?

Actually, that's up to you. When you choose File→Open, turn on "Ignore rich text commands" to make the document open up as HTML code. (To make this change permanent, turn on the same checkbox on the Open and Save pane of the TextEdit→Preferences dialog box.)

TextEdit Preferences

Most of the settings in the TextEdit Preferences→New Document pane have no effect on documents that are *already* open—only on documents you open or create. Most of the settings are self-explanatory; nonetheless, handy explanatory balloons appear if you point to an option without clicking. Here are a few settings that may not be immediately clear:

- **Font.** If Helvetica 12 doesn't float your boat, you can change TextEdit's starting font. In fact, you can set *two* default fonts—one for Rich Text documents and another one for plain text files.

Note: By definition, plain text files don't have any formatting. So whatever font you choose here for plain text files is for your viewing pleasure only. If you plan to send the file to anyone else, the font choice won't be saved with the document.

- **Window Size.** These settings have no effect unless you're in Wrap to Window mode, in which the text rewraps to fit the window width, as opposed to Wrap to Page mode. (You choose these options from TextEdit's Format menu.) If you *are* in Wrap to Window mode, then these dimensions determine the size of the window that appears each time you create a new TextEdit document.

- **Properties.** These boxes—Author, Company, and Copyright—are some of the tags Spotlight inspects when it searches your Mac. If you'd like to be able to round up your documents by these characteristics, fill them in here to specify the information you want to use for *most* documents. (To fill them in differently for individual documents, choose File→Show Properties instead.)

- **Options.** These are the on/off switches for the typing aids described in Chapter 6: smart quotes, data detectors, text replacement, and so on.

TextEdit's Other Writing Tools

TextEdit includes a few other useful document-editing tools:

- **Allow Hyphenation.** When you select this command from the Format menu, TextEdit breaks up words by syllable and inserts hyphens when necessary to create more visually pleasing line breaks.

Tip: It's a good idea to turn hyphenation on if your alignment is set to Justify, or if you create narrow columns. If it's turned off, TextEdit won't break up long words at the end of a line—even if it leaves big, ugly gaps.

- **Prevent Editing.** When you turn this option on (in the Format menu), you're locked out. You can select and copy text to your heart's content, but you can't change anything. Prevent Editing mode can be useful if you want to prevent yourself from making accidental changes to a file, but it's not much of a security feature. (All anyone has to do is choose Format→Allow Editing to regain full editing privileges.)

- **Spelling and Grammar.** These aren't TextEdit features; they're system-wide macOS features, and they're described starting on page 235.

Utilities: Your macOS Toolbox

The Utilities folder (inside your Applications folder) is home to another batch of freebies: a couple of dozen tools for monitoring, tuning, tweaking, and troubleshooting your Mac.

Tip: There's a menu command and a keystroke that can take you there. In the Finder, choose Go→Utilities (Shift-⌘-U).

Activity Monitor

Activity Monitor is designed to let the technologically savvy Mac fan see how much of the Mac's available power is being clicked at any given moment.

The list of processes

Even when you're running only a program or two on your Mac, dozens of computational tasks (*processes*) are going on in the background. The top part of the window, which looks like a table, shows all the different processes—visible and invisible—that your Mac is handling at the moment.

Check out how many items appear in the Process list, even when you're just staring at the desktop. It's awesome to see how busy your Mac is! Some are easily recognizable programs (such as Finder), while others are background system-level operations you don't normally see. For each item, you can see the percentage of the CPU being used, who's using it (either your account name, someone else's, or *root*, meaning the Mac itself), and how much memory it's using.

Or use the View menu to see views like these:

- **All Processes.** This is the complete list of running processes; you'll notice that the vast majority are little Unix applications you never even knew you had.

- **All Processes, Hierarchically.** In Unix, one process launches another, creating a tree-like hierarchy. For example, the Dock launches three mini-processes of its own, and the big daddy of them all is the process called *launchd*.

- **My Processes.** This list shows only the programs that pertain to *your* world, your login. There are still plenty of unfamiliar items, but they're all running to serve *your* account.

- **System Processes.** These are the processes run by *root*—that is, opened by macOS itself.

- **Other User Processes.** Here's a list of all *other* processes—"owned" by neither root nor you. Here you might see the processes being run by another account holder, for example (using fast user switching), or people who have connected to this Mac from across a network or the internet.

• **Active Processes, Inactive Processes.** Active processes are the ones actually doing something right now; inactive are the ones that are sitting there, waiting for a signal (like a key press or a mouse click).

• **Windowed Processes.** Now, *this* is probably what you were expecting: a list of actual programs with actual English names, like Activity Monitor, Finder, Safari, and Mail. These are the only ones running in actual windows, the only ones that are *visible*.

The System Monitor tabs

At the top of Activity Monitor, you're offered five tabs that reveal intimate details about your Mac and its behind-the-scenes efforts (Figure 11-38):

• **CPU.** As you go about your usual Mac business, opening a few programs, playing QuickTime movies, playing a game, and so on, you can see the CPU graphs rise and fall, depending on how busy you're keeping the central processing unit. You see a different graph color for each of your Mac's cores (independent subchips on

Figure 11-38:
The many faces of Activity Monitor.

Top: It can be a graph of your processor (CPU) activity, your RAM usage at the moment, your disk capacity, and so on. Usually, only the processes listed here with tiny icons beside their names are windowed programs—those with icons in the Finder, the ones you actually interact with.

The top-left Quit Process button (⊗) is a convenient way to jettison a locked-up program when all else fails.

Bottom: If you double-click a process's name, you get a dialog box that offers reams of data (mostly of interest only to programmers) about what that program is up to. (The Open Files and Ports tab, for example, shows how many files that program has opened, often invisibly.)

your processor), so you can see how efficiently macOS is distributing the work among them.

Tip: You may also want to watch this graph right in your Dock (choose View→Dock Icon→Show CPU Usage) or in a bar at the edge of your screen (choose Window→CPU Usage).

Finally, there's the Window→CPU History command. It makes a resizable, real-time monitor window float on top of all your other programs, so you can't miss it.

- **Memory.** Here's a glorious revelation of the state of your Mac's RAM at the moment.

 The graph shows "memory pressure"—how much your programs are straining the Mac's memory. If, when your Mac is running a typical complement of programs, this graph is nearly filled up, then it's time to consider buying more memory. Your Mac is suffocating.

- **Energy.** How much battery power is each of your programs responsible for sucking away? This fascinating tab tells all.

- **Disk.** Even when you're not opening or saving a file, your Mac's hard drive or flash storage is frequently hard at work, shuffling chunks of program code into and out of memory, for example. Here's where the savvy technician can see exactly how frantic the disk is at the moment.

- **Network.** Keep an eye on how much data is shooting across your office network with this handy tsunami of real-time data.

AirPort Utility

You use the AirPort Utility to set up and manage AirPort base stations (Apple's wireless Wi-Fi networking routers).

If you click Continue, it presents a series of screens, posing one question at a time: what you want to name the network, what password you want for it, and so on. Once you've followed the steps and answered the questions, your AirPort hardware will be properly configured and ready to use.

Audio MIDI Setup

This program has a split personality; its name is a description of its two halves:

- **Audio.** When you first open Audio MIDI Setup, you see a complete summary of the audio inputs and outputs available on your Mac right now. It's like the Sound pane of System Preferences, but with a lot more geeky detail. Here, for example, you can specify the recording level for your Mac's microphone, or even change the audio quality it records.

 For most people, this is all meaningless, because most Macs have only one input (the microphone) and one output (the speakers). But if you're sitting in your darkened music studio, humming with high-tech audio gear whose software has been designed to work with this little program, you'll smile when you see this tab.

There's even a Configure Speakers button, for those audiophilic Mac fans who've attached stereo or even surround-sound speaker systems to their Macs.

> **Tip:** Using the ✿ menu at the bottom of the window, you can turn your various audio inputs (that is, microphones, line inputs, and so on) on or off. You can even direct your Mac's system beeps to pour forth from one set of speakers (like the one built into your Mac), and all other sound, like music, through a different set.

- **MIDI.** MIDI stands for Musical Instrument Digital Interface, a standard "language" for inter-synthesizer communication. It's available to music software companies who have written their wares to capitalize on these tools.

 When you choose Window→Show MIDI Window, you get a window that represents your recording-studio configuration. By clicking Add Device, you create a new icon that represents one of your pieces of gear. Double-click the icon to specify its make and model. Finally, by dragging lines from the "in" and "out" arrows, you teach your Mac and its MIDI software how the various components are wired together.

Bluetooth File Exchange

One of the luxuries of using a Mac that has Bluetooth is the ability to shoot files (to colleagues who own similarly clever gadgets) through the air, up to 30 feet away. Bluetooth File Exchange makes it possible, as described on page 254.

Boot Camp Assistant

Since 2006, Macs have come with Intel chips inside, meaning Macs and PCs use exactly the same memory, hard drives, monitors, mice, keyboards, networking protocols, and processors. With just a little bit of setup, therefore, your Mac can run Windows and Windows programs!

Think of all the potential switchers who are tempted by the Mac's sleek looks, yet worry about leaving Windows behind entirely. Or the people who love Apple's productivity programs but have jobs that rely on Microsoft Access, Outlook, or some other piece of Windows corporateware. Even true-blue Mac fans occasionally look longingly at some of the Windows-only games, websites, or movie download services they thought they'd never be able to use.

Today, there are two ways to run Windows on a Mac:

- **Restart it in Boot Camp.** Boot Camp Assistant lets you *restart* your Mac into Windows. At that point, it's a full-blown Windows PC, with no trace of the Mac on the screen. It runs at 100 percent of the speed of a real PC, because it is one. Compatibility with Windows software is excellent. The only downsides: Your laptop battery life isn't as good, and you have to restart the Mac to return to the familiar world of macOS.

> **Tip:** What's cool, though, is that even when you're running Windows, you can still access your Mac files and folders, as described next.

- **Open Parallels or Fusion.** The problem with Boot Camp is that every time you switch to or from Windows, you have to close down everything you were working on and restart the computer. You lose two or three minutes each way.

There is another way: a utility called Parallels Desktop for Mac (*parallels.com*), or its rival, VMware Fusion (*vmware.com*). These two programs let you run Windows and macOS simultaneously; Windows hangs out in a window of its own, while the Mac is running macOS. You're getting about 90 percent of Boot Camp's Windows speed—which is plenty fast for everything but 3D games.

Having virtualization software on your Mac is a beautiful thing. You can be working on a design in iWork, duck into a Microsoft Access database (Windows only), look up an address, copy it, and paste it back into the Mac program.

You can even install Boot Camp *and* Parallels/Fusion. They coexist beautifully on a single Mac and can even use the same copy of Windows.

Both do require you to provide your own copy of Windows. Since Boot Camp comes with the Mac, here's a quick rundown.

Installing Boot Camp

To set up Boot Camp, you need the proper ingredients:

- **A copy of Windows 10.** It has to be the *64-bit version* of Windows, and it has to be a full installation copy—not an upgrade version. And you need the ISO (disk image) of the Windows installer. If you got Windows on a flash drive instead, download the ISO from Microsoft and use the serial number that came with the flash drive.

- **At least 64 gigs of free hard drive space** on your built-in hard drive, or a second internal drive. Windows is not svelte, and you can't install Windows on an external drive using Boot Camp.

- **The keyboard and mouse that came with your Mac.** You can also use a generic USB keyboard and mouse; what you *can't* use is a non-Apple cordless keyboard and mouse.

- **A USB flash drive, 16 GB or bigger.** The Boot Camp installer may require this, depending on your Mac model.

Before you install, Apple strongly recommends that you back up your Mac, make sure it's running the latest version of macOS, and acquire the latest version of Boot Camp (visit *apple.com/support/bootcamp*). If you're using a laptop, plug it in for the surgery.

The step-by-steps for installation are long, and they vary according to your Mac model and whether you're doing a fresh installation of Windows or upgrading to a newer version. Fortunately, Apple has written out detailed instructions for you here: *support.apple.com/en-us/HT201468*.

When it's all over, a crazy, disorienting sight presents itself: your Mac, running Windows. There's no trace of the desktop, Dock, or menu; it's Windows now, baby.

Using Boot Camp

At this point, your Mac is actually a true Windows PC. You can install and run Windows programs, utilities, and even games; you'll discover that they run *really* fast and well.

Most of your Mac's features work in Windows: Ethernet and Wi-Fi networking, audio input and output, built-in camera, brightness and volume keys, ⏏ key, multitouch trackpad gestures, Bluetooth, and so on. You'll also discover a new Control Panel icon and system-tray pop-up menu, as described later in this section.

Note: Once you're running Windows, you might wonder: How am I supposed to right-click? I don't have a two-button mouse or two-button trackpad!

Yes, you do. See page 233 for a panoply of options.

Figure 11-39:
Top: To choose your preferred operating system—the one that always starts up unless you intervene—choose ⌘→*System Preferences. Click Startup Disk, and then click the icon for either macOS or Windows. Next, either click Restart (if you want to switch right now) or close the panel. The same controls are available when you're running Windows.*

Middle: To open the Boot Camp Control Panel, choose its name from its icon in the Windows system tray.

Bottom: This display, known as the Startup Manager, appears when you press Option during startup. It displays all the disk icons or partitions that contain bootable operating systems. Click the one you want, and then click the up-arrow button.

Forth and back, Windows/Mac

From now on, your main interaction with Boot Camp will be telling it what kind of computer you want today: a Windows machine or a Mac.

Presumably, though, you'll prefer one operating system *most* of the time. Figure 11-39 (top and middle) shows how you specify your favorite.

Tip: If you're running Windows and you just want to get back to macOS right now, you don't have to bother with all the steps shown in Figure 11-39. Instead, click the Boot Camp system-tray icon and, from the shortcut menu, choose Restart in macOS.

From now on, each time you turn on the Mac, it starts up in the operating system you've selected. If you ever need to switch—when you need Windows just for one quick job, for example—press the Option key as the Mac is starting up. You'll see something like the icons shown in Figure 11-39 (bottom).

Keyboard translation guide

Now, if you really want to learn about Windows, you need a book like *Windows 10: The Missing Manual.*

But suggesting that you go buy *another* huge book would be tacky. So here's just enough to get by.

First of all, a Mac keyboard and a Windows keyboard aren't the same. Each has keys that would strike the other as extremely goofy. Still, you can trigger almost any keystroke that Windows is expecting by substituting special Apple keystrokes, like this:

Windows keystroke	Apple keystroke
Ctrl+Alt+Delete	Control-Option-Delete
Alt	Option
Ctrl key	⌘
Backspace	Delete
Delete (forward delete)	⌦ (on laptops, fn-Delete)
Enter	Return
Num Lock	Clear (laptops: fn-F6)
Print Screen (PrtScn)	F14 (laptops: fn-F11)
Print Active Window (Alt+PrtScn)	Option-F14 (laptops: Option-fn-F11)

The keyboard shortcuts in your programs are *mostly* the same as on the Mac, but you have to substitute the ⌘ key for the Ctrl key. So in Windows programs on the Mac, Copy, Save, and Print are now ⌘-C, ⌘-S, and ⌘-P.

Tip: You know that awesome two-finger scrolling trick on Mac laptops? It works when you're running Windows, too.

If you really want to understand how your Mac keyboard corresponds to a PC keyboard, don't miss Apple's document on the subject at *support.apple.com/kb/HT1167.*

Accessing Mac files from the Dark Side—and vice versa

When you've started up in one operating system, it's easy to access documents that "belong" to the other one. For example:

- **When you're running macOS,** you can get to the documents you created while you were running Windows, which is a huge convenience. Just double-click the Windows disk icon (called NO NAME or Untitled), and then navigate to the Documents and Settings→[your account name]→My Documents (or Desktop).

 You can only copy files *to* the Mac side, or open them without the ability to edit.

Tip: You can rename the Windows disk, if you want, so it doesn't say NO NAME the rest of its life—as long as you do it while you're running Windows.

- **When you're running Windows,** you can get to your Mac documents, too. Click Start→Computer. In the resulting window, you'll see an icon representing your Mac's hard drive partition. Open it up.

 You can see and open these files. But if you want to edit them, you have to copy them to your Windows world first—onto the desktop, for example, or into a folder. (The Mac partition is "read-only" in this way, Apple says, to avoid the possibility that your Mac stuff could get contaminated by Windows viruses.)

Tip: If you did want to edit Mac files from within Windows, one solution is to use a disk that both macOS and Windows "see," and keep your shared files on *that.* A flash drive works beautifully for this. So does a shared drive on the network, or an internet-based disk like Dropbox, Microsoft's OneDrive, or even Apple's iCloud Drive (page 210). You can make each of these show up in both Mac and Windows.

ColorSync Utility

If you use ColorSync, you probably know already that this utility is for people in the high-end color printing business. Its tabs include these two:

- **Profile First Aid.** This tab performs a fairly esoteric task: repairing ColorSync profiles that may be "broken" because they don't strictly conform to the *ICC profile* specifications. (International Color Consortium profiles are part of Apple's ColorSync color management system.) If a profile for your specific monitor or printer doesn't appear in the Profiles tab of this program when it should, then Profile First Aid is the tool you need to fix it.

- **Profiles.** This tab lets you review all the ColorSync profiles installed on your system. The area on the right side of the window displays information about each ColorSync profile you select from the list on the left.

For more on ColorSync, see page 609.

Console

Console is a viewer for all of macOS's logs—the behind-the-scenes, internal Unix record of your Mac's activities.

Opening the Console log is a bit like stepping into an operating room during a complex surgery: You're exposed to stuff the average person just isn't supposed to see. (Typical Console entries: "kCGErrorCannotComplete" or "doGetDisplayTransferBy-Table.") You can adjust the font and word wrapping using Console's Font menu, but the truth is that the phrase "CGXGetWindowType: Invalid window -1" looks ugly in just about *any* font!

Console isn't useless, however. These messages can be of significant value to programmers who are debugging software or troubleshooting a messy problem, or, occasionally, to someone you've called for tech support.

For example, your *crash logs* are detailed technical descriptions of what went wrong when various programs crashed, and what was stored in memory at the time.

Unfortunately, there's not much plain English here to help you understand the crash—or how to avoid it in the future.

DigitalColor Meter

DigitalColor Meter can grab the exact color value of any pixel on your screen, which can be helpful when matching colors in web page construction or other design work. After launching the DigitalColor Meter, just point anywhere on your screen. A magnified view appears in the meter window, and the RGB (red-green-blue) color value of the pixels appears in the meter window.

Here are some tips for using the DigitalColor Meter to capture color information from your screen:

- **To zoom in on the exact pixel** (and color) you want to measure, drag the Aperture Size slider to the smallest size: 1 pixel.

- **Press ⌘-X (View→Lock X)** to freeze your cursor at its current horizontal position; you can now move it only horizontally. Or press ⌘-Y (View→Lock Y) to freeze your cursor at its current vertical position. You can also lock the cursor in both directions by pressing ⌘-L (View→Lock Position). (Press the keystroke again to unlock.) The idea is to make it easier for you to snap to the pixel you want.

- **When the Aperture Size slider** is set to view more than one pixel, DigitalColor Meter measures the *average* value of the pixels being examined.

Disk Utility

This important program has two key functions:

- **It's a disk-repair program** that lets you repair, erase, format, and partition disks. You'll probably use Disk Utility most often for its First Aid feature, which solves many weird Mac glitches. But it can also be useful with more serious disk problems.

- **Disk Utility creates and manages *disk images*,** electronic versions of disks or folders you can exchange electronically with other people.

The following discussion tackles the program's two personalities one at a time.

Disk Utility, the hard drive repair program

When you first open Disk Utility, you see, at a glance, what kinds of files are eating up your disk space (see Figure 11-40).

Figure 11-40:
The left Disk Utility panel lists your hard drive and any other disks in or attached to your Mac at the moment.

The main welcome screen shows where all your disk space is going, color-coded by category.

When you click the name of your hard drive's mechanism, like "500 GB Hitachi iC25N0…" (not the "Macintosh HD" volume label below it), you see a cluster of buttons, one for each of the main Disk Utility functions:

- **First Aid.** This is the disk-repair part of Disk Utility, and it does a terrific job at fixing many disk problems. When you're troubleshooting, Disk Utility should be your first resort.

 To use it, click the icon of a disk and then click First Aid. After asking for confirmation (click Run), this function scours every single file on your drive, checking for corruption, flakiness, or trouble spots on the disk.

 If Disk First Aid reports that it's unable to fix the problem, *then* it's time to invest in a program like DiskWarrior (*alsoft.com*).

- **Partition.** With the Partition tools, you can erase a hard drive in such a way that you subdivide its surface. Each chunk will be represented on your screen by another hard drive icon (Figure 11-41).

 There are some very good reasons *not* to partition a drive these days: A partitioned hard drive is more difficult to resurrect after a serious crash, requires more navigation when you want to open a particular file, and offers no speed or safety benefits. And if you're using APFS (see the box on the next page), of course, creating new *volumes* is a much more modern, flexible way of subdividing your drive.

On the other hand, there's one very good reason *to* do it: Partitioning is the only way to use Boot Camp, described starting on page 464. When you're using Boot Camp, your Mac is a Mac when running off of one partition, and a Windows PC when starting up from another one. (But you don't use Disk Utility in that case; you use Boot Camp Assistant.)

Note: Partitioning is not the same thing as creating APFS volumes, described in the box below.

- **Erase.** Select a disk, choose a format—*always* APFS or macOS Extended (Journaled), unless you're formatting a disk for use on a Windows PC—give it a name, and then click Erase to wipe a disk clean.

Tip: Click Security Options to view a slider. It can strike four spots on the spectrum from the *speed* of the disk erasing to the *security* of it. At the far-left position, macOS erases the drive quickly, but a recovery app could recover the files. At the more secure settings, macOS performs various additional time-consuming scrubbing tasks, writing over your old files with randomized gibberish, making file recovery impossible. Something to remember if you sell your Mac!

GEM IN THE ROUGH

The Quiet Power of APFS

The *file system* is the underlying software that organizes all your documents, photos, mail, and so on—and by 2019, the file system driving the Mac was 21 years old. (It's called HFS+, if you're keeping score at home.)

So one of the biggest-ticket items in macOS is the Apple File System (APFS), developed for the new era of solid state drives and increased security threats. It's standard across all Apple's gadgets: macOS, iOS, tvOS, and watchOS.

All of this is very satisfying to programmers. But you, the average person, will probably notice only a couple of changes.

First, when you duplicate a file or folder on an APFS drive, it happens instantly. There's no progress bar, no waiting—and the copy takes up almost no space, at least until you make changes to it. Second, getting the size of a folder is also instantaneous.

APFS works on spinning hard drives or even Apple Fusion drives (which combine solid-state [SSD] technology with spinning drives for greater speed).

There are a few things to note as you enter the exciting new world of APFS, though. First, macOS and APFS require each

other. If you install macOS onto a solid-state drive (SSD), like the one on an Apple laptop, it gets converted to APFS automatically. Conversely, if you move an external APFS drive to a pre–High Sierra Mac, it doesn't show up on the desktop.

APFS is theoretically capable of great features like **snapshots**, where the current state of your entire drive is memorized in space-efficient format; if disaster befalls, you can "rewind" to that condition. Someday, Time Machine (page 260) will use this feature to save space; but at the moment, your Mac uses snapshots only when storing *local* snapshots (page 264), and, as always, only on SSDs.

APFS offers **space sharing**, too, where you can create sub-disks (APFS *volumes*) that all share space on the main disk, and flexibly grow or shrink as necessary. (To create one, click the + button in Disk Utility. Name it, click Size Options to specify a minimum and maximum size for its growth [Reserve and Quota] if you like, and then click Save.)

Overall, APFS is supposed to reduce wear on drives, make them faster, and make them more secure. Only some of it benefits you today, but Apple promises that APFS is the first step to a glorious disk-formatting future.

- **Restore.** You can create an exact replica of a volume. From the Sidebar, choose the target volume—the one that will become a replica of some other one—and then click Restore. Choose the volume you want to replicate, click Restore again, and then click Done.

Figure 11-41:
To add each new partition, click +.

Now drag the tiny round handles to adjust the dividers in the pie chart; that's how you specify the relative sizes of the partitions you want. Assign a name and a format for each partition in the Partition Information area, and then click Apply.

Partition Adjustments on the Fly

You can expand, shrink, or create partitions without having to erase the whole hard drive. If you're into partitioning at all, this is a *huge* convenience.

Expanding a partition. Suppose, for example, that your hard drive has two partitions: a main one (200 gigs) and a secondary one (50 gigs) that used to hold all your photos and movies. But you've outgrown the second partition and have moved all those photos and movies to their own external hard drive. Wouldn't it be nice to add the newly unoccupied 50 gigs to your main partition?

You can do that without having to erase the whole hard drive. (This process, however, nukes everything on the *second* partition, so make sure you're prepared to lose it all.)

Open Disk Utility. Click the name of the hard drive (for example, "Hitachi HTS541616J9SA00"–*not* "Macintosh HD"). Click Partition. You see a display like the one in Figure 11-41.

Click the second partition (or third, or whatever partition is *just after* the one you want to expand) and then click the — button below the list. Poof! It's gone.

Now you can drag the main partition's pie wedge larger (or type a new size into the Size box), expanding it into the free area. Take a deep breath, and then click Apply.

Shrinking a partition. In Figure 11-41, you can see that a portion of the first partition is colored. That section represents data; you can't shrink a partition so much that it crowds out your files. You can, however, shrink the partition to eliminate empty space. Just drag the lower edge of its map chunk upward.

Creating new partitions. Anytime there's leftover space on the hard drive, you can create *new* partitions from it. To do that, click the + button and proceed as described in Figure 11-41.

- **Unmount.** This button ejects whatever disk you've selected in the left-side list.

- **Info.** Click to view a little table of super-technical details about the selected drive.

Disk Utility, the disk-image program

Disk images are very cool. Each is a single icon that behaves precisely like an actual disk—a flash drive or hard drive, for example—but can be distributed electronically. For example, a lot of macOS apps arrive from your web download in disk-image form.

Disk images are popular for software distribution for a simple reason: Each image file precisely duplicates the original master disk, complete with all the necessary files in all the right places. When a software company sends you a disk image, it ensures that you'll install the software from a disk that *exactly* matches the master disk.

As a handy bonus, you can password-protect a disk image, which is the closest macOS comes to offering the ability to password-protect an individual folder.

It's important to understand the difference between a *disk-image file* and the *mounted disk* (the one that appears when you double-click the disk image). If you flip back to page 162 and consult Figure 5-2, this distinction should be clear.

Tip: After you double-click a disk image, click Skip in the verification box that appears. If something truly got scrambled during the download, you'll know about it right away—your file won't decompress correctly, or it'll display the wrong icon, for example.

You can create disk images, too. Doing so can be very handy in situations like these:

- **You want to create a backup of a CD.** By turning it into a disk-image file, you'll always have a safety copy, ready to burn onto a *new* CD. (This is a good practice for educational CDs that kids will be handling soon after eating peanut butter and jelly.)

- **You want to replicate your entire hard drive**—complete with all its files, programs, folder setups, and so on—onto a new, bigger hard drive (or a new, better Mac), using the Restore feature already described.

- **You want to back up your entire hard drive,** or maybe just a certain chunk of it, onto an iPod or another disk. (Again, you can later use the Restore function.)

- **You want to send somebody else a copy of a disk via the internet.** You simply create a disk image, and then send *that*—preferably in compressed form.

Here's how to make a disk image:

- **To image-ize a disk or partition.** Click the name of the disk in the list, where you see your currently available disks. (The topmost item is the name of your *drive,* like "484.0 MB MATSHITA DVD-R" for a DVD drive or "74.5 GB Hitachi" for a hard drive. Beneath that entry, you generally see the name of the actual partition, like "Macintosh HD," or the CD's name as it appears on the screen.)

 Then choose File→New Image→Disk Image from [the disk or partition's name].

- **To image-ize a folder.** Choose File→New Image→Image from Folder. In the Open dialog box, click the folder you want, and then click Choose. Either way, the next dialog box (Figure 11-42) offers some fascinating options.

Figure 11-42:
These two pop-up menus let you specify (a) whether you want your disk image password-protected, and (b) what kind of disk image you want. The latter option is great when you want to password-protect one folder without bothering with your entire Home folder.

- **Encryption.** Here's an easy way to lock private files away into a vault nobody else can open. If you choose one of these two AES encryption options (choose AES-128, if you value your time), you'll be asked to assign a password to your new image file. Nobody can open it without the password—not even you. On the other hand, if you save it into your Keychain (page 518), it's not such a disaster if you forget the password.

- **Image Format.** If you choose "read/write," your disk image file, when double-clicked, turns into a superb imitation of a hard drive. You can drag files and folders onto it, drag them off of it, change icons' names on it, and so on.

 If you choose "read-only," however, the result behaves more like a CD. You can copy things off of it but not make any changes to it.

 The "compressed" option is best if you intend to send the resulting file by email, post it for web download, or preserve the disk image on some backup disk for a rainy day. It takes a little longer to create a simulated disk when you double-click the disk image file, but it takes up a lot less disk space than an uncompressed version.

 Choose "DVD/CD master" if you're copying a CD or a DVD. The resulting file is a perfect mirror of the original disc, ready for copying onto a blank CD or DVD when the time comes. Finally, "hybrid image" is a combo format that can be used with file system standards such as HFS+, ISO, and UDF.

- **Save As.** Choose a name and location for your new image file. The name you choose here doesn't need to match the original disk or folder name.

When you click Save (or press Return), if you opted to create an encrypted image, you're asked to make up a password at this point.

Otherwise, Disk Utility now creates the image and then *mounts* it—that is, turns the image file into a simulated, yet fully functional, disk icon on your desktop.

When you're finished working with the disk, eject it as you would any disk (right-click or two-finger click it and choose Eject, for example). Hang on to the .dmg disk-image file itself, however. This is the file you'll need to double-click if you ever want to recreate your "simulated disk."

Grapher

This unsung little app is an amazing piece of work. It lets you create 2D or 3D graphs of staggering beauty and complexity.

When you first open Grapher, you're asked to choose what kind of virtual "graph paper" you want: two-dimensional (standard, polar, logarithmic, and so on) or three-dimensional (cubic, spherical, cylindrical, and so on). Click a name to see a preview; when you're happy with the selection, click Open.

Now the main Grapher window appears (Figure 11-43). Do yourself a favor. Spend a few wow-inducing minutes choosing canned equations from the Examples menu and watching how Grapher whips up gorgeous, colorful, sometimes animated graphs on the fly.

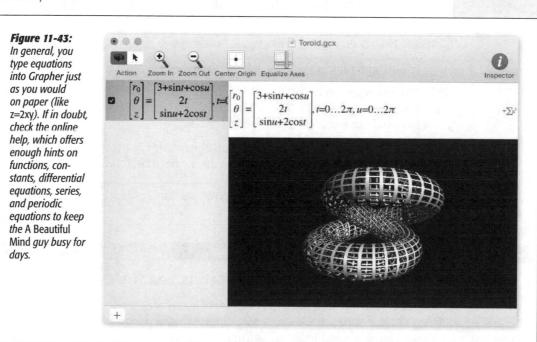

Figure 11-43:
In general, you type equations into Grapher just as you would on paper (like z=2xy). If in doubt, check the online help, which offers enough hints on functions, constants, differential equations, series, and periodic equations to keep the A Beautiful Mind *guy busy for days.*

When you're ready to plug in an equation of your own, type it into the text box at the top of the window. If you're not such a math hotshot, or you're not sure of the equation format, work from the canned equations and mathematical building blocks that appear when you choose Equation→New Equation from Template or

Window→Show Equation Palette (a floating window containing a huge selection of math symbols and constants).

Tip: *If you don't know the keystroke that produces a mathematical symbol like π or θ, you can just type* pi *or* theta. *Grapher replaces it with the correct symbol automatically.*

Once the graph is up on the screen, you can tailor it like this:

- **To move a 2D graph** in the window, choose View→Move Tool and then drag; to move a 3D graph, ⌘-drag it.

- **To rotate a 3D graph,** drag in any direction. If you add the Option key, you flip the graph around on one axis.

- **To change the colors, line thicknesses, 3D "walls," and other graphic elements,** click the ❶ button (or choose Window→Show Inspector) to open the formatting palette. The controls you find here vary by graph type, but rest assured that Grapher can accommodate your every visual whim.

- **To change the fonts and sizes,** choose Grapher→Preferences. On the Equations panel, the four sliders let you specify the relative sizes of the text elements. If you click the sample equation, the Fonts panel appears, so you can go to town fiddling with the type.

When it's all over, you can preserve your masterpiece using any of these techniques:

- **Export a graphic** by choosing File→Export.

- **Copy an equation to the Clipboard** by right-clicking or two-finger clicking it and choosing Copy As→TIFF (or EPS, or text, or whatever) from the shortcut menu. Now you can paste it into another program.

- **Export an animated graph** by choosing Equation→Create Animation. The dialog box lets you specify how long you want the movie to last (and a lot of other things).

Tip: *If you click the Orientation tab, you can Shift-drag the starting or ending images at the bottom to change their size.*

For Mathematicians (and Physicists, Scientists, and Students) Only

If you're into math, science, or studying math or science, Grapher is a tremendous addition to macOS. There's a whole lot to it—but if you're just getting started, here are a few features not to miss.

You can calculate values, intercepts, derivatives, and integrals (even indefinite integrals) by using the Equation→Evaluation and Equation→Integration commands.

Some useful ready-made equation components await in the pop-up button at the right side of the equation text box. Using the Sum and Product symbols, for example, you can quickly calculate summations and products.

That same pop-up menu can help you generate piecewise, parametric, and other specialized kinds of graphs (this means you, math students).

Finally, click Create Animation. After a moment, the finished movie appears. If you like it, choose File→Save As to preserve it on your hard drive for future generations.

Keychain Access

Keychain Access memorizes and stores all your secret information—passwords for network access, file servers, FTP sites, web pages, and other secure items. For instructions on using Keychain Access, see page 518.

Migration Assistant

This little cutie automates the transfer of all your stuff from another Mac, or even a Windows PC, to your current Mac: your Home folder, network settings, programs, and more. This comes in extremely handy when you buy a newer, better Mac—or when you need Time Machine to recover an entire dead Mac's worth of data. (It can also copy everything over from a secondary hard drive or partition.) The instructions on the screen guide you through the process (see page 768).

Screenshot

You know the fancy screen-capture feature macOS has? (If not, you can read up on page 612.) Well, behind the scenes, it's just this application at work. It opens when you press that Shift-⌘-5 keystroke.

Script Editor

This little program, formerly called AppleScript Editor, is where you can type up your own *AppleScripts*. You can read about these programmery software robots in the free online appendix to this chapter, "Automator & AppleScript." It's available on this book's "Missing CD" page at *missingmanuals.com*.

System Information

System Information (formerly called System Profiler) is a great tool for learning exactly what's installed on your Mac and what's not—in terms of both hardware and software. The people who answer the phones on Apple's tech-support line are particularly fond of System Information, since the detailed information it reports can be very useful for troubleshooting nasty problems.

There are actually two versions of System Information: a quick, easy snapshot and a ridiculously detailed version:

- **Snapshot.** Choose →About This Mac. You get a concise, attractive summary info screen that reveals your macOS version, your Mac's memory amount, its serial number, what processor it has inside, and so on (Figure 11-44, top).

Tip: If you click your macOS version number in the Overview box, you get to see its *build number*—something primarily of interest to programmers and people who beta-test macOS.

The tabs across the top reveal similarly precise details about your Displays and Storage. The Support tab offers links to various sources of online help, and the Service tab reveals your options for getting the Mac fixed.

- **Ridiculously detailed.** Open Applications→Utilities; double-click System Information. (You can also open the System Information program from inside the About This Mac dialog box shown in Figure 11-44 at top; just click System Report.)

Figure 11-44:
This dialog box gives you a plain-English display of the Mac details you probably care the most about: memory, screen, storage, serial number, macOS version, and so on. (Click the tabs across the top for more details.) To proceed from here to the full System Information program, click System Report.

When System Information opens, it tells you about your Mac in a list down the left side (Figure 11-45). The details fall into these categories:

- **Hardware.** Click this word to see precisely which model Mac you have, what kind of chip is inside (and how many), how much memory it has, and its serial number.

 If you expand the flippy triangle, you get to see details about which Memory slots are filled and the size of the memory module in each slot; what kind of Disc Burning your Mac can do (DVD-R, DVD+R, and so on); what PCI cards are installed in your expansion slots; what Graphics/Displays circuitry you have (graphics card and monitor); what's attached to your SATA bus (internal drives, like your hard drive); what's connected to your Thunderbolt, USB, and FireWire chains, if anything; and much more.

- **Network** details what Wi-Fi components you have, what internet connection Locations you've established, and so on.

- **Software** shows which version of macOS you have and what your computer's name is, as far as the network is concerned ("Pat's Computer," for example).

The Applications list documents every program on your system, with version information. It's useful for spotting duplicate copies of programs.

Similar information shows up in the Extensions panel. Extensions are the drivers for the Mac's various components, which sit in the System→Library→Extensions folder. Whatever is in that folder is what you see listed in this panel. Other categories include self-explanatory lists like Fonts, Preference Panes, and Startup Items.

Finally, the Logs panel reveals your Mac's secret diary: a record of the traumatic events it experiences from day to day. (Many of these are the same as those revealed by the Console utility; see page 468.)

Tip: If any of these screens is showing you more technical information than you'd like, then use the File→Show Less Information command to pare down the overload to just the human-recognizable items.

Figure 11-45:
Does your MacBook's chip run at 2 GHz or 2.6? What percentage of your external hard drive is filled up? What are the version numbers of every program installed on your Mac? Can your DVD burner burn dual-layer discs? Does your laptop have any open slots for extra RAM?

Terminal

Underneath its shiny skin, macOS is actually Unix, one of the oldest and most respected operating systems in use today. But you'd never know it by looking; Unix is a world without icons, menus, or dialog boxes. You operate it by typing out memorized commands at a special prompt, called the command line. The mouse is almost useless here.

Wait a minute—Apple's ultramodern operating system, with a command line? What's going on? Actually, the command line never went away. At universities and corporations worldwide, professional computer nerds still value the efficiency of pounding away at the little *C:* or *$* prompts.

You never *have* to use macOS's command line. In fact, Apple has swept it pretty far under the rug. There are, however, some tasks you can perform *only* at the command line.

Terminal is your keyhole into macOS's Unix innards. There's a whole chapter on it waiting for you on this book's "Missing CD" page at *missingmanuals.com*.

VoiceOver Utility

For details on this screen-reader software, see page 321.

Core Services: The Island of Misfit Apps

You thought the apps in Utilities were geeky? Wait till you meet the ones Apple has hidden away in the System→Library→Core Services→Applications folder. (That's the Library folder in your main hard drive window, not the hidden one in your own User folder.)

These are *very* specialized gizmos; most are primarily of interest to network administrators or Unix geeks obsessed with knowing what kind of computer-code gibberish is going on behind the scenes. In any case, here's what you'll find there.

About This Mac

Turns out that the information screen shown in Figure 11-44, which opens when you choose →About This Mac, is a standalone app. It's in your Library→Core Services→Applications folder.

Archive Utility

Here is the app that performs the zipping/unzipping functions described on page 103.

Directory Utility

On a corporate network, a network admin may use this app to manage the corporate directory servers—centralized databases and drives. If you are that person, you should read Apple's guide without delay: *support.apple.com/guide/directory-utility/*.

DVD Player

For the six people whose Macs still have physical DVD drives, Apple offers this ancient relic of a playback program.

Feedback Assistant

Apple tests out new versions of its operating systems on willing volunteers. Anyone who's interested can sign up for Apple's public beta-testing program at *beta.apple.com*. If you join, you'll get to try out upcoming versions of macOS before they're released to the teeming masses. Along the way, you'll probably encounter bugs, crashes, and other unfinished business.

When that happens, Apple hopes you'll use this app to submit reports of the problems you find. On its end, Apple's programmers collect all these bug reports, organize them, and set about fixing as many as they can in time for the public release of the software.

Folder Actions Setup

This app opens when you right-click or two-finger click a desktop folder and, from the shortcut menu, choose Folder Actions Setup. You're offered a list of folder actions—canned processes that run automatically every time you drop a file into this folder.

For example, maybe you want every graphics file in this folder automatically converted into PNG format. Or maybe you want every PDF document rotated 90 degrees. Or maybe you want the Mac to alert you every time someone puts a file into this folder.

All of this is part of Apple's ancient, technical, but (in some circles) beloved Apple-Script programming system. You can read more about it on this book's "Missing CD" at *missingmanuals.com*, in a document called "AppleScript & Automator."

Network Utility

You can find and open Network Utility with a Spotlight search, or from within System Information, described on page 477 (choose Window→Network Utility). It gathers information about websites and network citizens. It offers a suite of standard internet tools like netstat, ping, traceroute, DNS lookup, and whois—advanced tools, but ones that even Mac novices may be asked to fire up when calling a technician for help.

Otherwise, you probably won't need to use Network Utility to get your work done. However, Network Utility can be useful when you're doing internet detective work:

- **Use ping to enter an address** (either a web address like *google.com* or an IP address like 192.168.1.110), and then "ping" (send out a "sonar" signal to) the server to see how long it takes for it to respond to your request. Network Utility reports the response time in milliseconds—a useful test when you're trying to see if a remote server (a website, for example) is up and running. (The time it takes for the ping to report back to you also tells you how good your connection to it is.)

Figure 11-46:
The whois tool is a powerful part of Network Utility. First enter a domain that you want information about, and then choose a whois server (you might try whois.internic.net). When you click the Whois button, you get a surprisingly revealing report about the owner of the domain, including phone numbers and contact names.

- **Traceroute lets you track how many "hops"** are required for your Mac to communicate with a certain server (an IP address or web address). You'll see that your request actually jumps from one *trunk* of the internet to another, from router to router, as it makes its way to its destination. You'll learn that a message sometimes crisscrosses the entire country before it arrives. You can also see how long each leg of the journey took, in milliseconds.

- **Whois ("who is") can gather information** about the owners of any particular domain (such as *apple.com*)—including name and address info, telephone numbers, and administrative contacts. It uses the technique shown in Figure 11-46.

Screen Sharing

This app does the heavy lifting for the Screen Sharing feature described on page 550.

Storage Management

The "how to free up more space on your hard drive" feature described on page 102 is actually this little app at work.

Wireless Diagnostics

Here's a handy Wi-Fi troubleshooting trick: While pressing Option, open the 🛜 menu and choose Open Wireless Diagnostics. This app opens. It walks you through some Wi-Fi troubleshooting steps. A full guide is online at *support.apple.com/en-us/HT202663*.

Part Four:
The Technologies
of macOS

4

Accounts, Security & Gatekeeper

I n an era when *security* is the hottest high-tech buzzword, Apple was smart to make it a focal point for macOS. It was already virus-free and better protected from internet attacks than Windows. But macOS Catalina is the most impenetrable Mac system yet, filled with defenses against the dark arts. This chapter covers the whole range of them.

On the premise that the biggest security threat of all comes from other people in your home or office, though, the most important security feature in macOS is the *accounts* system.

Introducing Accounts

The concept of *user accounts* is central to macOS's security approach. Like the Unix under its skin (and also like recent versions of Windows), macOS is designed from the ground up to be a *multiple-user* operating system. That is, you can set up your macOS so that everyone must log in—click his name and type his password—when the computer turns on (Figure 12-1).

Upon doing so, you discover the Macintosh universe just as you left it, including these elements:

- **Your documents, files, and folders.**

- **Your preference settings** in every program you use: web browser bookmarks and preferred home page; desktop picture, screen saver, and language; icons on the desktop and in the Dock—and the size and position of the Dock itself; and so on.

- **Email account(s),** including personal information and mailboxes.

- Your personally installed programs and fonts.

- Your choice of programs that launch automatically at startup.

This system lets different people use it throughout the day, without disrupting one another's files and settings. It also protects the Mac from getting fouled up by mischievous (or bumbling) students, employees, and hackers.

If you're the only person who uses your Mac, you can skip most of this chapter. The Mac never pauses at startup time to demand the name and password you made up when you installed macOS, because Apple's installer automatically turns on something called *automatic login* (page 497). You *will* be using one of these accounts, though, whether you realize it or not.

Furthermore, when you're stuck in line at the Department of Motor Vehicles, you may find the concepts presented here worth skimming, as certain elements of this multiple-user system may intrude upon your solo activities—and figure into the discussions in this book—now and then.

Tip: Even if you don't share your Mac with anyone and don't create any other accounts, you might still be tempted to learn about the accounts feature because of its ability to password-protect the entire computer. All you have to do is turn *off* the automatic login feature. Thereafter, your Mac is protected from unauthorized fiddling when you're away from your desk or if your laptop is stolen.

Figure 12-1:
When you set up several accounts, you don't turn on the Mac so much as sign into it. A command in the menu called Log Out summons this sign-in screen, as does the Accounts menu described later in this chapter. Click your own name (or type the first couple of letters), and type your password (if any), to get past this box and into your own stuff.

The First Account

When you installed macOS, whether it was Catalina or an earlier version, you were asked for a name and a password. You were creating the first *user account* on your Mac. Since that fateful day, you may have made a number of changes to your desktop—adjusted the Dock settings, set up your folders and desktop the way you like them, added some bookmarks to your web browser, and so on—without realizing you were actually making those changes only to *your account.*

You've probably been saving your documents into your own Home folder, which is the cornerstone of your account. This folder, generally named after you and stashed in the Users folder on your hard drive, stores not only your own work, but also your preference settings for all the programs you use, fonts you've installed, your own email collection, and so on.

Now then: Suppose you create an account for a second person. When she turns on the computer and signs in, she finds the desktop exactly the way it was factory-installed by Apple—stunning Catalina desktop picture, Dock along the bottom, and so on. She can make the same kinds of changes to the Mac that you've made, but nothing she does affects *your* environment the next time you log in.

In other words, the multiple-accounts feature has two components: first, a convenience element that hides everyone else's junk; and, second, a security element that protects both the Mac's system software and everybody's work.

Creating an Account

Suppose somebody new joins your little Mac family—a new worker, student, or love interest, for example. And you want to make that person feel at home on your Mac.

Begin by opening System Preferences (Chapter 9). In the System Preferences window, click Users & Groups. You have just arrived at the master control center for account creation and management (Figure 12-2).

To create a new account, start by unlocking the Users & Groups panel. That is, click the 🔒 at lower left and fill in your own account password.

Now you can click + beneath the list of accounts. The little panel shown at bottom in Figure 12-2 appears.

Phase 1: Choose an Account Type

As though this business of accounts and passwords weren't complicated enough already, macOS offers several *types* of accounts. And you're expected to specify *which* type each person gets at the moment you create one.

To do that, open the New Account pop-up menu (Figure 12-2, bottom). Its five account types are described on the following pages.

Administrator accounts

If this is your own personal Mac, then just beneath your name on the Users & Groups pane of System Preferences, it probably says *Admin*. This, as you could probably guess, stands for Administrator.

Because you're the person who originally installed macOS, the Mac assumes that you are its *administrator*—the technical wizard in charge of it. You're the teacher, the parent, the resident guru. You're the one who will maintain this Mac. Only an administrator is allowed to do the following:

- **Install new programs into the Applications folder.**

- **Add fonts that everybody can use.**

- **Make changes to certain System Preferences panes** (including Network, Date & Time, Energy Saver, and Startup Disk).

- **Use some features of the Disk Utility program.**

- **Create, move, or delete folders outside of your Home folder.**

- **Decide who gets to have accounts on the Mac.**

Figure 12-2:
Top: The screen lists everyone who has an account. From here you can create new accounts or change passwords. If you're new at this, there's probably just one account listed: yours. This is the account macOS created when you first installed it. You, the all-wise administrator, have to click the 🔒 to authenticate yourself before you can start making changes.

Bottom: In the account-creation process, the first step is choosing which type of account you want to create.

- Open, change, or delete anyone else's files.

- Bypass FileVault using a recovery key (page 502).

The administrator concept may be new to you, but it's an important pill to swallow. For one thing, you'll find certain settings all over macOS that you can change *only* if you're an administrator—including many in the Users & Groups pane itself. For another thing, administrator status plays a huge role when you want to network your Mac to other kinds of computers, as described in the next chapter. And, finally, in the bigger picture, the fact that the Mac has an industrial-strength accounts system, just like traditional Unix and recent Windows operating systems, gives it a fighting chance in the corporations of America.

As you create accounts for other people who'll use this Mac, you're offered the opportunity to make each one an administrator, just like you. Needless to say, use discretion. Bestow these powers only upon people who are as responsible and technically masterful as yourself.

Standard accounts

Most people, on most Macs, are ordinary *Standard* account holders. These people have everyday access to their own Home folders and to the harmless panes of System Preferences, but most other areas of the Mac are off-limits. MacOS won't even let them create new folders on the main hard drive, except inside their own Home folders (or in the Shared folder described starting on page 504).

A few of the System Preferences panels display a padlock icon (🔒). If you're a Standard account holder, you can't make changes to these settings without the assistance of an administrator. Fortunately, you aren't required to log out so that an administrator can log in and make changes. You can just call the administrator over, click the padlock icon, and let him type in his name and password (if, indeed, he feels comfortable with you making the changes you're about to make).

Sharing Only accounts

This kind of account is extremely useful—*if* your Mac is on a network (Chapter 13).

See, ordinarily, you can log in and access the files on your Mac in either of two ways:

- In person, seated in front of it.

- From across the network.

This arrangement was designed with families and schools in mind: lots of people sharing a *single* Mac.

This setup gets a little silly, though, when the people on a home or office network each have their *own* computers. If you wanted your spouse or your sales director to be able to grab some files from you, you'd have to create full-blown accounts for them on *your* Mac, complete with utterly unnecessary Home folders they'd never use.

That's why the *Sharing Only* account is such a great idea. It's available *only* from across the network. You can't get into it by sitting down at the Mac itself—it has no Home folder!

Finally, of course, a Sharing Only account holder can't make any changes to the Mac's settings or programs. And since they don't have Home folders, you also can't turn on FileVault (page 511) for these accounts.

In other words, a Sharing Only account exists *solely* for the purpose of file sharing on the network, and people can enter their names and passwords *only* from other Macs.

Once you've set up this kind of account, all the file-sharing and screen-sharing goodies described in Chapter 13 become available.

Guest account

For years, macOS has offered a special account called the *Guest* account. It's great for accommodating visitors, buddies, or anyone else who's just passing through and wants to borrow your Mac for a while. If you let such people use the Guest account, your own account remains private and un-messed-with.

Note: The Guest account isn't listed among the account *types* in the New Account pop-up menu (Figure 12-2). That's because there's only *one* Guest account; you can't actually create additional ones.

But it's still an account type with specific characteristics. It's sitting right there in the list of accounts.

In the early days of the Guest account, there was a problem: Any changes your friend made—downloading mail, making web bookmarks, putting up a raunchy desktop picture—would still be there for the *next* guest, unless you painstakingly restored everything back to neutral. The Guest account was like a hotel room shared by successive guests. And *you* were the housekeeping staff.

Today, though, any changes your guest makes while using your Mac are automatically erased when she logs out. Files are deleted, email is nuked, setting changes are forgotten. It's like a hotel that gets demolished and rebuilt after each guest departs.

As noted, the Guest account is permanently listed in the Users & Groups panel of System Preferences. Ordinarily, though, you don't see it in the Login screen list; if you're normally the only person who uses this Mac, you don't need to have it staring you in the face every day.

So to use the Guest account, bring it to life by choosing Guest User and then turning on "Allow guests to log into this computer." You can even turn on the parental controls described on page 220 by clicking Open Parental Controls, or permit the guest to exchange files with your Mac from across the network (Chapter 13) by turning on "Allow guests to connect to shared folders."

Just remember to warn your vagabond friend that once he logs out (and acknowledges the warning), all traces of his visit are wiped out forever.

At least from your *Mac*.

Group

A *group* is just a virtual container that holds the names of other account holders. You might create one for your most trusted colleagues, another for those rambunctious kids, and so on—all in the name of streamlining the *file-sharing privileges* feature described on page 531. The box below covers groups in more detail.

Phase 2: Name, Password, and Status

All right. So you clicked the + button. And from the New Account pop-up menu, you chose the type of account you wanted to create. (If you chose a Managed with Parental Controls account, you've also specified the age of this person.)

Now, on the same starter sheet, it's time to fill in the most critical information about the new account holder:

- **Full Name.** If it's just the family, this could be "Chris" or "Robin." If it's a corporation or school, you probably want to use both first and last names.

- **Account Name.** You'll quickly discover the value of this Account Name, particularly if your name is, say, Alexandra Stephanopoulos. It's meant to be an abbreviation of your actual name.

POWER USERS' CLINIC

Creating Groups

Changing permissions settings on a networked Mac, or one with a lot of account holders, is a lot easier if you sweep all your minions into subsets called groups.

This process used to require a complicated series of Unixy steps that, if not performed carefully, could seriously foul up your Mac.

But in macOS, you can create a group as easily as you'd create an account. And in the same place: the Users & Groups pane of System Preferences.

Click the tiny 🔒 in the lower-left corner. When prompted, type in your administrator's name and password, and then click OK. The Mac is just making sure that somebody with a clue is at the helm.

Now click the + button as though you were about to create a new account. But from the New Account pop-up menu (shown at bottom in Figure 12-2), choose Group. Type a name for the new group (Accounting, Kids, or whatever), and then click Create Group.

Now you see something like the list shown here: checkboxes for all of this Mac's account holders. Turn on the checkboxes for the ones you consider worthy of being a part of this group.

You can create as many groups as you like. Later, when it comes time to share a folder or file, you'll save time by choosing a group name instead of setting these permissions one person at a time.

When you sign into your Mac in person, you can use either your full name or account (short) name. But when you access this Mac by dialing into it or connecting from across the network (as described in the next chapter), the short version is more convenient.

As soon as you tab into this field, the Mac proposes a short name for you. You can replace the suggestion with whatever you like. Technically, it doesn't even have to be shorter than the "long" name, but spaces and most punctuation marks are forbidden.

- **Password.** You're supposed to type this password twice, to make sure you didn't introduce a typo the first time. (The Mac displays only dots as you type, to guard against the possibility that somebody is watching over your shoulder.)

The usual computer book takes this opportunity to stress the importance of a long, complex password—a phrase that isn't in the dictionary, something that's made up of mixed letters and numbers. This is excellent advice if you create sensitive documents or work in a big corporation.

But if you share the Mac only with a spouse, or trusted colleagues in a small office, you may have nothing to hide. You may see the accounts feature more as a convenience (keeping your settings and files separate) than a protector of secrecy and security. In these situations, there's no particular urgency to the mission of thwarting the world's hackers with a convoluted password.

In that case, you may want to consider setting up *no* password—leaving both password blanks empty. Later, whenever you're asked for your password, just leave the Password box blank. You'll be able to log in that much faster each day.

(The first box says "Required," but it lies; no password is actually required. After setting up this new account and clicking Create User, the Mac asks if you're *sure* you don't want to make up a password; just click Continue and get on with your life.)

Tip: Actually, having *some* password comes in handy if you share files on the network, because Mac A can *store* your name and password from Mac B—and therefore you can access Mac B without entering your name and password *at all.* So consider making your password something very short and easy, like the apostrophe/quote mark—the ' key. It's a real password, so it's enough for Mac A to memorize. Yet when you *are* asked to enter your password—for example, when you're installing a new program—it's incredibly fast and easy to enter, because it's right next to the Return key.

- **Password Hint.** If your password is the middle name of the first person who ever kissed you, for example, your hint might be "Middle name of the first person who ever kissed me."

Later, if you forget your password, the Mac will show you this cue to jog your memory.

When you finish setting up these essential items, click Create User.

You then return to the Users & Groups pane, where you see the new account name in the list at the left side.

Three final decisions await your wisdom:

- **Allow user to reset password using Apple ID.** If this person ever forgets his password, he'll be offered, on the Login screen, a chance to recover it by entering his Apple ID. Nice little safety net. (Available only for accounts for which you've entered an Apple ID, of course.)

- **Allow user to administer this computer.** This checkbox lets you turn ordinary, unsuspecting Standard or Managed accounts into Administrator accounts. You know—when your kid turns 18.

- **Enable Parental Controls.** "Parental Controls" refers to the feature that limits what your offspring are allowed to do on this computer—and how much time a day they're allowed to spend glued to its screen. Details are on page 220.

Actually, if your Mac has a Touch Bar (page 227), a fourth option awaits, the most delicious of all: You can now log into the new account, open System Preferences→ Touch ID, and let its owner register a fingerprint. One touch on the Touch ID sensor built into the laptop's power button will now act as that person's security authentication, wherever fine passwords are requested. Page 366 has the details.

Phase 3: Choose a Picture

The usual sign-in screen (Figure 12-1) displays each account holder's name, accompanied by a little picture.

When you click the sample photo, you get the dialog box shown in Figure 12-3, where you choose a picture to represent you. It becomes not only your icon on the sign-in screen, but also your "card" photo in the Contacts program and your icon in Messages.

Figure 12-3:
The account-photo box offers you access to every photo on your Mac—and even to your Mac's camera (for taking a new shot). Once you've selected a photo to represent yourself, you can adjust its position relative to the round "frame," or adjust its size by dragging the slider. Finally, when the picture looks correctly framed, click Save.

If you'd rather supply your *own* graphic—a photo of your head, for example—use one of these options:

- **Defaults.** Apple starts you off with a selection of account photos, intended to represent various personalities: eagles, flowers, chalkboard math, basketball, and so on.

- **Camera.** Click Take Photo. The Mac takes the picture, while flashing the screen to add brightness. You can enlarge or shrink it, or drag to move it within the circular frame.

- **Photos.** Here you get access to your entire Mac photo collection, grouped just as it is in the Photos program (page 565).

- **Photo Booth.** And here are whatever zany funhouse photos you've taken with the Photo Booth app (page 437).

In each case, click Save to enshrine your account photo forever (or until you feel like picking a different one).

Phase 4: Login Items (Startup Items)

There's one additional setting that your account holders can set up for themselves: which programs or documents open automatically upon login. (This is one decision an administrator *can't* make for other people. It's available only to the person logged in at the moment.)

To choose your own crew of self-starters, open System Preferences and click Users & Groups. Choose your account. Click the Login Items tab. As shown in Figure 12-4, you can now build a list of programs, documents, disks, and other goodies that

Figure 12-4:
You can add any icon to the list of things you want to start up automatically. Click the + button to summon the Open dialog box, where you can find the icon, select it, and then click Add.

Better yet, if you can see the icon in a folder or disk window (or on the desktop), just drag it into this list.

To remove an item, click it in the list and then click the — button.

automatically launch each time you log in. You can even turn on the Hide checkbox for each one so the program is running in the background at login time, waiting to be called into service with a quick click.

Don't feel obligated to limit this list to just programs and documents, by the way. Disks, folders, servers on the network, and other icons can also serve as startup items, so their windows will be open and waiting when you arrive at the computer each morning.

Tip: Here's a much quicker way to add something to the Login Items list: Right-click or two-finger click its Dock icon and choose Open at Login from the shortcut menu.

- **Prevent the Dock from being modified.** Just what it says.

- **Use Simple Finder.** Use this option only if you're *really* concerned about somebody's ability to survive the Mac—or the Mac's ability to survive that somebody. Read on.

Editing Accounts

If you're an administrator, you can change your own account in any way you like.

If you have any other kind of account, though, you can't change anything but your picture, password, Apple ID, and login items. If you want to make any other changes,

POWER USERS' CLINIC

The Secret Account Options

Anyone who knows macOS very well might object to the sentence "If you're an administrator, you can change your own account in any way you like."

Because there's one aspect of an account that even an admin can't change: the account's *short name* (as opposed to the Full Name). Once that's created, it's yours forever, or at least until you delete the account.

Or at least that's what Apple *wants* you to think. There's a secret way to pick a different short name. You can't easily *change* the one you created originally, but you can create *another* one–shorter, or more memorable–that *also* works when you're logging in or authenticating yourself.

Advanced Options

User: "Casey Robin"

WARNING: Changing these settings might damage this account and prevent the user from logging in. You must restart the computer for the changes to these settings to take effect.

User ID: 502
Group: staff
Account name: casey
Full name: Casey Robin
Login shell: /bin/bash
Home directory: /Users/casey Choose...
UUID: 25F231D8-F9E3-4D5E-8112-6AC98B60DAC7 Create New
Apple ID: caseyrobin@icloud.com Change...
Aliases: caseyrobin@icloud.com
com.apple.idms.appleid.prd.456643526134632b455...

+ −

Cancel OK

To find it, right-click or two-finger click the account's name in the list at the left side of the Users & Groups panel in System Preferences. From the short-cut menu, choose Advanced Options. The strange and wonderful Advanced Options panel appears. Right in the middle is an "Account name" box, but don't bother editing that; it won't work.

Instead, click the + button below the Aliases list. You're offered the chance to type in an *alternate* account name. Do it and then click OK.

When it's all over, click OK. The next time you log in, you'll be able to use your new, improved short name instead of the old one. And rejoice that you lived to see the day.

you have to ask an admin to log in, make the changes you want made to your account, and then turn the computer back over to you.

Deleting Accounts

Hey, it happens: Somebody graduates, somebody gets fired, somebody dumps you. Sooner or later, you may need to delete an account from your Mac.

When that time comes, click the account name in the Users & Groups pane of System Preferences and then click the minus-sign button beneath the list. MacOS asks what to do with all the dearly departed's files and settings (Figure 12-5):

- **Save the home folder in a disk image.** This option represents the "I'll be back" approach. MacOS preserves the deleted account holder's folders on the Mac, in a tidy digital envelope that won't clutter your hard drive and can be reopened in case of emergency.

 In the Users→Deleted Users folder, you find a disk image file (.dmg). If you double-click it, a new, virtual disk icon named for the deleted account appears on your desktop. You can open folders and root through the stuff in this "disk," just as if it were a living, working Home folder.

Figure 12-5:
Top: This dialog box lets you know where to find the deleted account's material, should the need arise.

Bottom: The files and settings of accounts you deleted can live on in the Users→Deleted Users folder.

If fate ever brings that person back into your life, you can use this disk image to reinstate the deleted account. Start by creating a brand-new account. Then copy the contents of the folders in the mounted disk image (Documents, Pictures, Desktop, and so on) into the corresponding folders of the new Home folder.

- **Don't change the home folder.** This time, macOS removes the *account,* in that it no longer appears in the Login list or in the Users & Groups panel of System Preferences—but it leaves the *Home folder* right where it is. Use this option if you don't intend to dispose of the dearly departed's belongings right here and now.

- **Delete the home folder.** This button offers the "Hasta la vista, baby" approach. The account and all its files and settings are vaporized forever, on the spot. (And the "Erase home folder securely" option even records gibberish over the spot where that Home folder was, such that its contents couldn't be recovered even by the NSA.)

Note: If you delete a Sharing Only account, you're not offered the chance to preserve the Home folder contents—because a Sharing Only account doesn't *have* a Home folder.

Setting Up the Login Process

Once you've set up more than one account, the screen shown in Figure 12-1 appears whenever you turn on the Mac, whenever you choose →Log Out, or whenever the Mac logs you out automatically. But a few extra controls let you, an administrator, set up either more or less security at the Login screen—or, put another way, build in less or more convenience.

Open System Preferences, click Users & Groups, click the , enter an admin password to prove your worthiness, and then click the Login Options button (Figure 12-6). Here are some of the ways you can shape the login experience for greater security (or greater convenience):

- **Automatic login.** This option eliminates the need to sign in at all. It's a time-saving, hassle-free arrangement if only one person uses the Mac, or uses it most of the time.

 When you choose an account holder's name from this pop-up menu, you're prompted for his password. Type it and click OK.

 From now on, the screen shown in Figure 12-1 won't appear *at all* at startup time. After turning on the machine, you, the specified account holder, zoom straight to your desktop.

 Of course, everybody else must still enter their names and passwords. (But how can they, since the Mac rushes right into the Automatic person's account at startup time? Answer: The Automatic thing happens only at startup. The usual Login screen appears whenever the current account holder logs out—by choosing →Log Out, for example.)

- **Display login window as.** Under normal circumstances, the Login screen presents a list of account holders when you power up the Mac, as shown in Figure 12-1. That's the "List of users" option in action.

 If you're especially worried about security, however, you might not want even that list to appear. If you turn on "Name and password" (Figure 12-6), then each person who signs in must type both his name (into a blank that appears) *and* his password—a very inconvenient, but more secure, arrangement.

Figure 12-6:
These options make it easier or harder for people to sign in, offering various degrees of security. By the way: Turning on "Name and password" also lets you sign in as >console, an advanced geeky troubleshooting technique. It's also one way to sign in with the root account, if you're Unixy enough to know what that is.

- **Show the Sleep, Restart, and Shut Down buttons.** Truth is, the macOS security system is easy to circumvent. Devoted evildoers can bypass the standard Login screen in a number of different ways: restart in FireWire disk mode, restart at the Unix Terminal, and so on. Suddenly, these no-goodniks have full access to every document on the machine, blowing right past all the safeguards you've so carefully established.

 One way to thwart them is to use FileVault (page 511). Another is to turn off this checkbox. Now there's no Restart or Shut Down button to tempt mischief-makers. That's plenty of protection in most homes, schools, and workplaces; after all, Mac people tend to be *nice* people.

 But if you worry that somebody with a pronounced mean streak might restart simply by pulling the plug, then either use FileVault or set the *firmware password*, as described in the box on the facing page.

- **Show Input menu in login window.** If the Input menu is available at login time, it means people who use non-U.S. keyboard layouts and alphabets can use the login features without having to pretend to be American. (You can't use fancy non-Roman alphabets like Japanese or Russian for your password. But at least this option will let you enter your full name in the language of your choice. Greetings, Mr. Bond-san.)

- **Show password hints.** MacOS is kind enough to display your password hint ("Middle name of the first person who ever kissed me") after you've typed your password wrong three times when trying to log in. This option lets you turn off that feature for an extra layer of security. The hint will never appear.

- **Show fast user switching menu as.** The fast user switching feature lets you switch to another account without having to log out of the first one, as described on page 506.

If you do turn on fast user switching, a new menu appears at the upper-right corner of your screen, listing all the account holders on the machine. Thanks to this pop-up menu, you can now specify what that menu looks like. It can display the current account holder's full name (Name), the short name (Short Name), or only a generic torso-silhouette icon (Icon) to save space on the menu bar.

POWER USERS' CLINIC

The Firmware Password Utility

After all this discussion of security and passwords, it may come as a bit of a shock to learn that enterprising villains can bypass macOS's security features in 10 seconds. If you haven't turned on FileVault, their nefarious options include using the Unix console, single-user mode, FireWire disk mode, and so on.

But there is one way to secure your Mac completely: by turning on the very secret, little-known firmware password.

To find it, restart your Mac while pressing ⌘-R. That starts up macOS's Recovery console (page 779). Once you've chosen your language, choose Utilities→Startup Security Utility.

When you run this utility, click Turn On Firmware Password. Then make up a password—your firmware password—that will be required to start up from anything but the internal

drive, and then hit Set Password. A message tells you, "Firmware password protection enabled." Click Quit Startup Security Utility, and then choose →Restart.

From now on, whenever you attempt to start up in anything but the usual way, you're asked to type the firmware password.

Holding down N to start up from a NetBoot server, pressing T to start up in Target Disk Mode, pressing ⌘-Option-P-R to reset the parameter RAM, pressing Shift to enter Safe Mode—none of it works without the master firmware password.

The only way to reset this password, should you forget it, is to make an appointment at an Apple Store and beg for their mercy.

- **Accessibility Options.** If you benefit from the Mac's accessibility features (page 320)—like VoiceOver or Zoom if you're visually impaired, or Sticky Keys or Mouse Keys if you have motor-control problems—here's your chance to have them available to help you at the login screen.

- **Network Account Server.** If you work in a company big enough to use Microsoft's corporate server software (and rich enough to employ a hardworking network administrator), you might be told to click this button and enter a server address so that you'll be able to access things like the company address book and calendar.

Tip: Actually, there's one more, rather secret, login option—and if you're a laptop lugger, you might really like it. You can create a message that appears on the Login screen whenever you—or, rather, *not* you—turn on the computer. For example, it could be an "If found, contact…" message. Or a "$500 reward" message.

To set it up, open System Preferences→Security & Privacy→General. Click the 🔒, authenticate yourself, and then turn on "Show a message when the screen is locked." Click Set Lock Message, and then type your message. (Press Option-Return to create a new paragraph.) And hope whoever finds your laptop has a conscience.

Signing In, Logging Out

Once your account is set up, here's what it's like getting into, and out of, a Mac. (For the purposes of this discussion, "you" are no longer the administrator—you're one

GEM IN THE ROUGH

Automatic Login with the Apple Watch

If you own an Apple Watch, you're in for a treat. You never have to type in a password to unlock your Mac again!

The watch on your wrist can act as a wireless master key. (For security, it has a very short range—about 5 feet.)

The watch must be running watchOS 3 or later, the Mac must be a 2013 or newer, Watch and Mac must be associated with the same iCloud account, and Watch and Mac must both be passcode-protected.

Finally, you must have *two-factor authentication* turned on. That's Apple's security system for logging into things (page 508).

All that set? OK. On the Mac, open System Preferences→ Security & Privacy→General. Turn on "Allow your Apple

Cancel 9:03

Bryan's MacBook Pro

Double Click
to Approve

Watch to unlock your Mac." Enter your account password to prove you're you.

From now on, just waking your Mac logs you in, instantly and securely. In place of the usual password box on your Mac's screen, it says "Unlocking with Apple Watch." Your watch says "Mac Unlocked." And you're in.

In Catalina, in fact, that System Preferences setting also unleashes the new Approve with Apple Watch feature, in which the Watch can unlock the 🔒 icons that confront you in System Preferences panels, locked Notes, and other spots. Whenever you see one, double-click the side button on your watch to unlock that secure feature, using wireless magic. And to think that you lived to see the day!

of the lowly students, employees, or family members for whom a macOS account has been set up.)

Identifying Yourself

When you first turn on the Mac—or when the person who last used this computer chooses ⌘→Log Out—the Login screen shown in Figure 12-1 appears. At this point, you can proceed in any of several ways:

- **Restart.** Click if you need to restart the Mac for some reason. (The Restart and Shut Down buttons don't appear here if the administrator has chosen to hide them as a security precaution.)

- **Shut Down.** Click if you're done for the day, or if sudden panic about the complexity of accounts makes you want to run away. The computer turns off.

- **Log In.** To sign in, click your account name in the list. If you're a keyboard speed freak, you can just type the first letter or two—or press the up or down arrow keys—until your name is highlighted. Then press Return.

 Either way, the password box appears now, if a password is required. (Of course, if you're lucky enough to have a Touch ID sensor on your laptop, and you've taught it to recognize your fingerprint [page 365], then no password box appears. You can just touch your finger to the power button to log in, as shown in Figure 12-7.)

Figure 12-7:
Touch ID—the fingerprint reader on Macs with Touch Bars—really is the ultimate. You can wake your Mac and prove your authenticity simultaneously, with a single touch of the power button.

If you accidentally clicked the wrong person's name on the first screen, you can click Back. Otherwise, type your password, and then press Return (or click Log In).

You can try as many times as you want to type the password. With each incorrect guess, the entire password box shudders violently from side to side, as though shaking its head no. (If you see a ⇪ icon in the password box, guess what? You've got your Caps Lock key on, and the Mac thinks you're typing an all-capitals password.)

If you try unsuccessfully three times, your hint appears—if you've set one up. And if even that safety net fails, you can use your Apple ID as the key to resetting your password. See the box on the next page.

Once you're in, the world of the Mac looks just the way you left it (or the way an administrator set it up for you). Everything in your Home folder, all your email and bookmarks, your desktop picture and Dock settings—all of it unique to you.

Unless you're an administrator, you're not allowed to install any new programs (or, indeed, to put anything at all) into the Applications folder. That folder, after all, is a central software repository for *everybody* who uses the Mac, and the Mac forbids everyday account holders from moving or changing all such universally shared folders.

Logging Out

When you're finished using the Mac, choose →Log Out (or press Shift-⌘-Q). A confirmation message appears; if you click Cancel or press Esc, you return to whatever you were doing. If you click Log Out or press Return, you return to the screen shown in Figure 12-1, and the sign-in cycle begins again.

Tip: If you press Option as you choose →Log Out (or as you press Shift-⌘-Q), then the confirmation box doesn't appear.

The Forgotten-Password Survival Guide

Help—I forgot my password! And I never told it to anybody!

No problem. Your administrator can simply open up System Preferences, click Users & Groups, click your account name, and then click Reset Password to reestablish the password.

But you don't understand. I am the administrator! And I'm the only account!

Lucky for you, Apple has provided not one, not two, but three safety nets. None of them work, however, unless you, the administrator, turned them on in advance.

First: On your third attempt to type your password, the Mac shows you your password hint (if you have one, and if the administrator left the Hint option turned on).

Second: If the administrator has turned on the "Allow user to reset password using Apple ID" in System Preferences→ Users & Groups, then you can click the ? button right there in the Password box when you're logging in. A tiny message appears, letting you know that "If you forgot your password, you can reset it using your Apple ID."

To proceed, click the ○ button to bring up the Reset Password dialog box. Enter your Apple ID and password, and then click Reset Password. A message appears to let you

know changing your account password will also create a new Keychain (page 518). (The old one is still around, ready to be unlocked if you remember the old password at some point.) Click OK. Now enter a new password (twice) and a password hint, and then click Reset Password.

You've just reset your account password. Click Continue Log In to finish logging in with your new, improved, not-forgotten password.

Third: If the administrator has turned on FileVault, described starting on page 511, then you can use its recovery key to log in, in a pinch. It's the master password: a last-ditch, emergency-backup password.

If you have your recovery key, read on. (If not, and you opted to store it with Apple, call Apple tech support; they'll give it to you. If not, and you didn't store it with Apple, you're completely out of luck. Your hard drive is encrypted, and you can't do anything but erase it and kiss your files goodbye.)

Anyway, restart the Mac. On the Login screen, click your name; then click the ? button. If the hint appears and it helps you out, great. If not, click "Reset it using your Recovery Key," type in your recovery key, and then praise the Apple gods that this final safety net actually worked.

Logout Options

When you choose ⌘→Log Out and confirm your intention to log out, the Login screen appears, ready for its next victim.

But sometimes people forget. You might wander off to the bathroom for a minute, but run into a colleague there who breathlessly begins describing last night's date and proposes finishing the conversation over pizza. The next thing you know, you've left your Mac unattended but logged in, with all your life's secrets accessible to anyone who walks by your desk.

You can tighten up that security hole, and many others, using the options in the Security & Privacy→General panel of System Preferences:

- **Require password [immediately] after sleep or screen saver begins.** This option gives you a password-protected screen saver that locks your Mac when you wander away. Now, whenever somebody tries to wake your Mac after the screen saver has appeared (or when the Mac has simply gone to sleep according to your settings in the Energy Saver panel of System Preferences), the "Enter your password" dialog box appears. No password? No access.

 The pop-up menu here (which starts out saying "immediately") is a handy feature. Without it, the person most inconvenienced by the password requirement would be *you,* not the snitch from Accounting; even if you just stepped away to the bathroom or the coffee machine, you'd have to unlock the screen saver with your password. It would get old fast.

 Instead, the password requirement can kick in after you've been away for a more serious amount of time—5 minutes, 15 minutes, an hour, whatever. You can still put the Mac to sleep, or you can still set up your screen saver to kick in sooner than that. But until that time period has passed, you'll be able to wake the machine without having to log in.

- **Show a message when the screen is locked.** Whatever you type into this box will appear on the Login screen (where you click your name in the list) or the screen saver. It could be, "Getting coffee…" or your name and cellphone number, or anything you like.

- **Disable automatic login.** This is just a duplicate of the "Automatic login" on/off switch described on page 497. Apple figured that this feature really deserved *some* presence on a control panel called Security & Privacy.

- **Allow your Apple Watch to unlock your Mac.** You don't need a password to unlock your Mac anymore—if you're wearing an Apple Watch. It acts as a wireless master key that logs you in automatically, as described on page 313. This master switch for that glorious feature appears only if you've turned on two-factor authentication (page 508).

If you click the Advanced button (at the bottom of the Security & Privacy pane of System Preferences), you get these bonus tweaks:

- **Log out after [60] minutes of inactivity.** You can make the Mac sign out of your account completely if it figures out that you've wandered off (and it's been, say, 15 minutes since the last time you touched the mouse or keyboard). Anyone who shows up at your Mac will find only the standard Login screen.

- **Require an administrator password to access system-wide preferences.** Ordinarily, certain System Preferences changes require an administrator's approval—namely, the ones that affect the entire computer and everyone who uses it, like Date & Time, Users & Groups, Network, Time Machine, and Security & Privacy. If you're *not* an administrator, you can't make changes to these panels until an administrator has typed in her name and password to approve your change.

 However, once Mr. Teacher or Ms. Parent has unlocked *one* of those secure preference settings, they're *all* unlocked. Once the administrator leaves your desk, you can go right on making changes to the *other* important panels (Network *and* Time Machine *and* Security & Privacy) without the administrator's knowledge.

 Unless this "Require an administrator password" box is turned on, that is. In that case, an Administrative account holder has to enter her name and password to approve *each* of those System Preferences panes individually.

Sharing Across Accounts

It's all fine to say that every account is segregated from all *other* accounts. It's nice to know your stuff is safe from the prying eyes of your co-workers or family. But what about collaboration? What if you *want* to give some files or folders to another account holder?

You can't just open up someone else's Home folder and drop it in there. Yes, every account holder has a Home folder (all in the Users folder on your hard drive). But if you try to open anybody else's Home folder, you'll see a tiny red ⛔ icon superimposed on almost every folder inside, telling you "Look, but don't touch."

Fortunately, there are a couple of wormholes between accounts (Figure 12-8):

- **The Shared folder.** Sitting in the Users folder is one folder that doesn't correspond to any particular person: Shared. Everybody can freely access this folder, inserting and extracting files without restriction. It's Central Park, the farmers market, and the grocery-store bulletin board.

- **The Public folder.** In your Home folder, there's a folder called Public. Anything you copy into it becomes available for inspection or copying (but not changing or deleting) by any other account holder, whether she logs into your Mac or signs in from across the network.

- **The Drop Box.** And *inside* your Public folder is another cool little folder: the Drop Box (not to be confused with the free online Dropbox service). It exists to let *other* people give files to *you*, discreetly and invisibly to anyone else. That is, people can drop files and folders into your Drop Box, but they can't actually *open* it. This folder, too, is available both locally (in person) and from across the network.

Note: You can also share files in similar ways with people on *different* machines; start your journey on page 527.

Figure 12-8:

Top: In other people's Home folders, the Public folder is available for your inspection. It contains stuff other people have "published" for the benefit of their co-workers.

Middle: In the Public folder is the Drop Box, which serves the opposite purpose. It lets anyone else who uses this Mac hand in files to you; they, however, can't see what's in the box.

Bottom: Inside the Users folder (to get there from a Home folder, press ⌘-▲) is the Shared folder, a wormhole connecting all accounts. Everybody has full access to everything inside.

Fast User Switching

The account system described so far in this chapter has its charms. It keeps everyone's stuff separate, it keeps your files safe, and it lets you have the desktop picture of your choice.

Unfortunately, it can go from handy to hassle in one split second. That's when you're logged in, and somebody else wants to duck in just for a second—to check email or a calendar, for example. What are you supposed to do—log out completely, closing all your documents and quitting all your programs, just so the interloper can look something up? Then afterward, you'd have to log back in and fire up all your stuff again, praying that your inspirational muse hadn't fled in the meantime.

Fortunately, fast user switching lets Person B log in and use the Mac for a little while. All *your* stuff, Person A, simply slides into the background, still open the way you had it; see Figure 12-9.

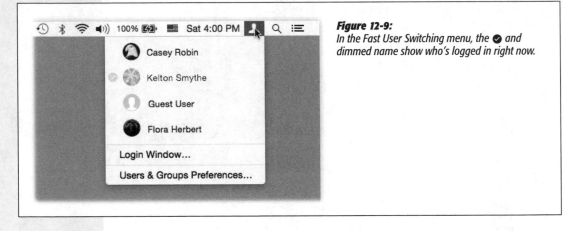

Figure 12-9:
In the Fast User Switching menu, the ⊘ and dimmed name show who's logged in right now.

When Person B is finished working, you can bring your whole work environment back to the screen without having to reopen anything. All your windows and programs are still open, just as you left them.

Do you see your own account name, or a human silhouette, in the upper-right corner of the screen (Figure 12-9)? That's a button that lists all account holders.

(If you don't see this Fast User Switching menu, open the Users & Groups panel of System Preferences; click the 🔒, if necessary, to unlock the panel. Click Login Options and turn on the "Show fast user switching menu as" checkbox. And while you're at it: You can change what this menu looks like by using the "Show fast user switching menu as" pop-up menu.)

Next time you need a fellow account holder to relinquish control so you can duck in to do a little work, just choose your name from the Accounts menu. Type your password, if one is required, and feel guiltless about the interruption.

Tip: If your Mac has a Touch Bar (page 227), and Person B has registered a fingerprint, then using fast user switching is even easier. All Person B has to do is click the Touch ID sensor (power button) at the right end of the Touch Bar. Boom: Accounts switched!

And now, the finer points of fast user switching:

- **To exit an open account,** choose →Log Out as usual. Or just choose Login Window from the Accounts menu. It ensures that you can get to your own account no matter whose is running at the moment.

- **Weirdly enough, a bunch of account holders** can be using the same program simultaneously in their own parallel universes.

- **You can't make changes to accounts** (in System Preferences) that are still logged in. You can't turn off fast user switching or turn on FileVault while other people are logged in, either.

- **If you try to shut the Mac down or restart it** while other people are logged in, a dialog box tells you "There are currently logged in users who may lose unsaved changes if you shut down this computer." And you're asked to type in an administrator's name and password to establish that you know what you're doing.

 Here's a moral dilemma for the modern age: If you proceed by typing the password and clicking Shut Down, you shut down all accounts that were open in the background *and* any open documents. If you click Cancel, you can't shut down the Mac until you hunt down the account holders whose stuff is still open in the background so they can log out.

Tip: You can avoid this awkward situation in either of two ways: (1) Trust one another completely, or (2) Save all your documents before you let anyone else cut in and send your account to the background.

- **Remember the Shared folder** (in the Users folder on the hard drive)? It's still the wormhole connecting all accounts. If you want to share a file with another account holder, put it there.

- **Your account isn't anesthetized completely** when it's switched into the background. In fact, it keeps on doing whatever you set it to doing. If you were downloading some big file, for example, it keeps right on downloading when the next guy logs in.

macOS and Security

The Mac has a spectacular reputation for stability and security. You hardly ever hear of a Mac virus. There's also no Windows-esque plague of spyware (downloaded programs that do something sneaky behind your back).

Here are a few of macOS's big-ticket defenses.

Two-Factor Authentication

These days, having a complicated password isn't enough to protect you from the bad guys. Even if your password is é$*@çg45e$+!!!>?!+r6ü, someone can still steal it. (There are all kinds of ways. An inside job. An FBI demand. Poor security on a company's servers. Social engineering, where someone calls up pretending to be you and saying, "I forgot my password.")

Impressively enough, security experts have come up with a way to keep baddies out of your account even if they've *got* your password. Figure 12-10 shows how it works.

If some Russian hacker does get your password, you won't care! He still can't get into your account, because the code will be sent to *your* machine, not his.

This ingenious system has earned the awful name *two-factor authentication*. (Let's call it 2FA to save paper.) These days, the setup process on new Apple machines pushes you hard to set it up.

Note: Just to make sure everybody is thoroughly confused, note that the 2FA system is not the same thing as Apple's previous system, which was called *two-step verification*. Not kidding. That earlier system was very similar but worked by sending the code as a text message.

2FA is better, because it can send the code not just as a text message, but also as a dialog box on your Mac or phone's operating system—or, in a pinch, in an automated phone call. 2FA also shows you a map that indicates *where* the login request is coming from.

If you've already signed up for two-step verification, you can keep on using it. But honestly 2FA is a lot better.

If you turn 2FA on, the odds of someone else being able to access your account (email, calendar, messages, movies, music, backups, photos, and so on) drop close to zero. They'd have to have your password *and* steal your laptop or phone *and* know your password on that device.

On one hand, an increasing number of Mac features require 2FA, like Apple Pay on the Web, Messages in iCloud, and Apple Watch unlocking (page 313). On the other hand, you can't turn off 2FA by yourself once you've turned it on. (You can call Apple Support and explain yourself, and they can turn it off for you.)

Now that you know what you're getting into, here's how to switch on 2FA.

Open System Preferences→Apple ID→iCloud→Password & Security. Next to Two-Factor Authentication, click Turn On. You're asked for your phone number, and you're sent one of the verification codes to type in.

Each time you use a new Apple device, or a new web browser, for the first time, you'll go through the setup process shown in Figure 12-10 (just once). Each time, you're adding to your list of trusted devices. At any time, you can look over a list of them in System Preferences→Apple ID→iCloud→Password & Security→Edit. (That's where you can set up a backup phone number or two, too.)

Note: All of this works pretty smoothly on gadgets and programs made by Apple. But other companies' programs—like non-Apple calendar and email programs—aren't part of it. They're locked out of your iCloud account just as though they were hackers.

Fortunately, you can go to *appleid.apple.com/account/manage* to generate an *app-specific* password. If you enter this 16-character password as your iCloud account password in your third-party calendar or email program, it will now be able to access your iCloud account as it did before.

Figure 12-10:
The first time you try to access any iCloud feature using a new gadget (a new laptop or phone, for example) or a new web browser, Apple instantly sends a notification to another Apple product you own (top), showing you the approximate location of the person making the attempt. If it's you, great—click Allow.

If you don't recognize the location, though, it's probably some hacker. Click Don't Allow to ruin his day and shut him down.

If you click Allow, Apple now sends a one-time code to a phone, tablet, or computer it knows you own. You need that code to get into your account. (And, of course, you need two Apple products to make this work, like a Mac and an iPhone.)

Gatekeeper

This security feature sends Eastern European teenage hackers into therapy.

Nasty programs aren't very common on the Mac. But unless you turn Gatekeeper off, downloading a program that's secretly designed to damage your Mac is virtually impossible. Gatekeeper won't even let you *install* programs that haven't been demonstrated to be safe (Figure 12-11).

To find Gatekeeper, you open System Preferences→Security & Privacy→General. At the bottom of this screen (Figure 12-11, top), you see two options. These two humble buttons are Gatekeeper.

Click the lock icon and enter your password to unlock this panel. Here are your choices, under "Allow apps downloaded from":

- **App Store.** This is the safest option. *Every* program that Apple allows into its Mac App Store is safe. Each has been tested by Apple to make sure that, among other things, it's both *sandboxed* (blocked from accessing parts of the Mac that it doesn't need) and *digitally signed* (set up to notify that Mac if it's been altered in any way since it left the software company).

So what happens if you try to download a program that didn't come from the App Store? The Mac won't let you install it, period.

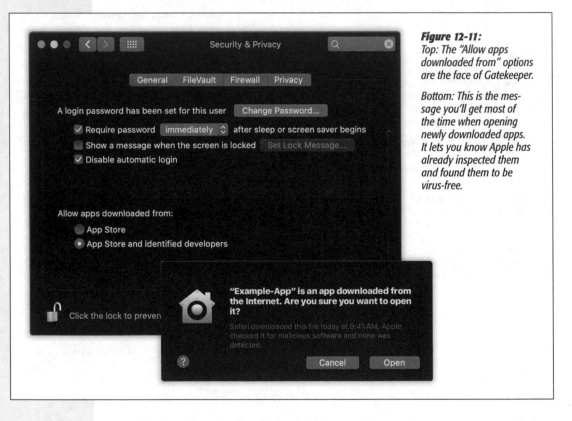

Figure 12-11:
Top: The "Allow apps downloaded from" options are the face of Gatekeeper.

Bottom: This is the message you'll get most of the time when opening newly downloaded apps. It lets you know Apple has already inspected them and found them to be virus-free.

- **App Store and identified developers.** This option, the factory setting, lets you download and install both App Store programs and those from "identified developers." That means software companies that have registered with Apple and received, in turn, an encrypted code (a "certificate") that's embedded in their programs.

This certificate lets Apple track who created the app, and also digitally signs it. Now, Apple may not know this software company, and Apple doesn't inspect its software. But if anybody reports that some program is actually a virus in disguise, Apple can instantly add that program to its blacklist—and prevent millions of other people from installing it. (MacOS updates its blacklist once a day.)

In Catalina, Apple has given Gatekeeper quite an upgrade. Apple has introduced the concept of *notarized* software—programs that may come from the App Store or an identified software company, which Apple has checked to make sure it's free of viruses and spyware.

The first time you open an app, therefore, you'll see one of three newly worded messages:

- **It's a notarized app, and it's clean.** The message (Figure 12-11) concludes: "Apple checked it for malicious software and none was detected." Click Open and go on with your life.

- **It's a notarized app, and it's infected.** The message says: "[App's Name] will damage your computer. You should move it to the Trash." Click Move to Trash, grateful to have dodged a bullet.

- **It's not notarized.** If you try to open an app Apple hasn't notarized, anything goes. Apple can't vouch for its safety—and so, in Catalina, it plays hardball: It *won't let you* open the app. Your only choices are Cancel or Move to Trash!

 OK, that's not entirely true. If you're willing to acknowledge that it's your problem if something bad happens, you can still open this app.

 Open System Preferences→Security & Privacy→General. There before you is a strange new message: "[App's Name] was blocked from use because it is not from an identified developer." Well, you already knew that.

 Click Open Anyway.

Note: Alternatively, you can right-click or two-finger click the app's icon; from the shortcut menu, choose Open.

Now an "Are you sure you want to open it?" dialog box appears. If you click Open, the app finally runs, and will run without any further hassle from now on. Apple just wanted to make sure you know what you're doing.

Overall, Gatekeeper is a pretty convincing barrier to a Windows-like nightmare scenario, where some virus breaks out into the wild and takes down hundreds of thousands of computers. If most people leave the factory setting selected—and they will—that outcome is virtually impossible.

FileVault

FileVault is one of macOS's most powerful security features. Understanding what it does, however, may take a little slogging.

As you know, the accounts system is designed to keep people out of one another's stuff. Ordinarily, for example, Chris isn't allowed to go rooting through Robin's email and files.

Until FileVault came along, though, there were ways to circumvent this protection system. A sneak or a show-off could start up the Mac in FireWire disk mode, for example, or even remove the hard drive and hook it up to a Linux machine or another Mac.

In each case, he'd then be able to run rampant through everybody's files, changing or trashing them with abandon. For people with sensitive or private files, the result was a security hole bigger than Warren Buffett's bank account.

FileVault is an extra line of defense. When you turn on this feature, your Mac automatically *encrypts* (scrambles) *everything* on your startup hard drive—not just what's in your Home folder. Every time you create or save a new file, it, too, is insta-encrypted.

Note: FileVault uses something called XTS-AES 128 encryption. How secure is that? It would take a password-guessing computer *149 trillion years* before hitting pay dirt. Or, put another way, slightly longer than two *Transformers* movies.

This means unless someone knows (or can figure out) your password, FileVault renders your files unreadable for anyone but you and your computer's administrator—no matter what sneaky tricks they try to pull. (You can, if you like, authorize other account holders to get in, too.)

You won't notice much difference when FileVault is turned on. You log in as usual, clicking your name and typing your password. Only a slight pause as you log out indicates that macOS is doing some housekeeping on the encrypted files: freeing up some space and/or backing up your home directory with Time Machine.

Here are some things you should know about FileVault's protection:

- **It's useful only if you've logged out.** Once you're logged in, the entire drive is unlocked and accessible. If you want the protection, be sure to log out before you wander away from the Mac.

- **An administrator can access your files, too.** According to macOS's caste system, anyone with an Administrator account can theoretically have unhindered access

UP TO SPEED

Password Hell

In macOS, you have quite a few different passwords to keep straight. Each one, however, has a specific purpose:

Account password. You type this password in at the normal Login screen. You can't get into anyone else's account with it—only yours. Entering this password unlocks FileVault, too.

Administrator password. You're asked to enter this password whenever you try to install new software or modify certain system settings. If you're the only one who uses your computer (or you're the one who controls it), your administrator password *is* your account password. Otherwise, you're supposed to go find an administrator (the parent, teacher,

or guru who set up your account to begin with) and ask that person to type in his name and password once he's assessed what you're trying to do.

Recovery key. Think of this password as a master key. If anyone with FileVault forgets her account password, the administrator who knows the master password can unlock the account. This master password also lets an administrator change an account's password right at the Login screen, whether FileVault is turned on or not.

Root password. This password is rarely useful for anything other than Unix hackery; you know who you are.

to his peasants' files—even with FileVault on—if that administrator has the master password (the recovery key) described in the box on the facing page.

- **FileVault relies on the Recovery HD partition.** You can read about this secret chunk of your hard drive on page 779. For now, the point is that if you've deliberately reformatted your hard drive in some nonstandard way, you may not be able to use FileVault.

- **FileVault can encrypt external drives, too—even flash drives.** The controls to do this, though, are in a different place—not in System Preferences at all. Instead, open Disk Utility (in your Utilities folder). Erase the external drive using Mac OS Extended (Journaled, Encrypted) format. (And, yes, you have to *erase* the drive before you can encrypt it.)

- **You can turn FileVault off at any time.** Just revisit the FileVault pane in System Preferences. (It takes time to decrypt your drive, but you can keep right on working.)

To turn FileVault on, proceed like this:

1. **In System Preferences, click Security & Privacy, and then click FileVault. Click the 🔒, authenticate yourself, and then click Turn On FileVault.**

 Now, remember, FileVault encrypts all your files. If you forget your Mac account password—well, that would be bad.

 Yeah, yeah, the peons with Standard accounts forget *their* account passwords all the time. But with FileVault, a forgotten password would mean *the entire hard drive is locked forever.* So Apple gives you, the technically savvy administrator, a back door, for use in that situation.

 It offers to let you use your iCloud password (your Apple ID) as the back door. That's a much more reasonable one than the alternative, the *recovery key*.

 The recovery key is a long, complicated override password like UK84-LVT5-YFX9-XN3K-LT53-PL9N. It gives you another way to unlock the encrypted drive, even without knowing the account holder's password.

2. **Choose the backdoor method you prefer: "my iCloud account" or "recovery key." Click Continue.**

 If you chose the recovery key, the Mac now shows it to you: a long, complicated string of numbers and letters and hyphens. Write it down and store it in a place you'll never lose it! Then click Continue.

 Either way, a list of account holders now appears (Figure 12-12, top). The button next to each one, Enable User, might sound like you're about to lead someone into drug addiction, but it's actually your chance to specify who else can unlock the disk by logging in.

Note: If an account has *no* password, you have to add one first. Click the Set Password button that appears.

3. **For each person you want to be able to log into this Mac with her own password, click Enable User. Type in that person's password and click OK. When you're finished, click Continue.**

(Anyone to whom you *don't* give access can still use the Mac—but only after persuading an administrator to come over and type in his name and password.)

4. **Click Restart.**

When you log in again, the Mac begins the process of encrypting your entire hard drive. This process takes a long time (the FileVault pane in System Preferences shows you the estimated remaining time), but you can keep using your Mac in the meantime. In theory, you won't feel much of a slowdown at all while the encrypting is going on. You can even restart or shut down the computer.

You shouldn't notice any speed hit as you *work* with an encrypted disk, either. You'll notice only a few small security-related changes. For example, you'll be asked for your password every time you wake the computer or exit the screen saver.

Figure 12-12:
Top: You have to explicitly give permission to each person you want to allow to log into your FileVault-protected Mac. Also, you won't get away with no-password accounts for this trick; Jane, shown here, won't be able to unlock the disk at all. Click Enable User to add a password to this account.

Bottom: Here's your recovery key: a skeleton key that can get you into your encrypted Mac even if the idiot administrator forgets his password. (You have no idea how often this happens.)

Note: Actually, there's one more change. When FileVault is turned on, you won't see the icon for the Recovery HD appear when you hold down the Option key at startup. It's still there, though, and you can still start up with the Recovery HD by pressing ⌘-R as your Mac starts up.

The Firewall

If you have a broadband, always-on connection, you're open to the internet 24 hours a day. It's theoretically possible for some cretin to use automated hacking software to flood you with data packets or to take control of your machine. MacOS's *firewall* feature puts up a barrier to such mischief. To turn it on, click the 🔒 on the Firewall pane in the Security & Privacy section of System Preferences, authenticate yourself, and then click Start.

Note: You don't need to turn on this firewall if your Mac connects to the internet through a wired or wireless router (including the AirPort base station). Virtually every router already has a built-in firewall that protects your entire network. (Similarly, if you're using the Internet Sharing feature described on page 653, then turn on the firewall only for the *first* Mac, the one connected right to the internet.)

In short: Use the firewall only if your Mac is connected *directly* to a cable modem, DSL box, or dial-up modem.

Fortunately, it's not a *complete* barrier. One of the great joys of having a computer is the ability to connect to other computers. Living in a cement crypt is one way to avoid getting infected, but it's not much fun.

Therefore, you can turn the firewall on by opening System Preferences→Security→ Firewall tab, authenticating, and then clicking Turn On Firewall. But you can also fine-tune the blockade.

To do that, click Firewall Options; you see something like Figure 12-13 at bottom. As you can sort of tell, macOS lets you allow or block internet connections individually for *each program* on your Mac. Here's what you'll find there:

- **Block all incoming connections.** This option might be better known as Paranoid Mode. You're allowed to do email and basic web surfing and a few other deep-seated services that macOS needs to get by. But all other kinds of network connections are blocked, including screen sharing, music sharing, and so on. This is a hard-core, meat-fisted firewall that, for most people, is more trouble than it's worth.

Tip: As you can tell from the wording of this item, macOS's firewall blocks only *incoming* connections, which covers most of the dangerous stuff. But if you'd also like your Mac to block *outgoing* internet connections, you can install a shareware firewall program like Little Snitch. It's available on this book's "Missing CD" page at *missingmanuals.com*.

- **[List of individual programs].** If the firewall is on but you haven't turned on "Block all," then the Mac uses this list of individual programs and features to determine what's allowed to accept network connections.

In this window (Figure 12-13, bottom), features of macOS itself are listed. They get added to this list automatically when you turn them on in System Preferences: File Sharing, Printer Sharing, and so on.

Figure 12-13:
Top: The macOS firewall starts with a simple button click. The fun stuff doesn't begin until you click Firewall Options.

Bottom: This pane lists the programs that have been given permission to receive communications from the internet. At any point, you can change a program's Block/ Allow setting, as shown here. You can also click the + button to navigate to your Applications folder and manually choose programs for inclusion.

Non-Apple programs can gain passage through your firewall, too. You can add one to the list manually by clicking the + below the list and choosing it by hand; or you can simply respond to the request box that pops up whenever a new program wants to accept incoming internet connections.

Click Allow for each such request (unless, of course, you see a request for an app called SneakyPoisonVirus or something). As you do so, their names get added to the list of programs in this dialog box.

For each program, you can use the pop-up menu beside its name to specify either "Allow incoming connections" or "Block incoming connections," depending on your level of paranoia.

Note: From time to time, some program will ask for permission to accept incoming messages from its mother ship online. If it's a program you trust, then click Allow.

- **Automatically allow built-in software to receive incoming connections** refers to the Apple apps that came with your Mac. Presumably, it's safe to let them talk to the internet.

- **Automatically allow downloaded signed software to receive incoming connections.** *Signed* software means programs Apple recognizes as coming from legitimate companies.

Note: OK, technically, a signed program is one whose authenticity is confirmed by a third party—a "certificate authority" company like Verisign or GoDaddy. A system of invisible *keys* (security numbers) confirms that the software did indeed come from the creators it claims it came from, no matter how many detours it took to reach you.

One more point: When you explicitly grant permission to a program, as described above, *you're* signing that program.

If this checkbox is *not* turned on, then each time you run a new program for the first time, you'll be interrupted so the Mac can ask if it's OK to permit internet connections. The "signed software" box cuts down on the interruptions, since well-known apps are assumed not to be viruses or spyware.

- **Enable stealth mode.** This is designed to slam shut the Mac's back door to the internet. See, hackers often use automated tools that send out "Are you there?" messages. They're hoping to find computers that are turned on and connected full time to the internet. If your machine responds, and they can figure out how to get into it, they'll use it, without your knowledge, as a relay station for pumping out spam or masking their hacking footsteps.

"Enable stealth mode," then, makes your Mac even more invisible on the network; it means your Mac won't respond to the electronic signal called a *ping.* (On the other hand, *you* won't be able to ping your machine, either, when you're on the road and want to know if it's turned on and online.)

Note: You might have noticed that there doesn't seem to be any option to turn on *firewall logging,* which creates a little text file where macOS records every attempt that anyone from the outside makes to infiltrate your Mac. Logging is available, though—in fact, it's turned on all the time. To view the log, open the Applications→ Utilities→Console program. In the left-side list, expand the */private/var/log* heading, and click *appfirewall.log.*

The Password Assistant

Plenty of software features require you to make up a password: websites, accounts, networked disks, and so on. No wonder most people wind up trying to use the same password in as many situations as possible. Worse, they use something easily guessable like their names, kids' names, spouse's names, and so on. Even regular English words

aren't very secure, because hackers routinely use *dictionary attacks*—software that tries to guess your password by running through every word in the dictionary—to break in.

To prevent evildoers from guessing your passwords, macOS comes with a good-password suggestion feature called the Password Assistant (Figure 12-14). It cheerfully generates one suggestion after another for impossible-to-guess passwords (*recharges8@ exchangeability*, anyone?).

Figure 12-14:
Anyplace you're supposed to make up a password, including in the Users & Groups pane of System Preferences, a key icon appears. When you click it, the Password Assistant opens. Use the pop-up menu and the Length slider to specify how long and unguessable the password should be. The Quality graph shows you just how tough it is to crack this password.

(In the Type pop-up menu, you might wonder about FIPS-181. It stands for the Federal Information Processing Standards Publication 181, which sets forth the U.S. government's standard for password-generating algorithms.)

Fortunately, *you* won't have to remember most of them, thanks to the Keychain password-memorizing feature described next. The only password you have to memorize is your account password.

The Keychain

The information explosion carries with it a colossal annoyance: the proliferation of *passwords* we have to memorize. Shared folders on the network, websites, FTP sites—each requires another password.

Apple has done the world a mighty favor with its *Keychain* feature. (It's an earlier, not-internet-based version of the iCloud Keychain described on page 729.) Whenever you log into macOS and type in your password, you've typed the master code that tells the computer, "It's really me. I'm at my computer now." From that moment on, the Mac *automatically* fills in every password blank you encounter, whether it's a website in Safari, a shared disk on your network, a wireless network, an encrypted disk image, or an FTP (File Transfer Protocol) program like Transmit or Cyberduck. With only a few exceptions, you can safely forget *all* your passwords except your login password.

All kinds of programs and services know about the Keychain and offer to store your passwords there. For example:

- **In Safari, when you type your name and password** for a web page and then click OK, a dialog box asks: "Would you like to save this password?" (See Figure 12-15, top.)

Note: This offer is valid only if, in Safari→Preferences→AutoFill tab, "User names and passwords" is turned on. If not, the "Would you like to save this password?" message never appears.

Note, too, that some websites use a nonstandard login system that doesn't produce the "Would you?" message. Keychain can't help you there.

Figure 12-15:
Top: Safari is one of several internet-based programs that offer to store your passwords in the Keychain; just click Save Password. The next time you visit this web page, you'll find your name and password already typed in.

At any time, you can see a complete list of the memorized web passwords by choosing Safari→ Preferences→Passwords.

Bottom: When you connect to a server (a shared disk or folder on the network), just turn on "Remember this password in my keychain."

- **When you connect to a shared folder or disk** on the network, the opportunity to save the password in your Keychain is equally obvious (Figure 12-15, bottom).

- **You also see a "Remember password (add to Keychain)"** option when you create an encrypted disk image using Disk Utility.

- **Mac email programs, like Mail and Outlook,** store your email account passwords in your Keychain. So do FTP programs; check their Preferences dialog boxes.

- **Your iCloud account information** is stored in the Keychain, too (as you entered it on the iCloud pane of System Preferences).

- **A "Remember password" option appears** when you type in the password for a wireless network or an AirPort base station.

- **The Music, TV, and Podcasts apps memorize** your iTunes Store password, too.

Locking and unlocking the Keychain

If you work alone, the Keychain is automatic and generally wonderful. Login is the only time you have to type a password. After that, the Mac figures, "Hey, I know it's you; I'll fill in all your other passwords." You've *unlocked* your Keychain by logging in.

But there may be times when you want the Keychain to *stop* filling in all your passwords, perhaps only temporarily. Maybe you work in an office where someone else might sit down at your Mac while you're getting a candy bar.

Of course, you can have macOS lock your Mac—Keychain and all—after a specified period of inactivity (page 504). But if you want to lock the Keychain *manually,* so that no passwords are autofilled until you unlock it again, you can use any of these methods. Each requires the Keychain Access program (in your Applications→Utilities folder):

- **Lock the Keychain manually.** In the Keychain Access program, choose File→Lock Keychain "login" (⌘-L), or just click the big lock picture in the toolbar (shown in Figure 12-16).

- **Lock the Keychain automatically.** In the Keychain Access app, choose Edit→Change Settings for Keychain [your name]. The resulting box lets you set up the Keychain

Figure 12-16:
In the main Keychain list, you can double-click a listing for more details about a certain password– including the actual password being stored. To see the password, turn on "Show password." The first time you try this, you're asked to prove your worthiness by entering your Keychain password (usually your account password). If you then click Always Allow, you won't be bothered for a password-to-see-this-password again.

to lock itself, say, five minutes after the last time you used your Mac, or whenever the Mac sleeps. When you return, you're asked to reenter your account password in order to unlock the Keychain, restoring your auto-password feature.

Whenever the Keychain is locked, macOS no longer fills in your passwords.

Managing Keychain

To take a look at your Keychain, open the Keychain Access program in Applications→ Utilities. By clicking one of the password rows, you get to see its attributes—name, kind, account, and so on (Figure 12-16, bottom).

Tip: The primary purpose of the Keychain is, of course, to type in passwords for you automatically. However, it's also an excellent place to record all kinds of private information just for your own reference: credit card numbers, ATM numbers, and so on. Simply choose File→New Password Item (if it's a name and password) or File→New Secure Note Item (if you want to type a blob of very, very private text).

No, the Mac won't type them in for you automatically anywhere, but it will maintain them in one central location that is, itself, password-protected.

Multiple Keychains

By choosing File→New Keychain, you can create more than one Keychain, each with its own master password. On one hand, this might defeat the simplicity goal of the Keychain. On the other hand, it's conceivable that you might want to encrypt all your business documents with one master password and all your personal stuff with another, for example.

If you do have more than one Keychain, you can view all of them by clicking the little Show Keychains button at the lower-left corner of the Keychain Access window; now you see a list of all your Keychains (including some maintained by macOS itself). Click their names to switch among them.

Keychain files

Keychains are represented by separate files in your Home→Library→Keychains folder. Knowing that can be handy when you want to delete a Keychain or to copy it to another Mac—your laptop, for example. (Then again, the File→Export command may be even more convenient.)

16 Privacy Shields

In Apple's mind, there's a difference between *security* (protecting your Mac) and *privacy* (protecting your information from distribution).

The Privacy tab in the Security & Privacy pane of System Preferences harbors a list of privacy-related options. Each represents one hunk of your Mac's hardware or software that some app might seek to use—and lets you allow or disallow your apps' access.

The complete list: Location Services, Contacts, Calendars, Reminders, Photos, Camera, Microphone, Speech Recognition, Accessibility, Input Monitoring, Full Disk Access, Files and Folders, Screen Recording, Automation, Analytics, and Advertising.

During your first few days in Catalina, you get a lot of weird messages about one or another of these. You're told that a program you're about to open would like access to your camera, or microphone, or location, or screen recording, and so on.

It's plausible, for example, that a weather app would like access to your location, that Skype wants access to your contacts, and that QuickTime Player wants to use your camera and microphone.

If it's a program you've installed and you've opened, it's safe to proceed about 99.99 percent of the time. Apple is just proceeding with super-abundant caution here. In case it turns out that Beekeeper Pro was accessing your to-do list and it becomes a big public scandal, at least Apple can say it warned you.

But Svetlana's Exxtra Hot Love Game, which you downloaded from the Dark Web, asks for access to your location, contacts, calendar, and photos—well, probably not.

The last two items in this list are slightly different:

- **Analytics.** These checkboxes permit your Mac to send data to Apple (and relevant software companies) about what's going on with your Mac and your iCloud activity. (Anonymously, of course—Apple doesn't know it's you.) The transmissions include details about crashes and freezes, what programs and hardware you use, what software versions and peripherals you have, and so on.

- **Advertising.** "Limit Ad Tracking" doesn't mean you'll see fewer ads on the web—but they'll have less to do with your interests, because advertisers will have a harder time knowing what your interests are. (And just in case, Reset Advertising Identifier deletes whatever data advertisers already have on you; you appear as a newly hatched, anonymous webster.)

 Three Apple apps sometimes display ads right within them: News, Stocks, and the App Store. These ads are chosen just for you—and other people in your city, with your kind of Mac, who perform your kind of App Store searches, and who read your kind of articles in News and Stocks. (If you ever want to know why Apple thinks you'd be interested in a certain ad, click the little Ad logo on it.)

 Hit View Ad Information to see what kind of data Apple has collected about you for this purpose.

Networking, File Sharing & Remote Access

Networks are awesome. Once you've got a home or office network, you can copy files from one machine to another—even between Windows PCs and Macs—just as you'd drag files between folders on your own Mac. You can send little messages to other people's screens. Everyone on the network can consult the same database or calendar, or listen to the same music collection. You can play games over the network. You can share a single printer or cable modem among all the Macs in the office. You can connect to the network from wherever you are in the world, using the internet as the world's longest extension cord back to your office.

In macOS, you can even do *screen sharing,* which means that you, the wise computer whiz, can see what's on the screen of your pathetic, floundering relative or buddy elsewhere on the network. You can seize control of the other Mac's mouse and keyboard. You can troubleshoot, fiddle with settings, and so on. It's the next best thing to being there—often, a lot *better* than being there.

This chapter also explores various advanced methods of manipulating your Mac from the road, including *remote access* technologies like FTP, SSH, and virtual private networking (VPN).

Wiring the Network

Most people connect their computers using one of two connection systems: Ethernet or Wi-Fi.

Note: Apple used to have its own name for Wi-Fi: AirPort. That's what it said in System Preferences→Network, for example, and that's what the 📶 menulet was called. *AirPort* was a lot cleverer , wordplay-wise, than the meaningless "Wi-Fi." Unfortunately, not many people realized that AirPort was the same thing as what the rest of the world called Wi-Fi. So at least in its onscreen references, these days, Apple gives AirPort a new name: Wi-Fi.

Ethernet Networks

Every desktop Mac has an Ethernet jack (Figure 13-1). Apple laptops don't have Ethernet jacks built in, but you can add one in the form of an adapter that plugs into one of your USB jacks.

Figure 13-1:
Every desktop Mac has a built-in Ethernet jack (left). It looks like an overweight telephone jack. It connects to an Ethernet router or hub (right) via an Ethernet cable (also known as Cat 5 or Cat 6), which ends in what looks like an overweight telephone-wire plug (also known as an RJ-45 connector).

Ethernet jack

Ethernet hub

If you connect all the Macs and Ethernet printers in your small office to a central Ethernet hub, switch, or *router*—a compact, inexpensive box with jacks for five, ten, or even more computers and printers—you've got yourself a very fast, very reliable network. (Most people wind up hiding the hub in a closet and running the wiring either along the edges of the room or inside the walls.) You can buy Ethernet cables, plus the hub, at any computer store or, less expensively, from an internet-based mail-order house; none of this stuff is Mac-specific.

Tip: If you want to connect only two Macs—say, your laptop and your desktop machine—you don't need an Ethernet hub. Instead, you just need a standard Ethernet cable. Run it directly between the Ethernet jacks of the two computers. Then connect the Macs as described in the box on the facing page.

Or don't use Ethernet at all; just use a person-to-person Wi-Fi network.

Ethernet is the best networking system for many offices. It's fast, easy, and cheap.

Wi-Fi Networks

Wi-Fi, known to the geeks as 802.11, means wireless networking. It's the technology that lets laptops get online at high speed in any Wi-Fi "hotspot." Hotspots are everywhere these days: in homes, offices, coffee shops, hotels, airports, and thousands of other places.

When you're in a Wi-Fi hotspot, your Mac has a very fast connection to the internet, as though it were connected to a cable modem or DSL.

Every Mac has Wi-Fi circuitry. It lets you connect to your network and the internet wirelessly, as long as you're within about 150 feet of a *base station* or (as Windows people call it) an *access point.* That box must in turn be physically connected to a network and internet connection.

The base station can take any of these forms:

- **AirPort base station.** Apple's sleek, white, squarish base stations ($100 to $200) come in two flavors, Express and Extreme, and permit as many as 50 computers to connect simultaneously. All of them have USB ports to connect printers, and you can also hook up an external hard drive to the AirPort Extreme.

- **A Time Capsule.** This Apple gizmo is exactly the same as the AirPort base station, except that it also contains a huge hard drive so that it can back up your Macs automatically over the wired or wireless network.

- **A wireless broadband router.** Linksys, Belkin, and lots of other companies make less expensive Wi-Fi base stations. You can plug the base station into an Ethernet router or hub, thus permitting 10 or 20 wireless-equipped computers, including Macs, to join an existing Ethernet network without wiring. (With all due non-fanboyism, however, Apple's base stations and software are more polished and satisfying to use.)

Tip: It's perfectly possible to plug a Wi-Fi base station into a regular router, too, to accommodate both wired and wireless computers.

- **Another Mac.** Your Mac can also *impersonate* an AirPort base station. In effect, the Mac becomes a software-based base station, and you save yourself the cost of a separate physical base station.

GEM IN THE ROUGH

Networking Without the Network

In a pinch, you can connect two Macs without any real network at all. You can create an Ethernet connection without a hub or a router—or an AirPort connection without a Wi-Fi base station.

To set up the wired connection, just run a standard Ethernet cable between the Ethernet jacks of the two Macs. (You don't need to use an Ethernet crossover cable, as you did in days of old.) To set up a wireless connection, from your 🛜 menulet, choose Create Network. Make up a name for your little private network, and then click OK. On the second Mac, choose 🛜→Join Network, enter the same private network name, and then click Join.

At this point, your two Macs belong to the same ad hoc micronetwork. If you've shared some folders on the first Mac, its name (like "Casey's iMac") now appears in the Sidebar of the second Mac. Click it to see what's on it.

From here, proceed exactly as described on page 537.

• **A modem.** A few, proud people still get online by dialing via modem, which is built into some old AirPort base station models. The base station is plugged into a phone jack. Wireless Macs in the house can get online by triggering the base station to dial by remote control.

Tip: If you connect through a modern router or AirPort base station, you already have a great firewall protecting you. You don't have to turn on macOS's firewall.

You use the AirPort Utility (in your Applications→Utilities folder) to set up your base station; if you have a typical cable modem or DSL, the setup practically takes care of itself.

Whether you've set up your own wireless network or want to hop onto somebody else's, page 647 has the full scoop on *joining* Wi-Fi networks.

Cell Networks

If you have an iPhone or a similar cellphone, you may be able to get your Mac online even when you're hundreds of miles from the nearest Ethernet jack or Wi-Fi hotspot. Thanks to *tethering,* your phone can act as an internet antenna for your laptop, relying on the slow, expensive, but almost ubiquitous *cellular* network for its connection. Details are on page 650.

FireWire Networks

Apple is busily phasing out the convenient, fast *FireWire* jacks on its Macs. But if you have two FireWire-equipped Macs, you can create a blazing-fast connection between

UP TO SPEED

802 Dot Whatever: Better Every Year

Over the years, networking gear has come in several flavors, each offering different degrees of speed, distance, and compatibility. They have such appetizing-sounding names as 802.11a, 802.11g, 802.11n, and 802.11ac.

In general, each generation of Wi-Fi gear improves the speed and range of your hotspot. (Note that you never get the "up to" speed printed on the box; in fact, you'll usually get around half that speed, since a wireless network uses a lot of the bandwidth for such network housekeeping chores as correcting transmission errors.)

The current standard is 802.11ac, which offers better speed *and* better range than its predecessors (thanks to multiple antennas). Remember, though, you won't get the better speed unless both your base station *and* your networking cards "speak" ac.

Meanwhile, keep in mind that faster equipment doesn't speed up your email and web activity. A cable modem or a DSL box delivers internet information at a fraction of the speed of your home or office network. The bottleneck is the internet connection, not your network.

Instead, the speed boost you get with newer Wi-Fi gear is useful only for transferring files *among computers on your network,* streaming video or audio *between computers* (or PCs and your TV), and playing networked games.

Finally, the great thing about wireless networking is that it all works together, no matter what kind of computer you have. There's no such thing as an "Apple" wireless network or a "Windows" wireless network. All computers work with any kind of access point.

them with nothing more than a FireWire cable. Details are in the free downloadable appendix to this chapter called "FireWire Networking." It's available on this book's "Missing CD" page at *missingmanuals.com*.

File Sharing: Three Ways

When you're done wiring (or not wiring, as the case may be), your network is ready. Your Mac should "see" any Ethernet or shared USB printers, in readiness to print (page 579). You can now play network games or use a network calendar. And you can now turn on *file sharing,* one of the most useful features of all.

In file sharing, you can drag files back and forth between different Macs (or even Windows PCs) on the network, exactly as though the other computer's folder or disk were a hard drive connected to your own machine.

The thing is, it's not easy being Apple. You have to write *one* operating system that's supposed to please *everyone,* from the self-employed, first-time newbie to the network administrator for NASA. You have to design a networking system simple enough for the laptop owner who just wants to copy things to a desktop Mac when returning from a trip, yet secure and flexible enough for the network designer at a large corporation.

Clearly, different people have different attitudes about the need for security and flexibility.

That's why macOS offers *three ways* to share files, striking three different positions along the simplicity-to-flexibility spectrum:

- **The easiest way: AirDrop.** This feature is dreamy—if there are other people in your house or office who have Apple stuff (Macs, iPhones, iPads, iPod Touches). Imagine this: You open the AirDrop folder, where you see everybody else's icons. To give someone a file, you drop its icon on that person's face. Done.

- **Slightly harder way: the Public folder.** Every account holder has a Public folder. It's free for anyone else on the network to access. Like a grocery store bulletin board, there's no password required. Super-convenient, super-easy.

 There's only one downside, and you may not care about it: You have to move or copy files *into* the Public folder before anyone else can see them. Depending on how many files you want to share, this can get tedious, disrupt your standard organizational structure, and eat up disk space.

- **The flexible way: any folder.** You can also make *any* file, folder, or disk available for inspection by other people on the network. This method means you don't have to move files into the Public folder, for starters. It also gives you elaborate control over who is allowed to do what to your files. You might want to permit your company's executives to see *and* edit your documents, but allow the peons in Accounting just to see them. And Andy, that unreliable goofball in Sales? You don't want him even *seeing* what's in your shared folder.

Of course, setting up all those levels of control means more work and more complexity.

The following pages tackle these three methods one at a time.

AirDrop

AirDrop is one of macOS's star attractions. It's a breakthrough in speed, simplicity, and efficiency. There's no setup, no passwords involved. It lets you copy files to someone else's Mac, iPhone, iPad, or iPod Touch up to 30 feet away, instantly and wirelessly; you don't need an internet connection or even a Wi-Fi network. It works on a flight, a beach, or a sailboat in the middle of the Atlantic. It also works if you're on a Wi-Fi network, doing other things online.

Sending by AirDrop

Usually, you begin the sending process in one of two ways:

- **From the Finder.** Right-click or two-finger click the file's icon. From the shortcut menu, choose Share→AirDrop. The box shown in Figure 13-2 appears.

Note: Here's a second way to send something in the Finder: Open the AirDrop *window*. (It's listed in the Sidebar at the left side of every Finder window. Or choose Go→AirDrop, or press Shift-⌘-R.) Drag the icon(s) you want to send onto the icon of the receiving device (Figure 13-3).

- **From an app.** When you're looking at whatever you want to send, click the ⬆ button. From the shortcut menu, choose AirDrop.

 And where is that ⬆ button? Everywhere. It's at the top of every Finder window and at the top of every Quick Look window. It's in Open and Save boxes. It's available on every page in Safari, map in Maps, photo in Photos, contact in Contacts, and note in Notes. Lots of non-Apple apps offer that ⬆ button, too. (See page 258 for more on the Share button.)

 In each case, you should now proceed as shown in Figure 13-2.

Figure 13-2:
The icons of nearby AirDrop-friendly Apple gadgets and Macs show up in this fun-sized window. You've already said what you want to send; now you just have to specify who gets it. Click the destination device's icon.

A message appears on the other gadget's screen, asking if the owner wants to accept your file. If she chooses Accept, then the transaction is complete. Quick, effortless, wireless, delightful.

Note: At one time, you and your recipient's Mac both had to have their AirDrop windows open. That's no longer true; AirDrop works whether that window is open or not.

Figure 13-3:
If there are other recent Macs within about 30 feet, you see their logged-in owners' icons here. Usually, the icons display the Mac owners' account pictures; but if they have facial photos in your Contacts, then you see those instead.

Reasons AirDrop Might Seem Not to Work

Miraculous though AirDrop may seem when it's working, certain stars do have to be in alignment. If AirDrop isn't working as advertised, here are some things to check:

• **The recipient may have AirDrop turned off or restricted.** If he's got an iOS device, ask him to open his Control Center and long-press the Wi-Fi button cluster, and then tap the AirDrop icon. If he's on a Mac, have him open the AirDrop window.

In each case, he can control who can AirDrop him: Off (nobody), Contacts Only (people in his address book), or Everyone. It's supposed to be a security precaution, but Everyone is a perfectly fine choice; after all, you have to approve every file individually, so it's not as though some passing hacker can shove evil files down your throat.

• **AirDrop requires both sending and receiving devices** to be on (awake).

• **Both sender and receiver must have Bluetooth and Wi-Fi turned on.** They also have to be within about 30 feet of each other.

• **AirDrop doesn't work with really old Apple models or operating systems.** It does work with Apple products made since about 2010. On the Mac, AirDrop requires macOS Lion or later. On an iPhone, iPad, or iPod Touch, it requires iOS 7 or later.

- If your Mac can't seem to "see" other nearby, older Macs (pre-2012 models)—either when sending or receiving an AirDrop file—the process may require an extra step. If you've right-clicked or two-finger clicked an icon or used the ⬆ button in a program, click "Don't see who you're looking for?" at top right (see Figure 13-2) and then click Search for an Older Mac.

 The "Don't see who you're looking for?" link also appears in the AirDrop *window* in the Finder (you can see it in Figure 13-3). Here again, only by clicking Search for an Older Mac will you see the icons for pre-2012 Mac models show up.

 And, by the way: When your Mac is seeing those *older* Macs, it can't see *newer* ones—and vice versa.

- If you don't see the AirDrop icon in your Finder's Sidebar, it's because somebody turned off its checkbox in Finder→Preferences→Sidebar. (You can still use AirDrop, though.)

- AirDrop doesn't work if you've turned on "Block all connections" in your firewall (page 515).

Receiving a File by AirDrop

If someone's sending *you* a file by AirDrop, the steps depend on whether you're using a Mac or an i-gadget:

- **Receiving on the Mac.** You get a notification (see Figure 13-4).

Tip: Actually, if you're sending something to *yourself*—from your phone to your Mac, for example—this notification is slightly different, in that it offers an Open button. Apple notices that both devices are signed into the same iCloud account and figures you don't need protection from *yourself*.

The file winds up in your Downloads folder. This folder generally sits on the Dock, so it's easy to find. But you can also choose Go→Downloads, or press Option-⌘-L, to jump there.

Figure 13-4:
A file arriving on your Mac via AirDrop announces itself with a notification. You can click either Decline (you don't want the file) or Accept. If you click Accept, the file transfer proceeds automatically. The transfer is encrypted, so evildoers nearby have no clue what you're transferring (or even that you're transferring). It winds up in your Downloads folder.

- **Receiving on an iPhone/iPad/iPod Touch.** A message says "[Other person's name] would like to share [the file's name]." Tap Decline or Accept.

 If your iOS device knows what to do with the file, it opens automatically in the appropriate app (a photo in Photos, a web page in Safari, and so on).

If you're the one receiving a file, you can cancel a half-finished transfer by clicking the ⊗ on the progress bar that wraps around the sender's icon in the AirDrop window.

Note: AirDrop also works from an iPhone *to* a Mac, of course. For directions on sending a file in that direction, see page 307.

Sharing Your Public Folder

All right. If AirDrop is so great, why doesn't it wipe out all other forms of file transfer and save this book a bunch of pages? Because (a) it works only on Macs and Apple devices, (b) it works only wirelessly, and (c) it's a one-way street. Other people can't take files from your Mac—you have to shove the files to them.

This next method eliminates those limitations. It's the Public-folder method.

Inside your Home folder, there's a folder called Public. (Inside *everybody's* Home folder is a folder called Public.) Anything you put into this folder is automatically available to everyone else on the network. They don't need a password, they don't need an account on your Mac—they just have to be on the same network, wireless or wired. They can put files here *or* copy things out.

To make your Public folder available to your networkmates, you have to turn on the File Sharing master switch. Choose System Preferences→Sharing, and then turn on File Sharing (as shown in Figure 13-5).

Now round up the files and folders you want to share with all comers on the network and drag them into your Home→Public folder. That's all there is to it.

Note: You may notice that there's already something in your Public folder: a subfolder called Drop Box. It's there so that other people can give *you* files from across the network, as described on page 535.

So now that you've set up Public folder sharing, how are other people supposed to access your Public folder? See page 537.

Sharing Any Folder

If the Public-folder method seems too simple and restrictive, you can graduate to the "share any folder" method. In this scheme, you can make *any* file, folder, or disk available to other people on the network.

The advantage here is that you don't have to move your files into the Public folder; they can sit right where you have them. And this time you can set up elaborate *sharing*

privileges (also known as *permissions*) that grant individuals different levels of access to your files.

This method is more complicated to set up than that Public-folder business. In fact, just to underline its complexity, Apple has created two different setup procedures. You can share one icon at a time by opening its Get Info window; or you can work in a master list of shared items in System Preferences. The following pages cover both methods.

The Get Info Method

Here's how to share a Mac file, disk, or folder disk using its Get Info window. The following steps assume you've turned on System Preferences→Sharing→File Sharing, as shown in Figure 13-5.

Figure 13-5:
Here's the master switch that makes your Public folder (and any other folders you designate) available to other people on the network. You can edit the Computer Name, if you like. Your Mac will appear on the network with this name. Make it nice and descriptive, such as Front Desk iMac.

1. **Select the folder or disk you want to share. Choose File→Get Info.**

 The Get Info dialog box appears (Figure 13-6). Expand the General panel if it's not already visible.

Note: Sharing an entire disk means every folder and file on it is available to anyone you give access to. On the other hand, by sharing only a folder or two, you can keep *most* of the stuff on your hard drive private, out of view of curious network comrades. Sharing only a folder or two does *them* a favor, too, by making it easier for them to find the files they're supposed to have. This way, they don't have to root through your entire drive looking for the stuff they actually need.

2. **Turn on "Shared folder."**

If file sharing isn't turned on, you're asked to confirm; click Enable. Enter your administrator password, if necessary.

Tip: To help you remember what you've made available to other people on the network, a banner labeled "Shared Folder" appears across the top of any Finder window you've shared. It even appears at the top of the Open and Save dialog boxes.

OK, this disk or folder is now shared. But with whom?

3. **Expand the Sharing & Permissions panel, if it's not already visible. Click the 🔒 icon and enter your administrator's password.**

The controls in the Sharing & Permissions area spring to life and become editable. At the bottom of the Info panel is a little table. The first column can display the names of individual account holders, like Casey or Chris, or *groups* of account holders, like Everyone or Accounting Dept.

The second column lists the *privileges* each person or group has for this folder.

Now, the average person has no clue what "privileges" means, and this is why things get a little hairy when you're setting up folder-by-folder permissions. But read on; it's not as bad as it seems.

Figure 13-6:
The file-sharing permissions controls are here, in the Get Info box for any file, folder, or disk.

4. Edit the table by adding people's names. Then set their access permissions.

At the moment, your name appears in the Name column, and it probably says Read & Write in the Privilege column. In other words, you're currently the master of this folder. You can put things in, and you can take things out.

If you just want to share files with *yourself,* so you can transfer them from one computer to another, you can stop here.

If you want to share files with *other* people—well, at the moment, the privileges for Everyone are probably set to "Read only." Other people can see this folder, but they can't do anything with it.

Your job is to work through this list of people, specifying *how much* control each person has over the file or folder you're sharing.

To add the name of a person or group, click the ✚ button below the list. The list shown in Figure 13-7 appears.

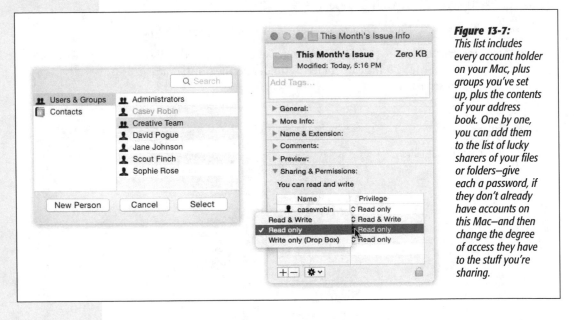

Figure 13-7:
This list includes every account holder on your Mac, plus groups you've set up, plus the contents of your address book. One by one, you can add them to the list of lucky sharers of your files or folders—give each a password, if they don't already have accounts on this Mac—and then change the degree of access they have to the stuff you're sharing.

Now click a name in the list. Then, from the Privilege pop-up menu, choose a permissions setting:

- **Read & Write** has the most access of all. This person, like you, can add, change, or delete any file in the shared folder, or make any changes she likes to a document. Give Read & Write permission to people you trust not to mess things up.

- **Read only** means "Look, but don't touch." This person can see what's in the folder (or file) and can copy it, but he can't delete or change the original. It's a good setting for distributing company documents or making source files available to your minions.

- **Write only (Drop Box)** means other people can't even open the folder. They can drop things *into* it, but it's like a mail slot: The letter disappears into the slot, and then it's too late for them to change their minds. As the folder's owner, you can do what you like with the deposited goodies. This drop-box effect is great when you want students, co-workers, or family members to be able to *turn things in* to you—homework, reports, scandalous diaries—without running the risk that someone else might see those files. (This option doesn't appear for documents—only disks and folders.)

- **No access** is an option only for Everyone. It means other people can see this file or folder's icon but can't do a thing with it.

Tip: Usually, you'll want the privileges for the folder to also apply to everything *inside* it; it would be a real drag to have to change the sharing privileges of the contents one icon at a time. That's why the ✿ menu at the bottom of the Get Info box has a command called "Apply to enclosed items."

5. **Close the Get Info window.**

 Now the folder is ready for invasion from across the network.

The System Preferences Method

It's very convenient to turn on sharing one folder at a time, using the Get Info window. But there's another way in, too, one that displays *all* your shared stuff in a handy master list.

To see it, choose System Preferences→Sharing→File Sharing (and make sure it's turned on). Now you're looking at a slightly different kind of permissions table, shown in Figure 13-8. It has *three* columns:

- **Shared Folders.** The first column lists the files, folders, and disks you've shared. You'll probably see that every account's *Public* folder is already listed here, since they're all shared automatically. (You can turn *off* sharing for a Public folder, too, just by clicking it and then clicking the − button.)

 But you can add more icons to this list. Either drag them into the list directly from the desktop or a Finder window, or click the +, navigate to the item you want to share, select it, and then click Add. Either way, that item now appears in the Shared Folders list.

- **Users.** When you click a shared item, the second column sprouts a list of *who* gets to work with it from across the network. You're listed here, of course, since it's your stuff. There's also a listing here for Everyone, which really means "everyone *else*"—that is, everyone who's not specifically listed here.

 You can add to this list, too. Click + to open the person-selection box shown in Figure 13-7. It lists the other account holders on your Mac, and some predefined groups, as well as the contents of your Contacts.

Note: Most of the Contacts people don't actually have accounts on this Mac, of course. If you choose somebody from this list, you're asked to make up an account password. When you click Create Account, you've actually created a *Sharing Only* account on your Mac for that person, as described in the box below. When you return to the Accounts pane of System Preferences, you'll see that new person listed.

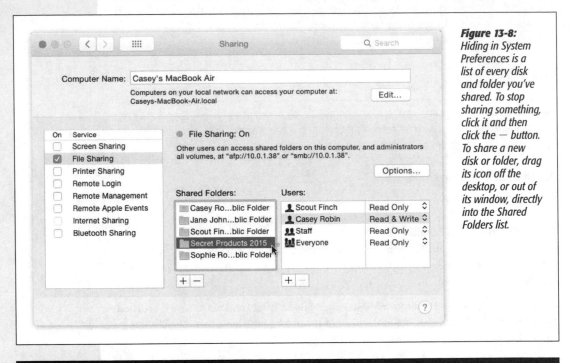

Figure 13-8:
Hiding in System Preferences is a list of every disk and folder you've shared. To stop sharing something, click it and then click the — button. To share a new disk or folder, drag its icon off the desktop, or out of its window, directly into the Shared Folders list.

GEM IN THE ROUGH

Sharing-Only Accounts

In the bad old days, you couldn't share your files with other people unless you first created full-blown accounts for them on your Mac. You know: a Home folder, Music and Movies folders, and so on. That was an awful lot of disk space sacrificed, just so other people could visit your Mac over the network.

Nowadays, you can create a Sharing Only account for them.

This way, you don't even have to set up a Home folder for them on your Mac, and they don't have to learn another name and password.

To set this up, open Contacts. Make sure there's a card for the person who will be visiting your Mac over the network.

Now visit System Preferences→Sharing. Click File Sharing. As shown in Figure 13-17, click the +. In the panel that appears, click Contacts, and then double-click the name of the prospective visitor. You're asked to enter a screen-sharing password for this person (twice) and then click Create Account.

That's the setup. (If you check the user list in System Preferences→Users & Groups, you'll see the new "Sharing Only" account in the list.)

When attempting to connect to your Mac, your guest can log in—even without a full-blown Home-folder account on your Mac!

Double-click a person's name to add her to the list of people who can access this item from over the network, and then set up the appropriate privileges (described next).

To *remove* someone from this list, just click the name and then click the — button.

- **User permissions.** This *third* column lets you specify how much access each person in the *second* column has to this folder. Your choices, once again, are Read & Write (full access to change or delete this item's contents); Read Only (open or copy, but can't edit or delete); and Write Only (Drop Box), which lets the person put things *into* this disk or folder, but not open it or see what else is in it.

 For the Everyone group, you also get an option called No Access, which means this item is completely off-limits to everyone else on the network.

And now, having slogged through all these options and permutations, your Mac is ready for invasion from across the network.

Accessing Shared Files

The previous pages have described *setting up* a Mac so people at other computers can access its files. There's an easy, limited way (use the Public folder) and a more elaborate way (turn on sharing settings for each folder individually).

Now comes the payoff for both methods: sitting at another computer and *connecting* to the one you set up. There are two ways to go about it: You can use the Sidebar, or you can use the older, more flexible Connect to Server command. The following pages cover both methods.

Connection Method A: Use the Sidebar

Suppose, then, you're seated in front of your Mac, and you want to see the files on another Mac on the network. Proceed like this:

1. **Open any Finder window. Click Network.**

 The Network icon appears in the Locations category of the Sidebar at the left side of the window. It reveals icons for all the computers on the network. See Figure 13-9.

Tip: The same Sidebar items show up in the Save and Open dialog boxes of your programs, too, making the entire network available to you for opening and saving files.

 If you don't see a certain Mac's icon here, it might be turned off, it might not be on the network, or it might have File Sharing turned off.

Note: Or it might not have the right file-sharing *type* turned on. To check, open System Preferences→Sharing; click File Sharing and then Options. You'll see checkboxes for AFP and SMB; your computers can't see each other if they don't have one of these options in common.

If you don't see any computers at all in the Network "folder," then *your* computer might not be on the network. Or maybe you've turned off the checkboxes for Connected Servers and Bonjour Computers in Finder→Preferences→Sidebar.

Tip: If the other Mac is just asleep, it still shows up in the Sidebar, and you can wake it up to get at it. How is that possible? Through the miracle of the Wake for Network Access feature described on page 347.

Figure 13-9:
Top: Click Network in the Sidebar. Macs appear in the Sidebar with whatever names they've been given in System Preferences→Sharing. Their icons usually resemble the computers themselves.

Bottom: When you open a computer's icon, you see whatever shared folders it contains—starting with a Public folder for each account holder.

If you're on a corporate-style network that has the sub-chunks known as *workgroups*, you may also see any "network neighborhoods" (limbs of your network tree). For example, you may see the names of network zones (clusters of machines, as found in big companies and universities).

Or, if you're trying to tap into a Windows machine, open the icon representing the *workgroup* (computer cluster) that contains the machine you want. In small office networks, it's usually called MSHOME or WORKGROUP. In big corporations, these workgroups can be called almost anything—as long as the name is no more than 15 letters long with no punctuation. (Thanks, Microsoft.)

If you *do* see icons for workgroups or other network "zones," double-click until you're seeing the icons for individual computers.

Note: If you're a network nerd, you may be interested to note that macOS can "see" servers that use the SMB/CIFS, NFS, FTP, and WebDAV protocols running on macOS Server, Unix, Linux, and Windows servers (NT, 2000, XP, Vista, and Windows 7, 8, or 10). But the Sidebar reveals *only* the shared computers on your *subnet* (your local, internal office network).

2. Double-click the computer whose files you want to open.

In the main window, you now see the Public Folder icons for each account holder on that computer: Mom, Dad, Sissy, whatever, as shown in Figure 13-9. (They *may* have shared other folders with you as well.) If you have an account on the other computer, you'll see a folder representing *your* stuff, too. At this point, you're considered a guest.

Note: This amount of access depends on a setting in System Preferences→Users & Groups. Click the Guest account to see it: "Allow guests to connect to shared folders." That checkbox is usually turned on—but it's something to check if you can't seem to connect.

From here, the remaining instructions diverge, depending on whether you want to access *other* people's stuff or *your* stuff. That's why there are two alternative versions of step 3 here:

3a. If you want to access the stuff that somebody else has left for you, then double-click that person's Public folder.

Instantly, that folder's contents appear in the Finder window.

POWER USERS' CLINIC

What You Can See

Precisely which other folders you can see on the remote Mac depend on what kind of account you have there: Guest, Standard, or Administrator (see the descriptions starting on page 487).

If you're using the Guest account, you can see only the Public folders. The rest of the Mac is invisible and off-limits to you. (You may see additional folders if somebody turned on sharing for them.)

If you have a Standard account, you can see other people's Public and Drop Box folders, plus your own Home folder. (Again, somebody may have made other folders available.)

If you're an administrator, you get to see icons for the account holders' Public folders and the hard drive itself to which you're connecting. In fact, you even get to see the names of any other disks connected to that Mac.

If you, O lucky administrator, open the hard drive, you'll discover you also have the freedom to see and manipulate the contents of the Applications, Desktop, Library, and Users→Shared folders. You can even see what folders are in other people's Home folders, although you can't open them or put anything into them.

Finally, there's something called the root user. This account has complete freedom to move or delete any file or folder anywhere, including critical system files that could disable your Mac. It also requires a degree in Unix.

In this situation, you're only a guest. You don't have to bother with a password. On the other hand, the only thing you can generally see inside the other person's account folder is his Public folder.

Tip: Actually, you *might* see other folders here—if the account holder has specifically shared them *and* decided that you're important enough to have access to them.

One thing you'll find inside the Public folder is the Drop Box folder. This folder exists so you can *give* files and folders to the other person. You can drop any of your own icons onto the Drop Box folder—but you can't open the Drop Box folder to see what *other* people have put there.

If you see anything else at all in the Public folder you've opened, it's stuff the account holder has copied there for the enjoyment of you and your networkmates. You're not allowed to delete anything from the other person's Public folder or make changes to anything in it.

You can, however, open those icons, read them, or even copy them to *your* Mac— and then edit *your* copies.

Tip: Every now and then, you'll click the name of a Mac in the Finder Sidebar, hoping to see its contents—and instead of seeing a list of the shared Public folders, you'll get a Not Connected or Connection Failed message at the top of your window.

In that case, go to the shared Mac and do this: Open System Preferences→Sharing. Click File Sharing and then Options. Turn off "Share files and folders using SMB." Close System Preferences. Often, that's all it takes to make your Mac visible and connectable from other Macs on the network. (If not, then try restarting the shared Mac to make the SMB change stick.)

Figure 13-10:
You can sign into your account on another Mac on the network (even while somebody else is using that Mac in person). Click Connect As (top right) and enter your name and password. Turn on "Remember this password in my keychain" to speed up the process for next time. No matter which method you use to connect to a shared folder or disk, its icon shows up in the Sidebar.

3b. **To access your own Home folder on the other Mac, click the Connect As button (Figure 13-10). Sign in as usual.**

When the "Connect to the file server" box appears, you're supposed to specify your account name and password (from the Mac you're tapping into). This is the same name and password you'd use to log in if you were actually sitting at that machine.

Type your account name (long or short version) and password. And if you didn't set up a password for your account, leave the password box empty.

Tip: The dialog box shown in Figure 13-10 includes the delightful and time-saving "Remember this password in my keychain" option, which makes the Mac memorize your password for a certain disk so you don't have to type it—or even see this dialog box—every darned time you connect. (If you have no password, though, then "Remember this password" doesn't work. You'll have to confront—and press Return to dismiss—the "Connect to the file server" box every time.)

When you click Connect (or press Return), the other Mac's icon shows up in your Sidebar, and its contents appear in the main window. (The other Mac's icon may also show up on the desktop, if you've turned on the "Connected Servers" option in Finder→Preferences→Sidebar.)

Note: Once you've connected to a Mac using your account, the other Mac has a lock on your identity. You'll be able to connect to the other Mac over and over again during this same computing session, without ever having to retype your password.

In the meantime, you can double-click icons to open them, make copies of them, and otherwise manipulate them exactly as though they were icons on your own hard drive. Depending on what permissions you've been given, you can even edit or trash those files.

Tip: There's one significant difference between working with "local" icons and working with those that sit elsewhere on the network. When you delete a file from another Mac on the network, either by pressing the Delete key or by dragging it to the Trash, a message appears to let you know that you're about to delete that item instantly and permanently. It won't simply land in the Trash "folder," awaiting the Empty Trash command.

GEM IN THE ROUGH

Faster Ways to Connect Next Time

If you expect that you might want to access a shared disk or folder again later, take a moment to make an alias of it. The easiest way is to press Option-⌘ as you drag it out of the window where it first appears. Next time, you can bring it back to your screen just by double-clicking the alias. And if you turned on "Remember this password in my keychain," you won't even be asked for your name and password again.

Similarly, if you put an alias like this onto the Dock, you can bring it back to your screen later just by clicking its icon.

You can even drag the alias into the Login Items window described on page 494. Now the disk appears on your desktop automatically each time you log in—the most effortless arrangement of all.

You can even use Spotlight to find files on that networked disk. If the Mac across the network is running Leopard or a later Mac version, in fact, you can search for words *inside* its files, just as though you were sitting in front of it. If not, you can still search for text in files' names.

Connection Method B: Connect to Server

The Sidebar method of connecting to networked folders and disks is practically effortless. It involves nothing more than clicking your way through folders—a skill that, in theory, you already know.

But the Sidebar method has its drawbacks. For example, the Sidebar doesn't let you type in a disk's network address. As a result, you can't access any shared disk *on the internet* (an FTP site, for example), or indeed anywhere beyond your local subnet (your own small network).

Fortunately, there's another way. When you choose Go→Connect to Server, you get the dialog box shown in Figure 13-11. You're supposed to type in the address of the shared disk you want.

Figure 13-11:
The Sidebar method of connecting to shared disks and folders is quick and easy, but it doesn't let you connect to certain kinds of disks. The Connect to Server method entails plodding through several dialog boxes, but it can find just about every kind of networked disk.

For example, from here you can connect to the following:

- **Everyday Macs on your network.** If you know the IP address of the Mac you're trying to access (you geek!), you can type nothing but its IP address into the box and then hit Connect. Or you can just type its Bonjour name, something like this: *afp://upstairs-PowerMac.local/*.

Tip: To find out your Mac's IP address, open the Network pane of System Preferences. There, near the top, you'll see a message like this: "Wi-Fi is connected to Tim's Hotspot and has the IP address 192.168.1.113." That's your IP address.

To see your Bonjour address, open the Sharing pane of System Preferences. Click File Sharing. Near the top, you'll see the computer name with ".local" tacked onto its name—and hyphens instead of spaces—like this: Little-MacBook.local.

After you enter your account password and choose the shared disk or folder you want, you're connected exactly as though you had clicked Connect As (Figure 13-10).

The next time you open the Connect to Server dialog box, macOS remembers that address, as a courtesy to you, and shows it pre-entered in the Address field.

- **Windows machines.** Find out the PC's IP address or computer name, and then use this format for the address: *smb://192.168.1.34* or *smb://Cheapo-Dell.*

After a moment, you're asked to enter your Windows account name and password, and then to choose the name of the shared folder you want. When you click OK, the shared folder's contents appear in the window, ready to use, and the computer's icon appears in your Sidebar. (More on sharing with Windows PCs later in this chapter.)

Tip: If you know the name of the shared folder, you can add that after a slash, like this: *smb://192.168.4.23/ sharedstuff.* You save yourself one dialog box.

- **NFS servers.** If you're on a network with Unix machines, you can tap into one of their shared directories using this address format: *nfs://Machine-Name/pathname,* where *Machine-Name* is the computer's name or IP address, and *pathname* is the folder path to the shared item you want.

- **FTP servers.** MacOS makes it simple to bring *FTP servers* onto your screen, too. (These are the drives, out there on the internet, that store the files used by websites.)

In the Connect to Server dialog box, type the FTP address of the server you want, like this: *ftp://www.apple.com.* If the site's administrators have permitted *anonymous* access—the equivalent of a Guest account—that's all there is to it. A Finder window pops open, revealing the FTP site's contents.

GEM IN THE ROUGH

Hello, Bonjour

Throughout this chapter, and throughout this book, you'll encounter rituals in which you're supposed to connect to another Mac, server, or printer by typing in its IP address (its unique network address).

But first of all, IP addresses are insanely difficult to memorize (192.179.248.3, anyone?). Second, networks shouldn't require you to deal with them anyway. If a piece of equipment is on the network, it should announce its presence, rather than making you specifically call for it by name.

So you can appreciate the beauty of Bonjour, an underlying macOS networking technology that lets networked gadgets

detect one another on the network automatically and recognize one another's capabilities.

It's Bonjour at work, for example, that makes other Macs' names show up in your Music program so you can listen to their music from across the network. Bonjour is also responsible for filling up your Bonjour buddies list in Messages automatically, listing everyone who's on the same office network; for making shared Macs' names show up in the Sidebar's Shared list; and for making the names of modern laser printers from HP, Epson, or Lexmark appear like magic in the list of printers in the Print dialog box.

If you need a password for the FTP site, however, you're now asked for your name and password.

Tip: You can eliminate that password-dialog-box step by using this address format: *ftp://yourname:your-password@www.apple.com.*

Once you type it and press Return, the FTP server's icon appears in the Sidebar. Its contents appear, too, ready to open or copy.

- **WebDAV server.** This special web-based shared disk requires a special address format, something like this: *http://Computer-Name/pathname.*

 In each case, once you click OK, you may be asked for your name and password.

And now, some time-saving features in the Connect to Server box:

- **Once you've typed a disk's address,** you can click + to add it to the list of server favorites. The next time you want to connect, you can just double-click its name.

- **The clock-icon pop-up menu lists Recent Servers**—computers you've accessed recently over the network. If you choose one of them from this pop-up menu, you can skip having to type in an address.

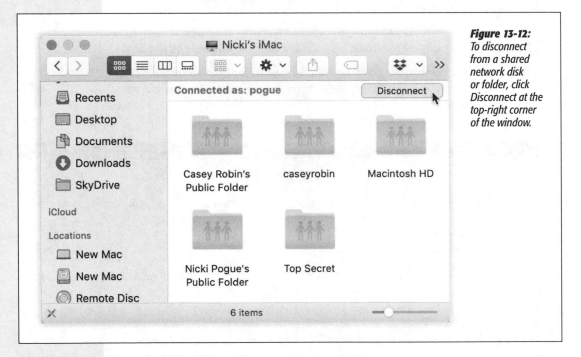

Figure 13-12:
To disconnect from a shared network disk or folder, click Disconnect at the top-right corner of the window.

Note: Like the Sidebar network-browsing method, the Connect to Server command displays each connected computer as an icon in your Sidebar, even within the Open or Save dialog boxes of your programs. You don't have to burrow through the Sidebar's Network icon to open files from them, or to save files onto them.

Disconnecting Yourself

When you're finished using a shared disk or folder, you can disconnect from it as shown in Figure 13-12.

Disconnecting Others

In macOS, you really have to work if you want to know whether other people on the network are accessing *your* Mac. You have to choose System Preferences→Sharing→ File Sharing→Options. There you'll see something like "Number of users connected: 1."

Maybe that's because there's nothing to worry about. You certainly have nothing to fear from a security standpoint, since you control what others can see on your Mac. Nor will you experience much computer slowdown as you work, thanks to macOS's prodigious multitasking features.

Still, if you're feeling particularly antisocial, you can slam shut the door to your Mac. Just open System Preferences→Sharing and turn off File Sharing. If anybody is, in fact, connected to your Mac at the time (*from* a Mac), you, the door-slammer, get to see the dialog box in Figure 13-13, which sends a little warning message to whomever's connected to your Mac.

If nobody is connected right now, your Mac instantly becomes an island once again.

Figure 13-13:
This dialog box asks you how much notice you want to give your co-workers that they're about to be disconnected.

There may be users connected to this computer.
Enter the number of minutes before file sharing is turned off.

5 Minutes

Cancel OK

Networking with Windows

Macs and Windows PCs can see one another on the network, with no special software (or talent) required. In fact, you can go in either direction. Your Mac can see shared folders on a Windows PC, and a Windows PC can see shared folders on your Mac.

It goes like this.

Seated at the Mac, Seeing the PC

Suppose you have a Windows PC and a Mac on the same wired or wireless network. Here's how you get the Mac and PC chatting:

1. **On your Windows PC, share some files.**

 This isn't really a book about Windows networking (thank heaven), but here are the basics.

 On a PC with Windows 8 or Windows 10, there may be nothing to it. All your personal files probably come preshared. You can skip to step 2.

 If step 2 doesn't seem to work, then maybe your PC files aren't already shared, and you have some reading ahead of you:

 Just as on the Mac, there are two ways to share files in Windows. One of them is super-simple: You just copy the files you want to share into a central, fully accessible folder. As long as nobody has turned off the Guest access feature, no passwords, accounts, or other steps are required.

 In Windows Vista, that's the Public folder, which appears in the Navigation pane of every Explorer window. (In Vista, there's one Public folder for the whole *computer*, not one per account holder.)

 In Windows 7, there's a Public folder in each library. That is, there's a Public Documents, Public Pictures, Public Music, and so on.

 Note: There is no system of Public folders in Windows 8 and later—but if you upgraded your PC from an earlier Windows version, then the Public folders are still there and work the same way.

 The second, more complicated method is the "share any folder" method, just as in macOS. In Vista, you right-click the folder you want to share, choose Properties from the shortcut menu, click the Sharing tab, and then turn on "Share this folder on the network."

 In Windows 7, use the Share With menu at the top of any folder's window; in Windows 8 or later, use the Share tab on the Ribbon at the top of any Explorer window at the desktop.

 Repeat for any other folders you want to make available to your Mac.

2. **On the Mac, open any Finder window.**

 The shared PCs appear as individual computer names in the Sidebar (Figure 13-14).

 (If you work in a big company, you may have to click the All icon to see the icons of their *workgroups*—network clusters. Unless you or a network administrator changed it, the workgroup name is probably MSHOME or WORKGROUP. Double-click the workgroup name you want.)

Tip: You can also access the shared PC via the Connect to Server command, as described on page 542. You could type into it *smb://192.168.1.103* (or whatever the PC's IP address is) or *smb://SuperDell* (or whatever its name is) and hit Return—and then skip to step 5. In fact, using the Connect to Server method often works when the Sidebar method doesn't.

3. Click the name of the computer you want.

If you're using one of the simple file-sharing methods on the PC, as already described, that's all there is to it. The contents of the Shared Documents or Public folder now appear on your Mac's screen. You can work with them just as you would your own files.

If you're using one of the "shared folder" methods, read on.

4. Click Connect As.

This button appears in the top-right corner of the Finder window. Now you're asked for your name and password (Figure 13-14).

Note: In Windows 8 and later, there are two ways to log into a computer—two kinds of user accounts. You can sign in with a *Microsoft ID* (which is just like an Apple ID) or with a regular *local* account. (Microsoft pushes you very hard to use a Microsoft ID; many features of Windows won't work without it.)

If you're trying to connect to a Windows account with a Microsoft ID, be sure to use *that* as the account name in this step (it looks like an email address), along with the corresponding password. If you enter the account's human name, you won't be able to connect.

Figure 13-14:
Click the PC's name in the Network folder of the Sidebar (top). If it's part of a workgroup, click your workgroup name first.

Next, enter the account name and password you'd enter if you were seated at the PC—your regular login password (bottom).

When you click Connect, you get to see all your PC files in the Finder window.

5. **Enter the name and password for your account on the PC, and then click OK.**

The contents of the shared folder on the Windows machine appear in your Finder window, just as though you'd tapped into another Mac. The icon of the shared folder appears on your desktop, too, and an Eject button (⏏) appears next to the PC's name in your Sidebar.

From here, it's a simple matter to drag files between the machines, open Word documents on the PC using Word for the Mac, and so on—exactly like you're hooked into another Mac.

Tip: Finally, for heaven's sake, make an alias of the Windows folder you've finally opened. That way, you can just double-click to open it next time!

TROUBLESHOOTING MOMENT

When the Mac Doesn't See the PC

Are you having trouble getting your PC's icon to show up in your Finder's Sidebar?

Now, you can probably connect to the PC using the Mac's Go→Connect to Server command, but the Sidebar would be a lot more convenient.

And the problem is probably that the Mac doesn't know anything about Windows *workgroups*.

Even a lowly home PC is part of a workgroup (a corporate cluster), whether it knows it or not. And until your Mac is part of that very tiny club, it won't be able to see your PCs, and they won't be able to see it.

So if you're having no luck with this whole Mac-PC thing, try this. First, find out what your PC thinks its workgroup is. (It's usually either WORKGROUP or MSHOME.) Windows 8 and later: Right-click the Start-menu icon (⊞); from the shortcut menu, choose System. Scroll down if necessary to see the workgroup's name.

Older Windows versions: Click Start, and then right-click Computer. From the shortcut menu, choose Properties. In the resulting info screen, you'll see the workgroup's name.

To find out the Mac's idea of its workgroup, open System Preferences→Network. Click the connection you're using (like Wi-Fi or Ethernet)→Advanced→WINS.

Now you see the peculiar controls shown here. Make sure that the Workgroup box shows the same name as the one on the PC. Click OK, and then click Apply.

Now your Windows PCs should show up in the Sidebar, like magic.

If they're *still* not showing up, then your PCs' firewall software is probably turned on. Make sure it's turned off—and turn off your Mac's firewall, too (page 515). You can't do much connecting if there's a virtual wall between the computers.

Seated at the PC, Seeing the Mac

Cross-platformers, rejoice: MacOS lets you share files in *both directions.* Not only can your Mac see other PCs on the network, but they can see the Mac, too.

On the Mac, open System Preferences→Sharing. Click File Sharing (make sure File Sharing is turned on), and then click Options to open the dialog box shown in Figure 13-15.

Figure 13-15:
Prepare your Mac for visitation by the Windows PC. It won't hurt a bit. The system-wide On switch for invasion from Windows is the first checkbox shown here, in the System Preferences→Sharing→File Sharing→Options box.

Next, turn on the individual accounts of people you want to allow to connect from the PC. You'll be asked to enter their account passwords, too. Click Done when you're done.

☑ Share files and folders using SMB

Number of users connected: 0

☑ Share files and folders using AFP

Number of users connected: 0

Windows File Sharing:

Sharing files with some Windows computers requires storing the user's account password on this computer in a less secure manner. When you enable Windows sharing for a user account, you must enter the password for that account.

On	Account
☐	Casey Robin
☑	David Pogue
☐	Jan Paulson

Done

Turn on "Share files and folders using SMB." Below that checkbox, you see a list of all the accounts on your Mac. Turn on the checkboxes to specify *which* Mac accounts you want to be able to access. You'll have to type in each person's password, too. Click Done.

Now you're ready to open your Mac files on the PC.

If your PC has Windows Vista, then choose Start→Network; if it's Windows 7 or later, then expand the Network heading in the Sidebar of any desktop (File Explorer) window. If you've sacrificed the proper animals to the networking gods, your Mac's icon should appear in the network window, as shown in Figure 13-16, top.

Double-click the Mac's icon. Public-folder stuff is available immediately. Otherwise, you have to sign in with your Mac account name and password; Figure 13-16, middle, has the details.

In the final window, you see your actual Home folder—on the Windows PC! You're ready to open its files, copy them back and forth, or whatever (see Figure 13-16, bottom).

More Mac-Windows Connections

The direct Mac-to-Windows file-sharing feature of macOS is by far the easiest way to access one another's files. But it's not the only way. Chapter 6 offers a long list of other options, from flash drives to the third-party service Dropbox.

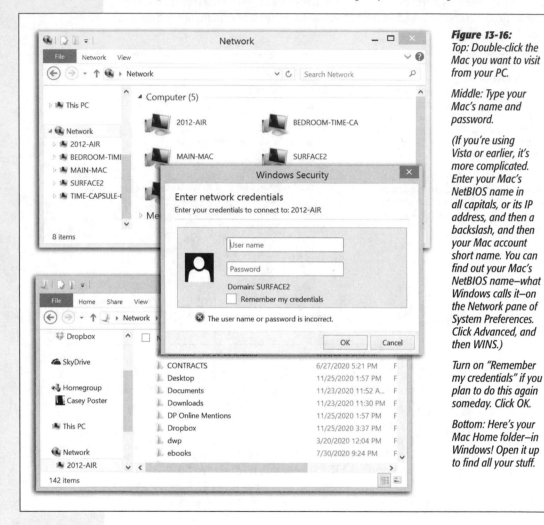

Figure 13-16:
Top: Double-click the Mac you want to visit from your PC.

Middle: Type your Mac's name and password.

(If you're using Vista or earlier, it's more complicated. Enter your Mac's NetBIOS name in all capitals, or its IP address, and then a backslash, and then your Mac account short name. You can find out your Mac's NetBIOS name—what Windows calls it—on the Network pane of System Preferences. Click Advanced, and then WINS.)

Turn on "Remember my credentials" if you plan to do this again someday. Click OK.

Bottom: Here's your Mac Home folder—in Windows! Open it up to find all your stuff.

Screen Sharing

MacOS has answered the prayers of baffled beginners and exasperated experts everywhere. Now, when a novice needs help from a guru, the guru doesn't have to run all the way downstairs or fly to Omaha to assist. Thanks to macOS's screen-sharing feature, you can see exactly what's on the screen of another Mac, from across the network—and even seize control of the other Mac's mouse and keyboard (with the newbie's permission, of course).

Anyone who's ever tried to help someone troubleshoot over the phone knows *exactly* how helpful this is. If you haven't, this small example may suffice: "OK, open the Apple menu and choose About This Mac." Pause. "What's the Apple menu?"

Nor is playing Bail-Out-the-Newbie the only situation when screen sharing is useful. It's also great for collaborating on a document, showing something to someone for approval, or just freaking people out. It can also be handy when *you* are the owner of both Macs (a laptop and a desktop, for example), and you want to run a program you don't have on the Mac in front of you. For example, you might want to adjust the playlist selection on the upstairs Mac that's connected to your sound system.

Or maybe you just want to keep an eye on what your kids are doing on the Macs upstairs in their rooms.

The controlling person can do *everything* on the controlled Mac, including running programs, messing around with the folders and files, and even shutting it down. You can press keystrokes on *your* Mac—⌘-Tab, ⌘-space, ⌘-Option-Escape, and so on—to trigger the corresponding functions on the *other* Mac.

MacOS is crawling with ways to use screen sharing. You can do it over a network, over the internet, and even during a Messages chat.

Truth is, the Messages method, described starting on page 758, is much simpler and better than the small-network method described here. It doesn't require names or passwords, it doesn't require the same macOS version on both Macs, it's easy to flip back between seeing the other guy's screen and your own, and you can transfer files by dragging them from your screen to the other guy's (or vice versa). Then again, the small-network method described here is built right into the Finder and doesn't require logging into Messages.

In modern macOS screen sharing, you can log into a distant Mac and control it as though you were logged into your own account—*while somebody else is using it* and seeing a totally different screen! Read on.

Other Mac: Give Permission in Advance

Trying to understand concepts like seeing one Mac's screen on the monitor of another can get confusing fast. So in this example, suppose you're seated at Your Mac, and you want to control Other Mac.

Now, it would be a chaotic world if any Mac could suddenly take control of any other Mac. Fortunately, though, nobody can share your screen or take control of your Mac without your explicit permission. To give such permission, sit down at Other Mac. Choose System Preferences→Sharing, and then turn on Screen Sharing.

At this point, there are three levels of security to protect Other Mac against unauthorized remote-control mischief:

- **Secure.** If you select All Users, *anyone with an account on your Mac* will be able to tap in and take control anytime they like, even when you're not around. They'll just have to enter the same name and password they'd use if they were sitting in

front of your machine. If "anyone" means "you and your spouse" or "you and the two other fourth-grade teachers," that's probably perfectly fine.

• **Securer.** For greater security, though, you can limit who's allowed to stop in. Click "Only these users" and then click the +. A small panel appears, listing everyone with an account on your Mac. Choose the ones you trust not to mess things up while you're away (Figure 13-17).

Figure 13-17:
Your Mac is now ready to be observed and even controlled by other machines across the network. The people listed here are allowed to tap in anytime they like, even when you're not at your machine.

GEM IN THE ROUGH

Screen Sharing with Windows and Other Oddball Machines

The beauty of Apple's screen-sharing technology is that it *isn't* Apple's screen-sharing technology. It's a popular open standard called VNC (Virtual Network Computing).

Once you've turned on Screen Sharing, any computer on earth with a free VNC client program—sort of a viewer program—can pop onto your Mac for a screen share. VNC clients are available for Windows, Linux, older Macs, and even some cellphones. (Not all VNC programs work with the Catalina version of screen sharing, alas; some require updates.)

To prepare your Mac for invasion, open the Sharing pane of System Preferences. Click Screen Sharing, and then click Computer Settings. Turn on "VNC viewers may control screen with password," and then make up a password. (VNC doesn't know anything about macOS account passwords, so you're making up one password for sharing your whole Mac.)

Give that password to the lucky few who have your trust. Let them plug your Mac's public IP address into their VNC clients—or let them connect over your office network, using the address displayed on the Screen Sharing pane (*vnc:// MacBook-Pro,* for example)—and let the sharing begin.

Tip: You can permit people to see your Mac's screen remotely by entering their Apple ID and passwords. That's a lot simpler and uses less disk space than before, when each person had to have a full-blown *account* on your Mac, complete with Pictures folder, Movies folder, and so on. To set this up, see the box on the facing page.

- **Securest.** If you click "Only these users" and then don't add *anyone* to the list, then only people who have Administrator accounts on your Mac (page 488) can tap into your screen.

Alternatively, if you're only a *little* bit of a Scrooge, you can set things up so they can request permission to share your screen—as long as you're sitting in front of your Mac at the time and feeling generous.

To set this up, click Computer Settings and then turn on "Anyone may request permission to share screen." Now your fans will have to request permission to enter, and you'll have to grant it (by clicking OK on the screen) while you're there to watch what they're doing.

Your Mac: Take Control

All right, Other Mac has been prepared for invasion. Now suppose you're the person on the other end. You're the guru, the parent, or whoever wants to take control.

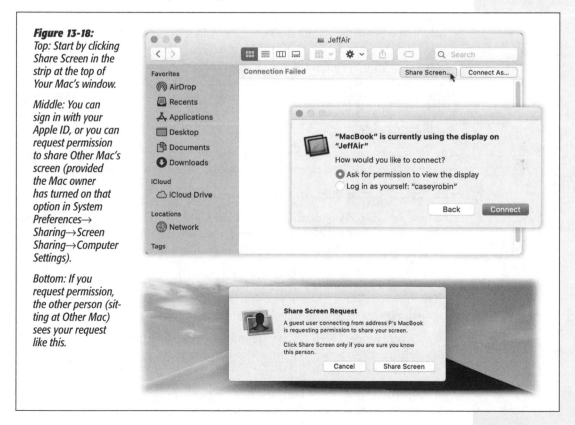

Figure 13-18:
Top: Start by clicking Share Screen in the strip at the top of Your Mac's window.

Middle: You can sign in with your Apple ID, or you can request permission to share Other Mac's screen (provided the Mac owner has turned on that option in System Preferences→Sharing→Screen Sharing→Computer Settings).

Bottom: If you request permission, the other person (sitting at Other Mac) sees your request like this.

Sit at Your Mac on your home or office network, and proceed like this:

1. **Open a Finder window. Expand the Locations list in the Sidebar, if necessary, to see the Network icon. Double-click it, and then double-click Other Mac's icon.**

 The strip at the top of the main window displays a button that wasn't there before: Share Screen (Figure 13-18, top).

2. **Click Share Screen.**

At this point, one of three things may happen.

- **If you and Other Mac** are both signed into the same Apple ID, that's it: You're in! That's super-convenient if the other Mac basically *is* your Mac.

- **If you don't pop right into Other Mac,** you get the box shown at middle in Figure 13-18. It offers two ways for you to prove you're not some German teenage hacker.

 If somebody is working on Other Mac right now, you can choose "Ask for permission to view." Other Mac's current operator gets a message asking if it's OK for you to take over. If that person grants permission, that's it; Other Mac's screen image appears on *your* screen.

- **But what if nobody is seated at Other Mac to grant permission?** If you have an account on Other Mac, you can choose "Log in as yourself." When you click Connect, you're taken to the standard login screen. Click your account and log in, exactly as though you were seated in front of Other Mac.

Tip: In theory, you can also connect from across the internet, assuming you left your Mac at home turned on and connected to a broadband modem, and assuming you've worked through the port-forwarding issue described on page 559.

In this case, though, you'd begin by choosing Go→Connect to Server in the Finder; in the Connect to Server box, type in *vnc://123.456.78.90* (or whatever your home Mac's public IP address is). The rest of the steps are the same.

And now a weird and wonderful sight appears. As shown in Figure 13-19, your screen now fills with a *second* screen—from Other Mac. You have full keyboard and mouse control to work with that machine exactly as though you were sitting in front of it.

Well, not *exactly*. There are a few caveats and options:

- **The indicator.** The ⊡ icon appears on both screens, so you're both reminded that somebody is rooting around on somebody else's computer.

- **Full Screen mode.** There it is, in its customary upper-left spot: the green ⊗ button. If you click it, your view of Other Mac expands to fill your screen, edge to edge; now there's *no sign at all* that you're actually using a different computer.

- **The speed-vs.-blurriness issue.** You're asking Other Mac to pump its video display across the network—and that takes time. Milliseconds, in fact.

So ordinarily, the Mac uses something called *adaptive quality,* which just means that the screen gets blurry when you scroll, quit a program, or do anything else that creates a sudden change in the picture. You can turn off this feature by choosing View→Full Quality. Now you get full sharpness all the time—but things take longer to scroll, appear, and disappear.

- **Mismatched screen sizes.** If the other screen is *smaller* than yours, no big deal. It floats at actual size on your monitor with room to spare. But if it's the same size as yours or larger, Other Mac's screen gets shrunk down to fit in a window.

If you'd prefer to see it at actual size, choose View→Turn Scaling Off, or click the "Scaling Off" and "Scaling On" buttons on the Screen Sharing toolbar (shown at top left in Figure 13-19). Of course, now you have to *scroll* in the Screen Sharing window to see the whole image.

Figure 13-19:
Don't be alarmed. You're looking at Other Mac's desktop in a window on the Your Mac desktop. You have keyboard and mouse control, and so does the other guy (if he's there); when you're really bored, you can play King of the Cursor.

- **Observe Mode.** In Observe Mode, you give up all your typing and clicking powers. In other words, you're playing "Look but don't touch." (To enter this mode, choose View→Switch to Observe Mode, or click the corresponding toolbar icon.)

This is a handy option when the person at Other Mac just wants to give you a slideshow or a presentation, or when you just want to watch what he's doing when you're on a troubleshooting hunt, or when he's freaked out by having you move the mouse or type stuff by remote control. Your cursor is now a ◌; when you click anywhere on the screen, there's a momentary magnification bubble on both screens, so the Other Mac person can see what you're "pointing to"—during, for example, a tech-support session.

- **Share the Clipboard.** You can actually *copy and paste* material from the remote-controlled Mac to your own—or the other way—thanks to a freaky little wormhole in the space-time continuum. Whenever Use Shared Clipboard is turned on (in the Edit menu or on the toolbar), you can copy and paste freely between Your Mac and Other Mac. If you want to do such inter-Mac copying more manually, you can also choose Send Clipboard to put what's on your Clipboard onto Other Mac's Clipboard, or Get Clipboard to copy Other Mac's Clipboard contents onto yours. Breathe slowly and drink plenty of fluids, and your brain won't explode.

- **Dragging files between computers.** You can transfer files from one Mac to the other, just by dragging their icons. Drag the icon from Other Mac clear out of its window, and pause over your own desktop until your cursor sprouts a green icon. When you let go, the files get copied to Your Mac.

- **Quitting.** When you hit the ⌘-Q keystroke, you *don't* quit Screen Sharing; you quit whatever program is running on Other Mac! So when you're finished having your way with the other computer, choose Screen Sharing→Quit Screen Sharing to return to your own desktop (and your own sanity).

The Toolbar

If you don't see the screen-sharing toolbar, you can summon it by choosing View→Show Toolbar. It starts out with buttons for Control Mode, Observe Mode, Scaling Off, Scaling On, and Clipboard.

But if you right-click or two-finger click the toolbar, you're offered a shortcut menu containing the usual controls over how the toolbar buttons appear (Icon and Text, Icon Only, Text Only, and so on), plus a Customize Toolbar command. It opens a box where you can move the toolbar buttons around by dragging, change the assortment of available buttons, add gaps between the buttons (drag a space or a flexible space into position), and modify how the buttons appear.

Variations on Screen Sharing

The previous steps guide you through screen sharing between two Macs running OS X 10.5 or later. But screen sharing is based on a standard technology called VNC, and macOS is bristling with different permutations.

Screen sharing through Messages

Two people who both have OS X 10.5 or later can perform exactly the same screen-sharing stunt *over the internet.* No accounts, passwords, or setup are required—only the granting of permission by the other guy. Just initiate a Messages chat, and then proceed as described on page 758. It's really awesome.

Screen sharing the manual way

Screen Sharing is an actual, double-clickable program, with its own icon on your Mac. (It's in the System→Library→CoreServices→Applications folder.) When you double-click it, you can type in the public IP address or domain name of the computer you want to connect to, and presto: You're connected!

Connecting from the Road

If you have a full-time internet connection, a special thrill awaits. You can connect to your Mac from anywhere in the world via the internet. If you have a laptop, you don't need to worry when you discover you've left a critical file on your desktop Mac at home.

MacOS offers several ways to connect to your Mac from a distant location.

FTP

FTP (file transfer protocol) sites store pieces of software that can be accessed from the internet. If you've heard of FTP at all, it was probably under one of two circumstances—either you've downloaded software from an internet FTP site, or you've created and maintained your own website.

Uploading and downloading from FTP sites

Hooking into an FTP site generally requires an FTP *client program* that runs on the kind of computer you use (Mac, Windows, or whatever). On macOS, popular FTP client programs include the shareware programs Transmit, Cyberduck, Fetch, Interarchy, and Captain FTP, and the free RBrowser (which is available from the "Missing CD" page at *missingmanuals.com*).

Using these programs, web designers, for example, can view a list of all the text and graphics documents, sitting there on an internet-connected computer somewhere, that make up their web pages. The effect is shown in Figure 13-20.

Figure 13-20:
Top: To access your macOS machine from across the internet, fire up a program like RBrowser and use the address ftp://111.222.33.4 (or whatever your public IP address is).

Bottom: Once you're looking at an FTP server's contents, you can drag files from your desktop into the list, copy them to your Mac by dragging them out of the list onto your desktop, or open them by double-clicking.

When they want to update one of those pages, they add it to this list; to delete a web page, they remove it from this list.

Downloading from FTP sites

If you're just going to *look at* and *download* files (but not upload or delete any), you don't even need a special FTP program. You can get to the files much more directly using one of these two methods:

- **Any old web browser will work.** Open Safari, for example, and type *ftp://ftp.apple. com* (or whatever the address is) into the address/search bar. A dialog box asks for an account name and password, if they're required. Once you're in, you switch to the Finder and see the contents of the FTP site as a window full of file icons. (In other browsers, you may see the list of the FTP site right in the browser window.)

- **Using the Finder's Go→Connect to Server command,** you can mount read-only FTP volumes right on your desktop. In other words, they appear just like any other disk icons.

 In the Connect to Server dialog box, just enter the address of the file server you would like to mount—*ftp://ftp.apple.com,* for example. You'll soon see the *ftp.apple.com* icon appear on your desktop, looking just like your other disks. Open it up and drag out whatever you want to download.

Remote File Sharing

You can also connect to your Mac's regular File Sharing feature (page 527) from over the internet. This feature is a blessing to anyone who travels, whether with a laptop or to a branch office, because you'll never be up a creek without a paddle if you discover that you left an important file at home.

You can also set up a remote file-sharing system on your own. Start by setting up the home-base Mac for file sharing, as directed in Chapter 13; then figure out your Mac's public IP address, as described in the box on the facing page.

Figure 13-21:
The Connect to Server dialog box lets you type in the IP address for the shared Mac you want to access. (Ensuring that the shared Mac is turned on and connected to the internet is the network administrator's problem.)

Finally, once you're on the road, go online and proceed like this:

1. **Choose Go→Connect to Server.**

 The Connect to Server dialog box appears, as shown in Figure 13-21.

2. **Type in the public IP address of the Mac to which you want to connect, and then click Connect (or press Return).**

3. **Enter your name and password, and then click Connect.**

 From here, it's just as though you were connecting to another computer on your office network (Chapter 13), although it's a good bit slower. But when you're in Hong Kong and need a document from your Mac in Minneapolis, you may not care.

UP TO SPEED

The IP Address Mess: Port Forwarding

There are so many ways to connect to your Mac from another computer. You can use SSH, file sharing, screen sharing, and so on. They're easy to use—when you want to connect across your home or office network. When you want to connect from across the *internet*, though, things get complicated fast.

In that case, you need to know your home Mac's *IP address*. (IP stands for Internet Protocol.) An IP address is always made up of four numbers separated by periods, like 192.168.1.104. Every computer on earth that's directly connected to the internet has its own unique IP address.

Now, if you have only one Mac, and it's connected directly to your broadband modem, no big deal. You can find out its IP address by opening System Preferences, clicking Sharing, and turning on File Sharing.

Unfortunately, your Mac at home probably *isn't* connected directly to the internet. If you're like most people, it's connected to a router, or maybe an AirPort base station, so that several computers in your house can share the same internet connection. In this setup, the *router* (or base station) has a unique IP address—not the Macs connected to it.

(The router doles out private IP addresses to each computer in your house or office, usually beginning with 192 or 10. If you check your Mac's IP address in System Preferences, you'll find out only its *private* address—not the public one that's accessible from the internet. To find out that information, you have to check your router or base station's configuration screen; check the router's manual for instructions.)

All right: How are you supposed to connect to one particular Mac if it's connected to a router and doesn't have a true, "public" IP address? Your best bet is to turn on a router feature called *port forwarding*. It makes the router pass signals intended for a specific port to one particular computer on the network. For example, you could direct all port-80 communications to the Mac doing web serving and all port-548 traffic to the Mac doing file sharing.

The point is that, even with port forwarding, you still can't access two different machines using the same port. (For some services, including SSH and Timbuktu, you can work around this limitation by logging into the machine specified for port forwarding, and then from that machine, logging into the others on the rest of the network.)

Turning on port forwarding doesn't require a programming degree, but it's not simple by any means. For starters, the steps are different for every router model.

Fortunately, you can find guided tutorials on the web. You can use Google to search for your particular router model, or check *portforward.com*, which offers free step-by-steps for hundreds of router models, including Apple's AirPort base stations. Even so, try to arrange the assistance of someone who knows networking.

In this chapter, the term "your IP address" means your *public* IP address. If you have only one Mac, that's its IP address. If you have a router or wireless network, use *that* device's IP address—as passed along by port forwarding.

Remote Access with SSH

If you're willing to dive into some technical underbrush, SSH (Secure Shell) is an extremely powerful tool. It lets you connect to your Mac from anywhere—from across the network or across the internet. And once you're connected, you can take complete control of it, copying files, running commands, rearranging folders, or even shutting it down, all by remote control. For step-by-steps, see the free PDF appendix to this chapter called "Remote Access with SSH" on this book's "Missing CD" page at *missingmanuals.com*.

Virtual Private Networking

Even though the methods on the preceding pages work fine if you're dialing into your *home* machine, they'll probably fail miserably when you want to connect to a corporate network. There's one enormous obstacle in your way: internet security.

The typical corporate network is guarded by a team of steely-eyed administrators, for whom job one is preventing access by unauthorized visitors. They perform this job primarily with the aid of a super-secure firewall that seals off the company's network from the internet.

So how can you tap into the network from the road? One solution is to create a hole in the firewall for each authorized person—software that permits incoming internet traffic only from specified IP addresses like your Mac's. Unfortunately, this setup isn't bulletproof, security-wise. It's also a pain for administrators to manage.

Back in the dial-up modem days, you could dial directly into the corporate network, modem-to-modem. That was plenty secure, but it bypassed the internet and therefore wound up being expensive. (Want proof? Make a call from the Tokyo Hilton to the Poughkeepsie Sheet Metal home office. Have a look at your hotel bill when you check out.)

Fortunately, there's a third solution that's both secure and cheap: a *virtual private network,* or *VPN.* Running a VPN allows you to create a super-secure "tunnel" from your Mac, across the internet, and straight into your corporate network. All data passing through this tunnel is heavily encrypted; to the internet eavesdropper, it looks like so much undecipherable gobbledygook.

And it's free—whether you're accessing the internet via your home DSL, a local ISP number from a hotel, or wirelessly from your stool at Starbucks.

Remember, though, that VPN is a corporate tool, run by corporate nerds. You can't use this feature without these pieces in place:

- **A VPN server.** If your tech department tells you it doesn't have one, then that's that—no tunneling for you.

 If they do have one, then you'll need to know what type of server it is. MacOS's VPN software can connect to VPN servers that speak *PPTP* (Point-to-Point Tunneling

Protocol), *L2TP/IPSec* (Layer 2 Tunneling Protocol over IP Security), or Cisco IPSec. Most corporate VPN servers work with at least one of these protocols.

You'll also need to know the internet address of your VPN server (for example, *vpn.ferrets-r-us.com*).

- **An account on the remote network that allows VPN access.** Your remote network can be set up in many different ways, but in every case, you'll still need to confirm with your network administrator that your account on it allows VPN access.

- **All necessary account information.** Make sure you have all the scraps of connection information you'll need to dial in. That would include your user (account) name, at the very least. You may also need a Windows Domain name; VPN servers are often part of Microsoft Windows Server networks, which won't let you in until you know this domain name.

 Some networks also may require that you type in the currently displayed password on an RSA SecurID card, which your administrator will provide. This James Bondish, credit card–like or flash drive–like thing displays a password that changes every few seconds, making it rather difficult for hackers to learn "the" password. (If your network doesn't require a SecurID card, then you'll need a standard password instead.)

 Finally, if your office offers L2TP connections, then you'll need yet another password called a Shared Secret to ensure that the server you're connecting to is really the server you intend to connect to.

Setting up the VPN connection

If you're lucky, your company's network geek has already provided you with a VPN settings file, a little double-clickable icon that automatically opens the Network pane of System Preferences and fills in the blanks for you. If not, you can do all that manually:

Note: OpenVPN is a free, very popular VPN program. If your VPN uses OpenVPN, then you'll need to get some connection software from your company's network geeks.

1. **Open System Preferences. Click Network. Click the + below the list of connections at the left side.**

 The "Select the interface" sheet appears.

2. **From the pop-up menu, choose VPN.**

 Now a new pop-up menu appears, called VPN Type; you're supposed to choose either L2TP over IPSec (Layer 2 Tunneling Protocol over IP Security), PPTP (Point-to-Point Tunneling Protocol), or Cisco IPSec (IP Security). Find out which system your company's network uses.

Note: MacOS can't connect to all Cisco setups; in some cases, you'll still have to use Cisco's own connection software to dial in.

3. **After you choose the type of VPN from the VPN Type pop-up menu, type a name for this connection (it can be anything you want). Click Create.**

 You return to the main Network pane, where the settings boxes for your VPN are waiting (Figure 13-22).

4. **Fill in the server address and account name. Click Authentication Settings to specify your password and other security settings.**

 Here, for example, is where you indicate that you have one of those SecurID cards.

5. **Click Connect. Turn on "Show VPN status in menu bar."**

 That checkbox makes the VPN menulet (▥) appear; it's your ticket to getting connected (Figure 13-22, top).

Figure 13-22:
You're on your way to joining the corporate network—from thousands of miles away. Virtual private networking is ideal for the paranoid (because it's very secure) and the cheap (because you're using the internet as a giant wire connecting you to your office).

Tip: If you always connect to the same VPN, you can turn on VPN on Demand. It autoconnects you to your corporate VPN every time you direct your web browser to a website, file server, or resource that requires the VPN connection, saving you some steps.

To set this up, click Advanced. (You can see this button in Figure 13-22.) Click VPN on Demand; click +. Enter the corporate VPN domain. You're good to go—as long as you've got your network geek's permission. (Some of them get understandably nervous about you storing your network password in your Keychain. It's convenient, yes, but it could open up your company's entire network to the evil intentions of whoever walks up to your laptop while you're away from your desk.)

Close System Preferences. You're ready to connect.

Connecting to a VPN

Connect the way you normally do—via cable modem, DSL, office network, modem, AirPort, or whatever. Once you're online, choose your VPN's name from the ▥ menulet. You'll be asked for your credentials: your password, for example, or the code displayed on your SecurID card.

If all goes well, several status messages go by. The last one says "Connected To" and gives the IP address of the network equipment you've reached out and touched.

At this point, you're connected to the corporate network. You can perform the same network tasks you could if you were actually in that office: check your email, view internal corporate web pages, access internal FTP servers, make printouts on laser printers thousands of miles away, and so on.

Depending on your network, you might even be able to use your Sidebar to view a list of the other computers on the office network or see a list of networked printers.

If not, to access these services, you must know their IP addresses. For example, to connect to a shared folder on another computer, choose Go→Connect to Server, type its network address, and press Return.

Tip: To connect to a shared folder on a Windows machine, the address looks like this: *smb://111.222.33.4/ sales-docs*. Of course, you'd substitute the correct IP address for the dummy one shown here and insert the actual name of the shared folder. (You can also use its *DNS name* instead of the IP address, if you know it, like this: *smb://big-blue-server.ferret-lan.com/sales-docs.*)

When you're finished accessing the remote network, choose Disconnect from the VPN menulet. (Accessing other websites can be slow while you're on a VPN.)

The fine points of VPN

For all the wonders of VPN, here are some possible complications:

- **If you're using a *router* at home** (page 524), it might not be able to handle the tunneling protocols, or it might not have that feature turned on. Check its manual, or ask its manufacturer for more information.

- **If the corporate network** doesn't seem to like your name and password, you might need to add your NT domain name and a backslash to the beginning of your account name (like this: *dom01\msmith*).

- **If you're able to make the connection** but experience trouble reaching services by their DNS names (for example, *big-blue-server.com*), then your Mac could be having difficulty finding the right DNS server. Working with your network administrator, open the Network pane of System Preferences. Click VPN, then Advanced, and then DNS; enter the desired DNS server addresses in the DNS Servers box. Click OK, then Apply, and then try the VPN connection again.

- **If you're still having problems using the VPN,** look at the *logs* (automatically kept technical records) for clues to share with your network administrator. To view these records, open the Console program (in Applications→Utilities). Click Show Log List, expand the */var/log* section, and click *ppp.log*.

Photos

A pple loves introducing or standardizing some new technology, persuading us to use it—and then abandoning it the minute a better tech comes along. (The floppy drive, CD burner, 30-pin connector, headphone jack...)

And sure enough. It replaced the beloved but aging iPhoto with a new Mac app called Photos, updated for the modern age of phone photos. And in Catalina, it has overhauled Photos yet again, to make it look and work more like the iPhone/iPad version.

The Top Controls

The controls along the top of the window come and go, depending on the mode you're using. But you may as well meet the most common ones:

- **The slider at top left** controls the size of the thumbnails. (You can also pinch or spread two fingers on your trackpad, if you have one.)

- **The ⓘ button** opens an information panel. For a single photo, it reveals the date, time, shutter speed, file size, and other photographic details; for a group of photos, it shows you how many there are, their date range, and how much storage they're eating up.

- **⬆ opens the Share sheet.** This is where you can *do* something with this photo besides just staring at it. You can use it as your Mac's wallpaper, print it, copy it, text it, send it by email, use it as somebody's headshot in your Contacts list, and so on.

- **Favorite (♡).** When you find a picture you love—enough that you might want to call it up later to show people—click ♡. This photo or video now appears

in the Favorites folder (in the left-side list), so it's easy to find with your other prize-winners.

- **The Auto-Enhance button** ($\ast$) appears whenever you've opened a photo. It does a very good job at fixing the color, exposure, and contrast values for a photo with one click—and now you don't have to heave into Editing mode to apply it to a photo, or a whole batch of them.

- **The search box** might seem odd. How can you search for a blob of pixels? How does the Mac know what's *in* a picture?

 Artificial intelligence, people. Apple has given Photos the ability to recognize what's *in* your pictures and videos. You can search for "dog," or "beach," or whatever. You can search by who's in the pictures, what the event was (concerts, festivals), by month or season or year, by business or museum, and so on. Or combine all those into one search.

Tip: For simple queries, it's usually faster to request such photos by voice, using Siri: "Show me all the photos from Texas in 2018." See page 287.

- **The Showing pop-up menu** at top right appears in some thumbnail views. It lets you filter your view by Favorites, photos you've edited, only movies, only stills, and so on.

The Sidebar

The Sidebar list, which lists your albums and other useful categories, isn't hideable in macOS Catalina (at least until you enter Full Screen view). Its buttons correspond precisely to the ones you'd see on the iPhone or iPad in the Photos app. Here's what it contains.

Photos

At the left side of the Photos screen, as in so many other Apple apps, there's a sidebar list. The first one is the most important: Photos. It's the only button that reveals your entire photo collection.

On the Photos tab, iOS groups your photos intelligently into sets that are easy to navigate.

The Years, Months, and Days tabs (top of the screen) are extraordinary displays. Each presents representative photos chosen by artificial intelligence (Figure 14-1). These displays aren't cluttered up by screenshots, receipts, or duplicate photos, and the AI crops each thumbnail to show only the important part of the photo it represents.

You can switch among the views by clicking the Years, Months, and Days buttons, of course. (Or press the keystrokes ⌘-1, ⌘-2, ⌘-3, and ⌘-4.) But it's much more fun to

spread with two fingers on your trackpad, if you have one (or double-click) to zoom in from Years to Months to Days. Pinch with two fingers to go the other direction.

In any of these views, press your arrow keys to scroll up or down.

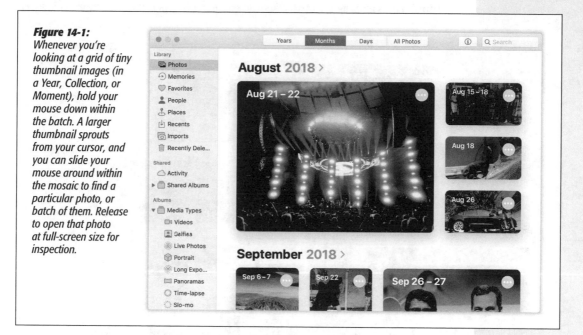

Figure 14-1:
Whenever you're looking at a grid of tiny thumbnail images (in a Year, Collection, or Moment), hold your mouse down within the batch. A larger thumbnail sprouts from your cursor, and you can slide your mouse around within the mosaic to find a particular photo, or batch of them. Release to open that photo at full-screen size for inspection.

What's cool is that as you zoom into finer time increments, you remain on the same key photo. For example, if a photo of you doing a belly flop is the sample photo for 2019, zooming into Months reveals the same photo in the context of July of that year, and zooming into Days reveals the same photo on July 15. (If you zoom in still more, you actually open that photo and start enlarging it.)

- **Years view** presents one handsome photo for each year; it starts out showing you a photo from *this time of year* each year. Scrolling through them is like a photo-graphic time machine.

- **Month view** *isn't* one photo per month. There *are* month headings, but the photo thumbnails are grouped by Moments—that is, photos taken in one place at one time (all the shots at the picnic by the lake one weekend, for example). The phone even uses its GPS to give each cluster a name: "San Francisco, California (Union Square)," for example.

- **Days view** is a grid of beautiful photos. You can, of course, click one of the pictures or videos to open it full-screen, but the photo grid is almost as good as a slideshow right there.

Note: As you scroll through these displays, videos and Live Photos play silently in place. It's a lovely effect.

- **All Photos** carries over from previous macOS versions. It's a massive, chronological, endlessly scrolling sheet of tiny photo thumbnails (Figure 14-2).

 Double-click any image within the batch to open it at full-window size. Or, if a thumbnail is already selected, click the space bar to open it (and again to close it).

Figure 14-2:
In All Photos view, you can see your photos either as correctly proportioned miniatures (front)—or as identical perfect squares, cropped to show you what Photos believes to be the most important element of each photo (back).

You hop between them using the ⬚ or ⬚ at top left. And you can enlarge or shrink the thumbnails either with the top-left slider or by spreading/pinching two fingers on a trackpad.

Memories

Memories are automatically selected groups of pix and videos from certain time periods or trips—which, with a click, become gorgeous, musical slideshows. Photos creates three new ones a day, which often dredges up delightful photos of events you'd nearly forgotten about. Most people are pleasantly surprised at how coherent and well-created these are, even though they're totally automatic. Photos, short pieces of your videos, and even scrolling panoramas are all first-class citizens in these slideshows.

Right off the bat, you see a few of Photos' suggestions, represented as clearly labeled billboards ("Cape Cod Summer," "Best of Last Week"...). Memories can auto-recognize and auto-build slideshows of your pets, babies, outdoor activities, performances, weddings, birthdays, and games.

Double-click to open a Memory; at this point, you can scroll down to see more about what's in it. You'll see the photos in it, as well as who's in them (People), and where the photos came from (Places).

At the very bottom, you'll see these options:

- **Delete Memory.** Vaporizes this computer-generated collection (does not touch the originals).

- **Add to Favorite Memories.** Adds this slideshow to a folder on the Albums tab called Favorite Memories, for quick access later.

- **Block Memory.** This command sounds like a parody of a psychological technique, but it actually does what it says: It prevents Photos from ever reminding you again, in Memories, of this day, place, or person. (When you click Block Memory, a shortcut menu identifies the factors Photos used to create this Memory—Person, Place, or Day—so you can tell it which of those three is causing you the psychic pain.)

Note: If, after years of therapy, you can face those painful memories again, click Photos→Preferences→General→Reset Blocked Memories.

Anyway, the real fun begins when you click ▶ to start an instant slideshow. It's usually fantastic.

During the slideshow, you can click ✿ (at the right end of the playback panel) for some quick editing options. You can change the animation/music style (Dreamy, Sentimental, Gentle, Chill, and so on) or the slideshow length (Short, Medium, Long).

When you come back to your senses, note that you can move the mouse off the image to make the playback controls (pause, skip, adjust volume, exit, and so on) hide.

Note: On the Mac, you can't edit which photos and videos appear in a Memory, as you can on the iPhone or iPad.

You can create a Memory using your own choice of photos, too. Open any album and click Show as Memory in the header.

Favorites

Any time you spot a photo you might want to return to later, click the ♡ that appears on its thumbnail. Then click this folder in the Sidebar, and boom—there they all are. Handy even for temporary "set-asides"—for example, when you're choosing photos to include in a photo book, slideshow, or calendar.

People

Photos can auto-group the people in your photos, using facial recognition. For example, all pictures of your mom appear in a clump. This feature is fantastic to remember the next time someone—a potential date, the kindergarten teacher, the Passport Bureau—requests a photo of you or someone in your circle.

To see it at work, click People in the Sidebar. Here are thumbnails representing the faces Photos has found and grouped. Click beneath a thumbnail to edit that person's name. Double-click the thumbnail to see all the photos of this person, laid out exactly like a Memory, described earlier.

Tip: The two buttons at top right, Photos and Faces, control what the thumbnails show—the *entire* photos containing this person, or a zoom-in of just that person's face.

If you see "There are additional photos to review," Photos is informing you that, upon further reflection, it thinks there may be some more pictures of this person. Click Review to begin the process of confirming or denying (and, in the process, improving Photos' discernment skills).

At the bottom, you get options like Remove from People Album (great when this person dumps you) and Confirm Additional Photos (does the same thing as the Review button just described).

Note: This feature doesn't work until the Mac has *analyzed* your photos, which can take a day or more. Apple proudly points out that all this analysis is done on your Mac. (That's in contrast to services like Google Photos, which offers similar features but requires Google to access your photo library.)

You can even drag your favorites into the top of the screen for quick access later.

Places

Every photo you take with a smartphone (and a few very fancy cameras) gets *geo-tagged*—stamped, behind the scenes, with its geographical coordinates. When you click Places in the Sidebar, you see a map, dotted with clusters of photos that you took in each place. Double-click repeatedly to drill down until you're looking at the individual photos taken in a certain spot.

Recents

This folder rounds up all photos that have entered your universe electronically. It includes pictures you took with your phone that got synced to your Mac with iCloud Photos, as well as photos and videos shared by other people.

Imports

Any old photos-management program can show you the most recent batch of photos you've imported (from a camera card or the desktop, for example). But what's great about Photos is that this is a *scrolling* display. It shows *older* batches of imported photos, stretching back in time. Sometimes, that feature makes it super-easy to find a photo or video you're looking for.

Recently Deleted

Even after you think you've deleted a photo or video, you have 30 days to change your mind. Deleted pictures and videos sit in this folder, quietly counting down to their own doomsdays.

If you wind up changing your mind about them, you can open Recently Deleted, click a photo you'd condemned, and click Recover. The photo pops back into its rightful place in the Photos app, saved from termination.

On the other hand, you can also zap a selected photo into oblivion immediately using the Delete Item button. If nothing is selected, you can hit Delete All.

Activity

This is like a Facebook news feed—if it were populated only with shared photos among you and your friends. Here are the photos you've each shared, along with comments; see page 576.

Shared Albums

A list of all the photo albums you've shared electronically (page 575).

Media Types

Here are specialized buttons for the kinds of photos the iPhone and iPad can take, like Videos, Selfies, Live Photos (three-second photo/video hybrids), Portraits (blurry-background photos taken with two- and three-lens iPhones), Panoramas, Time-lapse, Slo-mo, Bursts, and Screenshots. Handy when you're trying to show someone your latest time-lapse masterpiece, for example; now you know where to look for it.

My Albums

You can easily create photo "folders" called albums, for your organizing pleasure. A single photo can appear in as many albums as you like, without using any more disk space. If you delete a photo from an album, you're not removing it from Photos—only from this virtual grouping. You can drag thumbnails around in an album to rearrange them.

Tip: If you drag a photo into several albums, editing it changes that photo everywhere. But if you copy and paste a photo into a different album, you can edit the two independently. And yet, amazingly enough, you're still not using any more disk space.

You can't move very far without finding another way to make an album: Choose File→New Album and then drag thumbnails into it. Or select some thumbnails and then choose File→New Album with Selection. Or click the ➕ that appears when you point to the My Albums in the Sidebar, and then fill it with photos.

If your photo collection came from iPhoto or Aperture, you also see an album (in a folder called, for example, iPhoto Events) for each iPhoto Event or Aperture Project you had in the older program. (Yes, you can also create folders to hold your albums.)

My Projects

This Sidebar item houses the photo books, cards, calendars, prints, and slideshows you've created. To start one, select the photos you want to include, and then choose from the File→Create submenu.

Opening Photos

To open any selected thumbnail so you can see it at full size, press the space bar. (Press it again to close the photo.)

While the photo is open, you can zoom in or out—either drag the top-left slider or use two fingers on your trackpad (pinch or spread them). If your Mac has a Touch Bar (page 227), you can click or drag your finger through it to scroll through the photos in this set.

Tip: You can pop back and forth between actual size and a zoomed-in view by clicking the Z key.

You can open a video this way, too. Play it by clicking ▶ or hitting Option-space, or trim off the dead ends using the ✿→Trim command. For slo-mo videos from the iPhone, you can even adjust the start and stop points for the slow effect.

Tip: You can walk through a video one frame at a time—if you know the secret. On the playback panel, open the ✿ menu and choose Show Frame Stepping Buttons. Sure enough: Now the playback panel has one-frame-at-a-time buttons.

Editing Photos

Before reading about editing in Photos, first absorb this: All the changes described on these pages are *nondestructive*. That is, Photos never forgets the original photo. At any time, hours or years later, you can select a photo and then choose Image→Revert to Original, thus undoing any changes you've ever made. In other words, your edits are never really permanent.

Tip: You can do your editing in Photoshop (or any other external program), too. Just right-click or two-finger click a photo and, from the shortcut menu, choose Edit With→Photoshop (or whatever). Or use the Image→Edit With command. When you're done editing in the other program, hit Save, and marvel as the changes show up in Photos.

The changes you make in the external app are nondestructive—you can undo *them* at any time, too. In other words, you can use Photos for its superior organizational and sharing tools, but Photoshop for editing.

Auto Enhance

The quickest way to fix the color and contrast for a photo is to click the ✺ button. It's so important that it appears at the top of the window when you're viewing any photo, even before you've entered Edit mode. When you click this magical button, Photos analyzes the relative brightness of all the pixels in your photo and attempts to "balance" it. After a moment, the app adjusts the brightness and contrast and intensifies dull or grayish-looking areas. Usually, the pictures look richer and more vivid as a result.

You may find that Auto Enhance has little effect on some photos, only minimally improves others, and totally rescues a few. In any case, if you don't care for the result, you can click ✸ again to turn Auto Enhance off.

To make more fine-tuned corrections to a photo (either an open one or its thumbnail), press the Return key. The Edit mode appears, where three tabs greet you at the top, listed here from right to left:

Crop

When you click this tab, you get a crazy editing screen where you can adjust the size, shape, and angle of the photo.

First, Photos automatically analyzes whatever horizontal lines it finds in the photo—the horizon, for example—and uses them as a guide to straightening the photo automatically. You can reject the proposal (click Reset), or tilt the photo more or less (drag across the round scale).

If you want to rotate the photo more than 90 degrees—for example, if the camera is displaying it sideways—click ◼ as many times as necessary to turn the picture upright.

The other work you can do in this mode is cropping. Cropping means shaving off unnecessary portions of a photo. Usually, you crop a photo to improve its composition—adjusting where the subject appears within the frame of the picture. Cropping is also useful if your photo needs to have a certain *aspect ratio* (length-to-width proportion), like 8 × 10 or 5 × 7.

To crop a photo you've opened, drag any edge or corner of the white border; press Return when the proposed crop looks good. Or use the canned proportions at the right—Square, 3 × 2, 3 × 5, 4 × 3, and so on—to limit the cropping frame to preset proportions.

Filters

Filters are effects that make a photo black and white, oversaturated, or washed out, for example. Click each to see what it looks like on your photo; finish up by clicking Done.

Adjust

On this tab, the right-side panel contains a huge list of Photoshop-style adjustment sliders. For your learning-curve pleasure, they correspond exactly to the ones on the iPhone and iPad (Figure 14-3). For example:

- **Light, Color, Black & White.** When you click one of these categories, you see a "filmstrip" below or beside your photo. You can drag your finger across it, watching the effect on your photo.

 As it turns out, each of these sliders controls a handful of variables, all of which it's changing simultaneously, and each of which you can adjust manually. For example, the Light category includes Brilliance (a slider that, Apple says, "brightens dark areas and pulls in highlights to reveal hidden detail"), Exposure (adjusts the brightness of all pixels), Highlights (pulls lost details out of very bright areas),

Shadows (pulls lost details out of very dark areas), Brightness (like Exposure, but doesn't brighten parts that are already bright), Contrast (heightens the difference between the brightest and darkest areas), and Black Point (determines what is "black," shifting the entire dark/light range upward or downward).

Figure 14-3:
The Edit window offers a zillion expandable control tiles, each with its own sliders and menus. It can get pretty technical— fortunately, each also has an Auto button.

- **Retouch.** This very special brush can instantly and seamlessly paint out a minor flaw—a zit, a stray hair, or a dust speck or scratch on an old photo. All you have to do is dab away at the blemish with the mouse. Use the slider (or press the [and] keys) to resize your cursor until it's slightly bigger than the thing you want to remove.

- **Red-eye.** Devilish, glowing-red pupils in your subjects' eyes has ruined many an otherwise great photo. It's a reflection of the camera's flash off the blood-red retinal tissue at the back of the eyes.

 When you click this button, a message says, "Click each red-eye to correct." Do what it says: Click inside each eye that has the problem. The app turns the red in each eye to black.

Tip: It helps to zoom in first. Use the slider at top left, or press ⌘-plus.

At any point, you can compare your edited photo with the original by holding down the M key, or by clicking the top-left icon (■|□).

More Control Sliders

There's another book's worth of editing power in Photos. The other sliders include White Balance (the color of light in the shot—warmer, cooler, and so on); Levels (individual histograms—graphs—showing the distribution of red, green, and blue pixel densities in the photo, with handles that let you shift that distribution); Curves (lets you draw your own pixel-distribution graphs); Definition (adds clarity by adjusting the contrast of the photo's midtones); Selective Color (adjusts the intensity and shade of individual colors, like yellow or red); Noise Reduction (attempts to minimize "grain," or speckles); Sharpen (slightly de-blurs the entire image); and Vignette (darkens the corners of the image, focusing the attention on the center).

Most of these controls come with sliders, pop-up menus, and other tweaks that let you specify the effect. Most also offer an Auto button, which spares you from having to know what you're doing.

Tip: The Extensions button ●, in Edit mode, gives you access to plug-ins from Apple and other companies that let you do even more with your photo retouching. The one called Markup comes with macOS; it lets you draw or type right onto your photos, exactly as described on page 597.

Shared Albums

Shared Albums (formerly iCloud Photo Sharing) is like a tiny Instagram network of your very own, consisting solely of people you invite. You send photos or videos to *other* people's gadgets. After a party or some other get-together, you could send your best shots to everyone who attended; after a trip, you could post your photographic memories for anyone who might care.

The lucky recipients can post comments about your photos, click a "like" button, and even submit pictures and videos of their own.

In designing this feature, Apple had quite a challenge. There's a lot of back-and-forth among multiple people, sharing multiple photos, so Shared Albums can get complicated. Stay calm and keep your hands and feet inside the tram at all times. Here's how it works.

Note: Before you start, ensure that System Preferences→[your name]→iCloud→Photos is turned on.

Share Some Photos

To share some of your masterpieces with your adoring fans, do this (Figure 14-4):

1. **Choose the photos and videos.**

 You can open just one photo, open an album, or ⌘-click to select any bunch of pictures.

2. Create the album.

Click 📤. On the Share sheet, choose Shared Albums. Hit New Shared Album and give it a name.

3. Specify the audience.

Click ⊕ and choose the iCloud phone number or email addresses of your audience members. Add a comment about the pix, if you like.

4. Click Create.

Your recipients now get a notification that you've shared some pictures with them!

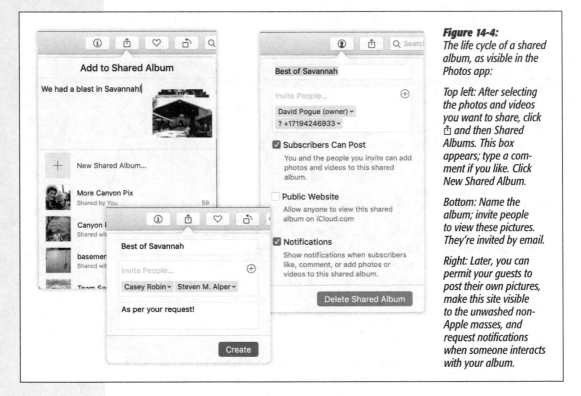

Figure 14-4:
The life cycle of a shared album, as visible in the Photos app:

Top left: After selecting the photos and videos you want to share, click 📤 and then Shared Albums. This box appears; type a comment if you like. Click New Shared Album.

Bottom: Name the album; invite people to view these pictures. They're invited by email.

Right: Later, you can permit your guests to post their own pictures, make this site visible to the unwashed non-Apple masses, and request notifications when someone interacts with your album.

At any time, you can look over the Activity in the left-side list. Here, for your amusement, is a visual record of everything that's gone on in Shared Photo Album Land: photos you've posted, photos other people have posted, comments back and forth, likes, and so on. It's your personal photographic Facebook.

Shared-Photo Management

To add more photos to a shared album, click its album's name and then "Add photos and videos."

All other forms of shared-album management require clicking the album's name and then clicking ⊙ to open the settings panel. Here's what's there:

- **Change who can see this album.** Click a name and press Delete to remove; click ⊕ to add someone new.

- **"Subscribers can post"** means your subscribers can contribute photos and videos of their own. That's a fantastic feature when it contains pictures of an event where there was a crowd: a wedding, show, political rally, picnic, badminton tournament. Everyone who was there can enhance the gallery with shots taken from their own points of view with their own phones or cameras.

- **Public Website** lets even people who aren't members of the Apple cult see these photos. The invitees will get an email containing a web address. It links to a hidden page on the iCloud website that contains your published photos.

- **Notifications** makes your Mac notify you each time someone adds photos or videos to your album, clicks the "Like" button for a photo, or leaves a comment.

- **Delete Shared Album.** If the whole thing gets out of hand, you can slam the door in your subscribers' faces by making the entire album disappear, using this button.

My Photo Stream

Over the years, Apple has experimented with two different ways to sync all your photos across all your gadgets. In the beginning, there was My Photo Stream. Later, there was iCloud Photos (described next). In Catalina, you can't have them both—so read about each before deciding which you want.

My Photo Stream is free, and it works like this: Every time a new photo enters your life—when you take a picture with an i-gadget, for example, or import one onto your Mac—it gets added to your Photo Stream and appears automatically on all your *other* iCloud machines.

It's reasonable to assume that Apple plans to kill off Photo Stream one of these days. Already, it's not even an option for newly registered iCloud accounts. And in Catalina, you can't use it simultaneously with iCloud Photos.

The best thing about My Photo Stream, besides being free, is that it doesn't count against your 5 GB of free iCloud storage.

The not-so-great features: My Photo Stream maintains only the most recent 1,000 photos you've taken—and no videos or Live Photos. The iCloud servers store your photos for only 30 days. And it doesn't sync over the cellular airwaves. It sends photos around only when you're in a Wi-Fi hotspot or connected to a wired network.

Still, as long as your gadgets go online at least once a month, they'll remain current with the My Photo Stream. And once a photo arrives, you can save it to your Camera

Roll, where it's permanently and automatically saved. (To save it on the iPhone or iPad, tap the Share button (⬆) and choose Save Image.)

To find your Photo Stream, open the Photos app on your phone, tablet, Apple TV, or Mac. There it is, in the Albums list: an "album" called My Photo Stream. (On a Windows PC, you'd get a Photo Stream folder in your Pictures folder.)

iCloud Photos

Apple offers yet *another* online photo feature: iCloud Photos (formerly iCloud Photo Library). The idea this time is that *all* your Apple gadgets will keep *all* your photos and videos backed up online and synced. The advantages:

- **All your photos and videos** are always backed up—not just the last 1,000. They don't self-delete after 30 days, or ever.

- **All your photos and videos** appear identically on all your Apple machines.

- **You can access** all your photos and videos at *icloud.com*, from any computer or phone.

- **You can reclaim** a lot of storage space. There's an option to offload the original photos and videos to iCloud but leave small, phone-sized copies on your phone.

There's a sizable downside to iCloud Photos, too:

- **Your entire iCloud account** comes with only 5 gigabytes of free storage. If you start backing up your photo library to it, you'll almost certainly have to pay to expand your iCloud storage. Photos and videos eat up a lot of space.

If you decide to dive in, choose Photos→Preferences→iCloud and turn on iCloud Photos.

While you're here, you'll be offered this important choice:

- **Optimize Mac Storage.** If you turn this on, your original photos and videos get backed up to iCloud—but on your Mac, you'll be left with much smaller versions that are just right for viewing on the screen (but not high enough resolution to, for example, print). This arrangement saves you a *ton* of space on your Mac.

 You'll rarely even perceive that the originals aren't actually on your Mac, apart from a brief downloading progress bar when you try to edit or share them.

- **Download Originals to this Mac** leaves the big originals on your computer.

Finally, the uploading process begins. If you have a lot of photos and videos, it can take a long time. But when it's all over, you'll have instant access to all your photos and videos everywhere: all Macs, iPhones, and iPads logged into your iCloud account, as well as *icloud.com*.

Printing, Scanning, Fonts & Graphics

T he Mac may be only the 10 percent solution in the mainstream business world, but in the graphics and printing industries, it's the 800-pound gorilla. You'd better believe that when Apple designed macOS, it worked very hard to keep its graphics and printing fans happy.

This chapter tackles printing, scanning, fonts, graphics, ColorSync, and PDF, which macOS uses as an everyday exchange format—one of the biggest perks of using a Mac.

Mac Meets Printer

MacOS used to come preloaded with the printing software for every conceivable printer model from every conceivable printer company—Epson, HP, Lexmark, Canon, and others—several gigabytes' worth. Most people wound up with wads of printing software they'd never use.

When you install macOS these days, though, you get *only* the drivers for the printers you actually have, or are nearby on the network. If you ever encounter a different printer model later, macOS offers to download it for you on the spot.

Setting Up a Printer

Setting up a printer is incredibly easy. The first time you want to print something, follow this guide:

1. **Connect the printer to the Mac, and then turn the printer on.**

 Inkjet printers and laser printers hook up either to your USB jack or to your network (Ethernet or wireless).

2. **Open the document you want to print. Choose File→Print. In the Print dialog box, choose your printer's name from the Printer pop-up menu (or one of its submenus, if any, like Nearby Printers). See Figure 15-1.**

 Cool! Wasn't that easy? Very nice how the Mac autodiscovers, autoconfigures, and autolists almost any USB, FireWire, Bluetooth, or Bonjour printer.

 Have a nice afternoon.

 Oh—unless your printer *isn't* listed in the Printer pop-up menu. In that case, read on.

Note: "Nearby Printers" refers to printers that aren't connected directly to your Mac but are accessible anyway: a printer connected to an Apple Time Capsule or an AirPort base station, certain network printers that speak Bonjour, or printers connected to other Macs that you've shared, as described later in this chapter.

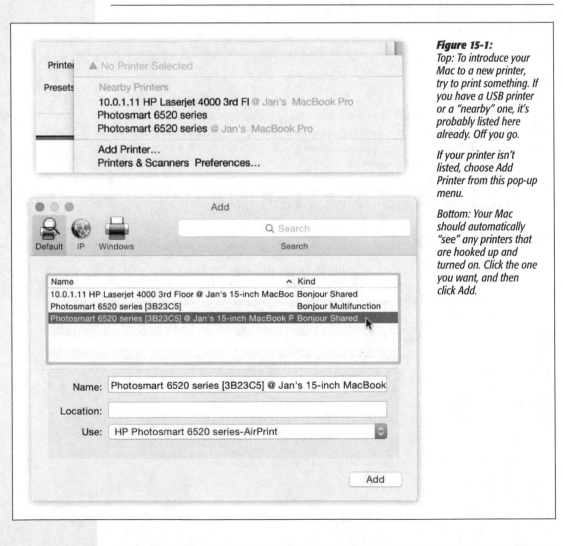

Figure 15-1:
Top: To introduce your Mac to a new printer, try to print something. If you have a USB printer or a "nearby" one, it's probably listed here already. Off you go.

If your printer isn't listed, choose Add Printer from this pop-up menu.

Bottom: Your Mac should automatically "see" any printers that are hooked up and turned on. Click the one you want, and then click Add.

3. **From the Printer pop-up menu (Figure 15-1, top), choose Add Printer.**

 A special setup window opens (Figure 15-1, bottom), which is even better at auto-detecting printers available to your Mac. If you see the printer's name here, click it and then click Add.

 You're all set. The End.

 Unless, of course, your printer *still* isn't showing up. Proceed to step 4.

4. **Click the icon for the *kind* of printer you have: Default, IP, or Windows.**

 Default usually does the trick, especially if you have an inkjet printer. Choose IP if you have a network printer that's not showing up in Default. And choose Windows if there's a Windows-only printer out there on your office network.

 After a moment, the names of any printers that are turned on and connected appear in the printer list. For most people, that means only one printer—but one is enough.

5. **Click the name of the printer you want to use.**

 As an optional step, you can open the Use pop-up menu at the bottom of the dialog box. Select Choose a Driver, and then, in the list that appears, choose your printer's model name, if you can find it. That's how your Mac knows what printing features to offer you when the time comes: double-sided, legal size, second paper tray, and so on.

6. **Click Add.**

 After a moment, you return to the main Printer Browser window, where your printer now appears. You're ready to print.

Note: If you still don't see your printer's name show up, ask yourself these questions: Is my Mac on a corporate network? Does the network have an LPR (line printer remote) printer? If you and your company's network nerd determine that the printer you want to use is, in fact, an LPR printer, click IP Printing at the top of the Printer Browser dialog box. Fill in the appropriate IP address and other settings, as directed by your cheerful network administrator.

Printer Preferences

If you're lucky enough to own several printers, just repeat these steps for each one. Eventually, you'll have introduced the Mac to all the printers available to it, so all their names show up in the printer list.

To see the printer list so far, open System Preferences→Printers & Scanners. You can have all kinds of fun here (Figure 15-2):

- **Choose a default printer.** As indicated by the "Default printer" pop-up menu, macOS intends, conveniently enough, to use whichever printer you used for the last printout for the next one. Most people, after all, don't switch printers much.

Still, you can choose one particular printer from this pop-up menu to set it as the default printer—the one the Mac uses unless you intervene by choosing from the Printer pop-up menu in the Print dialog box.

- **Create desktop printer icons.** *This* handy, little-known feature gives you drag-and-drop access to your printers.

 From the Printers & Scanners pane of System Preferences, just drag a printer's icon out of the window and onto the desktop (or wherever you like). Repeat for your other printers. From now on, you can print a document on a certain printer just by dragging the document's icon onto the appropriate icon.

- **Check the ink level.** Click a printer, and then click Options & Supplies, to see how your inkjet ink or laser-printer toner level is. That way you won't be caught short when you're on an urgent deadline and your printer is out of ink. You also get a bright-yellow "low ink" warning in the dialog box that actually appears when you print.

Figure 15-2:
You know that stuff you read about earlier? Setting up printers from the Print dialog box? You can do the same work here. Click the + button below the left-side list.

Making the Printout

You can't miss the Print dialog box. It appears, like it or not, whenever you choose File→Print in one of your programs.

The options you encounter depend on the printer you're using. They also depend on whether you *expand* the dialog box by clicking the Show Details button. That reveals a lot of useful options, including a handy preview; see Figure 15-3.

After you expand the box, the options you find vary by printer. But here are the common ones:

- **Printer.** If you have more than one printer connected to your Mac, you can indicate which one you want to use for a particular printout by choosing its name from this pop-up menu.

- **Presets.** Here's a way to preserve your favorite print settings: Once you've proceeded through this dialog box, specifying the number of copies, which printer trays you want the paper taken from, and so on, you can choose Save Current Settings as Preset from the pop-up menu and then assign your settings set a name (like "Borderless, 2 copies"). Thereafter, you'll be able to recreate that suite of settings simply by choosing its name from this pop-up menu.

- **Copies.** Type the number of copies you want printed.

- **Pages.** You don't have to print an entire document—you can print, say, only pages 2 through 15.

Tip: You don't have to type numbers into both the From and To boxes. If you leave the first box blank, the Mac assumes you mean "From page 1." If you leave the second box blank, it understands that you mean "To the end." To print only the first three pages, in other words, leave the first box blank and type *3* into the second box. (These page numbers refer to the physical pages you're printing, not any fancy numbering you've set up in your word processor. As far as the Print dialog box is concerned, the first printed page is page 1, even if you've told your word processor to label it "page 455.")

Figure 15-3:
Left: Most of the time, all you want is one darned copy of what's on your screen. So the standard Print dialog box is basic: a preview, page controls, and a Print button.

Right: But when you click Show Details, you get a new world of options: orientation, magnification, and so on.

- **Paper Size, Orientation.** Somebody at Apple finally realized how frustrating it was to have to open the Page Setup dialog box to change the paper-size and orientation settings and then open the Print dialog box for other settings. Now, in most programs, these controls are duplicated right in the Print dialog box for your convenience.

- **PDF.** You can easily save any document as a PDF file instead of printing it—a truly beautiful feature that saves paper, ink, and time (see page 587).

 Apple has added a long list of additional PDF options (like password-protected PDFs, emailed ones, and so on). But it faced a design quandary: How could it offer a list of PDF-related options without junking up the Print dialog box?

 Its solution was a strange little item called a pop-up *button,* shown in Figure 15-3, left. Use it like a pop-up menu. The command you'll use most often is probably Save as PDF, which turns the printout into a PDF file instead of sending it to the printer.

If you examine the unnamed pop-up menu just below the Orientation buttons, you'll find dozens of additional options. They depend on your printer model and the program you're using, but here are some typical choices:

- **Layout.** You can save paper and ink or toner cartridges by printing several miniature "pages" on a single sheet of paper.

- **Paper Handling.** You can opt to print your pages in reverse order so they stack correctly, or you can print just odd or just even pages so you can run them through again for double-sided printing.

- **Quality & Media** (inkjet printers only). Here's where you specify the print quality you want, the kind of paper you're printing on, and so on. (The name of this panel varies by manufacturer.)

- **Paper Feed.** If you chose the correct printer model when setting up your printer, this screen already knows about your printer's various paper trays. Here's where you specify which pages you want to come from which paper tray. (By far the most popular use for this feature is printing the first page of a letter on company letterhead and the following pages on blank paper from a second tray.)

- **Collation.** This controls the printing order for the pages. For example, if you print two copies of a three-page document, the Mac generally prints the pages in this order: 1, 2, 3, 1, 2, 3. If you turn off Collated, on the other hand, it prints in this order: 1, 1, 2, 2, 3, 3.

- **Cover Page.** Yes, that throwaway info page has made its way from the fax world into the hard-copy world.

- **Scheduler.** This option lets you specify *when* you want your document to print. If you're a freelancer, sitting at home with an inkjet on your desk, you might not immediately grasp why anyone wouldn't want the printouts *right now.* But try printing a 400-page catalog in a big office where other people on the network might conceivably resent you for tying up the printer all afternoon, and you'll get the idea.

- **ColorSync.** Most color printers offer this panel, where you can adjust the color settings—to add a little more red, perhaps. This is also where you indicate whose *color-matching system* you want to use: Apple's ColorSync (page 609), your printer manufacturer's, or none at all.

Then, below the light-gray line in this pop-up menu, you'll find a few options that are unique to the chosen printer or program. Some HP printers, for example, offer Cover Page, Finishing, and other choices. A couple of other likely guest commands:

- **[program name].** Whichever program you're using—Mail, Word, Pages, or anything else—may offer its own special printing options on this screen.

- **Summary.** This command summons a text summary of all your settings so far.

Printing

When all your settings look good, click Print (or press Return) to send your document to the printer.

Managing Printouts

After you've used the Print command, you can either sit there until the paper emerges from the printer, or you can *manage* the printouts-in-waiting. That option is attractive primarily to people who do a lot of printing, have connections to a lot of printers, or share printers with many other people.

Start by opening the printer's window. If you're already in the process of printing, just click the printer's Dock icon. If not, open System Preferences→Printers & Scanners, click the printer's name, and then click Open Print Queue.

At this point, you see something like Figure 15-4. The printouts that will soon be sliding out of your printer appear in a tidy list.

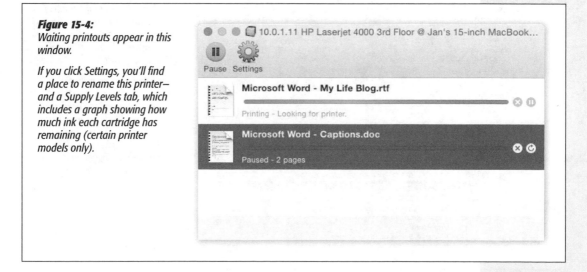

Figure 15-4:
Waiting printouts appear in this window.

If you click Settings, you'll find a place to rename this printer—and a Supply Levels tab, which includes a graph showing how much ink each cartridge has remaining (certain printer models only).

Here are some of the ways in which you can control these waiting printouts, which Apple collectively calls the *print queue*:

- **Delete them.** By clicking the tiny ✕ icon to the right of the document you want to delete, you remove that item from the list of waiting printouts. Now it won't print.

- **Pause them.** By clicking the tiny ❙❙ icon to the right of the document, you pause that printout. It doesn't print until you click the ⊙ button. (Other documents continue to print.) This pausing business could be useful when, for example, you need time to check or refill the printer, or when you're just about to print your letter of resignation as your boss drops by (maybe to offer you a promotion).

- **Halt them all.** You can stop all printouts from a printer by clicking Pause. (They resume when you click the button again, which now says Resume Printer.)

Tip: As you now know, the icon for a printer's queue window appears automatically in the Dock when you print. But it also *stays* in the Dock for the rest of the day; it doesn't disappear when the printing is complete. If you wish it would, right-click or two-finger click the printer's Dock icon; from the shortcut menu, choose Quit.

Printer Sharing

Printer sharing is for people (or offices) with more than one Mac connected to a network, who'd rather not buy a separate printer for each machine. Instead, you

Figure 15-5:
Top: On the Mac with the printer, open the Sharing panel of System Preferences. Turn on Printer Sharing, and then turn on the checkboxes for the printers you want to share. Switch to the Printers & Scanners pane, and turn on "Share this printer on the network" for the printers you want to share.

Bottom: To use a shared printer elsewhere on the network, open the document you want to print, and then choose File→Print. In the Print dialog box, the shared printer is identified under the Nearby Printers heading.

connect the printer to one Mac, flip a couple of software switches, and boom: The other Macs on the network can send their printouts to the printer—even wirelessly, if they're on a Wi-Fi network.

Note: Of course, this feature is most useful when you're sharing printers that can hook up to only one Mac at a time, like USB inkjet photo printers. Office laser printers are often designed to be networked from day one.

Setting up printer sharing is easy; see Figure 15-5, top. To make a printout from across the network, see the instructions in Figure 15-5, bottom.

Tip: You can control *which* account holders on your network are allowed to use the printer you've shared. You know that idiot in Accounting who's always using up your cartridges by printing 200-page documents? Cut that sucker off! Just add the lucky guests' names to the Users column in System Preferences→Sharing→Printer Sharing, as shown in Figure 15-5, top.

If your PC-wielding friends install Bonjour for Windows (a free download from this book's "Missing CD" page at *missingmanuals.com*), they can print to your Mac's shared printer, too.

Note: Of course, your Mac (the one actually attached to the printer) must be turned on in order for the other computers to print. In part, that's because the documents-in-waiting from other people pile up on *your* hard drive.

PDF Files

Sooner or later, everyone with a personal computer encounters PDF (portable document format) files. These, of course, are Adobe documents that anyone can view, read, and print using either Preview (page 589) or the free Adobe Reader included with every PC and Mac operating system. Many a software manual, ReadMe file, and downloadable "white paper" come in this format.

In macOS, you can turn *any document* (in any program with a Print command) into a PDF file—a trick that once required a $250 program called Adobe Acrobat Distiller.

But why would you want to create PDFs? What's the big deal about them? Consider these advantages:

- **Other people see your layout.** When you distribute PDF files, rather than files in their original programs, your recipients see precisely the same fonts, colors, page design, and other elements you put in your original document. And here's the kicker: They get to see all this even if they don't *have* the fonts or the software you used to create the document.

 Contrast that with the alternative: Say you're sending somebody a Microsoft Word document. If your correspondent doesn't have precisely the same fonts you have, he'll see a screwy layout. And if he doesn't have Word or another program that can open Word files, he'll see nothing at all.

- **It's universal.** PDF files are very common in the Mac, Windows, Unix/Linux, and even smartphone worlds. When you create a PDF file, you can distribute it (by email, for example) without worrying about what kinds of computers your correspondents are using.

- **It has very high resolution.** Professionally produced PDF files print at the maximum quality of any printer. A PDF file prints great both on cheapo inkjets and on high-quality image-setting gear at professional print shops. (Right now you're looking at a PDF file that was printed at a publishing plant.)

Note: MacOS creates *screen-optimized* PDF files: compact, easy-to-email files that look good onscreen but don't have high enough resolution for professional printing. For high-end purposes and more optimization for specific uses (web, fancy press machines, and so on), you still need a program like Adobe Acrobat Pro, Illustrator, or InDesign.

- **You can search it.** A PDF file may look like a captured graphic, but behind the scenes, its text is still text; Spotlight can find a word in a PDF haystack in a matter of seconds. That's an especially handy feature when you work with electronic software manuals in PDF format.

Opening PDF Files

There's nothing to opening a PDF file: Just double-click it. You can also highlight its icon in the Finder and tap the space bar for a Quick Look at it.

Creating PDF Files

Opening, schmopening—what's really exciting is the ability to create your *own* PDF files. The easiest way is to click the PDF pop-up button in the standard Print dialog box (Figure 15-6). When you click it, you're offered a world of interesting PDF-creation possibilities. Several of them convert whatever document you're on the verge of printing into a frozen PDF file that opens into Preview, sends in Mail as an

Figure 15-6:
The PDF button is crawling with neat ways to process a document while it's still open—and you can add to this pop-up button's list, too, by choosing Edit Menu.

For example, you can create even more elaborate pathways for documents you want to print or convert to PDF using an Automator workflow you've built yourself—if you're that kind of technical.

attachment, adds itself to the Books app for reading, saves to your iCloud Drive, or sends via Messages. A few merit further explanation:

- **Save as PDF** saves your document to the disk as a PDF instead of printing it.

- **Save as PostScript** gives you a PostScript file instead of a PDF. (PostScript is a format preferred by some designers and print shops. It consists of highly precise "what to draw" instructions for PostScript laser printers.)

- **Save to Web Receipts** is one of the simplest and sweetest features in all of macOS.

 You use it when you've just ordered something on a website, and the "Print this receipt" screen is staring you in the face. Don't waste paper and ink—and, later, time trying to find it! Instead, use this command. You get a perfectly usable PDF version of the receipt, stored in your Home→Documents→Web Receipts folder, where you can use Spotlight to find it later, when you need to consult because your gray-market goods never arrived.

Note: You may see other commands here, too, as you install other companies' software.

Preview

Preview is macOS's scanning software, graphics viewer, fax viewer, and PDF reader. It has always been teeming with features that most Mac owners never even knew were there.

Tip: Preview can open Microsoft Office documents (Word, PowerPoint, Excel) and iWork documents (Pages, Numbers, Keynote). You can't edit them in Preview, but you can read them, search them, and print them. No longer must you pay homage to Microsoft's bottom line just to have a look at the documents people send you.

Scanning

If you own a scanner, chances are good that you won't be needing whatever special scanning software came with it. Instead, macOS gives you *two* programs that can operate any standard scanner: Image Capture (page 417) and Preview. In fact, the controls are identical in both programs.

Open Preview, choose File→Import from Scanner→[your scanner's name], and put your photos or documents into the scanner.

Note: You can share a scanner on the network, if you like, by turning on Scanner Sharing in System Preferences→Sharing. That's sort of a weird option, though, for two reasons. First, what do you gain by sitting somewhere else in the building? Do you really want to yell up to whomever's sitting next to the scanner, "OK! Put in the next photo!"?

Second, don't forget that anyone else on the network will be able to see whatever you're scanning. Embarrassment may result. You've been warned.

Now you have a couple of decisions to make:

- **Separate and straighten?** If you turn on "Detect separate items" in the Scan Size menu, macOS will perform a nifty little stunt indeed: It will check to see if you've put *multiple* items onto the scanner glass, like several small photos, as shown in Figure 15-7. (It looks for rectangular images surrounded by empty white space, so if the photos are overlapping, this feature won't work.)

 If it finds multiple items, Preview automatically straightens them, compensating for haphazard placement on the glass, and then saves them as individual files.

Figure 15-7:
When you use the Show Details button, you get a new panel on the right, where you can specify all the tweaky details for the scan you're about to make: resolution, size, and so on. See how the photos have dotted lines around them? That's because Detect Separate Items is turned on. These will be scanned into two separate files.

- **Where to file?** Use the "Scan to" pop-up menu to specify where you want the newly scanned image files to land—in the Pictures folder, for example. You have some other cool options beyond sticking the scans in a folder; for example, you can send the resulting images to Photos or Mail.

Once you've put a document onto or into the scanner, click Scan. The scanner heaves to life. After a moment, you see on the screen what's on the glass. It's simultaneously been sent to the folder (or post-processing task) you requested using the "Scan to" pop-up menu.

More power to you

As you can see, Apple has tried to make *basic* scanning as simple as possible: one click. That idiotproof method gives you very few options.

If you click Show Details before you scan, though, you get a special panel on the right side of the window that's filled with useful scanning controls (Figure 15-7).

Opening the Details panel has another handy benefit, too: It lets you scan only a *portion* of what's on the scanner glass. Once you've put the document or photo into the scanner, click Overview. Preview does a quick pass and displays on the screen whatever is on the glass. You'll see a dotted-line rectangle around the entire scanned image—unless you've turned on "Detect separate images," in which case you see a dotted-line rectangle around *each* item on the glass.

You can adjust these rectangles until you've enclosed precisely the portion of the image you want scanned. For example, drag the rectangles' corner handles to resize them; drag inside the rectangles to move them; drag the right end of the line inside the rectangle to rotate it; preview the rotation by pressing Control and Option.

Finally, when you think you've got the selection rectangle(s) correctly positioned, click Scan to trigger the actual scan.

Importing Camera Photos

Preview can import pictures directly from a digital camera (or iPhone), meaning that there are now *three* macOS apps that can perform that duty—Photos (page 565) and Image Capture (page 417) are the other two. It's sometimes handy to use Preview for this purpose, though, because it has size/resolution options and format conversion options that no other built-in software has. Choose File→Import from [your camera's name], and off you go.

Multiple Pages, Multiple Views

One hallmark of Preview is its effortless handling of *multiples:* multiple fax pages, multiple PDF files, batches of photos, and so on. The key to understanding the possibilities is mastering the Sidebar, shown in Figure 15-8. The idea is that these thumbnails let you navigate pages or graphics without having to open a rat's nest of individual windows.

Tip: You can drag these thumbnails from one Preview window's Sidebar into another. That's a great way to mix and match pages from different PDF documents into a single new one, for example.

To control the Sidebar, choose one of these commands from the View menu:

- **Hide Sidebar.** Gets the Sidebar out of your way.

- **Thumbnails.** This standard view (Figure 15-8, left) offers a scrolling vertical list of miniature pages or photos. Click one to see it at full size in the main window. Make the thumbnails larger or smaller by dragging the window/Sidebar dividing line.

- **Table of Contents.** If you're looking over photos, this option turns the Sidebar into a scrolling list of their names. If you've opened a group of PDFs all at once, you see a list of them. Or, if you have a PDF that contains chapter headings, you see them listed in the Sidebar as a table of contents.

- **Highlights & Notes.** Preview is a better PDF editor than ever. If you add comments and highlighting to a PDF document, as described later in this section, you can view all of them in this tidy list—and click one to jump to it.

- **Bookmarks.** Here you can see any bookmarks you've added to a PDF, as described later in this section.

- **Contact Sheet.** When you choose this view, the *main* window scrolls away, leaving you with a full screen of thumbnail miniatures. It's like a light table where you can look over all your photos or PDF pages at once. Make them bigger or smaller using the magnifying glass buttons at top left.

Tip: You can also change among these views by pressing Option-⌘-1, -2, -3, -4, -5, and -6.

Figure 15-8:
The Sidebar can display thumbnails, a table of contents, or annotations, or it can appear as a full-screen array of thumbnail images. Drag the central scroll bar to make the Sidebar bigger; drag the lower-right corner of the Sidebar to make the whole Preview window bigger.

Preview as Graphics Viewer

Preview can display and manipulate pictures saved in a wide variety of formats, including common graphics formats like JPEG, TIFF, PICT, and GIF; less commonly used formats like BMP, PNG, SGI, and TGA; and even Photoshop, EPS, and PDF graphics.

Tip: Don't miss the Tools→Show Magnifier command. It gives you a loupe: a magnifying circle (or, in a PDF document, a magnifying rectangle) that lets you inspect part of your graphic or PDF file more closely.

Bunches o' graphics

If you highlight a group of image files in the Finder and open them all at once (for example, by pressing ⌘-O), Preview opens the first one but lists the thumbnails of the whole group in the Sidebar. You can walk through them with the ▲ and ▼ keys, or you can choose View→Slideshow (Shift-⌘-F) to open a full-screen slideshow.

Tip: You can change the order of the photos just by dragging them around in the Sidebar, in any of its views.

Cropping graphics

To crop graphics in Preview, drag across the part of the graphic you want to keep. To redraw, drag the round handles on the dotted rectangle or, to proceed with the crop, choose Tools→Crop. (The keyboard shortcut is ⌘-K.) Since Preview is an Auto Save program, you can always return to the original if you change your mind.

Tip: You can also rotate an image—even a PDF document—in 90-degree increments and then flip it vertically or horizontally, using the commands in the Tools menu. In fact, if you select several thumbnails in the Sidebar first, you can rotate or flip them all simultaneously.

Fixing up photos

Preview is no Photoshop, but it gets closer all the time:

- **Choose Tools→Show Inspector.** A floating palette appears. The tabs here depend on whether you've opened a PDF file or a photo, but they may include General Info (the photo's name, its pixel dimensions, and so on); More Info (camera settings like the lens type, ISO setting, focus mode, whether the flash was on, and so on); Keywords (add keywords so you'll be able to search for this image later using Spotlight); Crop (dimensions and selection size); and Annotations (markings that have been made to an image—maybe by you—using the Tools→Annotate function).

POWER USERS' CLINIC

Scaling and Resampling

When you're fooling around with a picture's size and resolution in the Adjust Size dialog box, you might find that a couple of the options take a little explaining.

If "Scale proportionally" is turned on, then Preview changes the Height number proportionally when you change the Width number, and vice versa. In other words, it won't let you change the *shape* of the photo; that's why a little padlock (🔒) icon appears to bracket the Height and Width boxes.

If "Resample image" is turned off, Preview adjusts the image's size by making the existing dots bigger or

> **Image Dimensions**
> Fit into: Custom ▾ pixels
> Width: 6
> Height: 6.67 🔒 inches ▾
> Resolution: 72 pixels/inch ▾
> ☑ Scale proportionally
> ☑ Resample image
>
> **Resulting Size**
> 52.8 percent
> 93 KB (was 253 KB)
>
> Cancel OK

smaller—but never changes the *number* of dots. (That's why a 🔒 now bracket links all three boxes together. For example, you can make the image larger—but you'll lower the number of dots per inch.)

If "Resample image" is turned *on*, you're giving Preview permission to add or subtract pixels as necessary to scale the photo up or down. Of course, it can't create detail that wasn't there in the original, but if you are scaling the picture *up*, it does a decent job of generating new pixels by averaging the colors of the neighboring ones.

- **Choose Tools→Adjust Color.** A translucent, floating color-adjustment palette appears, teeming with sliders for brightness, contrast, exposure, saturation (color intensity), temperature and tint (color cast), sharpness, and more. See Figure 15-9.

Figure 15-9:
Humble little Preview has grown up into a big, strong mini-Photoshop. You can really fix up a photo if you know what you're doing, using these sliders. Or you can just click the Auto Levels button. It sets all the sliders for you, which generally does an amazing job of making almost any photo look better.

- **Choose Tools→Adjust Size.** This command lets you adjust a photo's resolution, which comes in handy a lot. For example, you can scale an unwieldy 10-megapixel, gazillion-by-gazillion-pixel shot down to a nice 640 × 480 JPEG that's small enough to send by email. Or you can shrink a photo down so it fits within a desktop window, for use as a window background.

 There's not much to it. Type in the new print dimensions you want for the photo, in inches or whatever units you choose from the pop-up menu. If you like, you can also change the resolution (the number of pixels per inch) by editing the Resolution box.

Tip: Here's a Photoshoppy feature you would never, ever expect to find in a simple viewer like Preview: You can extract a person (or anything, really) from the background. That's handy when you want to clip yourself out of a group shot to use as your Messages portrait, when you want to paste somebody into a new background, or when you break up with someone and want him out of your photos. See the free PDF appendix to this chapter, "Cutting People from Photos with Preview." It's on this book's "Missing CD" page at *missingmanuals.com*.

Converting file formats

Preview doesn't just open all these file formats—it can also convert among most of them. You can pop open some old Mac PICT files and turn them into BMP files for a Windows person, pry open a TIFF file from a scanner and turn it into a JPEG for use on your website, and so on.

Tip: What's even cooler is that you can open raw PostScript files right into Preview, which converts them into PDF files on the spot. You no longer need a PostScript laser printer to print out high-end diagrams and page layouts that come to you as PostScript files. Thanks to Preview, even an inkjet printer can handle them.

All you have to do is open the file you want to convert and choose File→Export. In the dialog box that appears, choose the new format for the image using the Format pop-up menu (JPEG, TIFF, or PNG, for example); if you press the Option key, you're offered even more file types. Finally, click Save to export the file.

Preview as PDF Reader

Preview is a nearly full-blown equivalent of Adobe Reader, the free program used by millions to read PDF documents. It lets you search PDF documents, copy text out of them, add comments, fill in forms, click live hyperlinks, add highlighting, circle certain passages, type in notes—features that used to be available only in Adobe's Acrobat Reader. You can even fill out *PDF forms*, typing into boxes on the electronic document.

Tip: Don't forget that Preview is one of macOS's certified full-screen apps, as described on page 173. That means you can also flip through the pages of a PDF using the "next page" gesture: a two-finger swipe on the trackpad.

Here are the basics:

• **Zoom in and out** using ⌘-plus and ⌘-minus.

Tip: Another way to get a closer look: Press the ` key (upper left of your keyboard), or choose Tools→Show Magnifier. Now a big magnifying glass follows your cursor; you can even press + or − to zoom in or out within it. Dismiss the magnifier by pressing ` again.

• **Use the View menu commands** to control how the PDF document appears: as two-page spreads, as single scrolling sheets of "paper towel," with borders that indicate ends of pages, and so on.

• **Press the space bar to page through a document** (add Shift to page *upward*). The Page Up and Page Down keys do the same thing.

Tip: Some PDF documents include a table of contents, which you'll see in Preview's Sidebar, complete with flippy triangles that denote chapter headings. Use the ▲ and ▼ keys to walk through these chapter headings, and then expand one that looks good by pressing the ▶ key. Collapse it again with the ◀ key. In other words, you expand and collapse flippy triangles in Preview just as you do in a Finder list view.

- **Bookmark your place** by choosing Bookmarks→Add Bookmark (⌘-D). You'll be able to return to that spot by choosing its name—the page number and the first several words on the page—from the Bookmarks menu.

 These remain living, editable entities even after the document is saved and reopened. And they're full-blown Acrobat annotations; they'll show up when your PDF document is opened by Acrobat Reader or even on Windows PCs.

- **If you want to copy material out of a PDF document**—for pasting into a word processor, for example, where you can edit it—click the Text tool (the Aa⏐ on the toolbar) or choose Tools→Text Selection. Now you can drag through some text (and even graphics) and then choose Edit→Copy, just as though the PDF document were a web page. You can even drag across page boundaries.

- **To find a word or phrase** somewhere in a PDF document, press ⌘-F (or choose Edit→Find→Find) to open the Find box—or just type into the 🔍 box on the right of the toolbar, if it's open. Proceed as shown in Figure 15-10.

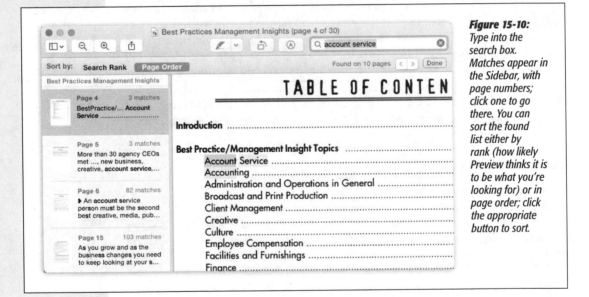

Figure 15-10:
Type into the search box. Matches appear in the Sidebar, with page numbers; click one to go there. You can sort the found list either by rank (how likely Preview thinks it is to be what you're looking for) or in page order; click the appropriate button to sort.

The search results show a snippet of the actual text surrounding each "find," along with the number of matches per page, and even a thumbnail of the page itself. It's all about context, baby.

- **You can save a single page from a PDF** as a TIFF file to use it in other graphics, word-processing, or page-layout programs that might not directly recognize PDF.

 To extract a page, use the usual File→Export command, making sure to choose the new file format from the pop-up menu. (If you choose a format like Photoshop or JPEG, Preview converts only the currently selected page of your PDF document.

That's because there's no such thing as a multipage Photoshop or JPEG document. But you already knew that.)

Tip: You can also scan a new page directly into an open PDF document, or use a page you shot on your i-gadget. Choose File→Import from [your device].

- **Add keywords to a graphic or PDF** (choose Tools→Show Inspector; click the 🔍 tab; click the **+** button to fill them in). Later, you'll be able to call up these documents with a quick Spotlight search for those details.

Annotations and Drawing Tools

Preview has become the Godzilla of PDF editing programs. It is, in fact, a full-blown drawing program now, with a choice of shapes, colors, lines, arrows, and text boxes to dress up a PDF document. These are identical to the drawing tools in Mail, so they're worth getting to know.

You can type notes (in a box or a bubble), add clickable links (to web addresses or other spots in the document), or use circles, arrows, rectangles, strikethroughs, underlining, or colored highlighting to draw your PDF readers' attention to certain sections. You can dress up photos this way, too. In fact, you can even use your laptop's trackpad to draw on a document—or to sign one.

To highlight text in a PDF document, click the ✒ button on the toolbar, and then drag across the text. Use the pop-up menu next to the ✒ to choose a different highlighter color, or to choose underlining or strikethrough styles.

For the more ambitious annotation styles, like signing a document or drawing on it, open the Markup toolbar, shown in Figure 15-11. To do that, click Ⓐ on the toolbar. At this point, the icons on the toolbar offer these features:

- **Aa‖ Text Selection, ⬚ Rectangular Selection.** These toggles let you highlight text in a document (so you can copy it, for example) or select a chunk of a graphic.

- **⤴ Sketch.** This remarkable tool lets you draw freehand in your document—and marvel as Preview cleans up your lines. For example, if you draw what's more or less a diagonal line, Preview straightens it and makes it a perfect 45 degrees. If you draw what seems to be a box or a circle, Preview zaps it into perfection. Use the ≡⌄, ▢ ⌄, and ⬚ ⌄ buttons to specify the line thickness, add a colored border, or fill the interior with a background color. Figure 15-11 shows the process.

- **⬡⌄ Shapes.** Use this pop-up menu to choose what kind of perfect shape you want to draw: line, arrow, circle, square, and so on. It will use whatever thickness and color you've chosen from the ≡⌄ and ▢ ⌄ pop-up menus. Once you've selected a tool, drag diagonally on your document to place the shape.

 The two icons at the bottom of this palette are unusual for a drawing program but handy when you want to draw attention to some part of a document or photo.

 At lower left in the Shapes pop-up menu, the Mask dims out the entire document except the rectangular portion you enclose. The tool at lower right, the loupe,

magnifies a circular area to draw the viewer's eye to it (Figure 15-11, bottom). Whatever attention-flagging markings you enclose using these tools become part of the finished, exported PDF or graphic.

Figure 15-11:
As you draw a freehand shape (top), macOS helpfully straightens your straight lines and makes your curved ones perfect (middle).

If you actually prefer your imperfect original, you can click the original (or any other variation) from the little floating palette shown at left in the middle illustration.

The Shapes pop-up menu (⬡˅) offers a range of fascinating drawing options. They include the classic Speech Bubble and the loupe, which produces a magnified view of one circular area (bottom).

While you're editing a loupe, you see a tiny green dot. Drag it to adjust the magnification inside the circle; drag the blue one to change the circle's size.

- ⊤ **Text.** Click to place a text box on the image. You can drag it or reshape it—and, of course, you can replace the word "Text" inside it with much superior words of your own. Use the *A* ˅ pop-up menu to choose a font, color, size, and style; use the ▢ ˅ and ▱ ˅ buttons to add a colored border or fill the interior with a background color.

- ℐ˅ **Sign.** See the next section for details.

- 🖼 **Note.** Click to place a virtual Post-it note onto the document. As you type or paste into it, the note expands; you can't otherwise control its size or shape. But when you click outside the note, it collapses down into a little square button. At this point, you can change the note's background color (right-click or two-finger click; choose a color from the shortcut menu), drag the little square to move the note, or reopen the note by double-clicking.

Tip: Later you can view a tidy list of all your notes and highlighted passages by choosing View→Highlighting and Notes. On the resulting panel, Preview ordinarily displays each text note with your name and the date. If you'd rather not have that info added, choose Preview→Preferences, click PDF, and then turn off "Add name to annotations."

- ☰ﹸ **Shape Style.** This palette governs the thickness and style of whatever line or shape you're drawing (or you've selected). There are some cool options here, including dashed lines, shadowed ones, chalky-looking ones—and ones with arrowheads.

- ▢ﹸ **Border Color,** ▱ﹸ **Fill Color.** These palettes affect the border color (line color) and interior background color of whatever shape you're drawing (or have selected).

- *A* ﹸ **Text Style.** Here are your font, size, and style commands for whatever text you're about to type (or have selected).

Once you've made an annotation, you can drag it around, drag its blue control dots to change its shape, edit the text inside it, and so on.

Signing PDF Documents with Your Real Signature

Of macOS's 47,000 features, few are quite as slick or useful as the PDF signature option (Figure 15-12). It lets your Mac memorize your signature, either by taking a picture of it or by letting you sign with your finger on your laptop's trackpad.

Once Preview has stored your signature, you can slap it into any PDF documents that come through your life.

The first step is to teach Preview what your signature looks like. On the Markup toolbar, click the Sign pop-up menu: ﹸ. In the resulting window, you're offered two tabs:

- **Trackpad.** If your Mac has a trackpad, this option lets you write out your signature with your finger! Click where it says "Click Here to Begin," and then draw away.

 Plan ahead; the width of the trackpad is all the space you've got. When you're done, press any key and then click Done. The result may not look exactly like your pen-and-paper signature, but it'll do for most purposes.

- **Camera.** Sign your name on a piece of white paper; hold it up to your Mac's camera, as shown in Figure 15-12. When the positioning looks good, click Done. You've just stored your signature. (You have to do this only once—per signature, anyway.)

Tip: As a handy bonus, whatever signatures you've saved this way also appear in Preview on all your *other* Macs. (At least those that are signed into the same iCloud account, are running Yosemite or later, and have iCloud Keychain turned on in Settings→iCloud.)

Now, then. When the time comes to sign a document, make the Markup toolbar visible. From the ✍⌄ pop-up menu, choose the signature's name (Figure 15-12, middle).

The signature appears in its own graphics box. Drag it to a new position, or drag the blue handles to resize it (Figure 15-12, bottom).

Tip: To delete a signature, open the ✍⌄ pop-up menu, point to the signature, and click the ⊗ next to it in the menu.

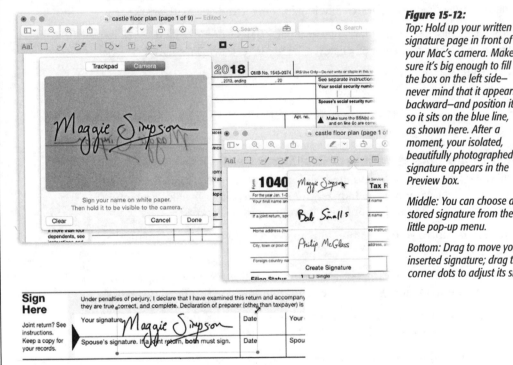

Figure 15-12:
Top: Hold up your written signature page in front of your Mac's camera. Make sure it's big enough to fill the box on the left side—never mind that it appears backward—and position it so it sits on the blue line, as shown here. After a moment, your isolated, beautifully photographed signature appears in the Preview box.

Middle: You can choose a stored signature from the little pop-up menu.

Bottom: Drag to move your inserted signature; drag the corner dots to adjust its size.

Fill in PDF Forms

Here's a feature that could save a lot of trees: fillable PDF forms.

Lots and lots of PDF documents are forms you're supposed to fill out—from IRS tax forms to school permission slips. Preview is smart enough to recognize boxes to fill in, lines to type on, and checkboxes to click, meaning that you don't have to print,

fill out, and then scan these things anymore. And it manages to find those lines, text boxes, and checkboxes on *any* PDF document, not just those that were originally designed to be filled in by PDF form-filling software. See Figure 15-13.

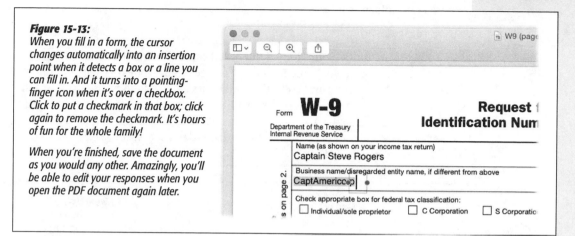

Figure 15-13:
When you fill in a form, the cursor changes automatically into an insertion point when it detects a box or a line you can fill in. And it turns into a pointing-finger icon when it's over a checkbox. Click to put a checkmark in that box; click again to remove the checkmark. It's hours of fun for the whole family!

When you're finished, save the document as you would any other. Amazingly, you'll be able to edit your responses when you open the PDF document again later.

The Toolbar

There's a lot you can do with Preview's toolbar. You can customize it (by choosing View→Customize Toolbar), rearrange its icons (by ⌘-dragging them sideways), and remove icons (by ⌘-dragging them downward).

Faxing

Apple giveth, and Apple taketh away. And Apple hath taken away faxing.

Apple has never been afraid to abandon technologies that strike it as obsolete, and faxing is one of them. Heck, macOS can't fax even if you have one of Apple's own USB fax modems.

If you still need to fax, you have a couple of options. First, you can sign up for a service like eFax or Faxaway, which lets you send and receive faxes online. Second, you're welcome to buy a non-Apple fax modem, some of which work fine. Whatever you buy comes with its own software and instructions.

Fonts—and Font Book

MacOS type is all smooth, all the time. Fonts in macOS's formats—called TrueType, PostScript Type 1, and OpenType—always look smooth onscreen and in printouts, no matter what the point size.

MacOS also comes with a program that's *just* for installing, removing, inspecting, and organizing fonts. It's called Font Book (Figure 15-14), and it's in your Applications folder.

Where Fonts Live

Brace yourself. In macOS, there are *three* Fonts folders. The fonts you actually see listed in the Font menus and Fonts panels of your programs are combinations of these Fonts folders' contents.

Here's a rundown:

- **Your private fonts (your Home folder→Library→Fonts).** This Fonts folder sits right inside your own Home folder. You're free to add your own custom fonts to it. Go wild—it's your font collection and yours alone. Nobody else who uses the Mac can use these fonts; they'll never even know you have them.

Note: Your Home→Library folder is ordinarily hidden. The quickest way to see it is to press Option as you choose Go→Library in the Finder.

Figure 15-14:
Each account holder can have a separate set of fonts; your set is represented by the User icon. You can drag fonts and font families among the various Fonts folders represented here—from your User account folder to the Computer icon, for example, making them available to all account holders.

- **Main font collection (Library→Fonts).** Any fonts in this folder are available to everyone to use in every program. (As with most features that affect everybody who shares your Mac, however, only the administrator can change the contents of this folder.)

- **Essential system fonts (System→Library→Fonts).** This folder contains the few dozen fonts the Mac itself needs: the typefaces you see in your menus, dialog boxes, icons, and so on. You can open this folder to *see* these font suitcases, but you can't do anything with them, such as opening, moving, or adding to them. Remember that, for stability reasons, the System folder is sealed under glass. Only the Unix entity known as the *superuser* can touch these files—and even that person would be foolish to do so.

With the exception of the essential system fonts, you'll find an icon representing each of these locations in your Font Book program, described next.

Note: And just to make life even more exciting, Adobe's software installers may donate even *more* fonts to your cause, in yet *another,* deeply hidden folder.

Font Book: Installing and Managing Fonts

One of the biggest perks of macOS is its preinstalled collection of more than 50 great-looking fonts—"over $1,000 worth," according to Apple, which licensed many of them from type companies. In short, fewer Mac fans than ever will wind up buying and installing new fonts.

But when you do buy or download new fonts, you're in luck. There's no limit to the number of fonts you can install.

Looking over your fonts

Right off the bat, Font Book is great for looking at samples of each typeface. For example, click Computer, click the first font name, and then press the ▼ key. As you walk down the list, the rightmost panel shows you a sample of each font (Figure 15-14).

You can also click any font family's flippy triangle (or highlight its name and then press ▶) to see the font *variations* it includes: Italic, Bold, and so on.

Tip: You can customize the type you see in the right panel. To see a full display of every character, choose Repertoire by clicking ⸬ in the toolbar or pressing ⌘-2. To type your own text, choose Custom by clicking AaI or pressing ⌘-3.

Eliminating duplicates

Since your Mac accesses up to three folders containing fonts, you might wonder what happens in the case of *conflicts.* For example, suppose you have two slightly different fonts, both called Optima, which came from different type companies and are housed in different Fonts folders on your system. Which font do you get when you use it in your documents?

The scheme is actually fairly simple: MacOS proceeds down the list of Fonts folders in the order shown on the previous page, beginning with your own home Fonts folder. It acknowledges the existence of only the *first* duplicated font it finds.

If you'd rather have more control, open Font Book. A dot next to a font's name is Font Book's charming way of trying to tell you that you've got copies of the same font in more than one of your Fonts folders. You might have one version of Comic Sans in your own Home→Library→Fonts folder, for example, and another in your Mac's main Fonts folder.

Click the one you want to keep, and then choose Edit→Resolve Duplicates. Font Book turns off all *other* copies, and the dot disappears.

Printing a reference sheet

You can print a handy, whole-font sampler of any font. Click its name and then choose File→Print. In the Print dialog box, click the Show Details button to expand the dialog box, if necessary.

As shown in Figure 15-15, you can use the Report Type pop-up menu to choose from three reference-sheet styles:

- **Catalog** prints the alphabet twice (uppercase and lowercase) and the numbers in each selected font; use the Sample Size slider to control the size. This style is the most compact, because more than one print sample fits on each sheet of paper.

- **Repertoire** prints a grid that contains every single character in the font. This report may take more than one page per font.

- **Waterfall** prints the alphabet over and over again, with increasing type sizes, until the page is full. You can control which sizes appear using the Sample Sizes list.

When everything looks good, click Print.

Figure 15-15:
From the Report Type pop-up menu, choose the style you want. The preview screen shows you each one before you commit it to paper. Type-size controls always appear in the lower right.

Adding, removing, and hiding fonts

Here's what you can do with Font Book:

- **Install a font.** When you double-click a font file's icon in the Finder, Font Book opens and presents the typeface for your inspection pleasure. If you like it, click Install Font. You've just installed it into *your account's* Fonts folder so that it appears in the Font menus of all your programs. (If you'd rather install it so that it appears in *all* account holders' Font menus, see Figure 15-14.)

- **Remove a font.** Removing a font from your machine is easy: Highlight it in the Font Book list, and then press the Delete key. (You're asked to confirm the decision.) Before taking such a drastic and permanent step, however, keep in mind that you can simply *disable* (hide) the font instead. Read on.

- **Disable a font.** When you disable a font, you're simply hiding it from your programs. You might want to turn off a font so that you can use a different version of it (bearing the same name but from a different type company, for example), or to make your Font menus shorter, or to make programs like Microsoft Word start up faster. You can always turn a disabled font back on if you ever need it again.

Tip: How's this for a sweet feature? MacOS can activate fonts *automatically* as you need them. When you open a document that relies on a font it doesn't have, macOS activates that font and keeps it available until that particular program quits.

Actually, it does better than that. If it doesn't see that font installed, it *searches your hard drive* on a quest to find the font—and then it asks you if you want it installed, so the document will look right.

To disable a font, just click it or its family name and then click the checkbox button in the toolbar (or press Shift-⌘-D). Confirm your decision by clicking Disable in the confirmation box. (Turn on "Do not ask me again" if you're the confident sort.)

The font's name now appears gray, and the word "Off" appears next to it, making it absolutely clear what you've just done. (To turn the font on again, highlight its name, and then click the now-empty checkbox button, or press Shift-⌘-D again.)

Note: When you install, remove, disable, or enable a font using Font Book, you see the changes in the Font menus and panels of your programs immediately.

Font collections

A font *collection*, like any of the ones listed in the first Font Book column, is a subset of your installed fonts. Apple starts you off with collections called things like PDF (a set of standard fonts used in PDF files) and Web (fonts you're safe using on web pages—that is, fonts that are very likely to be installed on the Macs or Windows PCs of your web visitors).

But you can create collections called, for example, Headline or Sans Serif, organized by font type. Or you can create collections like Brochure or Movie Poster, organized by project. Later, you can switch these groups of fonts on or off at will, or jump right to them in programs that use the standard Fonts panel, which saves you time wading through hundreds of fonts.

To create a new collection, click the leftmost + button to create a new entry in the Collection column, whose name you can edit. Then click one of the font storage locations—User or Computer—and drag fonts or font families onto your newly created collection icon. (Recognize this process from playlists in Music, or albums in Photos?) Each font can be in as many collections as you want.

To remove a font from the collection, click its name and then press Delete. You're not actually removing the font from your Mac—only from the collection.

Note: Each time you create a new font collection, macOS records its name and contents in a little file in your Home folder→Library→FontCollections folder.

By copying these files into the Users→Shared folder on your hard drive, you can make them available to anyone who uses the Mac. If your sister, for example, copies a file from the Shared folder into her own Home folder→Library→FontCollections folder, then she'll see the name of your collection in her own Fonts panel. This way, she can reap the benefits of the effort and care you put into its creation.

Smart collections

Font Book can create a collection *for* you, too. If you choose File→New Smart Collection, a new dialog box lets you specify criteria for this always-updated collection. For example, you might use the + buttons to specify "Kind is TrueType" and "Design style is Sans-serif." The effect is exactly like smart folders in the Finder (page 132) or smart playlists in Music (page 633): Once you set up the smartness, the set stays up to date as your font collection changes.

Font libraries

Don't get confused; a font *library* is not the same as a font *collection*.

A font library is a set of fonts *outside* Font Book that you can install or uninstall on the fly. They don't have to be in any of your Fonts folders; Font Book can install them from wherever they happen to be sitting on your hard drive (or even on the network). Font Book never copies or moves these font files as you install or remove them from libraries; it simply adds them to your Font menus by referencing them right where they sit.

Tip: That can be a handy arrangement if you periodically work on different projects for different clients. Why burden your day-to-day Font menu with the 37 fonts used by *Beekeepers Quarterly* magazine when you need to work with those fonts only four times a year?

Once you've added some fonts to a library, you can even set up collections *within* that library.

To create a library, choose File→New Library; the library appears at the top of the left side of Font Book under User. Now you can drag fonts into it right from the Finder.

Exporting fonts

Next time you submit a design project to a print shop or a graphics bureau, you won't have to worry that it won't have the right fonts. It's easy to collect all the fonts you used in a document and export them to a folder, ready to submit along with your file.

Use the Services→Font Book→Create Collection From Text command. Font Book opens and shows you the new collection it's created, containing all the fonts used in

your document. Click the collection and then choose File→Export Collection. The software prompts you to name and choose a location for the exported fonts folder.

Note: The Create Collection From Text command doesn't work in all programs, but you can always build and export a collection manually.

The Fonts Panel

Some existing Mac programs have simply been touched up—*Carbonized*, in the lingo—to be macOS-compatible. Choosing fonts in these programs works exactly as it always has on the Mac: You choose a typeface name from the Font menu or from a formatting palette.

Things get much more interesting when you use the more modern *Cocoa* programs, like TextEdit, iMovie, Pages, Keynote, Numbers, Photos, and Mail. They offer a standard macOS feature called the Fonts panel. If you're seated in front of your macOS machine now, fire up TextEdit or Pages and follow along.

Choosing fonts from the Fonts panel

Suppose you've just highlighted a headline in TextEdit and now you want to choose an appropriate typeface for it.

In TextEdit, you open the Fonts panel (Figure 15-16) by choosing Format→Font→Show Fonts (⌘-T). Just as in Font Book, the first column lists your Collections. The second column, Family, shows the names of the actual fonts in your system. The third, Typeface, shows the style variations—Bold, Italic, Condensed, and so on—available

Figure 15-16:
The Fonts panel, generally available only in modern programs, offers elaborate controls over text color, shadow, and underline styles.

See the handy font sample shown here above the font lists? To get it, choose Show Preview from the ✿ pop-up menu. Or use the mousy way: Place your cursor just below the title bar (where it says Fonts) and drag downward.

in that type family. (Oblique and Italic are roughly the same thing; Bold, Black, and Ultra are varying degrees of boldface.)

The last column lists a sampling of point sizes. You can use the Size slider, choose from the point-size pop-up menu, or type any number into the box at the top of the Size list.

Designing collections and favorites

At the top of the Fonts panel, the ⚙ menu offers a few useful customization tools:

- **Add to Favorites.** To designate a font as a favorite, specify a font, style, and size by clicking in the appropriate columns of the Fonts panel. Then use this command. From now on, whenever you click Favorites in the Collection column, you'll see a list of the typefaces you've specified.

- **Show Preview.** The Fonts panel is great and all that, but you may have noticed that, until you choose this option, it doesn't actually *show* you the fonts you're working with—something of an oversight in a window designed to help you find your fonts. See Figure 15-16 for details. (Choose this command again—now called Hide Preview—to get rid of the preview.)

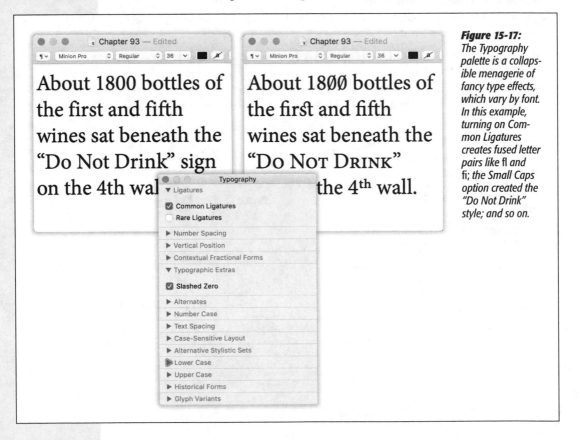

Figure 15-17:
The Typography palette is a collapsible menagerie of fancy type effects, which vary by font. In this example, turning on Common Ligatures creates fused letter pairs like fl and fi; the Small Caps option created the "Do Not Drink" style; and so on.

Tip: Once you've opened the preview pane, feel free to click the different sizes, typeface names, and family names to see the various effects.

- **Color.** Opens the Color Picker, so you can specify a color for the highlighted text.

- **Characters.** Opens the Character Viewer, so you can choose a symbol or emoji without having to remember the crazy keyboard combo that types it.

- **Typography.** Opens the Typography palette (see Figure 15-17).

- **Edit Sizes.** The point sizes listed in the Fonts panel are just suggestions. You can actually type in any point size you want. By choosing this command, in fact, you can edit this list so the sizes you use most often are only a click away.

- **Manage Fonts.** Opens Font Book, described starting on page 603.

ColorSync

As you may have discovered through painful experience, computers aren't great with color. Each device you use to create and print digital images "sees" color a little bit differently, which explains why the deep amber captured by your scanner may be rendered as chalky brown on your monitor yet come out as a fiery orange on your Epson inkjet printer. Since every gadget defines and renders color in its own way, colors are often inconsistent as a print job moves from design to proof to press.

ColorSync attempts to sort out this mess, serving as a translator for all the different pieces of hardware in your workflow. For this to work, each device (scanner, monitor, printer, digital camera, copier, proofer, and so on) has to be calibrated with a unique *ColorSync profile*—a file that tells your Mac exactly how it defines colors. Armed with the knowledge contained in the profiles, the ColorSync software can compensate for the quirks of the different devices and even the different kinds of paper they print on.

Most of the people who lose sleep over color fidelity are those who do commercial color scanning and printing, where "off" colors are a big deal. After all, a customer might return a product after discovering that the actual product color doesn't match the photo on a company's website.

Getting ColorSync Profiles

ColorSync profiles for many color printers, scanners, and monitors come built into macOS. When you buy equipment or software from, say, Kodak, Agfa, or Pantone, you may get additional profiles. If your equipment didn't come with a ColorSync profile, let Google be your friend; it shouldn't be hard to find. Put new profiles into the Library→ColorSync→Profiles folder.

Default Profiles

In professional graphics work, a ColorSync profile is often embedded right in a photo, making all this color management automatic. Using the ColorSync Utility program (in Applications→Utilities), you can specify which ColorSync profile each of your

gadgets should use. Click the Devices button, open the category for your device (scanner, camera, display, printer, or proofer), click the model you have, and then use the Current Profile pop-up menu to assign a profile to it.

Tip: In the Displays pane of System Preferences, you'll find a Color tab. Its Calibrate button is designed to create a profile for your particular monitor in your particular office lighting—all you have to do is answer a few fun questions onscreen and drag a few sliders.

More on ColorSync

If you ache to learn more about ColorSync, you won't find much in macOS's Help system. Instead, search the web. You'll find Googling *ColorSync* to be a fruitful exercise.

Graphics in macOS

Everywhere you look in macOS, you'll find visual effects that would make any other operating system think about early retirement.

For example: Menus are transparent. You can set Excel 3D graphs to be slightly transparent so they don't block other bars in a 3D graph. When you paste files into windows in icon view, their icons fade into view. When you open an especially long message in Mail, its text fades in from white. When you use Launchpad, it fades in and out. And when you switch accounts using fast user switching, your work environment slides off the screen as though it's pasted on the side of an animated cube.

All these visual goodies owe their existence to Quartz or its enhanced successor, Quartz Extreme (which is not available on older Macs).

Graphics Formats on the Mac

MacOS understands dozens of Mac and Windows graphics file formats. Better yet, its Preview program can open such graphics and export them in a different format, making it an excellent file-conversion program. You can confidently double-click graphics files—from a digital camera, scanner, or web download, for example—in any of these formats:

- **PICT files.** For almost 20 years, the PICT file was the graphics format Mac fans were most familiar with. It was the graphics format used by the Mac Clipboard. Unfortunately, no other kinds of computers could open these files, and so PICT is pretty much dead.

- **TIFF files** are high-quality, uncompressed *bitmaps*—that is, the Mac has memorized the color of each pixel in the file. Trying to enlarge one is like enlarging a fax: Make it too big, and the image breaks down into visible dots.

 Nonetheless, TIFF files are popular in the printing industry—the graphics in this book, for example, were stored as TIFF files. They print beautifully, work nicely in page-layout programs, and are understood by both Macs and Windows PCs.

- **JPEG files** are popular on the web, particularly for photos and other full-color art-work. What makes JPEG files ideal for online use is that they've been compressed (using a program like Photoshop). Just enough of the color data has been thrown out from the original file to make the image a quick download without noticeably affecting its quality.

- **GIF** stands for *graphics interchange format.* Today, GIF files are used almost exclu-sively on the web, usually for solid-colored graphics like cartoons, headlines, and logos. (A GIF file can have a maximum of 256 colors, which is not even close to the photorealism of, say, JPEG. That's what makes the GIF format inappropriate for photographs.) Crude, soundless *animated* GIFs have made a bit of a comeback lately, too.

- **PNG files.** As it turns out, one of the algorithms used by GIF files is, technically speaking, the property of a company called Unisys, which threatened to sue everybody who was creating GIF files. "No problem," said the World Wide Web Consortium. "We'll just come up with our own replacement—a file format that has no legal strings attached." What they created was PNG (Portable Network Graphics). You can save Photoshop and Preview documents in PNG format, and every web browser understands it. Screenshots you take in macOS are in PNG, too.

 PNG files don't lose quality when compressed, as JPEG files do. On the other hand, PNG files don't accommodate animation, as GIF files do. And when it comes to photos, they don't offer as impressive a size/quality balance as JPEG.

- **HEIF.** On iPhones and iPads, photos and videos occupy only half the space they used to—and look exactly the same. That's because Apple has adopted a format called HEIF (high efficiency image file format) for photos, and HEVC (high efficiency video coding) format for video. MacOS apps like Photos, Preview, and Quick Look can recognize and open these files, too.

- **Photoshop files.** If you're a graphic designer or webmeister, this one is kind of neat: MacOS can open (and Preview can even export) actual Photoshop files (except for so-called *16-bit RGB* files). In practical terms, the fact that macOS can open and display these files means you could use a Photoshop masterpiece, complete with layers and transparency, as, for example, a macOS desktop background.

- **BMP files.** You can think of this graphics format as the PICT of the Windows world. It's nice that macOS can open (and Preview can export) them, especially because you may occasionally find .bmp files on the web or attached to email messages.

- **Silicon Graphics, MacPaint, Targ.** You could go your whole life without ever seeing a graphic in one of these formats. Silicon Graphics is, unsurprisingly, the format created by Silicon Graphics computers. MacPaint is a black-and-white, 8 × 10–inch maximum, ancient Macintosh graphics format that disappeared from the scene in about 1988. And Targ (Targa) is the format once used by products from Truevision.

Screen Capture

If you're reading a chapter about printing and graphics, you may be interested in creating *screenshots*—captured images of the Mac screen. Screenshots are a staple of articles, tutorials, and books about the Mac (including this one). The Mac has a secret built-in feature that lets you make them—and in macOS Catalina, it's been beefed up to an astonishing degree. Here's how it goes.

The Screenshot Toolbar

For decades, the Mac has offered special keystrokes for taking digital pictures of the screen: Shift-⌘-3 to capture the entire screen, or Shift-⌘-4 to capture a rectangular piece of it. And those keystrokes still work.

But nowadays, your first thought when it's "I need to capture this" time should be this keystroke: Shift-⌘-5.

That combo opens the screenshot toolbar, which teems with options for capturing the screen (Figure 15-18).

Here's what you'll find on the screenshot toolbar, from left to right:

- **Entire Screen, Selected Window, Selected Portion.** These buttons specify what you want in your screenshot: the entire screen; only one open window (whichever you

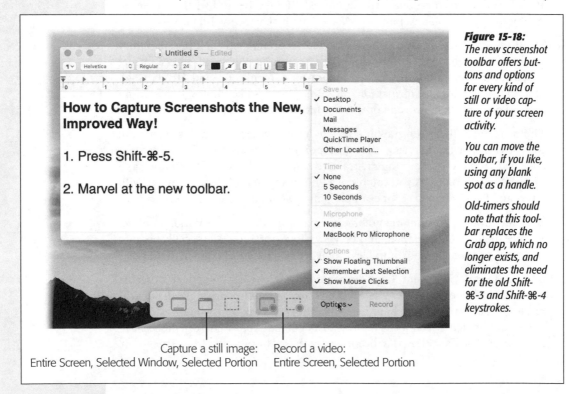

Figure 15-18:
The new screenshot toolbar offers buttons and options for every kind of still or video capture of your screen activity.

You can move the toolbar, if you like, using any blank spot as a handle.

Old-timers should note that this toolbar replaces the Grab app, which no longer exists, and eliminates the need for the old Shift-⌘-3 and Shift-⌘-4 keystrokes.

Capture a still image:
Entire Screen, Selected Window, Selected Portion

Record a video:
Entire Screen, Selected Portion

click); or a rectangular portion you choose by dragging the corners of the dotted-line rectangle and then pressing Return (or clicking Capture).

- **Record Entire Screen, Record Selected Portion.** This time, you're creating a *video* of all the action on the screen (or within the rectangle that you specify). Alas, these videos don't include sound. (For that, you'll have to buy a program like ScreenFlow.)

Begin the recording by selecting which video option you want and then clicking Record (far-right button on the toolbar); end it by clicking the ⊙ in your menu bar. (You can also press Shift-⌘-5 again to bring the toolbar back, and click the ⊙ button on *it*.) A thumbnail appears at the lower-right corner of your screen. If you click the thumbnail, you get the editing window described in the next section.

- **Options menu.** This icon offers powerful options for your screenshotting pleasure:

The **"Save to"** options specify where you want macOS to put the finished image file. Some of the options are folder locations, like Desktop and Documents. But don't miss the *apps* listed here, like Mail and Messages. They pre-attach your finished shot to an outgoing email or message, which can save you a few steps. The Other Location command lets you choose a folder (or app!) you prefer.

Timer gives you a five- or ten-second countdown before the Mac captures the screen. That's usually long enough for you to get everything positioned the way you like it: a menu open, for example, or certain text highlighted, or the cursor in the right place.

Microphone. When you're recording video of the screen activity, do you want to narrate? If so, which microphone should the Mac use?

Show Floating Thumbnail is the on/off switch for the whole "thumbnail in the lower-right corner of the screen" business described already. If you turn it off, then screenshots go straight to your desktop (or wherever you assigned them to go) as file icons, without the option to edit them. Basically you're back in 2017.

Remember Last Selection is useful for the "Selected Portion" option described previously. When it's turned on, then each time you select Selected Portion, the Mac will start out highlighting the same region you used last time. That's especially useful when you're trying to document something changing on the screen, step by step, screenshot by screenshot.

Show Mouse Clicks is for video recordings of the screen. It produces a little circle around the cursor each time you click, making it easier for future generations to understand when and where you were clicking. (Otherwise it would be hard to tell—there's no sound.)

In each case, after you snap the snap or record the video, a thumbnail image of your new screenshot appears in the lower-right corner of your screen. If you just smile and nod and go on working, then that thumbnail vanishes after about seven seconds, and the Mac creates a PNG-format graphics file. These files are named after the current time and date. They're called "Screenshot 2019-01-20 at 5.18.13 PM," "Screenshot 2019-01-20 at 5.18.32 PM," and so on.

Or, if you made a video, you get a QuickTime movie named, for example, "Screen Recording 2019-1-20 at 3.35.34 PM.mov."

If you click the thumbnail before it's gone, though, you open the screenshot into the screenshot-editing mode, described next.

The Screenshot Editor

If, after snapping a screenshot, you click the thumbnail that appears at the lower-right corner of your screen, you open the screenshot-editing window (Figure 15-19).

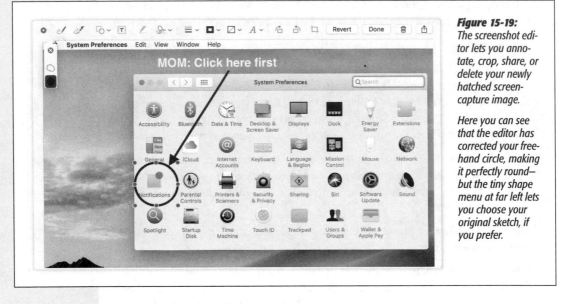

Figure 15-19:
The screenshot editor lets you annotate, crop, share, or delete your newly hatched screen-capture image.

Here you can see that the editor has corrected your free-hand circle, making it perfectly round—but the tiny shape menu at far left lets you choose your original sketch, if you prefer.

In this window, you can use any of the tools across the top. These are the standard macOS markup tools, as described on page 597: the Sketch pen, Shapes menu, Text tool, Highlight Selection, Sign pop-up menu, and controls for line thickness, line color, fill color, and font. (You can press ⌘-Z to Undo your last step, as you'd hope.)

Then come three buttons for rotating and cropping the image.

At the right end of that toolbar, you choose a fate for your edited screenshot. Click Revert to undo all the edits you've made, Done to preserve your work as a file saved on the desktop, 🗑 to delete the whole thing, or ⬆ to send your screenshot masterpiece to someone else.

For a video, the only buttons are Trim (makes the yellow trim handles appear, exactly as described on page 620), 🗑, and ⬆.

The Old Whole-Screen Keystroke

The screenshot toolbar offers tremendous flexibility—but the old ways of doing things are still around. You can still press Shift-⌘-3 to create a picture file, in PNG

format, that depicts the entire screen image. A satisfying camera-shutter sound tells you that you were successful.

Tip: It doesn't *have* to be Shift-⌘-3. You can change any of these screenshot keystrokes to anything you like. Open System Preferences→Keyboard→Shortcuts→Screenshots. Click the keystroke you want to change, press Return to highlight the current keyboard combo, and then press the new keystroke you prefer.

In Catalina, the thumbnail appears at the lower-right corner of your screen for editing, as described.

One Section of the Screen

Another long-standing combo is still around: You can capture a rectangular region of the screen by pressing Shift-⌘-4. Your cursor turns into a crosshairs with two tiny digital readouts—the horizontal and vertical coordinates of your cursor on the screen at this moment. (The numbers are in pixels, as measured from the upper-left corner of the screen, which has coordinates 0, 0.)

Now drag diagonally to capture a rectangular chunk of screen. When you release the mouse, you hear the camera-click sound, and the screenshot file appears in the lower-right corner of your screen—containing only the rectangle you enclosed.

But that's just the beginning. Once you've begun dragging diagonally, while the mouse is still down, you can press any of these keys for special manipulation effects:

- **Space bar.** While you hold down the space bar with one hand, your selection rectangle is frozen in size and shape. With your mouse, you can move the cursor with the selection rectangle attached, the better to fine-tune your positioning relative to your target.

- **Shift key.** When you hit Shift, you confine the dragging action of your mouse to a single dimension: horizontal or vertical. Which dimension depends on how you move your mouse after you hit Shift. For example, suppose you drag out a 2-inch square and then pause. With the mouse button still down, you press Shift. If you now continue to drag downward, the selected area maintains a fixed width; you're increasing only the rectangle's height.

- **Option key.** If you hold down Option after beginning to drag, you create a rectangular selection that grows from the center point outward. That is, it treats your initial click as the rectangle's center point, rather than as a diagonal corner.

- **Control key.** If you're pressing the Control key as you release the mouse, you copy the screenshot to your Clipboard, ready for pasting, rather than saving it as a new graphics file on your desktop. (In this case, you don't get the lower-right floating thumbnail.)

- **Esc.** If you change your mind about taking a screenshot, tap Esc. The darkened selection area disappears, and you've exited screenshot mode.

A Dialog Box, Menu, Window, or Icon

Why fuss with cleaning up a screenshot after you've taken it? Using this trick, you can neatly snip *one screen element* out from its background.

Make sure the dialog box, menu, window, or icon is visible. Then press Shift-⌘-4. But *instead of* dragging diagonally, tap the space bar.

Your cursor turns into a tiny camera. Move it so the misty-blue highlighting fills the window or menu you want to capture—and then click. The resulting picture file snips the window or menu neatly from its background.

Pressing Shift-⌘-4 and then the space bar also captures the Dock in one quick snip. Once you've got the camera cursor, click any *blank* spot in the Dock (between icons).

Tip: Here again, if you hold down the Control key as you click or drag, you copy the screenshot to your *Clipboard*.

Movies, Music & Sound

Macs have been capable of handling sound and graphics from day one, years before the word *multimedia* was even coined. MacOS's QuickTime technology, for example, plays digital movies and live "streaming" broadcasts from the internet; the new TV app is your window into Apple's online TV and movie stores; and the new Music app is what's left of the discontinued iTunes app for managing your music files (and shopping Apple's online music store).

This chapter covers all these multimedia apps, and describes recording audio, too.

QuickTime Player

A QuickTime movie is a playable video file, on your Mac or online. Like any movie, it creates the illusion of motion by flashing many individual frames (photos) per second before your eyes, while also playing a synchronized soundtrack.

The cornerstone of macOS's movie software is QuickTime Player, which sits in your Applications folder. Despite its name, QuickTime Player also lets you edit movies and even record new ones, either using your Mac's built-in camera or by recording screen activity. Finally, when everything looks good, you can post your masterpiece to YouTube, Facebook, Vimeo, or another online site.

You open a movie file by double-clicking it. When QuickTime Player opens, you get a borderless playback window. Just hit the space bar to play the movie.

There's a control toolbar at the bottom of the window (Figure 16-1), but it fades away after a few seconds—or immediately, if you move the cursor out of the frame.

The toolbar reappears anytime your mouse moves back into the movie frame. These are the controls:

- **Volume slider** (◀)...◀))). Click in the slider, or drag the dot, to adjust the volume—although it's actually easier to just tap the ▲ or ▼ keys.

Tip: To mute the sound, click the ◀ icon or press Option-▼. Press Option-▲ to make the volume slider jump to full-blast position.

Figure 16-1:
QuickTime Player displays this control bar only when you move your mouse into its window, or whenever playback is stopped.

- **Rewind, Fast-Forward** (◀◀, ▶▶). By clicking one of these buttons, you get to speed through your movie at double speed, backward or forward, complete with sound. Click again for 5x speed and again for 10x.

Tip: You don't have to keep your mouse button pressed on these. Just click once and let QuickTime Player do the work. Click ▶ or tap the space bar to stop scanning.

- **Play/Pause** (▶/❙❙). Click ▶ to start playback, ❙❙ to pause/stop. Or just tap the space bar for both functions.

- **Scrubber bar.** Drag the little vertical bar, or just click inside its track, to jump to a different spot in the movie. The counters at the beginning and end of the bar tell you, in "hours:minutes:seconds" format, how far your playhead cursor has moved into the movie and how far you are from the end. (Click the right-hand readout to see the total movie duration.)

Tip: You can also press the ◀ and ▶ keys to step through the movie one frame at a time. If you press Option-◀ or Option-▶, you jump to the beginning or the end of the movie. That's important to know, since there are no longer dedicated Jump to Start/Jump to End buttons on the control bar.

- **Window edges.** Drag any edge, or the lower-right corner, to make the window bigger or smaller. QuickTime Player always maintains the same *aspect ratio* (relative dimensions) of the original movie, so you won't accidentally squish it.

- **Share button** (⬆). Click for a pop-up menu of choices for passing on this video to your adoring fans: via Email, Messages, AirDrop, Facebook, YouTube, Vimeo, or Flickr. All of these options are described later in this chapter.

- **Full Screen** (⦿). Click to make the video fill your entire monitor, just as though you'd chosen View→Enter Full Screen. And what if the proportions of the movie don't quite match your screen? If you make the menu bar return by pointing to the top of your screen, you can handle this problem using one of the choices in the View menu, described next.

Note: When you enter Full Screen mode, the movie doesn't begin playing automatically (unless it was already playing, of course). You have to tap the space bar to get the show underway.

Fancy Playback Tricks

Playing one movie, start to finish, is kid stuff. Here's what else QuickTime Player can do:

- **Rotate or flip.** The Edit menu contains commands for Rotate Right, Rotate Left, Flip Horizontal, and Flip Vertical. Those commands can be handy when a movie turns out to be flipped or rotated—or when *you* want to flip or rotate it for creative purposes.

- **Change the screen size.** As noted already, you can drag the window to any size using the edges as handles. But the View menu commands are handy, too:

 Actual size represents the movie on your screen at its real size—no larger. (If it's truly huge, larger than your screen, then it may be scaled *smaller* to fit. But that's a rarity.)

 Fit to Screen fills your screen without cropping or distorting; the menu bar and other windows remain visible.

 Fill Screen is especially satisfying, because it turns your entire monitor into a movie playback area.

 Panoramic squishes the outer edges of the video, distorting them slightly, so that nothing gets chopped off *and* the movie fills the screen. (These last two options are available only in Full Screen mode.)

Tip: These same options are available via keyboard shortcuts: ⌘-1, ⌘-3, ⌘-4, and ⌘-5. There's even a little button on the control bar, second from right, that switches back and forth between Fit to Screen and Fill Screen. (This button appears only when you're already in Full Screen mode.)

Making the window larger may also make the movie coarser, because QuickTime Player simply enlarges every dot that was present in the original. Still, when you

want to show a movie to a group of people more than a few feet back from the screen, these larger sizes are perfectly effective.

Tip: You can make the movie window bigger or smaller by pressing ⌘-plus (+) or ⌘-minus (-).

- **Play picture-in-picture.** If your goal is to keep doing other things on the Mac while a video plays, no problem. In Catalina, you can shrink the video window to a little inset in the corner of your screen by clicking the 🖳 button on the playback controls. You can drag the picture-in-picture inset to any corner, or drag its edges to resize it.

- **Play more than one movie.** You can open several movies at once and run them simultaneously. (Of course, the more movies you try to play at once, the jerkier the playback gets.)

- **Loop the movie.** When you choose View→Loop and then click Play, the movie repeats endlessly until you make it stop.

- **Navigate chapters.** A few movies, like the ones you buy or rent from Apple, come with built-in chapter markers, just like a DVD. They let you jump around in the film at your whim.

Editing Movies

QuickTime Player is also QuickTime Editor. The program doesn't offer selection handles, so you might think there's no way to select a portion of the middle of a

Figure 16-2:

Top: To trim a video, choose Edit→Trim or press ⌘-T. Drag the yellow handles inward to isolate the chunk you want to preserve. (You can click ▶ or tap the space bar to check your work.) When everything looks good, click Trim or press Return.

Bottom: If you choose View→Show Audio Track, then you can use the sound waves as a guide to your precision editing.

movie (to chop it out, for example). But in fact, commands for trimming, splitting, and merging video clips let you perform just about any editing trick you can imagine:

- **Trimming video from the ends.** You can very easily trim dead space off the ends of a video. Figure 16-2 shows how.

 You don't have to worry about damaging the original video when trimming—you couldn't modify the original if you tried. The instant you use the Trim command, QuickTime Player peels off the shortened version as a new, untitled movie, which you'll have to name and save separately (choose File→Export As).

- **Splitting a clip.** *Clips* are subsections of a movie. To chop a movie in two, move the playhead to the spot where you want the movie to split, and then choose Edit→Split Clip. As shown in Figure 16-3, a clips map appears at the bottom of the window, showing the two resulting clips.

Figure 16-3:
The Split Clip command chops the video into two clips—and produces the map shown at bottom. If you click a clip and then press the space bar to play the video, you'll see the red vertical line that represents the playhead. To chop one of your clips up into further subclips, move that red line into position and then use the Split Clip command again.

- **Chopping video out of the middle.** If you want to trim some video from the *middle* of a movie, first open up the clips map. Then split the movie as described above. Once you've split a movie into a couple of clips, you can double-click one of the clips to produce trim handles just for it. In this way, you can cut unwanted sections from the *middle* of a video.

 Or just split the clip into three chunks—and delete the middle one.

- **Rearranging clips.** Once you've chopped a video into subclips using the Split Clip command, you can drag them around within the map. (If you don't see the map, shown in Figure 16-3, then choose View→Show Clips.)

 You can use the Cut, Copy, and Paste commands in the Edit menu, too, to move chunks around—even among different movies. (Just remember to first split the target movie at the spot where you want to paste the new clip. The pasted material appears just *after* whatever clip is currently highlighted.)

- **Combining movies.** Combining clips, as already described, is one way to merge videos together. But you can also merge entire movie files sitting in the Finder.

Start by opening the first movie. If you want the second movie to appear at the *end* of it, just choose Edit→Add Clip to End.

Tip: If you press Option, the command says Add Clip to Beginning. Sneaky!

The Open box appears. Find and open the clip you want to tack on. You can also drag movie clips' icons from the desktop right into a movie window. QuickTime Player adds them to the end of the existing movie.

If you want the second movie to appear somewhere in the middle of the first movie, then open up the clip map (View→Show Clips). Click the clip that appears right *before* the spot where the new movie will go. Choose Edit→Insert Clip After Selection; in the resulting dialog box, find and double-click the movie file you want to bring in.

Or drag a movie file from the Finder directly into the gap between two subclips.

Tip: QuickTime Player automatically shrinks or crops the incoming movies so they fit the same "screen size" as the original. If they're *not* the same size or proportions, you can use the Edit→Clip Alignment submenu (Top, Left, Center, and so on) to specify which edge of the movie frame the imported video should hug.

Recording Movies with QuickTime Player

QuickTime Player does more than *play* movies; it can also *record* them. Yes, your Mac is now a camcorder, and a darned handy one; you can pop out quick video greetings,

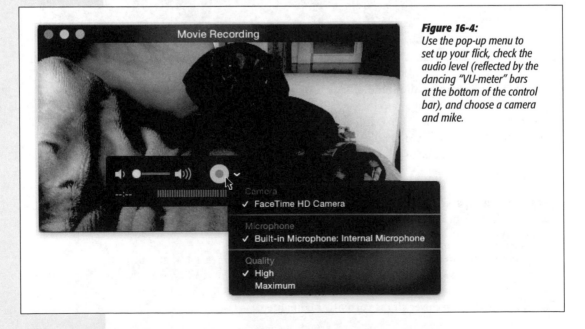

Figure 16-4:
Use the pop-up menu to set up your flick, check the audio level (reflected by the dancing "VU-meter" bars at the bottom of the control bar), and choose a camera and mike.

gross out your roommates, impress your co-workers with a dress rehearsal of your pitch, and so on.

Laptops and iMacs, of course, have a video camera built right in, above the screen. If you have another model, you can attach a webcam, an old iSight camera, or even a FireWire camcorder.

Then open QuickTime Player and choose File→New Movie Recording. The preview window appears. Use the pop-up menu shown in Figure 16-4 to specify what mike and camera you want to use (in the unlikely event that you have more than one) and what video quality you want.

Then, to record, click the red Record button (or press the space bar). Do your schtick. Press the space bar again to stop recording.

Your new video appears in its own playback window. Check it out, trim it if necessary, and then shoot it off to Vimeo, YouTube, or whatever.

Recording Screen Movies from the Mac

Why is it useful to capture screen activity as a video? Because you can make mini-tutorials for techno-clueless relatives. You can make video podcasts that show how to do things in software programs. You can preserve web animations that you used to think you had no way to capture.

The best way to go about making screen recordings is to use the ⌘-Shift–5 keystroke described on page 612.

The ancient way is to use QuickTime Player, which has limitations. Your movies won't include the Mac's own sounds (game soundtracks and so on), so forget about capturing videos playing on YouTube. (You can record from the *mike,* though, so you can narrate what you're doing.)

To record the Mac's screen, choose File→New Screen Recording. Use the pop-up menu on the resulting Screen Recording panel to turn the microphone on or off. Specify how much of the screen to record (Figure 16-5).

Figure 16-5:
This message appears when you tap the Record button. If you just click to start recording, you'll capture the entire monitor. But if you drag first, defining a rectangle, you'll capture only that area.

Click to record the full screen. Drag to record part of the screen.
End recording by clicking the stop button in the menu bar.

Tip: This pop-up menu also contains an option called Show Mouse Clicks in Recording. It helps your viewers understand when and where you actually clicked the mouse during the tutorial—by briefly displaying a little circle around the cursor each time you click. (It appears only in playback—not while you're recording.)

Finally, click the red Record button (or press Return).

Press Return, or click Start Recording, to begin the capture. When you finally click the Stop button in the menu bar, your finished movie appears in a regular playback window, ready to trim or to send away to your fans.

Recording Movies from an iPhone or iPad Screen

These days, it's easy to make screen videos right on iPhones and iPads.

But QuickTime Player offers an older way that's still useful, because it can record the iOS gadget's screen at times when it can't record its own screen—for example, when the phone is actually ringing. And this trick is equally handy when you want to project your iPhone/iPad demonstration for a crowd, using the Mac as a go-between.

To begin, connect the i-gadget to the Mac with its white USB cable. Open QuickTime Player. Choose File→New Movie Recording.

In the recording palette shown in Figure 16-4, click ∨ to open the pop-up menu; choose the iPhone's or iPad's name. In just a moment, the live image of the i-gadget now appears on your Mac. You can use this arrangement to show your phone activity to a crowd on the Mac's screen, or even click Record to record it as a movie.

Creating a Video from Stills

Here's a new one in Catalina: You can convert a folder full of still images—photos or drawings, for example—into a video.

Getting the folder full of individual images is up to you; if you're an animator, you probably have some idea how to go about that already. Just make sure they're numbered sequentially.

Then, in QuickTime Player, choose File→Open Image Sequence. Choose the folder that contains all the stills (or select the individual images you want). You'll be asked to specify resolution, frame rate, and encoding format of the result, and then boom: insta-flipbook movie!

Ways to Export Your Video

One of QuickTime Player's most important talents is *sharing* a video: posting it directly to Facebook, YouTube, Vimeo, Flickr, or your own website; converting it to the right format for an iPod, iPhone, or other cellphone; stashing it on your hard drive for easy transfer to your iPod/iPhone; handing it off to iMovie for further editing; saving it to the hard drive as a double-clickable movie; and so on.

Let us count the ways.

Post to YouTube, Vimeo, Flickr, Facebook

The Share button (⬆) offers one-click commands for posting to YouTube (the world's most popular and famous website for short videos), Vimeo (a less well-known, but classier, more high-def video-sharing site), Flickr (mainly a photo-sharing site, but it handles videos, too), or Facebook (the most visited website on earth).

All of these services require that you first sign up for a free account. You do that online, not in QuickTime Player.

Then, with your movie open in QuickTime Player, choose from the ⬆ menu. You're asked for your name and password for the service. If you turn on "Remember this password in my keychain," then you won't have to enter it the next time.

Finally, click Sign In. On the next screen (Figure 16-6), type a title and description for the movie. Enter keywords (search categories like "funny" or "sports") so people on that service will find your video when they search.

Work through the remaining upload screens; click Share. In a few minutes, your video will be live for the whole world to see—no charge.

Figure 16-6:
If you want to fit in with the rest of the YouTube community, be sure to misspell a lot of words, and never, ever put the apostrophe in the right place. Especially in the word "it's."

Send to email, Messages, AirDrop

To email your video, choose Mail from the ⬆ menu. QuickTime Player hands the movie file off to your email program, attaches it to an outgoing message, and sits there awaiting the email address and maybe a comment. Of course, many email systems have file-size limits, and movies are big; the recipient's email system may reject it on those grounds. You'll get a "bounce-back" message in that case.

The ⬆ menu also offers commands like Messages (which sends the movie to some-one's Mac, phone, or tablet via Messages) and AirDrop (which sends the movie to someone's Mac wirelessly, provided that it's within 30 feet of you; see page 528).

Saving the finished movie

After you've edited a movie (or not), you can use the Export command to specify a new name for your masterpiece—and, if you wish, to convert it to a different format, depending on what kind of machine will be playing it.

When you choose File→Export As, the Format pop-up menu offers these choices:

- **4K.** Ultra-high definition in H.264 format, with resolution up to 3840×2160 pixels.

- **1080p.** High-def video in H.264 format, resolution up to 1920×1080 pixels.

- **720p.** High-def video in H.264 format, resolution up to 1280×720 pixels.

- **480p.** Standard-definition video in H.264 format.

- **Audio Only.** Just the *audio* from a movie. That's handy if you want to listen on your phone, post an interview online, or use the audio track in another movie.

TV

This weird, hybrid app takes over the TV/movie skills from the dearly departed iTunes program. Although it's technically new in macOS Catalina, it's nearly identical to the TV app on the iPhone or iPad.

The tabs across the top offer these features:

- **Watch Now.** This screen (Figure 16-7, top left) is an App Store–ish page of sug-gestions for shows and movies available to watch. It includes movies you buy or rent from Apple, as you might have done in iTunes in days gone by; Apple TV+, Apple's paid streaming service ($5 a month for a few shows that Apple itself has produced); and other paid services, like HBO, Starz, Showtime, and CBS All Access.

- **Movies** and **TV Shows** are the new home for the old iTunes movies-and-TV-episodes store. The store offers a vast selection of downloadable TV episodes ($2 apiece, no ads) and movies (buy for $10 to $20, or rent for $3 to $5).

 Once you rent a movie, you have 30 days to start watching—and once you start, you have 48 hours to finish before it turns back into a pumpkin (it deletes itself from your computer or phone).

- **Kids** is a section of the TV and Movies store just for children.

- **Library** (Figure 16-7, lower right) lists TV shows and movies you've bought or rented from Apple, along with videos you've made yourself (in the Home Videos category). On the left side, the panel lets you view your collection by genre (Comedy, Documentary, and so on) or by file category (Downloaded, 4K & HDR, Recently Added, and so on).

How to Play a Video

When you click a video's thumbnail, it either opens up in the corresponding channel app—or, if it came from Apple, it opens a Details screen (plot summary, year of release, and so on).

If you see a ☁ on the Details screen, it means that this bought or rented movie is not actually on your Mac. If you have a good Wi-Fi signal, you can watch it right now by streaming it (instead of waiting for it to fully download).

If you don't see that icon, then the video file is actually on your Mac. You can play it by clicking ▶, or, if you need the space back, click ●●●→Delete From Library to delete the video. (Of course, you can always re-download it at no charge.)

When you're playing an Apple video, anything else on the screen is distracting, so Apple hides the video playback controls after a couple of seconds. Move the mouse to make them appear.

Here's what they do:

- ⊗. Tap to stop playback and return to the master list of videos.

- **Volume slider.**

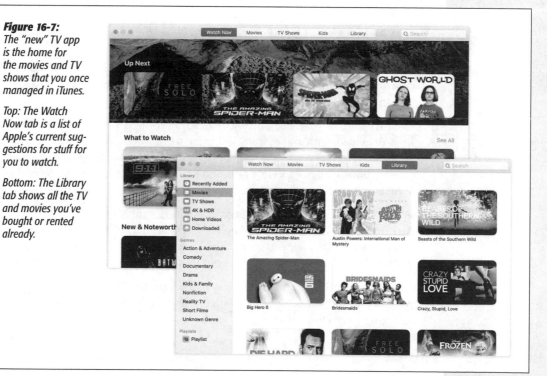

Figure 16-7:
The "new" TV app is the home for the movies and TV shows that you once managed in iTunes.

Top: The Watch Now tab is a list of Apple's current suggestions for stuff for you to watch.

Bottom: The Library tab shows all the TV and movies you've bought or rented already.

- **AirPlay** (⬜). This symbol appears if you have an Apple TV (or another AirPlay-compatible device). Tap it to send your video playback to the TV, as described on page 341.

- ⟲ or ⟳. Skips 15 seconds back (great if the actor mumbled) or forward (great if the next shot looks too grisly).

- **Scroll slider.** This progress indicator (bottom of the screen) shows the elapsed time, the remaining time, and a round handle that you can drag to jump forward or back in the video.

- **Play/Pause** (▶/❙❙). These buttons alternate playing and pausing.

If you're watching a movie from the iTunes Store, you may be surprised to discover that it comes with what were once called DVD Extras: chapter markers, deleted scenes, and so on. To see the Extras buttons for these goodies, tap the screen.

- **Language** (💬) summons subtitle and alternate-language soundtrack options.

- ▣ (**Unzoom**). Exits full-screen mode; now your video plays in a floating picture-in-picture window that you can drag to any corner of the screen. At that point, you can hit ▣ (Zoom) to make it jump to full screen again.

TV Output

When you crave a bigger screen, you can play your Mac's videos on a regular TV. You can do that either with a wire or without:

- **Get a cable.** The kind of cable depends on your Mac and your TV. A MacBook Pro connected to a modern HDTV, for example, needs Thunderbolt 3 on the Mac's end and HDMI on the TV set's.

- **Use AirPlay.** The Mac also offers wireless projection. AirPlay transmits music or high-def video, with audio, from your Mac to an Apple TV (or another AirPlay-equipped receiver) across the room. It's a fantastic way to send video, slideshows, presentations, games, FaceTime calls, and websites to your TV for a larger audience. Whatever is on the screen gets transmitted.

 When you're playing a video or music, open the ⬜ menulet to see a list of available AirPlay receivers. If you have an Apple TV, click its name. (If this is your first time, enter the four-digit code you see on the TV.) AirPlay receivers include the Apple TV and speakers, stereos, and receivers from Denon, Marantz, JBL, iHome, and so on.

 Everything on the Mac's screen now appears on the TV or sound system. You can use the ⬜ menulet to specify whether the TV image is a *mirror* of the Mac's screen or an *extension* of it.

Music

If you once knew your way around iTunes, the newly spun-off Music app should hold no surprises.

Apple Music

The Music app is, above all, the Mac's headquarters for the Apple Music service, which costs $10 a month (or $15 for a family of six). Here's what it offers:

- **Unlimited streaming music.** You can listen to any band, album, or song in the Apple Music library of 50 million songs—on demand, no ads. It's not like listening to a radio station, where someone else is programming the music; you program the music.

 On the other hand, this is not like Apple's traditional music store, where you pay $1 per download and then you own the song. If you ever stop paying, the music stops, too. You're left with nothing.

 If you do subscribe, you can tell Siri things like, "Play the top songs of 2010" or "Play some good running music" or "Play some Taylor Swift."

 But you're not obligated to do all your music programming manually. Apple Music comes with ready-made playlists, prepared by human editors, in all kinds of categories. There are sets of starter songs by various singers ("Intro to Sarah McLachlan"), playlists by genre and era, and playlists for specific activities like Waking Up, Running, Getting It On, and even Breaking Up.

- **Beats 1 radio.** Apple runs a "global, 24-hour internet radio station" called Beats 1. (It actually broadcasts live for 12 hours a day and then repeats.) Listening is free, even to nonsubscribers. Live DJs introduce songs and comment on the singers, just as on regular radio stations.

- **iTunes Match.** iTunes Match, which dates back to 2011, is a cloud-based version of your Music library, available to any of your Apple devices. For $25 a year, you can stream Apple's copies of any song files you actually own—ripped from CDs or even acquired illegally. The advantages: First, you save a lot of space. Second, you can play them on any Apple gadget you own. Third, the versions Apple plays are often of higher quality than your originals.

 iTunes Match continues as a separate service for non–Apple Music subscribers (the song limit is now 100,000 songs). But if you do subscribe to Apple Music, then in effect you get iTunes Match automatically.

- **iCloud Music Library.** This is a newer service, also part of Apple Music—a descendant of iTunes Match. This feature, too, matches all the songs in your collection with songs Apple has online, so you can play any of them on any Apple machine anywhere (once you've signed in). And if you have some songs Apple doesn't have, you can upload them to Apple and thereby add them to your locker.

The playback and volume controls are near the top left of Music (Figure 16-8). At the left side is a sidebar that lists different ways to dive into your music, topped by a search box that lets you pluck one track out of a haystack.

You may see wildly different things in the main window, depending on which of those groupings you've chosen. For example, if you click Songs, you see a huge alphabetical list; if you click Albums, you see a square grid of album covers.

The following pages take you through the many faces of Music, one by one. Note that most of the thumbnails on the For You, Browse, and Radio tabs are only ads that don't play anything *unless* you're an Apple Music subscriber (choose Account→Join Apple Music).

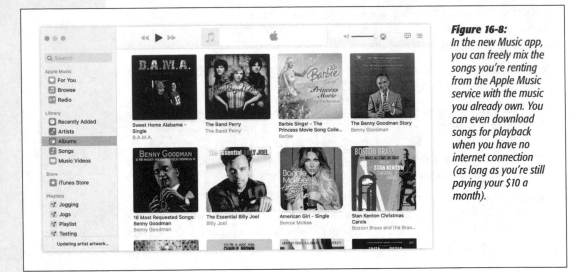

Figure 16-8:
In the new Music app, you can freely mix the songs you're renting from the Apple Music service with the music you already own. You can even download songs for playback when you have no internet connection (as long as you're still paying your $10 a month).

For You

Fifty million is a lot of songs. You won't live long enough to hear them all. So Apple has supplied the For You screen of the Music app (first in the left-side list) to present new songs, performers, and albums its algorithms think you'll like.

Scroll to see the playlists, albums, artists, and new releases Apple has chosen for you.

As you go through your life listening to music, you can always turn the ♡ button on or off to further fine-tune Apple's understanding of your tastes.

Browse

The Browse screen is for paying subscribers only. It's lists of lists.

Scroll down long enough, and you'll find lists like New Music, Playlists (music lists created by Apple's editors for particular activities, and moods), Music Videos, Top Charts, and Genres. Once again, the idea is to help you find new stuff you like.

Radio Tab

Your Mac includes an amazing gift: your own radio station. Your own empire of radio stations, in fact.

They come in three categories: free stations, ready-made stations for subscribers, and subscriber-only custom stations based on a "seed" song.

Free stations

If you're not an Apple Music subscriber, you're still free to listen to Beats 1 (the Apple live station).

You can also listen to any of the tens of thousands of free online streams of actual radio stations. Just search for the name in the top-left search box (for example, *WCBS*, *BBC Radio 1,* or *98.1 The Breeze*), and then click ▶ in the results.

Every internet radio stream also has a URL (web address). If you know one, you can paste it into File→Open Stream URL to start listening.

Subscriber stations

If you're an Apple Music person, this screen offers ready-made "radio stations" Apple has supplied for you. If you're a subscriber, they play; if not, they give you an ad inviting you to sign up.

You can hit ⏭ to skip a song you're not enjoying. And you don't hear any ads.

Custom stations

If you're a paid subscriber, the Radio service offers more than canned stations; you can create a new "station" instantly, based on any song, artist, or genre you choose.

You don't get to choose the exact songs or singers you want to hear; you have to trust Radio to select the music based on your chosen song, singer, or genre. For example, if you choose Billy Joel as your "seed," you'll hear a lot of Billy Joel, but also a lot of other music that sounds more or less like his.

To set up a new station of your own, find a song you like on any of the Library tabs. Right-click or two-finger click its name to open an Options menu, and click Create Station. Your new station's name shows up on the Radio tab, under Recently Played.

GEM IN THE ROUGH

AirPlay Audio

On page 341, you can read about the miracle of AirPlay—a wireless technology that sends video from your Mac to your Apple TV.

But even before there was AirPlay video, there was AirPlay audio. Your Mac can easily send audio to your Apple TV (or to your AirPort Express base station), and from there to what's presumably a better sound system than your Mac's puny built-in speakers.

The official way to do that: Open System Preferences→

Sound→Output. Click the name of the Apple TV or AirPort Express in the list of speakers.

But there are two faster ways:

Press Option as you open the ◀ɯ) menulet. The items in this menu magically sprout previously invisible choices—like Apple TV and your other AirPlay gear.

If you want to just play music, you can choose your Apple TV's name (or AirPort Express's name) from the ▱ pop-up menu in the top-left corner of the window.

The idea of a radio service based on a seed song isn't new, of course. It's the same idea as Pandora, the website and app that's been around for years. But Radio is built-in, it's incorporated with Siri, and it's part of Apple's larger ecosystem; that is, you can see the same set of "radio stations" on your PC, iPhone, iPad, and Apple TV.

Returning to a custom station

On the main Radio screen, the Recently Played list shows all the stations you've listened to (or recently created). Click to start playing.

Siri and radio

Truth is, there's an easier way to create a custom radio station: Just let Siri do the work. You can say, for example, "Start a station from Whitney Houston." Boom: The music begins.

Actually, Siri comes equipped to recognize a slew of commands pertaining to radio. Here's a sampler; you don't have to use these precise wordings: "Play some Taylor Swift" (or any song, album, or artist). "Play the radio." "What song is this?" "Play more like this." "Don't play this song again." "Pause the music." "Resume the music." "Skip this song." "Add this song to my Wish List." "Stop the radio."

Library

Here's all the music you've chosen yourself.

In the old days, this meant "music files actually on your Mac." If you have an Apple Music membership, though, you'll also see online songs listed here that you've added to your personal catalog.

You can view them grouped by any of the categories you see: Recently Added, Playlists, Artists, Albums, Songs, Music Videos, or (if you subscribe to Apple Music) Downloaded Music. Below all that, in the Recently Added section, you get thumbnails for albums and playlists you've recently downloaded or built.

As you could probably guess, you operate the Library by drilling down—by clicking from category to album to song or whatever. (Click ‹ to backtrack.)

Four Ways to Fill Your Library

Music gives you at least four ways to get music and videos onto your computer—ready for transferring to your devices, if you want:

- **Import music files.** Choose File→Import to bring all your music files (MP3 or whatever) into the Music app for organizing. You're asked to find the folder that contains them on your drive.

- **Subscribe to Apple Music.** For $10 a month, you can listen to, and download, all the music you want from Apple's multimillion-song catalog.

- **Buy from the iTunes Store.** Another way to feed your library is to shop at the iTunes music store, buying songs to own them.

Note: The iTunes Store icon doesn't appear in the list, though, until you open Music→Preferences→General and turn on iTunes Store. Yes, Apple has literally hidden the iTunes music store. That's how much it hopes you'll subscribe to Apple Music.

- **Import music from a CD.** Music can also convert tracks from audio CDs into digital music files. Just start up Music and then stick a CD into your Mac's CD drive, if you have one. The program asks if you want to convert the songs to audio files for Music. (If it doesn't ask, click the CD icon at the top of the window.)

 The program downloads song titles and artist information from the CD and begins to add the songs to the Music library. (For more control over this process, choose Music→Preferences→General. Click "Import Settings" to see your options.

Playlists

A *playlist* is a list of songs you've placed into a set to play sequentially. For example, if you're having a party, you can make a playlist from the dance music in your library. Some people may question your taste if you, say, alternate tracks from *La Bohème* with Queen's "A Night at the Opera," but hey—it's your playlist.

To create a playlist in Music, press ⌘-N or choose File→New→Playlist. A new playlist, called "Playlist," appears twice: once in the lower-left list ("Playlists"), and once on the main screen before you, highlighted so you can rename it.

Type a name for it: "Cardio Workout," "Shoe-Shopping Tunes," "Hits of the Highland Lute," or whatever. Press Enter.

At this point, you've created a list, but there aren't any songs in it yet. The easiest way to fix that is to click one of the Library headings at left (like Songs or Artists), and *drag* song or album names onto the name of your empty playlist.

Tip: Instead of making an empty playlist and then dragging songs into it, you can work the other way. You can scroll through a big list of songs, selecting tracks as you go by ⌘-clicking—and then, when you're finished, choose File→New→Playlist from Selection. All the songs you selected immediately appear on a brand-new playlist.

When you drag a song title onto a playlist, you're not actually moving or copying the song. In essence, you're creating an *alias* or *shortcut* of the original, which means you can have the same song on several different playlists.

Smart playlists

Smart playlists constantly rebuild themselves according to criteria you specify. You might tell one to assemble 45 minutes' worth of songs you've rated higher than four stars but rarely listen to, and another to list your most-often-played songs from the '80s.

Tip: You can make a clickable row of five ratings stars appear on your Songs, Albums, and Artists screens (Music→Preferences→General; turn on "Star ratings"). You can then sort your songs by rating or make smart playlists by rating. Your ratings do not, however, affect the suggestions Apple Music makes. Ah, well.)

To make a smart playlist, choose File→New Smart Playlist (Option-⌘-N). The dialog box shown in Figure 16-9 appears. The controls are designed to set up a search of your music database. Figure 16-9, for example, illustrates how you'd find up to 74 minutes of Beatles tunes released between 1965 and 1968—that you've rated three stars or higher and that you've listened to no more than twice.

Figure 16-9:
A smart playlist is a powerful search command for your music database. You can set up certain criteria, like the hunt for particular Beatles tunes illustrated here. The "Live updating" checkbox makes Music keep this playlist updated as your collection changes, as you change your ratings, as your play count changes, and so on.

Editing and deleting playlists

A playlist is easy to change with just a little light mousework. Click the playlist's name. Now you can do any of these things:

- **Change the order of songs in the playlist.** Drag song titles up or down within the playlist window to reorder them.

- **Add new songs to the playlist.** Tiptoe through your Music list and drag more songs or albums into the playlist list.

- **Delete songs from the playlist.** If your playlist needs pruning, or that banjo tune just doesn't fit in with the brass-band tracks, you can ditch it quickly: Click the song in the playlist window and then hit Delete.

 That doesn't delete it from your Mac—just from this playlist.

- **Delete the whole playlist.** To delete an entire playlist, click its name among the playlists (far left) and then press Delete. Again, this zaps only the playlist itself, not any of the songs you had in it.

Authorizing Computers

Some old music files are still copy-protected. When you sign into Music with your Apple ID, you automatically *authorize* that computer to play copy-protected songs from the iTunes Store.

You can copy those songs onto a maximum of four other computers. To authorize each one to play music from your account, choose Account→Authorizations→Authorize This Computer. (Don't worry—you have to do this just once per machine.) It's Apple's way of making sure you don't go playing those music tracks on more than five computers, which would greatly displease the music studios.

When you've maxed out your limit and can't authorize any more computers, you may need to *deauthorize* one. On the computer you wish to demote, choose Account→Authorizations→Deauthorize This Computer.

Playing with Playback

To play a song, double-click it. Or click the Play button (▶) or press the space bar. The Mac immediately begins to play the selected files or playlists.

Tip: The central display at the top of the window shows not only the name of the song and the album, but also where you are in the song, as represented by the horizontal strip. Drag the handle, or click elsewhere in the strip, to jump around in the song.

As music plays, you can manipulate the music and the visuals of your Mac in all kinds of interesting ways. There are even playback controls on your Touch Bar, if you have one (page 227). Some people don't move from their Macs for months at a time.

Turning on the Visualizer

The Visualizer is an onscreen light show that pulses, beats, and dances in sync to the music. (For real party fun, invite some people who grew up in the '60s to your house to watch.)

To summon this psychedelic display, choose Window→Visualizer, or just press ⌘-T.

The app offers two options in the Window→Visualizer Settings submenu: Visualizer and Classic Visualizer. Check out the latter for that special early-aughts-style trippiness. The show begins immediately—although it's much more fun if you choose View→Enter Full Screen (Control-⌘-F) so the show takes over your whole monitor. True, you won't get a lot of work done, but when it comes to stress relief, Visualizer is a lot cheaper than a hot tub.

Playing with the graphic equalizer

If you choose Window→Equalizer, you get a handsome control console that lets you adjust the strength of each musical frequency independently.

Playing Sounds

You can have a lot of fun with digital sounds—if you know where to find them, where to put them, and how to edit them. You can play almost any kind of digitized sound files, even MP3 files, right in the Finder—if you put their windows into column view or gallery view (or use Quick Look). But that's just the beginning.

Controlling the Volume

Adjusting the volume of your Mac's speakers couldn't be easier: Tap the ◀) and ◀)) keys on your keyboard. (The ◀ is the Mute button—a wonderful feature when you find yourself trying to use the Mac surreptitiously in a library or a church.) Or use the ◀)) menulet on your menu bar (Figure 16-10).

Figure 16-10:
The tiny speaker silhouette in the upper-right corner of your screen turns into a volume slider when you click it. To make this sound menulet appear or disappear, open the Sound pane of System Preferences and use "Show volume in menu bar."

The Output tab of the System Preferences→Sound pane, by the way, is designed to let you adjust the left-to-right balance of your stereo speakers, if you have them. The stereo speakers on most Macs that have them (iMacs, laptops) are already perfectly centered, so there's little need to adjust this slider unless you generally list to one side in your chair. (You might find additional controls here if you have extra audio gear—an old iSub subwoofer system, for example.)

Tip: In the Audio MIDI Setup program (in Applications→Utilities), you can configure much fancier speaker setups, including 5.1 and 6.1 surround-sound systems.

Alert Beeps and You

Alert beeps are the quacks, beeps, or trumpet blasts that say, "You can't click here." (Try typing letters into a dialog box where a program expects numbers, for example.)

Choosing an alert beep

Open System Preferences→Sound→Sound Effects. Press the ▲ and ▼ keys to walk through the 14 sound snippets you can use as error beeps. The "Alert volume" slider adjusts the error-beep volume relative to your Mac's overall speaker setting.

Adding new alert beeps

MacOS's error beeps are AIFF sound files, a standard Mac/Windows/internet sound format—also the standard sound-file format for music CDs. (The abbreviation stands for *audio interchange file format*, if you're scoring at home.)

As with fonts, macOS builds the list of error beeps you see in the Sound pane of System Preferences from several folder sources:

- **System→Library→Sounds folder.** This folder contains the basic macOS set. Because it's in the System folder, it's off-limits to manipulation by you. You can't easily delete one of the original macOS error beeps or add to this collection.

- **Home→Library→Sounds folder.** It's easy enough to add sounds for your own use—just put them in this folder. (Your Home→Library folder is usually invisible; to open it, press Option as you choose Go→Library in the Finder.)

- **Library→Sounds folder.** If you, an administrator, want to make a sound file available to all account holders on your Mac, create a new Sounds folder in the main hard drive window's Library folder. Any sound files you put there now appear in every account holder's list of alert sounds.

The sound files you put into these folders must be in AIFF format, and their names must end with .aiff or .aif. Changes you make to these Sounds folders don't show up in the Sound pane until the next time you open it.

Voice Memos

This audio app, another one that Apple adapted from iOS, is ideal for recording lectures, musical performances, notes to self, and cute child utterances (Figure 16-11). It can even sync your recordings with your iPhone and other Apple gizmos automatically, courtesy of iCloud.

Click ⏺ to start recording from your Mac's built-in microphone (or whatever source you've chosen in System Preferences→Sound). You get to watch the actual sound waves as the recording proceeds (Figure 16-11, left).

You can pause the recording (⏸) at any time, and then click Resume to continue; hit Done when the recording session is over.

The recording shows up with a name based on your current location, like 200 Madison St. (You can turn off this place-naming convention in Voice Memos→Preferences. In that case, every new recording is called, for example, New Recording 35.) You can rename it easily enough: Double-click the temporary name and then type something better ("Baby's First Words," "Orch Concert," whatever).

When you click a recording in the list (Figure 16-11, left), a convenient set of controls appears. Here's what you can do here:

- **▶.** Click to play the recording. You can pause with the ⏸ button. (The space bar plays and pauses, too.)

- **Rewind, Fast Forward.** Drag the scrubber bar to skip backward or forward in the recording. It's a great way to skip over the boring pleasantries. Or click the ⏪ or ⏩ buttons to jump forward or back by 15 seconds. Or just click a spot to jump there.

- **⬆.** Click to open the standard Share menu. It gives you the chance to send your recording to someone else by AirDrop, email, or Messages—or to drop the audio file into a Notes page.

To delete a recording, click its name in the list and then press Delete. You're not asked for confirmation, but you do have a safety net: The deleted recording will sit in the Recently Deleted folder at the very bottom of the list for 30 days.

To see these recordings on death row, click Recently Deleted. Your options here are Recover All (rescue them from deletion), Erase All, or erase just one recording (select it, press the Delete key, and then click Erase to confirm).

Tip: In Voice Memos→Preferences→Clear Deleted, you can specify how quickly these deleted recordings disappear. Your choices are Immediately, After 1 Day, After 7 Days, After 30 Days, or Never.

Editing Your Recording

You might not guess that such a tiny, self-effacing app actually offers some basic editing functions, but it does. Click a recording, then Edit to open its Edit screen (Figure 16-11, right).

Here you have four options:

- **Record over it.** When the blue playhead line is parked at the beginning or middle of the audio, the big red button says Replace. Click it to record over part (or all) of

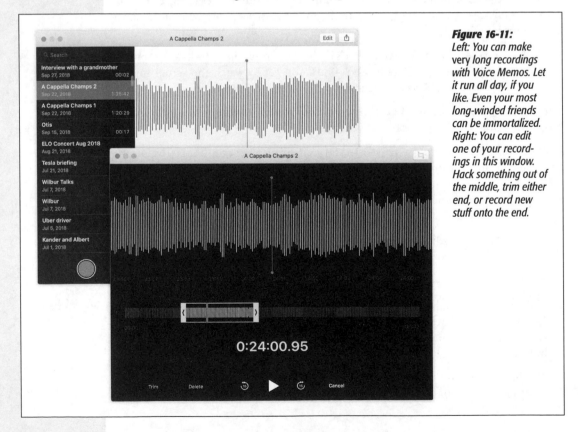

Figure 16-11:
Left: You can make very long recordings with Voice Memos. Let it run all day, if you like. Even your most long-winded friends can be immortalized. Right: You can edit one of your record- ings in this window. Hack something out of the middle, trim either end, or record new stuff onto the end.

your original recording. This is kind of handy. If you recorded a brilliant speech, but stumbled on the opening line (or any line, actually), you can replace it without having to redo the whole thing. Hit **❙❙** to stop.

- **Add onto it.** You can also add on more audio to your existing recording. Just park the blue playhead line at the end of the current sound waves, and then hit Resume. Hit **❙❙** to stop.

- **Trim it.** You can trim off the beginning or end of your audio clip—which is great, since that's where you'll usually find "dead air" or microphone fumbling before the good stuff starts playing.

 To do that, click the Crop button (⊟). At this point, the "map" of the entire sound recording (at the middle of the screen) sprouts yellow crop handles. Drag them inward to isolate the part you want to keep. When you're close, use the magnified area at top to fine-tune the trip points, using the vertical yellow lines. Play the sound as necessary to guide you (▶).

 Click Trim to shave away everything outside your selected area. If you like the result, click Save. If you'd rather try again, choose Edit→Undo. Or hit Cancel to forget the whole thing.

- **Cut out a chunk.** To cut something out of the middle, isolate the undesired audio using the crop and trim handles as described above. This time, though, hit the Delete button. You've just chopped the selection out of the middle.

 Here again, you can hit Save (to preserve the edit), or Cancel to back out of the entire operation.

The beauty of all of this, by the way, is that your audio recordings can now magically and wirelessly appear on all your other Apple machinery, just as though they're calendar appointments or Safari bookmarks. The on/off switch for this syncing is hiding away in System Preferences→iCloud→iCloud Drive→Options→Voice Memos.

Using the Microphone

You have many other options for recording sounds. Your microphone situation depends on the kind of Mac you have:

- **Laptop, iMac.** You have a built-in microphone, usually a tiny hole near the screen.

- **Mac Pro, Mac mini.** You can plug in an external USB microphone or use an adapter that accommodates a standard microphone.

The System Preferences→Sound→Input pane lets you choose which mike to use.

Tip: Actually, there's a quicker way to change audio inputs—if you know the secret. Option-click the ◀)) menulet, if you've installed it. The resulting menu lists all your audio inputs and outputs, making it simple to switch.

Making the Recording

Get some sound-recording software—like QuickTime Player, which is in your Applications folder. (GarageBand works, too, although it's a much beefier app.)

Choose File→New Audio Recording. Use the pop-up menu to specify the audio quality and sound source (Figure 16-12). Click the round, red Record button and begin to speak; click the square Stop button to finish up. Now you can use the volume slider and the ▶ button to listen to your masterpiece.

Tip: Don't adjust the tiny volume slider in the Audio Recording window unless you're wearing headphones. This slider lets you monitor the sound—and turning it up while the Mac's speakers are live risks producing the hideous shriek known as feedback.

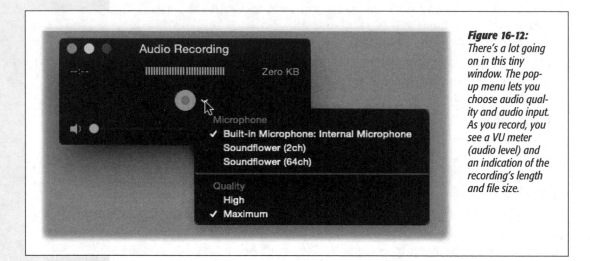

Figure 16-12:
There's a lot going on in this tiny window. The pop-up menu lets you choose audio quality and audio input. As you record, you see a VU meter (audio level) and an indication of the recording's length and file size.

Part Five: macOS Online

5

Internet Setup & iCloud

N o Mac is an island. Virtually all of them are connected to the internet—and therein lies the magic. So often do we think of our computers as windows to the web, email, and streaming entertainment that when we're not online— when the Wi-Fi goes down—many of us feel vaguely panicky.

There are all kinds of ways to get your Mac online these days:

- **Wi-Fi.** Wi-Fi hotspots are glorious conveniences if you have a laptop. Without stirring from your hotel bed, you're online at high speed. Often for free.

- **Cable modems, DSL.** Over 80 percent of the U.S. internet population connects over higher-speed wires, using *broadband* connections that are always on: cable modems, DSL, or corporate networks. (These, of course, are often what's at the other end of a Wi-Fi hotspot.)

- **Tethering.** *Tethering* is letting your cellphone act as a glorified internet antenna for your Mac, whether connected by a cable or a Bluetooth wireless link. You pay your phone company extra for this convenience.

- **Cellular modems.** A few well-heeled individuals enjoy the go-anywhere bliss of *USB cellular modems,* which get them online just about anywhere they can make a phone call. These modems are offered by Verizon, Sprint, AT&T, and so on, and usually cost around $50 a month.

- **Dial-up modems.** A few people still connect to the internet using a modem that dials out over ordinary phone lines. The service is cheap, but the connection is slow.

This chapter explains how to set up each of these. It also describes some of macOS's offbeat internet featurettes. And it tackles Family Sharing, which lets several computers

in the same household share a single broadband connection; the popular virtual wallet feature Apple Pay; and iCloud, Apple's suite of free online syncing tools.

Network Central and Multihoming

In this chapter, you'll be spending a lot of time in System Preferences→Network (Figure 17-1). This list summarizes the ways your Mac can connect to the internet or an office network—Ethernet, Wi-Fi, Bluetooth, cellular modem card, VPN (page 560), and so on.

Figure 17-1:
You set up your network connections here, and you can connect to and disconnect from them here. The listed network connections are tagged with color-coded dots. A green dot means turned on and connected to a network; yellow means the connection is working but some other setting is wrong (for example, your Mac can't get an IP address); and red means there's no connection or you haven't yet set up a connection.

Multihoming

The *order* of the network connections listed in the Network pane is important. That's the sequence the Mac uses as it tries to get online. If one of your programs needs internet access and the first method isn't hooked up, the Mac switches to the next available connection automatically.

In fact, macOS can maintain multiple simultaneous network connections—Ethernet, Wi-Fi, dial-up, even FireWire—with a feature known as *multihoming.*

This is especially relevant for laptops. When you open your web browser, your laptop might first check to see if it's plugged into an Ethernet cable, which is the fastest, most secure type of connection. If there's no Ethernet, then it looks for a Wi-Fi network.

Here's how to go about setting up the connection-attempt sequence you want:

1. **Open System Preferences→Network.**

 The Network status screen (Figure 17-1) brings home the point of multihoming: You can have more than one network connection operating at once.

2. **From the ⚙ pop-up menu, choose Set Service Order.**

 Now you see all the ways your Mac knows how to get online (Figure 17-2).

Figure 17-2:
The key to multihoming is sliding the network connection methods' names up or down. Note that you can choose a different connection sequence for each location. (Locations are described later in this chapter.)

Service Order:

AirCard 791L
Wi-Fi
Bluetooth PAN
Thunderbolt Bridge

Drag services to change order.

Cancel OK

3. **Drag the items up and down the list into priority order.**

 If you have a wired broadband connection, for example, you might want to drag your Ethernet connection to the top of the list, since that's almost always the fastest way to get online.

4. **Click OK.**

 You return to the Network pane of System Preferences, where the master list of connections magically re-sorts itself to match your efforts.

Your Mac will now be able to switch connections during a single internet session. If lightning takes out your Ethernet hub in the middle of your web surfing, your Mac will seamlessly switch to your Wi-Fi network, for example, to keep your session alive.

All right, then: Your paperwork is complete. The following pages guide you through the process of setting up these various connections.

Broadband Connections

If your Mac is connected wirelessly or, um, *wirefully* to a cable modem, DSL, or office network, you're one of the lucky ones. You have a high-speed broadband connection to the internet that's always available, always on. You never have to wait to dial.

Automatic Configuration

Most broadband connections require no setup whatsoever. Take a new Mac out of the box, plug in the Ethernet cable to your cable modem—or choose a wireless network from the 📶 menulet—and you can begin surfing the web instantly.

That's because most cable modems, DSL boxes, and wireless base stations use *DHCP*. It stands for *Dynamic Host Configuration Protocol,* but what it means is "We'll fill in your Network pane of System Preferences automatically." (Including techie specs like IP address and DNS server addresses.)

Manual Configuration

If, for some reason, you're not able to surf the web or check email the first time you try, it's remotely possible that your broadband modem or your office network *doesn't* offer DHCP. In that case, you may have to fiddle with the Network pane of System Preferences, preferably with a customer-support rep from your broadband company on the phone.

On the Network pane, click your internet connection (Wi-Fi, built-in Ethernet, cellular modem, whatever). Click Advanced; click TCP/IP. Now you see something like Figure 17-3. Don't be alarmed by the morass of numbers and periods—it's all in good fun. If you find TCP/IP fun, that is.

Note: *There's a bright side to having a* static IP address, *an internet address that's all your own and won't change: Because your Mac has this one reliable address, several cool macOS features are available to you. For example, it's easier to access your files from anywhere in the world, as described starting on page 557.*

Figure 17-3:
Here's the setup for a cable-modem account with a static IP address, which means you have to type in all these numbers yourself.

Ethernet Connections

The beauty of Ethernet connections is that they're superfast and secure. No bad guys sitting across the coffee shop, armed with shareware "sniffing" software, can intercept your email and chat messages, as they theoretically can when you're on wireless.

And 99 percent of the time, connecting to an Ethernet network is as simple as connecting the cable to the Mac. That's it. You're online, quickly and securely, and you never have to worry about connecting or disconnecting.

Wi-Fi Connections

Your Mac can communicate with a wireless base station up to 300 feet away. Doing so lets you surf the web from your laptop in a hotel room, for example, or share files with someone across the building from you.

Chapter 13 has much more information about *setting up* a Wi-Fi network. The real fun begins, however, when it comes time to *join* one.

Sometimes you just want to join a friend's Wi-Fi network. Sometimes you've got time to kill in an airport, and it's worth a $7 splurge for half an hour. And sometimes, at some street corners in big cities, Wi-Fi signals bleeding out of buildings might give you a choice of several free hotspots to join.

POWER USERS' CLINIC

The Secret Wi-Fi Menulet—and a Word About MAC Addresses

Here's something not one Mac fan in a thousand knows about: a secret diagnostic mode in the 🛜 menulet.

Turns out that if you press the Option key as you open the 🛜 menulet, you get a special treat: a faint gray *interior* menu that identifies some diagnostic details of your current wireless network. You get to see the hotspot's channel, your current data rate, and the BSSID (address of the base station you're using).

This secret menu also offers direct access to a hidden app called Wireless Diagnostics. It's for troubleshooting: It can capture network traffic, create a diagnostic report, or log all events for debugging purposes.

By the way: Some Wi-Fi networks aren't password-protected (there's no 🔒 next to their names), and yet they won't get you online. Why not? Because some hotspots are so restrictive that the network administrator has to register *each MAC address* that's allowed to use it.

A MAC address has nothing to do with Macintosh computers. It stands for media access control, although the equivalent term, Ethernet Hardware Address, is much more descriptive. It's a unique identifier for your networking card, whether it's your Ethernet card or your Wi-Fi circuitry.

MAC-address filtering is another, even more exclusive, way to keep the unwashed masses from using a hotspot.

Your Mac joins Wi-Fi hotspots like this:

- **First, it sniffs around for a Wi-Fi network** you've used before. If it finds one, it connects quietly and automatically. You're not asked for permission, a password, or anything else; you're just online. (It's that way, for example, when you come home with your laptop every day.)

- **If the Mac can't find a known hotspot,** but it detects a new hotspot or two, a message appears on the screen, displaying their names. Double-click one to connect.

Tip: If you don't *want* your Mac to keep interrupting you with its discoveries of new hotspots—it can get pretty annoying when you're in a taxi driving through a city—you can shut them off. In System Preferences, click Network, click Wi-Fi, and then turn off "Ask to join new networks."

- **If you're in the presence of a commercial hotspot**—one that requires payment or reading some kind of insipid legal agreement—macOS opens a miniature web page, shoving it right into your face, even if your web browser isn't open; see Figure 17-4.

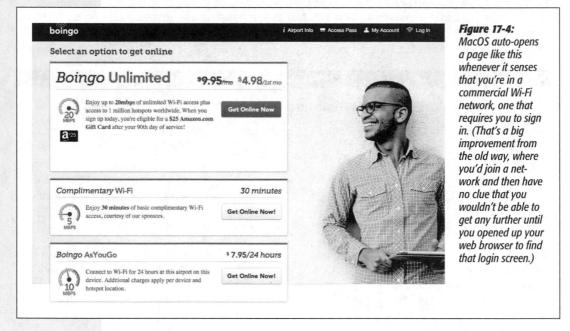

Figure 17-4:
MacOS auto-opens a page like this whenever it senses that you're in a commercial Wi-Fi network, one that requires you to sign in. (That's a big improvement from the old way, where you'd join a network and then have no clue that you wouldn't be able to get any further until you opened up your web browser to find that login screen.)

- **If you missed the opportunity to join a hotspot** when the message appeared, or if you joined the wrong one or a nonworking one, you have another chance. You can always choose a hotspot's name from the 🛜 menulet, as shown in Figure 17-5. A 🔒 icon indicates a hotspot that requires a password, so you don't waste your time trying to join it (unless, of course, you *have* the password).

Tip: It always takes a computer a few seconds—maybe five or ten—to connect to the internet over Wi-Fi. In macOS, the 🛜 menulet itself ripples with a black-and-gray animation to let you know you're still in the connection process. It's an anti-frustration aid. (Oh, and each hotspot's signal strength appears right in the menulet.)

Figure 17-5:
Top: Congratulations—your Mac has discovered new Wi-Fi hotspots all around you! You even get to see the signal strength right in the menu. Double-click one to join it. But if you see a 🔒 icon next to the hotspot's name, beware: It's been protected by a password. If you don't know it, then you won't be able to connect.

Bottom: Later, you can always switch networks using the Wi-Fi menulet.

Or, if you have an iPhone or cellular iPad with Instant Hotspot turned on (page 307), you can hop right onto your own private network.

> **None of your preferred networks are available.**
> Choose the Wi-Fi network you want to join from the list below.
>
> | Fontainebleau_Guest | 🔒 | 🛜 |
> | eNet 3 | | 🛜 |
> | hhonors | | 🛜 |
>
> ⟳ Scanning...
> ? Join Other Cancel Join

> 🖥 🕐 ✳ 🛜 🔊 100% 🔋 🏳 Sat 10:49 PM 👤 🔍 ☰
> Wi-Fi: On
> **Turn Wi-Fi Off**
>
> Personal Hotspot
> **P's iPad** ●●●○○ LTE 🔋 ⟳
>
> ✓ eNet 3 🛜
> guest 🔒 🛜
> Tonsberg 🔒 🛜
>
> **Join Other Network...**
> **Create Network...**
> **Open Network Preferences...**

POWER USERS' CLINIC

PPPoE and DSL

If you have DSL service, you may be directed to create a *PPPoE service*. (You do that on the Network pane of System Preferences; click the + button, choose PPPoE, select the connection you're using to PPPoE, and then click Create.)

It stands for PPP over Ethernet, meaning that although your DSL "modem" is connected to your Ethernet port, you still have to make and break your internet connections manually, as though you had a dial-up modem.

Fill in the PPPoE dialog box as directed by your ISP (usually just your account name and password). From here on in, you start and end your internet connections exactly as though you had a dial-up modem.

Before you get too excited, though, some lowering of expectations is in order. There are a bunch of reasons why your 🛜 menulet might indicate that you're in a hotspot but you can't actually get online:

- **It's locked.** If there's a 🔒 next to the hotspot's name in your 🛜 menulet, it's password protected. That's partly to prevent hackers from "sniffing" the transmissions and intercepting messages and partly to keep random passersby like you off the network.

- **The signal isn't strong enough.** Sometimes the Wi-Fi signal is strong enough to make the hotspot's name show up in your 🛜 menu but not strong enough for an actual connection.

- **You're not on the list.** Sometimes, for security, hotspots are rigged to permit only *specific* computers to join, and yours isn't one of them.

- **You haven't logged in yet.** Commercial hotspots (the ones you have to pay for) don't connect you to the internet until you've supplied your payment details on a special web page that appears automatically, as described in the next section.

- **The router's on, but the internet's not connected.** Sometimes a wireless router is broadcasting but its internet connection is down. It'd be like a cordless phone that has a good connection back to the base station in the kitchen—but the phone cord isn't plugged into the base station.

Commercial Hotspots

Choosing the name of the hotspot you want to join is generally all you have to do—if it's a *home* Wi-Fi network.

Unfortunately, joining a *commercial* Wi-Fi hotspot—one that requires a credit card number (in a hotel room or an airport, for example)—requires more than just connecting to it. You also have to *sign into* it before you can send so much as a single email message.

As shown in Figure 17-4, the Mac generally auto-opens the sign-up screen. Supply your credit card information or (if you have a membership to this Wi-Fi chain, like Boingo or T-Mobile) your name and password. Click Submit or Proceed, try *not* to contemplate how this $8 per hour is pure profit for somebody, and enjoy your surfing.

Tethering (Personal Hotspot)

Wi-Fi hotspots are fast and usually cheap—but they're *spots*. Beyond 150 feet away, you're offline.

Fortunately, if you have an iPhone, Android phone, or another smartphone, you've got a cellular modem in your pocket. Most smartphones nowadays offer *tethering*, where the cellphone passes the internet along to your laptop (or even your desktop computer). The phone connects to your laptop either with a USB cable or wirelessly (Bluetooth or Wi-Fi).

The nice part is that you can get online almost anywhere there's cellphone coverage. The less-nice part is that the connection isn't always blazing fast, and you usually have to pay your cell company extra for the privilege.

Here's a typical example: Suppose you have an iPhone. You open Settings→Personal Hotspot. You turn Personal Hotspot on. You use the password your phone has supplied or assign one to your private little hotspot.

Now, on your laptop, you choose your iPhone's name from the 🛜 menulet. (The menulet shows the iPhone's name even if it's asleep and Personal Hotspot is turned off.)

You enter your hotspot password (just this time—later, your laptop will remember), and presto: Your laptop is online. A bright blue "Personal Hotspot: 1 Connection" banner appears on your iPhone to remind you, and your 🛜 menulet changes to the International Symbol for Apple Tethering: ⌬.

Tethering eats up your phone's battery like crazy; you'll be lucky to get three hours out of it. So you probably shouldn't count on watching Netflix on your laptop via your phone.

But for email, emergency web checks, and other mobile crises, tethering is a convenient, useful feature. And when you're on the road for a couple of weeks, it's a heck of a lot cheaper than paying your hotel $13 a night for Wi-Fi.

Cellular Modems

The convenience of Personal Hotspot has nearly snuffed out the existence of cellular USB sticks or wireless MiFi pucks that let your laptop get online at high speed anywhere in major cities. They're the same idea as tethering. On one hand, you're not draining your phone's battery. On the other hand, the service is expensive—maybe $50 a month on top of your phone bill.

Dial-Up Modem Connections

Macs haven't come with built-in modems for years. You can get a non-Apple USB modem for $50, but clearly Apple is trying to shove the trusty dial-up technology into the recycling bin.

Still, millions of people never got the memo. Details on macOS's dial-up modem setup are in the free appendix to this chapter, "Setting Up a Dial-Up Connection." It's available on this book's "Missing CD" page at *missingmanuals.com*.

Switching Locations

If you travel with a laptop, you may find yourself frequently opening up System Preferences→Network so you can switch between internet settings: Ethernet at the office, Wi-Fi at home.

The simple solution is the →Location submenu, which appears once you've set up more than one location. As Figure 17-6 illustrates, all you have to do is tell it where you are. MacOS handles the details of switching internet connections.

Creating a New Location

To create a *location,* which is nothing more than a set of memorized settings, open System Preferences→Network and choose Edit Locations from the Location pop-up menu. Continue as shown in Figure 17-6 at bottom.

Tip: You can use the commands in the menu to rename or duplicate a location.

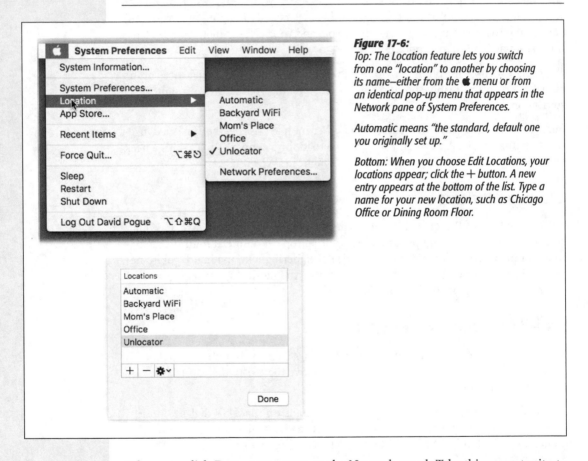

Figure 17-6:
Top: The Location feature lets you switch from one "location" to another by choosing its name—either from the menu or from an identical pop-up menu that appears in the Network pane of System Preferences.

Automatic means "the standard, default one you originally set up."

Bottom: When you choose Edit Locations, your locations appear; click the + button. A new entry appears at the bottom of the list. Type a name for your new location, such as Chicago Office or Dining Room Floor.

When you click Done, you return to the Network panel. Take this opportunity to set up the kind of internet connection you use at the corresponding location, just as described on the first pages of this chapter. If you travel regularly, you can build a *list* of locations, each of which "knows" the way you like to get online in each city you visit.

A key part of making a new location is putting the various internet connection types (Ethernet, Wi-Fi, Modem, Bluetooth) into the correct order. Your connections will be slightly quicker if you give the Modem connection priority in your Hotel setup, the Wi-Fi connection priority in your Starbucks setup, and so on.

You can even turn off some connections entirely. For example, if you use nothing but a cable modem when you're at home, you might want to create a location in which *only* the Ethernet connection is active. Use the Make Service Inactive command in the ✿ menu.

Conversely, if your laptop uses nothing but Wi-Fi when you're on the road, your location could include *nothing* but the Wi-Fi connection. You'll save a few seconds each time you try to go online, because your Mac won't bother hunting for an internet connection that doesn't exist.

Making the Switch

Once you've set up your various locations, you can switch among them using the ●→Location submenu, as shown in Figure 17-6. As soon as you do so, your Mac is automatically set to get online the way you like.

Internet Sharing

If you have cable modem or DSL service, you get terrific speed and an always-on connection. But, unless you take action, only one computer in your household or office can enjoy it.

It doesn't have to be that way. You can spread the joy of high-speed internet to every Mac (and PC) on your network in either of two ways:

- **Buy a router.** A *router* is a little box that connects to the cable modem or DSL box. In most cases, it has multiple internet jacks so you can plug in several Macs, PCs, and/or wireless base stations. As a bonus, a router provides excellent security, serving as a firewall to keep out hackers.

- **Use Internet Sharing.** MacOS's Internet Sharing feature is the software version of a router: It distributes a single internet signal to every computer on the network. But unlike a router, it's free. You just fire it up on the one Mac that's connected directly to the internet—the *gateway* computer.

The only requirement: The internet-connected Mac must have some *other* kind of connection (Ethernet, Wi-Fi, Bluetooth, FireWire) to the Macs that will share the connection.

Turning On Internet Sharing

To turn on Internet Sharing on the gateway Mac, open the Sharing panel of System Preferences. Click Internet Sharing, as shown in Figure 17-7.

Now set things up:

- **Share your connection from.** Using this pop-up menu, identify how *this Mac* (the gateway machine) connects to the internet—via Ethernet, Wi-Fi, cellular modem, or Bluetooth DUN (dial-up networking—that is, tethering to your cellphone or iPad).

- **To computers using.** Using these checkboxes, specify how you want your Mac to rebroadcast the internet signal to the others. (It has to be a *different* network channel. You can't get your signal via Wi-Fi and then pass it on via Wi-Fi.)

Now visit each of the other Macs on the same network. Open the Network pane of System Preferences. Select the network method you chose: Wi-Fi, Built-in Ethernet, or FireWire. Click Apply.

If the gateway Mac is rebroadcasting using Wi-Fi—by far the most common use of this feature—then you have one more step. In your 📶 menulet, you'll see a new "hotspot" that wasn't there before, bearing the name of the gateway Mac. Choose its name to begin your borrowed internet connection.

As long as the gateway Mac remains on and online, both it and your other computers, even Windows PCs, can get onto the internet simultaneously, all at high speed.

Tip: You can let a wired Mac share a *wireless* connection, too. Suppose, for example, that you and a buddy both have laptops in a hotel lobby. You're online, having paid $13 to use the hotel's Wi-Fi network. If you set up Internet Sharing appropriately, your buddy can connect to your Mac via an Ethernet cable and surf along with you—no extra charge.

Figure 17-7:
Ka-ching! You and your buddy are about to save money. In this example, an Ethernet wire is getting this Mac online. But it's sharing that internet connection with other Macs via Wi-Fi. They can get online, too.

Meet iCloud

If you have a Mac, you'll see frequent references to Apple's free iCloud service. It's a huge array of features designed to make you glad you belong in the Apple ecosystem. iCloud synchronizes information across all your Macs, iPhones, iPads, iPod Touches, across family members, across the world, wirelessly and automatically. It keeps track of every song, book, movie, app, and TV show you've bought from Apple, and you can download them onto any other gadget with an Apple logo on the back. It lets you find a lost Apple gadget. It gives you an email account. And a lot more.

The rest of this chapter details each of iCloud's goodies, one at a time. They're described in the order they appear in System Preferences→Apple ID→iCloud (Figure 17-8).

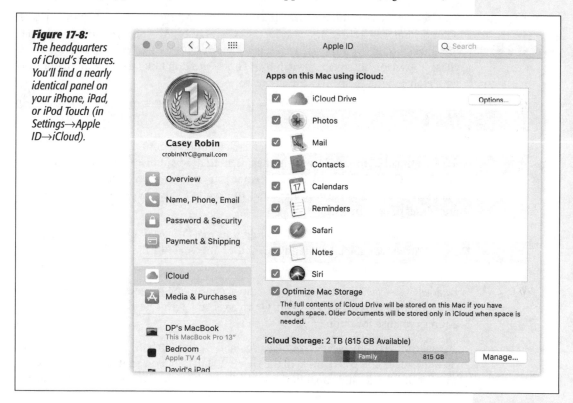

Figure 17-8:
The headquarters of iCloud's features. You'll find a nearly identical panel on your iPhone, iPad, or iPod Touch (in Settings→Apple ID→iCloud).

iCloud Drive

The iCloud Drive is Apple's version of Dropbox. It's a folder, present on every Mac, iPhone, iPad, and iPod Touch, that lists whatever you've put into it—an online "disk" that holds 5 gigabytes (more, if you're willing to pay).

The iCloud Drive is a perfect place to put stuff you want to be able to access from any Apple gadget, wherever you go. It's a great backup, too.

If you click Options next to iCloud Drive in System Preferences (shown in Figure 17-8), you find two tabs. The first, Documents, lists all the Mac apps that have stored files or preference settings on your Drive. Look Me Up By Email is a list of apps that permit other iCloud members to find you by looking up your address.

You can read more about iCloud Drive—and its offshoot, iCloud Desktop & Documents—starting on page 210.

Photos

For most people, pictures are extremely important data. iCloud takes the worry out of maintaining your collection by making sure they're all backed up and available online.

This feature is available in three flavors: Shared Albums, My Photo Stream, and iCloud Photos. All three are described in Chapter 14. All you need to know is that this checkbox, in System Preferences, is the master Off switch for all of it. It's a Break Glass in Case of Emergency switch for people who don't like the idea of any photos wirelessly leaving their Macs for any reason.

Mail

Apple offers an email address as part of each iCloud account. Of course, you already *have* an email account. So why bother? The first advantage is the simple address: *YourName@me.com*. (It may look like what you've got is *YourName@icloud.com*, but mail sent to *YourName@me.com* comes to exactly the same place. These addresses are aliases of each other.)

Second, *me.com* addresses are integrated into macOS's Mail program. You can also read your *me.com* email from any computer anywhere in the world, via the *icloud.com* website, or on your iPhone/iPod Touch/iPad.

Besides, it's always great to have a backup account, one you never enter on websites so it never gets overrun with spam. Or vice versa: Let this be your junk account, the address you use for online forms.

To make things even sweeter, your *me.com* mail is completely synced. Delete a message on one gadget, and you'll find it in the Deleted Mail folder on another. Send a message from your iPhone, and you'll find it in the Sent Mail folder on your Mac. And so on.

Contacts, Calendars, Reminders, Notes...

iCloud began life as a *synchronization* service. It can keep your calendar, address book, reminders, notes, bookmarks, and documents updated and identical on all your gadgets: Mac, PC, iPhone, iPad, iPod Touch. Also your web passwords and credit card numbers. And all your photos, rounded up from all your Apple gadgets.

It's a huge convenience—almost magical. It's one of the great payoffs of living within Apple's ecosystem of gadgets. It offers both the convenience factor—all your stuff is

always on all your gadgets—and a safety/backup factor, since you have duplicates everywhere.

iCloud works by storing the master copies of your stuff—email, notes, reminders, contacts, calendars, web bookmarks, and documents—on the web. (Or "in the cloud," as the product managers would say.)

Whenever your Macs, PCs, or i-gadgets are online, they connect to the mother ship and update themselves. Edit an address on your iPhone, and shortly thereafter you'll find the same change in Contacts on your Mac and Outlook on your PC. Send an email reply from your PC at the office, and you'll find it in your Sent Mail folder on the Mac at home. Add a web bookmark anywhere and find it everywhere else. Edit a spreadsheet in Numbers on your iPad and find the same numbers updated on your Mac.

Actually, there's even another place where you can work with your data: on the web. Using your computer, you can log into *icloud.com* to find web-based clones of Calendar, Contacts, and Mail.

Figure 17-8 shows the on/off switches for these sync features. They include these:

- **Contacts, Calendars.** There's nothing as exasperating as realizing the address book you're consulting on your home Mac is missing somebody you're sure you entered—on your phone. This option keeps all your address books and calendars synchronized.

- **Reminders.** This option refers to the to-do items you create in the phone's Reminders app; very shortly, those reminders will show up on your Mac (in Reminders, Calendar, or BusyCal) or PC (in Outlook). How great to make a reminder for yourself in one place and have it reminding you later in another one!

- **Safari.** If a website is important enough to merit bookmarking while you're using your phone, why shouldn't it also show up in the Bookmarks menu on your desktop PC at home, your Mac laptop, or your iPad? This option syncs your Safari Reading List, too.

UP TO SPEED

The Price of Free

A free iCloud account gives you 5 gigabytes of online storage. That may not sound like much, especially when you consider how big some music, photo, and video files are.

Fortunately, anything you buy from Apple—like music, apps, books, and TV shows—doesn't count against that 5-gigabyte limit. Neither do the photos in your Photo Stream.

So what's left? Some things that don't take up much space, like settings, documents, and pictures you take with your iPhone, iPad, or iPod Touch—and some things that take up a lot of it, like email, commercial movies, your iCloud Photo Library, and anything you put on your iCloud Drive.

You can, of course, expand your storage if you find 5 gigs constricting. You can expand it to 50, 200, or 2,000 gigabytes—for $1, $3, or $10 a month. You can upgrade your storage online, on your phone, or right on the Mac (in System Preferences→iCloud→Manage→Buy More Storage).

- **Notes.** This option syncs the notes from your phone's Notes app into the Notes app on the Mac, the email program on your PC, your other i-gadgets, and, of course, the iCloud website.

- **Siri.** Siri, in theory, gets better over time. She learns what you do, how you speak, what vocabulary you use when chatting. This checkbox lets Siri's knowledge of you synchronize to the other Apple machines you own (at least the ones you've signed into with the same iCloud account).

- **Keychain.** The iCloud Keychain keeps all your online name/password combinations synchronized across all your Apple machines, so you don't have to memorize them or even type them as you log into various sites. Credit card numbers, too. See page 518.

- **News, Stocks.** These checkboxes ensure that your preferences for news stories (page 428) and the contents of your stock portfolio (page 451) appear identically on all your Apple machines.

- **Voice Memos.** The audio recordings you make on your phone can be synced to the Voice Memos app on your Mac, and vice versa. But finding the On switch for this feature isn't easy. In System Preferences→iCloud, click Options next to iCloud Drive. *Here* is the Voice Memos switch.

To set up syncing, turn on the checkboxes for the items you want synced. That's it. There is no step 2.

Note: You may notice that there are no switches here for syncing stuff you buy from Apple, like books, movies, apps, and music. They're not so much synced as they are stored for you online. You can download them at any time to any of your machines.

Find My Mac, Find My iPhone

Did you leave your iPhone somewhere? Did your laptop get stolen? Has that mischievous 5-year-old hidden your iPad again?

You can check into *icloud.com* to see the exact location of your Mac, iPhone, iPad, Apple Watch, or AirPods (out of their case and near your phone); see Figure 17-9.

Or use the new Find My app, which is the same feature in app form. See page 413.

You can even make your device beep loudly for 2 minutes, so you can figure out which room of the house you left it in. If the missing item is an iPad or iPhone, you can make it beep even if the ringer switch is off, and even if the device is asleep. You can also make a message pop up on the screen; if you left the thing in a taxi or on some restaurant table, you can use this feature to plead for its return.

The bottom line: If you ever lose your Apple gear, you have a fighting chance at getting it back. (That's *if* you turned on Find My Mac in the iCloud panel of System Preferences.)

If an ethical person finds your Mac, you might get it back. If it's a person who says, "Hey, cool! A free MacBook!" maybe you can bombard him with so many of these messages that he gives it back in exasperation.

If not, you can either lock the gadget with a password (yes, by remote control) or even avail yourself of one more amazing last-ditch feature: Erase Mac (or iPhone or iPad).

That means *deleting your data by remote control,* from wherever you happen to be. The thief can do nothing but stare in amazement as the Mac, phone, or tablet suddenly erases itself, winding up completely empty.

Note: And by the way: That thief can't erase your stolen device himself, thanks to Apple's ingenious Activation Lock feature. It prevents the laptop, phone, or tablet from being erased without your Apple ID and password. Good luck with that, bad guy!

To set up your Mac so you can find it remotely, open System Preferences→iCloud. Make sure Find My Mac is turned on. That's all there is to it.

Later, if the worst should come to pass and you can't find your Mac, go to any computer and call up *icloud.com.* Log in with your Apple name and password. Click Find My Mac. If you're asked for your password again, type it; Apple wants to make sure it's really, *really* you.

The website updates to show you, on a map, the current location of your Macs (and iPhones, iPod Touches, and iPads); see Figure 17-9.

Note: If they're not online, or if they're turned all the way off, the map shows you the last known location (if that was within the past 24 hours). If it's been longer than 24 hours, you don't see their current locations. If they're just asleep—even if your laptop's lid is closed—you do.

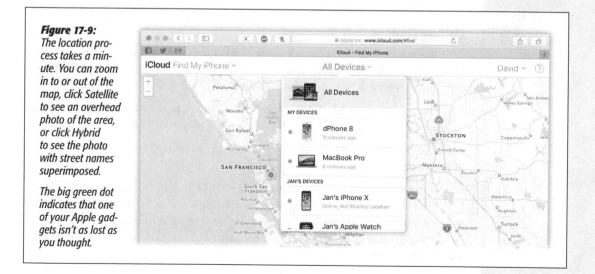

Figure 17-9:
The location process takes a minute. You can zoom in to or out of the map, click Satellite to see an overhead photo of the area, or click Hybrid to see the photo with street names superimposed.

The big green dot indicates that one of your Apple gadgets isn't as lost as you thought.

If just knowing where the thing *is* isn't enough to satisfy you, click the little pushpin that represents your Mac (or choose its name from the menu at top center), and try one of these three buttons:

- **Play Sound.** When you click this button, a very loud sonar-like pinging sound instantly chimes on your Mac, wherever it is, no matter what its volume setting. Even if your laptop is closed and asleep, it will chime. The idea is to help you find it in whatever room of the house you left it in.

 When it's all over, Apple sends an email confirmation to your *@me.com* address.

- **Lock.** What if you worry about the security of your Mac's info, but you don't want to erase it completely and just want to throw a low-level veil of protection over the thing? Easy: Lock it by remote control.

 The Lock button lets you make up a four-digit passcode (which overrides the one you already had, if any). Without it, the sleazebag can't erase your Mac, and can't even get into it.

 You're also offered the opportunity to type a message; it will appear on the Unlock screen, below the four boxes where you're supposed to type in the four-digit code. You might type something like "Thank you for finding my lost laptop! Please call me at 212-555-1003 for a delicious frosty reward."

- **Erase Mac.** This is the last-ditch security option, for when your immediate concern isn't so much the Mac as all the private stuff on it. Click this button, confirm the dire warning box, and click Erase All Data. By remote control, you've just erased everything from your Mac, wherever it may be. (If the Mac is ever returned, you can restore it from your Time Machine backup.)

 Once you've wiped the Mac, you can no longer find it or send messages to it using Find My Mac.

Offline Finding

This feature, new in Catalina, is insane. It lets Find My Mac work even if your lost Mac is offline! Incredibly, it turns the world's 1.4 billion other iPhones, iPads, and Macs into remote detectors for your lost laptop.

Suppose you left your MacBook in an Upper Peninsula restaurant where there's no Wi-Fi and no cell service. It's lying there, asleep, at the end of the booth where you sat.

Fortunately, it's still broadcasting an ever-changing ID number by Bluetooth, silently and invisibly.

The next day, a total stranger carrying another Apple device eats in the same restaurant. Unbeknownst to her, the sleeping iPhone in her purse picks up that Bluetooth signal, relays its location to Apple's servers, and from there back to you. You're at home in Madison, Wisconsin, using your iPad. You use Find My Mac on the iCloud website, and boom: You've found your Mac!

To make all this work privately and securely, Apple had to do some astonishing engineering. How can the feature transmit the location of your lost Mac without anyone else—not even Apple—finding out? How could Apple design this feature so nobody could use it to track somebody or intercept your lost phone's location before you get it?

Answer: That anonymous, constantly changing serial number broadcast by your phone is of no value to anyone but you, because only another Apple device owned by you can decrypt it. So the downside of this system is that it doesn't work unless you own two Apple devices.

The on/off switch for this feature is in System Preferences→Apple ID→iCloud→ Find My Mac→Options.

Family Sharing

Apple has finally acknowledged a fundamental fact of life: Many of us have *families*.

It used to be a hassle to manage your Apple life with kids. What if they wanted to buy a book, movie, or app? They had to use your credit card—and you had to reveal your iCloud password to them. Or what if they wanted to see a movie you bought? Should they really have to buy it again?

Family Sharing solves those problems. Once you've turned on Family Sharing and invited your family members, here's how your life will be different:

- **One credit card to rule them all.** Up to six of you can buy books, movies, apps, and music on your master credit card.

- **Buying permissions.** When your kids try to buy stuff, your phone pops up a permission request. You have to approve each purchase.

- **Younger Appleheads.** You can create Apple accounts even for tiny tots. (For regular Apple accounts, 13 is the age minimum.)

- **Shared purchases.** You all get instant access to one another's music, videos, Books books, and app purchases—again, without having to know one another's Apple passwords.

- **Shared subscriptions.** You can all share a single subscription to services like Apple Music ($10 a month for 5 million songs), Apple Arcade ($5 a month for hundreds of games), Apple News+ ($10 a month for hundreds of magazines), and Apple TV+ ($5 a month for Apple-produced TV shows).

- **Shared storage.** You can share any extra iCloud storage you've bought (page 657) with your fellow family members.

- **Find one another.** You can use your phone to see where your kids are, and vice versa (with permission, of course).

- **Find one another's devices.** The miraculous Find My Mac feature works for everyone in the family. If your daughter can't find her laptop, you can find it for her with yours.

- **Mutual photo album, mutual calendar, and mutual reminders.** When you turn on Family Sharing, your Photos, Calendar, and Reminders apps each sprout a new category that's preconfigured to permit access by everyone in your family.

Setting Up Family Sharing

You can turn on Family Sharing either on the Mac (in System Preferences; see Figure 17-10) or on the phone. Since this book is about the Mac, here are the steps to do it there:

1. **In System Preferences, click Family Sharing next to the Apple ID icon. (You can't turn on Family Sharing until you've signed in with an Apple ID.)**

2. **In the sidebar, click Family.**

 The very first time you click Family Sharing, you walk through some screens that explain the feature and confirm that you're about to become the Organizer—the one with the power, the wisdom, and the credit card.

 You're invited to share *your* electronic Apple purchases with the other family members, confirm the credit card that will be billed, agree to the inevitable legalese, and share *your* location with the other family members.

 Congratulations! You're the head of household.

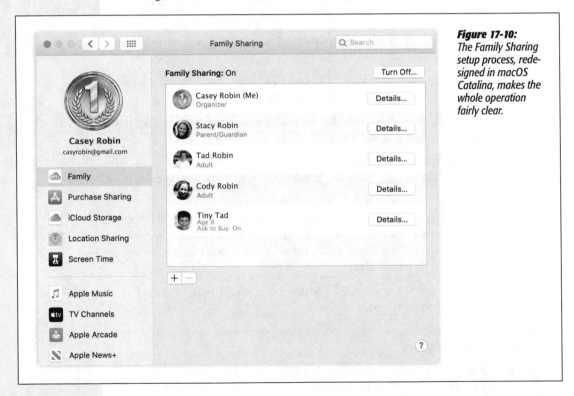

Figure 17-10:
The Family Sharing setup process, redesigned in macOS Catalina, makes the whole operation fairly clear.

3. **Now all you have to do is add up to five of your underlings. To begin, click the +** button at lower left. Then:

- **If the kid has an iCloud account:** Type in her name or email address. Your child's name must already be in your Contacts; if not, go add her first. (By the way, you're a terrible parent.)

 Apple now sends a numeric code to your Mac; type it into the box and then hit Next. And presto: An emailed invitation gets sent to your little darling, who must open it on her Apple gadget—in the Mail app, for example.

 When she hits Get Started and logs in, she can choose a picture to represent herself; tap Confirm to agree to be in your family; enter her iCloud password to share the stuff she's bought from Apple; agree to Apple's lawyers' demands; and, finally, opt in to sharing her location with the rest of the family.

- **If the kid is under 13:** Your kid doesn't have an iCloud account, because until Family Sharing came along, you had to be over 13 to get an iCloud account. No longer!

 Choose "Create an Apple ID for a child who doesn't have an account." Click Continue. On the screen that follows, you'll enter the kid's name and birth date.

 Make up a name and password for the new iCloud account. Decide whether you want the family to be able to see where the kid is at all times. Click Continue.

 On the Parent Privacy Disclosure screen, enter the security code for your credit card yet again (to prove that you're you, and not, for example, your naughty kid).

 On the next screen, you choose and answer three security questions for this new iCloud account. Click Continue. Then more legalese on two screens (click "I agree," and then "Agree").

 Once kids turn 13, by the way, Apple automatically gives them more control over their own lives. They can, for example, turn off Ask To Buy *themselves*, on their own Macs or phones. They can even express their disgust for you by leaving the Family Sharing group. (On her own phone, for example, your daughter can visit Settings→[her name]→Family Sharing, tap her name, and then tap Leave Family. Harsh!)

Note: Don't create a Child account just as an experiment. Once you've created one, you can't delete it until that kid, real or imaginary, is 13 years old! The only way to remove children from your account is by transferring them to another Family Sharing account. Children can be neither created nor destroyed, at least in macOS.

You can, of course, repeat this cycle to add additional family members, up to a maximum of six. Their names and ages appear on the Family screen.

Your Rights as the Organizer

As the designated ruler of the family, you can click someone's name and then Details to perform stunts like these:

- **Turn Ask To Buy on or off.** This option appears when you've selected a *child's* name. If you decide your kid is responsible enough not to need your permission for each purchase, you can turn this option off.

Note: If you turn off Ask To Buy for someone after she turns 18, you can't turn it on again.

- **Turn Parent/Guardian on or off.** This option appears when you've selected an adult's name. It gives Ask To Buy approval privileges to someone else besides you—your spouse, for example.

But you can also work with the headings at the left side of the preferences panel. For example:

- **Purchase Sharing.** Do you want the other family members to see and be able to download the stuff you've been buying? If this is turned on, your kids will see anything you buy. Keep that in mind when you download a book like *Tough Love: Sending the Unruly Child to Military School.*

 This is also where you can change the shared credit card.

- **iCloud Storage.** One of the perks of Family Sharing is that all of you can share the same pool of iCloud storage you're renting (page 657). Here you can see exactly how space-greedy each person is being.

- **Location Sharing.** Here you can specify exactly who can see your location from their own phones and Macs. If you need secrecy for the afternoon—Apple sweetly gives, as an example, shopping for a gift for your spouse—turn off the person you want to hide from. Now you're untrackable until you turn the switch on again.

- **Screen Time,** the new parental-controls feature in Catalina (page 216), summarizes your offspring's weekly Mac/phone/iPad activities here.

- **Apple Music, TV Channels, Apple Arcade, Apple News+.** These screens tell you whether you've signed up for the various Apple subscription services. Once you've subscribed, they're available to all family members. You can't block your teenage son from using Apple Arcade when he's grounded.

Your Rights as an Underling

If you're not the family organizer, you see all the same tabs at the left side of the System Preferences→Family Sharing window. You can see the iCloud Storage breakdown, the Screen Time reports, and so on. But you can *change* only two of those items:

- **Purchase Sharing.** Here you can stop sharing your purchases with individual family members. Your parents might ask you about it, though.

- **Location sharing.** You can specify exactly which family members are allowed to track you.

Life in Family Sharing

Once everything is set up, here's how you and your kids will get along:

- **Purchases.** Whenever one of your kids (for whom you've turned on Ask To Buy) tries to buy music, videos, apps, or books from Apple—even free items—he has to ask you. A notification appears on your screen (Mac, iPhone, iPad).

 When you hit Details, you open the appropriate app (for music, apps, or TV/movies). Here you can read about what your kid wants and then either Accept or Decline.

Tip: Anything you buy, your kids will see. However, you have three lines of defense. First, you can turn off purchase sharing entirely, as described on the previous page.

Second, you can hide only *certain* purchases so nobody sees them. In the Music or TV app, choose Account→ Family Purchases. In the Books app, click Book Store→Featured→Purchased→All. Point to the thing you want to hide, click the ⊗, and click Hide. (In the App Store app, click your name at lower left, and then point to the app you want to hide. From the ⦿ button, choose Hide Purchase.)

Finally, you can set up parental controls on each kid's Mac or phone, shielding their impressionable eyes from R-rated movies and stuff. See 220.

- **Where are you?** Use the Find My app (on Mac, iPhone, or iPad) to see where in the world your posse is right now. Or log into *icloud.com* and click Find iPhone.

- **Photos, appointments, and reminders.** In Photos, Calendar, and Reminders, each of you will find a new category, called Family, that's auto-shared among you all. You're all free to make and edit appointments in this calendar, to set up reminders in the Reminders app ("Flu shots after school!"), or to add photos or videos (or comments) to this album. Everyone else will see the changes instantly.

If you guys *really* don't get along, you can delete a family member. Click the person's name (in System Preferences→Family Sharing) and then click the — button. (You can't delete under-13-year-olds until they're 18. Apple is surprisingly rigid on that point.)

Apple Pay on the Web

Apple Pay (Figure 17-11) is a feature of recent iPhones. It lets you pay for things without cash, without cards, without signing anything, without your wallet: Just hold the phone up to the wireless terminal at most shops and restaurants. You don't have to open an app, don't have to enter a code, don't even have to wake the phone up; just hold your finger on the home button (it reads your fingerprint to make sure it's you) or look at the Face ID camera (on iPhones and iPads with that feature).

You can't do that with your Mac, although it sure would be fun to see someone hold an iMac up to the Starbucks cash register.

What you *can* do on the Mac is buy stuff in the Safari browser, on websites that accept Apple Pay. (About 200,000 do, including Apple, Seamless, StubHub, Airbnb, Fandango, Groupon, Ticketmaster, and so on.)

If you have a laptop with a fingerprint reader, you can complete those purchases with a tap on your Touch ID sensor. If not, you can use an Apple Watch or an iPhone as the identification authenticator; read on.

Figure 17-11:
Apple Pay lets you use the fingerprint reader or Face ID on your phone to confirm purchases on your Mac. Crazy! The only trick now is finding websites that offer Apple Pay as a payment method.

The Setup

To set up Apple Pay, you have to teach your Mac about your credit card (if you haven't already on your phone).

- **If your Mac has a fingerprint (Touch ID) sensor.** Open System Preferences→Wallet & Apple Pay. Click Add Card.

 If you've already set up a credit card with Apple (through the App Store, for example), all you have to do is supply the security code and then tap Next, Accept, and Done.

 If not, on the Add Card screen, you're asked to hold your Visa, Mastercard, or American Express card up to the Mac's camera. Hold steady until the digits of your card, your name, and the expiration date blink onto the screen, autorecognized. Cool! You can edit any of those four fields before clicking Next, Accept, and Done. (You can also choose Enter Card Details Manually and type in the numbers yourself.)

 Next, your bank has to verify that all systems are go for Apple Pay; it's generally instantaneous. (Most banks work with Apple Pay, but not all of them.) You'll see a notification when it's all ready.

- **If your Mac doesn't have a fingerprint sensor.** You can't set up Apple Pay without an iPhone or iPad. (Open Settings→Wallet & Apple Pay and turn on Allow Payments on Mac.)

As a final step, open Safari→Preferences→Privacy. Turn on "Allow websites to check if Apple Pay is set up."

The Shopping

Next time you're shopping at an Apple Pay–friendly website, and you're on the payment screen where the Buy with Apple Pay logo appears, click it.

A sheet appears where you can choose a different credit card (if you've registered more than one) and where you must authenticate. If you're using a Mac with a fingerprint reader, just touch your finger to it, and the whole thing is complete.

If you're shopping on a Mac that *doesn't* have its own fingerprint reader, a "Confirm on iPhone" or "Confirm on Apple Watch" message lets you know you can authenticate with your iPhone's fingerprint reader or Face ID, or with a double-press of the Watch's side button. The "OK, all clear" signal gets sent to your Mac automatically.

More iCloud Features

Not all of iCloud's goodies are represented as checkboxes in System Preferences. Don't forget that iCloud's online hub is waiting for you—available from any computer, tablet, or phone—at *icloud.com* (Figure 17-12).

And even *that's* not all there is to iCloud.

Automatic Backup

If you have an iPhone, iPad, or iPod Touch, iCloud can back it up, automatically and wirelessly (over Wi-Fi, not over cellular connections). It's a quick backup, since iCloud backs up only the changed data.

Continuity

The set of features Apple calls Continuity turn the iPhone into a part of the Mac. They let you make calls from your Mac as though it were a speakerphone. They let you send and receive text messages from your Mac—to any smartphone on earth. They let you AirDrop files between computer and phone, wirelessly. And more.

Continuity gets its own chapter (Chapter 8).

Books, Music, Apps, Movies: The Locker in the Sky

Apple, if you hadn't noticed, has become a big seller of multimedia files. It has the biggest music store in the world. It has the biggest app store, for both i-gadgets and Macs. It sells an awful lot of TV shows and movies. Its ebook store, Books, is no Amazon, but it's chugging along.

When you buy a song, movie, app, or book, you're allowed to download it to all your other Apple equipment—no extra charge. Even if one of your Family Sharing members buys something, same thing: Everyone in the family is welcome to it.

All they have to do is *find* it. To grab your downloads—or your family's downloads—on the Mac, open the appropriate app: App Store (for apps), TV (for movies and TV shows), Music, or Books. Then:

- **Books.** Click the Book Store tab, and then Purchased.

- **Music, TV.** Choose Account→Family Purchases.

- **Apps.** Click your name (lower-left corner).

Figure 17-12:
Top: Here's the iCloud home screen, showing the major online features of this service. All this stuff, of course, is an online mirror of what's on your Mac.

Bottom: Once you're in one of the modules—Mail, Calendar, Notes, or whatever—you can switch among iCloud features using the ∨ that always appears in the upper-left corner.

In each case, if you're part of Family Sharing, you can choose the person's name to see the purchases they've made.

There they are: all the items you've bought on your *other* machines using the same Apple ID, or all the stuff they've bought on their machines. To download anything listed here onto *this* machine, click the ⬇.

You can save yourself all that tapping by turning on Automatic Downloads within each app's Preferences. From now on, whenever you're on Wi-Fi, stuff you've bought on other Apple machines gets downloaded to this one *automatically*, in the background.

Mail & Contacts

I f you have an email address or two, you'll be happy to discover that macOS includes
Mail, a program that lets you get and send email without having to wade through
a lot of spam (junk mail). Mail is a surprisingly complete program, filled with
shortcuts and great features around every turn.

Setting Up Mail

Mail can't get your mail unless it knows the details of your email account. The first
time you open Mail, then, it asks you for your account information. It's kind of hop-
ing you use a common email service like Gmail, Yahoo, AOL, or Microsoft Exchange
(Figure 18-1), or a common internet provider like Verizon or Comcast. In those situ-
ations, all you have to do is type your email name and password. If Mail recognizes
the suffix (for example, *@gmail.com*), then it does the heavy lifting for you. Mail is
ready to go online.

Note: You can perform exactly the same account setup in the Internet Accounts pane in System Preferences.
There's no advantage of one method or the other, except that the System Preferences pane lets you enter
your account information for online calendars and address books, too.

Now, if you use a service provider that Mail doesn't recognize when you type in your
email name and password—you weirdo—then you have to set up your mail account
the long way. Mail prompts you along, and you confront dialog boxes, where you're
supposed to type in various settings to specify your email account. Some of this
information may require a call to your internet service provider (ISP).

If that happens to you, you'll have to enter details like your name, password, mail-server addresses (incoming and outgoing), and security settings.

When you've made it through the setup screens, turn on Take Account Online to make your new account "live." If you entered everything correctly, Mail checks for new mail right away.

Choose a Mail account provider...

○ **iCloud**

○ **E⊠ Exchange**

○ **Google**

○ **YAHOO!**

○ **Aol.**

○ Other Mail Account...

? Cancel Continue

Figure 18-1:
This dialog box lets you plug in the email settings provided by your internet service. If you want to add another email account later, choose Mail→Add Account and then enter your information in the resulting dialog box. (Or, if you like doing things the hard way, choose Mail→Preferences→Accounts tab, click the + in the lower-left corner of the window, and then enter your account information.)

Importing Old Mail

Mail also can import your email collection from an email program you've used before—Thunderbird, Netscape/Mozilla, Eudora, or even a version of Mail that's stored somewhere else (say, on an old Mac's hard drive). Importing is a big help in making a smooth transition between your old email world and your new one.

To bring over your old mail and mailboxes, choose File→Import Mailboxes. Mail offers to import your old email collection from just about any other Mac email program.

Checking Your Mail

You get new mail and send mail you've already written using the Get Mail command. You can trigger it in any of several ways:

- Click ⊠ on the toolbar.
- Choose Mailbox→Get All New Mail (or press Shift-⌘-N).

Note: *If you have multiple email accounts, you can also use the Mailbox→Get New Mail submenu to pick just* one *account to check for new mail.*

- **Right-click or two-finger click Mail's Dock icon and choose Get New Mail from the shortcut menu.** You can use this method from within any program, as long as Mail is already open.

- **Wait.** Mail comes set to check your email automatically every few minutes. To adjust its timing or turn this feature off, choose Mail→Preferences, click General, and then choose a time interval from the "Check for new messages" pop-up menu.

Tip: If you choose Automatically, you'll get incoming messages the instant they arrive—at least in any accounts that offer "push" email.

Now Mail contacts the mail servers listed in the Accounts pane of Mail's preferences, retrieving new messages and downloading any files attached to those messages. It also *sends* any outgoing messages that couldn't be sent when you wrote them.

Tip: If you'd like to monitor your mail progress in a separate window, choose Window→Activity or press Option-⌘-0. The Activity window gives you a Stop button, progress bars, and other useful information.

Also, if you're having trouble connecting to some (or all) of your email accounts, choose Window→Connection Doctor. There you can see detailed information about accounts that aren't responding. If your computer's internet connection is at fault, you can click Show Detail to try to get back online.

The Mailboxes List

The mailboxes panel, the leftmost list on the screen, lists all your email accounts' folders (and subfolders, and sub-subfolders) for easy access.

Tip: You can also collapse or expand the various sections of the mailboxes list by clicking the Hide or Show button next to each one. That button doesn't appear, however, until you *point* to the section title (like Smart Mailboxes or Google).

Under the Mailboxes heading, you may find these folders:

- **Inbox** holds mail you've received. If you have more than one email account, you can expand the triangles to see separate folders for each of your accounts. You'll see this pattern repeated with the Sent, Junk, and other mailboxes, too—separate accounts have separate subheadings.

Tip: If Mail has something to tell you about your Inbox (like, for instance, that Mail can't connect to it), a tiny warning triangle (⚠) appears on the right side of the Mailboxes heading. Click it to see what Mail is griping about.

If you see a wavy ◔ icon, that's Mail's way of announcing that you're offline. Click the icon to try to connect to the internet.

- **VIPs** displays messages from the most important people in your life—those you've designated as VIPs (page 702). This folder doesn't appear if you haven't identified any VIPs.

- **Flagged.** If you've flagged any messages, the flag headings appear here, too. (Flags are described starting on page 694.)

- **Outbox** holds mail you've written and tried to send but hasn't gone through yet (because you were on an airplane when you wrote it, for example). If you have no mail waiting to be sent, the Outbox disappears.

- **Drafts** holds messages you've started but don't want to send just yet.

- **Sent,** unsurprisingly, holds copies of messages you've sent.

UP TO SPEED

POP, IMAP, Exchange, and Web-Based Mail

When it comes to email, there are four primary flavors of *servers* (internet computers that process email): *POP* (also known as POP3), *IMAP* (also known as IMAP4), *Exchange*, and *web-based*. Each has its own distinct taste, with different strengths and weaknesses.

POP accounts (Post Office Protocol) are still pretty common. Your Mac downloads your incoming mail from a POP server to your hard drive before you read it, which works fine as long as you're using only one computer for email.

The problem with POP, of course, is that things get complicated when you have more than one machine—a phone and a Mac, say, or a laptop and a desktop. For example, if you usually use a desktop Mac, but you want to take your email along on the road on your laptop, you have to copy the Mail folder from your Home→Library folder into the corresponding location on your laptop's hard drive. That's the only way you'll see your messages and attachments when you open Mail on the laptop.

IMAP servers (Internet Message Access Protocol), a newer type, solve that problem. They keep all your mail online rather than making you store it on your hard drive; as a result, you can access the same mail regardless of the computer or phone you use. IMAP servers remember which messages you've read and sent, to boot. (With these accounts, you're not so much *downloading* mail as *synchronizing* your computer with what's online.) It's a great setup if, for example, you check your email during the workday on an iPhone, because the deletions and replies you process on the phone will be there on your Mac when you get home. (You can opt for a Gmail or AOL account to be an IMAP account, too.)

Exchange servers are popular in corporations and some schools. Most of the time, employees tap into these servers using a Windows program like Outlook. Corporate geeks like Exchange servers because they're easy to set up and maintain, and because they offer many of the same features as IMAP servers. Luckily, Mail can read and send email through Exchange servers as though your Mac were just another beige PC.

Free **web-based services** like Hotmail, Yahoo, and Gmail also store your mail on the internet, but you can use a web browser on any computer to read and send messages. They're slower and more cumbersome to use than "regular" email accounts, but they're usually free.

Unfortunately, Mail can't check accounts that are entirely web-based. Fortunately, the big-name web-based email services also offer POP or IMAP servers. If you have a Gmail account, for example, you'll find that you can read your email using either a web browser or Mail (see Gmail's help pages for details on making that work).

Conversely, more and more POP and IMAP accounts are also offering a *web-based* component. For example, whoever provides your internet service—EarthLink, Verizon, or MegaPath, for instance—probably provides both POP service and a web-based way of accessing your email, so you can access your mail either from home or an internet café in Bangladesh.

All Mail cares about, though, is whether your email account allows POP, IMAP, or Exchange access; what you do on the web is, as far as Mail is concerned, your own business.

- **Trash** works a lot like the Trash on your desktop, in that messages you put there don't actually disappear. They remain in the Trash folder until you permanently delete them—or until Mail's automatic trash-cleaning service deletes them for you.

- **Junk** appears when you use Mail's spam filter, as described starting on page 704.

Tailoring the Look of Mail

Apple put a lot of energy into exploiting the size and shape of your screen. In a program made for managing lists and reading messages, you need all the room you can get.

You've always been able to tweak Mail's look, layout, and proportions. In Catalina, the Classic layout has gained so much flexibility that Apple doesn't even call it Classic anymore. Figure 18-2 shows some of the layout variations, and here are some of the ways to get there:

- **Hide the folders list completely.** To do that, click the ⬚ icon above it. Now you have much more screen space to work with. (See the bottom examples in Figure 18-2.)

- **View all the header info on a single line.** That's the super-condensed message-list look shown in Figure 18-2 in the right-side examples. You get that by choosing View→Use Column Layout. (This is what was once called Classic view.)

- **Move the message pane under the list.** If you turn off View→Show Side Preview, then the message body appears below the message list instead of to the right of it (Figure 18-2, lower right).

Figure 18-2:
Mail's layout can be almost anything you want. You can see the list of folders (top examples) or hide it (bottom ones).

You can see a couple of lines of message preview (left examples) or all the info in a single line (right examples). You can have the message body appear beside the list (top right) or below it (bottom right).

- **Try Full Screen mode.** Click the green ⊙ dot in the upper-left corner to make the Mail window expand to fill your monitor. (See page 173 for details on Full Screen mode.) Full Screen mode is a natural for space-hungry email, especially on a small laptop screen.

Tip: When you click outside an open message, it collapses to the bottom of the screen, where only the title bar is visible. Now you're free to peruse other messages; the first one pops back up when you click its title bar.

Similarly, if you begin writing several messages, they can all be accessible at once; they sprout tabs across the top, just like Safari web pages do.

- **Install folders onto the Favorites bar.** You can drag any icon in the mailboxes list onto the Favorites toolbar, where it becomes a button or a pop-up menu. The button works exactly like a folder: For example, you can drag a message onto it to

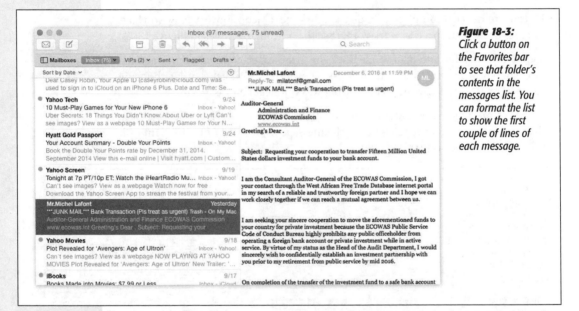

Figure 18-3:
Click a button on the Favorites bar to see that folder's contents in the messages list. You can format the list to show the first couple of lines of each message.

GEM IN THE ROUGH

Favorites Bar Keyboard Shortcuts

One of the best parts of the Favorites bar is that you have complete keyboard control over the buttons there. The keystrokes ⌘-1 through ⌘-9 "click" the first nine buttons on the Favorites bar. Press ⌘-1, for example, to see what's in the first mailbox you've installed on the Favorites bar.

Even cooler yet, if you add the Control key, you now know the keyboard shortcuts for moving selected messages to those

corresponding folders. For example, you can highlight a message and then press Control-⌘-3, confident that you've just filed that message away into your third Favorites-bar folder.

In other words, you can file messages using only the keyboard—and when you're in the thick of things, the less time you spend using the mouse, the better.

file it there, or you can click one of the folder buttons (or use its pop-up menu) to see what's inside.

As you can see in Figure 18-3, the Favorites bar comes with starter buttons already installed, like Inbox, Sent, Drafts, and so on. But you can, and should, install your *own* favorites there and remove the ones you don't want. (To move a button around, ⌘-drag it. To get rid of it, drag it away from the toolbar.)

You can also hide this Favorites bar when you feel the urge. Choose View→Hide Favorites Bar, of course.

Tip: Hey, here's a thought! Install the most important folders onto the Favorites bar, so you can get at them, and *then* hide the mailboxes list. Now you have easy access to the most important folders, but your mailboxes list isn't eating up a lot of screen space. This glorious, space-efficient result is shown in the bottom examples of Figure 18-2.

- **Label the toolbar buttons.** Out of the box, the buttons on the toolbar (✉, 🗑, and so on) have no labels. But if you right-click or two-finger click the toolbar, you get a pop-up menu that offers you other styles for those buttons: Icon and Text, Icon Only, and Text Only (which is *very* space-efficient). From this pop-up window, you can also customize the toolbar, adding other handy buttons like Print, Add to Contacts, and Copy.

- **Change the type size/icon size for the folders in the mailboxes panel.** To do that, open System Preferences→General. Use the "Sidebar icon size" pop-up menu to choose Small, Medium, or Large.

Note: Whatever size you choose here also affects the font and icon sizes in the *Finder window Sidebar*. Apple figures that if you're that eagle-eyed (or that vision-impaired), you'll want the same size adjustment in both apps.

- **Redesign the New Message window.** Do you want the Cc and Bcc lines to show up? How about the Priority Field pop-up menu?

 You can make all these settings using the little ☰ ⌄ menu in the New Message window; see Figure 18-4.

- **Adjust the message window width.** Drag the very right edge of the window inward or outward to adjust the width of the message itself. Double-click the edge of the messages list to make it snap to what Mail thinks is its proper width.

- **Adjust the width of the mailboxes or messages list.** Similarly, you can drag the right edges of the first two columns to adjust their widths. Or double-click the right edge to make the column exactly as wide as Mail thinks it should be.

- **Change what morsels show up in the messages list.** The messages list (center column) usually shows the sender's name, subject line, and the first few lines of the message itself (an iPhone/iPad feature brought to the Mac). But you can add

additional info displays to the list—message size, contact photo, date and time sent, and so on—by choosing from the View submenu.

- **Change what details show up in the header.** The *header* is the top part of a message, where you see the details of how the message reached you. Ordinarily, Mail shields you from the geekiest details of the header; if you really want to see it all, choose View→Message→All Headers.

But you can tailor the standard header so Mail always shows you exactly the information you want. In Mail→Preferences→Viewing, use the "Show message headers" pop-up menu to choose Custom. Now you can add just the details you always want to see: Attachments, Bcc, Cc, Flag, From, Reply-To, Resent-Cc, and so on. (In macOS 10.15.1, the feature is broken, but that's how it's *supposed* to work.)

- **Control how many lines of preview text appear.** In Mail→Preferences→Viewing, you can use the List Preview pop-up menu to control how many lines of each message you want to appear, in light gray, as a preview of what's in the message itself. You can choose up to five lines, or choose None to hide the preview completely.

- **Sort the messages.** Use the "Sort by" pop-up menu above the messages list (by Date, Attachment, Unread, and so on). Use the bottom two commands—Oldest Message on Top or Newest Message on Top—to control which way the sorting goes.

Tip: If you click the "Sort by" bar above the messages list, you jump directly to the top—just like you do on the iPhone or iPad. Some ideas you just can't keep down.

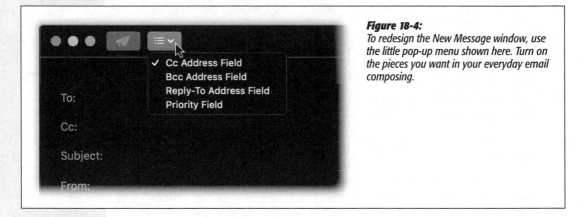

Figure 18-4:
To redesign the New Message window, use the little pop-up menu shown here. Turn on the pieces you want in your everyday email composing.

Dark Mode in Mail

As you know from page 152, Dark mode, which gives your Mac a deep-gray color for menu bars and windows, can look really cool. White type on black, however, may not be exactly what you want when reading email.

- **To make all messages appear with white backgrounds:** Choose Mail→Preferences→ Viewing→and turn off "Use dark backgrounds for messages." Now Mail still uses the dark look for menus, lists, and panels, but the actual message bodies are white.

- **To make one message appear with a white background:** Choose View→Message→ Show with Light Background. Only the currently open message goes white. (This command is available only if Mail is set to show dark backgrounds.) Choose View→Message→Show with Dark Background to restore the original look—or simply click off the message and back on it again. The light background is only a temporary feature.

The Toolbar

You have full control over the toolbar. You can rearrange or remove icon buttons (by ⌘-dragging them); add interesting new buttons (View→Customize Toolbar); change its display to show just text labels or just icons (choose View→Customize Toolbar, and then use the Show pop-up menu in the lower-left corner); or hide the toolbar entirely (using the View→Hide Toolbar command).

Tip: Even when the toolbar is hidden, you can still hit Option-⌘-F to use the search box. (Press ⌘-F by itself to search the *current message*.)

Writing Messages

To write a new email, click ✍ in the toolbar or press ⌘-N. The New Message form, shown in Figure 18-5, opens.

Note: The handsome, pre-designed templates known as Stationery are gone now.

Here's how you go about writing a message:

1. **In the To field, type the recipient's email address.**

 If somebody is in your Contacts, type the first couple of letters of the name or email address; Mail automatically completes the address. (If the first guess is wrong, then type another letter or two until Mail revises its guess.)

Tip: If Mail constantly tries to autofill in the address of someone you don't really communicate with, you can zap that address from its memory by choosing Window→Previous Recipients. Click the undesired address, and then click Remove From List.

 As in most dialog boxes, you can jump from blank to blank (from To to Cc, for example) by pressing Tab. To send this message to more than one person, separate the addresses with commas: *bob@earthlink.net, billg@microsoft.com,* and so on.

Tip: If you send most of your email to addresses within the same organization (like *reddelicious@apple.com, grannysmith@apple.com,* and *winesap@apple.com*), Mail can automatically turn all *other* email addresses red. It's a feature designed to avoid sending confidential messages to outside addresses.

To turn this feature on, choose Mail→Preferences, click Composing, turn on "Mark addresses not ending with," and then type the "safe" domain (like *apple.com*) into the blank.

2. To send a copy to other recipients, enter their addresses in the Cc field.

Cc stands for *carbon copy*. Getting an email message where your name is in the Cc field implies: "I sent you a copy because I thought you'd want to know about this correspondence, but I'm not expecting you to reply."

Tip: If Mail recognizes the address you type into the To or Cc box (because it's someone in your Contacts, for instance), then the name turns into a shaded, rounded button. In addition to looking cool, these buttons sprout a ∨; when you click there, you get a list of useful commands (including Show Contact Card). The buttons are also drag-and-droppable. For example, you can drag one from the To field into the Cc field, or from Contacts to Mail.

3. Type the topic of the message in the Subject field.

It's courteous to put some thought into the subject line. Use "Change in plans for next week," for instance, instead of "Yo." On the other hand, don't put the *entire* message into the subject line.

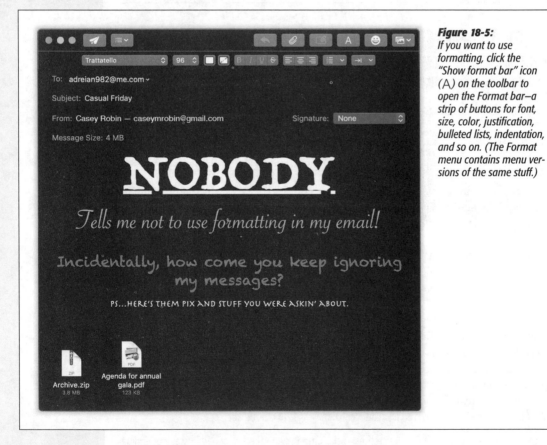

Figure 18-5:
If you want to use formatting, click the "Show format bar" icon (A) on the toolbar to open the Format bar—a strip of buttons for font, size, color, justification, bulleted lists, indentation, and so on. (The Format menu contains menu versions of the same stuff.)

4. Specify an email format.

There are two kinds of email: *plain text* and *formatted* (which Apple calls Rich Text). Plain text messages are faster to send and open. And even though the message itself is plain, you can still attach pictures and other files. But formatted messages, of course, let you use fonts, styles, and colors to design your message.

To control which kind of mail you send on a message-by-message basis, choose from the Format menu either Make Plain Text or Make Rich Text. To change the setting for *all* new outgoing messages, go to Mail→Preferences→Composing; choose from the "Message format" pop-up menu.

(But note: Even if you choose Rich Text, Mail sends a plain-text email if you don't actually *use* any formatting—choose a new font, size, or whatever.)

Tip: If you plan to send formatted mail, remember that your recipients won't see the fonts you use unless their machines have the same ones installed. Bottom line: For email to Mac and Windows owners alike, stick to universal choices like Arial, Times, and Courier.

Bcc, Reply To, and Priority

A blind carbon copy (Bcc) is a secret copy. This feature lets you send a copy of a message to somebody secretly, without any of the other recipients knowing that you did so. To view this field when composing a message (if it's not already visible), choose View→Bcc Address Field.

You can use the Bcc field to quietly signal a third party that a message has been sent. For example, if you send your co-worker a message that says, "Chris, it bothers me that you've been cheating the customers," you could Bcc your supervisor to clue her in without getting into trouble with Chris.

The Bcc box is useful in other ways, too. Many people send email messages (corny jokes, for example) to a long list of recipients. You, a recipient, have to scroll through the long list of names the sender placed in the To or Cc field. But if the sender used the Bcc field to hold all the recipients' email addresses, you won't see anybody else's names at the top of the email. In the To box, you might see the sender's name, or "undisclosed recipients," or nothing at all. (Spammers have also learned this trick, which is why it usually looks like you're the only recipient of a junk message when there are actually millions of other people who received the same message.)

Another hidden field you can add to your messages is *Reply To.* (Choose View→Reply-To Address Field.) That field has one simple purpose: to make the recipient's email program reply to a different email address than the one you sent the message from. For example, if your business email address isn't working but you absolutely *have* to send a field report to your boss, you can send the message from your personal email account but put your business address in the Reply To field. That way, when your boss emails you back to congratulate you, the email goes to your business account.

Finally, if you click the ☰∨ on the left side of an email message, you can enable one more header option: Priority. A pop-up menu with an exclamation point will appear, letting you set the importance of your email messages on a three-tiered scale.

The good part about this system is that it lets your recipient see that an email you've sent is, for example, urgent. The bad part is that not every email program displays the priority of email—and even if your recipient's email program *does* display your message's priority, there's no guarantee that it'll make him respond any faster.

5. **Type your message into the message box.**

You can use all standard editing techniques, including dictation, copy, paste, drag-and-drop, and so on. If you selected the Rich Text style of email, you can use word processor–like formatting (Figure 18-5).

Tip: And don't miss the Emoji browser at the top right of your message window. It opens a tidy palette containing thousands of emoji symbols, organized by category.

As you type, Mail checks your spelling, using a dotted underline to mark questionable words. You can read much more about macOS's built-in spelling/grammar checker (and typing expander) starting on page 235.

Tip: If you think what this message needs is a photo of something (or a scan of a document or a fun sketch), and your iPhone is handy, choose File→Insert from iPhone→Take Photo (or →Scan Document or →Add Sketch). Your phone awakes, ready to snap a pic, scan a doc, or draw a sketch, as described on page 310. It magically appears on your Mac, in the outgoing message. (This also works if you have an iPad nearby instead of an iPhone.)

If you're composing a long email message, or if it's one you don't want to send until later, press ⌘-S or choose File→Save. You've just saved the message into your Drafts folder. It'll still be there next time you open Mail. To reopen a saved draft, click the Drafts icon in the mailboxes column and then double-click the message you want to work on.

6. **Click ⤴ (or press Shift-⌘-D).**

Mail sends the message.

Tip: To resend a message you've already sent, find it in your Sent folder, click it, and then choose Message→ Send Again, or press Shift-⌘-D.

If you'd rather have Mail place each message you write in the Outbox folder instead of connecting to the net when you click Send, choose Mailbox→Take All Accounts Offline. While you're offline, Mail refrains from trying to connect, which is a great feature when you're working on a laptop at 39,000 feet and don't feel like paying for Wi-Fi. (Choose Mailbox→Take All Accounts Online to reverse the procedure.)

Attaching Files to Messages

Sending little text emails is fine, but sometimes you want to send somebody a photograph, a sound, or a Word document.

To attach a file to a message you've written, use one of these methods:

- **Drag the icons you want to attach directly off the desktop** (or out of a folder) and into the New Message window. There your attachments appear with their own hyperlinked icons (visible in Figure 18-5), meaning that your recipient can simply click to open them.

Tip: Exposé was *born* for this moment. Hit ⌘-F3 to make all open windows flee to the edges of the screen, revealing the desktop. Root around until you find the file you want to send. Begin dragging it; without releasing the mouse, press ⌘-F3 again to bring your message window back into view. Complete your drag into the message window.

Mail makes it look as though you can park the attached file's icon (or the full image of a graphics file) inside the text of the message, mingled with your typing. On the receiving end, however, all the attachments might end up clumped together at the end of the message (depending on which email system your correspondent uses).

- **Drag the icons you want to attach from the desktop onto Mail's Dock icon.** Mail dutifully creates a new outgoing message, with the files already attached.

- **Click ⌘ on the New Message toolbar,** choose File→Attach Files, or press Shift-⌘-A. The Open File sheet appears so you can find the files you want to include. (You can choose multiple files simultaneously in this dialog box. Just ⌘-click or Shift-click them as though you were selecting them in a Finder window.)

Once you've selected them, click Choose File (or press Return). You return to the New Message window, where the attachments' icons appear, ready to ride along when you send the message.

To remove an attachment, drag across its icon to highlight it, and then press Delete.

Mail Drop: Sending Huge Attachments

You're about to discover what may be one of the best features in the history of email.

Since the dawn of email, we, the downtrodden masses, have been told over and over again: Don't attach big files! Anything over about 5 megabytes is too much for most email systems. Best case, your entire message will bounce back to you; worst case, you'll clog the recipients' inboxes so they can't receive any more mail.

So the world has slogged along with workarounds—sites like *SendThisFile.com* or services like Dropbox.

UP TO SPEED

All the Little Symbols

The left edge of the messages list shows little symbols that let you know at a glance how you've processed certain messages. The most common one is, of course, the blue dot, which means "new message." (After reading a message, you can mark it once again as an *unread* message by choosing Message→Mark as Unread [Shift-⌘-U]—or by right-clicking or two-finger clicking the message's name and then choosing Mark as Unread from the shortcut menu.)

You might also see these symbols, which represent messages you've replied to (◀), forwarded (➡), redirected (➤), or flagged (🏳).

A well-guarded secret, however, is that the "replied to" and "forwarded" symbols aren't just indicators—they're also *buttons.* When you see one of these symbols next to your original message, click it to jump straight to your reply (or forwarded message). You're spared the trouble of having to search through all your mailboxes.

Today, that era is over.

If you use Mail in macOS, you'll probably never have to think about the file sizes of your attachments again. Go ahead—attach a whole video. Attach a gigantic Photoshop document, or several, or dozens. Attach a gigantic Keynote or PowerPoint file. Your file-size limit is now 5 *gigabytes*—about 1,000 times what it used to be.

The first time you attach a big file to an outgoing message and then click Send, Mail offers the message shown in Figure 18-6.

Note: Mail Drop is an iCloud feature. It works only if your Mac is currently signed into your iCloud account. (The files you send don't count toward your iCloud storage limit, though.)

Figure 18-6:
There's no reason not to use Mail Drop. In fact, there's no reason not to turn on "Don't ask again for this account," too. From now on, Mail Drop will work just like magic—invisibly.

You can attach a bunch of huge files to a single message, as long as the grand total is under 5 gigabytes.

The files' icons show up right in the body of the message.

Behind the scenes, Mail Drop uploads your file to iCloud's computers, where it sits for up to 30 days, waiting for your recipient to get a clue and download it.

If the recipient also has Mail (Yosemite or later), the attachment is quietly auto-downloaded in the background, so that it's on his Mac already when he opens the

message. He'll click, it'll open, and he'll probably never even consider the miracle of what just happened.

If you're sending to any other computer or mail program, your message contains an indication of the file's 30-day expiration date and a "Click to download" link. (Clicking it opens the recipient's web browser, where the file begins to download immediately.) It's one extra step, and a little waiting—but that's what people get for not drinking the Apple Kool-Aid.

And now Apple's entirely reasonable fine print:

- **Mail Drop allows you to send** a maximum of 200 messages a day, or messages to more than 1,000 recipients a day, from your iCloud account. A single message sent via iCloud can have a maximum of 100 recipients.

- **iCloud's online holding tank** for Mail Drop attachments doesn't hold more than 1 terabyte of files. In other words, once you've Mail Dropped that many attachments, you won't be able to send any more until those files have been downloaded (or 30 days have elapsed on some of them).

Mail Drop is fantastic.

Signatures

Signatures are bits of text that get stamped at the bottom of your outgoing email messages. A signature might contain a name, a postal address, a pithy quote, or even a scan of your *real* signature, as shown in Figure 18-7.

You can customize your signatures by choosing Mail→Preferences→Signatures. Here's what you should know:

- **To build up a library of signatures that you can use in any of your accounts:** Select All Signatures in the leftmost pane, and then click the + button to add each new signature (Figure 18-7). Give each new signature a name in the middle pane, and then customize the signatures' text in the rightmost pane.

Tip: If you ever get tired of a signature, you can delete it forever by selecting All Signatures→[your signature's name], clicking the − button, and then clicking OK.

- **To make a signature available in one of your email accounts:** Drag the signature's name from the middle pane onto the name of the account in the leftmost pane. In other words, you can make certain signatures available to only your work (or personal) account, so you never accidentally end up appending your secret FBI contact signature to the bottom of a birthday invitation.

- **To assign a particular signature to one account:** In the left pane, click an account; pick from the Choose Signature pop-up menu. Each time you compose a message from that account, Mail inserts the signature you selected.

Tip: To make things more interesting for your recipients, pick At Random from the Choose Signature pop-up menu; Mail selects a different signature each time you send a message. Or, if you're not *that* much of a risk-taker, choose In Sequential Order; Mail picks the next signature in order for each new message you write.

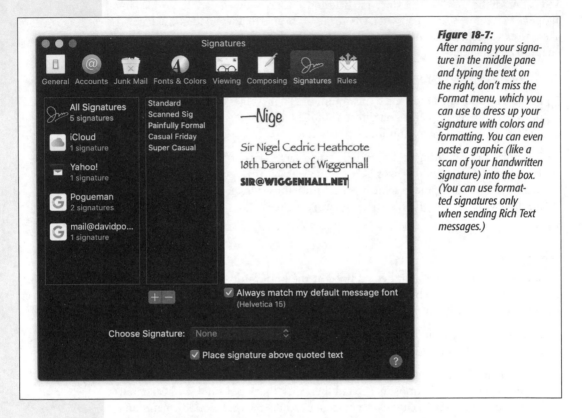

Figure 18-7:
After naming your signature in the middle pane and typing the text on the right, don't miss the Format menu, which you can use to dress up your signature with colors and formatting. You can even paste a graphic (like a scan of your handwritten signature) into the box. (You can use formatted signatures only when sending Rich Text messages.)

Remember that you can always change your signature on a message-by-message basis using the Signature pop-up menu in any new email message.

- **To use the signature feature as a prefix in replies:** Turn on "Place signature above quoted text." If you turn on this setting, your signature gets inserted *above* any text that you're replying to, rather than below. You'd use this setting if your "signature" said something like, "Hi there! You wrote this to me!"

Tip: If you're into consistent typographical styling, also turn on "Always match my default font." That setting makes sure that any messages you send contain the signature in the same font as the rest of the message, lending it an air of professionalism.

Marking Up, Signing, and Drawing on Attachments

You can mark up PDF and graphics attachments at the moment of sending them, too. You can add your signature to a contract, circle a typo on a document, draw arrows on a diagram, and so on.

All this magic awaits in the Markup toolbar—but finding it is a bit tricky. First, you have to attach a graphic—a photo, PDF file, or other kind of image—using any of the tricks described on page 680.

Once the image appears in your outgoing message, click to select it. At that point, the tiny ⌄ icon appears in its upper-right corner; from it, choose Markup (Figure 18-8).

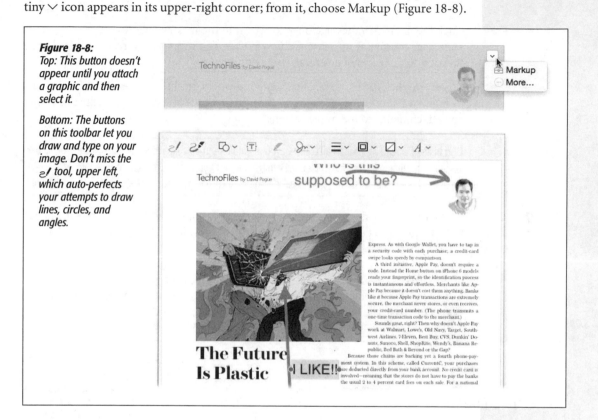

Figure 18-8:
Top: This button doesn't appear until you attach a graphic and then select it.

Bottom: The buttons on this toolbar let you draw and type on your image. Don't miss the ✐ tool, upper left, which auto-perfects your attempts to draw lines, circles, and angles.

What you'll quickly discover is that this entire markup feature is shared, pixel for pixel, with the markup feature in your Preview program. And it's described in detail on page 597.

Reading Email

Mail puts all incoming email into your Inbox; the statistic after the word *Inbox* lets you know how many messages you haven't yet read. New messages are also marked with blue dots in the main list.

Tip: The Mail icon in the Dock also shows how many new messages you have waiting; it's the number in the red circle. In Mail→Preferences→General, you can specify *which* mailbox it's tallying up—or have it tally up all of them.

Click the Inbox folder to see a list of received messages. If it's a long list, press Page Up and Page Down to scroll.

Tip: If you ⌘-click more than one mailbox folder, you can combine them (and their total-message counts) into one unified messages list.

Click the name of a message once to read it in the message window, or double-click a message to open it into a separate window. (If a message is already selected, then pressing Return also opens its separate window.)

When you click the name of a message in the messages list (or press the ▲ and ▼ keys to highlight successive messages in that list), you see the message itself, along with any attachments, in the message pane.

Tip: Instead of reading your email yourself, you might prefer to have macOS read it *to* you, as you sit back in your chair sipping a strawberry daiquiri. Highlight the text you want to hear (or choose Edit→Select All), and then choose Edit→Speech→Start Speaking. To stop the insanity, choose Edit→Speech→Stop Speaking.

At the top of a message, you see its *header*—date, subject, addresses, and some handy buttons that don't appear until you point to them (Figure 18-9).

Tip: New in Catalina: If you point to the sender's name and click ⌄, you're offered a Block Contact command. In Mail→Preferences→Junk Mail, you can specify whether future messages from this idiot get marked as read—or are trashed directly. In the same window, you can also view and edit the Blocked list. (It's a combined Blocked list of both email addresses and, from Messages, phone numbers.)

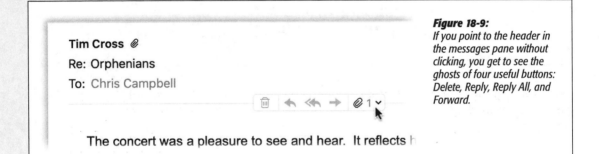

Figure 18-9:
If you point to the header in the messages pane without clicking, you get to see the ghosts of four useful buttons: Delete, Reply, Reply All, and Forward.

Once you've viewed a message, you can respond to it, delete it, print it, file it, and so on. The following pages should get you started.

Conversation View

Threading is one of the most useful mail-sorting methods to come along in a long time. It groups all messages that are part of the same back-and-forth conversation as a *single item* in the main messages list. (In this discussion, let's call that one item the *main message.* In Mail, it's always the most recent message in the conversation.)

Less sophisticated email programs figure out which messages go together by matching only their subject lines. But Mail is smarter; it also studies the message headers, senders, recipients, and dates. Even if someone changes the subject line along the way, Mail still knows that a conversation is a conversation.

As shown in Figure 18-10, Conversation view, as Apple calls it, hides all the usual awful indents, repetitions, forwards of forwards, and so on. You see only neatly numbered scrolling blocks, each representing the *newly added* text in each back-and-forth.

Note: When Organize by Conversation is turned on, you might be wondering: What happens to chronological order? In other words, if the messages in a certain thread took place over several days or weeks, where does Mail wind up listing them when it sorts your messages list by date?

Answer: They're all clumped together in the main message—the *most recent* message. That is, if the messages on a certain topic arrived on July 1, 4, 7, and 11, you'll find all four grouped with the July 11 message. They're essentially pulled *out* of the chronological list to join the latest one, for your reviewing pleasure.

Figure 18-10:
In Conversation view, the back-and-forths are represented concisely. (You can see the redundant stuff, if you really want to, by clicking the See More link at the bottom of each message.)

Inset: Click the tiny number, as shown here by the cursor, to view a list of the messages within the clump.

To turn on threading, choose View→Organize by Conversation. Each main message in the messages list sprouts a little numbered badge, like "3»," to indicate messages that have been clustered together (Figure 18-10, inset).

Here are some powerful ways to use threading:

• **View all the messages in a conversation** by clicking the main message in the messages list. In the message pane, you see all the back-and-forths, minus all the duplication and the replies to replies.

Tip: In macOS, the messages in a conversation appear chronologically, oldest at the top. It used to be the other way around—but Apple thinks this way makes more sense. (The latest message still appears when you click the thread's name.) If you prefer to see the messages from newest to oldest, then choose Mail→Preferences→ Viewing and turn on "Show most recent message at the top."

- **Expand a list of the messages in a conversation** by clicking the small blue number-of-messages badge—or by clicking the main message and then pressing the ▶ key. A tiny message-conversation list sprouts out of the one listed message, as shown in the inset in Figure 18-10. (Or you can make *all* conversations display their sub-messages like this; to do that, choose View→Expand All Conversations.)

 Once you've expanded the mini-list, you can walk through it (in the messages list) by pressing the up/down arrow keys. In the preview pane where the actual emails appear, you can press Option-▲ or Option-▼ to jump from one to the next.

- **Examine messages from multiple mailboxes.** Normally, conversations display only messages held in the *same* mailbox, but that's not especially convenient when you want to see, for example, the messages you've received (from your Inbox), as well as your replies (from your Sent box). To work around that problem, turn on "Include related messages" in Mail→Preferences→Viewing. This option means "Include messages in *other* mailboxes, too, like Sent messages—not just this one mailbox." Now your conversations seamlessly combine related messages from all mailboxes.

Note: When "Include related messages" is turned on, the related messages do *not* display the gray numbers in the corner; only the ones in the current mailbox sprout numbers.

- **Move all the messages in a conversation to a new mailbox** by dragging the main message. You might find this useful, for example, when you've just finished a project and want to file away all the email related to it quickly. You can even delete all the messages in a thread at once by deleting its main entry.

Note: If you drag a message to a different folder, it still appears in the conversation thread.

- **Send someone all the messages in a thread** by selecting the main message and then clicking Forward as usual. Mail automatically copies all the messages of the thread. You might find this useful, for instance, when you want to send your boss all the correspondence you've had with someone about a certain project.

- **Manipulate an individual message in a conversation** by first clicking it in the message-reading pane. For example, if you have five messages in a conversation, and you want to forward only the juicy one, which happens to be message #2, then click #2 and then use the Forward command—or Reply, Delete, or whatever. (You can also click one of the four light-gray buttons that appear when you point to the message header—Delete, Reply, Reply All, Forward.)

Tip: In Mail→Preferences→Viewing, you'll find a bunch of fine-tuning tweaks that apply to conversations. For example, you can ask that messages that are part of the same conversation show up highlighted in a color you choose—even when conversation grouping is turned *off*.

Filters

Mail offers one-click filters that hide or show all messages in the list of a certain kind—like ones you haven't yet read.

You might have to hunt for the ⊜ button, but it's there, atop the list of messages. When you click it, you automatically turn on the first filter: Unread. All the messages in the list that you have read are hidden—until you click the ⊜ button again to turn off the filter.

When the filter is on, you can click the word "Unread" to see a list of other ways to filter the list, as shown in Figure 18-11.

Figure 18-11:
Using the Filters pop-up menu, you can tell Mail to show you only messages you haven't read yet; only messages you've flagged; only messages to you (or that you were copied on); only the ones with attachments; or only the ones from people in your VIP list.

Adding the Sender to Contacts

When you choose the Message→Add Sender to Contacts command, Mail memorizes the email address of the person whose message is on the screen. In fact, you can highlight a huge number of messages and add *all* the senders simultaneously using this technique.

Thereafter, you'll be able to address a new message to somebody just by typing the first few letters of her name or email address.

Data Detectors

Data detectors are described on page 247. They're what you see when macOS recognizes commonly used bits of written information: a physical address, a phone number, a date and time, and so on. With one quick click, you can send that information into the appropriate macOS program, like Calendar or Contacts.

Data detectors are especially useful—*primarily* useful, in fact—in Mail. Watch for the dotted rectangle or gray triangle that appears when you point to an address, date, time, URL, or flight number.

Here's what's neat: If a Data Detector detects that there's discussion of an appointment in the body of a message, or if it finds somebody's contact information, it displays a banner strip at the top, as shown in Figure 18-12. With one click of the Add button, you can add that appointment to your Calendar, or that phone number to Contacts. (You see a similar banner if the person is *already* in Contacts but this message contains an additional or updated address or phone number.)

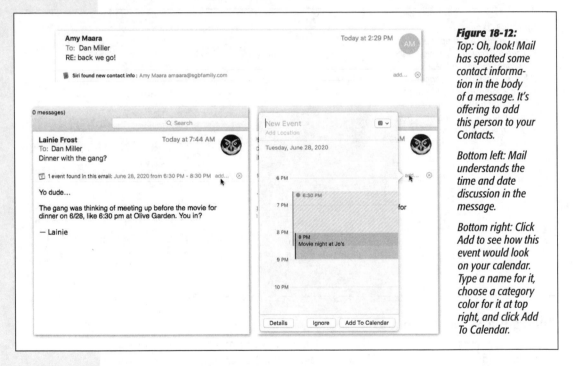

Figure 18-12:

Top: Oh, look! Mail has spotted some contact information in the body of a message. It's offering to add this person to your Contacts.

Bottom left: Mail understands the time and date discussion in the message.

Bottom right: Click Add to see how this event would look on your calendar. Type a name for it, choose a category color for it at top right, and click Add To Calendar.

Opening File Attachments

Just as you can attach files to a message, so can people send files to you. Sometimes they don't even bother to type a note; you wind up receiving an empty email message with a file or two attached. Only the presence of the file's icon in the message body (or the paper clip icon in the header) tells you there's something attached.

Mail stores downloaded files in a hidden folder on your hard drive. To bring them out into the open, you must proceed in one of these ways:

- **Go to File→Quick Look Attachments or press ⌘-Y.** You're treated to a nearly full-size preview of the file's contents. Yes, Quick Look has come to email. It works exactly as described on page 55.

Tip: If the attachments are pictures, launching Quick Look gives you the option to view a full-screen slideshow of every attached image. Click the ⊙ button in the upper-left corner, and a useful row of slideshow-control buttons appears along the bottom of the screen. Just press ▶ to view all the photos in a presentation.

- **Point your cursor at the message header without clicking,** and you'll see the ghost buttons shown in Figure 18-9, along with an additional button: a paper clip that lets you save the attachment to your Downloads folder, nestled within easy reach in the Dock. (It's a pop-up menu, which is handy if there's more than one attachment. You can either save *all* attachments at once or choose from the menu to save them individually.)

Tip: If you don't want to use the Downloads folder, you can choose a new autosave location for attachments by choosing Mail→Preferences→General→Downloads folder.

- **Drag the attachment icon** (it appears at the bottom of the message) out of the message window and onto any visible portion of your desktop or any visible folder.

- **Double-click the attachment's icon.** If you were sent a document (a photo, Word file, or Excel file, for example), it now opens in the corresponding program.

Note: After the attachment is open, use the File→Save As command to save the file into a folder of your choice. Otherwise, any changes you make to the document will be lost.

- **Right-click or two-finger click** the attachment's icon at the bottom of the message. From the shortcut menu, you can open it, save it, Quick Look it, and so on.

Replying to a Message

To answer a message, click the Reply (↰) button on the message toolbar (or choose Message→Reply, or press ⌘-R). If the message was originally addressed to multiple recipients, you can send your reply to everyone simultaneously by clicking Reply All (↰↰), choosing Message→Reply All, or pressing Shift-⌘-R.

A new message window opens, already addressed. As a courtesy to your correspondent, Mail places the original message at the bottom of the window, set off by a vertical bar, as shown in Figure 18-13.

Tip: If you highlight some text before clicking Reply, then Mail pastes only that portion of the original message into your reply. That's a great convenience to your correspondent, who now knows exactly which part of the message you're responding to.

The original sender's name is automatically placed in the To field. The subject is the same as the original subject with the addition of "Re:" (shorthand for "regarding"). You're now ready to type your response.

At this point, you can add or delete recipients, edit the subject line or the original message, attach a file, and so on.

Tip: Use the Return key to create blank lines in the original message. Using this method, you can splice your own comments into those paragraphs, replying point by point. The vertical line next to the original message (as well as its different-colored font) helps your correspondent keep straight what's yours and what's hers.

When you're finished, click Send (✐).

Figure 18-13:
When you reply to an email, your reply includes your correspondent's original message, marked in a special color (which you can change in Mail→Preferences→Fonts & Colors) and with a vertical bar to differentiate it from the text of your reply.

Forwarding Messages

Instead of replying to the person who sent you a message, you may sometimes want to pass the note on to a third person.

To do so, click the Forward (➡) toolbar button (or choose Message→Forward, or press Shift-⌘-F). A new message opens, looking a lot like the one that appears when

you reply. You may wish to precede the original message with a comment of your own, along the lines of: "Frank: I thought you'd be interested in this joke about your mom."

Finally, address it as you would any outgoing piece of mail.

Redirecting Messages

A *redirected* message is similar to a forwarded message, with one useful difference: When you forward a message, your recipient sees that it came from you. When you redirect it, your recipient sees the *original* writer's name as the sender. In other words, a redirected message uses you as a low-profile relay station between two other people.

Treasure this feature. Plenty of email programs don't offer a Redirect command at all. You can use it to transfer messages from one of your own accounts to another, or to pass along a message that came to you by mistake.

To redirect a message, choose Message→Redirect, or press Shift-⌘-E. You get an outgoing copy of the message—this time without any quoting marks. (You can edit redirected messages before you send them, too, which is perfect for April Fools' Day pranks.)

Printing Messages

Sometimes there's no substitute for a printout. Choose File→Print, or press ⌘-P to summon the Print dialog box.

Filing Messages

Mail lets you create new mailboxes (mail folders) in the mailboxes list. You might create one for important messages, another for order confirmations from web shopping, still another for friends and family, and so on. You can even create mailboxes *inside* these mailboxes, a feature beloved by the hopelessly organized.

Tip: You can drag mailbox folders up and down in the list to rearrange them. Sweet.

Mail even offers *smart mailboxes*—self-updating folders that show you all your mail from your boss, for example, or every message with "mortgage" in its subject. It's the same idea as smart folders in the Finder or smart playlists in Music: folders whose contents are based around criteria you specify (Figure 18-14).

Figure 18-14:
Mail lets you create self-populating folders. In this example, a smart mailbox will automatically display all messages from Momma Smythe that you've received in the past week.

The commands you need are all in the Mailbox menu. For example, to create a new mailbox folder, choose Mailbox→New Mailbox. To create a smart mailbox, choose Mailbox→New Smart Mailbox.

Mail asks you to name the new mailbox. If you have more than one email account, you can specify which one will contain the new folder. (Smart mailboxes, however, always sit outside your other mailboxes.)

Tip: If you want to create a folder inside a folder, then use slashes in the name of your new mailbox. (If you use the name *Cephalopods/Squid,* for example, then Mail creates a folder called Cephalopods, with a subfolder called Squid.) You can also drag the mailbox icons up and down in the drawer to place one inside another.

That trick doesn't work for smart mailboxes, however. The only way to organize smart mailboxes is to put them inside a smart mailbox *folder,* which you create using Mailbox→New Smart Mailbox Folder. You might do that if you have several smart mailboxes for mail from your co-workers ("From Jim," "From Anne," and so on) and want to put them together in one collapsible group to save screen space.

When you click OK, a new icon appears in the mailboxes column, ready for use.

You can move a selected message (or a group of messages) into a mailbox folder in any of four ways:

- **Drag it out of the messages list** onto a mailbox icon.

- **Click the Move button on the toolbar.** Most of the time it says "Move to" and lists all your mailboxes.

 Sometimes, though, the button shows the name of a certain mailbox. The idea here is that Mail has noticed where you filed a message from this person, or on this topic, in the past—and is trying to save you some time by proposing that folder as a one-click destination.

- **Choose from the Message→Move To submenu,** which lists all your mailboxes.

- **Right-click or two-finger click a message,** or one of several you've highlighted. From the resulting shortcut menu, choose "Move to," and then, from the submenu, choose the mailbox you want.

Of course, the only way to change the contents of a *smart* mailbox is to change the criteria it uses to populate itself. To do so, double-click the smart mailbox icon and use the dialog box that appears (Figure 18-14).

Flagging Messages

Sometimes you'll receive an email message that prompts you to take some sort of action, but you may not have the time (or the fortitude) to face the task at the moment. ("Hi there…it's me, your accountant. Would you mind rounding up your expenses for 2008 through 2018 and sending me a list by email?")

That's why Mail lets you *flag* a message, summoning a little flag icon in a new column next to the message's name. In fact, you can use seven differently *colored* flags.

These indicators can mean anything you like—they simply call attention to certain messages.

Once you've applied some flags, you can use their power in all kinds of ways. For example, you can view all of them in one place—in the Flagged folder that appears near the top of the mailboxes list.

You can also sort your mail list by flag color (choose Sort by→Flags at the top of the messages list). You can search for flagged messages using the search box. Better yet, you can view all messages with a certain flag color—magically rounded up from all your different accounts and mailboxes—by clicking the corresponding icon in the Flagged folder of the mailboxes list.

Tip: Just in case you don't find "Red," "Orange," "Yellow," and so on to be the most descriptive possible flag names, you can change them.

First, though, make sure you've applied a couple of flags to different messages already. That's necessary to make the Flagged mailbox appear in the mailboxes list. If you open the flippy triangle, you'll see the names of the flags you've applied so far. You can change a flag's name just the way you'd name a file—start by double-clicking it.

To flag a message in this way, select the message (or several messages) and then choose one of the colored flags in the Message→Flag submenu. Or right-click or two-finger click the message's name in the list and, from the shortcut menu, choose one of the seven flag colors. (To clear the flags, repeat the procedure, but use the Message→ Flag→Clear Flag command instead.)

If you're using only one flag to simply mean "flag this," and you don't need all the colors, you can also press Shift-⌘-L.

Mark as Read/Unread

Once you've looked at a message, Mail removes the blue dot from its name—the dot that tells you it's a new message. But what if you had only glanced at it, and you don't really consider it fully processed?

In that situation, you can use the Mark As Unread command, which basically means "Put the blue dot back." At that point, it turns into a Mark As Read command.

You'll find these commands in the Message menu, as well as in the shortcut menu that appears when you right-click or two-finger click a message or group of selected messages.

In fact, there's a swipey way to do the same job: On a trackpad or Magic Mouse surface, drag two fingers to the right across a message to mark it as read (or unread).

Finding Messages

The box in the upper-right corner of the main mail window is Mail's own private Spotlight—a fast, powerful search command. That's essential when you have to deal with masses of email (see Figure 18-15).

This search box incorporates the same pop-up suggestions lists and "search tokens" as regular file searching in the Finder. In fact, it understands plain-English search requests like "messages from Charlene about Halloween."

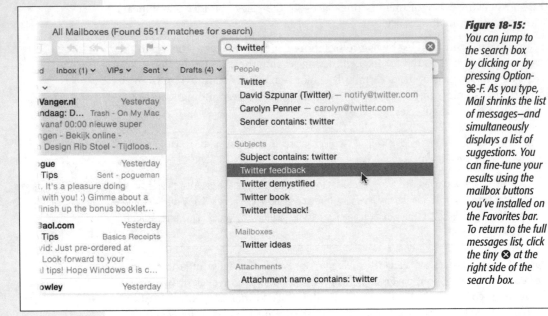

Figure 18-15:
You can jump to the search box by clicking or by pressing Option-⌘-F. As you type, Mail shrinks the list of messages—and simultaneously displays a list of suggestions. You can fine-tune your results using the mailbox buttons you've installed on the Favorites bar. To return to the full messages list, click the tiny ⊗ at the right side of the search box.

Here's how it works:

1. **Press Option-⌘-F (or click in the search box).**

 The cursor jumps up there.

2. **Start typing what you're looking for.**

 As you type, the messages list changes to show only the matching messages from all your mail folders.

 The first section of list results is called Top Hits. These are the results Mail thinks are most likely to be what you're looking for, based on factors like the age of the messages, whether you've read or replied to them, whether the correspondent is one of your VIP contacts, and so on.

 You can also type phrases that mention any combination of a person, time period, or subject. For example, you can type "mail from Casey last week," "mail to Alex last year," "messages about Italy yesterday," and so on.

Tip: Using the word "mail" or "messages" in these phrases might feel more plain English–like, but it's optional. Typing "from Casey last week" or "about Italy yesterday" finds exactly the same messages.

If you see the message you're looking for, great. Click it and off you go.

But this initial search is a pretty broad one. Mail is rounding up messages that match your search term *in any way.* If you type *veg,* you see messages from Murray Vegelstein, messages from vegan@militanteaters.org, and messages with the subject line "HOT DEALS IN VEGAS." All of them in one big stew.

To help you sort through it, Mail produces a Suggestions list, which sprouts from the search box. As in the Finder, it's Mail's way of asking what sort of *thing* your search term is. Is it a person? A subject? The status of a message? A date? Figure 18-15 shows the idea.

3. **Click the suggestion you want.**

 Mail filters the list. For example, if you click Murray Vegelstein, you'll see *only* the messages to or from Murray.

4. **Edit the search token.**

 The *search token* is the little bubble that appears in the search box after you've clicked one of the suggestions. You can click the little ▼ in the search token to change it. For example, if you've clicked somebody's name, that pop-up menu says To, From, or Entire Message (including the header and the body).

 You can also type more into the search box to add *another* search token. For example, the first token might limit the search to messages from one person; you could then create another one that limits the search to a certain date.

Tip: Once you've built up a complicated search like this, save yourself the effort next time by *saving* that search. Click the Save button just below the search box. You get the Smart Mailbox dialog box, shown in Figure 18-14, already filled out with the search setup you've specified. All you have to do is give it a name and click OK to transform your search into a smart mailbox that you can open anytime.

You've done a lot of refining of this search. But you still haven't limited your results by *account* or *folder.* Mail is showing you results from either *all* mailboxes, or from only the most recent mailbox you've searched. Fortunately, your Favorites bar has now sprouted two new buttons: one called All, and one that names the folder you most recently clicked.

5. **Click a button on the Favorites bar to change which mailbox is being searched.**

 The results list updates itself.

Tip: If you ⌘-click *several* mail folders before you search, you can limit the search to that particular *set* of mailboxes. (In that case, you see a button on the Favorites bar called Selected Mailboxes.)

When you're finished hunting around, you can empty out the search box—and get back to your regularly scheduled lists of email—by clicking any other mailbox or by clicking the ❎ button at the right end of the search box.

A few last notes on searching:

- **Mail searching is almost exactly like Finder searching,** right down to the saved-search mechanism. See page 119 for details.

- **You can also search for certain text *within* an open message.** Choose Edit→Find→ Find (or press ⌘-F) to bring up the Find dialog box (Figure 18-16).

Figure 18-16:
The Find box works just as it does in a word processor, except that the Replace function works only on messages you're writing—Mail doesn't let you change the words of received mail. Lawyers would have a field day with that one.

- **As with regular Spotlight, Mail matches your search term** by looking only at the *beginnings* of words. Searching for *flag* will find messages that contain the words *flagstone* and *flagellum,* but not *Redflag Incorporated*.

- **In Mail→Preferences→General, you can specify** whether you want Mail to include the Trash folder, Junk folder, and encrypted messages when you search all mailboxes.

Deleting Messages

Sometimes it's junk mail. Sometimes you're just done with it. Either way, it's a snap to delete a selected message, several selected messages, or a message that's currently before you on the screen. You can press the Delete key, click the Delete (🗑) button on the toolbar, choose Edit→Delete, or drag messages out of the list window and into your Trash mailbox—or even onto the Dock's Trash icon.

Actually, even that's not the end of the list of ways: You can also swipe leftward all the way across a message (with two fingers on your trackpad) to delete it; a red Trash button appears briefly during your swipe to let you know what's about to happen. It's the same way you'd do it on an iPhone.

Tip: If you delete a message by accident, the Undo command (Edit→Undo or ⌘-Z) restores it.

All these commands move the messages to the Trash folder. If you like, you can then click that Trash icon to view a list of the messages you've deleted. You can even rescue messages by dragging them back into a mailbox (back into the Inbox, for example).

Emptying the Trash folder

Mail doesn't vaporize messages in the Trash folder until you "empty the trash," just like in the Finder. You can empty the Trash folder in any of several ways:

- **Click a message (or several) within the Trash folder list,** and then click the 🗑 icon on the toolbar (or press the Delete key). Now those messages are *really* gone.

- **Choose Mailbox→Erase Deleted Items (Shift-⌘-Delete).** (If you have multiple accounts, choose Erase Deleted Items→In All Accounts.)

- **Right-click or two-finger click the Trash mailbox icon,** and then choose Erase Deleted Items from the shortcut menu.

- **Wait.** Mail will permanently delete these messages automatically after a week.

 If a week is too long (or not long enough), you can change this interval. Choose Mail→Preferences, click Accounts, and select the account name from the list at left. Then click Mailbox Behaviors and change the "Erase deleted messages" pop-up menu. If you choose "When quitting Mail" from the pop-up menu, then Mail will take out the trash every time you quit the program.

Archiving messages

There's another option for getting unwanted messages out of your hair: *archiving.* It just means "Get it out of my sight for now." Archiving sweeps the selected message into a folder called Archive, where it will stay until you deal with it further (by moving or deleting it). There's one of these folders per account.

To archive a selected message, a group of selected messages, or a conversation, choose Message→Archive, or click the Archive icon on the toolbar.

Exporting Mailboxes

Time Machine (page 260) keeps a watchful eye on your Mac and backs up its data regularly—including your email. If you ever delete a message by accident or otherwise make a mess of your email stash, you can duck into Time Machine right from within Mail.

But not everybody wants to use Time Machine, for personal reasons—lack of a second hard drive, aversion to software named after H.G. Wells novels, whatever.

TROUBLESHOOTING MOMENT

Rebuilding Your Mail Databases

Mail keeps your messages in your Home→Library→Mail folder. (Your Library folder is usually invisible, but you can jump to it by pressing Option as you choose Go→Library in the Finder.)

Over time, as you add and delete hundreds of messages from these database files, some digital sawdust gets left behind, resulting in general Mail sluggishness. You also wind up with *massive* message files hidden on your hard drive, which can consume hundreds of megabytes of disk space. That's a particular bummer if you like to copy your message databases to your laptop when you go on a trip.

Fortunately, it's easy enough to *rebuild the message databases.* Doing so cleanses, repairs, and purges your message files. As a result, you wind up with a much more compact and healthy database.

To rebuild a mailbox, highlight it in the mailboxes column in Mail. (Highlight several by ⌘-clicking, if you like.) Then choose Mailbox→Rebuild. MacOS takes several minutes (or hours, depending on the size of your mailboxes) to repair your database—but if you're experiencing Mail weirdness or slowness, it's well worth the sacrifice.

Yet having a backup of your email is critically important. Fortunately, there's a second good way to back up your email—*export it,* like this:

1. **In the mailboxes column, choose which mailbox or mailboxes you want to archive.**

 If you have multiple mailboxes in mind, then ⌘-click each one until you've selected all the ones you want.

2. **Right-click to get the pop-up menu and choose Export Mailbox.**

 You can also get to this command by choosing Mailbox→Export Mailbox.

3. **In the box that appears, navigate to the place you want to stash this cache of valuable mail, like a server, a flash drive, or a folder. Click Choose.**

 Your exported mailboxes are saved to the location you've chosen. You can now go back to work writing new messages.

 Later, if you need to pull one of those stashes back into duty, choose File→Import Mailboxes. Choose the Apple Mail option and then navigate back to the place where you stored your mailboxes.

Message Rules

Once you know how to create folders, the next step in managing your email is to set up a series of *message rules* (filters) that file, answer, or delete incoming messages automatically based on their contents (such as their subject, address, and/or size). Message rules require you to think like the distant relative of a programmer, but the mental effort can reward you many times over. Message rules turn Mail into a surprisingly smart and efficient secretary.

Setting up message rules

Here's how to set up a message rule:

1. **Choose Mail→Preferences. Click the Rules icon.**

 The Rules pane appears, as shown at top in Figure 18-17.

GEM IN THE ROUGH

The Email Answering Machine

If you're going on vacation, you can turn Mail into an email answering machine that sends a canned "I'm away until the 15th" message to everyone who writes you.

To do so, set the first set of pop-up menus in the Rules dialog box so they say Account and the name of your account. In the bottom half of the dialog box, select Reply to Message from the pop-up menu. Click "Reply message text," and then type your outgoing message in the resulting box.

Keep in mind, though, that mail rules work only when Mail is open and connected to the internet. If your computer is set to turn off after a certain period of time, therefore, make sure to disable that feature before you go on vacation.

Also: If you subscribe to mailing lists, set up another mail rule that intercepts and files them *before* your answering-machine rule kicks in. Otherwise, you'll incur the wrath of other internet citizens by littering their email discussion groups with copies of your autoreply message.

2. Click Add Rule.

Now the dialog box shown at bottom in Figure 18-17 appears.

3. Use the criteria options (at the top) to specify how Mail should select messages to process.

For example, if you'd like the program to watch out for messages from a particular person, you would set up the first two pop-up menus to say "From" and "Contains," respectively.

To flag messages containing *$$$$, XXX, !!!!,* and so on, set the pop-up menus to say "Subject" and "Contains."

You can set up *multiple* criteria here to flag messages whose subjects contain any one of those common spam triggers. (If you change the "any" pop-up menu to say "all," then *all* the criteria must be true for the rule to kick in.)

4. Specify which words or people you want the message rule to watch for.

In the text box to the right of the two pop-up menus, type the word, address, name, or phrase you want Mail to watch for—a person's name, or *$$$$,* in the previous examples.

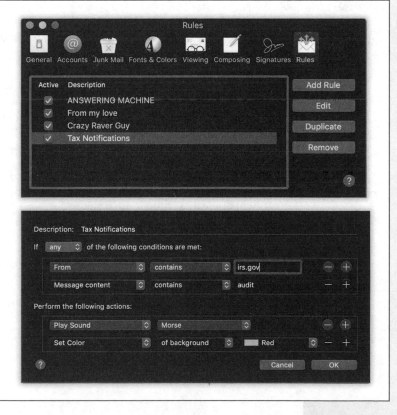

Figure 18-17:
Top: Mail rules can screen out junk mail, serve as an email answering machine, or call important messages to your attention. All mail message rules you've created appear in this list. (The color shading for each rule is a reflection of the colorizing options you've set up, if any.)

Bottom: Double-click a rule to open the Edit Rule dialog box, where you can specify what should set off the rule and what it should do in response.

5. **In the lower half of the box, specify what you want to happen to messages that match the criteria.**

If, in steps 1 through 4, you've told your rule to watch for junk mail containing *$$$$* in the subject line, here's where you can tell Mail to delete it or move it into, say, a Junk folder.

With a little imagination, you'll see how the options in this pop-up menu can do absolutely amazing things with your incoming email. Mail can colorize, delete, move, redirect, or forward messages—or even play a sound when you get a certain message.

By setting up the controls as shown in Figure 18-17, for example, you'll have specified that whenever your mother sends something to you that mentions a visit, you'll hear a specific alert noise—and the email will be highlighted in red, so it will jump out at you in the Inbox.

6. **In the very top box, name your mail rule. Click OK.**

At this point, Mail offers to apply your freshly minted rule to all the messages in the mailboxes that are currently selected. It's your one chance to go back in time—because from now on, the rule will apply only to *new* messages. Click either Apply or Don't Apply.

Now you're back to the Rules pane (Figure 18-17, top). Here you can choose a sequence for your rules by dragging them up and down. Here, too, you can turn off the ones you won't be needing at the moment but may use again one day.

Tip: Mail applies rules as they appear, from top to bottom, in the list. If a rule doesn't seem to be working properly, it may be that an earlier rule is intercepting and processing some messages before the "broken" rule even sees them. To fix this, try dragging the rule (or the interfering rule) up or down in the list.

VIPs

In the real world, VIPs are people who get backstage passes to concerts or special treatment at business functions (it stands for "very important person"). In macOS, it means "somebody whose mail is important enough that I want it brought to my attention immediately when it arrives."

So who should your VIPs be? That's up to you. Your spouse, your boss, and your doctor come to mind.

To designate someone as a VIP, follow the steps shown in Figure 18-18. From now on, lots of interesting things happen.

- **A new mailbox, called VIPs, appears in your mailboxes list.** Click it to see all the mail from all your VIPs (even messages you've deleted). Or click the flippy triangle to see your VIPs' names, each representing messages from that person.

- **A new menu button called VIPs appears on your Favorites toolbar.** Click to see all VIP messages, or click the ▾ to see a pop-up menu of all the VIPs' names. Here again, the point is that you can jump to the messages from just that person.

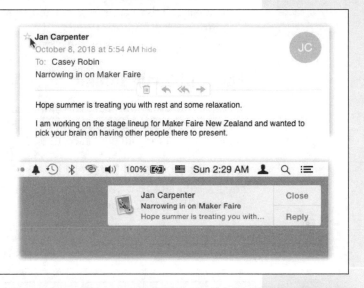

Figure 18-18:
Top: To designate a VIP, open a message she's sent you. Point to the spot to the left of her name. A hollow star appears; click there. The star darkens. (Or point to her name, and choose Add to VIPs from the ⌄ pop-up menu that appears next to her name.)

Note: If that person one day insults you, fires you, or dumps you, then you can remove her VIP status by clicking that same star again.

Bottom: MacOS can alert you when VIP messages arrive—and you can reply right on the spot.

GEM IN THE ROUGH

When You Want to Be Nudged About Incoming Mail

The Notification Center (page 376) consolidates all the different programs and features that might want your attention—Mail, Reminders, Twitter, Facebook, software updates, and so on—into a single tidy list.

But if a little Notification Center alert bubble appeared on your screen every time *any* new Mail message came in, you'd go quietly mad. Fortunately, a Mail setting lets you tell Mail, "Don't disturb me unless it's really important. Like if it's from my accountant."

Here's how to set up this useful filter. Choose Mail→Preferences→General. See the "New message notifications" pop-up menu?

Here you can choose Inbox Only (all incoming messages trigger alert bubbles); VIPs (perhaps the most useful option—only messages from these essential people produce alerts); Contacts (messages from anyone in your address book trigger alerts—just not messages from strangers); or All Mailboxes (every single incoming message flags you).

You can also choose the name of a smart mailbox, if you've created one. That's a pretty potent feature. It means that you can set up incoming messages to alert you only if they match whatever criteria your smart mailbox uses. For example, you might not want to be disturbed except when a message comes from one of your best friends *and* it has an attachment *and* it mentions "money I owe you."

You may have noticed, by the way, that there's no option here for "Don't show me Mail message bubbles at all." That's because you do that in System Preferences.

Open System Preferences→Notifications, click Mail, and turn off Show in Notification Center. Now you'll be left in peace when new mail arrives, no matter where it came from.

In macOS Catalina, you can also shut up all the notifications from a particular thread. It's a blessing when you're unwittingly copied on a Reply All hurricane.

Just select one of the messages, or a thread in the message list, and then choose Message→Mute. Ah, sweet silence!

- If you use iCloud, the same person is now a VIP on all your other Macs (running Mountain Lion or later), plus iPhones and iPads (running iOS 6 or later).

- Best of all, you can set up your Mac so that when a new message from a VIP comes in, an alert bubble appears in the top-right corner of your screen (Figure 18-18, bottom). That feature, of course, is part of the Notification Center, described in Chapter 10. See the box on the previous page for instructions on setting this up.

The Anti-Spam Toolkit

Spam, the junk that now makes up more than 80 percent of email, is a problem that's only getting worse. Luckily, you, along with Mail's advanced spam filters, can make it better—at least for *your* email accounts.

Using the Junk Mail Filter

You'll see the effects of Mail's spam filter the first time you check your mail: Certain message titles appear in brown. These are the messages that Mail considers junk.

Note: Out of the box, Mail doesn't apply its spam-targeting features to people whose addresses are in your Contacts, to people you've emailed recently, or to messages sent to you *by name* rather than just by email address. You can adjust these settings in the Mail→Preferences→Junk Mail tab.

During your first couple of weeks with Mail, your job is to supervise Mail's work. That is, if you get spam that Mail misses, then click the message and then click the Junk button on the toolbar. On the other hand, if Mail flags legitimate mail as spam, slap it gently on the wrist by clicking the Not Junk button. Over time, Mail gets better and better at filtering.

The trouble with this so-called Training mode is that you're still left with the task of trashing the spam yourself, saving you no time whatsoever.

Once Mail has perfected its filtering skills to your satisfaction, though, open Mail's Preferences, click Junk Mail, and then click "Move it to the Junk mailbox." From now on, Mail automatically files what it deems junk into a Junk mailbox, where it's much easier to scan and delete the messages en masse.

Tip: Don't miss the "Trust junk mail headers in messages" option in the Junk Mail pane of the Preferences window. If you turn on that checkbox, Mail takes your internet provider's word that certain messages are spam, giving you a *double* layer of spam protection.

The Unsubscribe Button

Every now and then, when you open a piece of mass-generated mail (usually from a store of some kind), Mail offers a line at the top that says: "This message is from a mailing list," and there's an Unsubscribe button. And sure enough: Clicking it (and then hitting OK) gets you off that mailing list.

Now, before you uncork the champagne, keep in mind that this button appears only on *some* pieces of commercial mail—from only the kindhearted, legitimate senders who have included an Unsubscribe link at the bottom of their messages already. All Mail does is move the Unsubscribe button to the top.

More Anti-Spam Tips

The Junk filter goes a long way toward cleaning out the spam from your mail collection—but it doesn't catch everything. If you're overrun by spam, here are some other steps you can take:

- **Rules.** Set up some message rules, as described on the preceding pages, that autoflag as spam messages that have subject lines containing trigger words like "Viagra," "Herbal," "Mortgage," "Refinance," "Enlarge," "Your"—you get the idea.

- **Create a private account.** If you're overrun by spam, consider sacrificing your current address, using it for the public areas of the internet, like chat rooms, online shopping, website and software registration, and newsgroup posting. Open a new, separate email account for person-to-person email.

 Spammers use automated software robots that scour every public internet message and web page, recording email addresses they find. (That's probably how they got your address in the first place.)

 Using this technique, at least you're now restricting the junk mail to a secondary mail account.

- **For goodness' sake, don't *order* anything sold by the spammers.** If only one person in 500,000 does so, the spammer makes money.

Contacts

Contacts is macOS's little-black-book program—an electronic Rolodex where you can stash the names, job titles, addresses, phone numbers, email addresses, and internet chat screen names of all the people in your life. It can also hold related information, like birthdays, anniversaries, and any other tidbits of personal data you'd like to keep at your fingertips (Figure 18-19).

The best part: It's *centralized.* This one address list appears everywhere: in Mail, Messages, and so on. And it synchronizes with your iPhone, iPad, Apple Watch, other Macs, and even Windows PCs (via iCloud).

Once you make Contacts the central repository of all your personal contact information, you can call up this information in a number of convenient ways:

- **You can open Contacts and then search for a contact** by typing just a few letters in the search box.

- **When you're composing messages in Mail,** Contacts automatically fills in email addresses for you when you type the first few letters.

Tip: If you choose Window→Previous Recipients from within Mail, you can browse the addresses of everyone you've ever corresponded with, without even launching the Contacts program. From here, you can delete one (so that Mail will quit autocompleting that address) or add it to Contacts.

Figure 18-19:
Contacts is meant to look like a physical address book. On the left, the full list of names; on the right, the card for the person whose name you've clicked. (You can hide the sidebar on the far left by choosing View→Hide Groups.)

- **When you use Messages to chat** with people in Contacts, the pictures you've stored of them automatically appear in chat windows.

- **Contacts can sync with an iPod Touch, iPhone, iPad, or Apple Watch,** giving you a "little black book" that fits in your pocket, can be operated with one hand, and comes with built-in musical accompaniment. You can have that happen wirelessly, using iCloud, when you connect your device to your Mac. (To set this up, open the Finder while your i-gadget is connected. Click the i-gadget's icon; on the Info tab, turn on "Sync contacts onto [device name].")

- **The free iCloud service can synchronize your contacts** to the web so you can see them while you're away from your Mac.

You can find Contacts in your Applications folder or in the Dock.

Importing Addresses

The easiest way to add people to Contacts is to import them from another service, like Yahoo or Exchange, or another program, like Microsoft Outlook (for Mac).

Importing from Yahoo, Google, Exchange, or another internet service

Contacts can synchronize its contacts with some online Rolodexes that may be very important to you: your Gmail (Google) contacts, your Yahoo contacts, your

iCloud address book, or your company's Microsoft Exchange master address book (Figure 18-20).

In Contacts, choose Contacts→Preferences→Accounts. There, staring you in the face, are checkboxes that let you sync your contacts with iCloud, Exchange, Yahoo, Google, and the like. Turn on "Enable this account" for each account you want, and Contacts is now synced with them. Change information in one place and it's also changed in the other. Even your contacts' photos, if your online address book has them, show up in Contacts!

Tip: You can also enter this information in the Internet Accounts pane of System Preferences.

If some other online service maintains your address book, Contacts can sync with it, too, as long as it uses one of the standard sharing formats (CardDAV or Lightweight Directory Access Protocol, known to the pros as LDAP). To teach Contacts about those, choose Contacts→Preferences→Accounts. Click the + button in the lower left, enter your account information on the resulting screen, click Sign In, and away you go.

Once you've set up a Contacts account, you can also change its settings, right there in the same Preferences dialog box. Specify how often you want your Mac to sync changes with the online account, for example.

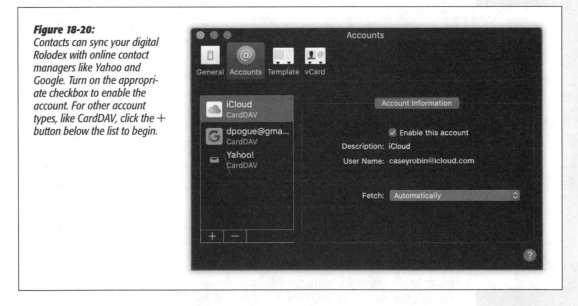

Figure 18-20:
Contacts can sync your digital Rolodex with online contact managers like Yahoo and Google. Turn on the appropriate checkbox to enable the account. For other account types, like CardDAV, click the + button below the list to begin.

Importing from another address-book program

Contacts can also slurp in contact info from other address-book or list programs, like Microsoft Outlook, Palm Desktop, Excel, and others. Not directly, of course; that would be too easy. But most of those programs can *export* their information as an intermediary file: vCard, archive, LDAP Interchange Format (LDIF), or a tab-delimited or comma-separated value (CSV) text file.

For example, Microsoft's programs can export addresses as vCards; Thunderbird can export in LDIF format; Excel can export tab-delimited or CSV files.

It's a fine art, this importing business; all kinds of things can go wrong. The fields (like Name, Street, Phone) may not be in the right order. Tab-separated export files may not have the right number of empty fields. And so on.

For best results, choose Contacts→Help and search for "Import contacts from other apps." The resulting page gives special tips for each kind of export/import file format. (Fortunately, if the fields are out of order, Contacts will offer you the chance to straighten them out.)

About vCards

Contacts exchanges contact information with other programs primarily through *vCards*. "vCard" is short for *virtual business card*. More and more email programs send and receive these electronic business cards, which you can identify by their .vcf file name extensions (if, that is, you've set your Mac to display these extensions).

If you ever receive an email with a vCard file attached, drag the .vcf file into your Contacts window to create an instant entry with a complete set of information. You can create vCards of your own, too. Just drag a name out of your Contacts and onto the desktop (or into a piece of outgoing mail).

Tip: In addition to letting you create vCards of individual entries, Contacts makes it easy to create vCards that contain several entries. To do so, ⌘-click the entries in the Name column that you want included, and drag them to the desktop. There they'll appear all together as a single vCard. You can even drag an item from the Group page to the desktop to make a vCard that contains all the group's entries.

Keep this trick in mind if you ever want to copy all your contacts from an old PC to a new Mac. By creating a single vCard containing all your contacts, you've made it trivial to import them into the copy of Contacts running on your new Mac.

Creating Address Cards

Each entry in Contacts is called a *card*—like a paper Rolodex card, with predefined spaces to hold all the standard contact information.

To add a new person, choose File→New Card, press ⌘-N, or click the + button to the right of the Name column. Then type in the contact information, pressing the Tab key to move from field to field, as shown in Figure 18-21.

Figure 18-21 shows some unusual fields you can plug into your address cards. The phonetic first/last name fields (shown at top) let you store phonetic spellings of hard-to-pronounce names. There's a "birthday" field and a place to store the Twitter handle, too. To add fields like these, choose from the Card→Add Field menu.

Tip: If you find yourself constantly adding the same fields to new cards, check out the Template pane of Contacts' Preferences (Contacts→Preferences). There you can customize exactly which fields appear for new cards.

Each card also contains a free-form Note field at the bottom, where you can type any other random crumbs of information you'd like to store about the person (pet's name, embarrassing nicknames, favorite Chinese restaurant, whatever).

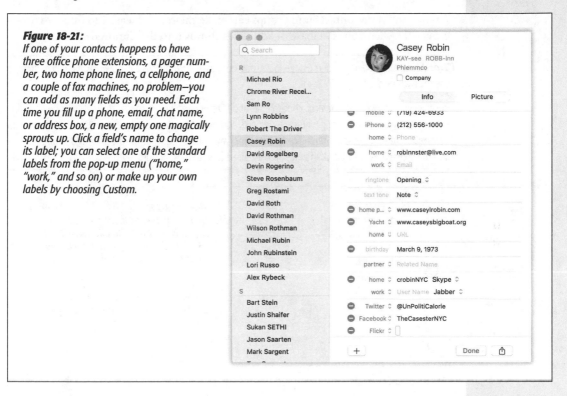

Figure 18-21:
If one of your contacts happens to have three office phone extensions, a pager number, two home phone lines, a cellphone, and a couple of fax machines, no problem—you can add as many fields as you need. Each time you fill up a phone, email, chat name, or address box, a new, empty one magically sprouts up. Click a field's name to change its label; you can select one of the standard labels from the pop-up menu ("home," "work," and so on) or make up your own labels by choosing Custom.

Editing an address

When you create a new address card, you're automatically in Edit mode, which means you can add and remove fields and change the information on the card. To switch into Browse mode (where you can view and copy contact information but not change it), click the Edit button or choose Edit→Edit Card (⌘-L). You can switch *out* of Browse Mode in the same ways.

Adding addresses from Mail

You can make new contacts right in Mail, saving you the trouble of having to type names and email addresses manually. Select a message in Mail, and then choose Message→Add Sender to Contacts. Presto: MacOS adds a new card to the Contacts, with the name and email address fields already filled in. Later, you can edit the card in Contacts to add phone numbers, street addresses, and so on.

Tip: If you enter some people's birthdays in Contacts, they can show up automatically in Calendar. To make that happen, open Calendar, and then choose Calendar→Preferences→General. Turn on "Show Birthdays calendar."

Groups

A *group* is a collection of related address cards, saved under a single descriptive name (see Figure 18-22).

Organizing your contacts into groups can make them much easier to find and use—especially when your database of addresses climbs into the hundreds.

Tip: When you send an email message to a group en masse, how does Mail know *which* email address to use for each person?

Because you've *told* it. In Contacts, choose Edit→Edit Distribution List. A special dialog box appears, listing everyone in each group, along with each person's complete list of email addresses. (Use the tiny pop-up menu above the list to choose Phone or Address; that way, you can also indicate the preferred phone number and mailing address.) Just click the preferred email address to make it bold.

Figure 18-22:
Groups are handy. If, for example, you regularly send out a family newsletter to 35 relatives, you might gather the address cards of all your assorted siblings, cousins, nieces, nephews, uncles, and aunts into a single group called Family. When addressing an outgoing message using Mail, you can type this group name to reach all your kin at once.

Your groups are displayed in the sidebar; if you've hidden the sidebar, choose View→Show Groups or press ⌘-1.

To create a group, click the + button at the bottom of the Contacts window and choose New Group from the pop-up menu, or choose File→New Group (Shift-⌘-N). Type a name for the newly spawned group icon in the sidebar.

Now you have to fill up the group with the appropriate subset of names. There are two ways to do that:

- **To turn a set of address cards into a group quickly,** select multiple entries from the Names column. You can do that either by Shift-clicking the names (to make contiguous selections) or by ⌘-clicking (for noncontiguous selections). Then

choose File→New Group From Selection. You end up with a new group containing all the selected names.

- **In the sidebar where your groups are listed,** click All Contacts at the top of the screen. Now your full names list appears on the right; drag names directly onto the group names to put them there.

Note: You're not *moving* those names; in essence, you're creating *aliases* of them, just as you might put songs in different playlists in Music.

Once you've created some groups, you can even add groups to *other* groups, as though you were nesting folders. You might find it useful to keep a Nieces group and a Nephews group, for example, but to keep both inside a master Family group. To do this, create the two groups. Then drag each onto the Family group. Now, whenever you select Family, you'll see both Nieces and Nephews listed among the rest of the cards; double-click either group to see its members.

Smart groups

The Finder has smart folders, Mail has smart mailboxes, and Music has smart playlists; inevitably, Contacts has smart *groups*.

Smart address groups, like smart folders in the Finder, automatically populate themselves with items that match criteria you specify. For example, you might create a

TROUBLESHOOTING MOMENT

Resolving Conflicts and Duplicates

Suppose you tell Contacts to sync its information with one of your online accounts. And suppose that someone is listed in both places—with a different phone number in each place. Which address-book information "wins"? What's the Mac supposed to do?

Ask you, of course. And that's exactly what it does.

The first warning you may see lets you know that the other address book is very different from the one on your Mac—more than, say, 25 percent different. If you know what you're doing, go ahead and click Sync Contacts. If you'd like to inspect the differences name by name, click Show Details instead. You'll see a summary box that indicates how many people need to be added to one list or the other, and how many people's information is different.

That "these two address books are radically different" warning isn't quite the same thing as the warning you may get about sync conflicts. That's when you've entered the same person into each address book source, but with different

information. Maybe one has a different phone number, for example. If you click Review Now, you're shown one conflict after another—the complete address cards—so that you can make a ruling on which version "wins."

One other problem may crop up when you're combining accounts: You may wind up with duplicates.

Fortunately, Contacts is ready for you here. Click the account with the problem (or All Contacts). Choose Card→Look for Duplicates.

The program lets you know about any duplicates it finds, even if only the name is the same and everything else is different. It even flags cards that have duplicate bits of information, like the same phone number twice. All you have to do is click Merge; Contacts merges the multiple cards into a single one, preserving all the details that are unique to each. (If there were duplicate photos, whichever one was on the first card becomes the new photo.)

smart group called "Apple Employees" that lists all your contacts with *apple.com* in their email addresses.

To create a smart group, choose File→New Smart Group (Option-⌘-N). Then use the resulting dialog box (which looks a lot like Mail's smart mailbox dialog box) to specify how you'd like the smart group to fill itself.

Once you're done, you can use your new smart group much like you'd use a regular group. You can't add contacts to a smart group yourself, but you can still send an email to all the members of a smart group, for example, or drag one to the Finder to create a composite vCard.

Removing someone from a group

To take someone out of a group, first click the group name, and then click the person's name in the Name column and press the Delete key. If you want to remove the person from Contacts *itself,* click Delete in the resulting dialog box. Otherwise, just click Remove from Group or press Return. Contacts keeps the card but removes it from the currently selected group.

Adding Pictures

You can dress up each Contacts entry with a photo. Whenever you're editing somebody's address book card, click the Picture tab and then single-click the circle bearing a +or the person's photo. You can choose from categories like Defaults (canned symbolic photos like animals and flowers); Camera (handy if this person is *with* you—take a new photo); Photo Booth (nutty pictures you've taken with this app); and Photos (your collection filed in handy folders, including Moments, Collections, Years, and so on). At that point, you can reposition or crop the photo. Click Save when you're done.

From now on, if you receive an email from that person, the photo shows up right in the email message—even on your phone or iPad.

Replacing and removing a picture

To replace a photo on an address card, click the profile picture where it says "edit." This opens up a panel where you can choose your new image. If you want to get rid of a picture without replacing it, select the card and then choose Card→Clear Custom Image (or, in Edit mode, select the picture next to your contact's name—not the editable profile picture—and then press Delete).

Finding an Address

You can search for a Contacts entry inside the currently selected group by typing a few letters of a name (or address, or any other snippet of contact information) in the search box. To search *all* your contacts instead of just the current group, click All Contacts in the sidebar.

Tip: You can press ⌘-F to jump directly to the search field and start typing. Your savings: one mouse click.

With each letter you type, Contacts filters your social circle and displays the matching records; the first of the matching card entries appears in the far-right pane, and the matching text itself appears highlighted in the matching card.

If Contacts finds more than one matching card, use the ▼ and ▲ keys, or Return and Shift-Return, to navigate through them.

Once you've found the card you're looking for, you can perform some interesting stunts. If you click the label of a phone number (see Figure 18-23), you see the Show in Large Type option: Contacts displays the number in a gigantic font, making it possible to read it from across the room. Or click the label of an email address to create a preaddressed email message, or click a home page to launch your browser and go to somebody's site. You can also copy and paste address card info into another program.

Tip: Once you find a street address in your Contacts, you can find those coordinates on a map by clicking the label (such as Home or Work) and, from the shortcut menu, choosing Open in Maps. The Maps app obediently leaps open to display the address.

Figure 18-23:
The options that become available when you click the field labels on an address card vary according to field type. Pop-up menus let you send email, open a web page, or view a map, depending on the type of field you've clicked.

If you have an iPhone, and it's on the same Wi-Fi network, you even see this Call option. It lets you use your Mac as a speakerphone, as described on page 304.

The Send Message command sends an iMessage to the phone number or email address whose label you've clicked—if, in fact, it's an iMessages-registered number or address.

And the Show Map button appears when you point to an address. It opens the Maps program and shows you this address on a map.

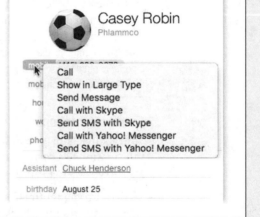

Changing the Contacts Display

You can't do much to customize Contacts' appearance, but the Preferences pane (Contacts→Preferences) gives you at least a couple of options in the General pane that are worth checking out:

• **Show first name.** Choose to have names displayed with the first name followed by the last name, or vice versa.

• **Sort By.** Sort the entries in Contacts by either first or last name.

Printing Options

When you choose File→Print and click Show Details, the Style pop-up menu offers three ways to print whatever addresses are selected at the moment:

- **Mailing Labels.** This option prints addresses on standard sheets of sticky mailing labels—Avery, for example—that you buy at office-supply stores.

Tip: As you manipulate settings, you can see your changes in the preview pane on the left. If the preview is too small for you to see, use the Zoom slider. (It doesn't affect your printout.)

- **Envelopes.** This feature is great if you have bad handwriting; rather than hand-addressing your envelopes, you can have Contacts print them out for you. Use the Layout pop-up menu to pick the size of your envelopes—it's usually listed on the outside of the envelope box.

Note: Both the Mailing Labels and Envelopes options print *only* the contacts for which you have, in fact, entered physical mailing addresses.

- **Lists.** If all you want is a paper backup of your Contacts entries, use this setting. In the Attributes list, turn on the checkboxes of the fields you want printed—just email and phone number, for example.

Tip: You can combine the smart-groups feature with the printing features in one clever way: to print yourself a portable phone book when you're heading off for a visit to a different city. That is, set up a smart group that rounds up everyone you know who lives in Chicago, and then print that as a list.

Contacts Backups

Your Contacts may represent *years* of typing and compiling effort. Losing all that information to a corrupted database or a hard drive crash could be devastating. Here are three ways to protect your Contacts data:

- **Back up your entire Contacts database.** Choose File→Export→Contacts Archive. Store the resulting backup file on another drive, if you like. Later, you can use the File→Import command to find that data and slurp it back in.

- **Turn on iCloud syncing.** An iCloud account has its privileges—and one of them is automatic synchronizing with the iCloud mother ship online.

- **Back up your whole Mac with Time Machine.** Page 260 tells you how.

Safari

S afari is the Mac's web browser. It's superfast and filled with great features. Here and there, you'll find certain sites or services that don't work in Safari (grrrr), which is why many Mac fans keep another browser, like Chrome or Firefox, on board just in case. Overall, though, Safari makes a slick, responsive window to the web.

The Unified Address/Search Bar

There are all kinds of ways to begin your web surfing session. Perform a search. Click a bookmark. On the following pages: a rundown of these starting points. Often, of course, you'll want to type in a web address; that's the purpose of the address/search bar identified in Figure 19-1. In Safari, a single, unified box serves as both the address bar and the search bar.

If you type a web address there, like *amazon.com,* then pressing Return takes you to that website; if you type anything else, like *cashmere sweaters* or just *amazon,* then pressing Return gives you the Google search results for that phrase, as described next.

Note: The address/search bar doesn't show the full address of the page you're on. You may be reading *http://www.nytimes.com/2019/2/28/us/politics/house-vote-moves-budget-deal-closer-to-approval. html,* but the address bar shows only *nytimes.com.* If you'd rather see the full address, then choose Safari→Preferences→Advanced and turn on "Show full website address."

A few important buttons come installed on the toolbar:

- **Back, Forward.** Click the Back button (<) to revisit the page you were just on. Keyboard shortcut: ⌘-◀ or ⌘-[, or a two-finger swipe left on the trackpad. (On an Apple Mouse or older Mighty Mouse, that's a *one*-finger swipe.)

Once you've clicked ‹, you can then click › (or press ⌘-▶, or ⌘-], or use a two-finger swipe to the *right*) to return to the page you were on before you clicked the Back button. Click and hold the ‹ or › button for a pop-up menu of *all* the web pages you've visited during this online session.

That pop-up menu lists the sites by name, as in "*The New York Times*—Breaking News, World News & Multimedia." To view the actual *addresses* instead, Option-click (and hold the mouse down on) the ‹ or › button.

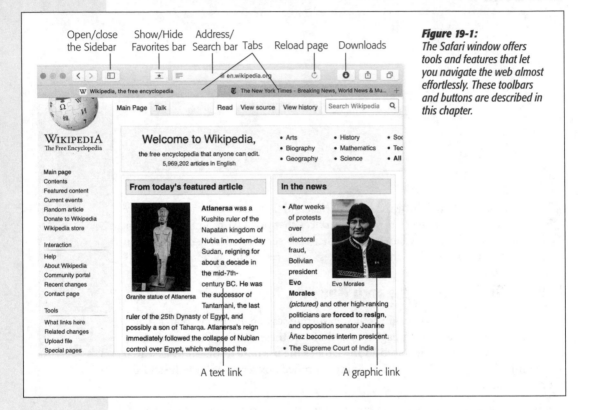

Open/close Show/Hide Address/
the Sidebar Favorites bar Search bar Tabs Reload page Downloads

A text link A graphic link

Figure 19-1:
The Safari window offers tools and features that let you navigate the web almost effortlessly. These toolbars and buttons are described in this chapter.

- **Sidebar** (▢). Click to show or hide the Sidebar, which offers lists of your bookmarks, Reading List, and RSS feeds. (All of this is described on the following pages.)

- **Reader View** (☰). This button appears at the left end of the address/search box, only when you're reading a web page article—a decent-sized block of text. See page 738 for more.

- **Add to Reading List** (⊗). This button appears only when you move your cursor to the far-left end of the address/search box. With one click, you add the current page to your Reading List (page 736). Or, if you hold down the mouse, you can add this page as a bookmark.

- **Stop/Reload.** Click the ✕ (or press Esc, or ⌘-period) to interrupt the download-
ing of a web page you've just requested—if you've made a mistake, for instance.

 Once a page has finished loading, the Stop button turns into a Refresh button (↻).
 Click it (or press ⌘-R) if a page doesn't look or work quite right, or if you want to
 see the updated version of it (like for a breaking-news site that changes constantly).
 Safari re-downloads the web page and reinterprets its text and graphics.

- **Share** (⬆) lets you send the current web page to the Reading List, install it as a
bookmark, send it by email or text message, or drop it into one of your apps. See
page 258 for details.

- **Show All Tabs** (⧉) displays all your open tabs at once, attractively arrayed as
miniatures; see page 734.

- **Downloads** (⬇). Here's Safari's awesome Downloads button (page 737). Click
to see everything you've downloaded, or *are* downloading.

Searching the Web

Press ⌘-L to deposit your insertion point inside the unified toolbar, type something
you're looking for—*phony baloney,* say—and then press Return. Safari takes you
directly to the results page of Google or whatever search site you've selected.

As Figure 19-2 makes clear, Safari offers plenty of assistance as you type, in the form
of Google suggestions, matching listings from your Bookmarks and History list, and
suggestions from Maps, Wikipedia, and other sources.

For example, if you type *empire state building* into the address bar, the first suggestion
may not be from the web—but instead from Maps. Click it to open the Empire State
Building's page in the Maps program. And if you type *small mouthed salamander,*
the first hit is likely to be a link to that critter's Wikipedia page, complete with a tiny
photo and the first lines of text.

Figure 19-2:
*As you type, Safari offers
autocomplete suggestions from
Wikipedia, Google's own Suggest
feature, and matching pages that
you've either bookmarked or
visited recently.*

*To save typing, click the correct
complete address with your
mouse, or use the ▾ key to reach
the desired listing and then press
Return.*

Tip: You can turn off the Google suggestions in Safari→Preferences→Search. Turn off "Include search engine suggestions."

Address/Search Bar Tips

Because typing internet addresses and searching for things are so central to the internet experience and such a typo-prone hassle, the address/search bar is rich with features that minimize keystrokes. For example:

- **You don't have to click there before typing;** just press ⌘-L.

- **You can highlight the entire address** (so it's ready to be typed over with a new one) by clicking anywhere inside the bar. Or press ⌘-L.

- **You don't have to type out the whole internet address.** You can omit the *http://* and *www* portions; Safari fills in those standard address bits for you. To visit *http://www.nytimes.com,* for example, a speed freak might press ⌘-L to highlight the address bar, type *nytimes.com,* and then press Return.

- **You don't have to use Google.** If you prefer to use Bing, Yahoo, or DuckDuckGo for searching instead of Google, then open Safari→Preferences→Search and use the "Search engine" pop-up menu. (DuckDuckGo is more limited than Google and its rivals. But it has gained a following among privacy fans because it doesn't store any information about its visitors or the searches they conduct.)

- **You can look up a word on a page.** If you right-click or two-finger click a highlighted word or phrase on a web page, you can choose Search with Google (or whatever your chosen search site is) from the shortcut menu to search for that text. And, even cooler, this trick works in *all* macOS programs—not just Safari.

Bookmarks, Favorites, and Top Sites

Another way to begin your web session is to click a bookmark. In any web browser, bookmarks are essential. They represent sites you want to visit again later. By picking

UP TO SPEED

Extensions

An extension is what, in another time, might have been called a plug-in. It's software from another company that plugs into Safari to add new features.

Maybe you've decided to install ClickToFlash, for example, a Safari extension that prevents animated ads from playing unless you click them. Or maybe you've installed a password-memorizing program like Dashlane. The Pin It button (a key to the popularity of Pinterest) is an extension, too.

To look over a catalog of available extensions, visit *extensions.apple.com.* Or open Safari→Preferences→Extensions and click More Extensions. The ones you find on Apple's extensions site are safe and solid. But they are intended to modify Safari, and it's possible that some extension, or some combination of them, will make Safari unstable.

So it's handy that on that same Preferences screen, you can find the list of all the extensions you've installed so far, complete with on/off switches and Uninstall buttons.

one from a list, you save yourself the trouble of searching the web or typing out an address.

Safari happens to be overrun with systems of adding and choosing bookmarks; you can't move your cursor without bumping into one. Read on.

Adding a Bookmark

When you find a web page you might like to visit again, do yourself a favor: Bookmark it. Here's how:

- **Press ⌘-D, or choose Bookmarks→ Add Bookmark.** Proceed as shown in Figure 19-3.

Figure 19-3:
When you add a bookmark, Safari offers to memorize this web page's name, or a shorter name that you specify for it.

You also have to specify where you want to save your new bookmark; Safari offers several options.

There's the Bookmarks menu, or any folders you've set up inside it.

There are the Favorites, a special set of bookmarks that you think you'll use a lot. They get their own special screen and their own special bar, as you'll read in a moment.

There are the Top Sites (page 724).

Finally, there's the master list, the Bookmarks list in the Sidebar; as you can see by (a) in Figure 19-4, this list lets you further categorize your bookmarks by putting them into folders.

- **Press Shift-⌘-D to add the page to the Reading List.**

- **Point to the far-left edge of the address bar; hold your cursor down on the ⊕ button that appears.** This time, you get a pop-up menu of the standard locations (Reading List, Favorites, Bookmarks Menu, and so on); choose where you want

this bookmark stored. This is a quick method, but it doesn't offer you the chance to rename the bookmark.

Organizing Bookmarks in the Sidebar

See the ⬚ button on the toolbar? It opens the Sidebar, the panel shown at left in Figure 19-4. (You can also choose Bookmarks→Show Bookmarks, or choose View→Show Bookmarks Sidebar, or press Control-⌘-1.)

Figure 19-4:
Here's "Bookmarks: The Missing Manual."

(a) Bookmarks (b) Open Sidebar (c) Drag to Favorites bar (d) Hold down the + button

(a) You can drag your favorite bookmarks up or down to organize them.

(b) Hide or show the Sidebar.

(c) You can drag a website's logo to the Favorites bar...

(d) ...or create and file a bookmark in one step.

At the top of this panel, two tabs await. On the first one, the ⬚ tab, you can really go to town with bookmark management. For example:

- **Rearrange bookmarks or folders** by dragging them up or down.

- **Create a folder** by choosing Bookmarks→Add Bookmark Folder. Or right-click or two-finger click anywhere in the list; from the shortcut menu, choose New Folder.

 Type a name for the folder, press Return, and then start filling it up by dragging existing bookmark names onto it.

- **To delete a bookmark or a folder**, right-click or two-finger click its name. From the shortcut menu, choose Delete.

- **To edit a bookmark's name,** right-click or two-finger click it, or hold your cursor down on it. From the shortcut menu, choose Rename.

- **To edit the web address a bookmark opens**, right-click or two-finger click its name. From the shortcut menu, choose Edit Address.

While you're poking around, you might notice a special folder that was here before you arrived. The Favorites folder lists the bookmarks you've installed on the Favorites screen described on the following pages; it's just another way to see, choose, and

organize those same items. The Bookmarks Menu folder performs that same function for the Bookmarks menu; it gives you an easy way to organize what's listed there.

Organizing Bookmarks in the Editor

Before the slick new Sidebar came along, there was an earlier way to organize bookmarks: the bookmarks *editor*. You can open this special, spreadsheety window by choosing Bookmarks→Edit Bookmarks or by pressing Option-⌘-B.

In the bookmarks editor window, drag the bookmarks up and down to rearrange them. You can edit a bookmark's name or underlying address by clicking it. Delete one by clicking it and then pressing Delete. There's a New Folder button at top right, too.

Tip: Safari is equipped to help you move out of other web browsers. If you've been using Chrome or Firefox, for example, then the first time you use Safari, your bookmarks and browsing history get imported from the other browser automatically. (You'll see a note to that effect at the bottom of the Favorites or Top Sites view; you can click either Keep or Don't Keep. You can always import them later, using the File→Import From→ Google Chrome or File→Import From→Firefox commands.)

If you have some other weirdo browser, like Internet Explorer or OmniWeb, then importing your bookmarks is only a little more complicated. Use that browser's Export feature to save them to a file, and then use Safari's File→Import Bookmarks command to save you the time of reentering the bookmarks by hand.

Favorites Bar

Safari lets you elevate a few special bookmarks to Favorites status. These are the sites you figure you'll open the most. And Safari gives you two ways to see them.

First, the Favorites bar is a horizontal strip just beneath the address bar (visible in Figure 19-4). If you leave this bar open, you have one-click access to a few very special sites.

To make this bar appear or disappear, choose View→Show Favorites Bar (Shift-⌘-B).

Tip: You can jump to the first nine bookmarks on your Favorites bar by pressing Option-⌘-1 through 9. That's one key more complicated than it used to be (in Yosemite, it was just ⌘-1, ⌘-2, and so on)—but those simpler keystrokes now switch to the first nine *tabs*.

Then:

• **Add a favorite.** You add a bookmark to this bar exactly as described on page 719— but for the new bookmark's destination, choose Favorites.

You can also drag your current web page's *name* from the address/search bar directly onto the Favorites bar. (Don't click first—just start dragging directly downward on the address bar.) You're offered the chance to type a shorter name for your new Favorite.

Tip: You can also drag a *link* from a web page (not just the tiny website logo) onto your Favorites bar. In fact, you can also drag a link directly to the desktop, where it turns into an internet location file. Thereafter, to open Safari and visit the associated web page whenever you like, just double-click this icon.

Better yet, stash a few of these icons in your Dock or Sidebar for even easier access.

- **Remove a button** from the Favorites bar by dragging it down and away.

- **Rearrange the buttons** by dragging them horizontally.

- **Edit a button** by right-clicking or two-finger clicking its name. From the shortcut menu, choose Rename or Edit Address.

Tip: Actually, you can rename a bookmark on the Favorites bar just by click-and-holding on its name. You'll see it highlighted; you can just retype. No right-clicking necessary!

The Start Page

Apple figures you'll often want to *begin* your surfing session with one of your Favorites. So whenever you open a new window, create a new tab, or click in the address bar (and don't type anything), you get Catalina's new Start page (Figure 19-5).

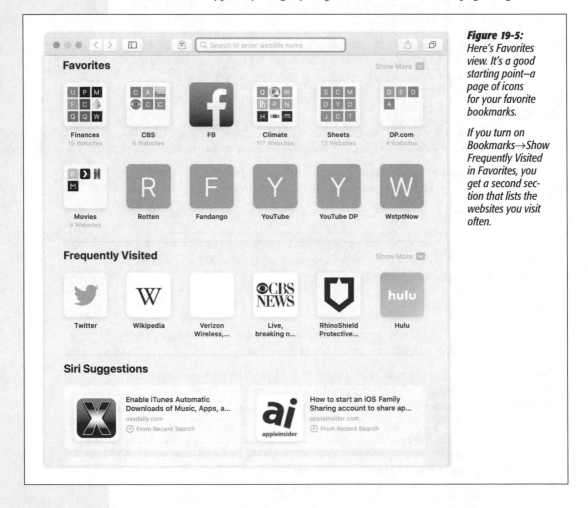

Figure 19-5:
Here's Favorites view. It's a good starting point—a page of icons for your favorite bookmarks.

If you turn on Bookmarks→Show Frequently Visited in Favorites, you get a second section that lists the websites you visit often.

Or just click the ⁝⁝⁝⁝ icon at the far left of the Favorites bar. (If that's not what you see when you open a new window or tab, you must have changed the settings in Safari→Preferences→General→"New pages open with" or "New tabs open with." From that pop-up menu, you should choose Favorites. Yes, even though this page is now called Start.)

At top, it shows a few of your Favorites (your very favorite bookmarked sites). Next on this screen, icons appear for some of your Frequently Visited sites. At bottom are Siri Suggestions—links to sites the Mac found in your Messages chats, recent Mail messages, and stories you've read in the News app.

You can edit the icons on the Start page, of course:

- **Rearrange them.** You can drag any icon to a new spot.

- **Remove them.** Drag an icon out of the main Favorites view window to make it disappear.

- **View them as folders.** If you put several bookmarks into a folder, it appears on the Favorites panel as a single icon filled with even tinier icons.

- **Add an icon.** When you find a page you'd like to add to the Favorites screen, choose Bookmarks→Add Bookmark (⌘-D); on the "Where" sheet that appears, choose Favorites. Click Add.

POWER USERS' CLINIC

Quick Website Search

This crazy and obscure feature lets you search *within* a certain site (like Amazon, reddit, or Wikipedia) right from within Safari's regular search bar.

For example, typing *wiki mollusk* can offer a one-click search of Wikipedia for its entry on mollusks. Typing *amazon ipad* can offer links to buy an iPad from Amazon. Typing *reddit sitcoms* can open *reddit.com* to its search results for sitcoms.

None of this works, however, until (a) the feature is turned on (Safari→Preferences→Search→Enable Quick Website Search), and (b) you've *manually* taught Safari how to search those sites one time each. To do that, pull up the home page of the site you'll want to search (let's say it's *reddit.com*)

and use its regular search bar. Search for anything. Close the window.

That site's name now appears in the list in Safari→Preferences→Search→Enable Quick Website Search→Manage Websites. (Usually. Many sites don't work with Quick Website Search.)

From now on, you can search that site by typing, for example, *reddit sitcoms* into the address bar. But before you press Return, look closely at the suggestions: The first one is a ready-to-click search for that item on that site, as shown here.

Click it to jump directly to that site's search results. You've saved yourself a few clicks and page-loads.

Top Sites

The Top Sites window (Figure 19-6) *used* to be the starting-out page in Safari. It's exactly the same idea as the Start page—it's a screen full of website icons—except that Safari chooses them, not you. It calculates which are your favorite websites according to *how often* and *how recently* you've visited them. The idea, again, is to save you time; the sites you're most likely to want to revisit are one click away.

Figure 19-6:
The Top Sites display is a little harder to get to than it was in previous versions of macOS. But if you've turned the feature on in Safari→Preferences→General→New windows open with→Top Sites, then you'll see it every time you open a new window or tab.

Ordinarily, the Top Sites change over time, as your activities change. But you can override Safari's attempt to curate this page in various ways. For example, you can pin a certain site so that it never leaves the Top Sites screen, or you can manually add a page.

Here's some of the other fun you can have:

- **Rearrange the thumbnails** by dragging them around.

- **Delete a thumbnail** by pointing to it; click the ✕ button that appears in the top-left corner after a couple of seconds. This page will never again appear in Top Sites.

- **Pin a site** so that it's always in Top Sites, even if you don't visit it much: Point to it and click the pushpin icon that appears in the top-left corner after a moment.

- **Add a new page to the Top Sites display.** You can drag a bookmark from the Sidebar (page 15) into the Top Sites window, or even onto the Top Sites icon (▦) on the toolbar, if you've installed it there. Or, when you choose Bookmarks→Add Bookmark (⌘-D) to bookmark an open web page, choose Top Sites as the location. You can also drag a web address wherever it may appear—an email, web page, or document, for example—into the Top Sites window or onto its toolbar icon.

Full Screen and Gestures

Once you enter Full Screen mode by clicking the green ⊗ at upper left (see page 173), using Safari is almost exactly like surfing the web on the iPad.

For example:

- **Zoom in and out with pinch and spread.** That is, put two fingers on your trackpad and spread them to magnify the web page, or pinch to zoom out. Great when the type is a little too small.

- **Magnify just a block with a two-finger double-tap.** Most web pages are subdivided into various rectangles of text and graphics. Just as on the iPhone/iPad, you can double-tap (with *two* fingers on your trackpad) to magnify a single block of text or graphics. Repeat the process to zoom back out to regular size. (Note that this is *tapping,* not *clicking.*)

- **Use a two-finger swipe for Back and Next.** This one's really juicy. With two fingers on your trackpad, swipe left or right instead of clicking the ⟨ or ⟩ buttons. The great part is that if you do this *slowly,* you pull the previous or next page onto the screen *gradually,* giving you a chance to peek at it without actually moving to it.

Tip: Each time you open Safari, it brings up whatever pages you had open last. It's part of macOS's auto-resume feature.

There's a grace note to all of this. Ordinarily, in Full Screen mode, the menu bar isn't the only thing that disappears; the main toolbar does, too (containing the Back/Forward buttons, the address bar, and so on). Every time you wanted to click one of its buttons, you had to move your mouse to the top of the screen so the bar reappeared.

No more! Now you can choose View→Always Show Toolbar in Full Screen to keep it visible all the time. Life is good again.

Scrolling

You'll rarely do more page scrolling than you do in a web browser. Scrolling is a *constant* activity.

Fortunately, Apple gives you about 11,339 different ways to do it.

You can use the regular scroll gesture (two fingers on the trackpad). You can also press your ▲ and ▼ keys to scroll one line at a time. Page Up and Page Down scroll in full-screen increments, while Home and End whisk you to the top or bottom of the current web page. And if your mouse has a scroll wheel, it works, too. (Hold Shift while you're rolling the wheel to scroll *horizontally*.)

But maybe the best way of all is to *tap the space bar* each time you want to see more. Press Shift-space to scroll *up*. (The space bar serves its traditional space-making function only when the insertion point is blinking in a text box or the address bar.)

Five Ways to Magnify a Page

If it seems as though a lot of websites are designed with type that's too small to read, it's not just you and your aging eyes. Often it has to do with the high resolution of today's screens, which work by packing their pixels together more tightly—and making everything look smaller.

Fortunately, Safari is well equipped to help you with this problem. In fact, it offers many solutions:

- **Enlarge the screen.** Press ⌘-plus or ⌘-minus to enlarge or reduce the entire web page. Or use the two-finger "spread" gesture on your laptop trackpad. Or use the Zoom button, if you've added it to your toolbar. The advantage of this method is that the whole web page's layout remains proportional.

- **Magnify a block.** Lightly double-tap (don't fully click) with *two fingers* on your trackpad to zoom in to one block of text or graphics on a page, as already described.

- **Blow up just the text.** If you add the Option key to ⌘-plus and ⌘-minus, the Zoom In and Zoom Out options become Make Text Bigger and Make Text Smaller, magnifying or shrinking *only the text* on your page. Graphics remain at their original size. You're now distorting the original layout, but you're maximizing the amount of reading you can do before you have to scroll.

- **Zoom in the usual way.** Remember the Control-key zooming technique described on page 321? It's not the same thing as the ⌘-plus or ⌘-minus tricks, which keep the window frame and menu at normal size. The Control-key zooming technique magnifies *everything*—the entire screen, menus and all. It also doesn't keep text as sharp as the ⌘-plus/⌘-minus trick.

- **Specify a minimum type size.** This may be the best option of all, because it saves you all that zooming. Open Safari→Preferences→Advanced and set the "Never use font sizes smaller than" option to, for example, 14 points. Now *every* web page shows up with legible text. (Except a few oddballs that use weird coding to prevent text-size changing.)

Customizing the Toolbar

There's no title bar in Safari. So the real estate on the bar that remains—the address/search bar, the one Apple calls the toolbar—is precious. Fortunately, you can summon or dismiss individual buttons on the toolbar, in effect customizing it (Figure 19-7).

Many of them, you'll recognize, but a few deserve some clearing up:

- **iCloud Tabs** open whatever browser windows and tabs you had open on your other Apple gadget, like an iPhone or iPad or another Mac. Thanks to the miracle of iCloud syncing, the last windows and tabs you had open on that other gadget (even if the gadget is turned off) show up here. (This is visible in Figure 19-13.)

- **Share.** Here's the standard macOS Share menu, for sending a web page to another person, or to your Notes app, for example.

- **Show/Exit Tab Overview.** See page 733.

- **Home.** Click to bring up the web page you've designated as your home page (in the Safari→Preferences→General tab).

- **History.** Click to open the list of websites you've visited recently in a window—a much easier-to-navigate display than the History *menu*.

- **Sidebar** shows or hides the Sidebar, the left-side column of bookmarks, saved articles, or RSS feeds.

Figure 19-7:
To summon this toolbar-tailoring screen, choose View→Customize Toolbar. Drag the buttons you want directly onto the address bar.

There's no way to summon text labels for these icons once they're on the toolbar. But all offer tooltip labels, which appear when you point to them.

Drag your favorite items into the toolbar...

Back/Forward	iCloud Tabs	Share	Show/Exit Tab Overview	Top Sites	Home
History	Sidebar	Bookmarks	AutoFill	Zoom	Mail
Website Preferences	Print	Web Inspector	Address and Search		
Ghostery Lite	Flexible Space				

... or drag the default set into the toolbar.

Back/Forward Sidebar Ghostery Lite Address and Search Share Show/Exit Tab Overview

Done

- **Bookmarks.** Hides or shows the horizontal toolbar that lists your favorite bookmarks (the equivalent of choosing View→Hide [or Show] Favorites Bar).

- **AutoFill.** Click this button to make Safari fill in web order forms with your name, address, and other information. See the next section.

- **Mail.** Opens a new, outgoing message in your email program. The subject line contains the *name* of the site you were visiting; the body contains the actual web page. But in the Send Web Content As pull-down menu, you can choose from three other ways to send the page: in Reader view, as a PDF, or a link only. You can address the message, add a comment ("Re: your claim that 'no expert' recommends trampolines for children"), and send it.

- **Website Preferences.** This button offers you some great options to configure how you interact with individual websites. See page 744.

- **Print.** You can add a printer icon to Safari for point-and-click paper action if you don't want to bother with ⌘-P.

Tip: Safari automatically shrinks your printouts, if necessary, by up to 10 percent, if doing so will avoid printing a second page with just one or two lines of text on it. Nice.

- **Web Inspector.** Opens a new window pane that displays the HTML code underlying the page you're reading.

- **Flexible Space.** This isn't really a button. It's an invisible "tile" you can drag between other buttons to adjust the button spacing on your toolbar.

Autofill: Your Name and Info

Every time you buy anything online or sign up for anything online, you have to type your name, address, and phone number. Over and over and over. This info doesn't change often—why can't someone invent a system to memorize it?

Figure 19-8:
Top: Safari can autofill your name and contact info.

Second from top: Safari can make up and memorize passwords, too. Click the 🔑 in any empty New Password box; click Suggest New Password.

Third from top: Here's Safari's proposed password. You won't care that all your passwords are gibberish like this; iCloud autosyncs them to all your other gadgets and fills them in there, too.

Lower right: When you return to this site, Safari can autofill both your login name and password.

Someone has. Visit the Safari→Preferences→AutoFill tab. Turn on "Using info from my contacts." Click Edit. From Contacts, find your own listing. You've just told Safari which name, address, city, state, zip code, and phone number belong to you.

From now on, whenever you're asked to input your details, you'll see a ⓘ icon in the typing box. Click it for a menu of your addresses (like Home and Work—see Figure 19-8, top), saving you no end of typing. (It works on *most* sites.) If there are extra blanks that AutoFill doesn't fill, you can press Tab to move your cursor from one to the next instead of tapping and scrolling manually.

Autofill: Your Passwords

Most of us are familiar with password hell. You're supposed to create a long, complex, unguessable password—capital and lowercase letters, numbers, and symbols, with a few Hindi characters thrown in if possible. For each site. And you can't reuse a password. Oh, and you have to change them all every month.

It's not possible. Not even security experts have that kind of memory.

Fortunately, Apple has come up with a system that comes very close to the ideal: complex, secure passwords—without your having to remember any of them!

When you're signing up for an account on some website, and you tap in the box where you're supposed to enter a password, Safari offers to make up a password for you. It's a doozy, too, along the lines of *23k2k4-29cs8-58384-ckk3322* (Figure 19-8).

UP TO SPEED

Website Notifications

MacOS can notify you when new email arrives. When a text message or phone call comes to your iPhone. When an alarm or reminder comes due. So why shouldn't websites be able to notify you just as easily—when new articles are posted, for example?

They can. Often, you'll arrive on some website and encounter a message like the one shown here: "The website would like to send you push notifications in Notification Center."

This is not the place to advise you on the wisdom of permitting such sites to vie for your attention during the workday. It is, however, a good idea to know how to turn these notifications on or off.

CNN

The website "CNN Breaking News" would like to send you push notifications in Notification Center.

Notifications can be configured in System Preferences.

Don't Allow Allow

In Safari→Preferences→Websites→Notifications, you'll find a list of every site that's ever asked for such permission. And you'll see how you replied to each one: Allow or Don't Allow.

Here you can change your mind. Or you can reset the slate by deleting some, so that you'll be asked again the next time you visit. Above all, you can make websites *stop* asking for permission altogether—by turning off "Allow websites to ask for permission to send push notifications."

From now on, you won't encounter any more pushy messages asking for permission to be even pushier.

You're not expected to remember that. Safari saves this password, so that it can enter it automatically on your next visit (Figure 19-8, lower right).

And if System Preferences→iCloud→Keychain is turned on, then your memorized passwords will be available on your other Apple machines (phones, tablets, Macs), too.

Note: If you have several accounts for the same site, you'll see a button for each one.

The master password list

You can view a master list of the actual memorized names and passwords. It waits for you at Safari→Preferences→Passwords. You have to prove your identity with your Mac password or Touch ID before you're allowed to see them.

On this screen, you can view a password by clicking its row (Figure 19-9). You can change any saved password, too; double-click it. To add a password manually, click Add. Or, if a login no longer pleases you, click it and hit Remove.

Figure 19-9:
Choose Safari→
Preferences→
Passwords (and
then enter your
Mac password)
to see the pass-
words Safari has
memorized. Click
a row to view the
corresponding
password.

This list, by the way, might display the occasional ⓐ symbol. That's flagging passwords you've used more than once, for different sites. Almost everyone does that, because who's really going to memorize 300 different passwords? But security experts frown on the practice, because it means once a hacker gets the password for one of your accounts (from some corporate data breach, for example), then he's got access to your other accounts, too. Since macOS can remember and fill in your passwords all by itself, you might as well avoid that fate.

Autofill: Credit Cards

When you buy something online, Safari can enter your credit-card information with one click, making shopping infinitely easier. It's as easy as 1, 2. Figure 19-10 shows you how to store your credit cards in Safari and how to use them to buy things online.

Figure 19-10:
Top: Teach Safari your credit card details by choosing Preferences→AutoFill. Click Edit to arrive at this list.

Click Add. Fill in a description for your card, the number, your name, and the expiration date. Click Done.

Bottom: Next time you're about to buy something, click inside the Card Number box). Safari shows this menu of your cards; click one to fill in all the boxes (except Verification Code).

This feature is a lot like the popular password/credit card keeper programs 1Password and Dashlane—better, really, because it's free, and because iCloud Keychain autosyncs your credit card information to your iPhones, iPads, and iPod Touches, too.

But in one way, it's worse: As yet another security layer, Safari doesn't memorize the security code, also known as the CVV or CV2 code, that you need to complete a credit card transaction. You have to fill that in yourself every time you buy something.

Autofill: Text-Message Authentication Codes

You know how, when you try to log onto certain websites, they first send your phone a text message to prove that you're you? (It's called two-factor authentication. Security experts love it. People hate it.)

Yeah, you get the notification that a text has come in. But then you had to either memorize the six-digit code they just sent you, or switch into Messages, find the text they sent you, and copy the code to your Clipboard. And then go back to Safari, tap in the "Enter code here" box, and paste it. Augh.

Not anymore! See Figure 19-11.

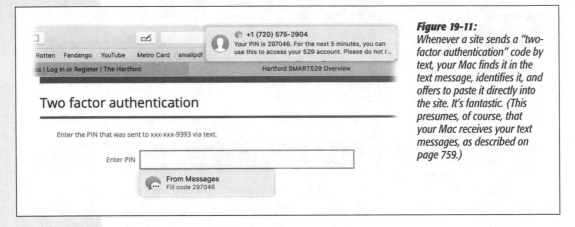

Figure 19-11:
Whenever a site sends a "two-factor authentication" code by text, your Mac finds it in the text message, identifies it, and offers to paste it directly into the site. It's fantastic. (This presumes, of course, that your Mac receives your text messages, as described on page 759.)

Tabbed Browsing

Beloved by hard-core surfers the world over, *tabbed browsing* is a way to keep a bunch of web pages open simultaneously—in a single, neat window. Figure 19-12 illustrates.

Turning on tabbed browsing unlocks a whole raft of Safari shortcuts and tricks, which are just the sort of thing power surfers gulp down like Gatorade:

- **When you ⌘-click any link on any page,** it opens into a new tab. (If, of course, the first checkbox in Safari→Preferences→Tabs is turned on.)

- **If there's a certain set of websites you like to visit daily,** put the bookmarks into one folder, using Bookmarks→Add Bookmark Folder and the Bookmarks organizer window. You can then load all of them into a single tabbed window, simply by selecting the resulting "folder" in the Bookmarks menu and choosing Open in Tabs from the submenu.

 The beauty of this arrangement is that you can start reading the first web page while all the others load into their own tabs in the background.

- **A variation on a theme:** When you have a bunch of pages open in tabs, you can drag the tabs across the window to rearrange the order. When you have them the way you want them, right-click or two-finger click a tab and then choose Add Bookmarks for "These [number] Tabs" from the shortcut menu. You can save your tabs to the Bookmarks bar and load all those pages with one click.

- **If you Option-click a tab's ✕ button,** you close all the tabs *except* the one you clicked. The same thing happens if you hold down Option and choose File→Close Other Tabs, or if you press Option-⌘-W.

- **If you Option-⌘-click a link,** it opens in a separate window, rather than in a new tab. (When tabbed browsing is turned *off*, just ⌘-click a link to open a new window.) If you find yourself with a bunch of separate browser windows all over your screen, you can consolidate them into one nicely tabbed Safari window by choosing Window→Merge All Windows.

- **If you Shift-⌘-click a link,** Safari opens that page in a tab *behind* the one you're reading. That's for when you're reading a web page and see a reference you want to set aside for reading next, but you don't want to interrupt what you're reading *now*.

- **If you have a lot of tabs open on your laptop**—so many that they don't all fit and some of them are getting stacked up at the right end—check out this trick: You can scroll through the open tabs on your trackpad. Position the cursor on the tab bar, and then swipe horizontally with two fingers.

- **If your Mac has a Touch Bar** (page 227), it shows tiny photos of all your open tabs. You can tap to jump to a tab, or just run your finger across them like a harpist.

- **Turn on favicons!** You can view favicons (tiny website logos) on each tab for quick visual identification. (You can see them in Figure 19-12.) To make them appear, visit Safari→Preferences→Tabs and turn on "Show website icons in tabs."

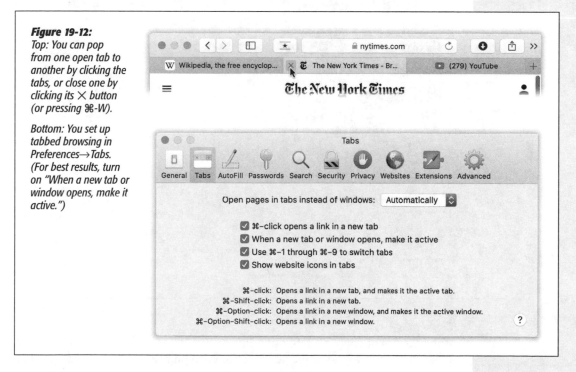

Figure 19-12:
Top: You can pop from one open tab to another by clicking the tabs, or close one by clicking its ✕ button (or pressing ⌘-W).

Bottom: You set up tabbed browsing in Preferences→Tabs. (For best results, turn on "When a new tab or window opens, make it active.")

Tab View

When you've opened a few tabs, their names, in titles across the top of your Safari window, get pretty cramped. Fortunately, there's also Tab view: Miniatures of all your

open tabs. To see it, click the Show All Tabs button on the toolbar (⬛)—or how about this? Just pinch two fingers on your trackpad. Figure 19-13 explains all.

Tip: Once you've opened Tab view, you can perform a cool trick: You can search all the open tabs at once (either for words in the web page's names, or text in their addresses). You don't have to click into any search box first; just type. As you type, Safari hides all but the matching tabs.

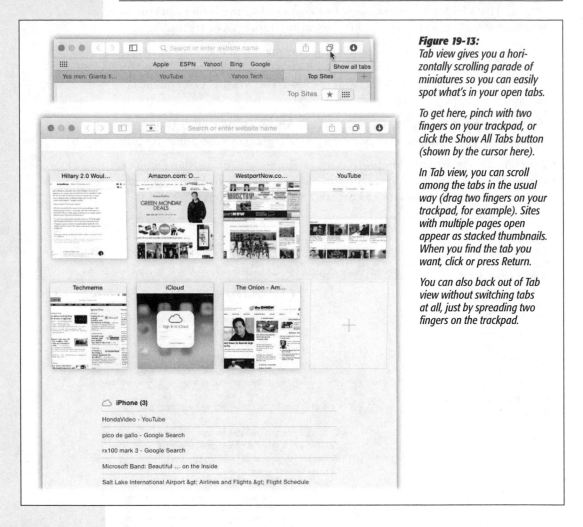

Figure 19-13:
Tab view gives you a horizontally scrolling parade of miniatures so you can easily spot what's in your open tabs.

To get here, pinch with two fingers on your trackpad, or click the Show All Tabs button (shown by the cursor here).

In Tab view, you can scroll among the tabs in the usual way (drag two fingers on your trackpad, for example). Sites with multiple pages open appear as stacked thumbnails. When you find the tab you want, click or press Return.

You can also back out of Tab view without switching tabs at all, just by spreading two fingers on the trackpad.

iCloud tabs

At the bottom of Show All Tabs view (Figure 19-13), a special treat awaits: A list of whatever browser windows and tabs you had open on your *other* Apple gadgets, like iPhones or iPads. Thanks to the miracle of iCloud syncing, the last windows and tabs you had open on that other gadget (even if the gadget is turned off) show up here.

The concept is to unify your Macs and i-gadgets into one glorious, seamless web-browsing experience. You're reading three browser windows and tabs on your phone—why not resume on the big screen when you get home and sit down in front of your Mac?

Amazingly enough, you can even *close* the tabs and windows on your other gadgets, by remote control—by clicking the ✕ button next to each one.

You won't see these tabs unless the Macs have Mountain Lion or later. And, of course, Safari has to be turned on in System Preferences→iCloud (on the Mac), or Settings→iCloud (on the phone or tablet).

Pinned Tabs

This feature is hard to describe but handy to have: *pinned* tabs. These are special, square, icon-only tabs at the far left end of your window that never go away, even when you close the window or quit Safari. (You can see three of them at the left end in Figure 19-14.)

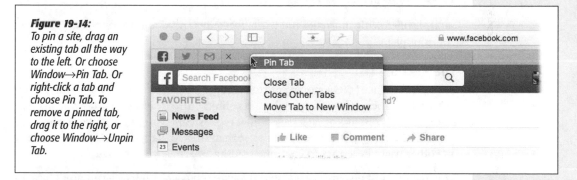

Figure 19-14:
To pin a site, drag an existing tab all the way to the left. Or choose Window→Pin Tab. Or right-click a tab and choose Pin Tab. To remove a pinned tab, drag it to the right, or choose Window→Unpin Tab.

GEM IN THE ROUGH

Mute Those Tabs

It's one of the most annoying situations in all of computing: Sound is blaring from some tab somewhere, and you don't know which one. You don't really care; you just want it to stop.

Safari can help: Whenever *any* tab is playing sound, a ◀) icon appears at the right end of the address bar, as well as any on tab that's playing sound. Click that icon to silence whichever tab is playing it, even if it's not the frontmost tab.

(The address bar says "Mute This Tab" if the frontmost tab is doing the playing, or "Mute All Tabs" if not.)

And what if *more than one* tab is playing audio? In that case, hold your mouse button down on the icon. The shortcut menu shows you the names of all the tabs now playing sound. Choose Mute Other Tab to silence the YouTube video or choose Mute This Tab to silence the *New York Times* video.

That might sound like the same thing as a bookmark, but there's a difference: When you click a bookmark, Safari takes a couple of seconds to fetch that web page and then display it. A pinned tab, on the other hand, is *already* loaded; Safari keeps its underlying page constantly updated.

That effect is especially useful for sites you check often throughout the day—sites like Facebook and Twitter, or mail sites like Gmail. Every time you click that pinned tab, the corresponding page appears, already loaded and up to date.

As a bonus, clicking a link on a pinned page opens up in a new tab, so the original page is waiting for you when you're done. When you're reading your Twitter feed, for example, you can click a link in someone's tweet to open the page he wanted you to see…you read it…you hit ⌘-W to close the tab…and you're right back in your Twitter feed, ready to click another link.

See Figure 19-14 for details on creating (and removing) pinned tabs.

Tips for Better Surfing

Safari is filled with shortcuts and tricks for better speed and more pleasant surfing. For example:

The Reading List

The Reading List (OO) stores entire web pages that you want to read later (Figure 19-15). These aren't just bookmarks (links); the Reading List downloads and stores the full contents of each page you've requested so you can read them when you don't have an internet connection. Better than that, actually: It stores that page *and* any other pages necessary to continue reading an article you've flagged.

The Reading List also makes it faster to flag a web page you like—you don't have to make up a name or a location for it, as with a bookmark. Also, the Reading List keeps track of what you've read; you can use the All/Unread buttons at the top of the list to view everything or just what you haven't yet read.

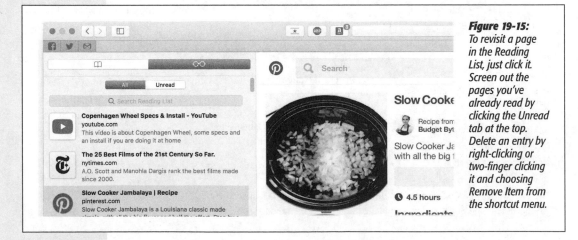

Figure 19-15:
To revisit a page in the Reading List, just click it. Screen out the pages you've already read by clicking the Unread tab at the top. Delete an entry by right-clicking or two-finger clicking it and choosing Remove Item from the shortcut menu.

You might treat the Reading List as a list of pages you'll want to read *once* later, and use bookmarks for pages you like to revisit *frequently*.

To make matters even sweeter, iCloud synchronizes your Reading List among your Mac, iPhone, iPad, and so on (if you've turned on Safari syncing in System Preferences→ iCloud). It's as though the web keeps your place as you move from gadget to gadget.

To add a page to the Reading List, use one of these techniques:

- **Shift-click a link.** That simple trick adds the linked page to the Reading List. You don't have to *visit* the page itself (only the link to it), or even open the Reading List first.

- **Click the ⊕ button.** This button appears only when you move your cursor to the left end of the address box.

- **Use the menu.** Choose Bookmarks→Add to Reading List, or press Shift-⌘-D.

- **Use the Share button.** You can also click 🔼 on the toolbar and choose Add to Reading List.

To view your saved pages, open the Sidebar (click ▣); then click the Reading List (◯◯) tab. Or just choose View→Show Reading List Sidebar (Control-⌘-2).

To read the pages in the Reading List, you can press Option-⌘-▼ or Option-⌘-▲ to move up and down your list.

Tip: If you're reading one article in your Reading List using the Reader feature (described in a moment), and then select another article, then it, too, will appear in Reader.

Keyboard Control

Efficiency freaks generally prefer keyboard shortcuts to using the mouse, so Safari is filled with them.

Press Tab to jump from one text box or pop-up menu to the next on your web page. Add the Option key to jump from one *link* to another (and when you highlight a link, press Return to "click" it).

Tip: For a shockingly complete list of Safari's keyboard shortcuts, open the Help menu. In the search box, type *safari shortcuts*. Wait a moment. Click "Safari keyboard and other shortcuts" in the list of Help topics.

The Download Manager

No browser has ever made tracking downloads simpler.

When you click a link to download something from a web page, it *visibly* flies to the upper-right corner of the Safari window, where the Downloads button (⊙) appears. You can then monitor the progress of the download at a glance—because the Downloads button *fills up* with blue as the download completes.

As Figure 19-16 shows, you can also view and manipulate a list of everything you've downloaded recently, all without leaving the comfort of whatever page you're on.

To pause downloading, click the ⊗ next to the download's name. Later, you can generally pick up from where you left off by clicking the Resume (↻) button.

Tip: In Safari→Preferences→General, you can opt to have your download listings removed from the Downloads window as soon as they've been successfully downloaded, maybe for privacy reasons.

Figure 19-16:
Click the Downloads (⬇) button to view this list of recent downloads. Double-click an icon to open the download. Drag it out of the list onto your desktop, or onto a folder on the desktop. You can even drag it onto a Dock icon to open that file with a particular program.

Click the ⊙ button to jump to the file wherever it's sitting in the Finder. To remove an item from the list, click it and then press Delete. (The Clear button erases the whole list.)

Status Bar

The status bar at the bottom of the window tells you what Safari is doing (such as "Opening page…" or "Done").

When you point to a link without clicking, the status bar also tells you which URL will open if you click it.

For those two reasons, it's a useful strip, but it doesn't appear when you first run Safari. You have to summon it by choosing View→Show Status Bar.

Reader

How can people read web articles when there's Times Square blinking going on all around them? The Reader button (☰) in the address/search bar is amazing. With one click (or press of Shift-⌘-R), it eliminates *everything* from the web page you're reading except the text and photos. No ads, blinking, links, banners, promos, or anything else.

The text also changes to a clean, clear font and size, and the background becomes plain white. Basically, it makes any web page look like a printed book page or a Kindle page, and it's glorious (Figure 19-17).

To exit Reader, press the same keyboard shortcut, or click ≡ again. Best. Feature. Ever.

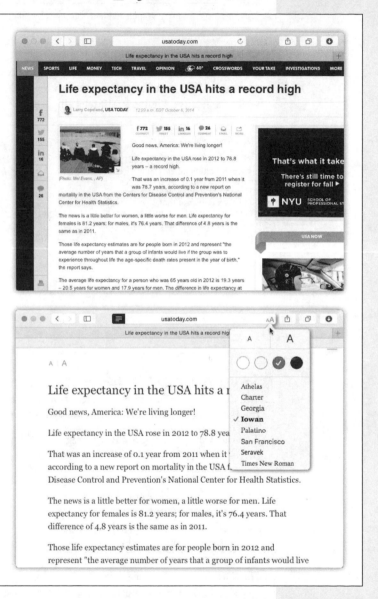

Figure 19-17:
Seriously, which way would you rather read an article? Like this (top)? Or in the calm peace of this (bottom)? Not only does Reader get rid of all the ads and clutter and blinking, it even knits multipage articles together into one seamless, scrolling page. Use the space bar or two fingers to scroll, as usual.

Using the ₐA button as a pop-up menu, you can change the typeface for your Reader view—or click one of the four circles to change the background color. Some people find that light text against a dark background is especially soothing.

Graphics Worth Saving

When you see a picture you'd like to keep, right-click or two-finger click it and choose Save Image to Downloads (or Add Image to Photos Library, or just Save Image As)

from the shortcut menu. Safari stores it as a new graphics file, freed from its birthplace on the web. (You can specify where Safari saves downloaded pictures on the Safari→ Preferences→General tab. In that case, the shortcut menu's wording changes to say, for example, "Save Image to 'Pictures.'")

Tip: You can also save a graphic to the desktop just by dragging it there, right out of the Safari window.

Expanding Web Forms

If the customer-service comment form on that corporate website doesn't give you enough room to rant properly, you can resize the text box right on the page—a *very* welcome feature. Figure 19-18 tells all.

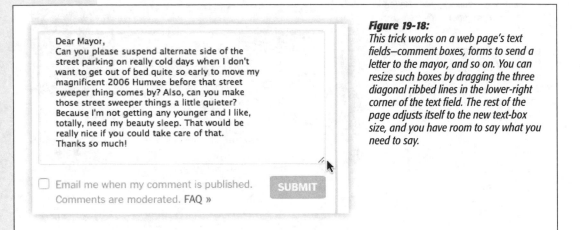

Figure 19-18:
This trick works on a web page's text fields—comment boxes, forms to send a letter to the mayor, and so on. You can resize such boxes by dragging the three diagonal ribbed lines in the lower-right corner of the text field. The rest of the page adjusts itself to the new text-box size, and you have room to say what you need to say.

Saving Web Pages to Disk

You don't have to be online to read a favorite web page; you can tuck it away for later, thanks to the Reading List feature described earlier in this chapter.

The old way of saving a page, though, is still around. You can save it to your hard drive—to archive it for good, or to send it to somebody, for example—by choosing File→Save As.

At that point, to save the *entire* page, along with all its images, movies, and so on, choose Web Archive from the Format pop-up menu. (Choose Page Source only if you intend to *edit* the raw HTML web documents and repost them, or if you just want to study the underlying code.)

Tip: When you buy something online, don't waste paper by printing out the "This is your receipt" page. Instead, just choose File→Print and, from the PDF pop-up button, choose Save PDF to Web Receipts Folder. Safari saves the page as a PDF file into a tidy folder (in your Home→Documents folder) called Web Receipts. Nice touch!

Sending a Page to a Friend

When you come across a particularly interesting news story, op-ed piece, or burrito recipe online, Safari is ready to help you tell a friend about it. While looking at a page, click ⬆ and choose Email This Page. Or, if you've installed the Mail button (✉) onto the toolbar, as described on page 726, click that instead. Once Safari has prepared your outgoing email message, you can add a comment if you want and then choose Reader (if it's available), Web Page, PDF, or Link Only to determine how your buddy will receive the page.

Note that *links* take only a split second for your recipient to download, and they're guaranteed to display properly in all email programs. All your recipients have to do is click the link to open it in their web browsers.

Tip: You can also just press ⌘-I. That keystroke sends a link to an outgoing email message.

By the way, here's a handy feature: At the *bottom* of the ⬆ menu, you see the names of people to whom you've recently sent web pages, and by which method. For example, you might see "Casey Robin, email" or "Kelly Swift, Messages." Those shortcuts make it incredibly easy to send more pages the same way, to the same people, again later.

Designate Your Start Page

What's the first thing you see when you open Safari? Is it the Apple news website? Is it the Top Sites display (Figure 19-6)? Actually, that's up to you.

Choose Safari→Preferences→General tab. Here the "New windows open with" pop-up menu offers choices like these:

- **Favorites.** Catalina's default Start page showing all your favorite sites (page 722) makes a great starting point.

- **Homepage.** If you choose this option, Safari will open up with whatever page you've specified in the "Homepage" box. Google—or its news page, *news.google.com*—is a good starting place. So is your favorite newspaper home page.

 If you're already *on* the page you like, just click Set to Current Page.

- **Empty Page.** Some people prefer this setup, which makes Safari load very quickly when you first open it. Once this empty window opens, *then* you can tell the browser where you want to go today.

- **Same Page** opens a new window that's a duplicate of whatever window you just had open.

Note: A nearly identical pop-up menu is available for "New tabs open with." That is, you can specify one starter-page preference for new *tabs* and another for new *windows*.

Finding Text on Web Pages

The address/search bar can help you find websites that match your keywords. But some pages are so long, dense, or poorly designed that finding the words *on* the page takes a whole 'nother search engine. Fortunately, Safari's search-within-the-page function shines a light on the word or phrase you're seeking.

To use it, press ⌘-F and then type your search word into the Find box (Figure 19-19). As Safari locates the word or words, it displays them within a bright highlight and dims the background of the rest of the page. The Find bar also tells you how many times the word or phrase occurs on the page; you can jump to each instance. Click the ⊗ to start over with new search terms, or click Done to close the Find box and return to your normal browsing activity.

Tip: When you use the Find command, are you looking for words on the page that *begin* with your search term, or that contain it *anywhere?* You can specify. Click the very tiny Q in the search box and choose either Contains or Starts With from the very tiny pop-up menu.

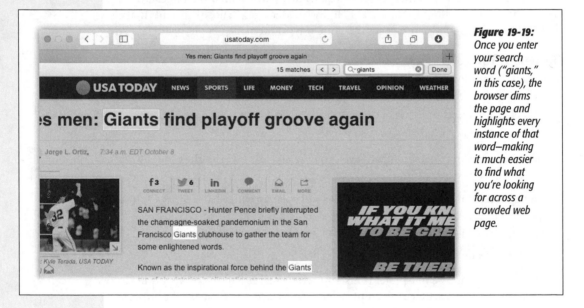

Figure 19-19:
Once you enter your search word ("giants," in this case), the browser dims the page and highlights every instance of that word—making it much easier to find what you're looking for across a crowded web page.

The History Menu

The History menu lists the websites you've visited in the past week or so, neatly organized into subfolders like Earlier Today and Yesterday. (A similar menu appears when you click *and hold* the 〈 or 〉 button.) These are great features if you can't recall the URL for a website you remember having visited recently.

Tip: See Safari's Help menu? It features a search box that lets you search all the menu commands in Safari—including Safari's History menu. That's just a *crazy* powerful feature. It means you can re-find a site without having to hunt through all the History submenus manually; just search for any word you remember from the title.

PDF Pages Online

PDF files are all over the web as, among other things, forms to download, online brochures, and scanned book pages. But they aren't always especially readable in a browser window.

Unless, that is, you're using Safari. The next time you're squinting at a PDF in a window, point to the bottom edge of the document; you'll see a toolbar like the one in Figure 19-20 appear. With these four icons, you can zoom out, zoom in, open the file in Preview, or save the PDF file to your Downloads folder.

Figure 19-20:
If you're having trouble reading the tiny type in a PDF, point your mouse to the bottom of it to invoke Safari's PDF toolbar. You can zoom out, zoom in, open the file in the Mac's Preview program, or even download it from the website with a well-placed click.

Picture-in-Picture Video

When you're watching a video, you can click a PIP icon (⧉) to detach it into a small, floating, movable window, so you can keep watching as you do other work. That floating mini-video window even hangs around when you switch Spaces (page 181).

Once it's on the screen, you can resize it (drag by the lower-right corner), move it to a different corner of the screen (drag the picture), pause it, or pop it full-screen (those buttons appear when you point to the video without clicking).

Alas, this feature doesn't work on every video you come across. It works only on videos that use HTML5, like those on Vimeo and ESPN. It does work on YouTube videos, but there's a trick to it (see Figure 19-21, bottom).

In Catalina, in fact, the Enter Picture-in-Picture command also appears in the tabbed window menu, too, as shown in the box on page 735.

Assessment: neat when it works—and if you can find the command.

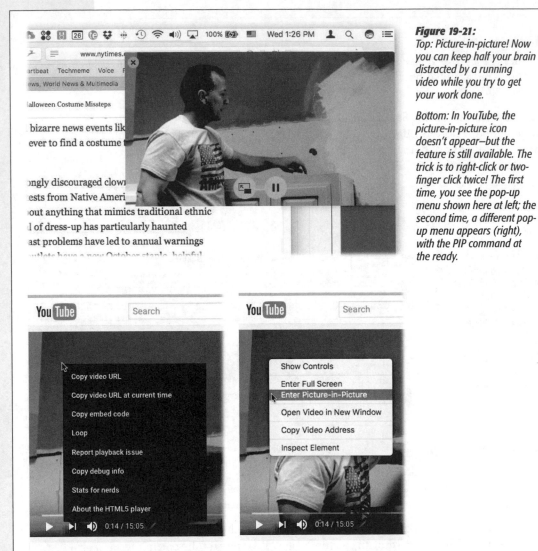

Figure 19-21:
Top: Picture-in-picture! Now you can keep half your brain distracted by a running video while you try to get your work done.

Bottom: In YouTube, the picture-in-picture icon doesn't appear—but the feature is still available. The trick is to right-click or two-finger click twice! The first time, you see the pop-up menu shown here at left; the second time, a different pop-up menu appears (right), with the PIP command at the ready.

Per-Website Settings

Here's one of the most useful features in Safari—and most people will probably never even know it's there.

Turns out you can now create different viewing settings for different sites. That is, each site can memorize your preferred page zoom, location services, notifications,

and ad blocker preferences. You might like *The New York Times* site to appear with larger text, *dilbert.com* to have ad blocking turned on, and so on.

To view your options, right-click or two-finger click in the address bar of the page you're on. A panel of options appears (Figure 19-22, right). You can choose to have this site open up in Reader view automatically (page 738); to turn on your ad blocker; to appear at a certain magnification size (Page Zoom); to prevent videos from auto-playing; from allowing the site access to your Mac's camera, microphone, or current location; and to block, permit, or ask your permission to use Adobe Flash, a famously unstable and battery-hungry plug-in.

Figure 19-22:
To view the settings Safari can store for each site (right), right-click or two-finger click in the address bar (left).

All of that is useful, but Auto-Play is *fantastic*. Its pop-up menu offers three options:

- **Allow All Auto-Play.** What you're used to: You open a web page, and some video starts blaring at you, unbidden.

- **Stop Media with Sound.** Videos can play automatically, but only if they have no soundtrack or if the sound starts out muted. (If it's muted, you're supposed to click the little speaker icon on the video controls to make it start playing.)

- **Never Auto-Play.** No videos will ever start playing automatically. That may be too strict for some sites—like when the site is *designed* for playing videos, like YouTube.

As you change these per-site settings, Safari thoughtfully logs them in Safari→Preferences→Websites, so that you can, at any time, change your mind about what you've done.

Privacy and Security Features

Every couple of months, there's another headline about some break-in where millions of credit card numbers are stolen by a hacker, sending panic into the hearts of the world's innocent web audiences. In macOS, Apple strikes back with some very clever privacy and security features indeed.

Erasing Your History

Some people find it creepy that Safari maintains a complete list of every website they've seen recently, right there in plain view of any co-worker who wanders by.

To delete just one particularly incriminating History listing, choose History→Show All History. In the resulting organizer window, highlight the offending address, and then press your Delete key. Choose History→Hide History to return to normal browsing. You've just rewritten History!

Or, to erase the entire History menu, choose History→Clear History. In the resulting box, you can specify that you want to erase only the *last hour's* worth of history, only *today's* history, the last *two days'* worth—or your *entire* history.

Of course, the History list isn't the only set of footprints you leave as you surf. But the Clear History command erases all other shreds of your activities: any cookies (web page preference files) you've accumulated, your list of past downloads, the cache files (bits of the web pages that a browser stores on your hard drive to save time when you return to the page they came from), and so on. This is good information to know; you might be nominated to the Supreme Court someday.

Private Browsing

Of course, that's a lot of work just to cover your tracks; it also erases a lot of valuable cookies, passwords, and History entries you'd probably like to keep. Is all that really necessary just so you can duck in for an occasional look at the Hot Bods of the Midwestern Tax Preparers' Association website?

No, it's not. *Private browsing* lets you surf without adding any pages to your History list, searches to your Google search suggestions, passwords to Safari's saved password list, or autofill entries to Safari's memory. (Apple says this feature is intended for use at public Macs, where you don't want to reveal anything personal to subsequent visitors. Ha!)

The trick is to choose File→New Private Window *before* you open the naughty site. (Your other Safari windows can stay open, in non-private mode.) A banner across the top of your new private window explains what's happening: Within this window, Safari records nothing while you surf. When you're ready to browse "publicly" again, just close the window.

In other words, what happens in Private Browsing stays in Private Browsing.

Cookie Control—and Privacy Control

Cookies are something like web page preference files. Certain websites—particularly commercial ones like *amazon.com*—deposit them on your hard drive like little bookmarks so they'll remember you the next time you visit.

Most cookies are perfectly innocuous—and, in fact, helpful, because they let websites remember your tastes, your name, and so on. But fear is widespread, and the media fan the flames with tales of sinister cookies that track your movements on the web.

To take some control, choose Safari→Preferences→Privacy tab (Figure 19-23), where your cookie preference settings await. "Block all cookies" means no cookies can come in, and no cookie information can go out. You'll have to reenter your information upon every visit to every web page.

Figure 19-23:
Cookies: the web's mysterious double-edged sword. Here you can specify whether or not you like them, although blocking all of them makes the web a pretty miserable experience.

If you don't use that checkbox, then Safari works as though you had the old "Only from websites I visit" option turned on. That is, you get cookies from sites you want to open, but not cookies deposited on your hard drive by sites you're *not* actually visiting—cookies that an especially evil banner ad gives you, for example.

The Manage Website Data button here reveals the complete list of all your cookies, and you can delete any scary ones. While you're in there, notice that there's other stuff websites have dumped onto your Mac. There are things like cache files and local storage files (data that web applications leave behind on your hard drive—a bit like cookies, except that websites can't retrieve this information later). All of it is available for your removal with a click on the Remove All button.

Also while you're in this box: "Prevent cross-site tracking" doesn't affect how many ads you see—but it does prevent advertisers from delivering ads *based on your interests* (as exhibited by your other web surfing). You'll just get less-targeted ads.

"Ask websites not to track me" signs you up for an online "Do not track" program. The problem is that this program is voluntary—so the sleazy operators just ignore it.

Finally, "Allow websites to check if Apple Pay is set up" appears only if your Mac has a Touch ID fingerprint reader, or if you have an iPhone or Apple Watch that works with Apple Pay. It permits shopping sites to show the Pay with Apple Pay button on product detail pages only if you do, in fact, have Apple Pay set up.

Stifle Pop-Ups and Pop-Unders

The world's smarmiest advertisers inundate us with *pop-up* and *pop-under* ads—nasty little windows that appear in front of the browser window or, worse, behind it, waiting to jump out the moment you close your current window.

If this kind of thing is driving you crazy, choose Safari→Preferences→Security→Block Pop-Up Windows. It's a war out there—but at least you now have some ammunition.

Tip: This feature doesn't block windows that appear when you *click a link*—only those that appear unbidden.

Messages

S omewhere between email and the telephone lies the joyous communication tool
called instant messaging. Plenty of IM programs run on the Mac, but macOS
comes with its very own instant messenger program called Messages. (It used to
be called iChat.) It's built right into the system and ready to connect to your friends
on Apple's iCloud network.

Note: At one time, the Messages app could handle chats on a bunch of different chat networks: AIM, Yahoo,
Facebook, Jabber, Gtalk, and so on. In macOS Catalina, though, Messages is primarily a gateway to Apple's
own chat network, called iMessages. It requires that both you and your chat partner have iCloud accounts
(Chapter 17). (The one exception: It can also show you regular text messages from your iPhone.)

This chapter covers how to use Messages to communicate by video, audio, and text
with your online pals.

Welcome to Messages

Messages does seven things very well:

- **Instant messaging.** Instant messaging combines the privacy of email and the
immediacy of the phone. You type messages in a chat window, and your friends
type back to you in real time.

 You can *keep* your text messages, too. They're not locked onto your phone, like
 regular text messages, and they don't scroll away forever, like regular text messages.
 You can archive them, search them, copy and paste them, print them, forward
 them, and so on.

- **Unified chat/text messages with phones (iMessages).** This is huge. If you and your conversation partner both have iCloud accounts, then you both can move freely from phone to tablet to Mac. Your conversation appears in real time on all your gadgets simultaneously. If you started texting someone on the train home, you can sit down at your Mac and open Messages—and pick up right where you left off.

 The messages, which Apple calls iMessages, are a lot more flexible than regular text messages. They can be much longer than 160 characters. They can include photos, movies, or other kinds of files. They give you feedback that lets you know when a message has arrived on the recipient's gadget.

 And they don't count as text messages. They're routed through the internet rather than the cellphone voice network. As far as your cellphone company is concerned, you're not texting at all, and therefore you don't have to pay for a texting plan.

- **Send text messages.** If you have an iPhone, you can also exchange text messages with *any* cellphone—from Messages, while seated at your *Mac*. That's a mind-bending violation of the usual rules that confine text messages to cellphones only.

- **Send audio clips.** Instead of just typing a line or two to somebody, you can speak it. That short recording winds up on the other person's Mac, iPhone, or iPad. It's like leaving a voicemail.

- **Free videoconferencing.** Messages can auto-open FaceTime, for those situations when having a face-to-face video chat (or a high-quality voice call) is more efficient than typing.

- **File transfers.** Got an album of high-quality photos or a giant presentation file that's too big to send by email? Forget about using some online file-transfer service or networked server; you can drag that monster file directly to your buddy's Mac, through Messages, for a direct machine-to-machine transfer. (It lands in the other Mac's Downloads folder.)

- **Screen sharing.** Next time your parents or neighbors are throwing themselves upon your mercy for tech support, remember this: Messages lets you see their screen, and even control it, from across the internet. Or you can volunteer your own screen for sharing, so you can demonstrate things to them.

When you open Messages for the first time, you're invited to sign into (or sign up for) your iCloud or Apple account. Take the opportunity to set this up; you'll be glad you did. (You may have to *authenticate* your account—prove it's really you—by entering a six-digit code that Apple sends to all the other gadgets on your Apple account, like your iPhone.)

Let the Chat Begin

If you've ever corresponded with someone in Messages before, you see that person's name in the left-side list of conversations, as shown in Figure 20-1. (Or, if you've got

a *lot* of conversations listed there, you can use the search box above the list to find that person.) Click the name and then start typing into the message box. The "conversation" with that person continues, even if the last exchange was months or years ago.

To start chatting with someone you've never corresponded with before, click the Compose button (🖉) next to the search box. The To field appears. As you type your buddy's name into it, Messages sprouts a list of matching names from your Contacts.

Some of them probably feature a blue speech bubble (💬). Those are people with iCloud accounts—with whom you can exchange iMessages, described next.

Note: An iMessage address can be either an email address or a phone number. Most people register both of those data bits as part of their iMessage setup, so that any message you send arrives on all your correspondent's Apple gadgets at once.

You can also click the ⊕ to get a pop-up version of your Contacts, complete with a search bar at the top.

Once you've selected your lucky conversation partner(s), just type what you want to say into the message box at the bottom of the window. As you correspond, the conversation appears in speech bubbles, scrolling up like a screenplay, making it easy to identify who said what—and to scroll back up to see what someone said earlier. (See Figure 20-1.)

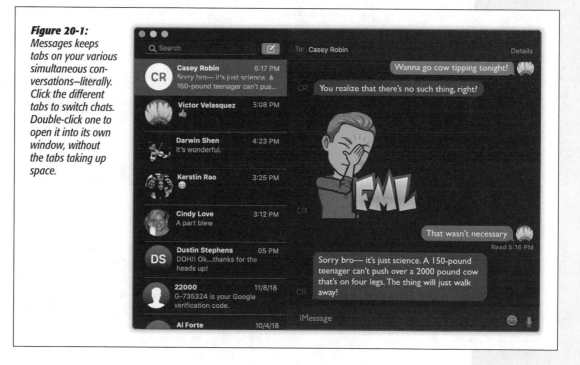

Figure 20-1:
Messages keeps tabs on your various simultaneous conversations–literally. Click the different tabs to switch chats. Double-click one to open it into its own window, without the tabs taking up space.

If someone invites *you* to chat, a notification appears in the top-right corner of your screen. If you point to it in time, you get a Reply button; see Figure 20-2.

If you click the notification instead, Messages opens automatically; click in the message box at the bottom and type your witty reply.

Figure 20-2:
When someone messages you, a bubble like this appears in the top-right corner of your screen. If you point to it before it vanishes, the Reply button appears, as shown here.

If you click it, you can type a quick response right there in the notification window (bottom), without having to fire up Messages at all.

iMessages

If the box where you type says "iMessage" in faint lettering, then you're about to chat with a fellow iCloud member—and you'll be sending iMessages. (Another clue: Your speech bubbles appear in blue, rather than green.) And you'll enjoy a long list of extra benefits as you chat (as compared with, for example, standard cellphone text messages).

For example:

- **Fancier, longer posts.** You can type outrageously long messages (unlike standard text messages, which are limited to 160 characters). And iMessages are unlimited and free.

- **Dressier chats.** You can use fonts and colors in your conversation.

- **Multigadget simulcasting.** If you have multiple Apple gadgets, and you've set up your iMessages email address or phone number identically in the Settings or System Preferences of each one, then your conversation appears simultaneously on all the gadgets. ("Simultaneously," however, is relative. If one of your devices has been offline for some time while you've been chatting on the other, it may take a few minutes to catch up. You'll see all the iMessages it missed pouring in.)

That's extremely useful, because it means you can (for example) start texting on your phone when you're out and about and pick up seamlessly on your Mac when you get home, enjoying the real keyboard and big screen.

- **Link previews.** When you send a web address in an iMessage, it appears on the recipient's screen as a little preview of the actual web page, for convenient identification. And if you send a video link, your buddy can play it right there in Messages, without having to lurch off to a web browser! (Click once to make the tiny video start playing; click a second time to make it stop. There's no scroll bar.)

Tip: And what if you *want* to lurch off to a web browser—for example, because you want to see that YouTube video bigger? In that case, click the label *beneath* the video thumbnail.

GEM IN THE ROUGH

Messages in iCloud

For years, it was a real hassle of Messages: You'd pick up one Apple gadget after doing a lot of texting on another—for example, switching to your iPhone after doing a lot of texting on your Mac during a flight. Then you'd have to wait a very long time for your phone's copy of Messages to catch up—to download all the conversations you had on your Mac.

In 2017, Apple introduced an optional feature that neatly solves that problem: Your message history would be saved online, in iCloud.

If you choose to turn on this feature, here's what you get:

Your text messages and iMessages (and all associated photos, videos, and attachments) are now stored online instead of on your iPhone, iPad, and Mac. Which means you save several gigabytes, or *many* gigabytes, of storage on every single device. That's storage that was duplicated on every machine—the same database stored in multiple places.

Your Mac, iPhone, and iPad backups are much smaller, because they no longer include your Messages database.

All your messages are synced. Delete a message or a conversation, and it's also deleted on all your other machines.

No more waiting for one device to "catch up." That should sound like a pleasant development to anyone who, for example, uses Messages on the MacBook on a plane ride—and then upon landing can't use Messages on the phone for 10 minutes because it's still syncing.

If you get a new Apple device, your entire history of text messages and attachments appears on it. (Without Messages in iCloud, your current and future messages appear, but you can't scroll to see past ones—at least not without restoring from a backup.)

There's one big downside of Messages in iCloud: Moving your database into your iCloud account online eats up space *there.* You're saving tons of space on all your Apple machines, but losing space on your iCloud account online—and that may cost you money (page 657).

If you decide it's worth doing, here's how to set it up.

First, you have to have two-factor authentication turned on, for security (page 508). Second, on each device, turn on Messages in iCloud:

On an iPhone or iPad, open Settings. Tap your name at the top, tap iCloud, and then turn on Messages.

On the Mac, open Messages→Preferences→iMessage, and turn on Enable Messages in iCloud.

It takes a few minutes for your devices to offload your entire Messages history; the phone/tablet must be plugged into power and on Wi-Fi before the process can begin.

Once that's done, you'll be treated to a technical but handy upgrade to your texting world.

- **Built-in suspense.** Whenever the other guy is typing, you see "..." in his balloon, so you know he's working on a response and not just ignoring you.

Tip: The ellipsis dots appear as soon as the other guy starts typing—and remain on your screen for 60 seconds, even if he *stopped* typing a long time ago. Conversely, they *disappear* from your screen after 60 seconds, even if he's still typing! Often you'll see the dots disappear shortly before you get a huge, long paragraph—because the other guy took longer than 60 seconds to write it.

- **Insta-file sending.** You can drag photos, movies, or other files (up to 100 megabytes!) into the typing box. They'll show up on the other guy's Mac, phone, or tablet just fine.

- **Easy switching to phone or video.** If you find that typing is losing too much emotional nuance, and you are signed into FaceTime on your Mac, you can jump into a voice call or video call at any point. For voice calls, you can choose either a FaceTime Audio call or a phone call; for video, the FaceTime app opens, and you can proceed as described on page 410.

 To jump into a voice call, click Details (top right); on the panel, click 📞; click FaceTime Audio. (Or, if you have an iPhone, you can click the person's phone number and make an actual phone call.) Once your invitation is accepted, you can begin speaking to each other. The bars of the sound-level meter let you know that the microphone is working.

 To switch to a video call, click Details at the upper right of the Messages window, and then click 🎥. A FaceTime call begins right away.

- **Tapbacks.** How many trillions of times a day do people respond to texts with repetitive reactions like "LOL" and "Awww" and "!!!!!"? Many. It's how you demonstrate to your chat partner that you appreciate the import of her text.

 But if you and your buddy are both using iOS 10 or macOS Sierra or later, you've now got a quicker, less cluttery, more visual way to indicate those sorts of standard

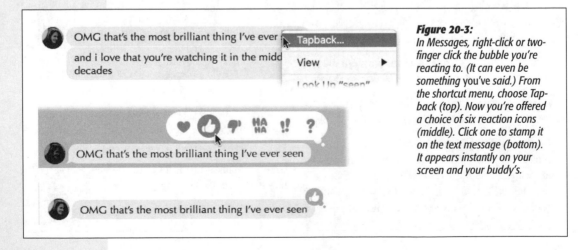

Figure 20-3:
In Messages, right-click or two-finger click the bubble you're reacting to. (It can even be something you've said.) From the shortcut menu, choose Tapback (top). Now you're offered a choice of six reaction icons (middle). Click one to stamp it on the text message (bottom). It appears instantly on your screen and your buddy's.

emotional reactions: what Apple calls tapbacks. Figure 20-3 shows you the ropes. Tapbacks take the form of six reaction icons: Heart, Thumbs Up, Thumbs Down, Ha Ha, Exclamation Points, and Question Mark. When you choose one, it appears instantly on your screen and your buddy's.

Tip: What's cool is that you can change your tapback icon later, if new information affects your reaction; just right-click or two-finger click again, and choose Tapback again, to bring up the same palette.

- **Incoming fanciness.** Messages on the Mac doesn't let you express yourself in all the ways Messages on an iPhone does. But it can *receive* some of the cool effects that your iOS friends send you, like handwriting, invisible ink, and stickers; see Figure 20-4.

Figure 20-4:
Among the cool Messages effects (from top): invisible ink (text that doesn't appear until you move your mouse across it—useful when the sender doesn't want to embarrass you), handwriting, and stickers (still or animated images your pal has dragged onto a message). You can't create these effects on the Mac, but you can receive them when they're sent by iPhones and iPads.

- **Big, plentiful emoji.** You can use the emoji pop-up menu (at the right end of the typing box) to insert emoticons and smileys.

 If you know the correct codes to produce the emoji you want—typing :) produces a yellow happy face, for example, and <3 produces a red heart—you can save time by typing them instead of using the pop-up menu. Messages converts them into smiley or heart icons on the fly, as soon as you send your reply.

 The emoji you transmit appear enormous—at three times their usual size—if you've typed three of them or fewer on a single line. (If, that is, your recipient is using an Apple device running iOS 10 or Sierra or later versions.)

Tip: If you have a Touch Bar (page 227), you'll find it much easier to enter emoji by tapping. Touch the ☺ button to see a row of frequently used emoji, any of which you can insert by tapping. Or you can tap the ☺ button to see a row of icons representing the other *categories* of emoji available to your fingertip.

- **Real-time feedback.** The tiny word "Delivered" appears beneath any message you send to let you know that your recipient's gadget has received it. If the recipient has

turned on "Send read receipts" (in Messages→Preferences→iMessage), you'll even see the word "Read" to let you know that the person has actually *seen* the message.

Tip: What about you? Do you want the other guy to know when you've seen his texts? You can turn "Send read receipts" on or off in Preferences, of course. But you can also turn it on or off for an *individual buddy*. You might want your primary love interests to know when you've seen their texts, for example, but you might not think your co-workers need to know.

Within a chat, click Details at the top right. And there it is: a Send Read Receipts checkbox for just this conversation partner (visible in Figure 20-5).

- **Individual attachments.** This one's really cool; see Figure 20-5.

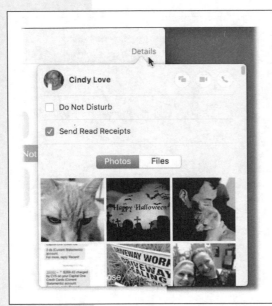

Figure 20-5:
If you click the Details button at the top right of the window, you get to see a mosaic of every attachment you've ever exchanged with this correspondent—files, photos, videos, whatever. Double-click one to open it. No more scrolling back through thousands of pages of typed text to find something you remember getting!

This Details panel also gets you access to buttons that begin screen sharing, video chatting, or phone calling with this lucky individual.

- **Type size.** Use the commands in the View menu to make all type larger or smaller—or just press ⌘-plus or ⌘-minus.

- **Sound clips.** A special 🎤 button appears whenever you're exchanging iMessages, just to the right of the typing box. It lets you quickly shoot over an audio bite as easily as you'd type something.

Just click the 🎤, say what you want to say, and then click the square Stop button. Now you can Cancel it or Send it.

What you said is instantly transmitted to your buddy as an audio recording.

If the recipient has an iPhone with iOS 8 or later, he can listen just by lifting the phone to his head. And then, get this: To reply, he doesn't have to touch anything or look at the screen. He just holds the phone to his head again and speaks! Once he lowers the phone, his recording shoots back to you.

Sometimes, an audio recording is just better than a typed message, especially when music, children, animals, or a lot of emotion in your voice are involved.

Tip: Audio eats up a lot more space than text. If you do a lot of audio messaging, then, over time, those audio snippets can fill up your storage. That's why Messages comes set to delete each audio message two minutes after you send it—unless you click Keep within that window of time.

- **Location mapping.** If you're chatting with an iPhone owner, that same Details panel might reveal a map that shows her current location in the world. (The map appears only if she's turned on "Share my location" on her phone.)

Messages blurs the lines between text messages, chats, and email. And it gives birth to this frequently asked question: "Are you on the phone or the Mac?" Now there's no way to know.

Group Chats

There's nothing to stop you from inviting several people to a single chat. Just click the Compose button (✐) as usual. Enter the desired chat partners' names one at a time in the To field, pressing Return or adding a space after each one.

Tip: If you've created a group in Contacts, you can also just enter the group's name. Everybody in it is instantly part of the chat.

Now you've got yourself a party line. Anything anyone types, everybody sees. Be careful what you say, won't you?

Many of the group-chat features are hiding in the panel that appears when you click Details at top right (Figure 20-6).

Figure 20-6:
If you click where it says "Add a group name," you can type a new name. That should make it easier to identify this conversation later in the list of chats at the left side of the window. (The Details button doesn't appear until somebody has actually said something in this chat.)

You can also add participants, even after the group chat is underway; click Add Member.

Do Not Disturb means new texts from this group won't trigger notifications on your Mac. And if the bickering becomes more than you can stand, you can excuse yourself and leave the chat by clicking "Leave this Conversation."

Audio and Video Chats

Messages no longer has audio-chat and video-chat features; that's the FaceTime app's job! Messages does, however, make it simple to jump from a typed chat directly into an audio or video call in FaceTime—involving as many as 32 people (see page 411).

If you're in a text chat, you can jump into audio or video in either of these ways:

- **Choose Buddies→FaceTime Audio** (or FaceTime Video).

- **Click Details**; on the panel, click either ☎ or ☐◁. (If you're making a voice call, a pop-up menu offers you either a FaceTime Audio call [page 413] or a regular speakerphone call through your iPhone [page 304].)

The call begins, courtesy of the FaceTime app, which opens automatically. (Unless you're making a cellular voice call, as noted above.)

Sharing Your Screen

As you've seen already, Messages lets you share your thoughts, your voice, and your image. And now, for its next trick, it lets you share…your computer.

Messages' screen-sharing feature is a close relative of the *network* screen-sharing feature described on page 550. It lets you not only *see* what's on a faraway buddy's screen, but also control it, taking command of the distant mouse and keyboard. (You can share your screen with the other guy, too.)

You can open folders, create and edit documents, and copy files on the shared Mac screen. Sharing a screen makes collaborating as easy as working side by side around the same Mac, except now you can be sitting in San Francisco while your buddy is banging it out in Boston.

And if you're the family tech-support specialist—but the family lives all over the country—screen sharing makes troubleshooting infinitely easier. You can now jump on your mom's shared Mac and figure out why the formatting went wacky in her Word

UP TO SPEED

The Chat Transcript

When you close a chat by clicking the ✕ in its tab, the conversation is gone forever. *Unless*, that is, you've opened Messages→Preferences→General and turned on "Save history when conversations are closed."

In that case, Messages autosaves the text of your conversations. Even if you close one, you can retrieve its contents by starting another chat with the same person; the history reappears.

Behind the scenes, your transcripts are saved in your Library→Messages→Archives folder. (To get to your Library folder, press Option as you choose Go→Library in the Finder.)

If you do have "Save history" turned on, and you wind up having a particularly incriminating chat, you can tell Messages *not* to save its transcript by pressing ⌘-Delete. Messages asks if you're sure. If so, that prose is hosed.

document, without her having to attempt to *explain* it to you over the phone. ("And then the little thingy disappeared and the doohickey got scrambled…")

Tip: Once you're controlling someone else's screen remotely, your keyboard shortcuts operate his Mac instead of yours. Press ⌘-Tab to bring up the application switcher, hit ⌘-Q to quit a program, use all the Mission Control and Spotlight shortcuts, and so on.

To make Messages' screen sharing work, you and your buddy must both be using an iCloud account, or be on the same Wi-Fi network (the Mac's Bonjour feature will make your Macs show up on each other's screens).

iCloud Screen Sharing

From within an iMessages conversation (that is, a chat between two iCloud members), you can share your whole Mac screen, right there in Messages. Both people have to be using Macs running Yosemite or later (not an iPhone, and not an older Mac).

There are other ways to share screens, of course (page 550)—but this is by far the easiest to set up.

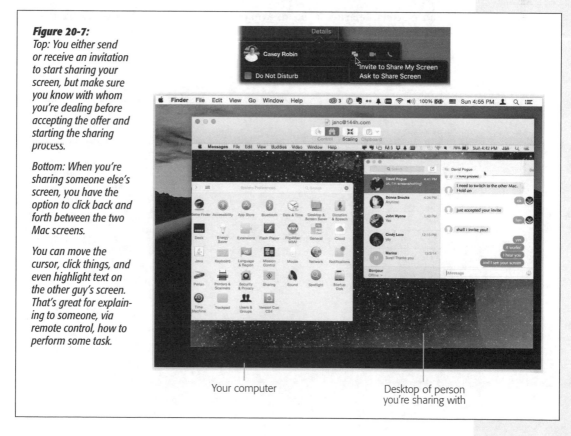

Figure 20-7:
Top: You either send or receive an invitation to start sharing your screen, but make sure you know with whom you're dealing before accepting the offer and starting the sharing process.

Bottom: When you're sharing someone else's screen, you have the option to click back and forth between the two Mac screens.

You can move the cursor, click things, and even highlight text on the other guy's screen. That's great for explaining to someone, via remote control, how to perform some task.

Your computer

Desktop of person
you're sharing with

Once a typed chat is underway, click Details (top right), and then click ⎘ (see Figure 20-7, top). If that icon is dimmed gray instead of blue, it's because the other person isn't using a Yosemite-or-later Mac.

The icon sprouts two choices: Invite to Share My Screen (meaning the other guy sees *your* screen) and Ask to Share Screen (you're going to see *his* screen). Click the one you want.

He receives an invitation. When he clicks Accept, the sharing is underway. He sees your screen on his Mac, or vice versa, as though some freaky cosmic wormhole has opened up.

Once the screen sharing is going, a new ⎘ menu appears at the top of your screen. It offers options like these:

- **Allow [other guy] to control my screen.** He can operate your mouse and keyboard—from his Mac, thousands of miles away.

- **Mute Audio.** During a screen share, Messages automatically turns on audio chatting, so you can explain stuff to each other. Mute Audio mutes the audio.

- **Pause Screen Sharing** is like drawing a privacy curtain when you want to duck into your email program to read something. The other guy sees only a "Paused" screen until you unpause.

- **End Screen Sharing.** You guessed it.

6

Part Six:
Appendixes

Installing macOS Catalina

If your computer came with macOS Catalina already installed, you can skip this appendix—at least for now. But if you're running an earlier version of the Mac operating system, this appendix is for you. It describes how to install the new OS on your Mac.

If you're new in these parts, you may be in for a shock: You can't buy macOS on a DVD. You download it from the Mac App Store.

There are some attractive elements to that system. For example, there's no copy protection and no serial numbers to type in. There's no cost to Apple for manufacturing or shipping, which may explain why Catalina isn't even $20 or $30—it's free.

There's no disc to hunt down when you want to install macOS again (onto a new Mac, for example). And when you do need a copy again, you'll download the latest version—10.15.3 or whatever it is—instead of having to install whatever updates have come out since you got your DVD.

(And what if you don't have a fast internet connection for downloading macOS? The world won't come to an end; read on.)

Hardware Requirements

For starters, you need to make sure you and your Mac have what it takes to handle Catalina. It has the same requirements as the previous version, Mojave:

- **A Mac that's not a geezer.** Catalina can run on any Mac laptop, iMac, or Mac Mini made since mid-2012, and any Mac Pro made since mid-2013.

- **Free storage space.** You need at least 12.5 GB free on your Mac if you're upgrading from El Capitan, Sierra, High Sierra, or Mojave; you need 18.5 GB or more if you have something older. More space, of course, is better.

- **A lot of memory.** Apple recommends at least 4 GB of memory, but macOS absolutely *loves* memory. For the greatest speed, install 8 gigabytes—more if you can afford it. (And these days, you probably can.)

- **A full backup.** It's a really, *really* good idea to back up your entire Mac before you begin this (or any) upgrade. Even if things go wrong for only, say, 0.01 percent of Mac owners, that's still thousands of people. If you don't have a second hard drive, this is your excuse to buy one; they're dirt cheap these days. You can use Time Machine (page 260) in your current version of macOS to make a complete, automatic backup of your Mac as it is now.

The Standard Installation

You may not have to do anything to get going with Catalina. You'll get a notification letting you know it's available, or you'll open System Preferences→Software Update and click Upgrade Now (Figure A-1).

Figure A-1:
Click More Info to read about all the wonders of Catalina. Or click Upgrade Now to begin the download, which takes maybe 20 minutes over a typical broadband connection.

POWER USERS' CLINIC

The Partitioning Question

Before you install Catalina, you might want to confront the issue of *partitioning* your Mac's hard drive—dividing its space so it shows up on your desktop with two different icons and two different names. You can keep Catalina on one and Mojave on the other, for example—and thereby keep all those older 32-bit programs and video files alive (page 163).

Now you can live like a king, enjoying all the advantages of having two hard drives.

The Mac even comes with a partitioning program: Disk Utility (page 469). And it doesn't require first erasing the drive completely; you can repartition on the fly, without disturbing whatever is already on the drive.

You can also open the App Store program on your Mac. If you don't see "macOS Catalina" advertised right there on the home page, you can find it by searching for *Catalina*. Click Get, and then click again when it changes to say Download.

Tip: If you don't have a fast internet connection, or if your internet provider imposes monthly data limits, you might not be thrilled about the prospect of waiting for an 8-gigabyte download.

Your best bet is to take your Mac to an Apple Store and use *its* free, fast Wi-Fi to download Catalina. (Or go to a friend's house, a library, a coffee shop…)

When the download begins, behind the scenes, the App Store puts a program called Install macOS Catalina into your Applications folder and onto your Launchpad, if you have it.

Tip: At this moment, you can duck out of the installer to make a safety copy of it, so you won't have to download it again the next time. See the box on the next page.

You'll know when the downloading is over, because the installer opens up automatically.

The procedure from here:

1. **Click Continue.**

 The installer begins its work (see Figure A-2). It will follow a pattern: Read the instructions, make a couple of choices, and then click Continue. As you go, a list on the left side of the screen reveals where you are in the overall procedure.

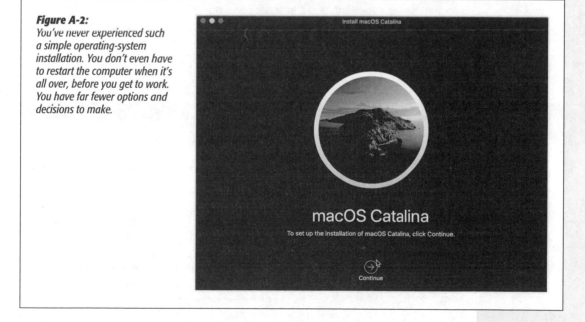

Figure A-2:
You've never experienced such a simple operating-system installation. You don't even have to restart the computer when it's all over, before you get to work. You have far fewer options and decisions to make.

2. **Click Agree to pass the License Agreement screen, and then click Agree again.**

 The license agreement requires you to agree with whatever Apple's lawyers say.

3. **Choose the disk or partition where you want to install macOS.**

 The installer proposes the obvious hard drive: the main one inside your Mac.

 If you have other drives, you can click Show All Disks to see their icons and choose one. Yellow exclamation-mark icons mean "You can't install here," for one technical reason or another. You can install Catalina only onto a blank hard drive, formatted as a Mac drive, or onto a drive that has Mavericks or later on it.

Note: If your Mac has a solid-state drive (SSD), it gets automatically formatted with the Apple File System (page 471). If you have a traditional hard drive, though, or if you're setting up an external drive, you're offered a choice of several formats for it. But you should stick with the factory setting, "Mac OS Extended (Journaled)." It turns on a background feature of macOS known as *file journaling*, which offers two benefits: a shorter startup time and better file safety in the event of a crash.

4. **Click Install. Enter an administrator's account name and password (page 488) when you're asked for it.**

 Now you're in for a 15- to 20-minute wait as the installer copies software onto your hard drive. (That's why, if you're using a laptop, the Mac will encourage you to plug it in.) At one point, the installer might ask you to hit Restart—and, if you don't respond, will just restart the Mac by itself and carry on.

MacOS 10.15 is now installed on your Mac. That, if you hadn't noticed, was a far less harrowing experience than in some previous operating system installations. You were never asked what kind of installation you wanted, which language translations or printer drivers you wanted installed, which optional components you wanted, and so on.

Still, you're not quite ready to dive in yet. Read on.

POWER USERS' CLINIC

Reinstalling: Tricks of the Trade

You can install macOS on as many Macs as you own. To install it on a second Mac, for example, open the App Store, find Catalina, and download it again.

That's what most people will do, anyway. Unfortunately, downloading the 8-gigabyte installer again and again takes a lot of time and eats up a lot of your monthly data allotment.

There is, fortunately, a trick that saves you the trouble of re-downloading Catalina over and over again: Copy the

Install macOS Catalina installer program from the *first* Mac to all your other Macs (over the network or on a flash drive, for example).

There's a tricky part to this trick: Ordinarily, installing Catalina on the first Mac *deletes* the installer program once it's finished, to save you the disk space. The trick to this trick, then, is to copy the installer to another Mac or drive (or at least to take it out of your Applications folder) *before* you install Catalina on the first Mac.

The Setup Assistant

What you see after installation depends on whether you installed Catalina onto an older macOS drive or an empty drive. Either way, it's called the Setup Assistant, and it's meant to interview you about which features you'd like turned on.

After Installing over an Older Version

If you installed onto a drive that already had Mac stuff on it—accounts, files, settings, and so on—then all you have to do is log in as usual.

You're asked for your iCloud name and password, or you can sign up for one now. If you have two-factor authentication turned on (page 508), you'll have to prove your worthiness by typing in a code Apple sends to your other Apple gadgets.

Next, you may be invited to share the data your Mac stores when it crashes with the programmers who are responsible, so they can fix it. Approve or deny.

Then, on the Choose Your Look screen, comes the big question: Do you want to turn on Dark mode? (See page 152).

You may also be invited to turn on standard Mac features like Screen Time (page 216), the True Tone display (page 340), and Siri (page 283).

Finally, you arrive at the desktop, where Apple invites you to explore the App Store. Welcome to Catalina!

After Installing onto a Blank Drive

If you installed Catalina onto an empty drive, the Setup Assistant is a little more involved.

Once again, you're in for a click-through-the-screens experience, this time with the aim of setting up your Mac's various options. After answering the questions on each screen, click Continue. The number of information screens you encounter may vary (see Figure A-3), but here are some of the possibilities:

- **Welcome.** Click the name of the country you're in.

- **Select Your Keyboard.** Different countries require different keyboard layouts. For example, if you choose the Canadian layout, pressing the] key on a U.S. keyboard produces the ç symbol. Click Continue.

- **Select Your Wi-Fi Network.** This is your chance to introduce the Mac to any networks in the vicinity. Click the name of the Wi-Fi hotspot you want to join, for example. If there's no wireless hotspot at all—hey, it could happen—then click Different Network Setup to specify, say, a wired or cellular network hookup.

- **Data & Privacy.** A declaration about how seriously Apple takes your data privacy, with a link to an even longer declaration about it.

• **Transfer Information to This Mac.** The Setup Assistant can suck all your old programs, files, folders, and settings from your old Mac to the new one—or even from an old *Windows PC* to your new Mac. This is the Migration Assistant.

Your choices here are From Another Mac (connect your old Mac to this one over a network, even a wireless one), From a Windows PC (ditto), From Time Machine or other disk (connect your new Mac to your backup drive), and Don't Transfer now.

Tip: You can always perform this sluggish task later. Just open the Migration Assistant program, in your Applications→Utilities folder, when it's a better time. See the box on the facing page for more on migrating from Windows.

If you choose one of the first options and then click Transfer, the data-copying process begins. It can take a *wicked* long time.

• **Sign In with Your Apple ID.** Here you're offered the chance to type in an Apple ID (an email address and password for all your Apple dealings), which is more essential in Catalina than ever before. If you don't have one, just click Continue; you can get one and fill it in later.

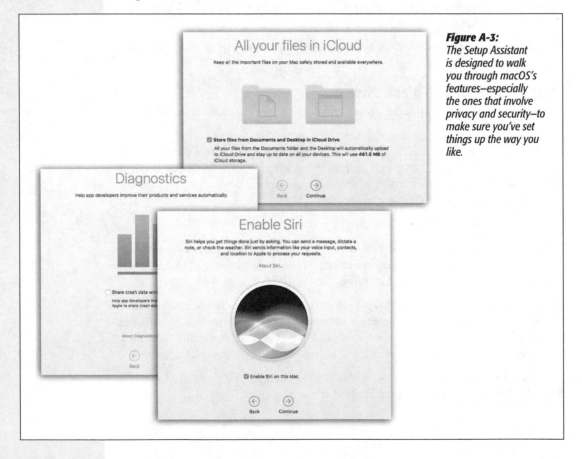

Figure A-3:
The Setup Assistant is designed to walk you through macOS's features—especially the ones that involve privacy and security—to make sure you've set things up the way you like.

Note: You'll be asked to enter a six-digit code sent to your phone. That's part of Apple's two-factor authentication process, as described on page 508.

- **Terms and Conditions.** Hello, Apple lawyers!

- **Create a Computer Account.** You're about to create your *account*—your Administrator account, in fact, as described on page 488.

 This is also where you can choose an account picture for yourself. Click the round starter icon, and then choose Defaults (an assortment of Apple-supplied images) or Camera (to take a photo of yourself to use as your account icon).

 Along the way, don't miss "Allow my Apple ID to reset this password." It's a useful bit of insurance in case you ever forget your Mac's password.

GEM IN THE ROUGH

Windows Migration

If, on the Transfer Information screen of the Setup Assistant, you choose From a Windows PC, you're treated to an unsung hero in macOS: the Migration Assistant. It's an automatic tool that copies all your important data from a Windows PC to your Mac.

When all is said and done, it transfers your email into Mail from Outlook or Windows Live Mail accounts (POP or IMAP); your address book into Contacts from Outlook contacts and the Contacts home folder on your PC; your calendar into Calendar from Outlook's calendar; your music collection from iTunes on Windows into Music for the Mac; everything in your Windows Home folder into the corresponding Mac folders (Music, Pictures, Desktop, Documents, and Downloads); your browser bookmarks and home page into Safari from Explorer, Firefox, and Safari for Windows; and your account settings like language and even your desktop wallpaper.

All of this winds up in a *new* account on your Mac. The migration program doesn't make any attempt to *merge* your Windows world into your existing Mac account.

For this to work, your Windows PC and Mac have to be on the same network; see page 545. To begin, you'll need the free Windows Migration Assistant program. It's waiting at *apple.com/migrate-to-mac.* On your PC, download, install, and then open this program. Click Continue.

The steps now depend on how you arrived at the Transfer Your Information screen on the Mac.

If you're in the process of installing Catalina: Click From a Windows PC and then click OK. Click your PC's name and then click OK.

If you're doing this later, using the Migration Assistant program in your Mac's Applications→Utilities folder: On the Mac, quit all programs. Click "From another Mac, PC, Time Machine backup, or other disk" and then click Continue. Authenticate yourself, and then click "From another Mac or PC." Click Continue; click the PC's name.

No matter how you got here, when the six-digit passcode appears on the Mac and PC screens, click Continue again.

After a while, the Mac shows you a list of all the stuff it can bring over from the PC. Turn on the ones you care about, and then click Continue.

The transfer may take a *long* time. When you finally start up your Mac again, you're asked to provide a name and password for the new account that the Migration Assistant created for your Windows-world-on-the-Mac. (If you didn't *want* your Windows stuff to wind up in a different account, you can always copy it back into your main account using the Users→Shared folder as a tunnel between the two accounts.)

- **iCloud Keychain.** Want Apple to memorize all your passwords (for the web and for networking), so you don't have to reenter them on multiple gadgets (Mac, iPhone, iPad, and so on)? Turn on iCloud Keychain and hit Continue. Your other Apple gadgets will suddenly sprout a confirmation box to prove you're the owner of them all.

- **Express Setup.** Turn on Siri, let Apple know your location (for use by Maps and other features), and share crash data with Apple. If you're opposed, then click Customize Settings to deny or approve these one at a time.

- **Screen Time.** Want to set up this new parental-controls feature (page 216)?

- **All your files and photos in iCloud.** Do you want to keep your Desktop and Documents folders online? It's a complicated question; see page 214.

- **FileVault Disk Encryption.** See page 511.

- **Touch ID.** If your laptop has a fingerprint sensor, here's where you train it to recognize yours.

- **Choose your look.** Do you want Dark mode? (See page 152.)

At last you wind up at the macOS desktop, just as described in Chapter 1.

POWER USERS' CLINIC

The Clean Install

For years, there were two ways to install a Mac operating system: the *automatic* way and the *clean install*.

The automatic way preserved everything on your Mac. Every program, setting, and file stayed exactly as you had it. In essence, this kind of installation just worked through your System folder, updating each component and disturbing nothing else.

The *clean install* was preferred by power users, especially in times of troubleshooting, because it erased the entire hard drive and *then* installed macOS. Any minor corruptions or ancient software crumbs were swept away, leaving you with a clean, perfect system.

The clean-install option is gone now; Apple says its automatic installation method is already perfect enough that the erase-and-install business is no longer useful.

Still, some people just like the idea of starting fresh. If that's you, start by making a *complete backup* of the Mac you

want to Catalina-ize. In case you missed it, the clean-install process *erases everything*.

Now make a homemade startup drive, as described starting on the next page. Use it to start up the Mac you just backed up.

The first thing you'll see is the Utilities screen; you can read more about this Recovery Mode in Appendix B. Click Disk Utility, and then click Continue. In Disk Utility, click the Mac's hard drive name at the left side; click Erase; choose "Mac OS Extended (Journaled)" from the Format pop-up menu; click Erase.

When the erasing is over, quit Disk Utility. You return to the Utilities screen.

Now click Reinstall macOS. Click Continue to trigger the Catalina installation described on these pages. At the end of it, you'll be offered the chance to copy everything from your backup back onto the empty hard drive.

The Homemade Installer Disk

MacOS's download-only shtick is incredibly convenient. But sometimes you'll miss having a physical disk with the installer on it. You might wish you had one if, for example, you want to install Catalina on a huge array of Macs, like the ones at a school or in a business.

You might also wish you had an installation disk for when your Mac starts acting up and the tricks described in Appendix B don't seem to work.

As it turns out, you can make an installation disk fairly easily. All you need is a hard drive or a flash drive (16 GB or larger), the Install macOS Catalina program that winds up in your Applications folder when you first get Catalina (see the box on page 766), and the free DiskMaker X app on this book's "Missing CD" page at *missingmanuals.com*.

Note: DiskMaker X is free, quick, and easy. But there's a more technical way to build the installer disk, too, using a Terminal command Apple has built right into macOS. For instructions, visit *http://j.mp/2MGNjto*.

Open DiskMaker X; when it finds the Catalina installer, click "Use this copy." Click either "A USB thumb drive" or (if you're using a hard drive) "Another kind of disk." The following screens ask you to choose the disk or partition that will become your installer—and warn you that that disk is about to be erased.

When the process is complete, you wind up with a Catalina flash drive or disk that you baked all by yourself.

How to Use Your Emergency Disk

When disaster strikes, and you need to repair or reinstall your Catalina installation, go find your emergency installer drive.

Turn off the Mac. Connect the emergency drive. When you turn the Mac back on, hold down the Option key so a choice of startup disks appears. Click your homemade installer to start up from it.

Now you can install macOS as usual or use any of the recovery features described in Appendix B.

Tip: If you discover right away that installing Catalina was a mistake—for example, some app you desperately need no longer runs—you have 24 hours to "rewind" to whatever you had before. See page 782.

Troubleshooting

Whether it's a car engine or an operating system, anything with several thousand parts can develop the occasional technical hiccup. MacOS is far more resilient than its predecessors, but it's still a complex system with the potential for occasional glitches.

Most freaky little issues go away if you just try these two steps, one at a time:

- **Quit and restart the wayward program.**
- **Log out and log back in again.**

It's the *other* problems that'll drive you batty.

Slowdowns and Fans

The biggest complaint you're likely to have about macOS Catalina comes right after you install it. Suddenly, the Mac slows to a crawl—and its fans are going so hard, it's alarmingly loud.

It's a feature, not a bug. And it will go away in about a day.

When you upgrade to Catalina, the Mac may reindex your drive so Spotlight and Siri can use it to find your files. Indexing a drive can take a long time, especially on big drives. Just let it run its course.

The enhanced Photos app may also share the blame. It likes to scan and study every single photo on your Mac so it can learn the faces of the people you take pictures of. This, too, takes time (and is processor-intensive).

Minor Eccentric Behavior

All kinds of glitches may befall you, occasionally, in macOS. A menu doesn't open when you click it. A program doesn't open—it just bounces in the Dock a couple of times and then stops. An app freezes.

When a single program is acting up like this, but quitting and restarting it does no good, try the following steps, in the following sequence.

First Resort: Repair the Disk

An amazing number of mysterious glitches arise because of tiny file corruptions on your hard drive.

When something doesn't seem to be working right, therefore, open your Applications→Utilities folder and open Disk Utility. Proceed as shown in Figure B-1.

This is a really, *really* great trick to know.

Figure B-1:
Click your hard drive's name in the left-side list, click the First Aid button, click Run, and then read an article while the Mac checks out your disk.

Second Resort: Look for an Update

If a program starts acting up immediately after you've installed macOS 10.15, chances are good that it has some minor incompatibility. Chances are also good that you'll find an updated version on the company's website.

Third Resort: Toss the Prefs File

A corrupted preference file can bewilder the program that depends on it.

Before you go on a dumpfest, however, try this simple test: Log in using a *different account* (perhaps a dummy account you create just for testing purposes). Run the

problem program. Is the problem gone? If so, then the glitch exists only when *you* are logged in—which means it's a problem with *your* copy of the program's preferences.

Return to your account. Open your Home→Library→Preferences folder, where you'll find neatly labeled preference files for all the programs you use. (To open the hidden Library folder, press the Option key as you open the Go menu; choose Library.)

Each preference file ends with the file name suffix .plist. For example, *com.apple.finder.plist* is the Finder's preference file, *com.apple.dock.plist* is the Dock's, and so on.

Put the suspect preference file into the Trash, but don't empty the Trash. The next time you run the recalcitrant program, it will build itself a brand-new preference file that, if you're lucky, lacks whatever corruption was causing your problems.

If not, quit the program. You can reinstate its original .plist file from the Trash, if you find that helpful as you pursue your troubleshooting agenda.

Remember, however, that you actually have *two* Preferences folders. In addition to your own Home folder's stash, there's a second one in the Library folder in the main hard drive window (which administrators are allowed to trash; this one contains system-wide preferences, like your network configuration).

In any case, the next time you open the sick program or log in, the Mac creates fresh preference files.

Fourth Resort: Restart

Sometimes you can give macOS or its programs a swift kick by restarting the Mac. It's an inconvenient step, but not nearly as time-consuming as what comes next. And it can fix problems that cropped up when you started the computer.

Last Resort: Trash and Reinstall the Program

Sometimes reinstalling the problem program clears up whatever the glitch was.

First, however, throw away all traces of it. Open the Applications folder and drag the program's icon (or its folder) to the Trash. In most cases, the only remaining pieces to discard are its .plist file (or files) in your Home→Library→Preferences folder, and any scraps bearing the program's name in your Library→Application Support folder. (You can do a quick search to round up any other pieces.)

Then reinstall the program from its original disk or installer—after checking the company's website to see if there's an updated version, of course.

Frozen Programs (Force-Quitting)

The occasional unresponsive application has become such a part of macOS life that, among the Mac cognoscenti online, the dreaded, endless "please wait" cursor has been given its own acronym: SBOD (spinning beachball of death). When the SBOD strikes, no amount of mouse clicking and keyboard pounding will get you out of the insubordinate program.

Here are the different ways you can go about *force-quitting* a stuck program (the equivalent of pressing Ctrl+Alt+Delete in Windows), in increasing order of desperation:

- **Force-quit the usual way.** Choose →Force Quit to terminate the stuck program, or use one of the other force-quit methods described on page 170.

- **Force-quit the sneaky way.** Some programs, including the Dock, don't show up in the usual Force Quit dialog box. Your next attempt, therefore, should be to open the Activity Monitor program (in Applications→Utilities), which shows *everything* that's running. Double-click a program and then, in the resulting dialog box, click Quit to force-quit it. (Unix hounds: You can also use the *kill* command in Terminal.)

- **Force-quit remotely.** If the Finder itself has locked up, you can't very well get to Activity Monitor (unless it occurred to you *beforehand* to stash its icon in your Dock—not a bad idea). At this point, you may have to abort the locked program from another computer across the network, if you're on one, by using the *SSH* (secure shell) command.

For a blow-by-blow description of how you might terminate a program by remote control in this way, see the free PDF appendix to this chapter called "Remote Access with SSH" on this book's "Missing CD" page at *missingmanuals.com*.

Tip: If all this seems like a lot to remember, you can always force-restart the Mac. On most Macs, you do that by holding down the power button for five seconds. If that doesn't work, press Control-⌘-power button.

Report to Apple

What the—I was working along in Safari, and all the sudden it just vanished! Poof! And all I got was this lousy dialog box about "reporting to Apple." What's going on?

Apple is trying to assimilate you.

Or, more accurately, it's trying to enlist your help in ferreting out all the little glitches that make modern computing so much fun.

If you're willing to click the Report button and type a few comments ("I was running Word, minding my own business, and when I clicked the Print button, the whole thing just crashed"), Apple will add your report to the thousands flowing in from everyone else.

The idea is that when its programmers get a moment, they'll study these reports, track down the patterns ("Hmm, we've received 50,000 reports about that Print button in Word"), and then chase down the software company responsible—and, presumably, get a fix underway.

The report you submit is full of technical info that helps the programmers figure out what was happening at the time of the crash, but no personal information goes along for the ride. So if you feel like doing some good for your fellow Mac fans, by all means submit the report (via the internet) whenever you're offered the chance.

Startup Problems

Not every problem you encounter is related to running applications. Sometimes trouble strikes before you even get that far. The following are examples.

Kernel Panic

When you see the cheerful, multilingual dialog box shown in Figure B-2, you've got yourself a *kernel panic*—a Unix nervous breakdown. (In such situations, *user panic* might be the more applicable term, but that's programmers for you.)

Figure B-2:
A kernel panic is almost always related to some piece of add-on hardware. And look at the bright side: At least you get this handsome dialog box. That's a lot better than the OS X effect: random text gibberish superimposing itself on your screen.

You need to restart your computer. Hold down the Power button for several seconds or press the Restart button.

Veuillez redémarrer votre ordinateur. Maintenez la touche de démarrage enfoncée pendant plusieurs secondes ou bien appuyez sur le bouton de réinitialisation.

Sie müssen Ihren Computer neu starten. Halten Sie dazu die Einschalttaste einige Sekunden gedrückt oder drücken Sie die Neustart-Taste.

コンピュータを再起動する必要があります。パワーボタンを数秒間押し続けるか、リセットボタンを押してください。

If you experience a kernel panic, it's almost always the result of a *hardware* glitch—most often a bad memory (RAM) board, but possibly an accelerator card, graphics card, or USB hub macOS doesn't like. A bad USB or FireWire cable can bring on a kernel panic, too.

If simply restarting the machine doesn't help, detach every shred of gear that didn't come from Apple. Restore these components to the Mac one at a time until you find out which one was causing macOS's bad hair day. If you're able to pinpoint the culprit, visit its manufacturer's website on a quest for updated drivers, or at least try to find out for sure whether the add-on is compatible with macOS.

Tip: This advice goes for your Mac itself. Apple periodically updates the Mac's *own* "drivers" in the form of a *firmware update.* You download these updates from the Support area of Apple's website (if indeed macOS's own Software Update mechanism doesn't alert you to their existence).

There's one other cause for kernel panics, by the way, and that's moving, renaming, or changing the access permissions for macOS's essential system files and folders—the Applications or System folder, for example. (See page 534 for more on permissions.) This cause isn't even worth mentioning, though, because nobody would be that foolish.

Safe Mode (Safe Boot)

In times of troubleshooting, Windows fans press an F-key to start up in Safe Mode. That's how you turn off all nonessential system-software nubbins in an effort to get a sick machine at least powered up.

Although not one person in a hundred knows it, macOS offers the same kind of emergency keystroke. It can come in handy when you've just installed some new piece of software and find that you can't even start up the machine, or when one of your fonts is corrupted, or when something you've designated as a login item turns out to be gumming up the works. With this trick, you can at least get the computer turned on long enough to uninstall the cranky program.

The trick is to *press the Shift key* as the machine is starting up. Hold it down from the startup chime until you see the words "Safe Boot," in red lettering, on the Login screen.

Welcome to Safe Mode. What have you accomplished?

- **Checked your hard drive.** The Shift-key business makes the startup process seem to take a very long time; as the progress bar suggests, macOS is scanning your entire hard drive for problems.

- **Brought up the Login screen.** When you do a safe boot, you must click your name and enter your password, even if you normally have Automatic Login turned on.

- **Turned off noncritical kernel extensions (drivers).** All kinds of software nuggets load during the startup process. Some of them you choose yourself, like icons you add to the Login Items list in the System Preferences→Accounts pane. Others are normally hidden, including a large mass of *kernel extensions*, which are chunks of software that add various features to the basic operating system. (Kernel extensions live in your System→Library→Extensions folder.)

 If you're experiencing startup crashes, some non-Apple installer may have given you a kernel extension that doesn't care for macOS 10.15—so in Safe Mode, they're all turned off.

- **Turned off your fonts.** Corrupted fonts are a chronic source of trouble—and because you can't tell by looking, they're darned difficult to diagnose. So just to make sure you can at least get into your computer, Safe Mode turns them all off (except the authorized, Apple-sanctioned ones macOS needs to run, which are in your System→Library→Fonts folder).

- **Trashed your font cache.** The font cache is a speed trick. MacOS stores the visual information for each of your fonts on the hard drive so the system won't have to read every single typeface off your hard drive when you open your Font menus or the Fonts panel.

 When these files get scrambled, startup crashes can result. That's why a Safe Boot moves all these files into the Trash. (You'll even see them sitting there in the Trash after the startup process is complete, although there's not much you can do with them except hold your nose and point.)

- **Turned off your login items.** Safe Mode also prevents any Finder windows from opening *and* prevents your handpicked startup items from opening—that is, whatever you've asked your Mac to auto-open by adding them to the System Preferences→Accounts→Login Items list.

 This, too, is a troubleshooting tactic. If some login item crashes your Mac every time it opens, you can squelch it just long enough to remove it from your Login Items list.

Tip: If you don't hold down the Shift key until you click the Log In button (after entering your name and password at the Login screen), you disable your login items but *not* the fonts and extensions.

Once you reach the desktop, some standard features may be inoperable. (The next time you restart, all this goodness will be restored, assuming you're no longer clutching the Shift key in a sweaty panic.)

In any case, the beauty of Safe Mode is that it lets you get your Mac going. You have access to your files, so at least the emergency of crashing-on-startup is over. And you can start picking through your fonts and login items to see if you can spot the problem.

Gray Screen During Startup

Confirm that your Mac has the latest firmware, as described earlier. Detach and test all your non-Apple add-ons. Finally, perform a disk check (read on).

Forgotten Password

If you or one of the other people who use your Mac have forgotten the corresponding account password, no worries: Just read the box on page 502.

Recovery Mode: Three Emergency Disks

When your Mac won't even start up, there's no DVD to insert as a backup startup disk. That's a scary place to be; if your hard drive is sick, everything on it may be inaccessible to you. What you need is an emergency drive that can repair the hard drive and get you back in operation.

Apple is way ahead of you. It offers *three* simulated repair disks: three ways to repair disks and system software in times of crisis.

The Recovery HD

Here's the sneaky surprise: When you install Catalina, it automatically creates an invisible hidden "hard drive" (a partition of your main drive that has its own icon) called Recovery HD. It's generally invisible to you. It's also invisible to Disk Utility, so even if you erase your hard drive, the Recovery HD is still there to help you.

But if you can't seem to start up your Mac properly, or if your hard drive is acting flaky, you'll be glad you have this "separate" startup disk. On it, Apple has provided some emergency tools for fixing drive or software glitches, restoring files, browsing the web, and even reinstalling macOS.

Note: The macOS installer creates the Recovery HD partition only if your startup drive is an internal drive. In certain other situations, it won't create the partition—for example, if you're installing macOS onto a RAID volume or one with a non-standard Boot Camp partition setup.

You can power up your Mac from the Recovery HD in either of two ways:

- **Hold down ⌘-R as the Mac is starting up.** You can let go when the Apple logo appears.

- **Hold down the Option key as the Mac is starting up.** When you see the Startup Manager (Figure B-3, top), let go. Click the up-arrow button below the Recovery HD icon.

Either way, you're asked to log in with an Administrator account, and then you wind up at the Utilities screen shown in Figure B-3, bottom.

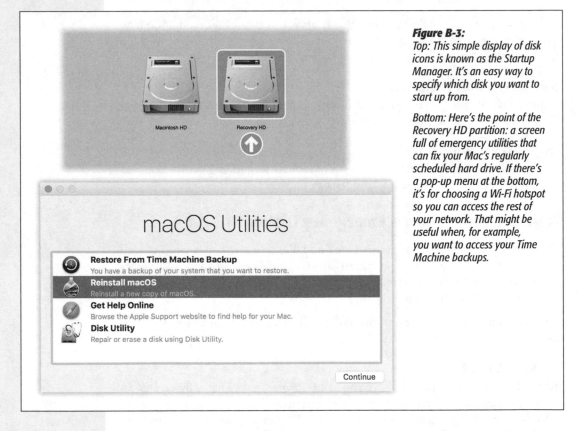

Figure B-3:
Top: This simple display of disk icons is known as the Startup Manager. It's an easy way to specify which disk you want to start up from.

Bottom: Here's the point of the Recovery HD partition: a screen full of emergency utilities that can fix your Mac's regularly scheduled hard drive. If there's a pop-up menu at the bottom, it's for choosing a Wi-Fi hotspot so you can access the rest of your network. That might be useful when, for example, you want to access your Time Machine backups.

Here Apple has supplied you with four important tools:

- **Restore From Time Machine Backup.** If your Mac is really hosed, this is the option you want. It restores your *entire* software world—programs, data, settings, macOS itself—from the Time Machine backup you carefully set up as you read Chapter 6.

You can use this feature to rewind a fresh Catalina installation to whatever you had before, as described on the next page. That's handy when you discover that some 32-bit app you really need no longer works.

This option *completely erases* your existing hard drive, so—you know. Be sure.

Once you choose this option, click Continue. You're now asked to choose the Time Machine drive, then the time-stamped backup you want to restore from and, finally, the drive or partition you want to wipe out. You get one more warning that you're about to wipe out the destination drive. When you click Continue, the restoration begins. When it's all over—usually a couple of hours later—the Mac restarts as though nothing ever happened.

- **Reinstall macOS.** You can use this option to install a copy of macOS onto any hard drive—for example, you could reinstall it on your main internal drive. This option will download the actual copy of Catalina from the internet—all 6.5 gigabytes of it. In other words, it requires an internet connection and patience.

Tip: Remember how all this started? You pressed ⌘-R to open the Recovery screen?

At this point, the "Reinstall macOS" routine will reinstall whatever macOS version you already had. But if you press *Option*-⌘-R to begin this process instead, you'll upgrade to the latest macOS version your Mac can handle. And if you press *Shift*-Option-⌘-R, you'll install whatever OS came on your Mac originally. Those Apple engineers think of everything, don't they?

- **Get Help Online.** This option opens your Safari web browser, which presents you with some helpful information about using the Recovery Mode you've fired up. You're actually online at this point, so you can also visit any other website you might find helpful.

 Quit Safari when you're finished browsing; you return to the main macOS Utilities window.

- **Disk Utility.** Use this option to open Disk Utility, the Mac's hard drive diagnostics-and-repair program. You can use it to check, fix, erase, or partition any of your hard drives. For example, you can repair the main startup disk, which is often the most useful option.

Those are the big-ticket items, but don't miss the menu bar. The commands here let you open the Firmware Password Utility (page 499), Network Utility (page 481), and Terminal (page 479).

Internet Recovery

OK, the Recovery HD concept is clever. And most of the time it's all you need. But what if your hard drive is *completely* hosed? What then, smart guy? You can't very well boot up from the Recovery HD if it's sitting on the same dead hard drive.

Or what if you've just installed a brand-new, bigger, or faster hard drive? It doesn't have macOS on it. It doesn't have Recovery HD on it. How are you supposed to install Catalina?

In those situations, Mac models released in 2011 and later offer an even cleverer option: Internet Recovery. This mode offers the same exact options that the Utilities screen of Recovery HD would have—but you're connecting to that software *online*, over a high-speed internet connection. You're literally starting up from *Apple's* hard drives, perhaps thousands of miles away.

So even if your hard drive is dead as a doornail, you can repair it, reinstall macOS, and get on with your life.

To fire up Internet Recovery, make sure your computer is in a Wi-Fi hotspot or connected to an Ethernet network. Then hold down ⌘-R as the computer is starting up. You can let go when you see the screen that asks you to choose a Wi-Fi network. Do that, and then enter the password for the network, if necessary.

Now your Mac downloads a disk image containing just enough software to get you to the Utilities screen described in the previous section.

Note: Once you're up and running, you can re-download the copies of Photos, iMovie, and GarageBand that came with your Mac. Just open the App Store program, log in with your Apple ID, click Purchases, and click Accept to download those iLife programs. You won't be charged for them.

Physical Recovery Disks

But what if the hard drive is so sick that you can't start up from the Recovery HD—*and* your Mac isn't new enough to offer the Internet Recovery feature? (Or what if it *does* offer that feature, but you'd rather repair your Mac a quicker way?)

The solution is to build yourself a bootable macOS flash drive or hard drive, as described on page 771. Not only is it capable of starting up or reinstalling macOS, but it also has a complete set of recovery tools on board.

To use this emergency disk, hold down the Option key as the Mac starts up. You wind up at the Startup Manager screen shown in Figure B-3, top. From the pop-up menu, choose your Wi-Fi hotspot.

Now click the up-arrow button below the Recovery HD icon. (You may even see *two* Recovery HD icons—one of them is the USB flash drive, and the other is the invisible partition on your hard drive. Either one works.) Your Mac is starting up from the flash drive! After a moment, you wind up at the Utilities screen described previously.

Note: The recovery flash drive you made will work only on the Mac model you used to make it.

Rewinding macOS

If you have a laptop, you have a secret safety net: MacOS has been quietly creating an hourly backup snapshot *of* the startup drive, *on* the startup drive (page 264). In case of disaster, you can open Time Machine and recover any file you've deleted or destroyed, even if you're on the road and far from any external backup drive.

But macOS Catalina offers a safety net: It also creates a snapshot of your drive's contents every time you install a macOS update—from 10.15.1 to 10.15.2, for example. If the new version does something bad to your Mac, you can rewind the whole thing.

Tip: You can also force the Mac to create a local snapshot on command. Open Terminal (page 479), type *sudo tmutil snapshot,* and press Return.

Here's the fine print:

- **Catalina creates these snapshots** only of APFS-formatted drives (that is, solid-state, or SSD, drives—like the one in every Mac laptop).

- **Your Mac creates these snapshots** only if there's enough disk space.

- **The Mac deletes the upgrade-moment snapshot** after 24 hours.

OK? Then here's how you perform the rewind:

1. **Start up the Mac in Recovery mode.**

 That is, press ⌘-R as it's starting up, so you see the dialog box shown in Figure B-3 at bottom. Log in with an Administrator account.

2. **Click Restore From Time Machine Backup. Hit Continue, and then Continue.**

 "But wait!" you protest. "I don't have a Time Machine backup! I don't have a backup drive! I never turned it on!" Never you mind. You're going to restore from one of those *local* snapshots.

3. **On the Select a Restore Source screen, click your startup drive; click Continue.**

 Now you're on the Select a Local Snapshot screen, where all your recent Time Machine local backups are listed. There may be only one.

4. **Click the most recent snapshot; click Continue. In the "Are you sure?" box, click Continue again.**

 The restoring process takes a few minutes. When it's over, the Mac restarts—and you may marvel to see that your Mac has de-upgraded from Catalina.

Fixing the Disk

The beauty of macOS's design is that the operating system itself is frozen in its perfect, pristine state, impervious to conflicting system extensions, clueless Mac newbies, and other sources of disaster.

That's the theory, anyway. But what happens if something goes wrong with the complex software that operates the hard drive itself?

Fortunately, macOS comes with its own disk-repair program. In the familiar Mac universe of icons and menus, it takes the form of a program in Applications→ Utilities called Disk Utility. In the barren world of Terminal and the command line

interface, there's a utility that works just as well but bears a different name: *fsck* (for file system check).

In any case, running Disk Utility or its alter ego *fsck* is a powerful and useful trouble-shooting tool that can cure all kinds of strange ills, including these problems:

- **Your Mac freezes during startup,** either before or after the Login screen.

- **The startup process interrupts itself** with the appearance of the text-only command line.

- **You get the "applications showing up as folders" problem.**

Method 1: Disk Utility

The easiest way to check your disk is to use the Disk Utility program. Use this method if your Mac can, indeed, start up. (See Method 2 if you can't get even that far.)

For best results, restart the Mac into Recovery Mode (page 779) and run Disk Utility from there. The process goes like this:

1. **Start up the Mac from the Recovery HD or a recovery flash drive.**

 You wind up, after some time, at the Utilities screen.

2. **Click "Disk Utility: Repair or erase a disk using Disk Utility."**

 After a moment, the Disk Utility screen appears.

3. **Click the disk or disk partition you want to fix, click First Aid, and then click Run.**

 The Mac whirls into action.

If you see the message "The volume 'Macintosh HD' appears to be OK," that's meant to be *good* news. Believe it or not, that cautious statement is as definitive an affirmation as Disk Utility is capable of making about the health of your disk.

Disk Utility may also tell you the disk is damaged but that it can't help you. In that case, you need a more heavy-duty disk-repair program like DiskWarrior (*alsoft.com*).

Method 2: *fsck* at the Console

Techier folk can boot into the Mac's raw Unix underlayer to perform some diagnostic (and healing) commands.

Specifically, you can run the Unix program *fsck,* for which Disk Utility is little more than a pretty faceplate.

Note: Even so, Apple recommends that you use Disk Utility if at all possible. Use *fsck* only if all else fails.

Like any Unix program, *fsck* runs at the command line. You launch it from the all-text, black Unix screen by typing *fsck* and pressing Return. (You can also use *fsck -f.*)

You can't, however, just run *fsck* in Terminal. You have to run it when the usual arsenal of graphic-interface programs—like the Finder and its invisible suite of accessory programs—isn't running.

Single-user mode (⌘-S at startup)

The Terminal program is the best-known form of macOS's command line, but it's not the only one. In fact, there are several other ways to get there.

In general, you don't hear them mentioned except in the context of troubleshooting, because the Terminal program offers many more convenient features for doing the same thing. And because it's contained in a macOS-style window, Terminal is not as disorienting as the three methods you're about to read about.

All these techniques take you into *console mode*, shown in Figure B-4. In console mode, Unix takes over your screen completely, showing white type against black, no windows or icons in sight. Abandon the mouse, all ye who enter here; in console mode, you can't do anything but type commands.

Figure B-4:
In console mode, your entire screen is a command line interface. Unix jockeys can go to town here. Everyone else can timidly type fsck -y *after the* localhost# *prompt—see that prompt on the very last line?—and hope for the best.*

```
Found old device 0x0cdea00
IOFireWireDevice,  ROM unchanged 0x0xcdea00
IOFireWireDevice  0x0xcdea00,  ROM generation zero
Got boot device =
IOService:/Core99PE/pc@f20000000/AppleMacRiscPCI/mac-
io@17/KeyLargo/ata-4@1f000/KeyLargoATA/ATADeviceNub@0/IOA
TABlockStorageDriver/IOATABlockStorageDevice/IOBlockStorageDr
iver/QUANTUM  FIREBALL  CX13.6A
Media/IOApplePartitionScheme/Untitled
@9
BSD root: disk0s9, major 14, minor 9
Rereading  ROM up to 25 quads
devfs on /dev
USB:    4.947. AppleUSBKeyboard[0xD0E80014::start   USB Generic
Keyboard @ 3 (0x18110000)
Mon Nov 19 23:18:53 EST 2001
Singleuser boot -- fsck not done
Root device is mounted read-only
If you want to make modifications  to files,
run '/sbin/fsck -y' first and then '/sbin/mount  -uw/'
localhost#
```

To get there in times of startup troubleshooting, press ⌘-S while the Mac is starting up. (If you're stuck at the frozen remnants of a previous startup attempt, you may first have to force-restart your Mac; hold down the ⏻ button for five seconds.)

Instead of arriving at the usual desktop, you see technical-looking text scrolling up a black screen as the Mac runs its various startup routines. When it finally stops at the *localhost#* prompt, you're ready to type commands. You're now in what's called *single-user mode*, meaning that the Unix multiple-accounts software has yet to load. You won't be asked to log in.

At the *root#* prompt, type *fsck -y* (note the space before the hyphen) and press Return. (The *y* means "yes," as in "Yes, I want you to fix any problems automatically.")

Now the file-system check program takes over, running through five sets of tests. When it's complete, you'll see one of two messages:

- **The volume 'Macintosh HD' appears to be OK.** All is well. Type *exit* and press Return to proceed to the usual Login screen and desktop.

- **File system was modified.** A good sign, but just a beginning. You need to run the program again. One *fsck* pass often repairs only one layer of problems, leaving another to be patched in the next pass. Type *fsck -y* a second time, a third time, and so on, until you finally arrive at an "appears to be OK" message.

Type *exit* at the prompt and press Return to get back to the familiar world of icons and windows.

Where to Get Troubleshooting Help

If the basic steps described in this appendix haven't helped, the universe is crawling with additional help sources. Apple's Support website is a great one. But the truth is you'll find more answers faster using Google than you ever will using individual help sites. That's because Google *includes* all those help sites in its search!

Suppose, for example, you've just installed the 10.15.2 update, and it's mysteriously turned all your accounts into Standard ones. You could go to one website after another, hunting for a fix—or you could just type *Catalina 10.15.2 standard accounts* into Google. You'll get your answers after just a few seconds of clicking.

Help Online

These websites contain nothing but troubleshooting discussions, tools, and help:

- **Apple Discussion Groups** (*discussions.apple.com*). The volume and quality of activity here dwarfs any other free source. If you're polite and concise, you can post questions to the multitudes and get more replies than you'll know what to do with.

- **Apple's help site** (*apple.com/support*). Apple's site includes downloadable manuals, software updates, frequently asked questions, and many other resources. Its search box is your ticket to the Knowledge Base, a collection of thousands of technical articles that Apple technicians themselves consult when answering calls for help.

Help by Telephone

Finally, consider contacting whoever sold you the component that's making your life miserable: the printer company, scanner company, software company, or whatever.

If it's a macOS problem, you can call Apple at 800-275-2273 (that's 800-APL-CARE). For the first 90 days after your installation of macOS, the technicians will answer your questions for free.

After that, unless you've paid for AppleCare for your Mac (a three-year extended-warranty program), Apple will charge you to answer questions. Fortunately, if the problem turns out to be Apple's fault, they won't charge you.

The Windows-to-Mac Dictionary

Maybe you love your iPhone and want to go all in with Apple products. Maybe you prefer the looks of today's Macs. Or maybe you've just endured one virus download too many. In any case, if you're switching to macOS from Windows, this appendix is for you. It's an alphabetical listing of common Windows functions and where to find them in macOS.

After all, an operating system is an operating system. The actual functions are pretty much the same—they're just in different places.

About [this program]

To find out the version number of the program you're using, don't look in the Help menu. Instead, look in the *application* menu next to the menu—the one that bears the name of the program you're in. That's where you find the About command for Mac programs.

Accessibility Options control panel/Ease of Access Settings panel

The features that let you operate the computer even with impaired vision, hearing, or motor control are called "Accessibility" in macOS. They're in System Preferences (see page 320).

Add Hardware control panel/Devices Settings panel

The Mac requires no program for installing the driver for a new external gadget. The drivers for most printers, mice, keyboards, cameras, camcorders, and other accessories are preinstalled. If you plug something into the Mac and find that it doesn't work immediately, just install the driver from the manufacturer's website.

All Apps

There's no Apps menu built into macOS, like the one on the Windows Start menu. If you'd like one, drag your Applications folder onto the end of the Dock. Now its icon is a tidy pop-up menu of every program on your machine.

Alt key

On the Mac, it's the Option key, although the key usually says "Alt" on it, too. (In some countries, it says *only* "Alt.") You can substitute Option for Alt in any keystroke in most popular programs. The Option key has a number of secondary features on the Mac, too: It hides the windows of one program when you click into another, and so on.

Backspace key

It's in the same place on the Mac keyboard, but it's called Delete.

BIOS

You'll never have to update or even think about the ROM of your Mac (the approximate equivalent of the BIOS on the PC). It's permanent and unchanging. The very similar *firmware* of your Mac does occasionally have to be updated in order to work with a new version of the Mac operating system or some dramatic new feature—once every four years, perhaps. You'll be notified on the screen when the time comes.

Calculator

The Calculator app in macOS is almost identical to the one in Windows. It sits in your Applications folder and is described starting on page 389. (And don't forget that you can type quick math equations into the Q Spotlight box.)

Camera and Scanner Wizard/Devices

When you connect a digital camera or scanner to your Mac, Photos opens and prepares to download the pictures automatically.

CDs and DVDs

In the unlikely event that you've outfitted your Mac with an external disc drive, you spit out the disc that's in it by holding down the ⏏ key on your Mac keyboard, or by right-clicking or two-finger clicking its desktop icon and then choosing Eject from the shortcut menu.

Character Map

This Windows program helps you find out what keys you need to press to trigger trademark symbols, copyright symbols, and other special characters. The equivalent on the Mac is called the Character Viewer (page 243).

Clean Install/Fresh Start

The macOS installer can give you a fresh copy of the operating system, just as the Windows installer can. Instructions are in Appendix A.

Clipboard

The Mac's Clipboard works much like the one in Windows. In the Finder, you can choose Edit→Show Clipboard to see whatever you most recently copied or cut.

Command line

In macOS, the command line is alive and well—but it speaks Unix, not DOS. You get to it by opening Terminal; see page 479.

Control Panel/Settings

The Settings app in macOS is called System Preferences, and you open it from your menu. As in older versions of Windows, you can view these icons either by category or in a simple alphabetical list: Just choose either Organize by Categories or Organize Alphabetically from the View menu.

Copy, Cut, Paste

When you're editing in a word processor or graphics program, the macOS Cut, Copy, and Paste commands work exactly as they do in Windows.

At the desktop, however, there are a few differences. You can indeed copy icons and paste them into a new window using the Copy and Paste commands—but *cutting* them out of a window works differently: After you've copied the icons from the first window, open the destination window. Then press the Option key, open the Edit menu, and choose Move Items Here.

Ctrl key

On the Mac, you generally substitute the ⌘ key in keystrokes that would involve the Ctrl key in Windows. In other words, the Save command is now ⌘-S instead of Ctrl+S, Open is ⌘-O instead of Ctrl+O, and so on.

Date and Time

To set your Mac's calendar and clock, open Date & Time in System Preferences.

Defragment and Optimize Drives

There's no such utility included with macOS; the system auto-defragments in the background. (A *defragmenting* program moves around the pieces of files on your hard drive to optimize their placement and speed of opening.)

Delete key (Forward Delete)

Most desktop Mac keyboards have a forward-delete key (labeled ⌦ or *Del*) exactly like the ones on PCs. On Mac laptops, and on Apple's aluminum keyboards, you trigger the forward-delete function by pressing the Delete key while simultaneously pressing the fn key.

Desktop

The Mac desktop is pretty much the same idea as the Windows desktop, with a few key differences:

- **You change the desktop picture** using the Desktop & Screen Saver panel of System Preferences. (Or just right-click or two-finger click the desktop.)

- **The Trash is an icon in the Dock,** not on the desktop.

Disks

Working with disks is very different on the Mac. Every disk inside, or attached to, a Mac can be represented on the screen by an icon. MacOS does have something like the This PC or My Computer window (choose Go→Computer), but the icons there reflect only the disks currently inserted in your Mac. You'll never see an icon for an empty drive, as you do in Windows, and there's no such thing as drive letters (because the Mac refers to *disks,* not to *drives*—and calls them by name).

Catalina doesn't display icons for disks on the desktop, as earlier Mac versions did—but you can bring them back by choosing Finder→Preferences→General and turning on the checkboxes for different kinds of disks.

Display control panel or Settings panel

The functions of the Windows Display control panel lurk in the macOS System Preferences program—just not all in one place. You set up your desktop picture and screen saver using the Desktop & Screen Saver pane and adjust your monitor settings using the Displays pane. (MacOS offers no equivalent to the Appearance tab in Windows, for changing the system-wide look of your computer.)

(My) Documents, (My) Music, (My) Pictures

The equivalent buckets for your everyday documents, music files, and pictures are the Documents, Music, and Pictures folders in your Home folder.

DOS prompt

There's a command line in macOS, but it's Unix, not DOS. For details, see page 479.

End Task dialog box

If some Mac program is hung up or frozen, you escape it pretty much the same way you would in Windows: by forcing it to quit. To bring up the Force Quit dialog box, press Option-⌘-Esc or choose →Force Quit.

Exiting programs

You can quit a program either by choosing Quit from the menu bearing the program's name (next to the menu), or by right-clicking or two-finger clicking its Dock icon and then choosing Quit from the pop-up menu.

Favorites

In macOS, there isn't one single Favorites menu that lists both favorite websites and favorite icons. The Bookmarks menu of Safari lists only websites, and the Sidebar at the desktop (page 15) lists only favorite files, folders, disks, and other icons.

File Explorer

The Mac has its own "tree" view of the files and folders on your hard drive: list view. By expanding the "flippy triangles" of your folders, you build a hierarchy that shows as much or as little detail as you like.

If you prefer the File Explorer effect of clicking a folder in *one* pane to see its contents in the next, try column view instead. Both views are described in Chapter 1.

File Sharing

See Chapter 13 for an in-depth look at the Mac's networking and file-sharing system.

Folder Options/File Explorer Options

The Folder Options control panel in older versions of Windows and File Explorer Options in Windows 10 is a collection of unrelated settings that boil down to this:

- **General tab.** Exactly as in Windows, it's up to you whether or not double-clicking a folder opens up a second window—or just changes what's in the first one. On the Mac, you make these changes using the Finder→Preferences command. There you'll find the option called "Open folders in tabs instead of new windows."

- **View tab.** Most of the options here don't exist on the Mac. For example, system files are *always* hidden on the Mac; you can't opt to make them visible (at least not with the built-in controls). You can, however, choose whether you want to see the file name extensions in your desktop windows (like .doc and .html). Choose Finder→Preferences→Advanced, and turn "Show all filename extensions" on or off.

- **File Types tab.** Just as in Windows, you can reassign certain document types so double-clicking opens them in the program of your choice. But on the Mac, you can reassign either a whole class of files at once, as in Windows, *or* one file at a time. To do it, use the Get Info window, as described on page 97.

- **Offline files.** There's no equivalent feature on the Mac.

Fonts

The Mac and Windows PCs both use TrueType, PostScript, and OpenType fonts. (In fact, your Mac can even use the exact font files you had in Windows.) On the Mac, however, there are actually three different folders that can contain them. A complete discussion starts on page 601.

Help and Support

At the desktop, choose Help→Mac Help. In other programs, the Help command is generally at the right end of your menus, exactly as in Windows.

Hibernation/Sleep

On a PC, hibernation cuts all power but remembers what programs and documents you had open for a faster restart later. The Mac's Sleep mode is more like Windows' own Sleep mode: It uses a little power but lets you restart where you left off instantly. See page 63.

Internet Explorer

Microsoft's most famous web browser doesn't exist on the Mac (or in Windows 10!). Apple would prefer, of course, that you try Safari, its own browser, but many a power user prefers Firefox or Chrome, which are nearly identical to the Windows versions.

Internet Options/Internet Properties

On the Mac, you find the options for your browser by choosing Safari→Preferences.

Java

This interpreter of tiny web page programs is alive and well in macOS. Java programs run fine in all Mac web browsers.

Keyboard control panel

You can make exactly the same kinds of settings—and more—on the Keyboard pane of System Preferences.

Logging in

The multiple-accounts feature of macOS is extremely similar to that of Windows. In each case, you can, if you wish, create a requirement to log in with a name and password before using the computer. This arrangement keeps separate the documents, email, and settings of each person who uses the computer. Chapter 12 tells all.

Mail control panel/Email & Accounts Settings panel

MacOS comes with its own email program (described in Chapter 18); all its settings are contained within the program.

Maximize button

On the Mac, clicking the Zoom button (the green ⊗ in the upper-left corner of a window) does something like the Maximize button in Windows: It shoots that program into *Full Screen mode,* where every last pixel of screen space is put to work displaying your document (page 173).

Menus

On the Mac, there's only one menu bar, always at the very top of the screen. The menus change depending on the program and the window you're using, but the point is that the menu bar is no longer inside each window you open.

Tip: Just because you don't see the little underlines in the menus doesn't mean you can't operate all the menus from the keyboard, as in Windows. See page 197 for details.

Minimize button

You can minimize a macOS window to the Dock, just the way you would minimize a Windows window to the taskbar. You do so by double-clicking its title bar, pressing ⌘-M, choosing Window→Minimize, or clicking the yellow Minimize button at the top left of a window. (Restore the window by clicking its icon in the Dock.)

Network Places

On the Mac, the "network neighborhood" is almost always on the screen: It's the Sidebar, the panel at the left side of every Finder window. All the Macs and PCs on your network are always listed here, in the Shared category (unless you turned this feature off in Finder→Preferences).

Notepad

Page 429 documents the Notes app, which is more powerful than the Notepad of old.

Phone and Modem Options control panel

To find the modem settings for your Mac, see the free appendix to this book, "Setting Up a Dial-Up Connection," available on its "Missing CD" page at *missingmanuals.com*.

Power Options

To control when your Mac goes to sleep and (if it's a laptop) how much power it uses, use the Energy Saver pane of System Preferences (page 344).

Printer Sharing

To share a USB inkjet printer with other Macs on the network, open the Sharing pane of System Preferences on the Mac with the printer. Turn on Printer Sharing.

To use the shared printer from across the network, open the document you want to print, choose File→Print, and choose the name of the shared printer from the first pop-up menu.

Printers and Faxes

For a list of your printers, open the Printers & Scanners pane of System Preferences. Faxing is no longer built into macOS.

PrntScrn key

You capture pictures of your Mac screen by pressing Shift-⌘-3 (for a full-screen grab) or Shift-⌘-4 (to grab a selected portion of the screen). There are many options available; see page 612.

Program Files folder

The Applications folder (Go→Applications) is like the Program Files folder in Windows—except that you're not discouraged from opening it and double-clicking things. On the Mac, every program bears its true name; Microsoft Word, for example, is called Microsoft Word, not WINWORD.EXE.

Properties dialog box

You can call up something very similar for any *icon* (file, folder, program, disk, printer) by highlighting its icon and then choosing File→Get Info. But objects in Mac *programs* generally don't contain Properties dialog boxes.

Recycle Bin

MacOS has a Trash icon at the end of the Dock. In general, it works exactly like the Windows Recycle Bin—and why not, since the Mac Trash was Microsoft's inspiration?—but there are a couple of differences. By default, the Mac never automatically empties it, for example (but see page 95 for directions on how to turn this advanced setting on). Usually, the emptying job is up to you: The simplest way is to right-click or two-finger click it, and then choose Empty Trash from the shortcut menu.

The Mac never bothers you with an "Are you sure?" message when you throw something into the Trash. It asks you for permission only when you choose File→Empty Trash. And you can even turn that confirmation off, if you like (in Finder→Preferences).

To put icons into the Trash, drag them there, or select them and then press ⌘-Delete.

Regional and Language Options control panel/Language Settings panel

The equivalent is the Language & Region panel of System Preferences.

Registry

There is no registry. Let the celebration begin!

Safe Mode

You can press the Shift key during startup to suppress the loading of certain software libraries, but macOS's "safe mode" isn't quite as massively stripped down as Windows' Safe Mode.

ScanDisk

Just like Windows, the Mac automatically scans and, if necessary, repairs its hard drive every time your machine starts up. To run such a check on command, open Disk Utility (located in the Applications→Utilities folder), click the name of your hard drive, and then click the First Aid button.

Scheduled Tasks

To schedule a task to take place unattended, use the *launchd* Unix command in Terminal (page 479), or one of the scheduling programs listed at *downloads.com*.

Scrap files

On the Mac, they're called *clipping files,* and they're even more widely compatible. You create them the same way: Drag some highlighted text, or a graphic, out of a program's window and onto the desktop. There it becomes an independent clipping file that you can drag back in—to the same window or a different one.

Screen Saver Gallery

The Mac's screen savers are impressive. Open System Preferences and click the Desktop & Screen Saver icon.

Search

In macOS, you have the ultimate file-searching tool: Spotlight (Chapter 3). Get psyched! To find websites, use the Google search box at the top of the Safari browser.

Shortcut menus

They work exactly the same as they do in Windows. You produce a shortcut menu by right-clicking—or two-finger clicking, or Control-clicking—things like icons, list items, and so on.

Shortcuts

On the Mac, they're known as *aliases*. See page 87.

Start menu

There's no Start menu in macOS. Instead, you stash the icons of the programs, documents, and folders you use frequently onto the Dock or into the Favorites section of the Sidebar at the left edge of every Finder window.

Exactly as with the Start menu, you can rearrange these icons within the Dock (drag them around) or remove the ones you don't use often (drag them away from the Dock and then release). To add new icons of your own, just drag them into place (applications go to the left of the Dock's divider line, documents and folders to the right).

Startup folder

To make programs launch automatically at startup, include them in the list of Login Items in the System Preferences→Accounts pane.

System control panel

The Mac has no central equivalent of the Windows System window. But its functions have analogs here:

- **Version number.** To find out your macOS version number and the amount of memory on your Mac, choose →About This Mac.

- **Computer name.** Open System Preferences, click Sharing, and edit your computer's network name here.

- **Hardware.** The closest thing the Mac has to the Device Manager is System Information (in your Applications→Utilities folder).

- **Advanced.** In macOS, you can't easily adjust your virtual memory, processor scheduling, or user profile information.

- **System Restore.** MacOS's Time Machine feature is like System Restore on steroids; see page 260.

• **Updates.** Open App Store→Updates.

• **Remote control.** MacOS's remote control is Screen Sharing, described starting on page 550.

Notification area

The macOS equivalent of the system tray (also called the notification area) is the row of *menulets* at the upper-right corner of your screen.

Taskbar

MacOS doesn't have a taskbar, but it does have something very close: the Dock (Chapter 4). Open programs are indicated by a small dot beneath their icons in the Dock. If you hold down your cursor on one of these icons (or right-click it, or two-finger click it), you get a pop-up list of the open windows in that program, exactly as in Windows.

On the other hand, some conventions never die. Much as in Windows, you cycle through the various open Mac programs by holding down the ⌘ key and pressing Tab repeatedly.

This PC or (My) Computer

The Mac's Computer window (choose Go→Computer) is very similar, in that it shows the icons of all disks (hard drives, CDs, and so on). On the other hand, it shows *only* the disks that are actually inserted or connected. (See "Disks.")

"Three-fingered salute"

Instead of pressing Control-Alt-Delete to jettison a stuck program, on the Mac you press Option-⌘-Esc. A Force Quit dialog box appears. Click the program you want to toss, click Force Quit, confirm your choice, and then relaunch the program to get on with your day.

Tooltips

Small identifying balloons pop up on the Mac almost as often as they do in Windows. Just point to a toolbar icon or truncated file name without clicking. (There's no way to turn these labels off.)

Uninstall or Change a Program control panel

Here's another one you just don't need on the Mac. Installing a program onto the Mac is described starting on page 162. Removing a program simply involves dragging its icon to the Trash. (For a clean sweep, inspect your Home→Library→Preferences and Library→Application Support folders to see if any preference files got left behind.)

User Accounts control panel/Accounts Settings panel

Like every Windows operating system since Windows 2000, macOS was designed to be a multiuser operating system, keeping each person's files, mail, and settings separate. You manage these accounts in System Preferences→Users & Groups (Chapter 12).

Windows (or WINNT) folder

MacOS's operating system resides in a folder simply called System, which sits in your main hard drive window. Exactly as in recent Windows versions, you're forbidden to add, remove, or change anything inside. Also as in Windows, most of it is invisible anyway.

Windows logo key

The Mac has no equivalent for the ⊞ key on most PC keyboards.

Windows Media Player

The Mac comes with individual programs for playing multimedia files:

- **QuickTime Player** (page 617) to play back and record movies and sounds.

- **Music** (page 628) to play CDs, internet radio, MP3 files, and other audio files.

Windows Messenger

MacOS's instant-messaging, audioconferencing, and videoconferencing software is called Messages, and it's described in Chapter 20.

WordPad

The TextEdit program (in the Applications folder) is a word processor along the lines of WordPad. It can even open and save Word files, as WordPad can. See page 452.

Zip files

Zip files exist on the Mac, too, and you create them almost the same way: Right-click or two-finger click a file or folder and choose Compress from the shortcut menu.

The Master Secret Keystroke List

Here it is, by popular, frustrated demand: the master list of keystroke in macOS, including all the keys you can press during startup. Clip and post to your monitor (unless, of course, you got this book from the library).

Note: For the most part, the following list doesn't include the keystrokes already listed in your menus, like ⌘-P for Print, ⌘-S for Save, and so on.

Keys to hold down at startup

N	Starts up from a NetBoot server
T	Puts the Mac into Target Disk mode
D	Starts up to diagnostic or hardware test mode
Option-D	Starts up to diagnostic or hardware test mode over the internet
⌘-R	Starts Recovery Mode
Option-⌘-R	Starts up from Recovery Mode over the internet
Option	Starts up to Startup Manager, which allows you to choose a startup disk
Option-⌘-P-R	Zaps the parameter RAM (PRAM) (hold down until you hear the second chime)
⌘-V	Shows Unix console messages during startup, logout, and shutdown

F12, mouse down, or trackpad button down	Ejects a stuck CD or DVD
Shift	Just after you hear the startup tone: Starts up in Safe Mode (page 778)
Shift	Just after logging in: Prevents Finder windows and startup items from opening (they'll return the next time you start up)

Speech recognition

Tap fn twice	Begin "speak to type"
Hold down ⌘-space	Summon Siri

In the Finder

⌘-space	Opens Spotlight search box
▶, ◀	Expands or collapses a selected folder in list view
Option-▶	Expands a folder in a list view *and* all folders inside it
Option-◀	Collapses a folder *and* all folders inside it
⌘-▲	Opens parent folder
⌘-▼ (or ⌘-O)	Opens the selected icon
Option-click the flippy triangle	Expands or collapses all folders within that window
Tab	Selects next icon alphabetically
Shift-Tab	Selects previous icon alphabetically
space bar	Opens Quick Look preview of highlighted icon(s)
space bar	During a spring-loaded folder drag, opens the disk or folder under the mouse immediately
Option-click Zoom button	Enlarges the window (but not into Full Screen mode)
Option-click Close button	Closes all Finder windows
Option-click Minimize button	Minimizes all windows (works in most apps)
Option	Changes Quick Look button to Slideshow button
⌘-drag	Rearranges or removes menulets or toolbar icons
⌘-click window title	Opens a pop-up menu showing the folder path

Menu

Option	Changes "About This Mac" to "System Information"
Shift-⌘-Q	Logs out
Shift-Option-⌘-Q	Logs out without confirmation box

Finder menu

Option	Eliminates the confirmation box from Empty Trash
Shift-⌘-Delete	Empties the Trash
⌘-Delete	Puts back a highlighted icon now in the Trash
Shift-Option-⌘-Delete	Empties the Trash without confirmation box
Option-Empty Trash	Empties the Trash without confirmation box
⌘-comma	Opens Preferences (also works in most programs)
⌘-H	Hide this program
Option-⌘-H	Hide other programs

File menu

⌘-N	New Finder window
⌘-T	New Finder tab
Shift-⌘-N	New folder
Control-⌘-N	New folder with selection
⌘-O or ⌘-▼	Open
Control-⌘-O	Open in new window
Option-click File menu	Changes "Open With" to "Always Open With"
⌘-W	Close window
Option-⌘-W	Close All
⌘-I	Get Info
Option-⌘-I	Show Inspector
Control-⌘-I	Summary Info (of selected icons)
⌘-D	Duplicate
Control-⌘-A	Make Alias
⌘-Y	Quick Look
Option-⌘-Y	Slideshow (of selected icons)
Option-Control-⌘-A	Show Original (of alias)
Control-⌘-T	Add to Sidebar
Shift-Control-⌘-T	Add to Dock

⌘-Delete	Move to Trash
⌘-E	Eject
⌘-F	Find
Shift-Control-⌘-F	Find by Name

Edit menu

⌘-Z	Undo
Shift-⌘-Z	Redo
⌘-C, ⌘-X, ⌘-V	Copy, Cut, Paste
Option-⌘-V	Move item here
⌘-A	Select All
Option-⌘-A	Deselect All
Control-⌘-space bar	Open Emoji & Symbols panel

View menu

⌘-1, -2, -3, -4	Icon, list, column, gallery views
Control-⌘-1, -2, -3, -4, -5, -6, -7	Sort by Name, Kind, Date Last Opened, Date Added, Date Modified, Size, Tags
Option-⌘-1, -2, -5, -6, -7	Clean up by Name, Kind, Date Modified, Size, Tags
Shift-⌘-T	Show/hide Tabs bar
Shift-⌘-\	Show all tabs
Shift-⌘-P	Show/hide preview pane
Option-⌘-P	Show/hide Path bar
Option-⌘-S	Show/hide Sidebar
Option-⌘-T	Show/hide toolbar
⌘-/	Show/hide status bar
⌘-J	Show/hide View Options palette
Control-⌘-F	Full Screen mode

Go menu

⌘-[, ⌘-]	Back, Forward
⌘-▲	Enclosing folder
⌘-K	Connect to Server
Control-⌘-▲	Enclosing folder in new window
Shift-⌘-F	Recents window
Shift-⌘-O	Documents window
Shift-⌘-D	Desktop window

Shift-⌘-H	Home window
Shift-⌘-L	Library window
Shift-⌘-C	Computer window
Shift-⌘-R	AirDrop window
Shift-⌘-K	Network window
Shift-⌘-A	Applications window
Shift-⌘-G	Go to Folder
Shift-⌘-I	iCloud Drive window
Shift-⌘-U	Utilities
Option	Makes Library Command Appear
Option-⌘-L	Downloads window

Window menu

⌘-M	Minimize
Option-⌘-M	Minimize All
⌘-`	Cycle through windows

Help menu

Shift-⌘-?	Opens help search box

Power keys

Control-⏻	Brings up dialog box for Shut Down, Sleep, or Restart
Option-⌘-⏻	Sleep
Control-Option-⌘-⏻	Shut Down
Control-⌘-⏻	Restart

The Dock

Shift-Option-click a Dock icon	Switches to new program and hides previous one
Option-⌘-D	Hides/shows the Dock
⌘-click a Dock or Stacks icon	Reveals its actual Finder icon
Option-⌘-click a Dock icon	Switches to this program and hides all others
Control-click a Dock icon	Opens a shortcut menu
⌘-drag an icon onto a Dock icon	Prevents Dock icons from moving, so you can drop your icon onto one of them
⌘-drag a Dock icon	Drags the actual item
Option-⌘-drag an icon onto the Dock	Forces a Dock program to open the icon you're dropping on it

Managing programs

Shift-Option-click a Dock icon	Switches to new program and hides the previous one
Option-click in a window	Switches to new program and hides the previous one
⌘-H	Hide this program's windows (works in most apps)
Option-⌘-H	Hide all *other* programs' windows (most apps)
Control-◄, ►	Previous/next Spaces screen
F9	Exposé: Shrinks and tiles all windows in all programs
Shift-F9	Exposé: Shrinks and tiles all windows in slow motion
F10	Exposé: Shrinks and tiles all windows in frontmost program
F11	Exposé: Flings all windows in all programs to edges of screen, revealing desktop
⌘-Tab	Press and release: Switches back and forth between current and previous open programs
⌘-Tab	Hold down ⌘: Displays floating icons of open programs. Press Tab repeatedly to cycle through them. (Add Shift to cycle *backward* through open programs.)
Option-⌘-Esc	Opens the Force Quit dialog box (to close a stuck program)
Shift-⌘-3	Captures the screen image as a PNG file on your desktop
Shift-⌘-4	Produces a crosshairs; drag to capture a selected portion of the screen as a PNG graphics file. (Press space to get the "camera" cursor that snips out just a menu, icon, or window.)
Shift-⌘-5	Opens a sophisticated set of options for screen captures
Control-space	Switches keyboard layout (if more than one is installed)

Dialog boxes

⌘-comma	Opens Preferences dialog box (any Apple program)
Esc	"Clicks" the Cancel button in a dialog box
Return	"Clicks" the OK button (or other blue, highlighted button) in a dialog box
Option-⌘-F	Moves the insertion point to the search box in most Apple programs
⌘-D, ⌘-R	"Clicks" the Don't Save or Replace button

Trackpad gestures

You can change many of these gestures, or turn them on and off, in the Trackpad pane of System Preferences. But here are the factory settings:

Two-finger click	Right-click
Two-finger drag up/down	Scroll up/down
Two-finger swipe left-/right	Move among open web or document pages
Two-finger swipe from right edge	Open Notification Center
Two-finger pinch or spread	Zoom in or out of a picture, PDF, or web page
Two-finger rotate	Rotate photo or PDF
Two-finger double-tap (not click)	"Smart zoom" into Safari or Preview page
Three-finger swipe up	Mission Control
Three-finger swipe down	Show all windows in this app (Exposé)
Three-finger swipe left/right	Previous/next Spaces screen or full-screen app
Three-finger drag	Move window
Three-finger tap (not click)	Look up this word in Dictionary
Four-finger pinch	Open Launchpad
Four-finger spread	Reveal desktop (Exposé)

Magic Mouse gestures

A few important gestures also work on the top surface of the Magic Mouse:

One-finger double-tap (not click)	"Smart zoom" into Safari or Preview page
Two-finger double-tap (not click)	Mission Control
One-finger swipe left-/right	Move between pages
Two-finger swipe left/right	Previous/next Spaces screen or full-screen app

Index

Index

MACOS CATALINA: THE MISSING MANUAL

Colophon

This book was written on a 13-inch MacBook Pro that remained attached to David Pogue like an appendage. It was updated from the Mojave edition of the same book, with substantial assistance from the typing-shortcut program TextExpander *(smileonmymac.com)*.

The book's screen illustrations were captured with macOS Catalina's screenshot toolbar, edited in Adobe Photoshop *(adobe.com)*, and overlaid with labels, lines, and circles in Adobe Illustrator.

The book was designed and laid out in Adobe InDesign CC. The fonts include Formata (as the sans-serif family) and Minion (as the serif body face). To provide the symbols (, ⌘, ⏏, and so on), Julie Van Keuren, Phil Simpson, and Judy Le designed custom fonts using FontLab Fontographer and TypeTool 3.

The book was then exported as Adobe Acrobat PDF files for final transmission to the printing plant.